The Camera Assistant:
A Complete Professional Handbook

The Camera Assistant:

A Complete Professional Handbook

Douglas C. Hart

Illustrations by Mary Mortimer

Focal Press
Taylor & Francis Group

NEW YORK AND LONDON

First published 1996

This edition published 2013
by Focal Press
70 Blanchard Road, Suite 402, Burlington, MA 01803

Simultaneously published in the UK
by Focal Press
2 Park Square, Milton Park, Abingdon, Oxon OX14 4RN

Focal Press is an imprint of the Taylor & Francis Group, an informa business

Copyright © 1996 by Taylor & Francis

All rights reserved. No part of this book may be reprinted or reproduced or utilised in any form or by any electronic, mechanical, or other means, now known or hereafter invented, including photocopying and recording, or in any information storage or retrieval system, without permission in writing from the publishers.

Notices
Practitioners and researchers must always rely on their own experience and knowledge in evaluating and using any information, methods, compounds, or experiments described herein. In using such information or methods they should be mindful of their own safety and the safety of others, including parties for whom they have a professional responsibility.

To the fullest extent of the law, neither the Publisher nor the authors, contributors, or editors, assume any liability for any injury and/or damage to persons or property as a matter of products liability, negligence or otherwise, or from any use or operation of any methods, products, instructions, or ideas contained in the material herein.

Library of Congress Cataloging-in-Publication Data
Hart, Douglas C.
    The camera assistant : a complete professional handbook / by
Douglas C. Hart.
      p.   cm.
    Includes bibliographical references and index.
    ISBN 0-240-80042-7 (hardcover)
    1. Cinematography—Handbooks, manuals, etc. I. Title.
TR850.H357 1995
778.5'3—dc20   95-31008
                                                                       CIP

British Library Cataloguing-in-Publication Data
A catalogue record for this book is available from the British Library.

ISBN 13: 978-0-240-80042-4 (hbk)

Transferred to Digital Printing in 2014

CONTENTS

Preface　xvii
　About This Book　xvii
　About the Author　xviii
　The Union　xx
　Trainee Program　xx
　Continuing Education　xx
　Workshops　xx
　Camera Assisting　xxii
　Technical Books　xxiii
　Preferences　xxiv
　Individuality　xxiv
　Teaching　xxv
　Intentions　xxvii
　Priorities and Attitude　xxviii

1　Introduction to Camera Assisting　1
　What is a Camera Assistant?　1
　Accepting Responsibility　3
　Preventing Mistakes　3
　Tell the Director of Photography　4
　Generalities　4

2　Responsibilities of the Camera Assistant　7
　Overview　7
　　Director of Photography　8
　　Camera Operator　9
　　First Camera Assistant　9
　　Second Camera Assistant　11
　　Still Photographer　12
　Compromises　12
　Additional Camera Crew Personnel　13
　Individuality　15

v

Geographic Differences   15
Other Departments   16
  Grips   17
  Sound   18
  Script   18
  Gaffer and Electrical Department   19
  Teamsters   20
  Assistant Director   21
  Production Manager   22
  Production Office Coordinator   22
  Others   22

3 Film Formats and Aspect Ratios   23
  Film Gauges   23
  Film Formats   24
  Anamorphic Systems   27
  Film Aspect Ratios   27
  Advent of Sound   27
  Wide-Screen Formats   28
  16mm Formats   29
  35mm Nonanamorphic (Spherical) Formats   30
  35mm Anamorphic Formats   33
  35mm Anamorphic and Horizontal Formats   33
  35mm Multistrip Systems   33
  65mm Nonanamorphic (Spherical) Formats   34
  65mm Anamorphic Formats   35
  Running Time for Various Film Gauges and Formats   35
  High Definition TV (HDTV)   35

4 The Camera Equipment Checkout   37
  The Importance of the Checkout   37
  Camera Equipment Rental Houses   38
  Before the Checkout   39
  Rental House Personnel   41
  The Philosophy of the Checkout   42
  Reserved Equipment Packages   44
  The Camera Equipment Checkout Checklist   47
  The Rental Contract   101
  Case Labeling   102

5 Shooting Tests During Checkout   103
  Tests   103
  Registration Tests   103
  Flicker Tests   109
  Ground Glass Markings Test   109
  Making Dailies Projection Leader   111
  Ground Glass Position   111

Lens Aberrations 113
Lens Sharpness 114
Lens Color 117
Emulsion Tests 118
Specifying Printing Lights 120
Filter Tests 122
Wardrobe and Makeup Tests 122
Actors' Screen Tests 123
Lab Continuity Test 123

6 Loading/Unloading 125
Manufacturer's Film Can Label 125
Changing Bags 131
Darkrooms 134
Camera Trucks 135
Magazine Maintenance 136
Loading Procedures 140
Recanned Raw Stock 143
Short Ends 145
Magazine Labeling 148
Magazine Case Labeling 150
Film Can Labeling 151
Multiple Film Stocks 153
Ordering Raw Stock 154
Storage of Raw Stock 155
Shipping of Raw Stock and Exposed Film 156
Dealing with Laboratories 158
Hand Tests ("Slop" Tests) 159

7 Lenses 161
Lenses in General 161
Prime Lenses 162
Anamorphic Lenses 162
Lens Mounts 163
Zoom Lenses 166
Special Lenses 166
  Macro Lenses 166
  Tele-Extenders 167
  Wide-Angle Adapters 168
  Proxars (Plus Diopters)/Split Diopters 168
Cleaning Lenses 170
Matte Boxes/Sunshades 170
Lens Flare 171
Transporting Lenses 174
Condensation on Cold Lenses 175
Changing Lenses 176

8 Filters 177
Sizes and Shapes of Filters 177
How Filters Work 177
Color Correction Filters 178
Color Compensation Filters 179
Neutral Density Filters 179
Graduated Filters 180
"Attenuator" Filters 181
Diffusion Filters 182
Polarizing Filters 183
Special Effects Filters 184
Behind-the-Lens Filters 185
Behind-the-Lens Diffusion 188
Multiple Filters 188
Filter Factors 189
Mired Shift Value 190
Cleaning Filters 190

9 Focus 193
Overview 193
Focus Theory 194
Circle of Confusion 196
f/ stops and T/ stops 198
Depth-of-Field 200
   Macro Lens Depth-of-Field 203
Depth-of-Focus 204
Hyperfocal Distance 205
Depth-of-Field Calculators and Charts 206
Camera Lens Depth-of-Field Calculator 212
Following Focus 212
Choices: Who Should be in Focus? 216
Splitting Focus 217
Four Categories of Shot Focus 219
Focus Marks 228
Eye vs. Tape Focus 232
Dolly Shots and Crane Shots 233
Camera Operators and Focus 234
Video Assist and Focus 235
Panavision "Blue Line" Lenses 235
Long Lenses 237
Zoom Lenses 240
Aperture Pulls 241
Plus Diopters 241
Split Diopter Lenses 243
Panatape 245

Rangefinders 246
Electronic Focus Gadgets 248

10 Setup and Maintenance 251
The Morning Routine 251
Warmup 252
Cleaning the Camera 253
   Viewfinder 254
Lubricating the Camera 255
Flange Focal Depth Checking/Film Gap Setting 256
Shutter Opening 257
Movement Phasing 258
Setting Up 260
Service Carts and Handtrucks 261
Bringing Equipment to the Set 263
Morning Chores 264

11 Shooting Procedures 265
Set Etiquette 265
Chain of Command 267
Never Distract Director or Actors 267
No Eye Contact with Actors 268
Never Leave Camera Unattended 268
Unplug and Cover the Camera 269
Moving the Camera 269
Scene Blocking 272
Directors' Finders/Real Lens Finders/Camera-as-Finder 274
Marking Actors 277
Hiding Marks 282
Numbering the Marks 282
   Removing the Marks 283
Color Charts and Gray Scales 284
Setting the Eyepiece 284
Keeping the Camera Quiet 285
   Lubrication 286
   Pitch Control 286
   Blimps and Barneys 286
Magazine Noise 287
Setting the Aperture 287
Camera Cases 290
Troubleshooting: What to Do When the Camera Stops 291
Once the Camera is Rolling 291
Following Focus 292
Zooming 292
Aperture Pulls 293
Shutter Changes 293

Simultaneous Moves 294
Filming in the Cold 295
Moving Cameras 296
   Dollies 296
   Cranes 296
   Insert Cars 298
Steadicam/Panaglide 298
Camera Reports 302
Safety on the Set 302
Checking the Gate 304
   Pull the Lens 307
   Through the Lens 308
   Pull the Gate 309
Cleaning the Gate 310
Reloading Etiquette 310
Film Break-Off 312
Recordkeeping—Shot Notebook 313
Multiple Camera Shooting 313
Efficiency on the Set 315
Looking at Dailies 315
Film Handling and Camera Problems 316
Raw Stock and Processing Defects 318

12 Slates and Slating 319
Why Slate? 319
Single System/Double System 321
Information on the Slate 322
Types of Slates 323
Roll Slates 324
Tail Slates 325
Second Sticks 327
False Starts 327
Silent Slates 327
Getting Started 328
Slating Procedure 330
Etiquette of Slating 332
Perspective and Timing 333
Documentary Slating 335
Time Code Slating 336
Commercial Slating 339
Multiple Camera Slating 340

13 Paperwork 343
No Shortage of Paperwork 343
Camera Reports 344

Identification   346
Contents   347
Instructions   351
Camera Reports for Short Ends   352
Daily Film Reports   353
Daily Film Inventory   354
Combination Forms   355
Purchase Orders   355
Time Cards   358
Equipment Lists   358
Call Sheets   359
Keep Copies of Everything!   359

14 Video Assist Systems   361
The Theory and Practice of Video Assist   361
Video Assist—Help or Hindrance?   364
Video Assist Flicker and Flicker-Free Video   364
Video Assist on the Set   365
The Video Assist Beamsplitter   366

15 Tools and Supplies   367
Assistant's Tool Kit   367
Essential Items   367
   Basic Tools   370
Optional Items   376
Assistant's Supplies   380
Travelling Heavy vs. Travelling Light   380

16 Education of a Camera Assistant, and Finding Work Afterwards   383
Film School   383
Equipment Rental Houses as Training Grounds   384
   Working at a Rental House   385
   Visit and Learn   385
Student Films   385
Ads in the Trade Press   386
Work as Production Assistant   386
Workshops and Seminars   386
Trainee Program   387
Finding Work   388
Freelancing   388
IATSE   389
Non-Union   390
Membership Procedure   391
Union Organizing   392
Did I Leave Something Out? Got a Better Way?   393
Send it to me for the Second Edition!   394

Appendix A: Bibliography   395
Appendix B: Expendable Supplies Shopping List   398
Appendix C: Camera Equipment Checkout Checklist   402
Appendix D: Useful Formulas and Charts   406
Appendix E: Film Magazine Takeup   410
Appendix F: Screen Time/Camera Running Time   411
Index   413

LIST OF ILLUSTRATIONS

| Figure P-1 | The Camera Assistants Workshop | xxii |

Figure 3-1	Horizontal/Vertical Formats	25
Figure 3-2	Anamorphic Systems	26
Figure 3-3	Screen Aspect Ratios	28
Figure 3-4	16mm Formats	29
Figure 3-5	35mm Formats	31
Figure 3-6	65/70mm Formats	34

Figure 4-1	Camera Equipment Checkout	43
Figure 4-2	Rental House Checkout Area	45
Figure 4-3	Mountain of Cases	46
Figure 4-4	Video Assist Adjustment	49
Figure 4-5	Crystal Checkers	51
Figure 4-6	Three Methods of Camera/Sound Synchronization	53
Figure 4-7	Power Cable Pin Configurations	61
Figure 4-8	Viewfinder Masks	70
Figure 4-9	Matte Slot and Matte Cutter	71
Figure 4-10	Cutting Gels for Gel Holders	73
Figure 4-11	Checking Lens Marks/In-Between Marks	81
Figure 4-12	Matte Box Masks with Telephoto Lenses	85
Figure 4-13	Lens/Matte Box Donuts	86
Figure 4-14	Magazine Scratch Testing	92
Figure 4-15	Camera Case Labeling	102

Figure 5-1	Registration Test—Grid	104
Figure 5-2	Registration Test—Moire	105
Figure 5-3	Registration Test—Marking Frame	106
Figure 5-4	Shooting Ground Glass Markings	110
Figure 5-5	Lens Sharpness Test	115
Figure 5-6	Exposure Test Setup	119

List of Illustrations

Figure 6-1	Film Manufacture—Origin of Emulsion Numbers	126
Figure 6-2	Film Can Label	128
Figure 6-3	Film Perforations	130
Figure 6-4	Changing Bag/Tent	132
Figure 6-5	Nitrogen Tank	137
Figure 6-6	Rubber Bulb Syringe/Dust-Off Can	138
Figure 6-7	Displacement Magazines	140
Figure 6-8	Dual Compartment/Coaxial Magazines	141
Figure 6-9	Attaching Film to Core	143
Figure 6-10	Recan Film Can Label	144
Figure 6-11	Short End Film Can Label	147
Figure 6-12	Loaded Film Magazine Label	148
Figure 6-13	Loaded Magazine/Exposed Film Can Label	149
Figure 6-14	Exposed Film Can Label	151
Figure 6-15	Rubber Stamp Labels	152
Figure 6-16	Camera Report/Purchase Order Envelopes	153
Figure 7-1	Anamorphic Photography	163
Figure 7-2	Panavision Lens Mount	164
Figure 7-3	Arriflex Lens Mount	165
Figure 7-4	Lens Tissue/Cleaning Lenses	169
Figure 7-5	Matte Boxes/Filter Holders	171
Figure 7-6	Lens Flares—Barn Doors and Black Wrap	172
Figure 7-7	Lens Flares—Grip Stands and Flags	172
Figure 7-8	Lens Flares—French Flags and Matte Box Extensions	173
Figure 8-1	Behind-the-Lens Gel Filters	186
Figure 9-1	Depth-of-Field	195
Figure 9-2	Circle of Confusion	197
Figure 9-3	Focal Length and Depth-of-Field	200
Figure 9-4	Aperture and Depth-of-Field	201
Figure 9-5	Distance and Depth-of-Field	202
Figure 9-6	Closer and Wider DOES NOT WORK!	203
Figure 9-7	Depth-of-Focus	204
Figure 9-8	Hyperfocal Distance	205
Figure 9-9	Depth-of-Field Charts	207
Figure 9-10	Depth-of-Field Wheel Chart	209
Figure 9-11	Samcine Mk. II Calculator	210
Figure 9-12	Camera Lens as Depth-of-Field Calculator	213
Figure 9-13	Camera Assistant Positioning	215
Figure 9-14	Split Focus—1/3 and 2/3 Rule	217
Figure 9-15	Favoring Focus	218
Figure 9-16	Type 1 Shot—Camera and Target Stationary	220
Figure 9-17	Type 2 Shot—Camera Stationary, Target Moving	221

Figure 9-18	Type 3 Shot—Camera Moving, Target Stationary	222
Figure 9-19	Type 4 Shot—Camera and Target Moving	224
Figure 9-20	In-Between Focus Marks	225
Figure 9-21	Dragline Focus Marks	226
Figure 9-22	Flashlight/Laser Pointer Focus Marks	227
Figure 9-23	Actors' Marks	229
Figure 9-24	Floor Marks	230
Figure 9-25	Lens Marks	231
Figure 9-26	Panavision Lenses—The "Blue Line"	236
Figure 9-27	Long Lens/Walkie Talkie Marks	238
Figure 9-28	P.A./Walkie Talkie Marks	239
Figure 9-29	Long Lens/Pointer and Dial Marks	240
Figure 9-30	Split Diopters	244
Figure 9-31	Panatape	245
Figure 9-32	Rangefinders	247
Figure 10-1	Movement Phasing	259
Figure 10-2	Hand Trucks	261
Figure 10-3	Camera Assistants' Service Cart	263
Figure 11-1	Gear Head Carry Rods	270
Figure 11-2	Camera, Head, and Tripod on Shoulder	272
Figure 11-3	Three Pound Finder	275
Figure 11-4	Hundred Pound Finder	276
Figure 11-5	Thousand Pound Finder	277
Figure 11-6	Actors' Marks—Start and End	278
Figure 11-7	Actors' Toe Marks—Four Styles	279
Figure 11-8	"Follow the Yellow Brick Road"	280
Figure 11-9	Other Actors' Marks—Sandbags, T-Marks, etc.	281
Figure 11-10	Numbering Marks	283
Figure 11-11	Eyepiece Marks	285
Figure 11-12	Two Lines Light? Where is That?	289
Figure 11-13	Dollies and Cranes	297
Figure 11-14	Insert Cars and Car Rigs	299
Figure 11-15	Steadicam	300
Figure 11-16	Camera Report Tin/Back of the Slate	303
Figure 11-17	Checking the Gate	305
Figure 11-18	Checking the Gate—Outside of Academy	306
Figure 11-19	Checking the Gate—Pull the Lens	307
Figure 11-20	Checking the Gate—Through the Lens	308
Figure 11-21	Checking the Gate—Pulling the Gate	309
Figure 11-22	Exposed Magazine in Case	311
Figure 11-23	Shot Notebook Pages	314
Figure 12-1	Sync Slate, Insert Slate, and Time Code Slate	320

Figure 12-2	Slates and Sync Sound	321
Figure 12-3	Slate Information	322
Figure 12-4	Tail Slate	325
Figure 12-5	M.O.S. I.D. Slate	328
Figure 12-6	Slate Perspective	334
Figure 12-7	Time Code "Smart Slate"	337
Figure 12-8	Commercial Slating	339
Figure 12-9	Common Marker	341
Figure 13-1	East and West Coast Camera Reports	345
Figure 13-2	Camera Report—Identification Section	347
Figure 13-3	Camera Report—Contents Section	348
Figure 13-4	Camera Report—Summary Section	350
Figure 13-5	Camera Report—Instructions Section	352
Figure 13-6	Daily Film Reports	353
Figure 13-7	Daily Film Inventory	354
Figure 13-8	Combination Film Report/Film Inventory Form #1	356
Figure 13-9	Combination Film Report/Film Inventory Form #2	357
Figure 14-1	Video Assist System	363
Figure 15-1	Swiss Army Knife/Tape Measures	368
Figure 15-2	Belt Pouch	369
Figure 15-3	Front Box and "Ditty Bag"	370
Figure 15-4	Larry Bag/Boat Bag	371
Figure 15-5	Precision Oilers	372
Figure 15-6	Flashlights and Magnifiers	373
Figure 15-7	Multimeter (Volt-Ohm-Meter)	375
Figure 15-8	Levels	375
Figure 15-9	Leatherman	377
Figure 15-10	Inspection Mirror/Lens Handle	377

Preface

About This Book

This handbook is an attempt at collecting all in one place the wide variety of theories, procedures, and tactics used by the Motion Picture Camera Assistants in the performance of their duties on the professional film set or location.

It will NOT be a camera instruction manual, detailing how to assemble and thread film into specific cameras. There are other books for that, books that go into incredibly minute detail about all of the bits and pieces of motion picture cameras and their associated magazines and accessories. It would be not only difficult but pointless for me to duplicate their efforts.

There are many more important things for the Camera Assistant to know than how to change the groundglass or adjust the magazine torque. This book is an attempt by a working Camera Assistant to describe and explain the more important facets of the Camera Assistants' job on the set; the theory behind the practice. This has never before been attempted on an advanced and sophisticated scale, to my knowledge.

I will be speaking in this book about the "software" of the Motion Picture Camera Assistant, if you will allow the analogy, rather than the "hardware."

The "focus" of the handbook will be primarily on theatrical feature films, but in general, the contents will apply, with minor alterations, to television commercials, episodic television, music videos, documentaries, student films, and other types of film projects as well.

"Features" are the top of the cinematic heap in the minds of many, because they generally have more money, more equipment, more time, and more personnel than the other forms, so it is easier to speak about feature procedures and practices, and then to estimate what would happen under less than these "ideal" circumstances.

About the Author

Perhaps this is the best place to insert some words "about the author," so my readers will know just who is presuming to publish such a book on such a subject.

First of all, I am a movie brat, having been raised in and around movie and television studios since I was old enough to walk. Secondly, I am a freelance Camera Assistant, and have been for nearly twenty-five years.

My father was, until his retirement a few years ago, a Construction Grip in New York City, building scenery for features and commercials for over three decades. I used to visit sets and locations with him as a child, and my first paying jobs in the industry were with him as a Grip, building and striking sets for commercials and feature films.

It quickly became apparent that the people having the most fun and making the most money were those closer to the camera than I was, so I started looking for a film school. I was already hooked on the business.

I attended the School of Visual Arts Film School, and started getting my hands on 16mm cameras there. After three years at SVA, during which I shot a lot of the student films directed by my classmates, I started freelancing as a Camera Assistant, getting work mostly on low-budget features, commercials, industrials and documentaries.

After building up a bit of a resume in nonunion film work, I applied to the Cinematographers' Union in New York, International Photographers Local 644, IATSE, and was eventually tested and accepted. There wasn't a lot of work for me in the beginning, but things gradually picked up, and after a few years of miscellaneous documentaries and commercials and work as additional crew for multiple cameras on features and concert films, I got a chance to work as Second Camera Assistant on a feature film shooting in New York City.

Unfortunately, despite having one of the all-time great film titles (*Baron Wolfgang von Tripps—Race Car Driver and Hero to Millions*), the picture was apparently never released in theaters, but at least I had one real picture under my belt. Many years later, I happened to see it on late-night television, with the title abridged to simply *The Baron*. Another job as Second Camera Assistant, on a TV movie, also retitled after shooting to *Sanctuary of Fear,* followed soon after, with a different camera crew.

The following summer I got a call from a Director of Photography I had worked with on some documentary and industrial films, including a National Geographic Special, who was about to do a made-for-TV movie in Bermuda, and who wanted me to work as his First Assistant. Naturally, I jumped at it, and it went very well, considering the stupid script and ridiculous story line (a giant sea turtle on the loose!). It starred Connie Sellecca (her first film) and still plays on obscure cable stations in the middle of the night.

After returning to New York, I went back to scattered TV commercials and multiple camera crew work on feature films. I did a few days as First Camera Assistant on the second camera for one sequence in *Manhattan,* where I met Director Woody Allen and Director of Photography Gordon Willis for the first time.

On Gordon's next picture, *Windows,* which he was directing as well as shooting, I got a call near the end of shooting to come in and replace the Second Camera Assistant, who was leaving to honor another commitment after *Windows* went beyond its original schedule. I worked as Second Assistant for a week or so, and then got bumped up to First Assistant when the First Assistant I had been working with also had to leave for a prior commitment. I finished the job as First Assistant, for about the last two weeks of shooting.

I must have done something right, because Gordon offered me his next picture for Woody Allen, *Stardust Memories,* as First Camera Assistant. I spent the next ten years working with Gordon—ten complete pictures, parts of four others, and over 100 television commercials.

These features included *A Midsummer Night's Sex Comedy, Zelig* (Gordon's first Oscar nomination, and not a winner, unfortunately), *Broadway Danny Rose, Purple Rose of Cairo* (these four also for Woody Allen), *The Lost Honor of Kathryn Beck, The Money Pit, The Pickup Artist, Bright Lights Big City*, and most recently *Presumed Innocent.*

During this ten-year stint with Gordon, I also served as First Camera Assistant for Director of Photography Robby Muller on *They All Laughed,* for Carlo DiPalma on *Hannah and Her Sisters* (again Woody Allen), for Laszlo Kovaks on the New York scenes for *Legal Eagles,* for Woody Omens on the New York scenes for *Coming to America,* and for Don Thorin on the New Jersey prison scenes for *Lockup.*

A quartet of made-for-TV movies (also known as "MOW's" or "Movies-of-the-Week") followed, named "Shadow of a Killer," "A Jury of One," "The Black Widow Murders," and "New Eden," and Second Unit work for the TV series "N.Y.P.D. Blue," all for Director of Photography Geoff Erb, who had been that First Camera Assistant who gave me my first job as his Second Assistant, on *Baron Wolfgang,* years earlier.

Other Second Units I have worked on include *The Hard Way* and *The Cowboy Way* (which sound like they should be related, I guess, but are not), and the TV series "Spencer for Hire" and "N.Y.P.D. Blue."

I have spent this past year working on NBC's new series, "The Cosby Mysteries," also for Geoff Erb. This is my first long-term job in episodic television; twenty hour-long episodes the first season. The strangest thing about episodic TV is the changing of directors for each episode. We had eleven different directors in the first thirteen episodes. By the time the crew gets used to the director's pace and style of working, a new director shows up. Most hour-long series shoot seven or eight days per episode, but on "Cosby" we are shooting nine days for each one-hour show. This helps keep the hours reasonable, but it also keeps our paychecks smaller.

There have also been hundreds of commercials (for Directors of Photography such as Dave Quaid, Conrad Hall, Caleb Deschanel, Mario Tosi, Ralf Bode, Jerry Cotts, Tom Houghton, Ed Barnett, Tom Ackerman, Ron Fortunato, Carl Norr and many others) and documentaries for IBM, National Geographic, Phillips Petroleum, and many others, and I have been fortunate to have travelled to and worked in forty-two of the fifty states, and in twenty-eight foreign countries, at last count.

The Union

I started getting active in my union (International Photographers of the Motion Picture and Television Industries, Local 644, IATSE) as well, first as Secretary, then as Vice-President, then as Executive Board member representing Camera Assistants, then Vice-President again, and a little over three years as President, 1990–1993. I am also proudly a member of Studio Mechanics Local 52, IATSE, as a Grip, and of International Photographers Local 666, IATSE, as a Camera Assistant.

I believe in unions, not only for the good of the people actually working to make the films, but also for the good of the industry itself. Film crews make better films when they are treated with respect and dignity by management, and are paid reasonably for their labors, and are protected from physical, moral, and even spiritual injustices through their union contracts. It's that simple.

More on unions, including a description of the membership application procedure, will be found at the end of this book. Unions are hardly ever mentioned in film schools, except in a derogatory way. I am doing my best to change this unfortunate view of one of the forces for good in our industry.

Trainee Program

When I first started working on feature films as a Camera Assistant, there were no trainee or apprentice programs for Camera Assistants in operation on the East Coast. About fifteen years ago, I helped start the Camera Trainee program in Local 644, in which new members work with feature crews to meet people and learn procedures, and since then have had some twenty-five or so trainees work with me on Feature Films. More on this Trainee Program later in this book.

Continuing Education

Also during this period, I went back to school at the School of Visual Arts and finished the requirements for my Bachelor of Fine Arts degree in Cinema Studies by taking night classes. I liked going back to school so much that I kept going, and got my Master of Arts degree in Communication Arts at the New York Institute of Technology.

I am now working on another Masters Degree, in Labor and Policy Studies, at Empire State College (part of the State University of New York). I may actually finish this program someday, and get my second Masters degree.

I also started teaching and getting involved in the Maine Photographic Workshops, now known as the International Film and Television Workshops.

Workshops

This book began as teaching notes for the Motion Picture Camera Assistants Workshops I began and continue to teach at the International Film and Television Workshops in Rockport, Maine, every summer. This series of summer Photography

Workshops began as one, and two-week still photography workshops with renowned professional photographers, and later expanded into motion pictures, with Workshops devoted to Directing, Editing, Steadicam, Lighting, Cinematography, Screenwriting, Video Production and Editing, etc., all taught by industry professionals.

After attending one Film Lighting Workshop as a student in 1980 (Vilmos Zsigmund was the instructor), I kept coming back year after year to help out with other workshops, as Assistant Instructor for the Camera Workshops and as Course Assistant and/or one of the Unit Managers for the Film Lighting Workshops.

After a few years of pushing, I think it is fair to say I was instrumental in persuading the directors of the Workshop that a Camera Assistants Workshop would be a good and profitable idea for them. The two major professional camera manufacturers for feature film worldwide, Arriflex and Panavision, were already involved in the Workshops, supplying their product lines and technical representatives, so it wasn't difficult getting the very best professional camera equipment from them to play with and train with. With the help of these and other sponsors, the Workshops have become world famous as a place to go and learn the craft and the art of the Cinema.

The Camera Assistants Workshop began as a two-day weekend workshop sandwiched between the week-long Camera and Lighting Workshops. With considerable favorable feedback from the participants, the Camera Assistants Workshop gradually expanded from two days to three, and then to a full week. As far as I know, it is the ONLY professional week-long Workshop in the country (possibly even in the world) devoted entirely to the Motion Picture Camera Assistant.

One of the most important things we tried to instill in the Workshop students is a respect for the equipment. One of the representatives from Panavision who helped us set up the course, Benjamin Bergery, used to describe this respect as "Equipment Zen." Learn to treat equipment as if it were alive and with proper respect. The equipment exists to help us make movies, but it can only do that if the equipment works properly and if the crew using that equipment knows what the capabilities and limitations of the equipment are.

When approaching an unfamiliar camera or other item of equipment, look before you touch. Think before you tinker. Don't force two pieces together, or try to wrestle a piece off. If it doesn't attach or detach easily, you're probably doing it wrong, it's not necessarily a fault in the equipment. Stop and think. Step back and consider what you are doing. Then try again. And above all, if there is any question about the equipment, or how things fit together, ASK someone who knows. That's what teachers and rental house personnel and manufacturer representatives are for.

One of the problems with equipment seminars and demonstrations is that in their eagerness to examine, probe, assemble and disassemble every new toy, students sometimes get carried away, causing what Benjamin described perfectly as a "Feeding Frenzy," just like with sharks when there is a wounded fish in the area. This is when new equipment gets damaged or someone gets hurt, simply through carelessness.

My teaching notes and transcribed lectures from the Workshop, combined with frequently asked questions from Workshop students, became the nucleus for this book. I had been recommending several technical books to Workshop students for

Figure P-1 The Camera Assistants Workshop. Author Doug Hart teaching at the Camera Assistants Workshop, one of the International Film and Television Workshops held in Rockport, Maine, twice every summer. This is the world's only intensive, hands-on, week-long Camera Assistants Workshop. Also visible are the Arriflex 535 and Panavision Platinum cameras, supplied by the Workshops' long-time sponsors, Arriflex and Panavision.

further reading and information, but I wanted a real Camera Assistants' textbook. I also realized that if I wanted one, I was going to have to write it myself.

I repeatedly complained in my classes and workshops that there was no Camera Assistants' textbook, and people kept telling me that I should be the one to write it, so here it is.

Camera Assisting

I will use the term "Camera Assistant" in this book as a general term to include both First Camera Assistants and Second Camera Assistants, using "First" and "Second" in such cases where delineation between the two is important.

I have stopped describing the job as "Assistant Cameraman," because of its sexist/chauvinist connotation but I refuse to use the clumsy compromise, "Assistant Cameraperson." The neutral description "Camera Assistant" should keep everyone happy.

With apologies in advance to my female readers, I will use, on occasion, the masculine pronoun "he," in my text, but only because "he/she" (or, even worse, "s/he") is very clumsy and time-consuming, and "it" is obviously not appropriate.

Until the English language gives birth to a better neutral pronoun than "it," I will use "he."

There are currently very few female Camera Assistants in this country in comparison to males, but the percentage of females gets higher every year. Historically, this job, as with nearly every other job in the movie industry, has been held by males, but there is absolutely no reason why it should continue to be so. Cameras are no longer the 150-lb. cast-iron monsters they used to be, and there are some fine female Camera Assistants working out there now. I'm proud to say that several of them have come from my Workshops, and that I call some of them to work with me when I can.

Technical Books

There are, of course, many technical manuals and books available to the aspiring Camera Assistant, which illustrate how the equipment works, and some of these even include a section about film can labeling or depth-of-field charts, but until now, there has been, to my knowledge, only one book devoted entirely to the Camera Assistant.

Although I began this book first, David Elkins, a West Coast Camera Assistant, beat me to the press with his book *The Camera Assistant's Manual*. David's book is much smaller and less technical than this one. I recommend David's book for beginning Camera Assistants, and then this one for when you get more advanced. Since both books come from Focal Press, I assume that the publishers intended this division as well. I couldn't find anything in David's book that was not already included here, but there is much more material in this book that is not in David's book.

Since there were no existing Camera Assistants' manuals when I began this book, and since I don't want this book to be simply another equipment manual, the going has been slow. I have had to resist the temptation to write about the specific equipment which I am most familiar with and prefer to work with, which may or may not still be around and popular when this book is read, or which may be upgraded and improved before I get this work into print.

Wherever possible I will resist using brand names for equipment, except where a specific point needs to be made. I would love to be able to never once mention a brand name of camera equipment, but I know this won't be possible.

Readers who need specific information about a particular camera should go first to that magnificent book, the *Professional Cameraman's Handbook*, and then if necessary to one of the other technical books listed in the Bibliography in the back of this book. David Samuelson's series of books in the Media Manuals series are particularly good, as is the famed *American Cinematographers Manual* (known to many in the industry as the "Bible," and for good reason). These books go into incredible technical detail on how to assemble specific cameras, and so on, and there is no point in my duplicating their work.

Two recently released books that every aspiring Camera Assistant MUST acquire are the *Panaflex Users' Manual*, by David W. Samuelson, and *The Arri 35*

Book, by my friend Jon Fauer. There are few, if any, technical questions on those camera systems left unanswered by these two books.

Preferences

Every Camera Assistant has his or her own preferences with respect to equipment, and I don't want this book to deteriorate into a comparison of existing equipment preferences. I don't want to write yet another "equipment manual"; I want this to be a "procedure" manual, which will be applicable to whatever particular brands and models of equipment, and whatever film gauge or format may be in use at the time.

Hopefully this book will transcend the equipment trends of the Industry, and will serve a generation of Camera Assistants, whatever brands of camera equipment happen to be in vogue.

Whatever brand of camera is in use, film stock will still have to be loaded into magazines, depth-of-field calculated, and focus adjusted. Scenes and takes will still have to be slated. Camera reports and purchase orders will still have to be filled out, production managers, laboratories and rental houses dealt with, and apertures set. Lenses will still be zoomed, focus followed, and cameras reloaded. Additional cameras and accessories will still have to be ordered and checked out, time cards filled in, and filters compensated for. In short, the job of the Camera Assistant transcends the particular brands of equipment in use.

Individuality

Since, until now, there were no textbooks or regular courses of instruction, new Camera Assistants have had to learn the job from established Camera Assistants, or just "wing it" and devise their own unique methods of solving the problems inherent in the job.

Every First Camera Assistant has his or her own way of working, their own systems of checking out and setting up, their own methods for marking actors and determining focus splits, their own preferences for film can and magazine labeling, and their own particular way of delegating responsibility to their Second Camera Assistants, Loaders, and Trainees.

Put a dozen Camera Assistants in a room and ask a technical or procedural question, and you will be likely to get a dozen different answers. Not only that, but each of the Assistants will likely insist that their own particular way is the best and only way to do the job, and that any other way is at best inefficient, and at worst incorrect, sloppy, or dangerous. Camera Assistants can be very intolerant when it comes to their jobs.

To make things even more difficult, every Director of Photography has ideas about what the Camera Assistants should be doing and how they should be doing it.

Directors of Photography who have come from still photography, or from directing or even from gaffing, and who have never worked as Camera Assistants, are generally easier to work for, in my experience, because they do not have preconceived ideas and prejudices on the specifics of how the Assistant should do his or her job. They are happy to leave the voodoo and witchcraft of camera assisting to the Assistant.

The down side is that these Directors of Photography sometimes do not realize how important the Camera Assistant is to the final product, and do not know how long things take to do correctly.

Directors of Photography who have been Camera Assistants obviously know what is involved and how long things take, but may have very specific demands on what should be done and how it should be done, which may or may not be compatible with the Camera Assistant's own training and experience.

Obviously, in either case, the basic rule for the Camera Assistant is:

**"Always Keep
the Director of Photography
Happy"**

To make matters even more difficult, Camera Assistants rarely get to see each other work. There is generally only one First Camera Assistant on a feature film, so there is no one to watch and learn from and share ideas with. In those instances where there is more than one camera in use, there will be other First Assistants on the job, but they will often be widely separated and are generally too busy to chat and show each other short cuts and tricks.

Second Camera Assistants who move around and work with different First Assistants have the best chance to see different approaches to the job and to learn from more than one First. Unfortunately (or fortunately—I'm not sure which) I only completed two pictures as a Second Camera Assistant before I started working as a First. I was probably a lousy Second Assistant. The good news is that I worked for two different Firsts, and I consider myself deeply indebted to each of them. I learned a great deal from each, both technical and procedural, for they were very different from each other in their routines, styles and priorities.

Teaching

The other essential way to learn the job is to listen to and remember "war" stories told by other Assistants, Operators, and Directors of Photography about their experiences on other jobs. Every job is unique, and will present the Camera Assistant with unique problems to be solved. The "war" stories of others often provide clues and suggestions on how to solve these problems. Unique solutions to unusual problems will rarely be found in books, no matter how thoroughly researched or well written, but might more easily be recalled from an interesting and remembered story.

Early in my career, I had the extreme good fortune and unforgettable pleasure of having as an instructor in Film School at the School of Visual Arts cinematographer David L. Quaid, ASC. Dave had known and worked with my father years earlier, when

Dave was a staff cameraman and my father was a staff carpenter at one of the very first television commercial production houses in the country, a New York production company called Transfilm.

When I decided to enter film school, almost purely by coincidence, there was Dave as an instructor (when he wasn't off shooting and directing commercials in some distant part of the world). He missed quite a few classes, of course, because of work, but he more than made up for those when he was there. He usually brought equipment with him that we would never otherwise have seen in Film School, and always had (and still has) the very best "war" stories, many of which I pass on to my students.

I asked him once why he bothered to teach, when he was so busy shooting and traveling, and I will never forget what he told me.

"There are two kinds of people in this business," he said, "those who say 'It took me twenty years to learn that—why should I give it to you for nothing?' and those who believe that 'If I die, knowing something unique, and have not passed it along, I die a failure. So, as soon as I discover or rediscover something, I tell everyone.'—I belong in the second group."

"This business has been very good to me," he went on, "and it is my duty and responsibility to give some of that back to the industry and to the next generation."

I have always believed as Dave does, and have done my best to pass on what I have learned. I learned a great deal from Dave in school, and then later on the learning experience continued attending some of Dave's seminars, and while working with him on fifteen or twenty commercials spread out over the last five years or so before Dave retired. One of the few regrets in my career is that I never got to work with Dave on an entire feature film. It would truly have been marvelous!

Gordon Willis was also one of Dave's Camera Assistants in those early Transfilm days. When Gordon first spoke to me about my working as his First Camera Assistant for *Stardust Memories*, I'm sure that my telling him that I had studied under Dave in film school and had worked for Dave on commercials played no small part in Gordon's deciding to give me a try. It definitely brought a smile to his face when he heard Dave's name (and still does).

A high point in my life and career came while working with Gordon on a commercial in Boston, near where Dave lives, and I managed to get Dave and Gordon and myself together for dinner at our hotel one night. What a night! Dinner with the two people I respect and admire most in the business. Four hours of nonstop stories! The maitre d' finally had to ask us to leave, as we were the last customers in the restaurant and they wanted to close up.

Dave is also at least partly responsible for this book. When I was first thinking about writing it, Dave was the first person I spoke to. He not only urged and encouraged me into actually sitting down at the word processor, but he put me in touch with the people at Focal Press.

Teaching is also good for the teacher. I have not taught a single class or workshop without learning something from one of the students, either prompted by a student's question into an explanation of a previously misunderstood event, or learning another possibly simpler, cheaper, or more efficient solution to a problem.

Any day that goes by without learning something new is a wasted day.

"Filmmaking is the art and science of solving problems," Dave once said. You'll find a lot of Dave's ideas and quotes in this book. Not only have I spent a lot of time (never enough) working with him and learning from him, but Dave is a born teacher, gifted with an intensity, energy level, and generosity of time and knowledge unsurpassed in the industry.

Dave is one of those guys that if you needed a piece of equipment that didn't exist, he would invent it. Dave's solutions to technical problems always seemed so simple and logical looking back, but at the time, were miraculous and exciting. Dave retired a few years ago, but still holds the occasional seminar and is now working on the definitive fluorescent light color correction system, soon to be published. I call and speak with Dave occasionally—I should do it more often. Anytime I mention "Dave" in this book you'll know who I'm talking about!

One of my treasured possessions is a copy of the *Professional Cameraman's Handbook*, for which Dave had written the Preface, inscribed to me by Dave, in which he referred to me as the "Best Camera Assistant in the World," an exaggeration, I know, but I feel terrific knowing that he thinks of me that way. A lot of that is due to the time I spent with him, in class, on the job, and just chatting.

Intentions

My intention with this book is to write about and pass on my own working system and procedures, and then to mention variations on procedures used by other Camera Assistants, if I know of any.

No one system is inherently better or worse than any other. Whatever you, as the Camera Assistant, feel comfortable with, and works for you, is right. Stick with it, until you feel the need to add or subtract or change something, and then do just that.

Every job is unique, with different equipment, personalities, schedules, budgets, and problems to solve. Different situations require different solutions.

Once I had the basics of the text, I distributed copies to a select group of Camera Assistants whose work I know and respect, and to certain Directors of Photography (the first copy went to Dave, the second to Gordon!) and technical people at equipment manufacturers and rental houses for their input, suggestions, and corrections.

This way I was able to include a wide range of systems and solutions, not just my own. I also intend to ask for feedback from readers so that subsequent editions and printings can be even more complete and valuable to future readers and Camera Assistants.

I have tried to resist the temptation to say things like "The rule is this . . .," or, "Always do this . . .," or, "Never do that . . .," etc., unless it really is necessary. I tried to give guidelines, but I don't want to be dogmatic about anything. There are too many variables and differences of opinion among professional Camera Assistants.

I also want the writing to be light, easy to read and understand, and above all, fun. A good sense of humor is an important trait for a Camera Assistant. You just can't let the people or the pressure or the hardware drive you crazy.

Whatever works is right, and what works in one situation may not work in another. Be flexible, be creative, and do whatever must be done to get the job done, and done well.

Priorities and Attitude

I do have a set of priorities that I would like to pass on. First of all, and by far most importantly, no job is worth getting hurt on; either yourself, or someone else. A basic rule of thumb heard in many industries is "One hand for the job, one hand for yourself." In other words, don't neglect your own safety while trying to do a job.

No matter what kind of hurry you're in, there's always time for safety. Never let anyone rush you into an unsafe situation. People get killed and injured every year making movies—don't be one of them. Having a movie dedicated to your memory in the opening credits is hardly a sought-after honor, nor is it worth the price. Safety must be the first priority.

Secondly, a professional does the very best job possible under the particular circumstances of the job. A professional gives 110%, not just 100%. That's what makes someone a professional. A professional takes pride in his or her work, and does the best job possible, for his or her own satisfaction, and only incidentally for the producer.

Thirdly, a professional gets paid for his or her efforts, as agreed at the beginning of the job. Sure, there are jobs that you will do that you will not get paid for, for charity, for your friends in the business, to build up a show reel for yourself or someone else, or just to meet some people who can help you later on in your career, but this should be your choice before the job begins, not the choice of a crooked producer who bounces a check on you and then leaves town. This is one reason why we have unions.

And lastly, have a good time. Film people work hard, so it's only fair that they should play hard, too. A lot of fun can be had on film sets and locations, if you don't forget the real reason why you are there.

Thus, my Professional Priorities:

- Safety
- Professionalism
- Money
- Fun

As for a professional attitude, I cannot put enough emphasis on the importance of this. You will be hired, and more importantly, re-hired or recommended to others, as a Camera Assistant, only partially for what you know, but mostly, in my opinion, for how you behave on the set.

This is what your employers and co-workers will remember. Professionals are quiet, efficient, confident, and they stay alert and can anticipate and solve problems before they become problems.

There are plenty of fragile egos and prima donnas on the set already. The very last thing the crew needs is another one. A Camera Assistant who has the time and the inclination to make a lot of small talk and chit-chat is probably not doing his or her job.

An inefficient Camera Assistant makes more work for himself and for those around him. If you have to get something from the camera truck, for example, take something back with you, such as a dead battery or exposed magazine. Planning ahead can save a lot of work and aggravation.

Confidence is important, as well. A nervous and uptight Camera Assistant only makes the job harder for himself or herself than it needs to be. Relax!

Anticipation of problems prevents them from becoming problems. You have all heard "Light Bulb" jokes about various social and ethnic and maybe even cinematic groups. My contribution to the litany:

Q: How many Camera Assistants does it take to change a light bulb?
A: Never mind, it's already done.

Therefore, my Attitude Attributes:

- Quiet
- Efficiency
- Confidence
- Anticipation

This professional attitude is far more important than being able to thread a Panaflex camera in eight seconds. No one is seriously impressed by that kind of childish show-boating.

In a way, the SECOND job you get as a Camera Assistant is more important than the FIRST, because how you behave and handle yourself the first time will determine whether or not you will be re-hired by the same producer, production manager, or Director of Photography, or recommended by them to others.

This business operates by reputation and word-of-mouth. A good-looking resume is not enough. The saying "You're only as good as your last picture" was originally coined about the film business in general, but certainly could have been aimed specifically at Camera Assistants. Your reputation is everything. You will come up against the same people over and over again in your career, and people will remember your name and your attitude and your demeanor far longer than they will remember how fast you can reload a camera. Knowledge and experience can only get you so far in the business. Attitude and professionalism get you the rest of the way.

It is also essential to stay healthy. A Camera Assistant on a feature film is a very important person, and continuity of performance is vital to the look of a film. Other departments, like the grips and electricians, usually have enough people that if someone gets sick they can be replaced without any noticeable bump or gap in the performance or efficiency of the department, but if ANY member of the Camera

Department gets sick and has to be replaced, the momentum is gone, and it takes a while to get it back.

I've been lucky—I've been out sick only five days in twenty-five years (six days, if you count one subpoenaed court appearance as a witness that I couldn't get out of), and on those five days I was so sick I couldn't get out of bed. But I wasn't so sick that I couldn't get on the phone and replace myself with another Camera Assistant so the job was not too severely inconvenienced. It's one thing to turn down work because you have something else you want to or have to do—that's one of the attractions of the freelance life—but once you accept the job, stick with it to the end!

Equally important is promptness. Better to be a half hour early than a half minute late. Give yourself enough time to get to location and to allow for the unforeseen (flat tires, traffic, weather, etc.). You are being paid to be there on time, so be there! Very little is worse for your reputation than to be habitually late, especially for a Camera Assistant.

Very often nothing else can happen on the set until actors get marked or the camera is set up and ready to look through. A Camera Assistant (First or Second) or even a Trainee who is habitually late will either be fired or will never again work with that particular crew.

Keeping in mind all of the above, I pass on to you

THE ONLY TWO ABSOLUTE RULES OF CAMERA ASSISTING:

Rule #1:
There are no rules.

Rule #2:
Never forget Rule #1.

CHAPTER 1

Introduction to Camera Assisting

What is a Camera Assistant?

A professional motion picture Camera Assistant is a very valuable commodity, all too often overlooked in the hustle and hype of contemporary motion picture production.

The Camera Assistant is the person closest to the camera on the motion picture set, usually standing quietly on the camera's left side, ever alert. The Camera Assistant is instantly recognizable by the roll of white camera tape hanging on one side of his or her belt, usually balanced by a small pouch of pens, markers, and small tools on the other side.

The Camera Assistant is wary as someone approaches the sacred machine, as watchful as a mother grizzly bear with her cubs. Yes, someone may touch the camera, may look through the eyepiece, may even change the direction the camera is pointing, but no harm shall befall that wondrous machine while the noble Camera Assistant is standing sentinel. No president, queen, or prime minister ever enjoyed protection as vigilant.

When hungry, the camera in the Assistant's charge shall be fed—film in magazines on top or on the back, electricity through cables plugged into the back or side, heat when necessary, lenses and filters in front, oil for the mechanism inside. When the camera moves to the next set or location, the Camera Assistant places a casual but resolute hand on the magazine or handle, and walks alongside in a procession of vigilance and confidence.

This delicate precision machine is to be kept safe, warm, and dry at all costs, even when the Camera Assistant may not be. It is not only the potential expense that keeps the Camera Assistant so protective, it is "the job."

The job of the professional motion picture Camera Assistant requires an unusual, demanding, and sometimes very personally satisfying and financially rewarding combination of talent and skill and luck and experience.

2 THE CAMERA ASSISTANT

The job involves technical expertise (an understanding of photography, mechanics, optics, electricity, and electronics), certain physical attributes (manual dexterity, quick reflexes, excellent peripheral vision, good judgment of time and speed and distance, physical strength, and considerable endurance), and considerable mental and attitude control (organizational ability, consistency, good memory, patience, extraordinary concentration under conditions of stress and distraction, common sense, flexibility, adaptability, a briskness of attitude and demeanor, boundless energy, and a good sense of humor).

The job may also involve considerable local and world travel, interesting and unique people, places and events, occasional excitement, meeting and working with "celebrities," substantial financial rewards for a few very good and very lucky ones, and the ever-present possibility for advancement to Camera Operator, Director of Photography, and maybe even Director.

That's the "up" side.

The "down" side is that the job all too often requires long hours, little sleep, low pay, unpredictable and seasonal freelance employment, stressful family and social life, minimal or nonexistent job security, unfair favoritism, more patience and tolerance than should be required of any mere mortal, working conditions of extreme heat, cold, wet, damp, dirt, mud, dust, smoke, etc., not even imaginable by most civilians (those outside the industry), occasional extremely hazardous situations, and the necessity to put up with the absolute dregs of humankind—the stupid, the arrogant, the dishonest, the incompetent, the criminal, and the asinine, all of whom seem to be attracted in droves to the film business.

We shoot in blizzards in winter, jungles in summer, inside coal mines and construction sites and land fills. And when it is not raining, we often make our own rain to work in.

I always tell the classes and workshops that I teach that if you can't go for 48 hours without sleep, 12 hours without food, or 8 hours without a bathroom or a phone, then stay out of this business, at least as a Camera Assistant.

Someone once summarized the motion picture production process this way—"Hours of Excruciating Boredom, Punctuated by Moments of Sheer Terror."

Still interested? Now comes the hard part—acquiring enough knowledge and experience to get yourself hired to this position, and to do the job once you are hired.

How does one prepare for a job as Camera Assistant? There are no classes in film school about Camera Assisting. I doubt if the Camera Assistant is even mentioned in most film schools. Film schools turn out directors, writers, editors, actors, and only rarely cinematographers and sound mixers. Other positions on the film crew, such as the Camera Assistants, are ignored and denigrated, if not downright slandered.

The reality is that the Camera Assistant is often, if not generally, the first one to start in the morning, the last one to finish at night, and has one of the highest responsibility levels on the set.

Accepting Responsibility

A prime requisite of the job of Camera Assistant is the ability to accept the responsibility thrust upon him or her by the job. Accepting responsibility sometimes means admitting mistakes.

If anyone else on the set makes a mistake you can usually see it right away—if an actor flubs a line, an electrician misses a light cue, a dolly moves too fast or runs over the director's foot, a microphone dips into the frame; everyone can see these things right away, and can try again.

If the Camera Assistant makes a mistake, it is quite likely that no one will see it until dailies are screened the next day. That makes these mistakes by Camera Assistants very costly to the production company because if something must be reshot because of that mistake, you have to go and set it all up again—go back to the location that you thought you were done with, relight, redress, bring in actors who thought they were wrapped, etc.

A missed focus pull, a bumpy zoom, a scratched negative, or hair in the gate can prevent the director from using the take he or she might have preferred because of an actor's performance. A mistake in film can or magazine labeling, or in inserting a filter, can mean a very expensive reshoot of an entire scene or perhaps even a whole day's work.

A Camera Assistant who is preoccupied or distracted or ill or tired can make a multithousand-dollar mistake in a second, and no one will be aware of it until the dailies screening, or until the panic phone call from the lab the next morning.

Preventing Mistakes

This is why on a set you will hear the Camera Assistants constantly asking each other if they have remembered to remove the 85 filter, or checked the amount of film left in the magazine, or called to order the high-speed camera for next week; a continual barrage of questions and reminders between them.

There are a great many things going on at any given moment, and the two Camera Assistants on the job can keep reminding each other about them. This is not a result of inexperience, or of not trusting each other, but is the mark of a professional. The airplane pilot has his checklist to run through before take-off to remind him of the hundreds of small items that can contribute to an airplane's flightworthiness, the Camera Assistants have each other.

A good Camera Assistant will never take offense at being asked if the filter has been changed, or what stock is in the magazine. It is that kind of constant dialogue and double-checking that minimizes mistakes. Directors of Photography and Camera Operators also sometimes get involved in this dialogue, especially if they have come up through the ranks and have spent any time as Camera Assistants themselves.

Everyone makes mistakes, even Camera Assistants. No one is immune. And there is nothing wrong with making mistakes. What is wrong, and potentially devastating, is failure to admit a mistake. If a mistake is made, no matter how trivial or large, the Assistant must immediately let the Director of Photography know what happened, and begin the process of repairing the damage.

Tell the Director of Photography

If something has to be reshot, it is cheaper and easier to reshoot it immediately, while the shot is still set up, or while the crew and equipment are on the same location, than to have to reschedule and reassemble everyone at a later date. The most important thing is to get the shot, regardless of the consequences.

If you do make a mistake while shooting, it's very important that you tell someone immediately—go to the Director of Photography and say "I messed up that take—I had the wrong filter in," or "I missed a focus mark," or "I zoomed the wrong way," or whatever the problem is.

But tell the Director of Photography immediately—I can't stress that strongly enough. The Director of Photography may have some harsh words for you, but you'll get the shot. Hopefully the Director of Photography will not make a spectacle out of it and embarrass you in front of the entire crew, but he may just call you over later and say emphatically, "Don't ever do that again!"

If the D.P. chooses to take you aside later and chastise you for your error, so be it, that comes with the job. We've all been yelled at, and we've all survived. But the shot is in the can, and that is the important thing. "The Show Must Go On!"

There must be a constant dialogue back and forth between the members of the Camera Crew. It's not that they don't trust each other, it's just an insurance or safety device, a mutual support system designed to minimize mistakes. Under "combat" conditions, it is all too easy to overlook some small yet vital aspect of the Camera Assistants' job. There are 100 things to remember at any one time. Only remembering 99 of them is not good enough. You've got to remember all 100 and you do that through the constant dialogue between the First and Second Assistants. It's an attempt at making the system foolproof.

When the Director of Photography asks for a lens or a filter, or gives the Assistant the lens aperture or frame rate to be set for the shot, the Assistant should repeat back the request out loud and in its entirety.

This is partly to let the D.P. know that the request has been heard correctly by the Assistant, and partly to give the D.P. one last chance to change his or her mind. Hearing the request back verbally (not just "Yes" or "OK") gives both the opportunity to decide if that is what they really want.

Generalities

A feature film, television movie, and television series will almost always have a First Camera Assistant and a Second Camera Assistant. A television commercial or documentary usually will have only one Camera Assistant, although more and more commercial shoots are beginning to realize the value of having a second pair of eyes, a second pair of hands, and a second brain next to that camera.

I have to keep qualifying my statements with "usually" and "almost always" because there are no hard and fast rules about this business, only generalities. I will try in this book not to use absolutes to avoid getting into trouble with my readers. So many of these decisions are based on the amount of money available in the budget, or on the working styles and experience of various individuals, that there are no hard and fast rules.

The Camera Assistant has a very large responsibility on any set, no matter how small or how large the set may be. I've invented a scale I call the "RSI"—the "Responsibility: Salary Index," and I have determined through careful research that the Second Camera Assistant has the highest Responsibility to Salary Index on the set. In other words, the Second Camera Assistant has got one of the highest levels of responsibility compared with his salary, and the First Camera Assistant is not far behind him.

The next chapter describes in detail the respective responsibilities of the Camera Assistants and other members of the Camera Department and other departments on the set or location.

CHAPTER **2**

Responsibilities of the Camera Assistant

Overview

The first logical step to take in a volume about professional motion picture camera assisting is to define what a Camera Assistant is and what a Camera Assistant does. In order to do this, however, we have to define what a lot of other people do as well, so it is clear how the Camera Assistant fits in to the team effort required for any motion picture project.

Filmmaking is a highly specialized undertaking. Neither the term "Art" nor the term "Business" describes the process adequately by themselves. The reality of filmmaking is that it is both an art and a business, and inseparably so. Perhaps "Industry" is the best description. Even the smallest, lowest-budget film involves many people performing a multitude of artistic, technical and administrative tasks.

The larger the budget and the more complicated the project, the more people are going to be directly involved in the manufacture of the product, and the more highly specialized they will be. This should be obvious to anyone who has sat through the ten minutes of screen credits found on typical recent theatrical motion pictures, especially the special effects action blockbusters we all love to watch.

Literally hundreds of different people work for months and even years on a particular project, rigidly divided into specific job titles and departments. Truly, the cinema is the most collaborative of arts. A painter or sculptor can lock himself or herself in a studio alone and produce a finished work. A writer can retreat to the beach or the mountains in solitude and return with a completed book or play. But you can't do that with a film. No one individual can hope to know or perform all of the work required for the completion of a motion picture.

Every individual motion picture project has its own individual circumstances and personalities involved, and will handle this specialization and crewing differently, so I can only generalize in the Division of Responsibility list that follows. Individual crews will inevitably work differently, and may draw the lines between the job responsibilities differently, but in general, the following represents a fairly complete and accurate listing of job responsibilities of the Camera Department for a typical motion picture production.

Such a list can never be completely and absolutely accurate for all productions, of course, because shooting styles and circumstances differ between productions, and because of the differences between the ways that different crews work together, especially if they have been working together for any length of time.

Crews that work job after job together evolve into living and breathing entities, fitting together like the pieces of a jigsaw puzzle, complementing each others' abilities and experiences, tuning in to each others' thoughts and needs, often nonverbally. It is a wonderful thing to experience!

The **CAMERA DEPARTMENT** on a typical theatrical feature-length motion picture in this country generally has five members for all principal photography when a single camera is in operation. (Notice all of the qualifiers in the previous sentence: "typical," "in this country," "generally," "principal photography," "single camera." You see what I'm up against?!)

Their titles and usual responsibilities are outlined below:

Director of Photography (also known as "First Cameraman" or "Lighting Cameraman," and abbreviated either as "D.P." or "D.O.P.")

Determine Photographic Style for Project
Maintain Photographic Continuity and Integrity
Work with Director, Production Designer, Costume Designer, and Makeup Artist in Determining the Visual Style of the Production
Select Camera Operator and First Camera Assistant and Refer them to Production Manager for Hiring
Select Gaffer and Key Grip and Refer them to Production Manager For Hiring
Determine with Production Manager and/or Assistant Director:
  Size of Crew Required
  Shooting Schedule
  Order in which Scenes Should be Shot at a Particular Location
  Order in which Shots Should be Filmed for a Particular Scene
Scout Proposed Shooting Locations with Director and Department Heads
Determine with Gaffer and Key Grip Electrical Power and Equipment Requirements for each Location
Specify Film Gauge, Format, and Aspect Ratio to be Used
Specify Camera Negative Film Stock(s) to be Used
Specify Film Laboratory to be Used
Specify Camera Equipment List
Specify Camera Equipment Rental House to be Used
Specify Lighting and Grip Equipment to be Used
Specify Lighting and Grip Equipment Rental House to be Used
Shoot Tests of Film Emulsions to be Used

Shoot Tests of Cameras, Lenses, and Filters to be Used
Shoot Tests of Wardrobe, Makeup, Hair Dressing, Scenery Elements, Props, Special Effects, and Process Components
Work with Director to Determine Actor and Camera Blocking for each Scene
Maintain Proper Action and Screen Direction
Specify Composition of Shots
Set up Shots:
    Specify Camera Position
    Specify Lens
    Specify Filters, Mattes, Diffusion
    Specify Dolly or Crane Move
Direct Lighting of Studio and/or Location Settings
Specify Aperture Setting and Exposure for each shot
Issue Instructions to Laboratory for Proper Handling and Development of Exposed Film
Issue Instructions to Laboratory for Proper Exposure and Color Timing/ Printing of Dailies Workprint and/or Video Transfer
Participate in Postproduction:
    Determine Release Print Stock Type to be Used
    Participate in Color Timing of Answer Print
    Ensure Contrast and Color Continuity of Release Prints
    Ensure Quality of First-Run Release Prints
    Participate in Video Transfer (for Television Movies, Commercials, Music Videos, and Videocassette Release of Theatrical Motion Picture)

Camera Operator
Execute Smooth Camera Movements
Maintain Composition Specified by Director of Photography and/ or Director
Certify each take as to Technical Requirements:
    Focus Sharp
    Camera and/or Dolly and/or Zoom Moves Smooth
    No Microphones, Lights, Stands, or Cables in Frame
    No Lens Flares During Shot
    No Unwanted Shadows During Shot
    No Unwanted Reflections on Glass or Metal Surfaces During Shot
Certify each take as to Artistic Requirements:
    Proper Composition Maintained
    Proper Headroom Maintained
    Actors' Movements Properly in Frame
    Actors' Sightlines Correct
Establish a Good Rapport with the Actors and Director

First Camera Assistant
Responsible for Care and Maintenance of Camera Equipment
Select Second Camera Assistant and Refer to Production Manager for Hiring

10 THE CAMERA ASSISTANT

- Select Film Loader (if Applicable) and Refer to Production Manager for Hiring
- Select (with Second Camera Assistant) a Camera Trainee (if Applicable) and Refer to Production Manager for Hiring
- Preproduction Equipment Check-Out:
  - Make Sure Equipment Inventory Complete
  - Make Sure All Equipment in Working Order
- Determine Expendable Supplies to be Purchased
- Order and Obtain Expendable Supplies
- Ensure Proper Gate, Mask, and Groundglass Installed in Camera
- Ensure Accuracy of Groundglass Markings
- Assemble, Warm Up, Balance, and Prepare Camera for Shooting
- Clean and Lubricate Camera Movement as Required
- Check Flange Focal Depth as Necessary
- Check Film Gap Setting as Necessary
- Check Shutter and Movement Phasing as Necessary
- Keep Camera Clean and Properly Lubricated
- Keep Camera as Quiet as Possible
- Check Parallax and Rack-over Status (if Necessary)
- Check for Camera and/or Magazine Scratches
- Ensure Camera is Running at Correct Speed
- Ensure Security of Mounted Camera
- Never Leave Camera Unattended
- Find Out from D.P. which Film Stock(s) are to be Used for Each Set or Location
- Thread Proper Film in Camera
- Determine Proper Focus Setting as Required
- Determine Split Focus Settings as Required
- Determine Depth-of-Field as Necessary
- Set Focus on Lens
- Set Aperture on Lens
- Prevent and/or Eliminate Lens Flares
- Execute Variable Shutter Changes as Required
- Execute Focus Changes (Follow Focus) During Shot as Required
- Execute Focal Length Changes (Zooming) During Shot as Required
- Execute Aperture Changes (Aperture Pull) During Shot as Required
- Execute Use of Color Correction Filters, Special Effects Filters, Graduated Filters, Mattes, and Diffusion Filters, as Required
- Clean Filters as Required
- Change Lenses
- Clean Lenses as Required
- Ensure that Lenses are Properly Supported on Camera
- Check Gate for Hairs, Film Chips, and Debris
- Keep Accurate Record of Lenses Used, Filters Used, Exposure, Shutter Settings, Focus, Aperture, and other Variables, if Required

Change Camera Batteries as Required
Ensure that Batteries are Properly Charged
Ensure that enough Film is Remaining in Magazine for Next Shot
Notify Assistant Director of Footage Remaining in Magazine and When Reloading is Necessary
Change Magazines and Rethread Camera
Notify Assistant Director when Reloading is Complete and Camera is Ready to Continue Shooting
Disassemble and Store Camera Equipment
Perform Routine Camera Maintenance
Order Special or Additional Camera Equipment as Required
Find Additional Camera Crew Personnel as Required and Refer to Production Manager for Hiring
Ensure that Entire Camera Crew is Notified of Next Day's Call Time and Location (don't trust the Production Staff to do this!)

Second Camera Assistant
Assist First Camera Assistant with above Duties
Maintain Inventory Control:
    Camera Equipment
    Unexposed Film (Raw Stock)
    Exposed Film
    Expendable Supplies
Order Raw Stock as Required, Maintaining Continuity of Emulsion Numbers Whenever Possible
Ensure Security of Camera Storage Facilities and/or Truck
Ensure Light-Tightness of Darkroom Facilities
Ensure Light-Tightness of Magazines
Clean Magazines as Required
Load, Unload, and Reload Film Magazines
Label Loaded Magazines
Set Actors' Marks
Operate Slate and Clapsticks
Keep Accurate and Complete Camera Reports
Check Takes to be Printed with Continuity Supervisor
Charge Camera Batteries as needed
Label, Pack, and Ship Exposed Film to Laboratory
Label Unexposed Short Ends and Recans
Keep Payroll Records for Camera Crew
Fill Out Weekly Time Cards for Camera Crew
Keep Meal Money/Per Diem Money Records for Camera Crew
Keep Petty Cash Records for Camera Crew
Maintain Telephone Contact with:
    Production Office
    Equipment Rental House

Laboratory
Editing Room
Union Office
Keep Copies of all Relevant Paperwork:
  Camera Reports
  Daily Film Reports
  Film Inventory Reports
  Laboratory Purchase Orders
  Equipment Rental Contracts
  Supply Purchase Orders
Relay Any Special Instructions from Director of Photography to Film Laboratory or Color Timer
Obtain Reports from Laboratory on Dailies and Relay to Director of Photography

On certain films, there may be employed an additional person in the Camera Crew, known as a **Film Loader** or **Camera Loader,** also occasionally known as a **Second Second Camera Assistant,** or a **Camera Trainee.**

Whatever the title, this additional Assistant helps out the Second Camera Assistant, especially in the darkroom and with the slating and paperwork. Various crews assign different responsibilities to this extra Assistant, so it is difficult to be specific.

Still Photographer
Shoot ALL Still Photographs Required for:
  Location Scouting
  Publicity
  Continuity (Action, Props, Wardrobe, Hair, Makeup)
  Photographic Props and Set Dressings
  Photographic Scenic Backdrops

Compromises

One Director of Photography I showed this list to laughed and told me that he rarely gets to choose the equipment rental house or film lab or to do some of the other things on the list. Obviously, this list represents the ideal job, with the ideal budget, the ideal producer, and the ideal production company. I know that such jobs are rare, and that often, because of financial or political reasons, deals and compromises have to be made.

When the production company owns their own film laboratory, or has a past relationship with a particular lab, for example, the D.P. may be pressured into using it instead of the laboratory of the D.P.'s choice, even if it means shipping the exposed film from distant locations. Some decisions may have been made and deals signed before the Director of Photography is even hired.

Just as there are some Directors of Photography who command higher salaries than others, some D.P.'s have more "clout" than others, and put some of these things into their individual contracts with the producer, such as the right to be there for the video transfer and the right to bring his or her favorite crew to location to work on the job.

But sometimes these decisions are already made, and usually for financial reasons. There may not be enough money in the budget for multiple cameras or cranes. The Director of Photography may be restricted to six days of Steadicam instead of the ten that the director and D.P. may want. Some scenes may have to be shot in real locations instead of on sets built in studios. Studios are usually easier to shoot in because of soundproofing, weatherproofing, and the ability to remove walls and/or ceilings of sets for ease of lighting and access, but they are also often more expensive to rent and build in than real locations.

There may not be time to shoot wardrobe tests, or to scout all of the locations. The company may have a long-standing relationship with a particular camera equipment rental house or laboratory. Some equipment companies refuse to rent equipment to certain production companies who may have been "slow" at paying their rental bills in the past.

These and other compromises have to be accepted as an inevitable part of the film business.

Additional Camera Crew Personnel

Most shooting is done by a single camera, known as the "A" camera with the "First Unit," the term used to describe the crew shooting scenes involving the principal actors and dialogue, or "principal photography."

The "Second Unit" describes the crew shooting scenes in a different location than the "First Unit," possibly with photo doubles or stunt doubles representing the principal actors (such as driving in cars, seen from a distance), or scenes with no actors at all (such as scenes with animals, or showing traffic jams, sunsets, ships in the harbor, or inserts of door-knobs turning and traffic lights changing), or footage establishing locations (such as panoramic scenic landscapes or city skylines), or elements for special effects matting use, such as scenes with models or of fire effects, or plates for front or rear projection uses, etc.

On days when Multiple Cameras are in use simultaneously on the same set or location, such as for scenes involving stunts, animals, children, or large numbers of extras, these extra cameras are labeled "B," "C," "D," etc., and there will be additional Camera Assistants and Camera Operators employed to work with those cameras, generally one First Camera Assistant and one Camera Operator for each additional camera, with additional Second Camera Assistants as required by the particular circumstances.

These multiple camera crews, often referred to as "Second Camera," or "B Camera" crews, will work with the main crew on the same set or location, will use equipment specially ordered for them or carried as "back-up" camera equipment by the primary, or "A Camera" crew, and will shoot film stock ordered and inventoried by the "A Camera" crew.

They may only work for part of the day, or even for only a single shot in a day. They will sometimes have their own call times for reporting to work, and may be wrapped early and sent home if circumstances permit, but otherwise, they are still considered part of the primary crew, or "First Unit."

This "B Camera" is used for additional simultaneous coverage of a First Unit scene, that is, two different shots accomplished simultaneously, with cameras positioned side-by-side, or in totally different areas, with the same or different focal length lenses, but still filming the same actors doing the same scene.

Sometimes the cameras will be set up to film a wide shot (or master shot) and a medium shot or a medium shot and a close-up simultaneously, or two close-ups of two different actors speaking to each other, or whatever other combination of shots will save the company time, energy, and money.

Depending on the personalities involved and the style of shooting involved, this "B Camera" crew may work every day of the production, getting those simultaneous shots whenever there is room for them in the set, or when it is convenient and efficient to do so.

When using a child actor, for example, most states have laws restricting the number of hours a child may work on the set, so if the crew can shoot the child's close-ups and medium shots simultaneously, more shooting can be completed each day, even within the restricted hours. Multiple cameras are often used when filming dance numbers, stunts, or when real events have been incorporated into the script, such as parades, concerts, horse races, sports events, or circuses.

It is not always possible or efficient to shoot with two cameras simultaneously. The sets or locations may be too small to allow two cameras with crews inside to shoot, or there may be lighting problems trying to shoot two different angles at once, or having two cameras may be too distracting for the performers. But when it is possible, this practice can save the company much time, and time means money in this business.

On jobs where there is a Second Unit filming at some other location from the First Unit, or where there is a Model Unit or Matte (or Process Plate) Unit or Special Effects Unit working on other portions of the film, obviously there will be additional Camera Assistants and Camera Operators employed, as well as other Directors of Photography.

These "Second" and other units will generally function as totally separate entities, with little or no exchange of personnel or equipment between each other or with the "First Unit." The Camera Assistants with these separate units will order their own camera equipment, do their own check-out, order their own film raw stock, keep separate paperwork, send their own exposed film to the lab, and in general, behave as if they were the ONLY camera unit on the production.

A Second Unit may also be split off from the First Unit, by sending the Camera Operator and the Second Assistant off to shoot the sunset while the rest of the camera crew loads up the truck for a company move to another location, for example. Once they have the shot they need, they could rejoin the First Unit.

The First Unit crew may not even know that a Second Unit exists. We once came in to work one cold December morning to find that a Second Unit crew we didn't even know was shooting on our film had raided our equipment truck in the middle of the night and used all of our nice, warm, fully charged batteries, leaving behind their cold, wet, discharged batteries. They did leave us a polite note of thanks, however.

We started a day's work with two cameras shooting outside in December in New York City with only two charged batteries until we could get some more delivered from the rental house when they opened two hours later. If the Second Assistant and I had not each taken a battery home with us for recharging, we wouldn't have had any. I had some well-chosen words for the production manager about this situation, needless to say. It never happened again, at least on that job. We also changed the combination to the padlocks on the camera truck doors, just to be sure.

Individuality

Specific Directors of Photography may have their own ways of delegating responsibility within the Camera Crew. For example, some D.P.'s do their lighting by eye, and then when they are done, send the First Assistant out into the set with a light meter to get an exposure reading.

Some D.P.'s will give to the First Assistant a basic exposure reading, and the First will have to calculate in any filter, frame rate, or shutter angle exposure factors to determine the correct shooting aperture; some D.P.'s will do their own calculations for these factors.

Some D.P.'s prefer to keep their own records of lenses, filters, exposure, shutter angle, etc. for each shot, anticipating a future reshoot or need to match something for a succeeding scene shot out of sequence; some prefer that the First Camera Assistant keep such records, and some prefer the Second Camera Assistant. Many D.P.'s keep no records at all.

Geographic Differences

There are also geographic differences in the way that crews divide responsibility. In Great Britain, for example, the Director of Photography is usually known as the Lighting Cameraman, and rarely even looks through the camera. The Camera Operator on the job works closely with the Director to compose and block scenes, while the Lighting Cameraman concerns himself with lighting the scene. In other words, they are splitting up the responsibilities of the American Director of Photography between two people, a Lighting Director and a Camera Operator.

Elsewhere in Europe, the decision NOT to employ a Camera Operator is often made, allowing (or requiring) the Director of Photography to operate the camera during filming. Sometimes in this country there is no Camera Operator on a job, but it is usually a budget consideration, rather than an artistic one, to have the Director of Photography operate the camera. Some European cinematographers claim they cannot do their job of ensuring photographic integrity unless they operate the camera themselves.

There's one well-known film director who joined the camera union so that he could operate the camera himself on pictures he was directing, claiming he could direct more efficiently looking through the camera during the shooting. It's just a matter of different approaches based on different training, experience, and personal preference.

When Directors of Photography from Europe or elsewhere used to operating their own camera, or used to the British system of being primarily involved in lighting the set and having the Camera Operator work closely with the director on blocking and composing the scenes, come to the United States to work on a film, they sometimes have problems adjusting to the "American" system described above, causing problems on the set until they get used to a different style of working.

None of these systems is inherently better or worse than any other system, and each has its advantages and disadvantages.

The "American" system, for lack of a better description, and the "British" system, while employing another person on the crew as Camera Operator, do allow the Director of Photography to concentrate on lighting and exposure, and allow him or her to watch the changing exterior light more carefully, and watch to see whether or not the actors hit their marks for their big close-up, while the Camera Operator can concentrate on watching for microphone shadows, bumpy camera dolly moves, maintaining proper composition and adequate headroom, etc.

It is also a faster and more efficient operation for the Camera Operator, First Camera Assistant, and Dolly Grip to be able to rehearse a complicated or difficult dolly move while the Director of Photography is still lighting, therefore being ready to shoot sooner than letting the D.P. finish with the lighting, and THEN starting to rehearse for the camera move, with the D.P. now in the role of Camera Operator.

Another advantage is that while the Camera Operator, director, and actors are rehearsing one setup with the Dolly Grip and Camera Assistants, the Director of Photography can often move ahead to the next setup with the Gaffer and Key Grip, and begin roughing in the lighting, or at least begin thinking about it.

The Camera Operator, by releasing the Director of Photography from total involvement in every shot, can be the factor which can bring in the production on time and on budget. A Camera Operator can easily save the company more money than they are paying him in salary and benefits. I cannot imagine a job where having a Camera Operator did not save a tremendous amount of time. A Camera Operator is one of the best investments a film company can make.

In Britain, First Camera Assistants are called "Focus Pullers" or "Focus Assistants." I've never liked these terms because Focus is only one of the many, many things that a Camera Assistant does, but it is a popular description in Britain and Europe. The English name for the Second Camera Assistant is even worse: "Clapper/Loader." The less said about that appellation, the better for all concerned.

Other Departments

It is also important to understand the relationships between other departments and the Camera Department, and the Camera Assistants in particular.

Obviously, not every member of the crew has direct or significant dealings with the Camera Assistants, but some crew members have very direct and very important interaction with the Camera Assistants on a daily basis.

Keeping in mind that different crews work differently with each other, and that regional geographic differences exist, please accept the following as a small sample of crew interaction. There is obviously more to each of the relationships described below, but you will get the idea from this brief summary.

Grips

Probably the most important one of these relationships is with the **Dolly Grip**. A good Dolly Grip is worth his or her weight in gold to the Camera Assistants. A bad Dolly Grip, or even worse than bad, an INDIFFERENT Dolly Grip, will be an endless nightmare. The First Assistant depends on the Dolly Grip to ensure camera security and to hit very specific marks with a dolly move.

The Focus calculations made by the First Assistant can only be accurate if the dolly is in the right place at the right time, in relation to the actors, who may also be moving. This shouldn't be a problem with an experienced Dolly Grip (although I've been surprised several times by sloppy moves by experienced grips who should be able to do better). The sloppiness I'm referring to may not even be visible on the screen, except when the focus is soft because the dolly winds up in the wrong position and the First is not paying close enough attention. Who gets the blame if the focus is soft because of the dolly being in the wrong place? I'll give you a hint—it's not the Dolly Grip!

It is vital to impress on ANY Dolly Grip at the beginning of the job the importance of hitting the marks accurately and with the proper timing. This can, and must be done diplomatically, of course. At the very least, get them to agree to letting you know immediately if they happen to miss the mark appreciably, so that you can make whatever focus adjustments might be appropriate.

This communication with the Dolly Grip can be done even before the scene is cut by the use of hand signals and gestures. Get in the habit of glancing over at the Dolly Grip after every move, to see if he needs to show you how far he missed the mark by. As an added precaution, the Assistant should also mark some visible part of the dolly and the floor as a check on the final dolly position.

A good relationship with the **Grip Department** in general can make the difference between a smooth job and a constant and exhausting battle. The grips, if they like you, can make the job of the Camera Assistants much easier, from helping out with moving the ton or so of camera equipment cases that we use daily, to anticipating the need of a flag to prevent lens flare before it is asked for, to the preparation of an umbrella for the Camera BEFORE it begins to rain.

Grips are especially useful to the Camera Department at the very beginning of the job, in working with the Carpenters in building a darkroom and shelves for the camera truck. On the East Coast the camera truck rarely remains a camera truck between jobs, unless it belongs to one of the camera equipment rental houses. Many productions just rent an empty truck. Each time a job begins, another truck needs to be rigged with darkroom and shelves. These are built and installed by the carpenters and grips already on the company payroll, and usually at the studio carpenter shop. A good relationship with them will guarantee a truck you will want to work out of, and after all, the camera truck becomes your "Home Away From Home" for months at a time.

I keep sketches and even photographs of various truck sizes and layouts, and copy these for the carpenters and grips once I know what equipment we will be carrying and what size truck we will have.

Camera Trucks on the West Coast are generally larger, fancier, and newer than on the East Coast, and often have many user-friendly amenities such as carpeted shelves, fluorescent lighting, and maybe even air conditioning for the darkroom, not usually found in the East.

Sound

The relationship with the **Sound Department** is also very important. On the East Coast, at least, the odds are about 100:1 that the Camera and Sound Departments will be sharing the same equipment truck, and like roommates everywhere, compromises will have to be made with allocating shelf space and floor or aisle space.

Think of it as eight or nine people (feature sound crews are usually three people) and two or three tons of equipment occupying a space not much bigger than a walk-in closet. Space is always going to be tight, no matter how big the truck is, and when it is raining, or cold, everyone will want to try and stay dry and warm between setups, and where better to do this than the camera truck? Winters are always the worst, because everyone wants to store their boots, heavy down coats, and rain gear on the truck, using up even more precious space.

The Sound Department has many of the same concerns and problems as the Camera Department—they also have expensive and fragile equipment that needs to be kept secure, warm, and dry. They keep very similar paperwork, need very similar supplies, etc. Video Assist also ties together Sound and Camera Departments, since both will have to deal with monitors and their cables, for picture and playback sound.

If Time Code slates are being used, these slates must be periodically "jammed" or fed with the correct clock signal from the sound recorder to ensure proper synchronization between picture and sound.

Script

The **Script Supervisor** (or **Continuity Supervisor**) is generally considered an honorary member of the Camera Department, because he or she is usually a one-person department on the set with no separate vehicle like the other departments, and needs a place to store boots, parka, folding chair, etc. The Second Assistant, especially, will spend a great deal of time in conversation with the Script Supervisor, getting the correct scene numbers to write on the slates, checking their lists of takes to be printed, and making sure that they know when we change camera rolls and lenses.

Script Supervisors will also have their own particular systems of operation. Sometimes all they want for the notes they keep is what camera roll we're on and what lens is up; sometimes they want everything—what filters we're using, what aperture we set, even what the focus settings are during the shot. Get used to their individual systems as soon as possible.

Sometimes they prefer to go over printed takes repeatedly throughout the day, usually immediately after each scene is completed. Others prefer to wait until the end of the day and go over the whole day's work at one time, with someone from the Sound Department present as well, since they require the same information for their sound reports.

Some script people prefer to write out lists of the takes to be printed and present copies to the Second Assistant and to the Sound Department. Others will even take the Camera Report sheets from the Second and circle all the takes to be printed themselves. Others will read out the printed take numbers to the Second, then check over the completed Camera Report sheets and initial them as correct.

Any of these systems is fine if it works consistently. There is very little more embarrassing than getting to dailies and discovering that a take the director wanted to see was inadvertently not printed. Unfortunately, this business thrives on "finger-pointing" and passing the blame. This is why the Second ALWAYS keeps one of the carbon copies of each Camera Report, to check over if a take intended to be printed is somehow not printed, to see where the blame lies—with the script person, with the Assistant, or with the lab itself. Childish? Of course, but also very common.

I also consider it the Script Supervisor's responsibility to chase down the Second Camera Assistant at the end of the day and confirm that the selected takes indicated on the Camera Reports for the day's work are correct and complete. But sometimes the Second needs to chase after the script person. Whoever does it, get those numbers right!

Gaffer and Electrical Department

The relationship with the **Gaffer and the Electrical Department** is usually of more importance for a location picture than a studio picture, but should never be neglected. Getting electrical power to the camera truck from the generator, or from the location power supply, should be a high priority, especially in the cold, because you will want to keep the truck and the darkroom as warm as possible, and you probably want to keep batteries on charge whenever convenient.

VERY IMPORTANT NOTE: Make sure that the power run to the truck is **Alternating Current (AC)** power, **NOT Direct Current (DC)**! All battery chargers I've seen and worked with require **AC** power, and their chargers tend to catch fire or even explode if fed **DC**! Lights and heaters will work just as well with **AC** or **DC**, but battery chargers need **AC**.

The Second should ask the Gaffer to delegate one of the electricians in his or her crew to run a power cable to the camera truck each time you arrive at location. Get them used to doing it immediately at each location. And keep checking with the

Electricians to make sure they are supplying you with AC and not DC. The best way to tell is by the kind of lights in use. Arcs use DC, HMI lights use AC, and Tungsten lights can use either one. And in the rain, or near water, DC is much safer to have on the set than AC. Many generator trucks and trailers are capable of supplying both AC and DC. Keep checking to make sure you are getting the right type of electricity. Having the same Electrician run power to the camera truck consistently is the best way.

The Electricians can also be of use to the Camera Department in the truck rigging at the beginning of the job, with installing power outlets, lights, heaters, and possibly even a battery lighting system. In some areas, the Electrical crew will also charge camera batteries overnight, if you want them to. Sometimes you will even get the batteries back the next morning, and sometimes they will actually be charged. Make sure you find someone dependable if you elect this option, and NEVER give them ALL of your batteries at the same time!

My favorite Second Assistant, the last crew member leaving the location one evening, spied the four camera batteries he had entrusted to one of the Electricians calmly sitting all by themselves in the grass at the side of the road. He took them home with him, charged them up, and never mentioned his discovery when coming in the next morning, except to me. By that time on that job, we were used to the Electricians forgetting to charge the batteries or forgetting to bring them in the next day. It took the offending electrician until after lunch that day to work up the courage to approach and confess his transgression. We all had a good laugh at his distress and embarrassment. It never happened again, at least not on that job.

One California cinematographer reacted very violently when he read in an early version of this manuscript that on the East Coast, electricians sometimes charge the camera batteries after the day's shooting. He declared that such "dereliction of duty" on the part of the Camera Assistants would be "grounds for instant dismissal" in Hollywood. Execution by firing squad perhaps?

This is yet another example of the geographic differences in the ways crews work, and also of a phenomenon known the world over as "Hollywoodism," the belief held by certain people (in Hollywood) that only in Hollywood are movies made correctly, and that in any other part of the world, there are no professional cinema technicians to be found. They seem to have forgotten that the movies were born on the East Coast, in and around New York City, and that a large segment of the Hollywood film population is transplanted East Coasters.

Teamsters

The **Camera Truck Driver (Teamster)** is a very important person to have on your side. The right driver can save you endless work, by getting the truck as close as possible to the shooting location, moving the truck periodically during the day to keep it close to the shooting location (especially at wrap time!), anticipating moves between locations, helping with the lift-gate, and opening up the back of the truck as soon as possible after a move or upon arriving in the morning.

The camera truck, because the darkroom is inside and the Second Assistant has to download and can out and prepare all the paperwork each night, is usually the last truck to leave the location after wrap, so a cooperative and pleasant driver is essential. I sometimes think the drivers get together at the beginning of the job and draw straws. The loser gets the camera truck.

Assistant Director

The **Assistant Director** is the prime source of information on the set. Unfortunately, he or she is also the prime source of misinformation. The A.D. knows, or should know, or at least could find out for you, where the next location is, what time wrap is likely to be, what time the dailies will be screened, where you are going to be next week, when the scene with the Steadicam is scheduled, when the "B Camera" will be required, when lunch will be, where the craft service table is, etc.

The A.D. is often also the person to talk to about moving the camera truck closer to the set, about how many shots are remaining, about when to start moving nonessential equipment back to the truck, about where the phones or the bathrooms are, etc.

In return, I try to let the A.D. know when we reach the point of having one or two more takes' worth of film in the magazine. Sometimes he or she has other things that need to be attended to, and if they know that a camera reload is coming after the next take, they can often get ready to do this other thing during that pause as well, such as getting the makeup or hair person ready to give the actors a check over, or to give the extras a bathroom break. I also make sure to let the A.D. know when the camera is reloaded and ready to continue shooting.

There is other information I can pass on to the A.D. during the day. I stand closer to the Director and Director of Photography than the A.D. does, usually, and hear things the A.D. doesn't. I can sometimes give the A.D. the framelines of the shot so he or she can begin clearing civilians or setting background extras or moving vehicles. I can let him or her know what the D.P. or the director wants to do for the next shot, or let him know that the D.P. or the Camera Operator has gone to the phone or bathroom, etc. I can also pass along information from my discussions with the D.P. about which locations or scenes will involve multiple cameras or cranes or Steadicam, etc.

A good A.D. is essential to a smooth-flowing shoot. A good A.D. will see everything that goes on and will make sure that everyone is ready before calling for a rehearsal or shot. A good A.D. will notice if the Camera Operator is discussing something with the Director or Director of Photography, or if the First is running the tape measure out to check a focus mark, or if the Second is changing the number on the slate or fetching a different filter to be used for the shot, and will wait until all these things are finished and all the necessary people are ready and in position before yelling "Roll Sound." You can spot an inexperienced A.D. immediately by how much attention he or she pays to what is going on around the camera.

Production Manager

The **Production Manager** (or **Unit Production Manager**) is rarely on the set, but is still vital to a smooth-flowing operation and a happy Camera Department. The Second will spend a lot of time on the phone with the Production Manager, especially at the beginning of the job. Usually anything to do with money must be cleared with the P.M., from renting an additional camera, to hiring additional Operators and Assistants, to ordering more or different raw stock, to ordering expendables, to getting reimbursed for petty cash expenditures, to arguing over the overtime hours on the time card. The Production Manager's job is a tough one, and his job is NOT to be generous.

Hopefully, long before the job starts, the individual salary and kit rental and per diem amounts and overtime guarantee and other such matters will have been settled to everyone's satisfaction, but it is not unusual to have to "discuss" these things further once shooting begins, especially after the first paycheck arrives. Production managers have a lot on their minds, and sometimes "forget" what you have agreed on in previous conversations. It helps to have a written and signed deal memo, if you can get one.

Production Office Coordinator

The **Production Office Coordinator** (P.O.C.), sometimes known as the **Production Secretary**, is the key person at the production office. They are the source and often the final destination of all paperwork: scripts, script updates and rewrites, shooting schedules, time cards, deal memos, petty cash forms, crew lists, film inventory forms, purchase orders, invitations to the wrap party, etc.

They will order film raw stock and have it delivered to you when you need it, will arrange for shipments of special equipment from out of town, and will telephone additional crew people to give them their call time and location for the next day, etc.

Many times they seem to be just a voice on the phone, almost never seen on the set. More than once I've gone through an entire job without ever seeing them in person, until the wrap party.

Others

There are, of course, many other people on the set who have an effect on the work of the Camera Assistant, but these mentioned above are the most important.

A happy crew is an efficient crew. You should constantly remind yourself that the crew is your "family"; even more than a family, since you will be with them more hours and under more pressure and intimacy than with your real family, at least for the length of the shoot. Make a real effort to get along with everyone, as difficult as it may be. It's very important to the job and to your own well-being.

TEAMWORK!

CHAPTER 3

Film Formats and Aspect Ratios

Film Gauges

Three general rules apply to cinematic image quality. The first is that the larger the original camera negative, the better the image quality. The second is that image quality deteriorates with each generation of printing. The third is that the larger the projected image, the poorer the image.

Putting these rules together, the better the original image, the better the screen image. The best images come from a large negative, and are seen on smaller screens from prints with few generations between negative and release print. In other words, film will rarely look better than it does in the Dailies Screening Room. Using a smaller gauge negative, or subjecting the image to repeated generations for optical or special effects work, or projecting the image onto a larger screen, all deteriorate the image.

There are currently four film gauges (widths) in common usage: 8mm, 16mm, 35mm, and 65/70mm.

8mm (Regular 8mm and Super 8mm) is almost exclusively an amateur gauge, and as such will not be discussed here, except to say that attempts have been made to use this film size professionally, or at least semiprofessionally, but these attempts have failed because the tiny negative could not be successfully enlarged for distribution. The picture quality was just too poor. The development and popularity of the hand held video "Camcorders" has pretty much wiped out Super 8mm film, much the way Super 8mm wiped out regular 8mm.

16mm film was originally designed back in the 1920s for amateur use, but advances in film stock and lens quality, and camera weight and size have made 16mm the medium of choice for most documentary films, industrial films, training films, etc., as well as for certain television commercials and lower-budget feature film production, and even a few bold television series. Many fine 16mm cameras and lenses are available from various manufacturers. 16mm negatives can also be enlarged ("blown up") for distribution in 35mm, especially when shot in the format known as "Super 16mm." For television usage, both in television series and commercials, 16mm photography is often difficult to distinguish from 35mm, when seen only on a 19-inch TV set.

35mm film is the worldwide industry standard for professional feature film production, and has been for many years. Originally developed and patented by Thomas Edison, this gauge has survived virtually intact for nearly 100 years. Several different formats and screen aspect ratios have enjoyed popularity using the same 35mm film. From the early silent hand-cranked cameras to the modern crystal-controlled production cameras, 35mm has been and continues to be used for every type of film production.

65/70mm film is described this way because the cameras use a 65mm width negative, and those negatives are printed on 70mm film for projection; the extra 5mm providing space for the soundtrack on release prints, and the absence of the extra 5mm providing considerable savings in camera raw stock costs, camera size and weight, laboratory costs, etc. While currently enjoying a resurgence, with several camera manufacturers building new 65mm cameras, 65mm photography is only rarely used for filming entire films, but is used instead on certain sequences in films, for scenes that will be involved in such image degrading postproduction processes as matting, split screen, superimposition, or other optical wizardry.

The larger the original camera negative, the better the image quality, so by starting with the largest negative available, the extra generations necessitated by the optical special effects process will cause the minimum of image quality loss. The resulting composite special effects scenes will at least equal, and generally excel, the image quality of the 35mm dialogue scenes with which they will be intercut.

Film Formats

Film normally runs through the camera vertically, exposing a series of pictures in sequence. The width of the exposed frame is determined by the width of the film material being used and by the size and placement of the perforations.

Regularly spaced perforations are found along one or both edges, and are used to propel the film through the camera between exposures, and to hold the film steady during exposure.

But it is also possible to move the film through the camera horizontally, resulting in a larger negative and often a wider picture shape because now the image height is determined by the width of the film instead of the image width. I have never heard of 8mm or 16mm film being run through the camera horizontally, but there are horizontal systems for both 35mm ("VistaVision," also known as "Lazy 8" because it stretches for 8 perforations and is "lying down" horizontally) and 65/70mm ("IMAX" and "OMNIMAX," both 15 perforations in width) currently in use.

Horizontal and Vertical Formats

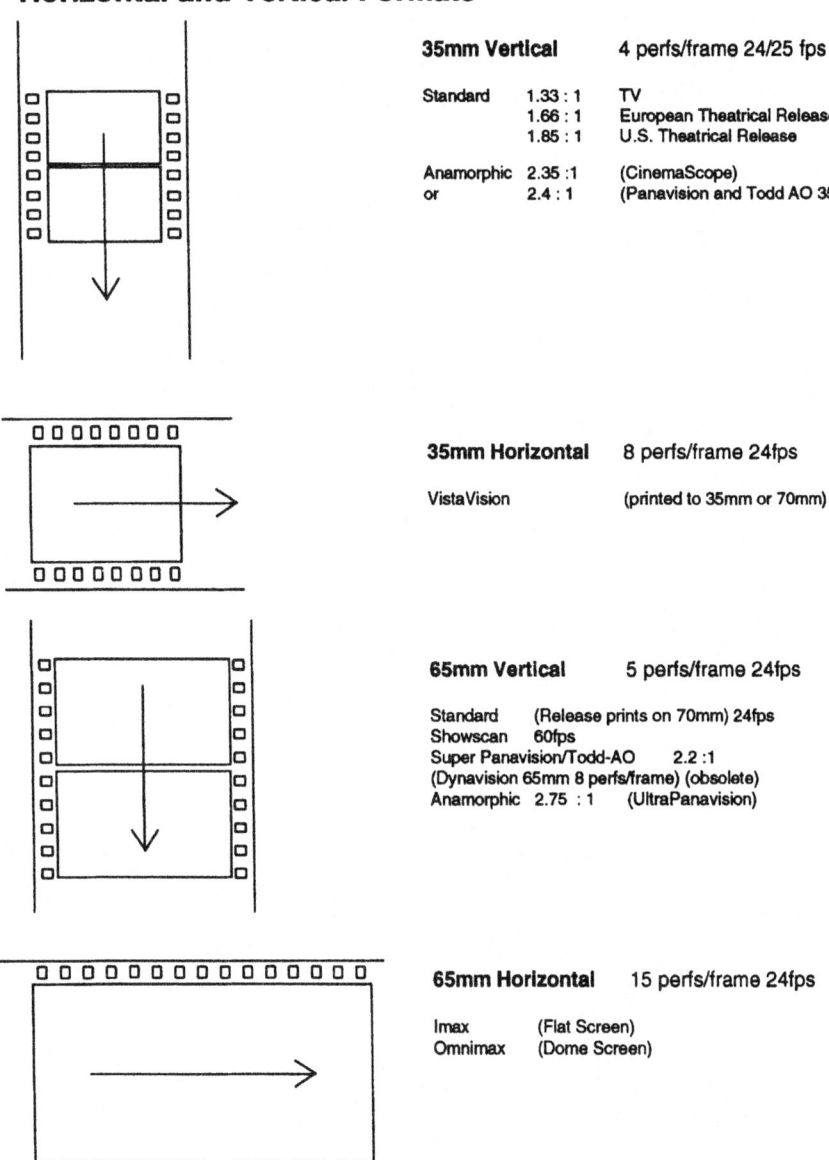

Figure 3-1 Horizontal/Vertical Formats. Film usually runs vertically through the camera, but there are horizontal systems for both 35mm and 65mm cameras.

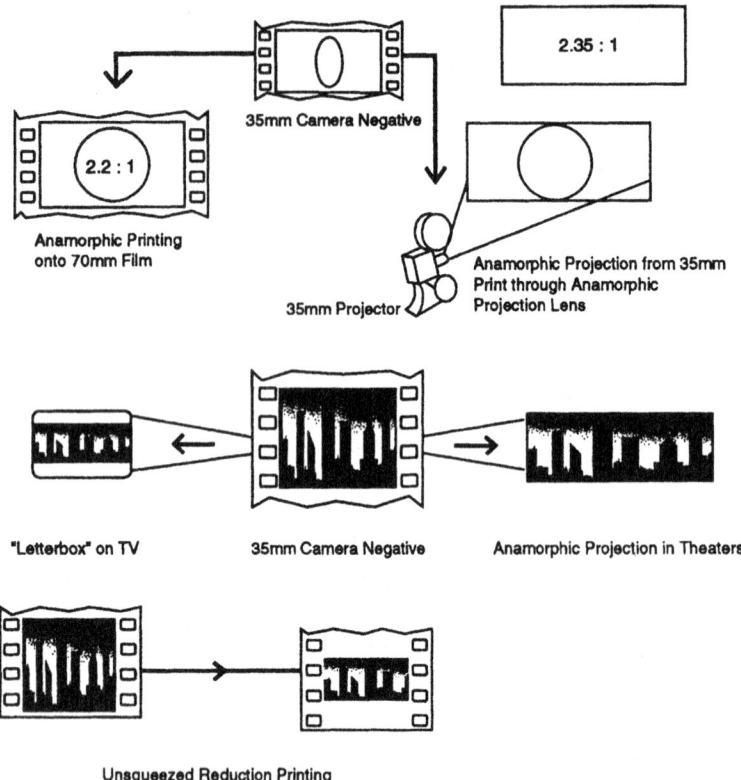

Figure 3-2 Anamorphic Systems. Anamorphic photography squeezes a wide-screen image onto a standard 35mm film negative. This squeezed negative can be used to make a 70mm unsqueezed print, or can make a squeezed 35mm print that can be unsqueezed during projection through an anamorphic projection lens.

Anamorphic Systems

It is also possible to squeeze more information into a standard negative using an anamorphic lens system, which squeezes the image horizontally without affecting the image vertically. These systems use either a lens specifically designed to be anamorphic, or a standard lens with a cylindrical or anamorphic element added either in front or in the rear.

These systems are used for wide-screen projection systems, either by projecting the anamorphic print through a matching anamorphic projection lens, or by unsqueezing the anamorphic image during release printing, sometimes during a "blow-up" to a larger gauge film.

There are 16mm anamorphic lenses made, but they are rarely used. 35mm anamorphic photography systems usually have the word "scope" in their names, such as "Cinemascope." A 65mm anamorphic system known as Ultra-Panavision enjoyed a brief popularity in the 1950s and 1960s.

Film Aspect Ratios

The "Aspect Ratio" refers to the shape of the image when projected. This rectangular projected image is described as the ratio of the image width to the image height. In the aspect ratio known as "1.85:1," for example, the image width is 1.85 times the image height. A screen ten feet high would have to be eighteen and one half feet wide to properly show a 1.85:1 film.

The first aspect ratio used in 35mm photography, called "Full Aperture" or "Silent Aperture," had an aspect ratio of 4:3, or 1.33:1. The negative image completely filled the space between the two rows of perforations, and an image height of four perforations was decided on. The standard gate in current production cameras is still this format—"Full Aperture," sometimes described as "Silent Aperture."

This four-perf image yielded sixteen frames per foot of film. Early handcrank cameras were geared so that one turn on the crank would expose one-half foot of film, or eight images. Turning the crank at the rate of two turns per second was a speed easy for early D.P.'s and Camera Operators to practice and to maintain, and the standard frame rate for the early silent films was established at that rate—sixteen frames per second.

Advent of Sound

The beginning of the sound era in motion pictures caused two problems for the camera designers, in addition to the problem of keeping the camera quiet. First of all, space was needed on the film for the soundtrack. Secondly, sixteen frames per second (one foot per second) was just not fast enough to satisfactorily reproduce the soundtracks.

The first problem was solved by proportionally reducing the size of the camera negative image but keeping nearly the same shape, leaving a blank strip for the

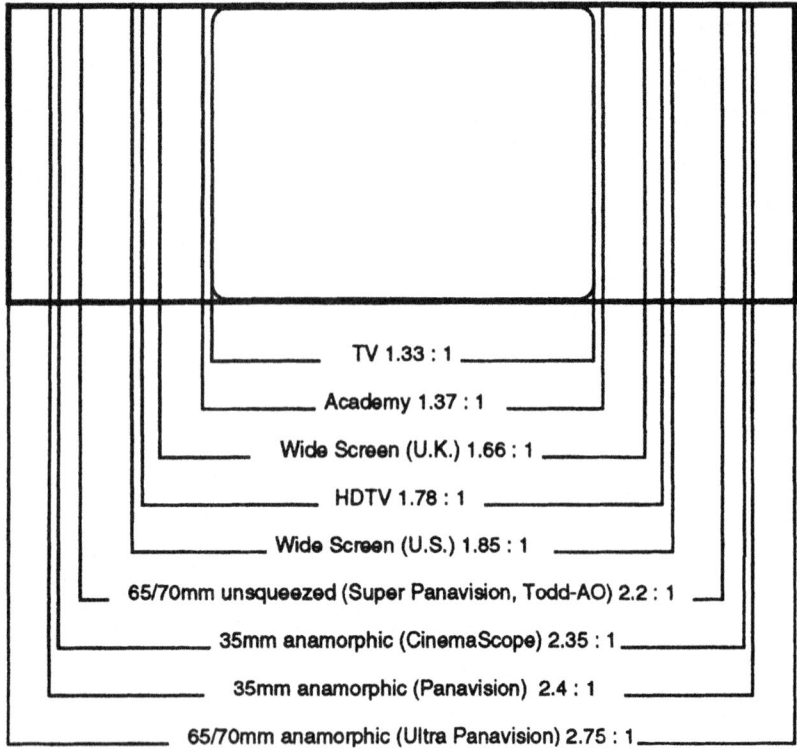

Figure 3-3 Screen Aspect Ratios.

soundtrack alongside the image between the perforations. Since the early filmmakers wanted to preserve the original proportions of the frame, the image height was reduced as well. This reduction of the image size while preserving the proportions had the added benefit of creating a wider frame line between frames, allowing the film editors to better hide their splices. The new format was called the "Academy" format, after the Academy of Motion Picture Arts and Sciences, a slightly wider rectangle than the Silent format, 1.37:1 as opposed to 1.33:1.

The second problem was solved by increasing the standard filming and projection speed from 16 to 24 frames per second, which used up more film stock, but greatly improved sound quality.

Wide-Screen Formats

Theatrical film presentations stayed with the Academy (1.37:1) format for many years, until the advent of broadcast television. When television sets started becoming common in American households, in the early 1950s, the Hollywood studio heads, fearing that people would stop going to movie theaters when they could watch television at home, searched for some special incentive to lure audiences into the theater. Their solution to the problem was "Wide-Screen" films, finally settling on the 1.85:1 format in the United States, while European audiences saw films projected in 1.75:1 and then 1.66:1.

Anamorphic wide-screen formats, which had been experimented with since nearly the birth of the motion picture, also became popular about this time, as well as more gimmicky formats such as Cinerama, various 3-D processes, and such bizarre oddities as "Smell-O-Vision."

The cost for this changeover to wide-screen and/or anamorphic processes was minimal, requiring only that the theater owners buy wider focal length (or anamorphic) projector lenses and new masks for the projectors, and mask off the top and/or bottom of the screens for the new wider formats. The audiences were persuaded, through clever studio advertising, that they were getting something extra for their theater admission.

Of course, color was a selling point in favor of the big screen as well, as color television was still a decade or more away. Color film processes had been around for a long time, but did not really become cost-effective and popular until the 1950s.

Personally, I don't think it would have made any significant difference. People, especially Americans, like going to the neighborhood movie theaters, and would have anyway, despite the presence of a TV set at home, and now the availability of movies on videocassette. Movies have been, and will continue to be, a chance to get out of the house, a place to send children on weekends and school vacations, a place for teenagers to begin dating, etc. Movies are here to stay!

Big Screen TVs, Cable TV, Satellite TV, VCRs and cassette rentals, and even HDTV, pose no serious threat to the motion picture theaters now or in the foreseeable future. I think the past forty years have proved me correct, and the future will continue to do so.

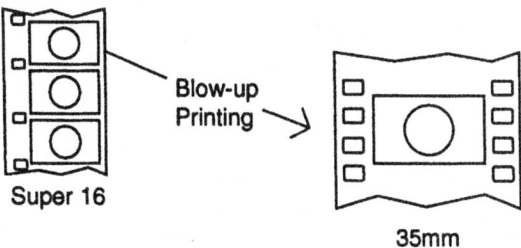

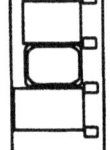

Regular 16mm (1.33 : 1) .295 x .404

16mm TV Transmitted & Safe Action areas

Super 16 Camera Aperture for 35mm 1.66 : 1 blow-up .295 x .492

Figure 3-4 16mm Formats.

16mm Formats:

Standard Format	* Standard Spherical Lenses
	* 1.37:1 Aspect Ratio
	* One perf per frame
	* Uses either Single or Double Perf film
Super 16mm	* Spherical Lenses (be careful to check that lens coverage fills the enlarged and recentered 1.66:1 Aspect Ratio frame)
	* One perf per frame
	* Requires Single Perf film (because image extends all the way to the edge of the film)
	* Cameras must be modified for larger gate and recentered lens axis
	* This format is intended to be "blown up" to 35mm for theatrical release, as it cannot be shown in 16mm format by standard projectors without being reduced to accommodate the soundtrack and wider image.
CIRCARAMA	* Multiple 16mm system used at Disneyland for 360° presentation
	* Eleven 16mm cameras arranged in a circle
	* Eleven Interlocked Projectors

35mm Nonanamorphic (Spherical) Formats:

Vertical Format (4 perforations per frame):

SILENT (1.33:1)	* First Format in common usage
	* Modern professional Cameras still have SILENT APERTURE (also known as FULL APERTURE) gates installed, allowing maximum flexibility in printing for different aspect ratios
ACADEMY (1.37:1)	* Worldwide Theatrical Release Format in 1930s and 1940s
THEATRICAL 1.85:1	* Current U.S. Theatrical Format
THEATRICAL 1.66:1	* Current European Theatrical Format
THEATRICAL 1.75:1	* Obsolete European Theatrical Format
TELEVISION	* Approximately 1.33:1
	* Usually seen with straight sides, top and bottom, but with rounded corners
	* Sometimes seen with "Pumpkin" shape, flat top and bottom, curved sides

PANAVISION SUPER 35
(also described as
"Super 1.85")

* Extends into soundtrack area for larger negative, useful for 1.85:1 projection, TV (1.33:1), or 1.66:1 projection
* Larger negative area theoretically should mean better quality, but some sources claim that these benefits are offset by the extra printing generation needed to make 35mm release prints from SUPER 35 negative
* Must be optically reduced for 35mm release print, to allow for soundtrack
* Also used for Television filming, allowing scanning for standard TV and HDTV formats from the largest possible negative

SUPERSCOPE (obsolete)

* RKO Radio Pictures system shot with normal lenses, but released in 35mm Anamorphic to yield 2:1 or 2.35:1 screen aspect ratio

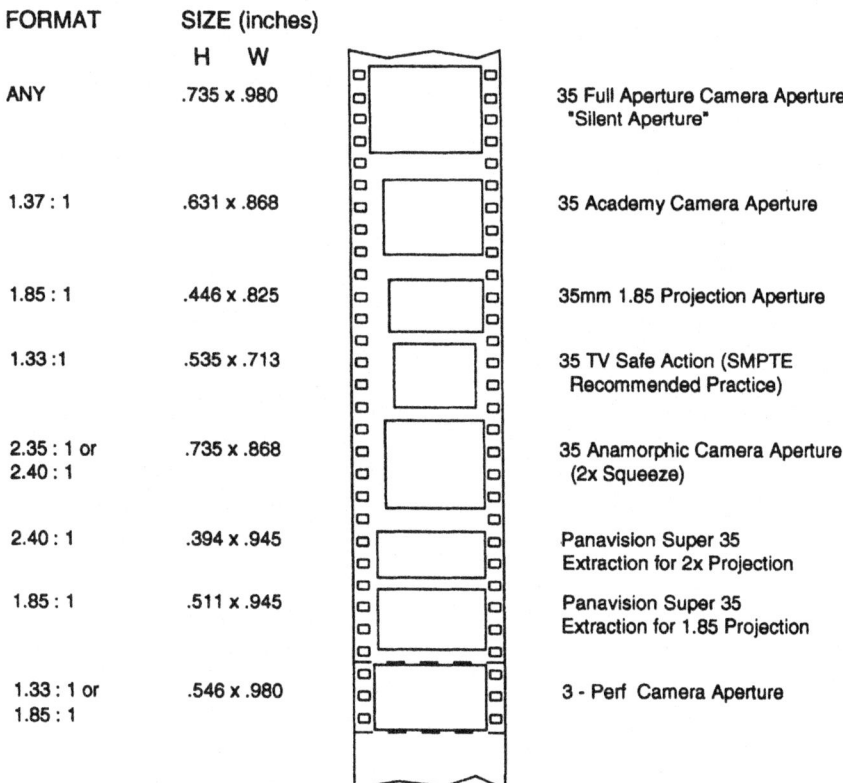

FORMAT	SIZE (inches) H W	
ANY	.735 x .980	35 Full Aperture Camera Aperture "Silent Aperture"
1.37 : 1	.631 x .868	35 Academy Camera Aperture
1.85 : 1	.446 x .825	35mm 1.85 Projection Aperture
1.33 : 1	.535 x .713	35 TV Safe Action (SMPTE Recommended Practice)
2.35 : 1 or 2.40 : 1	.735 x .868	35 Anamorphic Camera Aperture (2x Squeeze)
2.40 : 1	.394 x .945	Panavision Super 35 Extraction for 2x Projection
1.85 : 1	.511 x .945	Panavision Super 35 Extraction for 1.85 Projection
1.33 : 1 or 1.85 : 1	.546 x .980	3 - Perf Camera Aperture

Figure 3-5 35mm Formats.

32 THE CAMERA ASSISTANT

TECHNISCOPE
* Obsolete system used for some low-budget feature work in 1960s and 1970s
* 2 perforations per frame
* 50 percent savings in film stock and lab costs
* Poor image quality due to negative size
* Difficult to edit
* Specially modified cameras needed
* Yielded 35mm anamorphic release print with screen aspect ratio of 2.35:1

Vertical Format (3 perforations per frame):

3-PERFORATION FORMAT
* Used for 1.33:1, 1.66:1, or 1.85:1 projection, as well as TV and HDTV
* Saves 25 percent on film raw stock and laboratory costs with no noticeable quality loss
* Easy conversion of certain existing cameras—just change movement, groundglass, and electronic circuit boards
* Cannot be edited or projected in 3-perf form—must be transferred to videotape for editing
* Used mostly for episodic television series such as "Dallas," which has no need for projection release prints
* Good format for filming for HDTV scanning—Large negative, very close to HDTV shape (little waste)
* When used in conjunction with 30 fps speed, yields far better video transfer than 4-perf 24 fps systems, for approximately same cost—used this way for short-lived TV series "Max Headroom"

Horizontal Format (8 perforations per frame):

VISTAVISION
("Lazy 8")
* Now used mainly for matte and special effects photography, and for rear- or front-projection plate photography
* Originally used for normal production, reduced to standard 35mm release prints with 1.85:1 screen aspect ratio

Film Formats and Aspect Ratios **33**

* Reduction printing to 35mm meant reduced negative grain, increased sharpness, and better resolution
* Several new camera models built recently by special optical effects companies such as Industrial Light and Magic
* System uses 35mm still photography (Nikon) lenses to cover larger negative

35mm Anamorphic Formats:

CINEMASCOPE/
PANAVISION 35

* 2:1 Anamorphic squeeze ratio yielding 2.35:1 or 2.40:1 image (with optical soundtrack), or 2.55:1 picture (with 4-track magnetic soundtrack)
* Can be released on 70mm unsqueezed
* Can be released on 35mm anamorphic print film for use with 2:1 anamorphic projector lenses to unsqueeze image

35mm Anamorphic and Horizontal Formats:

TECHNIRAMA
(obsolete)

* 1.5:1 Anamorphic squeeze ratio yielding either
* 35mm reduction print with 2:1 screen aspect ratio, or
* 70mm unsqueezed release print with 2.2:1 screen aspect ratio

35mm Multistrip Systems:

CINERAMA
(obsolete)

* Three separate 35mm films shown side-by-side (slightly overlapping) from three projectors to make single wide-screen image on deeply curved screen
* 6 perfs per frame
* Combined Aspect Ratio 2.59:1
* Later printed together on single strip of 70mm film to eliminate seams between images
* Original Cinerama used 26 fps frame rate
* No Soundtrack on film—Sound on separate 35mm 7-track magnetic film
* Later productions shot on Anamorphic 65mm (1.25 squeeze ratio), then printed onto three 35mm prints for showing in Cinerama theaters

CINEMIRACLE (obsolete)	* Three strip 35mm process similar to above, but three projectors in same booth * Screen alignment accomplished by using mirrors for the two outside images	

65mm Nonanamorphic (Spherical) Formats:

Vertical Format (5 perforations per frame):

Standard 65mm 2.2:1 Aspect Ratio	* SUPER PANAVISION	*Exodus* *West Side Story* *Lawrence of Arabia*
	* TODD-AO	*Oklahoma* (six-track sound)
	* 70mm prints yield 2.25:1 screen aspect ratio with 4-channel sound, or 2:1 ratio with 6-channel sound	
	* Currently beginning a resurgence of popularity—Arriflex, Panavision, and Cinema Products are building new 65mm cameras and lenses	*Far and Away* *Little Buddha*
SHOWSCAN	* 60 frames per second * Used in amusement venues	
DYNAVISION (obsolete)	* 8 perfs per frame	

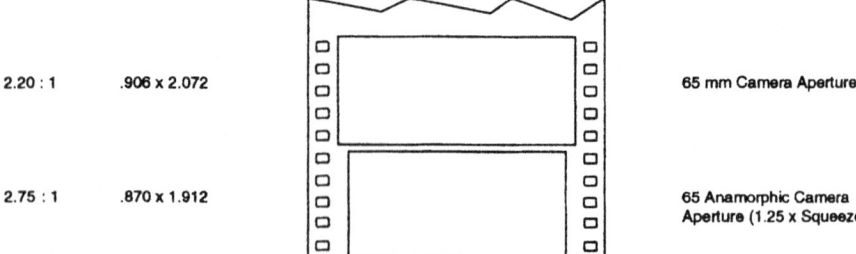

2.20 : 1	.906 x 2.072	65 mm Camera Aperture
2.75 : 1	.870 x 1.912	65 Anamorphic Camera Aperture (1.25 x Squeeze)

Figure 3-6 65/70mm Formats.

Horizontal Format (15 perforations per frame):

IMAX   * Shown on huge flat screen in places like Washington DC's **Smithsonian Institution**, and New York's **Museum of Natural History**

OMNIMAX   * Shown on domed screen

There is also a 3-D IMAX system in a very few specially constructed theaters. The 3-D effect is accomplished by having the audience wear light-weight goggle helmets which use infrared sensors and liquid crystal displays (LCD) to alternately block out one eye at a time in conjunction with alternating left-eye/ right-eye images from a matched pair of IMAX projectors. The effect is nothing less than stunning, the best 3-D presentation I've seen, by far. The screen is 80 feet high at the New York theater.

65mm Anamorphic Formats:

ULTRA PANAVISION   * 2.75:1 Aspect ratio
                                     * 1.25:1 Anamorphic squeeze ratio

CAMERA 65 (MGM)   * 3:1 Aspect Ratio
                                     * 1.33:1 Anamorphic squeeze ratio
                                     * Obsolete system used for
                                           1957 *Raintree County*
                                           1959 *Ben Hur*

Running Time For Various Film Gauges and Formats at Various Camera Speeds (in FPM— Feet per Minute)

Film Gauge & Format	Frames/ Foot	Running Time @ 24 fps	Running Time @ 25 fps	Running Time @ 30 fps
16mm/Super 16mm	40	36.0 fpm	37.5 fpm	45.0 fpm
35mm (4 perf)	16	90.0 fpm	93.75 fpm	112.5 fpm
35mm (3 perf)	21.33	67.5 fpm	70.3 fpm	84.4 fpm
35mm Vistavision	8	180.0 fpm	187.5 fpm	225.0 fpm
65/70mm (5 perf)	12.8	112.5 fpm	117.2 fpm	140.6 fpm
IMAX/ OMNIMAX	4.27	337.5 fpm	351.6 fpm	421.9 fpm

High Definition TV (HDTV)

It is too early to tell exactly how the HDTV revolution will affect the motion picture industry, but two things seem abundantly clear, from everything I've heard and read about HDTV.

First of all, originating on FILM will be the medium of choice, for a good many years yet. No other medium gives the quality, the resolution, the color fidelity, the interchangeability between whatever formats may be required in the future, and the archival protection of plain old 35mm movie film.

Yes, electronic (digital) image recording will eventually replace photochemical image recording, but not for a long time to come. Any television programming for which a film negative exists, no matter how old the negative, can be transferred to HDTV and be on your new HDTV monitor tomorrow, if need be, with a little cropping top and bottom, maybe, and this HDTV transfer will look as good as, if not better than, the original, because the required information is there on the film already.

Previous video transfers of filmed originals have not been able to use the full range of resolution, color, or tonality found in the film negative. Production originating on video, however, will look pretty poor transferred to HDTV, because the original image quality and resolution is just not good enough. Film projection technology is still light-years ahead in color rendition, brightness, contrast range, and resolution, of any video projection technology, even HDTV, for large-screen theatrical audiences.

A film negative can be transferred to any video format with far better end quality than transferring from one video format to another video format. We can even change the shape of the image by simply cropping and/or blowing up the image as required, although the artistic integrity of the original composition will, of course, be compromised.

The second immediate effect of HDTV will be that the 16:9 HDTV aspect ratio will cause more problems for Directors of Photography. This size, which divides out to 1.7777777 . . . to 1, or more commonly, 1.78:1, represents yet another variation and compromise to the growing list of formats that must be considered when composing a frame of film. The new HDTV format is a bit wider than Academy/ TV (1.37:1) and European theatrical release (1.66:1), but is narrower than U.S. theatrical release (1.85:1) and much narrower that CinemaScope (2.35:1).

A growing concern among filmmakers is just how many formats can a Director of Photography "protect for," and still deliver a quality image displaying his or her artistic vision for the project being filmed? It just doesn't seem fair.

For a while there was a push to standardize the HDTV format at 1.5:1 or 2:1, but these ideas seem to have faded away. The 16:9, or 1.78:1, format seems to be here to stay.

Camera manufacturers are busy making 16:9 groundglasses for their cameras, usually with 1.85:1 or 1.33:1 (standard TV) markings as well. The question is, how many other aspect ratios will have to appear on these groundglasses before we totally obliterate the viewfinder image with rectangles?

CHAPTER **4**

The Camera Equipment Checkout

The Importance of the Checkout

The importance of the preshooting equipment checkout cannot be overemphasized. This could easily be the most important thing that the Camera Assistant does on the job. A complete and thorough checkout can make the difference between an easy job and a nightmare.

It would be a rare occurrence, indeed, for a Camera Assistant to be hired and not allowed to have a checkout period, usually a single day for commercials or music videos, three days for a TV movie ("M.O.W."), and a week or two (or more) for a feature film. The only excuse that comes to mind as a reason for NOT having a checkout is if the entire camera equipment package belongs either to the production company or to the cinematographer, that the equipment is brand new and in perfect condition, and that no one else ever uses that equipment. Even then the Assistant should argue for a checkout, to familiarize yourself with the particular equipment before the shoot, to see what condition the equipment is in, to see how it is distributed and packed into cases, to see what accessories and back-up equipment there are, etc.

Anyone that rents equipment from a camera equipment rental house and does not give the Camera Assistant a chance to check it out thoroughly, is asking for trouble, and often gets it.

Camera Assistants are, of course, paid for the Camera Equipment Checkout by the production company. The Assistants are working for the company, ensuring that the equipment is in working order, and have to be paid for their efforts, just as other crew people are paid for preproduction work. Sometimes, especially on low-budget features, production managers will try to bargain down the money, trying to get the Assistants for half-pay on checkout days, or some other such discount. This is totally outrageous, and should be fought against tenaciously. This is another reason why we have unions.

First of all, the Checkout is a necessary part of the job, and should be paid for at proper rates, which is a full-day rate, not a half-day. As far as the Assistants are concerned, they are not available for other work on checkout days, so the day rate should be the same as for shooting days. There is no such thing as a half-day rate in any union contract that I know about.

In some parts of the country, Camera Assistants are expected to own a van or truck, and to pick up and transport all of the camera equipment on their own for the whole length of the job. This presents a number of concerns and dilemmas for the Camera Assistant. First of all, this practice is discriminatory against Assistants who do not own, or do not want to own, a van or truck. Other Assistants with vans will have an unfair advantage in hiring preference. This is wrong.

Secondly, there are security and insurance problems with Assistants being responsible for hundreds of thousands of dollars worth of camera equipment. Where do you park this van? What do you do with the equipment overnight? Do you spend an additional half hour loading it into your house or apartment every night, and then another half hour the next day loading it back into the van? Will you be paid for the extra time spent handling equipment? Is the company renting your van, and are they paying prevailing rates for such rental? What about insurance on the equipment in case of theft, fire, or other damage? As an Assistant, are you willing to take that risk?

At the very least the company must provide an insurance policy relieving the Assistant of any responsibility for the loss of the equipment through theft or other causes. Think hard about these things before you agree to pick up and transport the equipment yourself. Be very careful. So far I have been able to avoid being in this situation, but I know that many Assistants in other parts of the country face these problems often.

For a feature film or TV movie, there must also be at least one day at the end of shooting for an equipment "check-in" day to make sure everything on the rental contract is accounted for. This should also be a paid day for the Assistants. This check-in day also gives the Camera Assistants a chance to get an accurate film stock inventory, deal with unused expendable supplies, and to unload their personal equipment and tools from the camera truck.

Camera Equipment Rental Houses

Professional motion picture camera equipment rental houses exist because the camera equipment used to make movies is outrageously expensive, and because few companies or individuals shoot often enough to justify the tremendous cost of purchase, maintenance, storage, security, and insurance.

There is also the obsolescence factor for most equipment. Once purchased, the equipment immediately begins to depreciate and become outdated. The camera equipment rental houses are better suited than individuals to try and keep up with the changes in motion picture technology, which is advancing faster than the equipment can be manufactured. However, a rental house can only make the requested equipment available to the customer. They cannot guarantee with any degree of certainty its condition at the time of rental.

Despite the best efforts of a rental house—ANY rental house—to supply the required equipment in working order, the Camera Assistant who is going to be on the job MUST spend enough time with the equipment to check it thoroughly and become familiar with the specific items he or she will be responsible for when the shooting starts.

There are hundreds of things that can go wrong with equipment as complex and as exacting as the modern professional motion picture camera and the required lenses and accessories that go with it.

Keep in mind that these cameras and lenses work with optical tolerances of tenths of thousandths of an inch, a dimension much too small to see without sophisticated gauges. Mechanical tolerances are not much more forgiving. These are precision machines more complex than automobiles, and with more electronic components than television sets. An apparently healthy camera can be suffering from many maladies, some fatal.

The rental house does not know the shooting styles and preferences of the Director of Photography or of the Camera Assistant on the job. Every crew works differently, and uses different accessories and feels comfortable with different backup equipment. The Camera Assistant knows the way he or she wants to work, and it is part of the Assistant's responsibility to know or find out the personal preferences of the D.P., so the required equipment is available on the job and in proper working order.

The Camera Assistant wants to find out if something is not working at the rental house during the Checkout, not on the first day of shooting with a hundred people watching, although that has certainly happened many times, through no fault of the Assistant.

The Assistant will also try to ensure there are enough backups, spares, and alternates to get through most emergencies and contingencies. A good Camera Assistant always has a Plan B to go to if Plan A doesn't work, and sometimes even a Plan C and D.

In the last twenty-five years, I have been involved in probably five hundred equipment checkouts, and NOT ONCE has the pile of equipment ordered over the phone and assembled for the checkout been COMPLETE to my satisfaction, and/or FULLY FUNCTIONAL. Sometimes the problems are minor, such as a defective camera power cable, or a tripod whose leg lock slips. Sometimes it is considerably more serious, such as a lens with a defective diaphragm, or a magazine with a broken latch.

Sometimes the problems are really stupid and obvious, like having batteries of the wrong voltage, or a zoom lens without the proper support bracketry, or cables with the wrong plugs. Sometimes the problems are much more subtle and elusive, such as an intermittent zoom motor control.

Before the Checkout

The first thing to do when contacted about a job is to get as much information as possible about the shooting. How many days, what kind of locations, whether the shooting involves high-speed cameras, long lenses, shooting in the rain, Steadicam, what film stocks will be used, what filters will be needed, etc., anything that might affect the equipment list.

When a producer or production manager calls a rental house to reserve camera equipment, he or she doesn't list every cable or filter that you're going to need. The conversation probably lasts all of two minutes, and consists of mostly discussion about how big a discount off the catalog prices the rental house will allow on the rental. This is what the producer and P.M. are primarily interested in—how much it is going to cost. They are not particularly interested in what the camera crew needs or feels comfortable with to get the job done.

Production managers are rarely qualified to order equipment anyway. What they are doing is alerting the rental house that a complete order is forthcoming, and to tell the rental house the key items on the list to make certain they will be available for the period needed.

Don't let this be the only contact with the rental house before the shooting starts. The Director of Photography, or the Camera Assistant speaking for the Director of Photography, should follow through with a more detailed and specific order, based on location scouts and/or discussions with the Director.

When first contacted about the job, don't even bother talking to the production company about equipment—go directly to the Director of Photography. This is known as getting information "From the FRONT of the Horse." Speak to the Director of Photography as soon as possible, and then check in with the rental house to add to the preliminary list given them by the production company, adding lenses and magazines and batteries and filters and things not usually included in the preliminary order, and to find out if there will be an availability problem with any of the equipment specified.

By availability problem, I mean that if you need a high-speed camera for the 18th of the month, and the only high-speed cameras belonging to the rental house are booked on other jobs or down for repair on that day, then you have an availability problem.

The earlier you find out about equipment scheduling problems, the better the chance that the problem can be solved by substituting other more-available equipment, rerenting some items from another rental house, or by having additional equipment shipped from the manufacturer, supplier, or other dealer.

If none of these solutions works for you, maybe the shoot can be scheduled around the available equipment instead of the other way around. But however the problem is solved, the earlier the start on reserving the equipment, the better.

At this stage, the shoot may be weeks away, and the Camera Assistant is not even on the payroll yet, but the job is already off on the right foot.

I've been on feature checkouts where the company didn't want to pay the Second Camera Assistant to be there except for the last day to help load the truck. I always have an argument with them about that. The Second Assistant has to know where things are and how things go together—no two equipment packages are the same. The time saved by having the Second Camera Assistant helping out on the Checkout can either shorten the time needed for the Checkout, or can allow the

Camera Assistants to be more thorough in their equipment tests. Either duction manager and the company get their money's worth by having bc present for the entire Checkout.

Rental House Personnel

There are many camera equipment rental houses in the world, of varying sizes, completeness of inventory, and competency. People that work in camera equipment rental houses and actually handle the equipment and prepare the orders for the Camera Assistant to check out rarely have much, if any, production or set experience, and rarely get paid enough at the rental house to stay there long enough to learn much more than just the basics about cameras.

Many of these people are at entry level in the film industry, in their first job in the business, either recent film-school graduates or relatives of someone in the business, and are only working at the rental houses to learn the equipment and to make contacts for when they quit and enter the freelance market as Camera Assistants or in some other capacity.

Don't get me wrong, I have nothing against nepotism. I started that way, not in a rental house, but on the set, and many others have as well. Who better to enter this insane industry than the family of other industry professionals, family that has grown up exposed to the ups and downs, understanding the business from the inside? Give me a crew of Second Generation film professionals anytime! (Dave Quaid added a big "AMEN" to this!)

Some of the very best Camera Assistants have rental house background, heavy on equipment training when they become Assistants, but light on set experience. After a year or two preparing equipment orders and meeting people, they are ready to go after what they think are the big bucks in the freelance market.

They often apply to one of the film camera unions, take the examination, and pass with flying colors, because they work with the equipment every day. The entrance examination for the unions really tests only specific equipment knowledge, and rarely extends into much practical application on the set. Their first job as a Second Assistant or Camera Trainee is usually an eye-opener for them.

They have been used to eight-hour days, relatively low stress levels, regular meals, and minuscule paychecks. They are used to air conditioning in the summer, heat in the winter, staying dry, having bathrooms and telephones available nearby, and having the ability to call in sick so they can go to a baseball game. None of those things exist in the freelance world. You can always spot the new ex-rental house Camera Assistant on the job. They are usually breathing heavily, sweating, and they sit down a lot. But they get over it quickly, and become terrific Assistants.

The management at rental houses hate that short turnover in floor personnel, and sometimes have trouble filling those jobs when vacancies occur. Many rental houses ask job applicants to agree to stay there for eighteen months or two years, or some other definite period, before quitting to work freelance. They try various things to induce people to stay (reserved parking spaces, espresso machines, etc.), but they rarely try the most obvious solution—pay them more money.

As soon as these people find out they can earn more in one day as a freelance Camera Assistant than in a week at the rental house, they naturally want to move into the freelance market. Of course, a small steady paycheck is more desirable for some people than the irregular, undependable, and sometimes bouncing paychecks of the freelance Camera Assistant, especially if there is a family at home. It's a difficult choice.

Camera rental houses try hard to keep their customers happy, and the customer they see most often is the Camera Assistant. The Director of Photography rarely, if ever, appears in person at the rental house, and the producer or production manager will probably never show up, but the Camera Assistant is there for the checkout, and again for the check-in at the end of the job, and they will speak to the Assistant on the phone throughout the job. So even though the Camera Assistant doesn't sign the checks, he or she is the most visible representative of the production company that the rental house deals with.

A good relationship with the rental house is essential for the Camera Assistant. The willingness of the rental house to help out an Assistant in trouble is directly proportional to the amount that the rental house likes that Assistant, which in turn is directly proportional to how well that Assistant treats the equipment and the personnel at the rental house. This symbiotic relationship between the rental house and the Camera Assistant begins early in the Assistant's career.

Any new Camera Assistant needs to get acquainted with the equipment he or she is likely to encounter on the job. And where is that equipment, but in the rental houses?

The Philosophy of the Checkout

The Checkout accomplishes two goals for the Camera Assistant and for the job. First of all, it gives the Camera Assistant the opportunity to make sure the equipment list is complete; that everything needed for the job, down to the smallest screw and cable, will be there when needed, plus sufficient backup equipment for unplanned emergencies.

Secondly, the Checkout gives the Camera Assistant the opportunity to make sure that everything fits together the right way and is working the way it should be.

Renting a motion picture camera package is not like renting an automobile— get in, turn the key, and drive away. Instead of a fully assembled and ready-to-drive automobile, a camera equipment rental order is more like a pile of disassembled parts. It is comparable to renting a chassis, four wheels, a carburetor, an engine block, a steering wheel, a gas tank, a set of windshield wipers, etc., and trying to assemble all that into a working automobile, and then racing that car in the Daytona 500 the next day. Making sure that all of the separate parts fit together properly and work as expected is what the Camera Assistant is doing during the checkout.

As in many other aspects of the motion picture business and life in general, Murphy's Law plays an important role in the equipment checkout. We have all heard the primary codicil of **Murphy's Law, "Whatever Can Go Wrong, Will Go Wrong."** Actually, there are two corollaries comprising **Murphy's Law of Camera Equipment Checkouts**. Here they are:

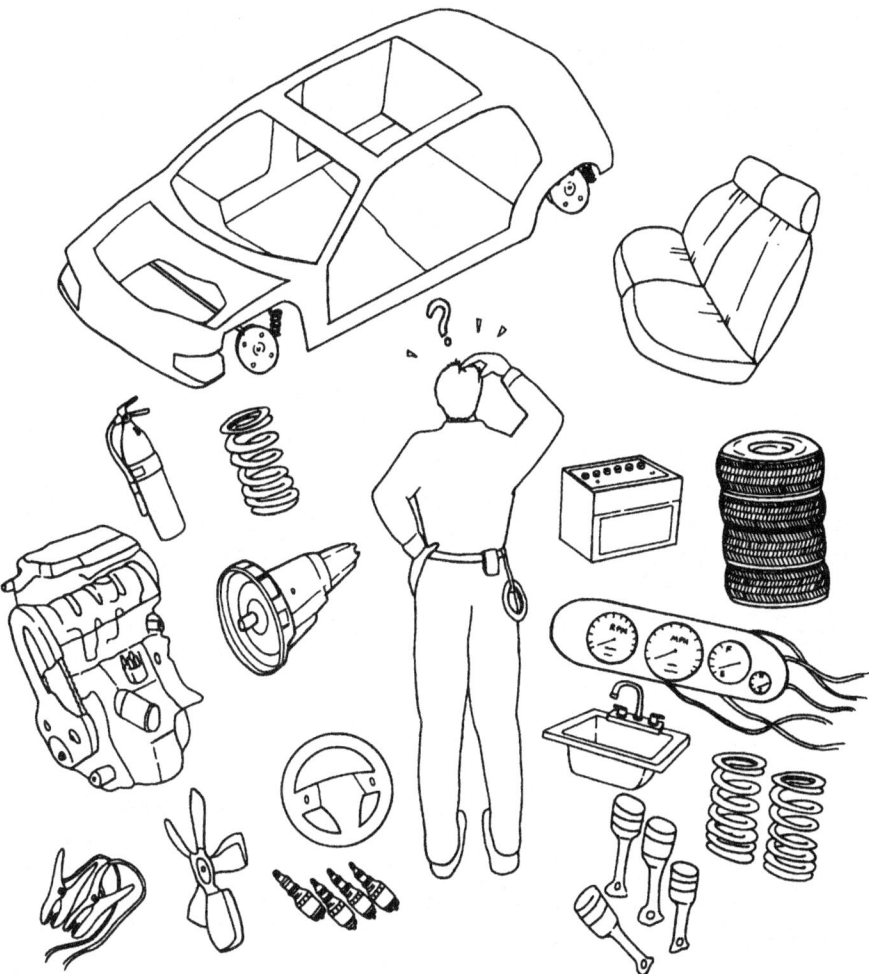

Figure 4-1 Camera Equipment Checkout. Renting a camera package is not like renting an automobile that is ready to get in and drive. Renting a camera package is more like renting a pile of auto parts, and trying to build a working automobile, and then racing that automobile at Daytona the next day.

MURPHY'S LAW OF CAMERA EQUIPMENT CHECKOUTS

1. **Whatever piece of equipment the Assistant does not look at during the Checkout, will fail during the job, and**
2. **No matter how thorough the Assistant is during the Checkout, something unexpected will fail during the job.**

Keeping in mind these two inescapable Laws, we can now begin the Checkout.

The modified preliminary camera equipment order, received by the rental house by phone from the production manager, will have been given to one of the floor people at the rental house, usually a day or two before the Camera Assistant is scheduled to come in for the Checkout. The equipment will be collected and piled together in the checkout area at the rental house in preparation for the Assistant's arrival.

Rental houses invariably have areas set aside for Camera Assistants to use for their equipment Checkout. Depending on the size of the house, the checkout area will vary, of course. Sometimes in a big rental house, there will even be separate checkout areas for Commercials and Features.

Commercial checkouts are almost always one-day affairs, and the equipment is packed up and shipped out the same day. Lately, half-day checkouts for television commercials, have become very common, and then the equipment (and the Camera Assistant) is transported to the studio that afternoon and often used for pre-lighting and camera blocking.

Movie-of-the-Week checkouts usually last for three days or so, and Feature Film checkouts a week or two or more, so finding an out-of-the-way place to leave equipment set up overnight and longer is important to the Camera Assistants. Some of the larger rental houses even have individual checkout rooms for feature films with lengthy checkouts.

A typical checkout area might include a high hat (tripod head mounting base) or old friction tripod head mounted on a work table, sometimes on wheels, a lens chart mounted on the wall, and some sort of light pointed at the chart, either regular tungsten movie lights on stands, or lights mounted on the ceiling or walls. Sometimes camera dollies are available to mount up on. Sometimes it is easier to use the tripods and heads you're taking with you on the job to check out on.

The other requirement is a lot of floor space. A typical camera equipment order (single 35mm camera with accessories and support gear) might have anywhere from ten to forty equipment cases, and they have to be put somewhere. One camera manufacturer (who shall remain nameless) typically puts each lens in a separate case for shipping. This makes for a veritable mountain of equipment cases to be moved and stored. The equipment cases often weigh more than their contents.

The rental house floor person has assembled, as completely as possible, the equipment package, based on the preliminary list ordered by phone. When the list is incomplete, the rental house will take an educated guess on how many and what size magazines, and how many batteries, what size filters, etc.; their guess is based on what limited information they have about the job, telephone conversations with the production company, Director of Photography, Camera Assistant, etc., and based on past experience with that company and/or crew.

The more work you do as an Assistant, the more the rental houses will get to know you, and the better they can anticipate your needs and wants.

Reserved Equipment Packages

If the Director of Photography works a lot, and uses the same rental house and the same basic equipment package every time, then the rental house, if they have the

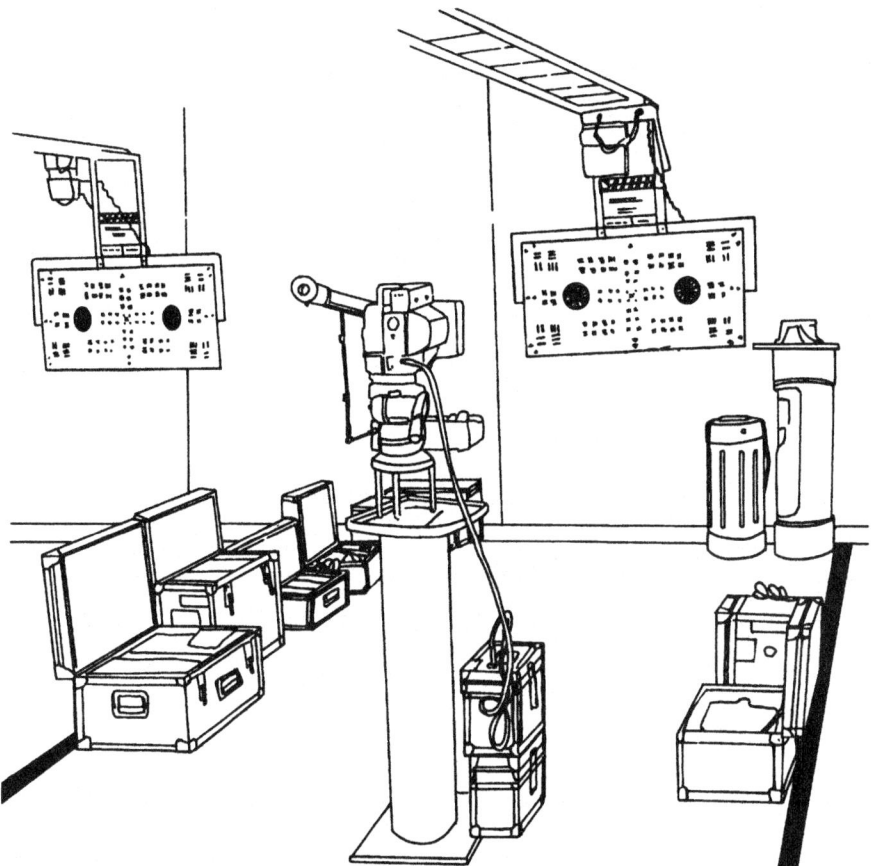

Figure 4-2 Rental House Checkout Area Camera Equipment. Rental Houses invariably have some floor space set aside for Camera Assistants to check out their equipment. A typical setup might include a pedestal or tripod to mount the gear head and camera on, a lens chart on the wall or on an overhead track, and enough space to open the cases and try out all the pieces.

floor space and the equipment to spare, will often try and keep the camera, the lenses, the gear head, the filters, etc., together, and reserve that package for that D.P.'s next job.

When the job is over and the equipment returned to the rental house, it is checked in, cleaned, maintained, and if that Director of Photography has another job scheduled in the near future, that entire package of equipment is set aside for that next job. This saves everyone a lot of work. The rental house doesn't have to keep assembling and separating the same package, the Camera Assistant has the same equipment package to look at on each checkout and work with on the job, and gets to know its idiosyncracies, and the Director of Photography gets to work with the same dependable camera, lenses, and support gear each time.

Figure 4-3 Mountain of Cases. Our hero, the intrepid Camera-Assistant-to-the-Stars, fearlessly faces a daunting mountain of camera equipment cases during the Checkout at the Rental House; equipment cases that must be carried up and down stairs, into and out of trucks, through the snow, mud, rain, sand, and underbrush; equipment that must be kept in working order at all times under the worst conditions. Cameras, accessories, gear heads, magazines, batteries, chargers, filters, tripods, cables, monitors, and, of course, lenses—many, many lenses—each in their own case sometimes. Good thing this job is only a two-day shoot!

This happens for both commercial and feature D.P.'s, but only if they work often enough. Obviously, if the camera package is just sitting in the rental house collecting dust, and the house needs a zoom lens, or a set of neutral density filters, or some additional batteries for a cash customer, then they will raid that reserved package, hoping that the equipment borrowed will be returned in time for the next time that the reserved package goes out. With luck, the rental house will remember which pieces have been used by other crews, and can tell the Camera Assistant, so those pieces can be more carefully checked before the next job.

If the Director of Photography doesn't work a lot, the equipment package will have to be assembled from scratch each time, and must be checked over more thoroughly by the Camera Assistant.

The first week of shooting on a Feature Film is the equipment shakedown week. The Assistant will spend a lot of time on the phone to the rental house, exchanging things and getting additional items. Despite a thorough checkout, once shooting begins, there will be changes. It is virtually impossible for the Camera Assistant to foresee ALL contingencies. But the more thoroughly the Assistant does his or her homework before the job starts, the less chaotic and traumatic the first week of shooting will be. The more the Assistant finds out about the job before shooting begins, from discussions with the production manager and the Director of Photography, the better he or she can anticipate the problems the job will present.

For a television commercial shoot, there is rarely any time for a shakedown period. Shooting only one or two days on average, everything had better work, and work the first time! Sometimes it is possible to take along back-up equipment for those unforeseen problems, but not always. On the other hand, most commercials are shot in studios or nearby locations, so getting replacement equipment from the rental house for something that has broken down is often possible without too much time lost.

I can't think of any feature film I have worked on that did not carry a back-up camera body, just for those absolute emergencies when the camera dies on its own or with help (such as being dropped!), or for those times when a second camera is wanted to run simultaneously and spontaneously with the prime camera. Too much money is flowing constantly on a feature set to be caught without a working camera. But a commercial shoot rarely carries a back-up body, unless the job is being shot high up in the Rockies or in the swamps in Florida, far from the nearest rental house.

Checkouts are never a breeze. An Assistant can never just walk in, look around, say, "This is great!" and then go home. The Assistant will have to set things up, plug in all the cables, try all the batteries, play with all the switches, scratch test the magazines, make sure the lenses are properly supported, check the focus scale on the lenses for accuracy, etc. Different cameras have different problems to be aware of and watch for.

The Camera Equipment Checkout Checklist

I wish there were a single, simple, complete one-page checklist available for the camera checkout, but it seems to be impossible to compile such a list. The best I could do is three pages. There is just too much equipment, and too many different possible combinations of equipment, and there are too many different ways of working and of getting the same shot. There are, of course, some very obvious things to look for, but every crew is going to have different priorities for the checkout.

The list is as complete as makes sense without it becoming a book of its own. Some of the items may not apply to the particular camera being checked out, but they can still serve as reminders and guidelines for the Checkout. I am sure there are omissions that should be added and obsolete items that should be omitted. Reader feedback will help to refine the list for future editions of this book.

The following Checklist should serve as a guide to the Equipment Checkout. The list is reprinted, without text commentary, in Appendix C at the end of this book, so you can photocopy it and bring it to the Checkout with you, crossing out the items as you check them.

Other sources suggest that the Assistant begin the Checkout "from the ground up," but I have found from my own experience and from watching other Assistants, that a far better approach is to begin at the "center" and work outward, and that you begin with the camera body itself. This holds true for every brand of equipment. Because time is often limited, practical common sense would dictate starting with the most important things first.

Long before you put on the first magazine or the first lens, there are several things about the camera body itself that must be checked. Also, there may be something basically wrong with the camera body (and this happens sometimes, no matter how carefully the camera has been prepped, no matter what brand of equipment you're working with, and no matter what rental house you are in).

That camera body may need to be replaced with another, or may need to be worked on in the repair shop. If so, then every other step of the checkout needs to be repeated with the new or reworked camera body, so finding out first if the camera body is working properly before proceeding on to other items can save the Camera Assistant hours of double work.

There will be plenty of "Dead Time" during the Checkout while waiting for replacement or additional equipment, or waiting for the dreaded video assist to be "tweaked," to thoroughly check out the heads, tripods, spreader, etc., "from the ground up."

CAMERA EQUIPMENT CHECKOUT CHECKLIST
I. The Camera Body
    A. Video Assist
        1. Acceptable Picture
        2. Cables—Power and Video
        3. Power—110 Volt or Batteries
        4. Adjusted for Picture Size and Shape
        5. Adjusted for Proper Contrast and Brightness
        6. Flicker-Free

Even before examining the camera body, set up the video assist system, on those jobs that use such a device. The video assist is simply a small video camera, usually black and white, although color systems are becoming more popular, mounted on the film camera, looking at the film camera's groundglass. This yields a video image identical to the film camera's viewfinder image, including the markings on the film camera's groundglass.

Virtually ALL television series and commercials use video assist, and an increasing number of feature films, as well. Set up and look at the video assist first, because it is the piece that is LEAST likely to be working, takes the LONGEST time to adjust and/or repair, and is the Camera Assistants' single BIGGEST headache on the job (after the Production Manager).

It's hard to believe that for nearly one hundred years, films have been made without video assist, and that practically overnight, it has become such a "necessity."

Many times I have shown up at a Checkout without having eaten breakfast, because I know that when the video technicians, with their screwdrivers and oscilloscopes and monitors begin trying to fix the damn thing, I can go out, have a leisurely breakfast, and get back in plenty of time to continue the Checkout.

I don't think I've ever met a Camera Assistant who doesn't hate video assist with a passion. In fact, the video assist is such a pain that I have given it its own chapter, later

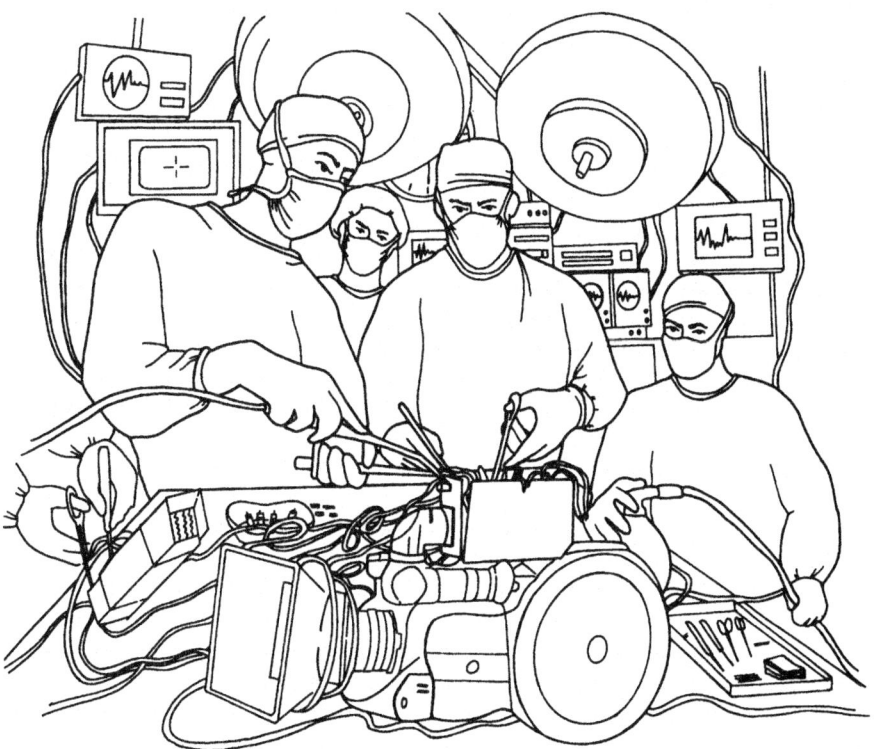

Figure 4-4 Video Assist Repair at the Rental House. Once the operation begins, you might as well go out for a big breakfast.

in the book, so no more about it here, except to say that I don't touch any other piece of equipment in a Checkout until the video assist is working.

    B. Check for Obvious Damage
        1. Broken or Missing Knobs and Switches
        2. Missing Screws

Once a minimally acceptable picture is obtained from the dreaded video assist, breathe a sigh of relief and proceed to the Camera Body. First look at the camera body exterior for any obvious damage or missing screws, switches or knobs.

    C. Run Camera

The next thing to do is inch the camera, and then plug it in and turn on the switch. If the wheels go 'round, you're on your way! It is always a good idea to inch the camera movement by hand first, before switching on the power, in case something is REALLY wrong with the camera body. Almost all cameras have some sort of inching knob to move the movement manually and facilitate threading. The knob should turn easily and silently. If the movement is jammed in some way, switching on the motor without first inching the camera may make it worse.

    D. Switches and Controls
        1. On/Off Switches
            a. Main Power Switch
            b. Remote On/Off Switch

Try all the switches and knobs to see if they do what they're supposed to do. Some cameras have more than one on/off switch, either mounted in a hand-grip or accessed through a remote cable that plugs into the body. Try them all. Some zoom motor controls also have a camera run switch. Try this one too.

        2. Tachometer steady
            a. Accurate at Crystal Speeds

Most modern cameras have some sort of out-of-sync warning signal, either a flashing light of some sort, either in the viewfinder visible to the Camera Operator, or on the camera body visible to the Camera Assistant, or some sort of audible beep signal, but how can one be sure that the warning system is operational without some sort of test?

Several hand-held meters are available for checking the accuracy of the camera speed control crystals. Generally these meters function by displaying a series of LEDs (Light Emitting Diodes) or LCD (Liquid Crystal Display) elements whose flashing rate is controlled by a crystal installed within the meter.

In the P.O.M. meter from Haflexx, for example, each of the LEDs flashes once per frame, or twenty-four times per second (some of these meters also operate at 25 and/or 30 frames per second), and in rotation sequence, one after the other. When the LED display is observed through the viewfinder of the running camera, a specific pattern of lit LEDs is seen, and that pattern should remain stable as long as the camera is running.

The Camera Equipment Checkout **51**

Figure 4-5 Crystal Checkers. Two examples of meters used to check the crystals installed in professional cameras. The P.O.M. ("Peace of Mind") from Haflexx allows the Assistant to compare the camera crystal with the crystal installed in the meter, or when connected by a cable, with the crystal installed in the sound recorder. The CINE-CHECK from Cinematography Electronics reads camera speed when the photocell is pointed through the camera eyepiece while the camera is running. The CINE-CHECK also measures flicker rate in HMI and other lighting units.

Whichever LEDs on the display are lit and are visible through the rotating mirror shutter of the camera viewfinder, should be lit each time the shutter is in the viewing position. The same pattern should be visible for each frame, creating the illusion that those LEDs are on continuously while the camera is running, and that other LEDs appear to be off, because they are lit only when the shutter is in the open (non-viewing) position.

This process compares the camera crystal with the crystal in the meter. A stable pattern indicates that the crystals are "in sync" and functioning properly. If the pattern appears to rotate or "travel," then the camera is running either faster or slower than the crystal in the meter, and the sync is not assured. By observing the direction of the travel, and the length of time it takes to make a full rotation, it is possible to compute the amount of drift and the direction of drift.

The first thing to check, in such a situation, is that the proper speed switches are set and cables are connected to the camera, and that the proper power voltage is being supplied to the camera. The next thing to check is the battery in the meter. Try again with a fresh meter battery before panicking. If the pattern still seems to travel, report the condition to the rental house experts.

The P.O.M. also permits the connection of the meter by cable to the sound recorder, allowing the crystal in the camera to be compared to the crystal in the sound recorder, for an even more accurate test. By connecting the cable to the recorder, the pattern of LEDs is controlled by the crystal in the recorder instead of the crystal in the meter. When I was working a lot in documentaries, we used to connect the P.O.M. meter to the sound recorder and film about a minute's worth of the meter every morning when we were on location in Africa or somewhere away from "civilization." This showed us that the crystals in the camera and the recorder were working properly, and that sync sound recording and filming was happening the way we wanted.

The P.O.M. meter may also be connected by cable and transformer to the power mains or generator, to judge whether the crystal control of the generator or the accuracy of the Alternating Current in the mains will permit the use of HMI lights without a flicker problem. HMI lights flash on and off at the frequency of the alternating current in the mains or generator power supply, and can cause a flicker effect to be photographed if the power supply is not accurately enough controlled in relation to the camera speed. Most modern generators are crystal controlled, and most modern mains power systems are accurate enough for no flicker filming, but checking periodically can't hurt.

The CINE-CHECK meter from Cinematography Electronics measures flicker rate, and can be used two ways by the Assistant. First, with the meter switch set to FPS (frames per second), the meter measures camera running speed when the photocell in the top of the meter is held to the camera eyepiece while the camera is running. The display on the meter shows the camera speed to two decimal places (to the hundredth of a frame per second) by measuring the flicker rate of the moving shutter. It helps to point the camera at a light source or bright sky or other bright background. Running the camera for a minute or so while looking at the meter display will let you know everything is working properly. Also for those cameras without a tachometer, this meter functions as a very accurate auxiliary tachometer.

The CINE-CHECK can also be used to measure the flicker rate of HMI, fluorescent, or other light sources, by setting the meter switch to "Hz" (for "Hertz", or "cycles per second"), and pointing the photocell at the light source. Many gaffers use this method to check the running speed and consistency of the generator or the accuracy of the alternating current available at a location.

While on the subject of crystal sync, perhaps a further discussion of the several methods of maintaining sync for filming purposes is in order.

There are three ways to maintain sync between the film camera and the sound recorder for double-system filming. The first is to plug both the camera and recorder into the same Alternating Power source, either from a generator or from the main power supply in a studio or location. Both the camera and recorder need to have AC synchronous motors, and both will run in sync, using the frequency of the AC power supply (60 Hz) as a common reference to run the camera motor at speed and to supply the 60 Hz sync signal for the recorder's sync track. The camera and recorder need not be connected directly to each other, but each must be connected to the same

The Camera Equipment Checkout 53

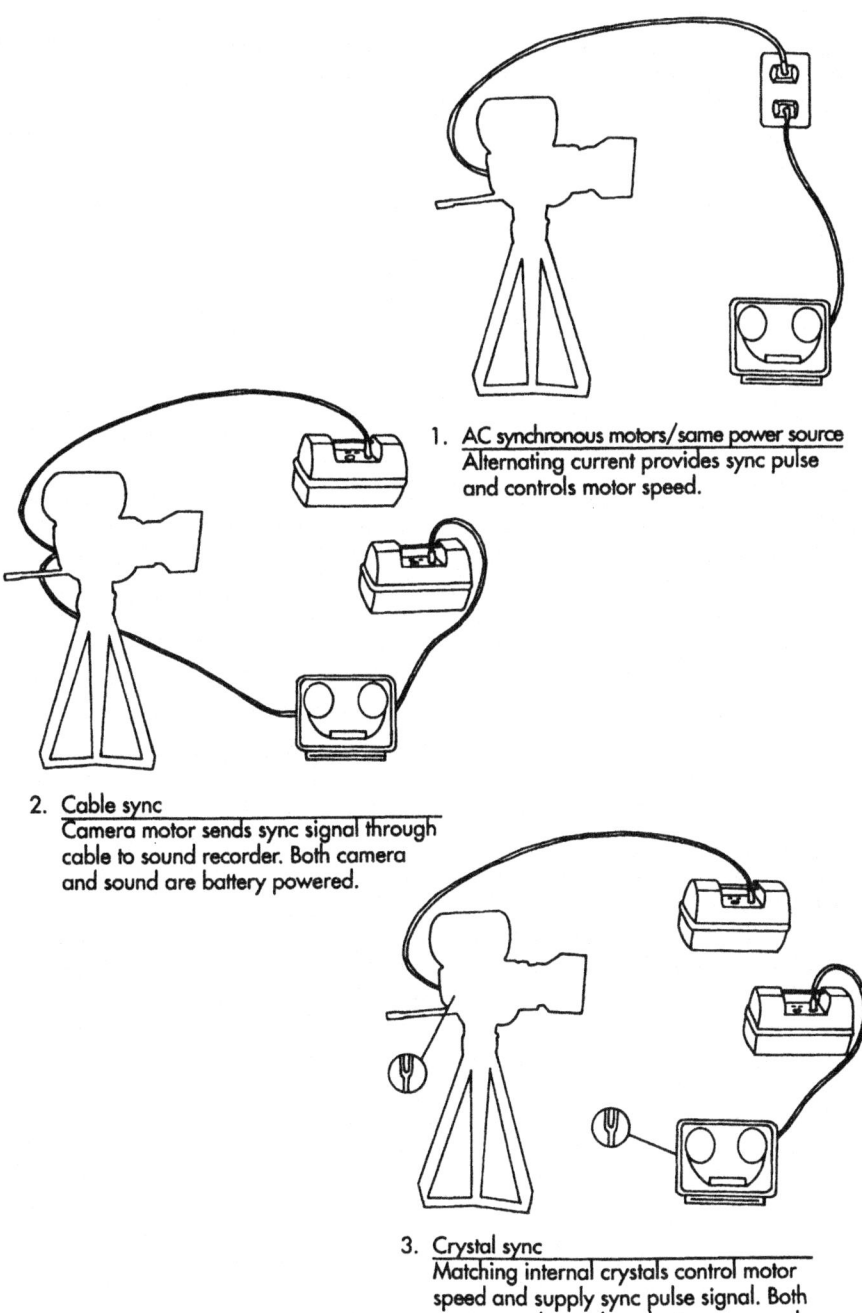

Figure 4-6 Three Methods of Camera/Sound Synchronization.

power source. Minor fluctuations in the power frequency will affect both together, and sync will be maintained.

The second method is to have the camera run on a Direct Current motor from batteries, and generate its own 60 Hz sync signal, which will be carried on a wire "Sync Cable" to the recorder, where the signal is recorded on the sync track. Both camera and recorder may run on batteries, eliminating the need for a generator or attachment to the main power supply, but they must be connected together by cable. These methods are rarely seen these days, now that crystal sync is so readily available, but if your crystal should fail in some remote location, understanding the principle of cable sync might save the show and permit further filming, if you have brought with you a sync cable, or if one can be constructed. Modern cameras and sound recorders still have the cable connectors for a sync cable, should the need for one arise.

The third, and presently most common method for maintaining sync between camera and sound recorder, is for each camera and sound recorder to be equipped with a matching crystal oscillator, which supplies a specific frequency when an electric current passes through it. This high-frequency signal, highly accurate, is divided electronically to provide a very stable and reliable 60 Hz signal to control camera speed and provide a signal for the sound recorder's sync track.

Crystal sync, as this process is called, has the advantage of untying the camera from the sound recorder. There need not be any connection between camera and sound, nor between camera and main power or sound recorder and main power. All are free and unencumbered. Crystal sync systems also have the advantage of being able to sync up any number of cameras with any number of sound recorders, as long as each camera and recorder have the same crystals installed, and that appropriate and adequate slating procedures are followed.

Absolute accuracy in camera running speed is essential when using intermittent lighting sources, such as HMI lights, with a rotating mirror shutter on a film camera. Only certain combinations of shutter angle and film running speed produce acceptable pictures. Other combinations will appear to flicker, because the flicker rate of the light source may be out-of-sync with the rotating shutter. Cinematography Electronics, a company that manufactures a wide range of electronic accessories for motion picture cameras, especially Arriflex cameras, publishes and distributes the best charts of shutter angle and frame rate data for flicker-free filming. For your own laminated chart cards, call or write Cinematography Electronics.

    b. Accurate Variable Speeds

Nearly all cameras have Tachometers (a dial or digital display that shows at what speed the camera is running, in frames per second), so if yours does, check it for accuracy with one of the several crystal checkers available. Also try out the variable speed mode, to see that you are getting the proper range of speeds.

    3. Footage Counter and Reset

An additive footage counter is not much use if it cannot be reset to zero for each new roll of film. The mechanical reset on the early Arriflex 35BL cameras was notorious for not working properly. The electronic digital counters are much more reliable (until they get wet or dusty). Some cameras require a small battery for the footage counters to remember footage readings when the main camera battery is unplugged for moving to another location or changing batteries, etc. Make sure the battery works, and that you have a spare.

4. Crystal and Hertz Settings

Most professional sync-sound cameras have some sort of switching system to change from 24 frames per second (U.S. standard) to 25 fps (European standard) and sometimes to 30 fps (increasingly popular frame rate for film destined for direct video transfers). There may also be a choice of 23.976 fps and/ or 29.97 fps, used when synching the camera with a television or video or computer monitor. They may also have a way of switching from 60 Hertz (cycles per second—U.S. standard) to 50 Hertz (European standard). Make sure you can get the combination you need for your job, and that you know how to change the settings if necessary.

5. Variable Speed Control
   a. Adjusts throughout Range
   b. Minimal Drift

If your camera has a variable speed control, the camera should hold the speed you set it at without significant drift one way or the other. If you do need to shoot something at some unusual speed, the camera should maintain that speed without constant adjustment for at least the length of the shot. Some of the newer and fancier cameras are crystal controlled at all speeds, and will hold these in-between speeds with great accuracy. Other cameras' speed controls are simple (noncrystal) rheostats that can and will drift as the battery depletes or as the film load shifts from the feed side to the takeup side of the magazine.

Not all cameras have a variable speed control as part of the camera body. Some cameras require a variable speed control accessory to be attached in order to change the camera's running speed.

Sometimes the camera has certain preset crystal-controlled speeds, with any other in-between speeds noncrystal. Sometimes, especially in the more modern state-of-the-art cameras, all speeds are crystal controlled, and digitally controlled and accurate to a tenth or even a thousandth of a frame per second. There may be an accessory precision speed control available for your camera, a separate unit connected to the camera by cable that supplies accurate crystal speed control for cameras not built with internal crystal speed control.

6. Variable Shutter
   a. Adjusts throughout Range
   b. Locks

If your camera has the variable shutter feature, you should not only check that the control knob moves, but physically look through the lens port (without a lens) and watch the shutter move as you change the dial setting. Inch the camera movement through its cycle, and make sure the shutter opening itself matches what the shutter dial reads. On some cameras, the shutter itself is marked with the degree settings, and these numbers are visible through the lens port as the shutter turns.

If your camera has a variable shutter, find out from the Director of Photography where he or she would like the shutter angle set for "normal" shooting. Every D.P. has his or her own idea what a "normal shutter angle" is. Some will ask you to set it for its maximum opening (typically 200 degrees for Panavision cameras, 180 degreees for Arriflex), while others will prefer a setting of 180 degrees, even if the camera shutter can be set at a wider opening, to yield a shutter speed of 1/48 second at 24 fps. This is what most light meters are set for. The difference between 180 and 200 degrees on the shutter is only 1/6 stop.

SHUTTER ANGLE AND EXPOSURE COMPENSATION (ROUNDED OFF)

Shutter Angle	Shutter Speed @ 24 fps	Exposure Compensation from 180°
200°	1/43 second	close 1/6 stop
180°	1/48 second	none
172.8°	1/50 second	open 1/10 stop
144°	1/60 second	open 1/3 stop
135°	1/64 second	open 1/2 stop
114°	1/76 second	open 2/3 stop
90°	1/96 second	open 1 stop
72°	1/120 second	open 1+1/3 stop
57°	1/152 second	open 1+2/3 stop
45°	1/192 second	open 2 stops

Another reason to change the shutter is for synching the camera to a television or computer monitor or to such intermittent light sources as HMI lights, or even for 25 fps filming for European use. For these purposes, a shutter angle of 144 or 172.8 degrees is sometimes desired.

Sometimes the variable shutter is used for exposure control without changing the depth-of-field, which would change if the lens aperture was changed. For example, if the D.P. wanted to cut down the exposure one stop without increasing the Depth-of-Field, the shutter could be changed from 180 to 90 degrees. This might be the best way to solve the problem of panning from shade into sunlight during a shot.

Panavision, Mitchell, and the new Arriflex 535 cameras allow shutter changes while the camera is running. Other cameras' shutters may only be changed when not running, by removing the lens and setting the shutter through the lens port, or by some other mechanical means requiring that the camera not be running.

Another possible reason to change the shutter angle would be to reduce the shutter speed of each individual frame if a freeze-frame effect was planned, making each frame sharper and less of a blur. Keep in mind that a shorter exposure time (shutter speed) is more likely to strobe during a pan or with a moving subject than a longer exposure time.

If a special tool is required for changing the shutter, as on some Arriflex cameras, make sure you have the proper tool (a 2mm metric screwdriver-type allen key) and know how to use it.

   E. Electrical System
     1. Buckle Trips (Stops and Resets)
     2. Fuses (Location and Spares)

The more sophisticated the camera, the more likely it will contain one or more Buckle Trip devices. These are simply switches that are normally on, but if the film should break or "buckle," or if the magazine takeup fails for some reason, and film begins piling up inside the camera, the switch will be moved by the film to the "off" position and the camera will be shut off. This is done to prevent permanent damage to the camera and to let the Operator and Assistant know as soon as possible that a film break has occurred. The buckle trips should move freely, should stop the camera immediately upon their activation, and should reset quickly and easily.

Like any electrical device, there are probably fuses somewhere to protect the camera from damage during power surges or short circuits. Find out where the fuses are, and get some spares to carry in your kit.

     3. Circuit Boards and Modules

Some cameras give you access to the primary electrical and electronics circuits by allowing you to easily change electronic circuit boards or electronic modules. The Panavision cameras come with spare (duplicate) circuit boards in the camera case, as well as a tool to open the motor cover and gain access to the boards. Obviously, you shouldn't change the boards unless it is really necessary, and there are two very important rules to follow if you DO have to change the boards.

First of all, **DISCONNECT THE POWER CABLE** to the camera to prevent short circuits and permanent damage while poking around on the inside, removing and inserting the boards.

And secondly, **IF YOU CHANGE ONE BOARD, CHANGE THEM ALL**. The boards, three or four in number depending on the particular camera model, are made to work as a set, and may or may not be compatible individually, depending when the camera was last worked on or repaired, so keep the boards working together as a set.

The boards should also be kept with the particular camera body they were shipped with. The boards should be marked with the serial number of the camera body, and the spare boards often have the serial number plus the letter "S" for "spare."

Some of the symptoms that would indicate some problem with a circuit board are failure to run at all, failure to maintain crystal sync speed, failure of the mirror shutter to stop in the viewing position, loss of variable speed control, and loss of tachometer and/or counter display.

     4. Battery Condition Meter

Not all cameras have battery condition meters, but if yours does, make sure it works and that you understand the codes that the meter is giving you. There are various combinations of red, green, and yellow lights possible, and you should know what they mean. To be of use, a battery meter should give plenty of warning before the battery runs down far enough to prevent the camera from maintaining sync speed. The newer Arriflex cameras show the actual voltage being put out by the batteries, and can be displayed while the camera is running. Find out from the rental house what the minimum voltage is for that model of camera.

5. Heaters
   a. Heater Power Cables
   b. Eyepiece Heater
   c. Magazine Heaters
   d. Heater Electrical Contacts

Not all cameras have internal heaters, but if you are shooting in the cold, it's a nice feature to have. Cameras don't like the cold, and a built-in heater can make a lot of difference. It's hard to check out a heater in a nice warm rental house, because you can't get the camera cold enough to activate the thermostat that turns on the heater, but there should at least be some sort of indicator that the heater circuit is getting power.

Generally you should use a separate battery for the heater whenever possible, because the heater will drain the battery a lot faster than the camera motor, and you certainly wouldn't want to ever be in a situation where you are ready to roll on a scene and the camera won't start because the heater has run the battery down so far that the camera will not maintain sync speed. When the Panavision Platinum cameras were first introduced, there was only one power cable for both the camera and heater systems. Enough complaints came in from Camera Assistants that the second power jack for the heater was installed in later versions of the Platinum cameras.

There may be other heater circuits available on some cameras, in the magazines themselves, in the eyepiece (to keep the eyepiece from fogging up), or elsewhere. Make sure you have the proper cables and enough batteries for the job. Also check the magazine heater electrical contacts to see that they are clean and corrosion free.

6. Magazine Torque Motor Electrical Contacts

If your camera has electrically driven torque motors in its magazines (as opposed to having gear-driven or belt-driven magazines), then the torque-motor electrical contacts should also be checked during the Checkout and periodically during the job to make sure they are clean. If the magazine should stop taking up the film during the shoot, this is the first place to look. Cleaning the electrical contacts with a pencil eraser will often solve the problem.

7. Motors
   a. Types
   b. Power Requirements

Most state-of-the-art professional cameras have a permanently mounted motor that runs on selected crystal speeds and sometimes also a limited range of noncrystal variable speeds. Older cameras often use interchangeable motors, giving you a choice between crystal, wild (variable), high-speed, and constant speed motors, in varying voltages. Be sure you have the right combination of motor speeds, cables, and batteries of the correct voltage necessary for the job. Also check on the motor mounting hardware and motor covers, to make sure they are sufficient and correct, and that you have the proper tools available in your kit to change the motors, if necessary.

8. Bulbs/LEDs
   a. Camera Running
   b. Sync Warning
   c. Battery Condition
   d. Film Jam Warning
   e. Low Film or Out-of-Film Warning
   f. Frame Marking
   g. Edge Marking

Many cameras have running lights, out-of-sync warning lights, and/or battery condition lights. Others may have film jam warning lights, or low film lights (warning that the roll of film is almost gone). Obviously, these lights need to be working properly to be of any value to the Camera Assistant. Some cameras have a "Test" button, which illuminates all of the warning lights so you can see that they are all working. Other systems work like the dashboard warning lights in an automobile. When the camera is first started up, all of the lights come on momentarily to indicate they are working, and then the lights go out if there are no problems.

Camera frame and edge marking bulbs are generally obsolete, used only when cable sync was in vogue before crystal motors were easily available, but are mentioned here just as a reminder in case you do have need of them.

9. Power Cables

Cameras generally come from the rental house with two power cables, but don't hesitate to order more if you would feel more comfortable. You might also want a long power cable if you think the camera might be mounted up high or in some other inconvenient place. You might also consider a long remote switch on a cable to turn the camera on and off from a distance, such as when the camera is mounted on a car hood. Longer cables also need to be heavier gauge wire, to minimize the voltage drop. Twelve-volt cameras with male and female four-pin Cannon XLR plugs on their cables have the advantage that the cables can be "daisy-chained" together to make your own long cable. This will not work with other camera types or voltages. In an emergency, I have borrowed a standard microphone cable with three-pin XLR plugs from the Sound Dept. to extend a 24V Panavision power cable. If shooting in extreme cold, avoid plastic or PVC power cables, and use only neoprene rubber-covered cables, which will better resist cracking.

10. Batteries/ Chargers

a. Correct Voltage
b. Adequate Amperage
c. Batteries Hold Charge

Another book could be written on the subject of batteries, but for this discussion we will limit ourselves to voltage, amperage, and quantity. There are also different types of batteries; Wet Cell, Gel Cell, Ni-Cad, Lead-Acid, Lithium, etc. Obviously, you need batteries of the correct voltage. Most professional cameras generally operate on either 12 or 24 volts, but there are a few 8 and 16 and 30 volt systems and even a 28 volt system still out there. Find out what voltage you need, not only for the camera but for the various accessories, such as heaters, video assists, and zoom motors. Many modern batteries are switchable from 12 to 24 volts, and can be used for either camera system. Just make sure the switch is in the right position BEFORE plugging in.

I once saw a video techie (described affectionately in the business as a "Vidiot") blow out a portable VHS video recorder by switching from 24 to 12 volts on a battery AFTER the 12 volt cable was plugged in to the recorder. There must have been a burst of 24 volt power through the 12 volt outlet as the switch was thrown. It resulted in a puff of smoke and an expensive repair.

In general, cameras of different voltages will use different plugs on their cables. Twelve volt cameras generally use 4-pin XLR (Cannon) plugs, but there are exceptions. There are 5-pin XLR cables and batteries for some 12 volt Arriflex cameras, as well as 4-pin XLR cables and batteries for the 24-volt Moviecam camera. All of the Panavision cameras are set up for 24 volts (except for a few of the older PSR cameras which use 30 volts), and use a 3-pin XLR plug. You would think that the industry could at least standardize on voltages and plugs, but no.

My vote would be for 4-pin XLR for 12 volts and 3-pin XLR for 24 volts, because Arriflex and Panavision are the most common systems. The 5-pin XLR 12-volt system should be discontinued and all 5-pin batteries and cables changed to 4-pin. Unfortunately, in some systems, the 5th pin is used in conjunction with other pins for battery charging and discharging and temperature sensors. Its prime function seems to be to infuriate Camera Assistants who wind up with 5-pin batteries and 4-pin cables, or vice versa. I made up a pair of short adapter cables to carry in my kit, to change 4-pin cables to 5-pin and vice versa.

On Arriflex's 4-pin 12 volt systems, pin 1 is negative and pin 4 is +12 volts; pins 2 and 3 are not used. The same configuration is used for the Aaton, Eclair, and other 16mm cameras. For 5-pin Arriflex 12 volt systems, pin 1 is negative and pin 3 is +12 volts.

All Panavision cameras are now set up for 24 volts. For Panavision's 3-pin 24 volt system, pin 1 is +24 volts and pin 2 is negative. I was not surprised to find that on the Arriflex 16SR3 and 535 cameras, which also use a 24 volt, 3-pin system, the polarity is reversed from the Panavision system. For the Arriflex 24 volt system, pin 1 is negative and pin 2 is +24 volts.

The Moviecam SuperAmerica and Moviecam Compact cameras also use 24 volts, but depending on which rental house the camera is rented from, it may be either a 3-pin or 4-pin system, and may be wired either for the Arriflex batteries or for the Panavision batteries. If you use the wrong battery or cable for that camera system, a fuse in the camera body will blow, and the camera will stop. Be very careful mixing cameras, cables, and batteries from different rental houses!

With the original Moviecam 4-pin 24 volt XLR connector system, pin 1 is negative and pin 2 is +24 volts, and supplies power to BOTH pins 2 and 4 at the camera end of the cable. A Moviecam running with Panavision 3-pin 24 volt batteries needs a cable with pin 1 at +24 volts (supplying pins 2 and 4 at the camera end of the cable) and pin 3 negative, connected to pin 1 at the camera. The same camera running with Arriflex 3-pin 24 volt batteries needs a cable with pin 1 negative and pin 2 supplying +24 volts to pins 2 and 4 at the camera.

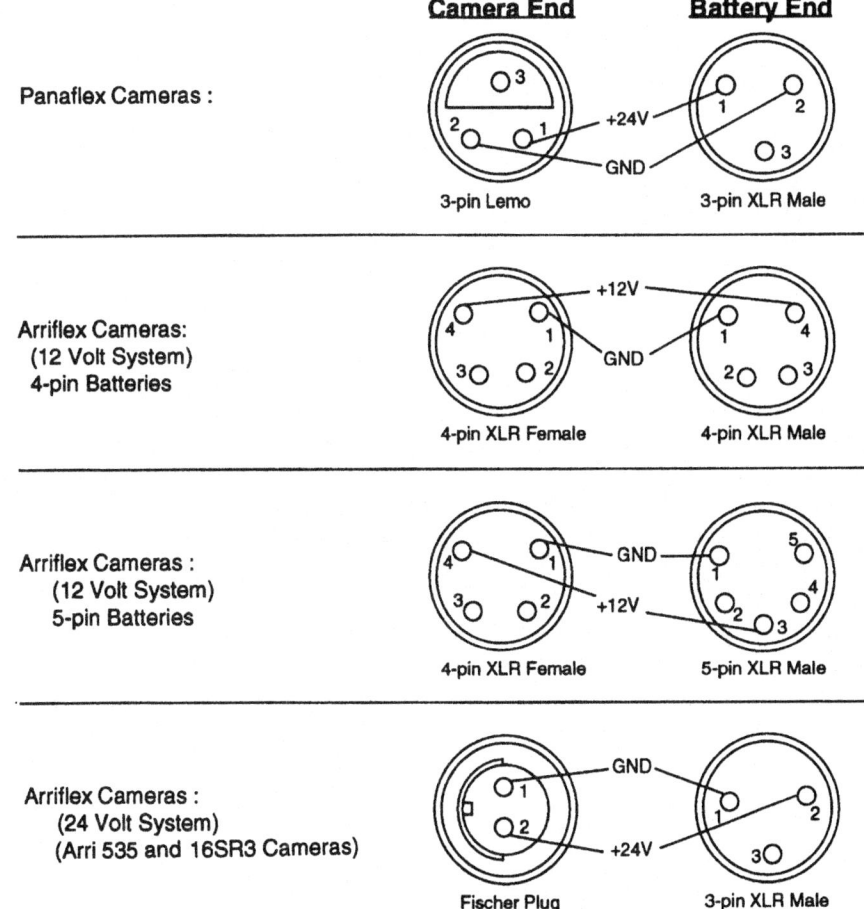

Figure 4-7 Power Cable Pin Configurations. Here are wiring diagrams for the most common camera power cables. All plugs are viewed from the pin side.

62 THE CAMERA ASSISTANT

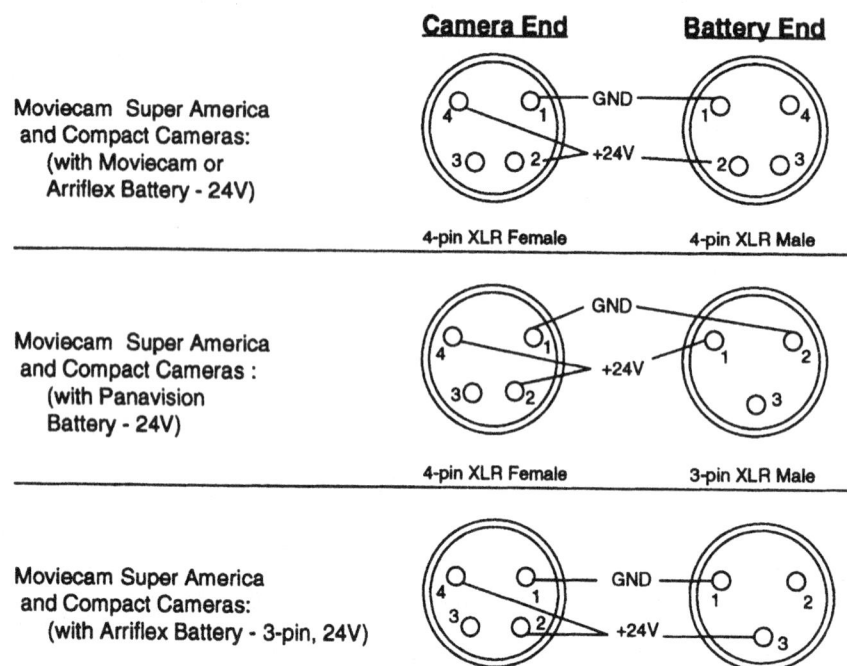

Figure 4-7 Continued.

As far as amperage goes, you don't need to know much except that any camera starts up with a surge of amperage drawn (especially in the cold), and then settles down to a lower amperage when it is running. The more accessories in use, especially heaters, video assist systems, and zoom motors, the more amperage will be drawn and the faster the battery will drain. Make sure you have enough batteries of sufficient amperage for the job. When in doubt, order more!

In the cold, when using belt batteries, the belt batteries can be worn by crew members under their heavy parkas, using the natural body warmth to keep them operating. Keeping batteries warm under your coat won't work with larger and heavier batteries, of course, but there are things you can do. First of all, keep batteries up off the ground. Place them on the dolly, or on an apple box, or in a plastic ice chest or cooler. This will help insulate the batteries and help them hold a charge longer. Wrap batteries in plastic or aluminum foil—anything to hold in the heat or at least slow the cooling.

Most batteries have fuses somewhere (get spare fuses!) that will blow if you try to draw out more amperage than the battery can handle. This is especially serious in the cold, with the higher amperage starting surge. If in doubt, switch off all accessories before warming up the camera, then switch on your video assist, zoom motors, etc. one at a time after the camera warms up a bit.

Also keep in mind that certain high-speed cameras require two separate batteries to operate, and that the amperage drawn will be generally greater at high speed than at sync speed.

Most modern batteries are of the Ni-Cad (Nickel-Cadmium) or Lead-Acid variety, and can be recharged over and over again. The chargers may either be built in to the battery, or may be a separate unit. Generally the batteries take 12 hours (at a charging rate of 1/8 the rated capacity) to 16 hours (at 1/10 of the rated capacity) for a full charge, and the chargers will drop down to a "trickle" or "maintenance" charge when a certain level of charge has been reached.

These systems are fairly "idiot-proof," but make sure you understand the charging procedure and follow two basic rules for getting the best life out of your batteries. First, do not overcharge. Unplug the charger when the batteries are charged.

Second, run the battery down quite a ways before recharging. If you only use the top 10% of your Ni-Cad battery, and then recharge, and repeat this procedure over and over again, the battery can "forget" that it still has another 90 percent and when you need it, you won't get it. Use your batteries until you get a warning light on your battery meter (discharging to about 1 volt per cell), and then recharge completely. This "exercising" or "deep-cycling" of your batteries will prolong their life and the Assistant's sanity.

The easiest way to remember to do this is to clearly number your batteries during the Checkout, rotate them during the shoot, and to use the same battery all day, or until the warning light on the camera tells you it is time to change. On even-numbered days, start the day's shooting with even-numbered batteries, with odd-numbered batteries used on odd-numbered days.

Depending on the type of camera and battery, and the temperature and type of shooting you are doing, you should get between four and ten magazines of film from a fully charged battery. If you are not getting at least four mags out of a battery, the battery probably has one or more bad cells, and needs to be checked by the technicians.

I realize that this is a very short summary of battery use. If you need or want further information, check the Bibliography for references.

11. Power Supplies/Battery Eliminators

If you are shooting in the studio, or on a location where you know there will be adequate and reliable electrical power, you might consider getting a Power Supply or Battery Eliminator. These are very useful devices, especially if you are shooting long takes, or high-speed takes, or if your video assist is on constantly all day long. They can save you many battery changing and charging headaches, but only if the power supply itself is in good condition. Make sure you have spare fuses.

Some power supplies have two or more power outlets, enabling you to run the camera and the video tap simultaneously, or to run both sides of a high-speed motor, but check it out carefully. Many units cause interference ("snow" or "noise") on the video screen when the camera is running, and some units cannot be used in place of two separate batteries for high-speed work. Don't assume that if there are two outlets, that you can use both simultaneously for any purpose.

F. Movement
   1. Clean

Obviously, the heart of the camera body is the movement. The movement is the sole purpose of the camera body; the movement of the film past the aperture, stopping only long enough to receive a short burst of light. The movement must be kept clean, and lubricated, and properly adjusted, in order to do its job. As with any delicate and intricate machinery, leave repairs to the professionals. More than once, well-intentioned but amateurish repair attempts have made the situation worse instead of better.

The movements of some cameras are removable, for easier cleaning, but make sure someone at the rental house shows you the right way to remove and reinsert the movement.

   2. Gate (aperture)
      a. Correct Aperture
      b. Easily Removable
      c. Clean
      d. No Rough Edges
      e. Locks Securely
      f. Gate Masks

The vast majority of cameras will come supplied with a "Full Gate" (also known as a "Silent Aperture" or "Full Aperture" gate), but there are other possibilities. Sometimes the producer or Director of Photography may want to shoot with a gate masked for Academy, or 1.66:1 aspect ratio (for European theatrical release), or 1.85:1 aspect ratio (for U.S. theatrical release). While the use of one of these other gates virtually guarantees proper projection framing by all but the most inept projectionists, it causes problems as well.

The Full Gate gives the Assistant a "safety zone" for debris and hairs found in the gate (which might well be outside of the Academy area). The smaller format gates make it far more likely that any foreign matter that works its way into the gate area will be photographed. The use of a smaller gate area also makes transfer to video format more difficult.

Another possibility is a slotted gate that accepts "mattes" or "inserts" that mask off part of the photographed negative. If you have such a gate, as in the Panavision Panaflex family of cameras and the Arri 535 camera, make sure the matte is not still in the slot from a previous customer, unless you want it there. Aperture masks or mattes are available in Academy, Super 35, 1.66:1, and 1:85:1 formats, but their use is rare. Aperture masks are not used for Full (Silent) Aperture or Anamorphic filming.

The gate itself is removable from most cameras to aid in cleaning and inspection. The gate should slide out easily and lock securely. Any dirt or build-up of emulsion may result in scratching of the film as it moves past, or may cause a jam. Obviously, any scratches in the metal or rough edges in the film path can be very detrimental to smooth operation.

Clean the gate area only with plastic or wooden tools, never metal, which may scratch the delicate aperture plate and make the situation worse than if you had left the gate dirty! An orange-wood stick or plastic skewer and lens tissue is often all you will need to clean and polish the gate.

3. Pressure Plate
   a. Easily Removable
   b. Clean
   c. No Rough Edges
   d. Locks Securely

The same considerations apply to the pressure plate, which is positioned on the back side of the film to help keep the film flat against the gate during exposure. It is generally held in place with a spring of some sort, and should be kept clean, using only plastic or wooden implements, and lens tissue.

4. Flange Focal Depth and Film Gap
   a. Checking
   b. Adjustment

Depth checking and setting will be discussed in depth later in this book. For now, just be aware that these dimensions are critical, and that on some cameras they are user-adjustable, and on some cameras they are not.

5. Shutter Sync (Timing)/(Phasing)

The synchronization between the shutter and the movement of the film is very critical. The film should be absolutely stationary when the shutter is open, should remain stationary throughout the exposure, and should not start moving to the next frame until the shutter has closed completely.

If the camera has registration pins, the pins should be fully retracted while the film is moving, and should enter the appropriate perforations only after the film has stopped. With a little practice, by slowly advancing the inching knob, which turns the movement manually, and observing the action of the shutter and registration pins, you should be able to determine if the synchronization is accurate. Another, better and more reliable method will be discussed later in this book, in the chapter on Setup and Maintenance.

6. Registration Pins
   a. Operational
   b. Retract Smoothly
   c. Registration Test

The registration test is discussed at length later in this book, in the chapter on Shooting Tests.

7. Lubrication

If your camera allows user lubrication (not all cameras do), find out from the rental house and/or manufacturer's instruction manual what types of lubrication should be used and where and how often lubrication should be performed, and whether there are different lubricants for different operating temperatures.

Some high-speed cameras require lubrication with every film reload or after every high-speed take. After such high-speed lubrication, run the camera with scrap film and then discard the oil-specked film, as the oil contaminates the film developer. If using a camera like the Mitchell S35R or Mark II, the dual compartment magazine allows the Assistant to open the magazine and quickly remove and discard the oil-specked film and reattach the new end of the roll to the hub. Check the manufacturer's recommendations.

It has been my experience that standard cameras which allow user lubrication should be oiled approximately every ten thousand feet of film; they should be oiled more often if shooting high-speed or if the temperature is either hot or cold; and even more often if shooting black-and-white film (which does not have the lubrication layer on the film that color negative film does have).

I generally oil the camera every morning, as part of my daily routine maintenance procedure, unless I know that very little film has been shot since the last oiling. If shooting a lot of film, a second oiling in the middle of the day may have to be done.

After any oiling, excess oil should be wiped off, with a Q-tip, or lens tissue, or some other absorbent (but lint-free) material.

8. Free Rollers

The rollers (or idlers) should all turn freely, and should not have any sharp edges.

9. Pitch Control
    a. Working
    b. Quiets Camera

It is hard to imagine why any professional camera today would be made WITHOUT a pitch control, but there are several. A pitch control is essential in keeping a modern sound camera quiet. The pitch control adjusts the length of the stroke between the pull-down claw and the registration pin. These two enter different perforations as they work, and tiny variations in the distances between perforations can make a tremendous difference in the noise produced in the camera. Changes in types of film stock, the age of the film stock, or even in the temperature and humidity, can stretch or shrink the film microscopically, but enough so that the camera will make more noise. The pitch control can greatly reduce that noise.

10. Scratch Test

The camera and magazine scratch tests will be discussed at length later in this chapter.

G. Viewing System
    1. Ground glass
        a. Correct Aspect Ratio Markings
        b. Accurate Markings

What is the intended audience for your production? Every application has a different shape screen, known as the aspect ratio (a ratio of two numbers representing the proportion of the width of the screen and the height). Theatrical release in the U.S. is generally 1.85:1 (the width of the screen being 1.85 times the height). European theatrical release is usually 1.66:1. Television (which includes video cassette releases of films shot in other ratios) is approximately 1.33:1, but is usually pictured with rounded sides or corners instead of as a rectangle, and is smaller in scale than Academy.

Ground glasses, those fragile, postage-stamp-sized, pieces of glass that the lens focuses an image on, usually come with multiple markings, generally Academy markings, which show the limits of usable picture area on the negative, plus one other format. The most common configurations of ground glasses are "Curved T.V./ Academy" (television screen markings with rounded corners), 1.66/Academy, and 1.85/ Academy. These ground glasses are quickly and easily changed with simple tools. There will often be a choice of frame center markings (a dot, a cross, or nothing).

There are also other formats available, such as Anamorphic (2.35:1, also variously described as Cinemascope, Panavision 35, etc.), and some new and different formats coming into the marketplace: "Super 1.85" or "Super 35" (which extends into what is normally the soundtrack area of the negative) and Three-Perf (with three perforations per frame instead of the normal four) to name but a few.

As far as accuracy of the ground glass markings goes, a procedure for testing the markings is discussed later in this book.

c. Illuminated Markings Correct

Certain cameras have a feature that illuminates the markings on the groundglass for easier operating at night or in dim surroundings. A black frameline is hard to see against a black sky or black street. This illumination is accomplished in the Panavision cameras by the Panaglow system, by means of a small lightbulb or LED (light emitting diode) inside the viewing system that reflects off mirrored groundglass markings. If your camera supports this feature, a special groundglass (in whatever configuration you might need) is required. These illuminated markings generally are controllable by a dimmer, and can be brightened or dimmed to the Director of Photography's or Operator's preference. The newer Arriflex cameras have the Arriglow system which is slightly different in principle, but still illuminates the frameline. Ask the rental house personnel to show you how to adjust the brightness and the timing of the Arriglow.

d. Installed Correctly

In some cameras there is only one way that the groundglass can be installed, but in others, like the Panavision cameras, it is possible to install the groundglass backwards. The rough side of the groundglass (the "ground" side) must face the mirror shutter and lens. If the groundglass is installed incorrectly (backwards), nothing that is in focus for the viewfinder will be in focus for the film, and vice versa, so be careful. If there is a significant difference between eye-focus and the markings on the lens consistently throughout the focus range of the lens in a Panavision camera, first check the orientation of the groundglass.

e. Depth Correct

The ground glass must not only be facing the right direction, but also be positioned at the precisely correct distance behind the lens as the film plane or else the focus will be different for the viewfinder and the film. Depth checking and setting will be discussed later in this book.

2. Clean

Obviously the viewfinder should be clean. There are some surfaces the Assistant can reach, and some he or she cannot, so if there is a lot of dust and/or fingerprints visible as smudges in the finder, clean the surfaces you can reach, and ask the rental house technicians to clean the ones you can't. Don't start taking things apart.

3. Stops in Viewing Position

Virtually all of the professional 16mm and 35mm cameras currently available are designed to stop with the mirror shutter in the viewing position. The exceptions include the Arriflex IIC, Arri IIIC, Arri 16S and 16BL cameras, and the Mitchell family of cameras, although some newer motors for these cameras do stop in the viewing position. If your camera is supposed to stop in the viewing position, but does not, it could indicate either a mechanical or an electronic problem. Have the rental house shop check it out.

4. Diopter Correction
   a. Working
   b. Adequate for Job

It is difficult to see through or operate the camera wearing eyeglasses, so virtually all camera viewing systems include some sort of diopter correction to allow viewers to dial in their particular eyesight peculiarities. Since there will be at least four people (Director of Photography, Director, Camera Operator, and Camera Assistant) who MUST look through the camera, and many more who will WANT to look through the camera, make sure the diopter correction is working, and that the range is suitable for the people who may have to use it.

This is not easy to check until you have all the people and the camera in the same place, but in general, the Assistant should know what his or her own eyesight is, and can judge what the range is in comparison. In other words, if you have good eyesight without glasses, your eyepiece mark should be approximately in the middle of the correction range to allow for the maximum correction for others, whether they are near- or far-sighted.

The range of correction is somewhat adjustable by service technicians, and can be adjusted to your request. I was once on a feature where the D.P.'s correction was nearly all the way in one direction, and the director's nearly all the way in the other direction, and the diopter correction range had to be adjusted several times to find the right setting for both. Our backup camera on that job was an identical model, but for some reason, the viewfinder could not be set to hold both the D.P.'s and the director's eyesight, so we set it for the D.P. and had the rental house set the lens cut from an old pair of the director's glasses into a removable mount on the eyepiece so that both could look through the camera.

I also have worked with two D.P.'s and a Camera Operator who have an astigmatism in their normal vision, and who have had a correction lens made for them that fits into the camera eyepiece and attaches magnetically in the proper orientation to correct the astigmatism.

    5. Illuminated Groundglass Dimmer

If your camera has the illuminated groundglass feature mentioned above, there will also be a dimmer for that feature. Find out where it is and see if it is working. Set it for the Operator's preference when you use this feature on the shoot. I have never heard of a case where the illuminated groundglass feature was so bright that the film was fogged, but I suppose it is possible, especially with the new faster color emulsions.

    6. Viewfinder Magnifier
    7. Contrast Viewing Glasses
       a. Correct Filters
       b. Clean

Many modern cameras have built into their viewing systems a magnifier for the groundglass image used for critical focusing and contrast viewing glass(es) used by the Director of Photography to aid with lighting. These should be checked by the Assistant to see if they are functioning properly, and are clean. There should not be a visible focus shift between viewing through the magnifier and without. The contrast glasses are changeable, to the D.P.'s preference. Usually they are set up for two different densities of neutral density filters, but they can be changed in the rental house shop, should you need, for example, a black-and-white viewing glass or an even darker neutral density filter instead. Find out from the Director of Photography what he or she needs for the particular job at hand.

    8. Eyepiece Extension
       a. Functional
       b. Clean

Some cameras have a basic eyepiece for hand-held use and an extension viewfinder for use when the camera is on a gear head. The Assistant should check that the various glass surfaces are clean and that the Eyepiece Diopter Correction marks do not shift when using the built-in magnifier. The pieces should also attach together quickly and securely, and if required, the internal viewfinder prism should flip over correctly when the extension is added or removed. The rental house personnel will show you how to do this.

    9. Periscope
   10. Video Assist Door
   11. Rotating Eyepiece
       a. Functional
       b. Clean

These should be self-explanatory. Some cameras allow the use of a periscope finder for the Operators' comfort. If you have one, make sure it is clean and functional. If your camera has a separate camera door for the video assist, check the optical viewfinder on this door as well as the standard door. If the eyepiece is supposed to rotate, make sure it does, that the image remains upright as the eyepiece rotates (if it is supposed to), and that it locks in position when you want it to.

12. Viewfinder Masks

Some Directors of Photography like to use viewfinder masks when shooting certain aspect ratios so as to restrict what can be seen through the viewfinder. These masks affect only the viewfinder—not the image being photographed. For example, inserting a 1.85:1 mask into the matte slot next to the groundglass in the viewfinder restricts the viewfinder to only the 1.85:1 frame. This is often used for lighting the scene and rehearsing, to give the D.P. and the director a better idea of what will appear on the screen, without distractions.

The 1.85 mask is generally removed prior to shooting so that the Operator can see the full Academy frame, or more if the viewfinder shows more outside of Academy, so that microphones, lights, and other obstacles can be seen before they enter the frame.

Sometimes the Operator prefers to have an Academy mask installed, blacking out everything outside of the Academy frame, so that anything seen in the finder will definitely be photographed. This allows the Operator to concentrate more on the Academy frame.

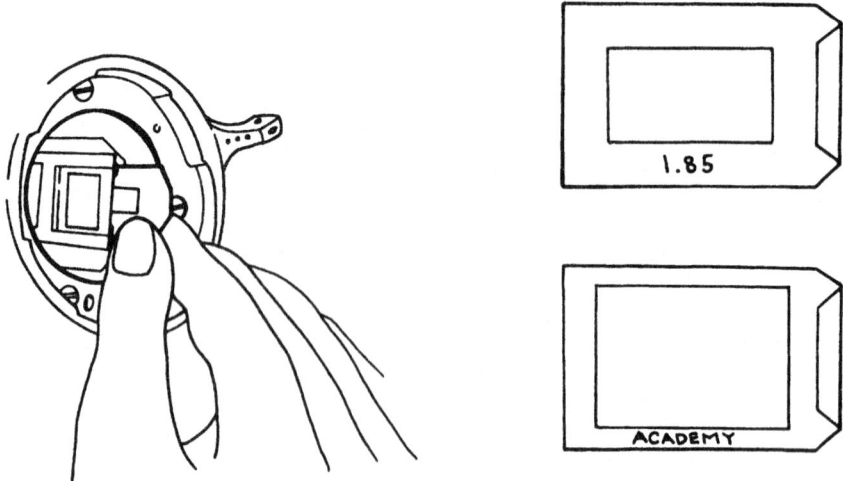

Figure 4-8 Viewfinder Masks. Viewfinder Masks can be inserted into the Matte Slot next to the Groundglass of the Panavision Panaflex cameras to block out unwanted areas from the viewfinder. Two of the most common are the "1.85:1" and "Academy" masks.

In the heat of battle, a light or microphone might be seen briefly in the corner or edge of the frame, and the Operator may be watching for so many other things that he or she may be unsure whether the unwanted object was inside Academy or outside. With the Academy mask in place, if he saw it, so did the Academy frame on the film.

Find out from your Director of Photography and Operator what their preferences are. Using the masks can remove a lot of distractions, but the Operator may prefer being able to see the obstacles and potential intruders outside the frame before they enter Academy.

13. Matte Slot

If you are shooting background plates, or special effects mattes, make sure your camera has a matte slot immediately adjacent to the groundglass and that the mattes cut from the film strip by the accessory matte cutter you should add to the equipment list do indeed fit in the slot.

deed fit in the slot.

H. Miscellaneous
1. Door Latches and Seals

Check to see that the door latches, seals, and hinges are clean and tight, and that the door locks securely to the camera body. Some cameras use a rubber "O-Ring"

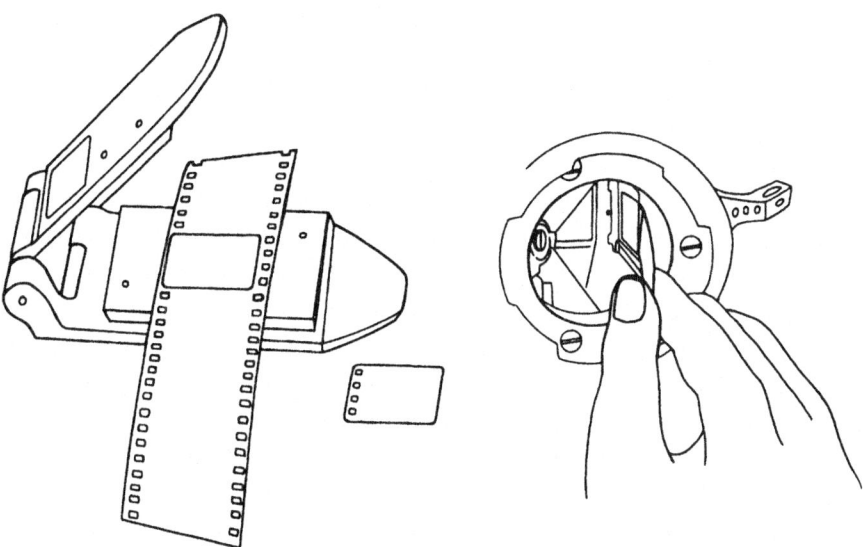

Figure 4-9 Matte Slot and Matte Cutter. The Panavision Matte Cutter is used to cut a single frame from a previously shot and printed strip of film. This single frame, or "matte" is inserted into a slot in front of the groundglass in the camera to aid in positioning foreground elements or actors for "matting" into previously filmed footage of the background.

around the inside of the door as part of the light and sound seal. Check to see that this is not worn or frayed, and make sure it is sitting properly in its slot.

    2. Gel Filter Slot
        a. Slot Empty
        b. Gel Holders
        c. Cut Gels for Holders

If your camera has a slot for behind-the-lens gelatin filters, make sure the slot is empty, that the gel holders frames fit into the slot, and that you have the proper gelatins to cut to fit the holders. Ask the Director of Photography which filters to mount in holders. Generally only type "85" filters and Neutral Density (and the 85/Neutral Density combinations) will be needed, but sometimes others will be used, such as the 85B or 81EF series, or the "CC," or "Color Compensation" filters.

The Panavision gel holders come in a box of twelve, and Assistants generally cut at least three of each filter needed. Properly cared for, they will last quite a while, but always check them for dust and fingerprints before inserting them into the camera. Dust may be blown off, but if fingerprints are present, use another gel and replace the smudged one. Forget about trying to clean them; gels are too fragile and will scratch too easily.

Panavision makes a gel filter punch for this shape holder, but I have found that a small sharp pair of scissors and some paper tape is all that is needed. If you are careful, four gel holders can be filled from a single 3"x 3" gel filter. A tiny piece of paper masking tape (NOT cloth camera tape—too thick!) or Scotch Magic Mending Tape will secure the cut gel into the holder. Take great care in making sure that the filter holders are properly labeled.

Using gels behind the lens is a somewhat controversial issue for some D.P.'s, and is discussed at length in the chapter on Filters.

    3. Camera Lockdown Screw

This may seem like a silly item to include in this list, but should be checked anyway. First check the threads on the tripod head screw, and look at the threads in the camera mounting hole, to be sure they are neither worn nor stripped. Look to see how long the camera lockdown screw of your tripod head protrudes above the mounting plate. Then measure the depth of the hole in the bottom of the camera. The screw should be long enough to mount the camera securely, but not too long. If this screw is too long for the camera mounting hole, you run the risk of damaging the delicate camera movement or electronic circuit boards in the bases of some cameras, especially the Arriflex 16SR. If the screw is too long, or too short, it can usually be adjusted or simply replaced with a longer or shorter one. Ask the rental house to show you how.

    I. Accessories
        1. Hand-Held Accessories

Make sure you have the proper handgrips, shoulder rests, bracketry, etc., if you are planning any hand-held shooting. Also check any camera power switches that may be built into the handgrips to make sure they function correctly.

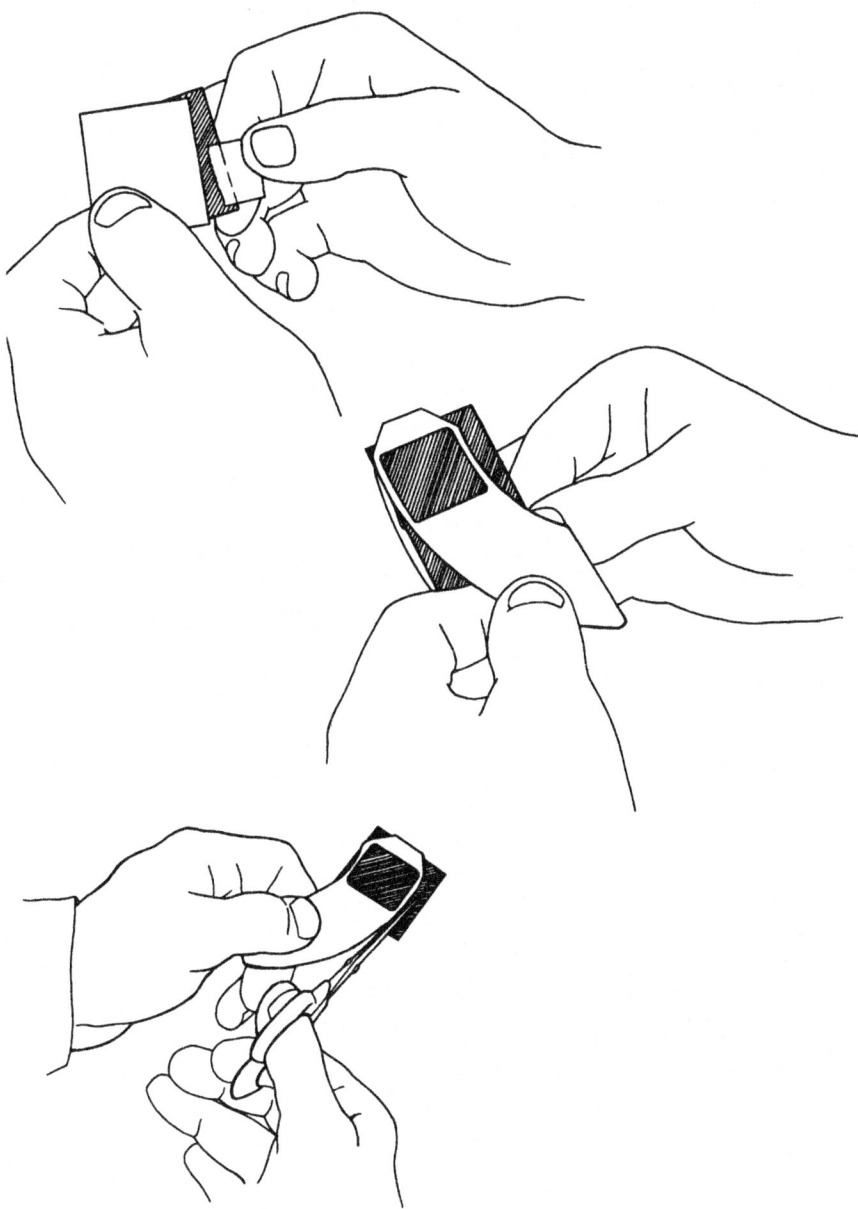

Figure 4-10 Cutting Gels for Gel Holders. Cutting gels for the Panavision Gel Holders takes some time and some practice. After cutting the 3" x 3" gels in quarters (keep the gel inside the white tissue paper it is packaged with until after cutting). A small piece of tape makes the best handle and attaches the gel to the inside of the gel holder. Once the gel is taped to the holder, scissors can be used to trim the waste around the exterior of the holder.

2. Speed Control Accessories
   a. Variable Crystal Speed Controllers
   b. Time Lapse/Single Frame Controllers
   c. High Speed Controls

These are all "black boxes" that plug into the camera body to perform special functions. If you need any of them, check them out thoroughly, make sure you understand completely the principles and the procedures involved, and then take backups anyway, especially of any cables that might be needed.

Variable Crystal Speed Controllers allow the user to adjust the running speed of the camera. The range of adjustment varies from model to model, and also depends on what camera it is attached to, but four frames per second to sixty or one hundred and twenty frames per second is a typical range. Some of these units are accurate to a thousandth of a frame per second, and provide accurate crystal speed control at all speeds.

Time lapse (single frame) controllers, also known as Intervalometers, expose one frame at a time, at specific intervals, such as six frames per minute, or twelve frames per hour, or whatever might be required for what you are trying to film. They are used for filming flowers blooming, grass growing, speeding up sunrises or sunsets, etc. Make sure you understand the programming procedure, and that you know the exact exposure time (the length of time the camera shutter remains open) for each possible frame rate. Time-lapse filming presents various other problems as well. Sometimes in bright exterior filming, and with certain camera systems, the lens must be "capped" between exposures. Wind buffeting of the camera during time-lapse filming is much more severe on the screen, so great care must be taken to firmly secure the camera and brace it off during filming. Check with your D.P. for other requirements for this type of filming.

Any speed over 24 frames per second is considered a high speed, which slows down the action. The main sync-sound-capable production camera will rarely go faster than 30 to 50 frames per second. Other easily obtainable cameras will go as fast as 120 frames per second. For any speed above 120 fps, special cameras are available, and much care must be taken. Special training for these cameras is a must. Threading and lubrication on these special high-speed cameras is very critical, and should not be attempted without thorough training and practice.

EXPOSURE COMPENSATION FOR CHANGES IN CAMERA SPEED (ASSUMING 24 FPS STANDARD SPEED)

Camera Speed	Exposure Change	Camera Speed	Exposure Change
6 fps	−2 stops	30 fps	+1/3 stop
8 fps	−1 2/3	36 fps	+1/2
10 fps	−1 1/3	40 fps	+2/3
12 fps	−1	48 fps	+1
16 fps	−2/3	60 fps	+1 1/3
18 fps	−1/2	72 fps	+1 1/2
20 fps	−1/3	96 fps	+2
24 fps	0	120 fps	+2 1/3

A negative number on the chart means to give the film LESS exposure by STOPPING DOWN the lens to a smaller stop (larger T/ number). A positive number means to give the film MORE exposure by OPENING UP the lens to a larger stop (smaller T/ number).

3. Sync Control Accessories
   a. Field/Frame Synchronizers
   b. Projector Synchronizers84
   c. Television/Monitor Synchronizers

Field/Frame and Television/Monitor synchronizers allow the production camera to film television and computer monitors of various scan rates without the annoying and distracting "roll bar" which would result from straight filming at 24 frames per second. Even if the monitor is very small, the roll bar in the background of the scene can be very distracting to the audience.

Properly used, and in conjunction with a variable shutter, these units can reduce the width of the bar to near zero, and freeze it just off the visible screen of the monitor. The shutter setting can reduce the roll bar in width, and the frame rate can freeze it off the screen. Certain combinations of shutter angle and frame rate will work. Two of the best combinations are listed below:

SHUTTER OPENING		**FRAME RATE**
180 degrees	at	29.97 fps
144 degrees	at	23.976 fps

23.976 frames per second is close enough to 24 to permit sync sound filming without a noticeable pitch change for projects destined for the big screen, while 29.97 fps is a perfect rate for direct video transfer, for television commercials, and for other television projects.

Another option is to use the services of one of the several companies who use the "24-Frame Video" process, permitting the filming of video monitors with real video pictures, at 24 frames per second at a 180 degree shutter angle.

Computer monitors, depending on the brand of the computer and the particular software being used, run at various frame rates between 29 and 30 frames, and can be filmed at specific frame rates determined by test. Some monitors scan much faster, and must be filmed at 40 or more frames per second. The best description of the testing process can be found in the *American Cinematographer Manual.*

Projector Synchronizers allow the filming of an image projected on a screen by a specially equipped motion picture projector for front- or rear-projection process filming. In effect, the camera is connected to the projector by a cable, and the camera shutter is "slaved" to the projector shutter. Both shutters are open at the same time and closed at the same time, resulting in synchronization between projector and camera and pictures without flicker. When shooting front- or rear-projection, the projectionist who comes to the studio with the equipment will generally be a specialist in such work, and will make sure the camera and projector are properly hooked up together.

4. Eyepiece Levelers

The Eyepiece Leveler supports the rotating eyepiece when the camera is mounted on a geared head or fluid head, and holds it in more or less a stationary position as the camera is tilted up or down. It is essential to remember to release the eyepiece brake lock whenever the leveler is in use. This makes it much easier and more comfortable for the Operator to keep his or her eye to the viewfinder while tilting the camera. Years ago, with cameras with fixed eyepieces, the Camera Operators had to be contortionists to keep their eye to the finders on some shots, and some planned shots were just not possible to do, because of the human body's inability to follow the eyepiece of a moving camera.

Take an eyepiece leveler whenever you have a rotating eyepiece, and a gear head or fluid head that accepts the leveler.

5. Weather Protectors/Rain Covers

The weather protectors and rain covers help keep the camera dry and warm in bad weather. The weather protector, theoretically, at least, lets you operate the camera during bad weather, with holes for the eyepiece and gear head wheels, and clear plastic windows so that the Assistant can see the lens marks for following focus. I emphasize "theoretically" because while it may be POSSIBLE to shoot with this raincoat on, it is not easy.

The cover gets caught and pulls on the camera, the "clear" plastic windows get scratched and dirty and then fog up so the Assistant can't see through them. The Assistant cannot see the tach or footage counters, cannot hear when the film runs out, and in general the cover is almost more of a hindrance than a help, but it is better than nothing. Barely. Ask the grips to rig an umbrella or tent for the camera, instead. In really severe weather, a six-foot section of parallel (scaffolding) wrapped in a tarp and surrounding the camera just cannot be beat.

6. Matte Punch

Not all cameras have a matte slot, but if yours does, and you plan to use it, then remember to take a matte punch, to correctly cut the desired frame out of the strip of film. If you need to shoot through a matte, make sure the lab sends over to the set strips of film long enough to work with, at least two to three feet. It is also desirable to have both negative and positive images of the frames to be matted, and it is also a good idea to have printed several different densities of print of the scene to be matted. Having these options will enable you to select a frame for matte cutting and inserting that gives the operator the best chance of seeing what needs to be seen through the frame, both the live image and the print.

7. Lens Lights

These are very useful worklights for the Assistants, allowing them to see the lens focus and aperture scales in a dark studio or night exterior location. They are also useful for threading the camera—much better than holding a flashlight in your teeth. These lights might either be powered by the camera battery through their connection to the camera or might contain their own penlight (AA) batteries.

8. On-Board Video Monitor

Some cameras have an on-board video monitor for use when there is a video assist system in use. This is occasionally useful to an Assistant, mostly in showing the Assistant what actual target is being photographed, and when the target enters and/or leaves frame, and in positioning the slate in frame, but not often otherwise. They are much too small to be used for focus. Mostly they drain batteries, cause eyestrain, and attract tourists.

9. Carrying Handles

There is a long camera carrying handle, often called a "Hollywood" handle, that is made for the Panaflex cameras, but that, for some unfathomable reason is not automatically supplied as an accessory. You have to ask for it, and pay extra rental for it. But it is by far the best way to carry the Panaflex camera. This handle attaches to the rear magazine port and to the back of the lens support rod holders, and with that two-point purchase, is very strong. There are two models for use with and without an on-board video assist camera. Make sure to ask for it, and the extended long rod bracket that it attaches to it.

The Arriflex 35BL family of cameras sport the ideal handle, built right in to the top of the camera body. This handle is comfortable, well balanced, and perfect for carrying the camera. Unfortunately, the video assist camera mounts directly in front of this handle and extends back over this handle, often preventing the Camera Assistant from being able to use it without swinging the video assist out of the way (if your model video assist allows this), which would mean resetting it again before filming. Bad planning, fellas!

The Moviecam Compact offers an incredible array of handle options and configurations. All the pieces should come as standard equipment with the camera.

II. Lenses and Filters
A. Lens Mount

Obviously, all the lenses should have the same mount, and that mount should be the same as is found on the camera. Unfortunately, this is another area that the industry has been unable (unwilling) to standardize. There are more than half a dozen different mounts available for professional cameras. There are occasionally adapters to change one mount to another, but not all combinations can be adapted, because of diameter of the mount or rear element or because of differences in the flange focal depth (the distance between the lens mount and the film plane).

Lenses and mounts will be discussed further elsewhere in this book, but for purposes of the Checkout, the lenses should fit into the mount with the aperture, focus, and zoom markings visible to the Assistant, should lock securely into the mount, release easily, and the surfaces of the lens mount and the camera body mount should be clean, dry, and dust free.

Before inserting a new lens for the first time into a camera body, inch the mirror shutter out of the way. After mounting the lens, always inch the camera mechanism by hand several turns, making sure that the rotating mirror shutter does not come into contact with the back of the lens. Some lenses, generally wide-angle lenses, extend so far into the camera body that they have to be specially bevelled (cut at an angle) to clear the mirror. If your lens is cut this way, there will be a locating pin or notch to prevent the lens from being attached in any other orientation than the correct one. Do not attempt to bypass this feature! Serious damage can result.

Other lenses can be attached to the camera in several orientations, allowing the Assistant to position the focus, aperture, and zoom indices to a convenient orientation. Some lens focus scales are marked in feet and inches on one side, and meters on the opposite side. Choose which scale you want to use, rotate the lens and insert into the camera accordingly.

Sometimes the Camera Assistant must work on the camera's right side (known as the "Dumb Side" because there are usually no switches, displays, or other filming aids on that side, and also because the Assistant cannot communicate as easily with the Camera Operator), because of the lighting or other obstacles, and being able to rotate the lens in the mount allows the focus, aperture, and zoom scales to be visible on the Dumb Side of the camera. Some lenses have scales marked on both sides, but not all. The Panavision Platinum and Arri 535 cameras have a second display on the right side of the camera, making the Assistant's job a bit easier.

    B. Lens Support
        1. Adequate Support
        2. Correct Rods
        3. Correct Brackets

Heavy Zoom Lenses and some long Telephoto Lenses require support. Make sure everything fits, that the support rods are of the right length, and that you can still mount follow-focus gear and matte boxes when the support and lens are installed. These support rods are often called "support bars" in England and "iris rods" by some people, although they have absolutely nothing to do with the lens iris. (Dave Quaid suggests that this term goes back to the silent film days when an additional "iris" mechanism was mounted in front of the lens for in-camera "iris in" and "iris out" effects.) Don't assume that the rods and brackets that are in the case with the lens actually fit the lens. Try them and see.

    C. Iris
        1. Moves Smoothly
        2. Leaves Flat and Regular
        3. Minimal Play

One of the most common lens problems is a broken iris. The iris is a collection of thin metal leaves connected together to form a variable diameter opening. If one of those leaves becomes loose, it can either block too much of the opening or leave too big a hole. Either will throw off your exposure. The iris leaves can be knocked off their tracks by a sudden shock or fall. If you look at the iris from the back of the lens each time you put the lens on the camera, you should be able to notice if any of the leaves are out of line. The opening should be smooth-edged and regular, or symmetrical. The same amount of each leaf should be visible at all times. Depending on the manufacturer and model of the lens, the opening might be round, hexagonal, octagonal, or even triangular, but the opening will always be regular.

Get in the habit of always looking at the rear of the lens before inserting it into the camera. Look for two things—that the rear element is clean (smudge free and dust free), and that the iris is working properly. It wouldn't hurt to also check the lens mount on the camera and the mount on the lens. It only takes a few seconds to check. You will never be in that much of a hurry.

When turning the iris ring on the lens, there should be very little "slack" or "play" before the iris starts to move, especially on the newer lenses. There will always be a little bit of "play," and to compensate for any possible errors resulting from that "play," you should always set the aperture from the same direction.

In other words, always stop down the lens when changing stops. Turn the iris from a larger stop (lower number) to a smaller stop (higher number), always coming from the same direction. If you need to open the aperture before shooting, open the iris of the lens past your destination on the iris, and then stop down to your destination from the wider aperture. This will help make the exposures more consistent throughout the shoot.

    D. Focus
       1. Infinity

Focus is, of course, one of the most important responsibilities of the Camera Assistant, so accurate focus marks on the lenses are an absolute necessity. If you have no time for anything else on your checkout, do check the focus marks on the lenses. If the infinity mark is good, and two or three other marks are good, then the odds are pretty good that the rest of the scale is accurate.

The best and fastest way to check the infinity mark is with a collimator. Rental houses nearly always have a big bench collimator, and if you have any doubts about the infinity mark on the lens, ask the technicians to put your lens on their collimator.

If a collimator is not available, just look out the window, if you can find one. Find a distant target, like a city skyline, look through the camera and lens combination, and focus normally. If the lens focus scale reads infinity, or close to it, the lens scale infinity mark is probably all right. Unfortunately, for security and blackout reasons, most rental houses' checkout rooms do not have windows, so you may have to go elsewhere in the building to find a window or rooftop or out into the parking lot to conduct this test.

       2. Focus Marks
          a. Enough Marks
          b. Marks Accurate
          c. Feet/Meters

Once you have established to your satisfaction an accurate infinity mark, you need to check the other marks. Set up a target in front of the camera, either a lens chart or any high-contrast, easily readable target, set the target at a specific distance with your tape measure, moving either the camera or the target until the distance is correct, and then focusing on the target through the eyepiece, with the lens wide open, and with the magnifier on, if your camera viewfinder has one. Find the sharpest focus by eye, and compare with the distance mark on the lens. Try this several times, and compare your results.

If the eye focus and tape measure focus marks disagree to any significant degree, try another lens of the same focal length by the same manufacturer. Repeat this procedure with other marks at other distances, and with each of your lenses. After some practice, you will be able to complete this procedure very quickly, and you will begin to see a pattern emerging. You will understand the peculiarities of your particular lenses.

If there are not enough marks on your lenses, add your own. A narrow strip of white or yellow chart tape (available in art supply stores) on the lens will give you the space to add your own marks. For example, if there is a six-foot mark and an eight-foot mark but no seven-foot mark, and you would feel more comfortable with a seven-foot mark, set your focus target at exactly seven feet from the film plane. Focus is always measured from the film plane—most cameras have a post or a hook for the end of your tape measure mounted in line with the film plane on one side of the camera or the other, or sometimes both sides. Focus as accurately as you can by eye at seven feet, and mark the chart tape. Try this at least twice more to see if you getting the same mark each time. Repeat the process for any other in-between marks you might want to add.

Needless to say, you must be aware of the difference between feet and meters. Some lenses are marked only in feet, some only in meters, and some, especially zoom lenses, with both feet and meters, usually in different colors. Some lenses have feet on one side and meters on the other. Don't confuse the two. I usually cover the metric scale with white or yellow chart tape, which I use for my own focus marks.

3. Follow Focus Gear
    a. Mounts Correctly on Lenses
    b. Smooth over Full Range
    c. Minimal "Play"

Virtually all professional cameras have some sort of follow focus knob connected by gears to the lens focus ring. This knob should be free turning and not have excessive "play" or "slop." There may be a white plastic disk for marking focus moves. There might be a right hand knob as well, or a focus extension, or a handle (sometimes called a "speed-crank" or "L-handle"). If you have these pieces, make sure they all fit and work the way they are supposed to. Focus extensions are particularly useful for those times when the Assistant cannot stand within arm's reach of the camera. I often take two of these on a job, because they can be attached in line together for an even longer reach. There will be more discussion on this subject in the chapter on Focus.

For Louma Crane and Steadicam use, remote focusing devices have been made, both "hard-wire" and "wireless." Test these devices thoroughly, and take plenty of back-ups and batteries.

4. "Blue Line" Lenses

Certain Panavision lenses may have a second focus index (in blue) near the main focus index (in white). These "Blue Line" lenses are designed in such a way that at the widest apertures, there are differences between eye focus and tape focus. These alternate indices are to compensate for those differences. Ask the rental house

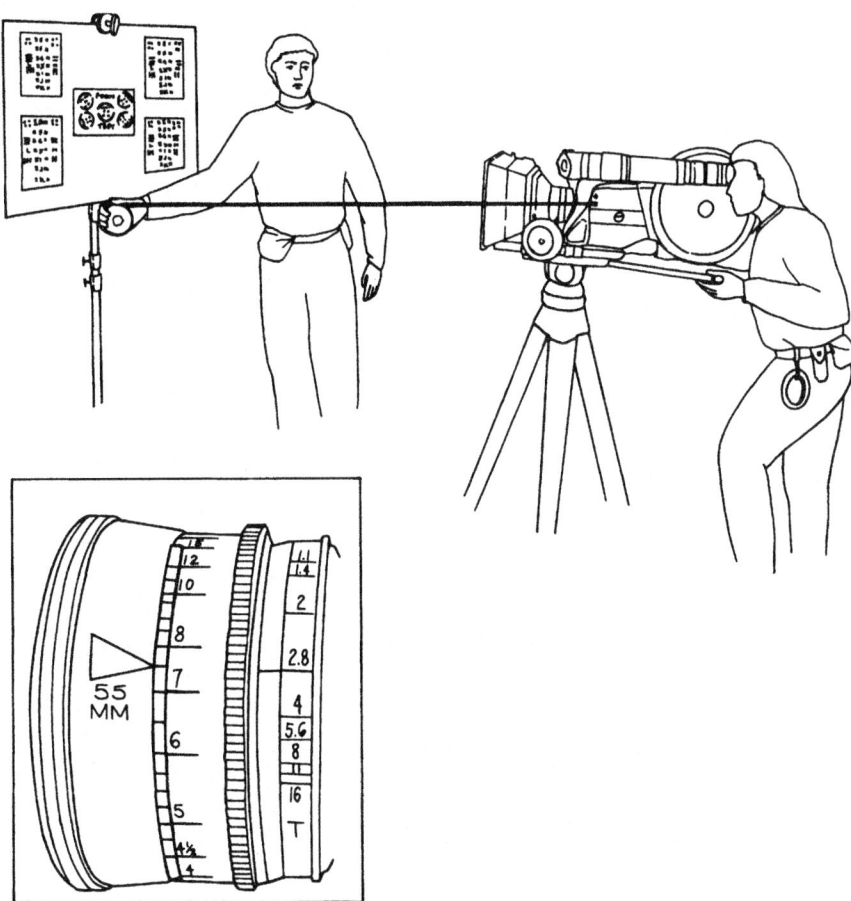

Lens with focus scale and in-between marks on chart tape

Figure 4-11 Checking Lens Marks/In-Between Marks. Checking the Focus Scale and getting some in-between marks is much faster and easier with two people; one to run the tape measure and move the chart, and the other to look through the camera and dial in the eye focus for each chart position. Check the focus with the lens wide open and with the viewfinder magnifier in position, if the camera has one. Eye focus should match tape focus for each mark on the focus scale.

personnel to show you how to use these marks. More discussion on this issue will be found in the chapter on Focus.

   5. Sharp Across Frame

The lenses you are using should, of course, photograph sharp images, images equally sharp from top to bottom of the frame, and from side to side and corner to corner. Wide-angle lenses, in particular, will have problems being sharp across the frame at wide apertures. Generally, once the lens is stopped down to T/4 or so, the lens will be at its optimum for contrast, definition, and flatness of field. If your lenses are not equally sharp in all parts of the frame, ask for another lens in that focal length to compare, and select the best one.

  E. Zoom Lenses
   1. Tracking Straight
   2. Holds Focus throughout Zoom Range

The first thing to look at on a zoom lens is the tracking. At full telephoto, line up the crosshair on a specific target. With the pan and tilt controls of the head locked off, look through the camera while zooming back slowly. The crosshair should remain on the same spot on the target and not deviate. But most zoom lenses will deviate some. That deviation may be up, down, left, right, diagonal, or even spiral. Decide for yourself if your zoom's tracking error is acceptable, or if you want another one. A tracking error in a zoom lens will not necessarily degrade your photographed images, but it will make it more difficult for the camera operator to maintain proper composition during a zoom.

While doing this, you can also check as to whether the focus holds during zooming. Focus carefully at full telephoto, with the aperture wide open, then zoom out slowly. Does your target remain sharp? A "true" zoom lens should hold focus throughout the zoom range. If your lens does not, that is, when the lens is focused at full telephoto, and zoomed out, if the target is no longer in focus at full wide on the lens, then the lens is probably not mounted correctly or seated correctly in the camera lens mount. Depth-of-focus is more critical with wide-angle lenses, so if the depth is off even a little because of a faulty mount, then it might be within the depth-of-focus requirements at the long end of the zoom, but not at the wide end.

There is another type of lens, called a "variable focal length" lens, which is not a true zoom, and the focus must be reset for each focal length. These lenses, generally long telephotos, were obviously designed for still photography rather than motion picture photography, where each frame can be set up and focused separately. But some of these lenses have been adapted for motion picture work, and are especially used in wildlife photography and other filming where long telephotos are used.

   3. Zoom Motors
      a. Smooth at all Speeds
      b. Smooth throughout Zoom Range
      c. Mounting Bracket and Rods Correct
      d. Lens Gears Correct and Solid
      e. Power—Correct Voltage

1. Batteries/Chargers
2. Power From Camera Body
   a. Power Available from Body
   b. Cables and Back-ups

These days an electric zoom motor is virtually required whenever a zoom lens is used. The motor should be quiet, smooth at all speeds, should have the proper brackets and cables, and should be responsive to your slightest touch. Slow speeds are more important than faster speeds. You can always do faster zoom by hand, without the motor, and never notice a slight unevenness on the screen, but the slower the zoom required, the more noticeable any unevenness and the more the zoom motor is needed.

Check especially the starts and stops, which need to be very smooth. Bumps or hangups in the starts or ends of zoom moves are very jarring on the screen, and should be avoided. Practice easing into the zoom move by slowly increasing pressure on the zoom motor control until you reach the speed you need, and then easing off just before the end in order to come to a smooth stop.

There are several brands of zoom motor controls available. Try them all. You will soon develop a favorite. Some of these controls also have a camera run switch. Make sure these are operating properly, as well.

The motor might be powered from the camera battery through the camera body, by a separate battery, or by internal batteries in the zoom control itself. If you have the internal battery type, there will also be available a "bypass" cable for powering directly from another battery should the internal batteries run down. Have plenty of back-ups, and check the motor especially carefully at very slow zooming speeds. Some zoom controls have a "Fast/Slow" speed switch in addition to the variable speed rheostat control.

F. Coatings

Check the front and rear surfaces of your lenses to see the condition of the coatings. The coatings help minimize lens flare, and help with color matching between lenses. If the coatings are scratched or worn, ask for another lens. Rental houses send bills to customers for damaged coatings when the lenses come back from a rental, so the Assistant has to examine the coatings at least as carefully as the rental houses do, at the beginning of the job as well as at the end.

Years ago I had a zoom lens on a job, with a small worn spot right in the center of the lens where the coating had worn away, probably because some previous Assistant had mounted a filter on the lens in contact with the front element, or had set the lens down on a table somewhere, with the front element actually touching the surface of the table. The spot was so small I thought it was negligible. Besides, it was the only lens of that type available from the rental house at that time.

We shot with that lens for weeks with no problems, but then one day we had a shot toward a brightly lit window, and there in dailies was a bright blue circular "ghost" right in the center of the frame. It looked like a U.F.O.! The lens had flared from the bright background, and the lens coating had successfully eliminated the flare everywhere except for that small spot in the center where the coating was worn away. Fortunately, one of our takes was without the "flying saucer," and we did not have to reshoot. We shot with that lens another few weeks before we were able to exchange it, but we were a lot more careful about lens flares. I learned new respect for lens coatings that day, and another thing to check for during the checkout.

- G. Filters
  1. Materials
  2. Sizes
  3. Types
- H. Sunshades/Filter Rings
  1. Sizes
  2. Quantities

More on filters and sunshades in the chapter on Filters. For purposes of the Checkout, check to be sure that the filter sizes ordered actually fit into the matte box and do indeed cover the full frame of the wide lenses (don't forget the wide end of your zoom lenses) without cutting into the frame at the corners (known as "vignetting"). Also check to see that the filter rings fit the lenses, and that the sunshades and matte boxes clear the frame edges and corners of the wide lenses.

- I. Matte Boxes
  1. Sizes
  2. Support Rods
  3. Holders for Filters
  4. Adapters for Different Size Filters

The matte boxes you will take on your job will depend mostly on what size filters you have, what type and size lenses you will have, and how many filters you plan to use simultaneously. If you have different size filters, make sure to have the proper adapter holders to use them in your matte box.

If you need to be able to use graduated filters, it is important that at least one of the filter stages in the matte box is able to rotate and to slide up and down and lock securely to correctly position and orient the grad line in the frame.

Check to see that the frame is clear (no vignetting) with the matte box and filter holders in position, especially for the wide lenses and the wide end of the zoom lenses, and that the support rods are long enough for the proper attachment of the matte box to the camera. It may be necessary to stop down the lenses in order to see the vignetting in the corners.

  5. Motorized and Geared Matte Box Trays

When graduated filters are to be used, it is sometimes necessary to slide a graduated filter into or out of the frame during the shot. For this purpose, some matte boxes have filter trays geared like a follow focus, with a manual knob to turn to raise or lower the filter in front of the lens. Some of the fancier models are electric motor driven, and use a motor control similar to a zoom motor control.

  6. Tilting Filter Stages

Sometimes when more than one glass filter is used in front of the lens, internal reflections between the filters are visible in the viewfinder as "ghosts" of headlights, street lights, practical lamps, etc. A tilting filter stage is necessary to eliminate them. More about this in the chapter on filters.

7. Extensions
8. Masks

Matte box extensions, also known as "hoods" and "eyebrows," help cut down on lens flare by keeping the sun and/or overhead lights from hitting the filters and out of the matte box. They also reduce sky flare and protect the lens from rain or splashed water. Some of these systems include side flaps, sometimes called "ears," which help eliminate flares coming from the sides.

Matte box masks, checked and labeled for use with individual focal length lenses without vignetting, also reduce lens flare by reducing the size of the front opening in the matte box, according to the focal length of the lens.

9. Check for Cutoff with Wide Lenses

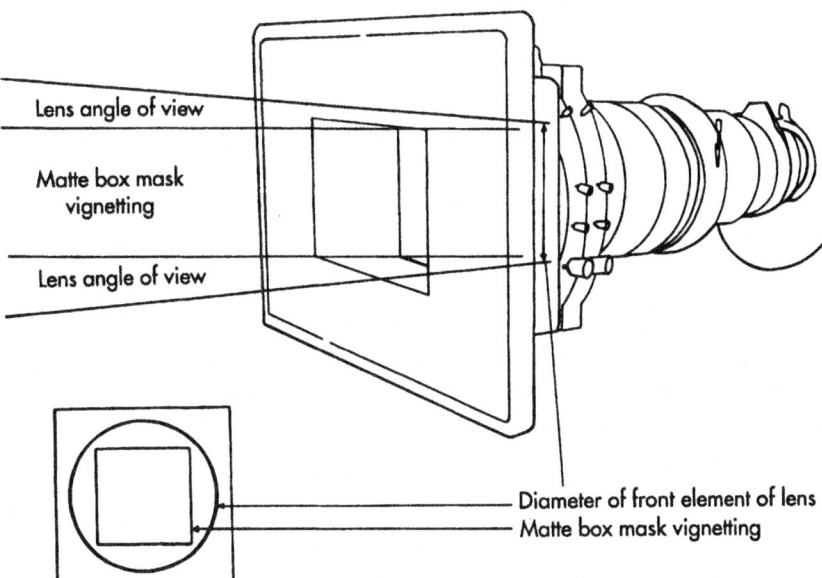

Figure 4-12 Matte Box Masks with Telephoto Lenses. A matte box mask shown used with a telephoto lens with a large diameter front element. When a mask is used that is smaller than the diameter of the front element of the lens, the mask vignettes, or cuts out light that should be entering the lens. With a long telephoto lens, you probably will not be able to see this vignetting in the viewfinder, because it is so far out of focus. That vignetting results in underexposure, as much as a stop or more. Never use a mask with an opening smaller than the diameter of the front element of any lens!

It is very important to check for matte box cutoff or vignetting with your wide-angle and zoom lenses. Put the lens and matte box on the camera, focus as close as you can, and stop down the lens to increase the depth of field. If there is going to be cutoff or vignetting, you will see it now. Check the matte box masks the same way. With the matte box and mask on the camera, focus close and stop down to see any cutoff from the masks.

With fast telephoto lenses with large diameter front elements, be very careful about using masks on the matte box. The longer the lens and the larger diameter the front element, the harder it will be to see any cutoff, but that cutoff may be there, and be so out-of-focus that you can't see it. This cutoff can show up as underexposure.

I was on a job once where we used a fast, large diameter long lens, a Nikkor 300mm, for much of the filming. We wanted to use the matte box so we could use effects filters and grads, and I had placed a 50mm mask on the front of the matte box. That should have been fine, right? A 50mm mask on a 300mm lens. Well, it wasn't. The dailies were at least a stop underexposed, and it took a long time to figure out why. The mask was cutting off light from the edges of the lens, but the cutoff was so far out of focus we couldn't see it through the finder. But the film saw it, and the difference was over a stop in exposure. Don't mask long lenses with large diameter front elements! As a rule-of-thumb, never use a matte box mask with an opening smaller than the diameter of the front element of the lens.

10. Swing-Out Matte Boxes

Matte boxes are a lot easier to use if they swing out of the way when you want to change lenses or check the gate after a shot. Most modern matte boxes do swing out, but there are still a lot of older ones that don't. If the matte box does not swing out of your way, then you have to remove the matte box from the support rods and set it down someplace while changing lenses or checking the gate. Not much fun in the rain, or in a moving car, or on a crane. Ask for a swing-away matte box if possible.

J. Donuts for Lenses

Donuts for lenses are disks of thick rubber foam with a center hole that fits snugly around the front housing of the lens. Their purpose is to prevent light coming from behind the camera from sneaking past the lens, entering the matte box from the rear, between the lens and the matte box, bouncing off the filter, and reflecting back into the lens, creating a photographable reflection on the film.

Once the donut is in place, close the matte box right up to the donut, making a light-tight seal. You need a donut for each size (diameter) lens.

You do not need donuts when not using filters, or not using matte boxes (such as when using a round filter in a screw-in filter ring/lens shade, or when using a matte box equipped with a tightly fitting expandable bellows-type lens seal). Many Assistants, including myself, use the donut anyway, in case the D.P. requests a filter just before shooting. This is a good routine to follow. Ask your Second to hand you the lens, the donut, the matte box mask and the rods (if they need to be changed) every time a lens is changed.

The Camera Equipment Checkout 87

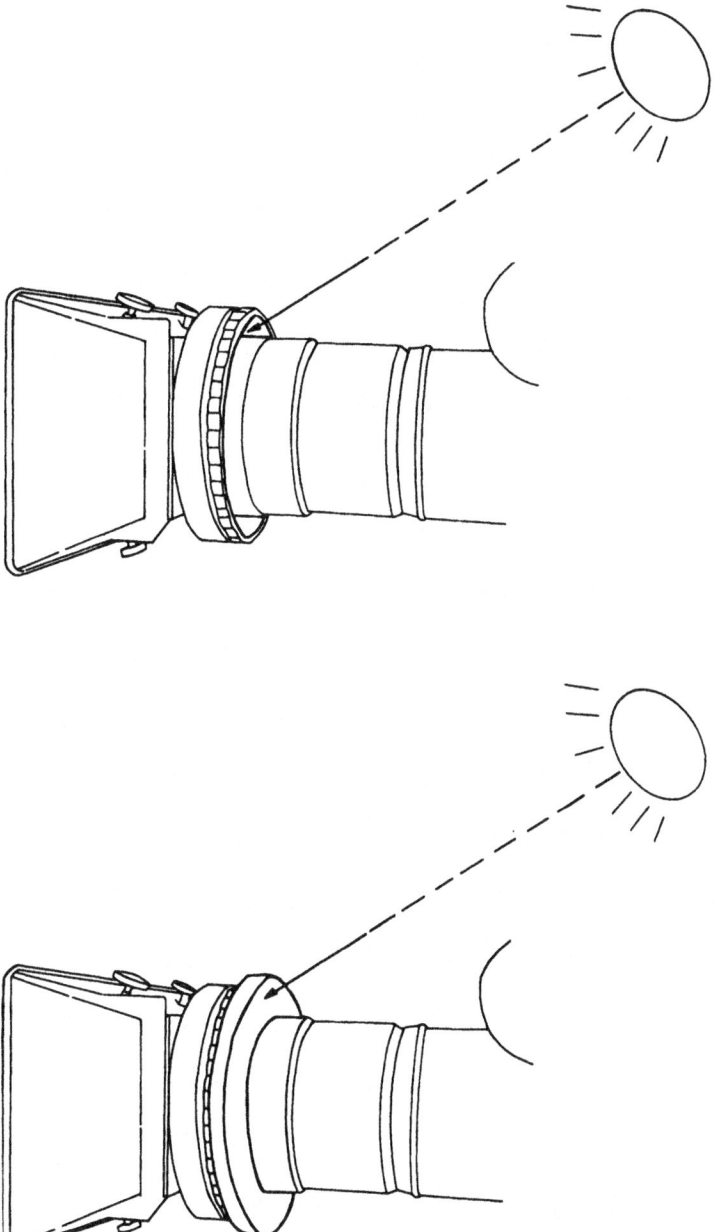

Figure 4-13 Lens/Matte Box Donuts. The rubber donut, when placed on the front of the lens just behind the matte box, blocks light from entering the matte box from the back, between the lens and the matte box. This stray light could reflect off the back of a filter in the matte box and bounce back into the lens, showing up on the film as a flare or irregular reflection. The donut is not necessary when no filter is in use or when the matte box contains an internal donut that closes tight to the lens.

K. Lens Housing

Once upon a time, long ago and far away, in a futile attempt to keep the early Arriflex 35BL Cameras (models 1 and 2) quiet, lens housings were required on the camera, and had to be changed sometimes when changing lenses. These lens housings were built for prime and zoom lenses, and had rubber gaskets and optical flat glasses mounted in front to minimize the noise, which was projected out the front of the camera like a megaphone projects a voice. The housings were built to accept metal or plastic strips marked with aperture and focus marks, because the little windows built to look into the housing at the markings on the lens itself were so inadequate.

If you are unlucky enough to have to use one of these early 35BLs with the lens housings, my sympathies. I did a feature once with two of these cameras, and I found it faster and easier to leave the zoom lens mounted in its housing and on one camera body, and to use the other camera body only for the prime lenses. That zoom lens remained on that camera for three months. I even had a special camera case built to accommodate the body and lens housing together. It was easier and faster to change camera bodies when we wanted the zoom lens than to dismantle the zoom housing and lens and remount the prime lens housing and lenses. There are still a lot of those cameras out there, but fortunately fewer every year.

III. Magazines
    A. Sizes
    B. Quantities

Most modern cameras will accept more than one size magazine. Deciding what size magazines to take, and how many of each size, will depend on what kind of shooting you are planning. In 35mm the standard size is 1000 feet. With studio shooting, and most location shooting, 1000-foot magazines are the best choice—they give you just over eleven minutes of filming at 24 fps and minimize reloading and darkroom time. Panavision recently introduced a 2000-ft. magazine, mainly for use on television situation comedies filmed before a live audience. If you are planning to shoot hand-held, or with the Louma Crane or Steadicam, or shooting in small rooms, or in and around cars, smaller magazines might be a better choice. Most modern cameras have a 400-ft. size (500 ft. for Panavision) and maybe even a 200-ft. size (250 ft. for Panavision).

If you have only one film stock, five or six 1000-ft. magazines is an average order. With more than one type of film stock, or if multiple cameras are to be used, you will need more magazines, or else you or your Second will constantly be in the darkroom changing over one stock for another. With multiple film stocks, having eight or ten or even more 1000-ft. magazines is not unusual. Also keep in mind that high-speed filming burns up film faster. Magazine compatibility is also a consideration. Obviously, magazines from one manufacturer will not be suitable for cameras from another manufacturer (although there are exceptions to even this—Arri 35BL magazines are used with a Mitchell camera in the Wescam remote camera system, and Arriflex magazines are used in one model of the Vistavision camera!). But even within a specific brand of cameras, there are often several models of cameras and magazines, and they are not mutually interchangeable in all cases.

Magazines from the same manufacturer are generally "downwardly" compatible, but not often "upwardly." In other words, magazines from a newer camera may work on an older model camera body, but older magazines may not work on the newer body. For example, magazines from the Arri 35BL-1 and -2 should not be used on 35BL-3, -4, or -4s cameras, but magazines for the 35BL-3, -4, and -4s cameras will be fine with the older cameras.

For Panavision cameras, Panastar magazines will work on the Panaflex Platinum and Gold (GII) cameras, but not vice versa. If you are taking a different (older) model of your main camera to use as a back-up, as is commonly the practice, make sure that magazines are compatible. On one job, we were using both the Panaflex Gold II and Panastar cameras every day, and rather than carrying two complete sets of magazines, we took only Panastar magazines, which would work on both cameras without problems.

    C. Locks Securely on Camera Body
    D. Clean
    E. Latches and Seals

The magazines should lock securely onto the camera body, they should be clean, and the latches and seals should be tight and secure. Just to be sure, most Camera Assistants tape over the latches of loaded magazines, and sometimes tape around the seams where the lid joins the body, for added security and light-tightness.

    F. Torque Motors/Belts/Brakes
    G. Clutch Tension Adjustment

There are three types of magazine take-up systems: electric-driven, gear-driven, and belt-driven. Be sure your take-up system is working, whichever system you have. If the clutches need adjustment, the technicians at the rental house will show you how, or the equipment manuals may describe the process. If you have belt-driven magazines (as on Mitchell cameras), make sure you have spare belts (either leather or plastic), and know how to repair or replace the belt. There are different belts to use for different size magazines, and still other belts to use when running the camera in reverse. Some of these cameras also require magazine brakes, either mounted permanently on the magazine and requiring periodic adjustment, or separate pieces attached and detached from the magazine before and after use. Sometimes the brake is just a cord or leather thong with a rubber band or metal spring for tension.

    H. Footage Counters
        1. Working
        2. Accurate
        3. Feet or Meters
        4. Additive or Subtractive

Most magazines have some sort of footage counter to tell you how much film you have shot and/or how much film remains. Some of these are rollers on arms that ride along on the outside edge of the film roll and measure the diameter of the roll. These are notoriously inaccurate, but are better than nothing. They should read "zero" on their scales when resting on an empty film core. Check this during the Checkout, and have the counter arm adjusted if necessary. Sometimes these counter arms must be manually lowered into position on top of the roll of unexposed film during the loading procedure. Others are positioned automatically when the lid of the magazine is closed.

Other magazines' counters need to be swung into position for a reading, but only when the camera is not running. Still other magazines have cute little electronic digital footage counters that make the magazines heavier, that help drain the batteries on the camera, and that are practically certain to screw up as soon as it rains or the temperature or humidity fluctuates. You must also remember to reset these counters during reloads.

Whatever type of counter you have, be sure it works, and be sure to notice if it is scaled in meters or in feet, and if it is additive (counting up) or subtractive (counting down), which means whether it is counting the footage already used or the unexposed footage remaining in the magazine.

    I. Heaters
       1. Electrical Contacts Clean
       2. Indicator Lights

Heaters were mentioned earlier, in the section on the camera body. The same considerations apply to magazines with heaters. Clean the electrical contacts with a pencil eraser, if necessary. There may be an indicator light to let you know that the heater element is receiving power, or maybe only when the thermostat is on.

    J. Hand-Held Capability
       1. Light Weight
       2. Sizes
    K. Steadicam/Panaglide/Louma/Hot Head Capability
       1. Extension Throats
       2. Light Weight
       3. Sizes

If you are expecting hand-held, Steadicam, Louma, or other remote camera system shooting on your project, check with the Director of Photography, Operator, or Steadicam or Louma Operator about sizes and weight factors with magazines, and also whether there are special batteries, cables, or brackets that will be needed. Sometimes you can substitute plastic magazines for the standard metal magazines to reduce the weight of the camera for Steadicam or hand-held use. There are extension throats available for the Arriflex IIC and III camera magazines, that move the magazine to the back of the camera, lowering the camera/magazine profile and center of gravity. Arriflex also manufactures a coaxial rear-mount magazine for the Arri III camera. These are required, or at least desired, for some remote camera applications.

    L. Scratch Testing

All magazines should be scratch tested during the Checkout, both on the camera body they will be used on and at the running speeds that you expect to be shooting at. Load each magazine with a roll of scrap film obtained from the rental house or that you have brought with you. Always save the small short-ends, 50 to 200 feet, that are too short to be of use while filming, but that are perfect for magazine scratch testing. The rental houses will love you forever if you make a habit of sending them these short rolls of scrap film. Just leave them in the magazines at the end of the job, when the equipment is being returned to the rental house (tape the ends of the rolls so they don't unroll during transport). It is important that this film be "virgin" film (never run through a camera), that it be from the same manufacturer as the film you intend to shoot (Kodak, Fuji, Agfa, etc.), and that it not be too old (older film tends to dry out and shrink, and may not show a tendency to scratch even if new, fresh film will).

Running twenty-five or thirty feet of film (more if shooting high speed) at the expected running speed should be enough to indicate a tendency to scratch. When finished, remove the "exposed" film from the take-up side of the magazine. I usually remove the film from the magazine, leaving the film threaded in the camera, in case I have to run the test again with that magazine. Examine both sides of the film under a strong light. There should not be any scratches or abrasions, or any other indication that the film has been run through the camera.

Some Camera Assistants use a flashlight and magnifying glass, or some sort of illuminated magnifier, to examine the film, but I have found that stretching out an arm's length of film, pointing the far hand at a ceiling light, window, or other light source, and sighting along the length of film looking at the reflection of the light on the surface of the film, sufficient to see any scratches. While stretched out this way, it is easy to turn the film over to check the other side. Check both sides of the film at several places in the roll.

If any scratches or abrasions are visible, blow out the camera, remove and clean the gate (with lens tissue, chamois cloth, or just your finger). If the gate is really dirty, use a plastic or wooden tool to scrape off any emulsion build-up, and rewipe. I have tried not to use the word "never" in this book, but NEVER NEVER NEVER use any metal tools near the gate surface!!!!

Thread that magazine again, and try the test once more. This time, before removing the film from the camera, mark the film with a pen or marker in four places: where the film exits the magazine, where the film enters the gate, where the film exits the gate, and where the film reenters the magazine. Now when the film is removed from the camera and examined, if the scratches are still present, it should be possible to determine where in the camera the scratches begin, by comparing the start of the scratch with the marks you made on the film. The three most likely places for scratches to begin are in the feed side of the magazine throat, in the gate area, and in the take-up side of the magazine throat.

If the scratches originate in the gate area, and cleaning the gate did not solve the problem, take your camera to the repair shop and get it fixed. Show the technician the scratched film. If the scratch starts in the magazine throat, get another magazine and try again.

Obviously, scratches outside the perforation area, or scratches on the base side of the film are less serious than scratches on the emulsion side of the film between the perforations, but ideally, a camera should not scratch film at all, anywhere, ever.

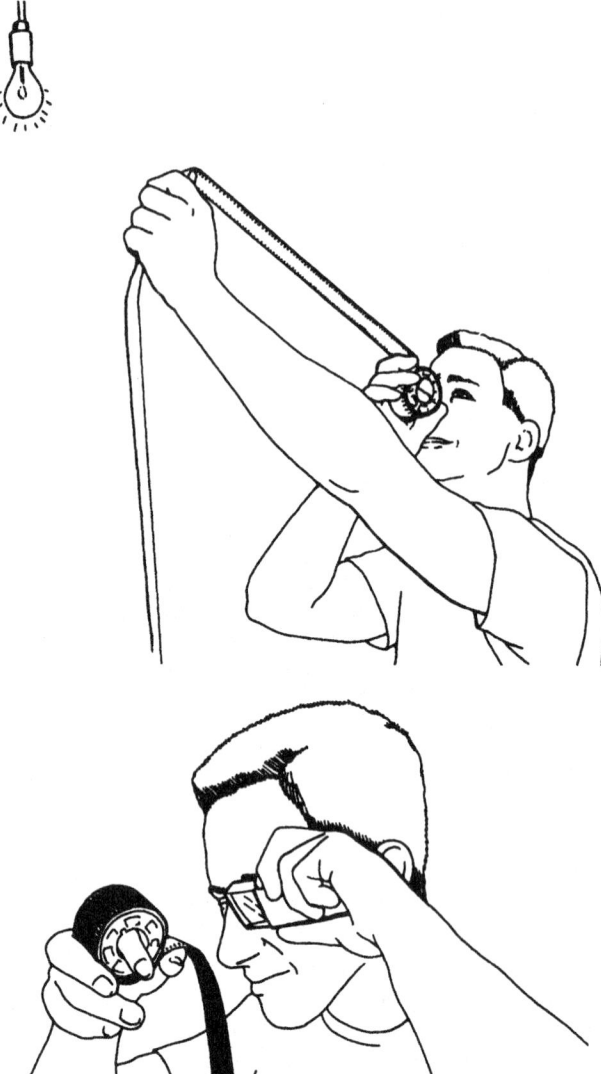

Figure 4-14 Magazine Scratch Testing. Two methods of scratch testing film magazines. After running 20 to 30 feet of film through the camera, remove the film from the magazine. Sighting along the film held up to the eye and pointing to a light source will show any scratches. Examination of the film with an illuminated magnifier will also show scratches. Remember to check both sides of the film, and several places in the roll.

If you find a magazine that scratches, return it to the technicians at the rental house and tell them what is wrong with it. If necessary, show them the scratched film. But make sure someone knows that the magazine is scratching the film. Otherwise it will end up back on the shelf for the next checkout. The next guy may not be as thorough as you are.

At a checkout, always ask for a replacement for a defective piece of equipment, rather than trying to fix something yourself. The technicians can probably fix whatever it is faster and easier than you can, and they have the right tools, parts, training, and experience. You certainly don't have the time, and probably not the energy, either.

    M. Cores or Core Adapters

If your magazines require empty cores for film take-up (such as Mitchell or Panavision magazines), make sure you have enough (one for each magazine, and some spares). Each roll of film you shoot out to the end will give you an empty core for the next roll to take up on, but if you have to change emulsions or can out a short end you will need spare cores. Empty cores, as well as empty film cans and black bags, are available from the film laboratory, normally without charge.

Other magazines (such as Arriflex magazines) have "core adapters" on the take-up side which eliminates the need for empty cores. Just make sure that when these core adapter magazines are unloaded, that you do not send the core adapter to the laboratory with the film. This is a common, but nonetheless embarrassing mistake made by new Camera Assistants, especially with 16mm cameras.

Somehow, the unnecessary practice got started of Camera Assistants placing an empty core back into the hole in the center of the roll before packing up to send to the lab. First of all, it is sometimes not easy to get the core back into the roll, and even if it could be done, what purpose would it serve? Don't waste your time or energy. The labs don't care whether there is a core in the roll or not.

    IV. Support Equipment
        A. Heads
            1. Types
                a. Geared
                b. Fluid
                d. Friction
                e. Special
                    1. Underslung
                    2. Remote Control
                f. "Dutch" Head

Check with the Director of Photography or Operator to find out their preference concerning tripods and heads. Almost all feature films shot in this country use a gear head (Panahead, Arrihead, Worrall, Mitchell, Mini-Worrall, etc.) as their primary head, but will always have a back-up or additional fluid head nearby for particularly difficult or hard to reach shots, or shots involving a very fast pan or tilt move, or just to quickly set up an additional camera on. These back-up fluid heads are most commonly O'Connor, Sachtler, or Ronford heads. Europeans are less fond of the gear heads, and use fluid heads almost exclusively.

A few Camera Operators own their own gear heads or fluid heads, and will expect their personal heads to be used on the job, at least until it starts raining, or there is danger of salt spray or sand, or some other hazard. Then they are willing to use a rental head. A new gear head costs up to $30,000, so there are not many Operators who will buy their own.

There is nothing that REQUIRES the Operator on an American feature to use the "wheels" of a gear head, but most do. It depends on Director of Photography and Camera Operator preference. Before the checkout begins I generally telephone the Camera Operator just to check in with him or her, asking their particular preferences in gear and fluid heads, and so on. The Camera Operators like to feel they are involved in the process from the beginning. Most of them are ex-Camera Assistants, after all.

One last note on gear heads: when shipping, or even just when returning them to their cases, all pan and tilt locks should be unlocked, and the pan and tilt gears should be in neutral. This will prevent damage while shipping.

A "Dutch" head is a second fluid head mounted on the main fluid head so that its tilt axis is perpendicular to the tilt axis of the main head, allowing the camera to be tilted to the left or right, adding a third dimension of movement. This tilted view of the world is becoming very popular for music videos and TV commercials. To take full advantage of the three axis, a second tripod handle is used. The operator can pan and tilt up and down with the main handle, and tilt left and right with the "Dutch" head handle. I don't know where the description "Dutch" came from—I hope it is not derogatory in some way to people from Holland.

    2. Camera Mounting
       a. Quick Release
       b. Balance Adjustment
       c. Camera Attachment Screws

Many gear heads and fluid heads have a "quick release" mechanism built in. The theory is that the camera needs to be quickly detached and moved or taken into the action for hand-held work. The mechanism may be a sliding dovetail mount, or a spring-loaded dovetail plate. Make sure the mechanism is compatible to the various cameras you may want to mount on that head, and that the mechanism locks securely and cannot be released accidentally.

Most gear heads have some kind of camera balancing slide, which should be adjusted whenever lenses or magazines are changed, or whenever some accessory is added to or subtracted from the camera. The slide should operate smoothly. If not, a drop or two of silicone, or a spray of silicone or teflon should loosen and smooth the slide action. Try to keep the slide surfaces clean and lubricated.

If the camera mounting mechanism is just a simple 3/8" screw, then there is still something to check. Make sure that the screw extends far enough to secure the camera, but not so far that it will exceed the depth of the threaded hole in the base of the camera and damage the camera interior or the delicate electronics that may be hidden in the base of the camera (especially in the Arriflex 16SR cameras).

3. Controls
   a. Locks Securely in all Positions
   b. Drag/Tension Adjustment
   c. Spring Settings
   d. Smooth Gear Shifting
   e. Balancing Ability

To minimize Camera Operator grumbling on the first day of shooting, check out the head(s) thoroughly. Make sure the pan and tilt are smooth, that the locks do lock the head securely, and that the tension or drag controls function well.

For the Camera Assistant, the most important thing about the head is the security, solidity, and safety of the mounting plate, tilt plate, mounting screws, slide locks, etc. You certainly don't want the camera to fall off the head in front of the whole crew. Also check the camera sliding balance mechanism, which should be smooth (lubricate sparingly with silicone if necessary), and the tilt plate, if your gear head has one. This is an adjustable wedge plate to enable you to increase the angle of the tilt either up or down. The tilt wedge locks should also be secure. These plates generally allow the camera to be mounted pointing straight up or straight down, which is useful for certain shots.

Always turn the camera over to the Director of Photography or Operator in a properly balanced state, and keep adjusting the balance. As the film runs from the feed side to the take-up side of a displacement magazine, the balance will shift to the rear. As you change lenses or add or remove filters, the balance will shift. Keep checking the balance and adjust when necessary.

4. Mounts
   a. Mitchell Standard
   b. Ball Leveling

As with many other aspects of the motion picture equipment industry, nothing is standardized. This applies to tripod mounts, as well. The closest thing to a standard mount is the Mitchell plate. All dollies and cranes are set up for this flat circular mount. But there are other mounts as well; several ball-type leveling mounts that vary in diameter from manufacturer to manufacturer and from head model to head model. Make sure that you have the same mount on all of your heads, tripods, high hats, dollies, and cranes, or that you have the proper adapters.

B. Tripods and High Hats
   1. Mounts (Topcasting)
      a. Matches Casting of Heads to be Used
      b. Ball Level Adapters (If Needed)
   2. Materials
      a. Wood
      b. Fiberglass
      c. Carbon
      d. Stainless Steel
   3. Sizes
   4. Smooth Length Adjustment

    5. Locks
    6. Head Lockdown Screw Fits
 C. Bridge Plates/Risers/Geared Wedges/Rocker Base
 D. Spreaders/Rugs
    1. Matches Legs
    2. Smooth
    3. Locks

Often overlooked at the checkout, many problems have come from inappropriate or defective tripods. Make sure everything fits and everything works. Tripod legs and spreader runners should slide smoothly and lock in all positions. The tripod leg points (all size tripods) should fit the spreader, and lock there securely. A spreader without locks for the tripod legs is not a good idea, although there are many like that out there. The spring-loaded spreader locks are the fastest ones to use. Many Camera Assistants, including myself, prefer a piece of carpet about three feet square to keep the tripod legs under control, but take the spreader anyway.

Most modern gear heads have a tilt wedge built in, extending the tilt range to allow the camera to be pointed straight up or straight down. Sometimes when using other heads, increased tilt is desired, and a tilt wedge or geared wedge is what you need. Ask to see what the rental house has.

For low-angle filming, sometimes it is desirable to take the camera off of the geared head and mount up on a device called a "rocker-base" or "rocker-plate," which is placed on the floor but still allows some tilt and pan control. Panavision's is called the "Panarock," of course.

 E. Dollies

Dollies are the grip's responsibility, but sometimes when they come from the same rental house as the camera, and the grips don't come in for the checkout on a commercial or short job, I give them a once-over. Make sure they track in a straight line, that they shift from crab (four-wheel) to conventional (two-wheel) steering easily, that the brakes work, and that the hydraulic riser system works, as well as the compressor. If that particular dolly comes with sideboards ("running boards"), risers, or other accessories, get them as well. An offset plate (or "ratchet head") is a particularly useful item for positioning the camera.

 F. Autobase

The Panavision Autobase secures the Panaflex family of cameras to the various car mount rigging provided by the grips. The Autobase provides a secure base for mounting the camera, as well as a plate for the top of the magazine secured to the base plate with sturdy turnbuckles. This rig ties the camera together and provides an extra measure of protection against damage from stress, vibration, "g" forces, etc.

The Autobase works with the various size magazines, and specially modified brackets permit the use of the video assist systems. If you plan on car rig shooting, definitely take an Autobase, and make sure to get a long camera power cable and a long remote switch, so the camera can be powered and turned on and off from inside the vehicle, if necessary.

V. Miscellaneous Accessories
   A. Changing Bag

I usually take a changing bag from the rental house in addition to my own, but just as a back-up, in case mine gets wet or damaged. If you do take one from the rental house, make sure that it is clean, that it has not got too many patches or repairs, that it seems to be light-tight, that the zippers or Velcro closures are in good condition, and that the elastic around the armholes is in good condition. Even if you expect to be shooting in a studio with a darkroom, or on location with a truck that has a darkroom, ALWAYS have a changing bag with you! You may have to split off a Second Unit crew, or the darkroom may spring a light leak or get flooded, or who knows what else. A changing bag is too essential and inexpensive an item to be without. It is the cheapest insurance possible.

   B. French Flag

The French Flag, so called, apparently, because they are made in Italy (by the Ianiro company), is a black, metal, rectangular flag or cutter, mounted on an articulating arm which is in turn attached to a clamp of some sort. It is attached to the camera and is used to shield the front of the lens from stray light.

   C. Slate

New slates are almost always purchased for feature films, but they are available for rental, as well. More discussion about the various types of slates in the chapter on Slates and Slating.

   D. Barney

A Barney is a soft, padded, leather or nylon soundproofing cover for the camera. It often attaches to the camera with zippers or Velcro, wrapping around either the magazine or the camera body, in an attempt to muffle some of the noise. Barneys often have a layer of lead foil inside, which further reduces noise. They are clumsy and cumbersome, and often have to be removed and then reattached whenever the camera is reloaded, but they do eliminate some of the noise.

   E. Lens Light

In order to follow focus or set the aperture, the Camera Assistant needs to be able to see the marks on the lens. This is not always possible in dark studios, or on night exterior locations. Working with a flashlight in one hand is inconvenient, and in one's mouth is uncomfortable. To solve this problem, many Camera Assistants tape a gooseneck flashlight to the camera body or viewfinder, with the adjustable neck of the flashlight pointed at the side of the lens.

A better solution is offered by some camera manufacturers, with a device known as a "lens light." This is a small gooseneck lamp mounted somewhere on the camera body, and getting its power through the camera body and camera power cable. There is usually a dimmer on the lamp, to keep the light from being a distraction to either the actors or the Camera Operator. If there is a lens light made for your camera, ask for it.

F. "Real-Lens" Finders

Some directors and Directors of Photography prefer using the actual camera lenses mounted in a viewing device for setting camera positions. This viewing device consists of a camera eyepiece, a groundglass with the same aspect ratio markings as the main camera, and a lens mount to accept the camera lenses. Arriflex, Panavision, Mitchell, and others make them (Panavision's is called the "Panafinder"). Check out the viewfinder, groundglass and lens mount just as you would on a camera body. More on this and similar equipment in the chapter on Shooting Procedures.

G. Spray Deflectors

Various types and models of spray deflectors are available for motion picture cameras. The spray deflector is simply a matte box with a glass disk inside that spins with an electric motor, to deflect any rain or splashed water that may strike the glass in front of the lens. It is based on the spray deflectors found on ships' bridges. It will require its own battery and cables. If you are expecting to be shooting in the rain, either real or fake "movie" rain, suggest to the Director of Photography that a deflector get added to the list. It isn't cheap, but it does work. One disadvantage is that the unit makes quite a bit of noise; a high-pitched whirring sound.

H. On-Board Lights

Various "On-Board" (or "O.B." or "Obie") lights are available for mounting on the front of the camera above or below the lens. These lights mount on the matte box, on the lens support rods, or on the magazines themselves, and often include shutters or dowsers that operate with a knob to dim the light output without changing the color temperature, during the shot, if necessary. They usually have some sort of gelatin filter holders or slot to allow the use of diffusers or color correction gels. If you have one of these units, make sure it works, that you have a spare bulb, and that you can still balance the camera with the extra weight up front.

I. Dynalens and Image Stabilizer

The Dynalens is an image stabilizing device mounted in front of a standard camera and lens, with two glass panes containing a liquid-filled chamber. The liquid has an optical clarity and density similar to glass. The two glass panes are independently controlled by gyroscopes, one with a vertical axis and one with a horizontal axis. The gyros react to vibration, and attempt, quite successfully, to cancel out horizontal, vertical, or combination movements of the camera, by deflecting the light path in the opposite direction to the vibration. The system is adjustable to frequency sensitivity, and has its own battery system. Limitations to the system include the diameter of the chamber, which restricts the lens choice to approximately 35mm and above (for 35mm filming), and the maximum deflection limits of plus and minus six degrees. The system takes a minute or so to come up to speed, and makes a whining sound while running, but it works quite well. The device is not made anymore, but you may be able to find one on a dusty shelf at a rental house. I am surprised they are not more popular.

Other image stabilizers that use gyroscopes to minimize camera shake during hand-held, dolly, or camera truck moves are not common, but they do exist if you can find them. Order well in advance if you want them. They do work quite well, if properly installed and adjusted.

J. Low-Angle Prism/Inclining Prism

The Low-Angle or Inclining Prism is a device that attaches to the lens support rods in place of the normal matte box, allowing the camera to be placed near the floor, but the image appears as if the camera were located below the floor line. There is theoretically no loss of image quality. There are a couple of different models to choose from, and there is an exposure compensation required when using one.

K. Panatape

This is a device made by Panavision for the Panaflex series of cameras. It is an infrared ranging system using technology originally developed for the Polaroid autofocus instant picture cameras. It looks like a standard matte box with two cylinders mounted on top. One is the sender and the other the receiver, of infrared pulses that measure the distance to the subject, the distance being digitally displayed on the side of the matte box. Further discussion of the Panatape will be found in the chapter on Focus.

L. Arri Varicon/Panaflasher

The Arri Varicon and Panavision Panaflasher are two different approaches to a similar problem, that of decreasing image contrast, building in shadow detail, and subtly overlaying a color tint into the shadow areas of the frame. Both operate by giving the film a basic exposure below the "toe" of the sensitometric curve.

The Varicon, formerly called the Lightflex before it was acquired and reengineered by Arriflex, is a matte box addition which adds a controlled light and/or color to the frame while you are shooting, reducing contrast and slightly tinting the shadow areas of the picture. This extends the photometric range of the film, providing more apparent detail in shadow areas without increasing the grain. The light source is adjustable in intensity and color temperature. With a bit of practice and many tests, the effect may be viewed through the camera and set by eye to the desired effect. The latest model of the Varicon fits into the Arri matte box like a double-thick 6.6" x 6.6" filter (needs a double filter slot).

If you are using one of these units on a job, get checked out on its operation by qualified rental house personnel, take lots of notes, and shoot lots of tests. Keep accurate notes during filming, in case you need to reproduce a specific effect for connecting scenes shot out of sequence.

The effect of the Varicon is similar in appearance to the effect of pre- or postflashing the negative, but with the advantages over flashing of being able to set the effect by eye through the camera, being able to change the intensity and/or color from shot to shot, and even being able to change the intensity of the effect during the length of the shot. Pre- and postflashing at the laboratory has to be done to the entire roll of negative at one time, with a single setting for the roll.

The Panaflasher is a device that attaches to the unused magazine port on the Panaflex cameras, either in the rear when the magazine is top-loaded or on top if the magazine is rear-loaded. The device consists of a variable light source, a filter slot, and a light meter, and provides a controllable low-level, filterable, "flash" to the film. The flash can be considered a "preflash" or a "postflash," depending on where the unit is mounted in relation to the film gate. The filter slot allows color to be added to the flash. The flash can also be adjusted for intensity, even while the camera is running. The Panaflasher is small and light enough to be used while hand-holding.

M. Panatate and Pananode

The Panatate and Pananode units together allow the positioning of the Panaflex camera so that the lens axis is the central axis for a rotatable camera mount, so that the camera can be spun about its lens axis while running, for an interesting special effect. The rotating Panatate camera mount itself mounts directly on the standard Panahead.

N. Water Box ("Shallow Water Housing")

Sometimes in filming near water, the director or Director of Photography would like to get the camera as close to the waterline as possible, possibly placing the waterline itself in the frame. The Water Box is just the device needed for such a shot. It is a waterproof metal box, large enough to place the camera with lens and magazine inside, and with a window at one end to film through. The box is open on top, and floats because of its natural buoyancy, so weights might be needed to sink the box to the level desired. The box is high enough that water will probably not slosh inside, except from the highest waves, and with the extension viewfinder rotated up, the Operator can see what is going on. The top of the box should be covered when filming, so that no light can strike the window glass from the inside, causing unwanted reflections of the camera in the window.

The Rental Contract

Before escaping from the rental house, the dreaded equipment rental contract must be prepared, listing each and every piece of equipment; every cable, every filter, every support rod and bracket; all the little pieces that hopefully when assembled will produce a working camera system. All of these items must be listed, and serial numbers, where applicable, recorded on paper.

During the checkout, hopefully the rental house technician working with the Camera Assistant will have started preparing the contracts, at least listing the items to be taken, but possibly leaving out the serial numbers until after the Camera Assistant is satisfied with the condition of the various parts.

Once the Camera Assistant is satisfied, the serial numbers may be inserted into the form, and before removing the equipment from the building, the Camera Assistant is often asked to sign each page, acknowledging receipt of the listed equipment. I usually hope for the teamster to sign, but sometimes this is not possible.

If the Camera Assistant is asked to sign, it is common to sign the contract with your signature, and then add "for John Smith Productions," or whatever the name of the production company is. While I have never heard of a Camera Assistant being held personally accountable for the equipment signed for, it doesn't hurt to be cautious, and add this disclaimer. The Camera Assistant is merely an agent of the company paying his or her salary, and the company is renting the equipment, not the individual Camera Assistant.

After signing, make sure to get a complete and legible copy of each page of the contract. Unfortunately, it is often the case that there are so many carbon copies of the contract that the bottom copy, the one usually given to the Camera Assistant, often has no writing on it at all, or at least is difficult to read. When this happens, request a photocopy of the top or original copy, for better legibility. The Camera Assistant is at least entitled to a clear, legible copy of the contract, and it will make the job and the check-in much easier if you have one.

This contract needs to be accurate, for this will be used again at the end of the job to check-in all of the equipment being returned. The company will be billed for anything missing or damaged, so care must be taken by the Camera Assistant to make sure the list is complete and accurate. It is a primary duty of the Camera Assistants to minimize this "Missing and Damaged" list at the end of the job. The best way to do this is to keep accurate records of any new equipment added, or equipment returned or replaced during the job.

Changes in the equipment inventory that occur after the job begins, from damaged or nonfunctioning equipment that is returned for repair or replacement, or extra equipment taken out, will have their own contract paperwork, and the Camera Assistant is responsible for making sure that everything taken out is returned intact. The Camera Assistant is not responsible, of course, for normal wear and tear on the equipment, but only for equipment damaged through neglect and/or abuse.

Case Labeling

One last thing to do before leaving the rental house is to label the cases with a brief description of the contents in large letters, generally on the handle side of the case, and also on the sides of the case that will be facing the aisle when the case is on the shelf on the camera truck, and on the top of the case for when the case is lying on the floor. Labeling will not only make it easier for the Assistants to find things, but will also make it easier to send a production assistant or trainee or even a grip back to the truck or equipment staging point to fetch something. Labels are of no use, however, if you can't read them.

After a while, a Camera Assistant will be able to recognize instantly a case from just a glimpse of the outside, from the color or from the dimensions, but for unfamiliar equipment or for the benefit of the less experienced Camera Trainee, label the cases.

If there is more than one camera in your package, color coding the cases may make it a bit easier to keep the appropriate accessories with the correct camera, and

102 THE CAMERA ASSISTANT

to keep them separate from other similar accessories. The accessories themselves need to be color coded, as well. Camera tape is available in many colors, and is ideal for the purpose.

Once combat begins (some people call it "filming"), accessories and pieces of cameras are scattered everywhere. Color coding the various pieces will make it easier to sort everything out at the wrap, so that when combat begins the next day, each contestant begins with a full assortment of weapons and ammunition.

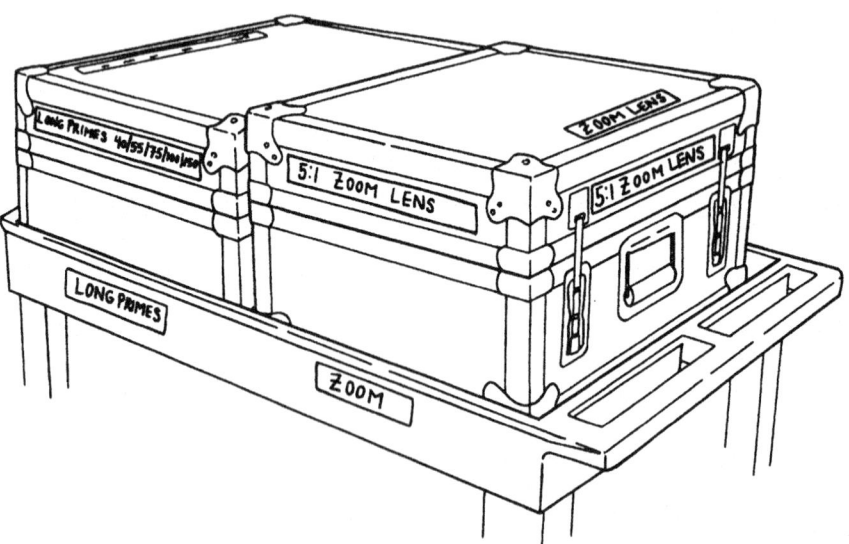

Figure 4-15 Camera Case Labeling. Camera equipment cases labeled on top, ends, and sides make finding things much easier.

CHAPTER 5

Shooting Tests During Checkout

Tests

There are a lot of tests that might be shot during the checkout period, if the crew is given enough time and money and raw stock, but I will only attempt to describe and discuss the procedures and the reasons for the most common tests that might be shot for a feature film.

Some of these tests might be done by the Camera Assistant alone; others will require the presence of the Director of Photography; still others will require additional crew and cast members.

Try and find out in advance what tests the Director of Photography wants to shoot, and when he or she will be available to shoot them. The list of tests to be done will be different for every job.

Registration Tests

Probably the most important test the Camera Assistant might shoot during the Checkout is a camera registration test. This is a test of the camera movement's ability to hold a single frame of film absolutely steady during exposure, and then repeat that process for each and every succeeding frame of film, holding the film not only still during exposure, but in register with the perforations on the film for each successive frame.

This means that the spatial relationship between the framelines, picture position, and perforations is consistent, frame after frame, so that the projected film will appear steady on the screen.

The way to test this is to run a strip of film through the camera twice, photographing an image on the first pass, then shifting the camera aim slightly, both horizontally and vertically, so that the second image photographed on the second pass through the camera is slightly offset from the first photographed image.

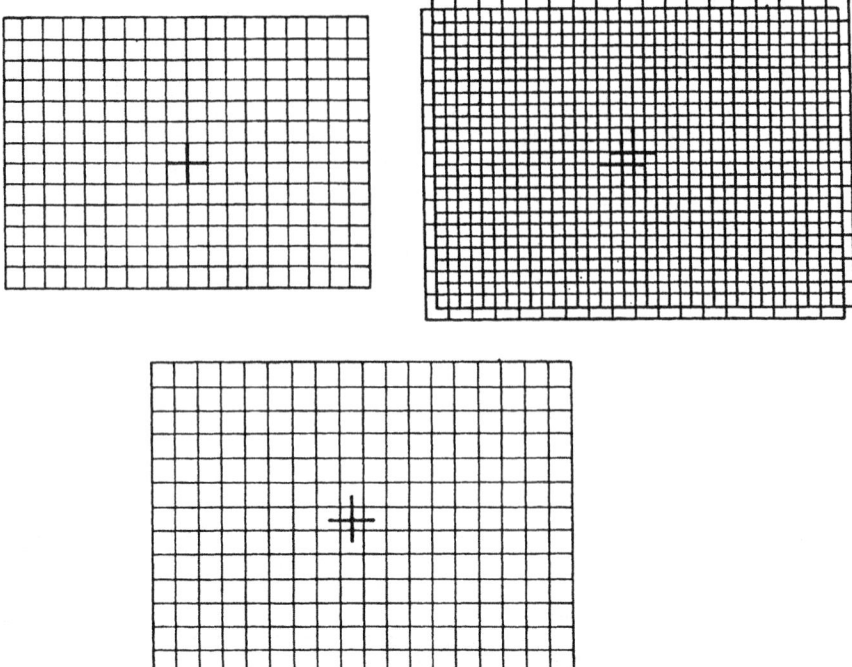

Figure 5-1 Registration Test—Grid. For the first pass through the camera, align the crosshairs of the ground glass directly over the intersection of two of the grid lines. For the second pass, put the crosshairs in the center of one of the open boxes of the grid. This vertical and horizontal displacement will show up in the double exposure as a grid with boxes one-half the original size, and any movement between the first pass grid and the second pass grid will show up clearly as one set of lines will move in relation to the other set.

The film is rewound and rethreaded carefully, so that the framelines are exactly the same for both passes. It is very important that the registration pins enter the same perforations on the second pass as on the first.

The registration pins enter every fourth perforation on 35mm film; one perf for every frame photographed. (A dual-registration-pin camera has one registration pin on each side of the film, and each pin enters every fourth perf on its side of the film.)

This test shows up on the developed and printed film as a superimposition or double exposure of the two images. When the negative or print of this superimposition is projected on a screen, it should look like a single image; that is, there should not be any "wobbling" or fluctuation of one image against the other. Ideally, the superimposition of the two images should appear as a single image, with no movement of one image in relation to the other.

The test target is usually a "checkerboard"-style grid of straight horizontal and vertical lines, lines fine enough to position quite a few of the boxes in the frame. For the second pass, the grid is photographed again, but offset horizontally and vertically,

Shooting Tests During Checkout **105**

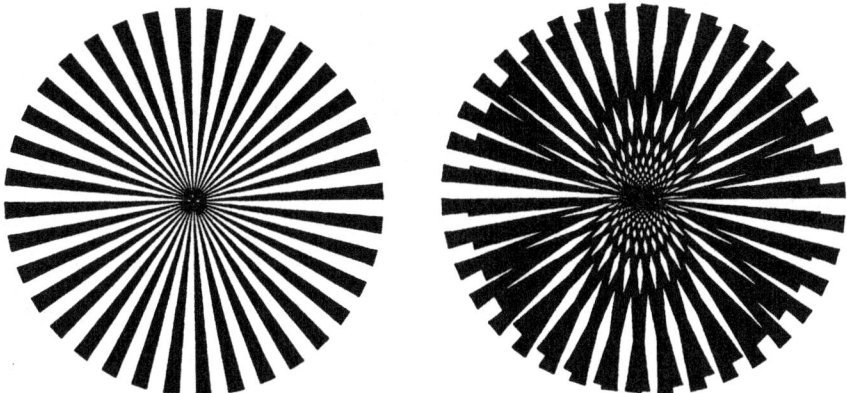

Figure 5-2 Registration Test—Moire. The Siemen's Star can also be used for a registration test. Film the chart in two passes, panning or tilting slightly between passes. The resulting double-exposure shows a "figure 8" pattern called a "Moire" pattern. If there is a registration problem with the camera, the Moire pattern will appear to move, rotate, or wobble.

so that the second grid image bisects the first grid, making a grid of squares half the size of the original grid, when the strip of film is projected.

Another type of target finding some use for registration tests is a circular pattern of radiating lines called a "Siemen's Star." The two superimposed images reveal moving Moire patterns if there is a registration problem with the camera.

Set up the camera on as solid a mount as possible. I usually use a tripod and fluid head for the registration test, because they will lock off more securely than a geared head on a dolly or wheeled checkout table. Lock off everything as solidly as you can, and when you are actually shooting, ask that other people in the room not walk around, because any movement of the camera such as the floor shaking as someone walks by or slams a door during either pass will be indistinguishable from legitimate camera registration problems. Use sandbags on the spreader and legs of the tripod if possible.

Do not look through the camera eyepiece during the filming. Even the pressure of the forehead against the eyepiece can introduce an unwanted movement or vibration. Close off the eyepiece light trap, if the camera has one, and/or place a piece of black tape over the eyepiece.

Use a medium focal length prime lens for the test, and position the chart so that the frame is filled with the grid pattern. For the first pass (and first pass only) label the chart with the serial number of the camera being tested, making sure the label is in the frame. If you have more than one camera to test, you will need the serial numbers displayed to tell one test from the others. After the first pass, remove the label before the second pass, to prevent superimposing two label images from two passes one on top of the other and making the label unreadable.

For 16mm cameras, shooting this test is very easy. There is only one perforation per frame, so the positioning of the film for the second pass is automatic. For

35mm (and 65mm), however, because there is more than one perforation per frame (4 perfs/frame for standard 35mm, 5 perfs/frame for 65mm), the positioning of the film for the second pass becomes critical. You want the same four or five perforations for each frame of the second pass that you had for the first, so the film must be positioned exactly, to the exact perforation, for the second pass.

Unless you are using a camera that will run in reverse, and the film will never have to be unthreaded and threaded again, and since there are no visible frameline markings on the film, you have to put them there yourself.

Once the camera is threaded, remove the lens and look through the lens port at the film in the gate. Use the inching knob to advance the mirror and shutter out of the way, and mark the frame of film in the gate with a pen or marker by drawing a large "X" on both diagonals from corner to corner. I usually inch the camera ahead by hand and mark at least three consecutive frames with "X"s, because this makes it easier to find them when setting up for the second pass, and easier to check the alignment after threading for the second pass.

For the second pass, when threading up the camera, you will position these "X"s precisely the same way as when the "X"s were drawn, looking through the lens port at the film, inserting the registration pin into the film only when the entire "X" is visible in the gate.

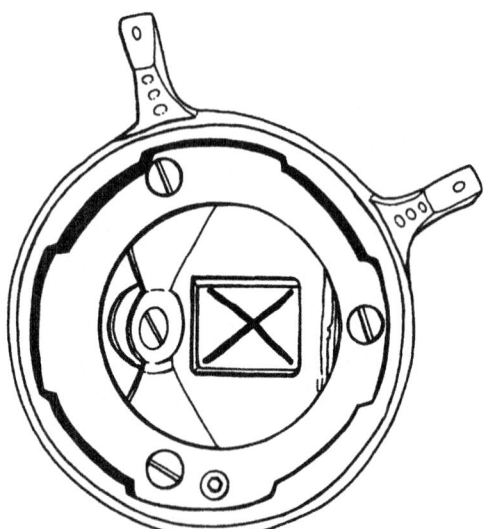

Figure 5-3 Registration Test—Marking Frame. In order to guarantee that the two passes of the film are photographing the same frames each time (that the registration pins are entering precisely the same perforations on each pass through the camera), the film should be marked when first threaded into the camera, by removing the lens, inching the shutter out of the way, and drawing an "X" with a felt-tip pen on the film frame in the gate. When the film is rewound and threaded for the second pass, place the "X" in the gate, making sure the complete "X" is seen in the gate, then continue threading normally.

If you have marked more than one frame with an "X," continue inching the movement and check to see that each successive "X" fills up the frame and that the film is properly positioned.

Once the film is threaded for the first pass, and the frames marked, reinsert the lens, and focus on the chart, either by eye or with a tape measure. Light the grid target as evenly as possible, and take a normal exposure reading of the target. Since you are going to be exposing the same strip of film twice, remember to divide the exposure in half by closing down one stop from what your meter reads. If the meter reads f/4, shoot each pass at f/5.6, to get a normal exposure.

If you are shooting a black grid on a white background, you might want to close down another half-stop or so, to darken the lines so they will be easier to see when the film is projected.

Some Assistants shoot the test with white lines on a black background, or project the negative (not a print), so that the lines show up better. I have found that either way is fine for the test purposes, white on black or black on white.

Once your focus and aperture are set, check the framing one last time, make sure the label with the camera's serial number is visible, close off the eyepiece light trap (there is no need to operate the camera and the presence of an operator with head up against the eyepiece may jostle the camera enough to render the test useless).

Announce to others in the room you are about to roll, and ask them to remain still while rolling. Slate the roll, indicating that this is a registration test of camera so-and-so, for such-and-such a company, so the lab knows where this film is coming from and why, and knows who to send the bill to.

Shoot at least one minute's worth of film (about 100 feet in 35mm) on the target. Any less and you may miss seeing an intermittent problem, and any more is very boring in the screening room.

Once the first pass is completed, stop the camera and check the framing once more. If nothing has moved, you are now ready to rewind the film for the second pass. If you are fortunate enough to have a camera which runs in reverse, put the lens cap on, close the eyepiece trap again and run in reverse back to the head of the roll. Not many cameras run in reverse these days, so the odds are that you will have to remove the film from the camera and rewind the film either on editors' rewinds in the darkroom, if you have them, or by hand, if you don't.

Don't panic at the thought of rewinding film in the dark. It's easier than it sounds. Just remove the roll of film from the take-up spindle and rewind it onto the feed side by hand. There are so many different cameras and magazines you might be testing that I can't give you step-by-step directions here, but try it out with an empty magazine and a roll of scrap film first.

Once you have rewound the film and threaded the magazine again, winding as little film as possible onto the take-up side (so that the "X"s you marked on the film are still on the feed side) come out of the darkroom (hopefully you won't be doing this with only a changing bag). You now have to find where the "X"s were drawn. Slowly pull film out of the magazine feed side until the "X"s are visible. Then thread the film into the camera with the "X"s visible in the gate as described above.

Then proceed with the second pass, setting the focus and aperture to the same settings, and repositioning the second image slightly so that the superimposition will be slightly offset. The easiest way to do this is to position the crosshair on the ground glass precisely on top of one of the grid line intersections for the first pass, and then in the middle of one of the squares away from the grid line intersections for the second pass. Remember to remove the camera serial number label for the second pass. Close the eyepiece, and shoot the same amount of film for the second pass, again asking the others in the room to stand still while you are shooting.

When finished, announce that you have "Cut" the camera, and run off some additional film as "safety" or "leader" before proceeding to the next test. If you have shot the registration test first on the roll, nothing prevents you from continuing with other tests on the rest of the roll. Otherwise you should break off the roll at this point and can it out for the lab.

Some people arrange with the lab to project the negative instead of the print, thereby eliminating one possible source of registration inaccuracy, the printer that is making the print, but I have found this to be unnecessary.

If there is a registration problem with the projected test, it can come from three sources. The first possible source is the camera itself. If one grid pattern seems to be moving in relation to the other, then the camera appears to be at fault. Return to the rental house and inform the repair department that your particular camera body has flunked the registration test. Ask that they check out the movement or give you another camera body.

If the entire superimposed grid pattern seems to be moving in relation to the frameline of the negative, that would indicate a registration problem in the printer at the lab. Inform the lab people that their printers are "weaving." This problem is sometimes easier to see if you ask the projectionist to frame either up or down so that the frame line is visible on the screen. If the frameline bounces around the screen with the grid pattern, blame the projector.

A further test would be to ask the projectionist to remove the mask from the projector, allowing the perforations to be projected on the screen as well. If the perforations seem to be bouncing around with everything else, then the projector is at fault.

Another use for the registration test grid is to graphically demonstrate the "axial drift" inherent in a zoom lens. Every zoom lens has some drift during zooming—as the focal length is changed, the crosshairs shift slightly. This drift may be horizontal, vertical, diagonal, or a combination. This drift is one of the things the Assistant will look for during the equipment checkout, by looking through the lens, aligning the crosshairs precisely on a small target, locking down the pan and tilt locks, and running through the entire zoom range. The crosshairs will be seen to drift off the target at some point during the zoom, and sometimes will come back to the target further along the zoom.

In order to see this drift on the screen, the registration grid chart can be used. Somewhere in the middle of the zoom range of the lens, line up the crosshairs exactly on an intersection of grid lines and shoot thirty seconds or so of film. Then without releasing the pan and tilt locks, rewind the film as in the registration test discussed above, and shoot a second pass while slowly zooming from full wide to full telephoto and back again.

When the test is projected, the grid lines will be seen to separate and come together. The magnitude and the direction of the shift can be clearly seen. Let the D.P. decide whether the drift is acceptable or if you need to search for another zoom lens in that range. The lens may make perfectly acceptable images, but a lens with excessive drift makes it more difficult for the Camera Operator to maintain proper composition while zooming.

Flicker Tests

The flicker test is simply a test of the shutter/ movement timing (also known as "phasing"). The Camera Assistant simply shoots a minute or so of a plain white or light gray card, and looks at the film in the screening room to see that the exposure is equal all over the card.

I always put a small label in the frame with the serial number of the camera. This serves to identify the particular camera body if you are testing several, but it also lets the lab know that this piece of film is a test, and not just clear leader. It also gives the projectionist something to frame and focus on. If you keep the label relatively small in the frame, it will not obscure or interfere with the test, but will still serve the above purposes.

If the projected test frame is not of uniform brightness top to bottom, then there may be a shutter/movement timing problem with the camera. If either the top or bottom of the frame is darker than the rest, this is a symptom of the shutter and the movement of the camera being out of sync. The film may therefore still be moving through the gate during exposure, instead of being held motionless during exposure, meaning that all parts of the frame are not receiving the same amount of light.

Ground Glass Markings Test

This test, also described as "Projector Line-Up Leader," serves two purposes. First of all, this test compares the markings on the ground glass in the camera with the projector mask in the projector that will be projecting the dailies (and theoretically, by extension, the masks in the projectors of the many movie theaters that will be showing the finished film). The test also, as a by-product, produces projection leader to facilitate proper framing and focusing for dailies.

The ground glass is that small piece of glass inside the camera generally just to the right of or just above the lens port where the lens image is focused when the mirror is in place behind the lens. The image is focused alternately on the film in the gate and on the ground glass, depending on the position of the rotating mirror shutter.

The test is filmed by simply locking off the camera to prevent any movement during the test, tracing out on a white card the exact markings found in the ground glass, labeling the markings appropriately, and filming the card.

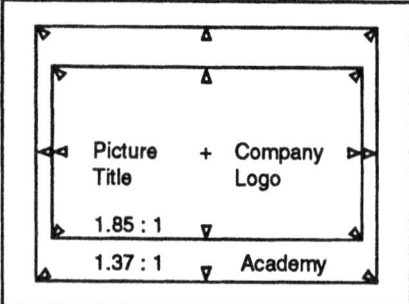

Corners and Sides of Frame indicated with Triangles of Tape

Figure 5-4 Shooting Ground Glass Markings. Filming a chart matching the ground glass markings in the camera will result in projection leader that can be used for the dailies, and also tests the mask in the projector used to screen the dailies. An improper mask in the projector will alter the original composition of the film. If too much or too little of the frameline markings is seen during projection, then the projector mask does not match the camera ground glass.

Set up the camera on a tripod or dolly, six feet or so in front of and perpendicular to a flat wall, on which you have placed a white card or paper. Using a 50mm or 75mm lens, fill the frame with the white card. Lock off the camera securely.

There are two methods of tracing out the ground glass markings. If there is a second person available to help out, then you can look through the camera and lens at the white card and direct the other person to place a pencil mark at the corners of the frame markings in the viewfinder, and then just connect the marks with solid lines. If you have available a small tungsten lighting unit, such as an "Inky," then it is possible to shine this light through the eyepiece of the camera, projecting the ground glass markings through the camera optical system and lens, and onto the white wall, using the camera as a projector, the way the very first motion picture cameras were used. The corners of the ground glass markings can then simply be marked where they fall. If your ground glass has an "X," or "crosshairs," in the center of the frame, mark this on the card as well.

Most ground glasses show multiple frame markings, such as 1.85:1 and Academy, or TV Safe Action and Academy. Mark the corners of all of the frames displayed in the finder, as well as the crosshairs. Once the corners are marked, use a straightedge to connect the corners, reproducing the ground glass markings. Make the markings dark enough and thick enough to photograph clearly, either with a felt-tip pen or with thin strips of tape.

With small triangles of tape, indicate the inside of the corners of the frame markings and the centers of the straight sides of the frame markings. These triangles will help the projectionist frame and center the projected image on the screen, and will help show just how much of the proper image is being cropped or cut off, or how much extra frame outside the ground glass markings is being shown by an improper projector gate mask.

It is common practice to label the markings with the appropriate aspect ratio, such as "1.85:1" or "TV Safe Action." You may also want to write out the title of the film, production company, and year, or include the film's title graphic or logo, if there is one available.

Shoot at least one hundred feet (just over one minute in 35mm), to give the projectionist time to focus and frame as accurately as possible, and to allow close inspection of all sides and corners of the frame, to see how closely the projector mask matches the ground glass. If other masks are available, it is sometimes possible to find one which is a closer match. Once a proper match is found, or once the closest one has been filed or machined out to become a close match, then make sure that your dailies are projected on that particular projector through the appropriate mask. If more than one projector is to be used, check the masks in all projectors.

A properly sized and shaped projection mask is necessary to see proper framing, composition, and headroom in dailies. If the dailies are properly projected, then the finished release prints should also be properly framed in theaters. Of course, this is only theoretical. Actual projection in neighborhood movie houses is abysmal, especially in those ten- or twelve-screen multiplexes with only one projectionist on the payroll. Movie theater projection is certainly the weak link in the motion picture chain. No matter how carefully the D.P., Camera Operator, and Camera Assistants are in capturing the perfectly lit, composed, exposed, and focused image on the negative, at some point the release prints have to be turned over to local theater projectionists. You'll be lucky to get an image on the screen, let alone one that is framed, in focus, or bright enough to see. But at least the dailies will look good.

Making Dailies Projection Leader

Once the ground glass markings test has been projected and it is deemed satisfactory, many productions arrange to have some of this footage attached to the head of each roll of dailies footage. Turn the ground glass markings test negative over to the assistant editor of the job. The assistant editor can then order multiple prints from the lab, and can attach twenty feet or so to the head of each dailies roll, to allow the projectionist to properly frame and focus the dailies.

Don't trust the dailies leader supplied by the laboratories, as it has probably been printed and duped so many times that the markings are no longer accurate. Also, what could possibly be more accurate than shooting the markings from the production's own camera ground glass?

Ground Glass Position

The easiest and fastest way to determine accurate ground glass positioning (distance from the lens mount flange) is with a collimator. A collimator, or more properly, autocollimator, is an optical device with a light source, target reticle (the pattern being projected), lens, and beamsplitter prism, which creates an artificial infinity target. With a wide-angle lens focused to infinity on the camera, look through the collimator eyepiece with the collimator switched on and positioned along the lens axis pointed into the camera lens.

The collimator target reticle image will be projected by the collimator light source "from infinity," through the collimator beamsplitter, through the collimator objective lens, through the camera lens, and reflected by the shutter mirror to the camera ground glass. The target will then be reflected back along the same path and deflected up to the collimator eyepiece by the beamsplitter.

By turning the focus ring of the lens, the viewed target image can be sharply focused. If the lens focus ring is at or very near the infinity mark, then the ground glass is correctly positioned. Try this with several lenses. A brighter image may be obtained by turning the ground glass over, using the smooth side of the glass to reflect off of instead of the ground side, if your camera allows this (Panavision and Mitchell cameras). Don't forget to turn the glass back again!

It used to be that the collimator could be used to verify correct flange focal depth in precisely the same way. Set up the collimator again, but turn the camera inching knob so that the mirror shutter is out of the way. You can then view the target image as reflected back from the frame of film in the gate rather than from the ground glass.

If the focus scale on the lens reads infinity, then the camera depth is correct. By then turning the camera inching knob to bring the mirror shutter back, the infinity mark derived from looking at the film could be easily compared with the infinity mark derived from looking at the ground glass. Obviously they should match very closely.

An even better test would be to run the camera with fresh scrap film while looking through the collimator, viewing the target image on the surface of running film. Running film is actually what you want to be focusing on, after all. With the collimator, the viewer can actually see the effect of turning the lens focus ring on the image projected by the lens on the film surface. It was a very fast and easy way to reassure yourself that the camera/lens system is working properly. After a plane trip, or a long bumpy truck ride, or even worse, a fall, the camera could be easily and quickly checked out to make sure that everything was in order. Fresh scrap film is essential for this purpose, as older film dries out and becomes less flexible, affecting the curvature found in the gate area.

Unfortunately, this is no longer feasible, or even possible, in many cases. The philosophy of focal flange depth has changed. After a hundred years of sharp pictures, the new thinking is that focusing the lens image on the surface of the film is not good enough. The image must now be focused below the surface of the film, in an attempt to optimize the image focus for all three of the emulsion's color-sensitive layers, not just the top layer.

This works just fine, except that the collimator cannot see below the top surface layer. The ground glass is still in the same place, and may be viewed normally using the collimator, but the image reflected back into the collimator from the top surface of the film will not be in focus, and cannot be brought into focus. This severely limits the collimator's usefulness to the Camera Assistant in the field.

On the other hand, the new Camera Assistant need no longer wonder if he or she should purchase one. It just isn't necessary to own one any more. I haven't used mine in years. If in doubt about the ground glass in your camera, ask the rental house to check it on their large shop collimator, which is more accurate than the smaller field models anyway.

Lens Aberrations

Before discussing Lens Testing, a mention of the types of lens aberrations (abnormalities or irregularities) sometimes found in lenses is in order. Many different types of things can be wrong with photographic lenses. Aside from physical damage to the glass elements or to the lens barrel or internal mechanisms, there exist several design flaws that you may encounter when trying to choose a set of lenses for a job. You should be familiar with some of the terminology in order to describe what you are seeing, in order to discuss these aberrations intelligently with the rental house personnel.

Field Curvature   is probably the most common problem with cinema lenses. When a lens forms an image that is sharp in the center and soft in the corners, or sharp at the corners and soft in the center, this lens has a field curvature problem. The image formed by this lens is only sharp along a curved surface. This is a problem because the film is held flat during exposure. A good image cannot be obtained from this lens, and stopping down the aperture will not help.

Chromatic Aberration   is what we call it when a lens focuses different colors of light at different distances behind the lens. Different colors bend to different angles in the lens. This can result in color fringing around objects in the frame, easily seen with a collimator or lens projector.

Spherical Aberration   occurs when light rays at the edges of a lens are bent more than rays closer to the center of the lens, and are therefore focused closer to the lens than rays at the center. This makes the image appear to be soft in focus, although stopping down the lens may help, by eliminating the rays at the edges of the lens.

Astigmatism   causes a lens to focus a horizontal line in a different plane than a vertical line. Many human eyes suffer from this problem also. This is seen at the edges of the image, and is also decreased when the aperture is stopped down.

Coma   causes rays that pass at an angle through a lens to be focused at a different place than rays passing perpendicularly through the lens. It makes a bright point in the image appear like a comet, or to have a tail or halo. Stopping down the lens can help.

Curvilinear Distortion   (also known as Geometric Distortion) is a description that covers both "Barrel Distortion," in which parallel lines seem to curve outward on the image, and "Pincushion Distortion," in which parallel lines seem to curve inward on the image. This aberration is usually corrected by designing a lens with multiple elements, and with an internal diaphragm.

Lens designers try to eliminate such aberrations by combining several elements with opposite aberrations so that their individual faults cancel each other out. This works with various degrees of success. All lenses have these aberrations to some degree.

Most of these aberrations are more pronounced when the lens is wide open, and are less of a problem if the lens is stopped down a stop or two from wide open. When shooting wide open on a lens, these aberrations, present in most lenses, limit the lens sharpness.

Your job, as Camera Assistant, is to find a set of lenses with minimal faults.

Lens Sharpness

This is one of the most important tests to be done during the checkout. Choosing the best set of lenses available to be used in the production is vital. Rental houses have many lenses on their shelves. Most rental house lenses have been evaluated at some point in their rental life using the MTF (Modulation Transfer Function) system, a comparison of the contrast of a particular lens with its resolving power. The *American Cinematographer Manual* calls this an "objective measure of sharpness," but cautions that this test does not account for all distortions or aberrations that may be present in that lens. Even identical lenses from the same manufacturer have minute differences in contrast, color rendition, resolution, and focus scale accuracy.

Lenses, despite the best care and maintenance, get worn through use, and are sometimes abused by other rental customers. Rental lenses get dropped, get dusty, get wet, and get exposed to high heat, cold, and humidity.

The lens test philosophy is simple. Shoot several lenses of each focal length desired, and choose the best of each size. Since lens quality is such a subjective matter, lenses can best be judged in relation to other lenses of similar focal length and manufacturer. Other criteria to consider in your evaluation are image sharpness at the center of the frame as well as the corners and edges, contrast, flare, vignetting, and image distortion.

Once you have a complete list of the lenses requested by the Director of Photography, ask the rental house to assemble for you three or four lenses of each focal length. Physically examine each lens, and reject those with worn lens coatings, or scratched elements, or too much play in the iris or focus rings. Once you have made the obvious rejections, shoot a test of the remaining lenses. Hopefully you will still have at least three lenses left in each focal length.

There are many lens charts available, with complex procedures laid out to measure resolving power, contrast, etc. But for most purposes, what looks good on film is what you need, not necessarily the maximum resolving power. Some charts require that you place the chart at a specific distance from the film plane, such as twenty-six times the focal length of the lens, and examine the resulting developed negative under a microscope, in order to accurately compute resolving power.

It seems more useful to me to place the chart at a reasonable distance from the camera, at a distance commonly used in motion picture photography, and that you will often be shooting at. Six or eight feet are convenient, comfortable distances for testing almost all lenses except long telephotos, and they are distances that are most likely indicated on the focus scale of the lenses.

I generally set up the camera with the widest lens to be tested, at eight feet from the wall, and use as many lens charts as may be required to fill the frame. Remember, it is not only the center of the frame that needs to be sharp, but also the sides and corners. If several commercial lens charts are not available, photocopies can be used, if they are clear and sharp copies, or any printed pages may be used, if they contain high-contrast graphics or text. Magazine pages are best, on slick glossy paper, especially the advertisements, because they often contain large, crisp, clear, black text and graphics. Newspaper is not as good as magazine pages, because of the lower contrast and duller paper finish. Tape or staple up on the wall enough charts or pages to fill the frame of the widest lens, and all lenses of higher focal length will be covered without having to move the camera.

Light the wall as evenly as possible to a light level yielding an f/stop likely to be used during shooting, and hopefully one which can be used for all, or at least most, of the lenses to be tested. Find out from the Director of Photography what stops are likely to be used during filming, and what stop he or she would like to see the lens test shot at. Generally T/2.8 is a stop that is available on normal prime lenses except for long telephotos, and is a commonly used stop for interior filming.

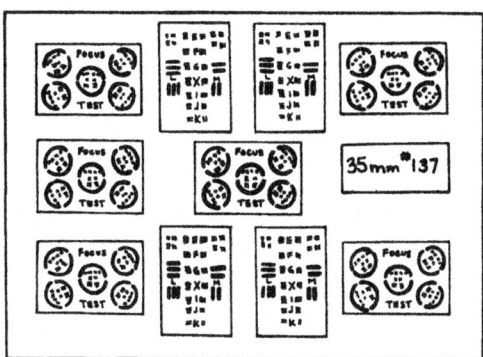
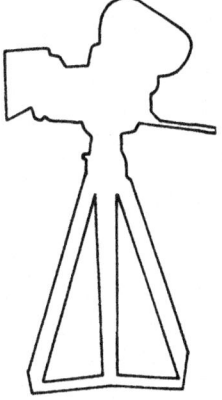

Lens serial number and focal length placed on chart before shooting

Figure 5-5 Lens Sharpness Test. Camera Assistants will almost certainly want to shoot a lens sharpness test during the checkout for any long job. Set up the camera at a reasonable distance (eight feet is a good distance for almost any lens) from the lens chart or charts, make sure the lighting is as even across the chart as possible, and shoot about twenty feet of film on each of several lenses of the same focal length, making sure that the lens is correctly identified by serial number somewhere in the frame.

Since time is often limited during the checkout period, lighting to a stop that can be used with all or most lenses to be tested eliminates having to relight several times for different lenses. If zoom lenses or long telephoto lenses are to be tested, additional light may be needed for those lenses, as they are generally slower lenses than primes.

If enough time and film stock are available for the checkout period, and if the particular production calls for it, tests might be shot at a stop like f/2.8 or f/4, and again at the widest open aperture for each lens, to see how the lenses perform under those conditions.

It is a basic law of lens design that lenses look and perform better closed down a stop or two than they do wide open, so if the Director of Photography is planning a lot of low-light filming, with the lenses at their maximum aperture, you might want to shoot a test of them that way. It is not uncommon for a lens that looks great at f/2.8 or f/4 to look not-so-great wide open, when the corners go soft in relation to the center or vice versa.

Once the chart wall is evenly lit at the chosen aperture, and fills the frame of the widest lens to be tested, shooting may begin. If eight feet from the chart is the chosen distance, then set eight feet on the focus scale of the lens, and set the correct aperture for your lighting and film stock. Be sure to accurately repeat these settings for each lens tested. Close off the camera eyepiece to prevent light entering the eyepiece and possibly fogging the film as it runs through the camera, and be sure the camera is set for the correct frame rate and has no unwanted filters inside.

A lens test is useless if the individual lenses cannot be identified on the screen, so prepare slates or cards to be placed in frame, of suitable size and position and lettering to be clearly and easily read on the projected test, showing the focal length and serial number of each lens to be tested. Slate the roll to indicate to the lab the roll number, the job title, production company, date, etc., and begin.

Shoot twenty to twenty-five feet of film (in 35mm) for each lens, changing only the cards indicating focal length and serial number of the lens, when you change lenses. Keep all of the lenses of each focal length together, shooting in sequence. When the test is projected, it should be a simple matter to pick out the sharpest lens of the group for each focal length. Run the film several times, if necessary. Beware of running the film backwards through the projector while watching, as this often requires a projector focus adjustment. The serial numbers of the best lenses will be right there on the screen, and all you need do is list the numbers of the lenses you like, or circle them on the camera report for that test roll.

If you are really interested in the actual resolving power of the particular lenses, there is another type of lens sharpness test that can be performed. Using a real lens resolution chart placed at the proper distance from the film plane according to the directions on the chart, shoot just a few seconds of film for each lens, placing a small ID tag with the serial number of the lens somewhere in the frame, so you know which lens you are looking at.

When the film is developed, examine the negative (no need to have a print made—just process the negative) under a microscope or other powerful magnification device, and determine which set of numbered lines on the chart you can "resolve" by eye (see the difference between pairs of lines and the blank spaces between the lines). The number next to the closest lines that can be resolved represents the resolving power of the lens; the higher the number (the closer together the line pairs) the better the lens. Simply pick out the best resolving lenses in each focal length you will need for the job.

A short cut to this test would be to put each lens on a lens projector, if your rental house has one. This projector is much like a slide projector, but with the proper lens mount to allow attaching your camera lens. The resolving chart projected through the lens will appear on the wall or screen and will allow you to examine the lens not only for sharpness, but also for other lens aberrations, such as astigmatism (better resolution with vertical line pairs than with horizontal pairs, or vice versa), flatness of field (sharper in the center than at the corners, or vice versa), vignetting (darker at the corners than in the center), curvilinear distortion (barrel or pincushion distortion—parallel lines curving outward or inward instead of remaining straight and parallel), color fringing, low contrast, and with zoom lenses, minimal axial drift when zooming. Using the lens projector obviously requires that the rental house have one (not all rental houses have one available), and that they have the time and personnel available to run through the test with you.

Lens Color

Once the sharpest lenses have been selected, a simple test will show how close in color they are. Obviously, it is an advantage if all the lenses show the same colors the same way on the screen as in real life, but not all lenses do. Differences in glass chemistry and coatings can make differences in color.

Modern lens design has pretty much solved these problems, and you can generally count on prime lenses from the same manufacturer giving you the same colors, but if you are mixing lenses from different makers, or using primes from one manufacturer with a zoom lens from another, there may be subtle color differences which can make intercutting a problem, and final color timing much more complicated and expensive.

All you have to do to find out for sure about your lenses' color rendition is shoot a white card with each selected lens in sequence and look at the projected test. The white will change color if one or more of the lenses is a little off. If you shoot short enough pieces, five to ten feet each, then on the screen you will see quite easily when one shows up a little more yellow, or a bit more blue, than its neighbors.

Be sure you place a small label somewhere in the frame showing the focal length and serial number of the lens being tested so you can immediately identify the offender. Shoot the zoom lens, too, as well as your long telephotos. The label will also give the projectionist something to frame and focus on, and will show the lab that this material is a test and not just clear leader.

If there is one lens slightly off in color, you might consider going back to your sharpness test and testing your second sharpness choice for color to see if it is a closer match to the rest of the set.

If this is not acceptable, you might consider attaching a complementary colored gelatin filter to the lens to correct the color shift. For example, I once had a set of lenses that looked great together except for the 40mm, which was a bit yellow in comparison to the others. The Director of Photography had me attach a CC05B (very pale blue) gelatin to the lens, which brought this 40mm into a very close color match to the others. I had to change the gel about once a week, but we shot the whole movie this way, and it looked fine.

If the color shift is minor, the Director of Photography may choose to go with that lens anyway, and let the color timing correct for any mismatch, but it is still better to know about these things in advance, and make a decision based on all of the facts.

A more objective test of lens color would be to shoot a few feet of gray card with each of the lenses you would like to use, under the same lighting conditions, and then to place the negative under the densitometer at the laboratory, and obtain an objective reading of the color for each lens. By examining the readings obtained, you will see how closely matched your lenses are for color rendition.

This test, and all of those listed and described above, can be done by the Camera Assistant alone, without the Director of Photography present, unless for some reason the Director of Photography wants to be present. For the following tests, the Director of Photography will generally want and need to be present.

Emulsion Tests

The Director of Photography will almost always want to test the particular emulsions being used in the shooting. There are many things the D.P. might want to look at.

First of all, the emulsions need to be tested to make sure there is not some manufacturing defect in the film, such as scratches or a perforation problem. I have had film direct from the manufacturer with two deep scratches directly down the center of the frame, and another time with one perforation missing every foot. The camera tried to punch its own perforations, and made a lot of noise and tore the film doing that. Sometimes these things happen, despite the best intentioned quality controls at the manufacturer. Fortunately they are rare.

The D.P. will also want to know if the film conforms somewhat to the exposure index recommended by the manufacturer. Film stocks can vary from batch to batch, and finding the true speed of the particular stock you want to use is important. The Director of Photography can do this by shooting a "normal" situation with "normal" lighting and "normal" exposure using the "normal" recommended speed rating, and having the lab make a "normal" print.

By looking at the printing lights from the lab, a Director of Photography can approximate the true speed of the particular batch of film. If the numbers are in the middle of the scale, then the D.P. can use the manufacturer's speed rating safely with that batch of film. If the numbers are at the low end of the printer scale, then the manufacturer's ASA rating should be decreased accordingly. If the numbers are high, then the rating index should be increased.

The Director of Photography will probably also want to test the exposure latitude of the particular stocks intended for use in the production; to see how the stocks perform under various degrees of under- and overexposure.

Depending on the D.P., this might be a series of exposures of a test subject, usually a person sitting in front of a black and white background, with or without a gray scale and/or color chart, exposed first "Normal," then progressively underexposed at set intervals, usually one-half stop or one stop. The test may continue with a similar series of overexposures.

Once the background and lighting are set, and a suitable model is positioned, with whatever charts and gray scales are required, and the scene is lit to the Director of Photography's satisfaction, twenty feet or so can be shot at a normal exposure.

Figure 5-6 Exposure Test Setup. Before shooting begins on a feature film, the Director of Photography will probably want to shoot a test of the various film emulsions that will be used on the job. The D.P. needs to know how that particular batch of film responds to color, contrast, overexposure, and underexposure. A typical test setup might include black and white background, a gray scale and/or color chart, and a real live person for skin tone and to make it more interesting to watch in the screening room. Prominently displayed are the emulsion type and a card showing the exposure variation—NORMAL, 1/2 STOP OVER, 1/2 STOP UNDER, 1 STOP OVER, 1 STOP UNDER, etc., usually to about 3 stops overexposed and 3 stops underexposed.

Be sure to place in the frame somewhere a slate of information: the type of stock, the emulsion number, possibly the production name or company name, a date (in case the test is done more than once on different days), and, most importantly, a prominent label for "NORMAL" exposure. All that needs to be changed for the following exposures are the exposure labels; to "1/2 Stop Under," "1 Stop Under," "1 Stop Over," etc., as required.

A typical series of tests might run from normal to three stops under in 1/2 stop increments, then from normal to three stops over, and then normal again. If the exposure labels are prominent and legible in the frame, then the projected test will be very informative to the Director of Photography.

Some Directors of Photography will change the exposure of subsequent parts of the test by simply changing the aperture on the lens; stopping down for underexposure and opening up for overexposure, without changing the lighting. Others prefer to leave the aperture set (so as not to increase or decrease the Depth-of-Field, and risk becoming distracted by the changes in focus during the test), and prefer to change the lighting by adding nets or scrims to the lights for subsequent passes, or even better, to change exposure by adding neutral density filters and/or by changing the variable shutter on the camera, on those cameras that allow such changes.

This has the advantage of leaving the aperture set for a constant Depth-of-Field, leaving the lighting set to save time and provide constant highlight and shadow areas.

For example, if your basic "Normal" exposure is f/2.8, at 180 degree shutter angle, then for "1/2 Stop Under" all you have to change is the shutter, from 180 to 135 degrees, leaving the lens at f/2.8. For "1 Stop Under," either change the shutter to 90 degrees, or reset to 180 degrees and add an N3 (Neutral Density 0.30) Filter to the lens. For "1 1/2 Stops Under," use the N3 filter PLUS set the shutter at 135 degrees. This process can be continued through the range of underexposure desired, usually up to "3 Stops Under," which would be using an N9 (Neutral Density 0.90) Filter, with the shutter at 180 degrees, still leaving the aperture set at f/2.8.

For the overexposure part of the test, the aperture of the lens must either be opened, or the lighting must be increased. A clever D.P. might have set the lighting so that for the overexposure part, all that needs to be done is to remove scrims or nets, without moving the lighting units themselves. Generally, however, the underexposure series is much more important to the Director of Photography than the overexposure series, to see how the shadow areas will behave on film.

This type of test will need to be repeated for each type of film stock intended for use in the production. If daylight balance stocks are used, the Director of Photography might want to recreate this test outdoors, under daylight conditions, or indoors using HMI lighting. If special lighting conditions are to be encountered, such as shooting in a stadium with mercury vapor lighting, or in a factory with fluorescent lighting, then a test series might be done at that location as well, time and money permitting.

Specifying Printing Lights

Some Directors of Photography use this emulsion test to choose the printing lights for that emulsion, to be used for printing all dailies from negatives of that emulsion.

Most Directors of Photography send printing instructions to the Timer at the laboratory either by phone each day or by having the Camera Assistant write the instructions on the Camera Reports submitted for each roll of film, or both. These printing instructions give the Timer an idea of what the Director of Photography is looking for in each scene or location, and allow the Timer to help out, adding or subtracting a bit of color, or changing the overall density of the print. Typical instructions might be "Print for Early Morning," "Print for Blue Moonlight effect," "Print for Late Afternoon Sun," "Print for Candlelight," or whatever else might be required.

A few Directors of Photography don't want any help from the lab. They want to have total control of the image at the camera, through filters, lighting, and original exposure. All they want from the lab is for the lab to do exactly the same thing every day, with every roll of film.

If they want a blue cast to the scene, they prefer to do it with blue gel on the lights, balanced by eye on the set, rather than having the Timer add blue to the print. The Timer cannot know the precise shade or amount of blue the D.P. has in mind for a particular shot. If they want a low-key scene, they prefer to do it through original exposure of the negative, rather than having the Timer increase the density of the print.

These D.P.'s will choose a set of Printing Lights for each emulsion type being used, at the beginning of the job, or possibly several sets for different locations or lighting situations, and the Camera Reports will read simply "Print at 32-28-36," or whatever those numbers might be.

By sending the lab the exposure test described above, and asking the Timer to make a "Normal" print, the Director of Photography can look at the projected test print, make whatever changes he or she thinks appropriate, reprint and rescreen the test until it is correct to the D.P.'s satisfaction, and then use that set of printer light numbers for that emulsion. The process is repeated for each emulsion being used.

These sets of numbers will be given to the Camera Assistant for adding to the Camera Reports. It is not unusual for the Assistant to have a list of half a dozen sets of numbers for different stocks under different conditions. The Assistant should check with the D.P. for each scene or location to make sure that the correct printing lights are added to each Camera Report.

This process has the advantage of making the eventual color timing of the finished film very easy, as there should be only very few and very minor corrections needed. It also makes the dailies consistently better, because there is no subjective and potentially misunderstood communication necessary between the Director of Photography and the Color Timer. The Director of Photography knows what he wants, and does it, directly on the negative.

There is no chance that the Timer might inadvertently add too much blue, or make the print too light or too dark. The Director of Photography is in total control, specifying the color and density of each area of each frame to his or her satisfaction on the set, instead of depending on an overall correction in color and density later on at the lab.

Not many Directors of Photography work this way, but some do. Few D.P.'s know enough about the exposure, negative densitometry, and lab chemistry processes to work this way. Most D.P.'s like and need the help of the Color Timer to get the effect they want.

It is difficult to accurately and exactly describe a mood or feeling to another person who is not present on the set, by telephone or by adding a few notes on the bottom of a Camera Report. The exact effect may not be communicated the first time, and the dailies might need to be reprinted darker, or with more blue, and maybe a third time, to get the desired effect. This is expensive, time-consuming, and annoying to a Director and Director of Photography who need to see immediately what a scene looks like.

Filter Tests

Depending on the Director of Photography and the subject matter or mood of the script, there might be filters to test. It seems that every year there are new diffusion filter series in vogue among D.P.'s, or new colored graduated filters, or new stockings to be attached behind the lenses. Camera Assistants often refer to these as "Fad Filters" or "Filters du Jour."

The Director of Photography will certainly want to conduct these tests himself or herself, possibly with the actual actresses or actors from the cast. For Diffusion Filters especially, the D.P. needs to see the effect on the real cast members. This often means involving the makeup artist and hair stylist, as well as a gaffer and grip in attendance for the test.

Diffusion filters generally come in sets of four or five different strengths or densities, and will need to be tested to find the right lens focal length/filter strength combinations that will be used in the shooting.

For the Camera Assistant, a test of this type generally only means having the proper filters available for testing, having several magazines loaded with film, and making sure that the specific filters used are slated before and/or during the test, usually on a card or slate prominently visible in the frame, and noted carefully on the camera report for that test roll. A clipboard mounted in a grip stand in one corner of the frame, with cards added to indicate which filters are in use, is an easy and common solution.

Wardrobe and Makeup Tests

Close to the start of filming, there may be wardrobe and/or makeup tests to be done. These will probably not be done at the rental house, and will require studio space, with dressing rooms, extensive lighting setups, a larger crew, etc.

A typical test would consist of the actual cast members, made up and in costume, starting in a full figure shot facing the camera, turning completely around to show all sides of the costumes, and then walking toward the camera, ending in a medium or medium close shot, and turning again, showing profiles and back. The test might be repeated with a different color shirt, or with a different hat, or whatever. The changes should be slated, and someone, hopefully one of the wardrobe or makeup people, should be taking notes of what exactly has been changed between takes. A typical slate might contain the actor's name and consecutive numbers for the different clothes or makeups worn.

If you do have to do makeup and wardrobe tests for a production, prepare yourself for a long and boring day's work, mostly spent waiting for the cast to change clothes and have their makeup redone. Also be prepared to shoot a lot of film.

Actors' Screen Tests

Sometimes you might be involved in screen tests for actors. The process is similar to the wardrobe tests described above, but might be even more involved, filmed on actual sets or locations, complete with dialogue recording, dolly moves, scene coverage such as close-ups, etc. Other screen tests might just be shot in an empty studio using very basic settings and props like a chair and a table. Others might just be "talking-head" close-ups, or simple scene readings in front of the camera. As above, be prepared for a long day and shooting a lot of film.

Lab Continuity Test

This test is rarely needed, but when used never ceases to surprise me with its results. The only Directors of Photography who use this test seem to be those who specify printing lights to be used by the lab. The test is simply a method of determining how accurately and consistently the lab is handling the film sent in to them.

The process is simple. A setup similar to the emulsion test described above is used, a person standing or sitting in front of a black and white background, possibly with a color scale or gray scale. A long roll of film, 500 to 1000 feet, is then run continuously through the camera on this scene, at a normal exposure. This magazine is then unloaded in the darkroom and divided into rolls of approximately 100 feet each, and each of these small rolls placed in a separate film can. These test rolls are then labeled and stored, and are sent to the laboratory on different days, maybe every other day or twice a week.

These rolls are as identical as possible; same original roll of film, same camera, same lens, same lighting, same exposure, same subject; everything exactly the same. The only thing that will change is the laboratory processing and printing. If the laboratory is doing the same thing to the film every day, then every one of these test rolls should look exactly the same. But they never do.

After the last of the rolls have been sent in to the lab and processed and printed, then the prints are spliced together in the sequence they were sent in. The prints should be cut down to, say, twenty feet or so of each day's test, so the changes can be seen in rapid succession. This assembled collection of several days' tests should then be screened. Be prepared for a surprise.

Each day's negative/print combination will look slightly different, either in density differences or color shifts, or both. There may also be visible contrast or grain differences. This test will mostly demonstrate differences in dailies (positive) printing.

A further test often done is to cut short lengths of the various days' negatives together and to make a single print from this assembled negative. This will more clearly show differences in day-to-day negative development. These tests are always interesting and fun to watch!

Some D.P.'s ask the lab for densitometer readings of a sample strip of film exposed and processed by the laboratory, on a regular basis, to monitor laboratory performance. For this process, the Camera Assistant sends over to the laboratory a short end (100 to 200 feet) of the stock type being used, unexposed. The laboratory periodically takes short lengths of this unexposed film, exposes them to a standardized test, and develops this test strip with the dailies negative. The resulting developed negative is then scanned in a densitometer, and readings are obtained, and compared with readings from other test strips on other days.

CHAPTER **6**

Loading/Unloading

Between the manufacturer and the laboratory the Camera Assistant is the only person to actually touch the film. Others may handle the cardboard boxes of film or handle the sealed aluminum film cans, but only the Assistant touches the film itself.

On a normal feature film, the responsibility for loading and unloading the film magazines belongs to the Second Camera Assistant. On a television commercial, or a documentary, or even some low-budget features, there may only be one Camera Assistant, responsible for all of the duties of the First and Second Camera Assistants. In some cases there may also be a film loader on the payroll, or a trainee, who can help the Second Assistant with the loading, but it is generally the Second Assistant who does all of the loading and unloading of the film magazines.

The film is handled at least twice by the Camera Assistant, once before exposure in the camera, and once after. In addition to physically handling the film, the Camera Assistant also has "spiritual" control of the film, from its delivery from the manufacturer, through its exposure in the camera, to its shipping to the lab. Each and every roll of film, as it arrives at the studio or location and is placed in the Assistant's charge, becomes part of the living inventory maintained by that Assistant.

Manufacturer's Film Can Label

Each roll of film leaves a trail in the Assistant's paperwork, from virgin roll, to loaded magazine, to exposed roll and short end. At any given moment in time, the Assistant should be able to track down any particular roll, or remnant of a roll. The roll's "fingerprint," which makes this tracking possible, is the label on the film can, beginning with the manufacturer's label, and continuing with the Assistant's labels. There can be no such thing as a can of film without a label. If the manufacturer's label no longer applies, the Assistant has replaced it with a handwritten label, but the label must always be kept up-to-date.

126 THE CAMERA ASSISTANT

There is a great deal of information available on a film can label. First, of course, is the type of film contained in that can. Each type of film available from a manufacturer is identified by a four-digit emulsion type number, usually found in nice large prominent numerals on the label. Smaller numbers tell more of the story.

The second set of numbers is called the "emulsion number" or "batch number." Every batch of film made by the manufacturer varies slightly, so it is to everyone's advantage if all of the film needed of a particular type comes from the same batch. Just as in knitting a sweater, you want all of your "yarn" to be from the same batch because of the minor variations in color, contrast, and speed (sensitivity). This may not always be possible, but it is desirable. Eastman Kodak now claims that the quality control in the manufacture, distribution, and processing of the new "EXR" color

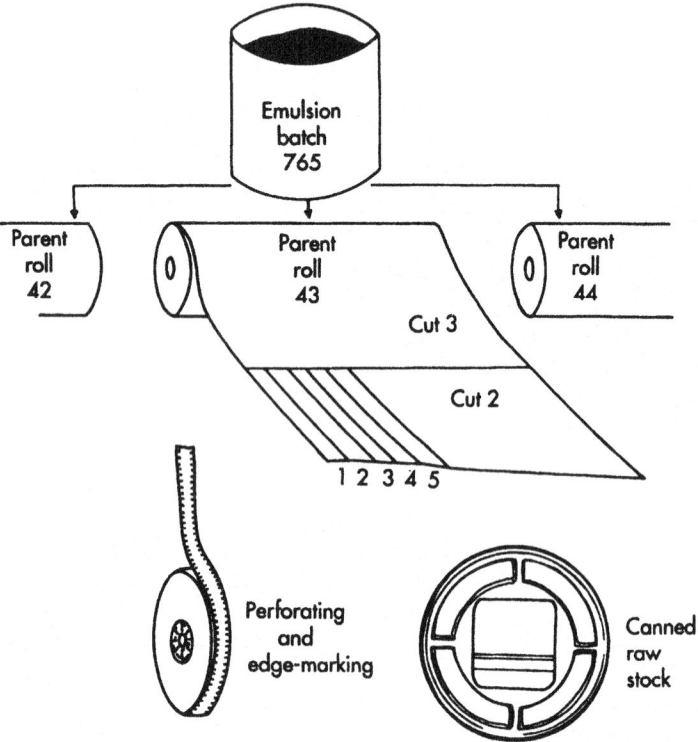

Figure 6-1 Film Manufacture—Origin of Emulsion Numbers. For our example, Emulsion Batch 765 of our type 5247 emulsion is used to make several "parent rolls." Parent Roll 43 is cut to 400 foot lengths, and this 400 foot Cut 2 (the second cut from the beginning of the roll) is then slit to 35mm width rolls, perforated on both sides, and rolled up around plastic cores. This film is thus labeled 5247-765-432, and the small adhesive label showing the "slit" or "can" number is then placed on the can. This "serial" number, describing the ancestry of that particular roll, follows that roll wherever it goes—magazine, short end, exposed film can, camera report, etc.

negative films has reached the level of consistency that it is no longer necessary to order film from a single batch in order to match color, contrast, and speed; but for now, however, I believe that D.P.'s will still prefer to order raw stock from the same batch. It is a tradition based on experience and common sense!

Think of the manufacturing process as making film in large, wide rolls, which are then slit into 35mm or 16mm, or whatever gauge you have purchased. According to Eastman Kodak, a "batch" is sufficient for from five to fifty "parent" rolls each approximately 4000 feet long and 54 inches wide. All parent rolls made from the same batch of emulsion will have the same batch number. All rolls slit off the same large parent roll will have the same batch and parent roll numbers. All camera rolls cut from the same "slit" will have the same batch, parent, and slit numbers.

A 54-inch parent roll is sliced into either thirty-eight "slits" of 35mm film, numbered from 1 to 38, or 78 "slits" of 16mm film, numbered from 1 to 78. Each of these 4000 foot slits is then cut into the appropriate lengths, and numbered starting with 1. This third number is called the "cut" number.

A feature film might shoot anywhere from 200 to 500 thousand feet of film, and there is nowhere near enough film available in a single parent roll for that much film, (38 slits times 4 rolls of 35mm film from each parent roll = 152 1000-foot rolls maximum for each parent roll) so a typical feature film order would include film from several parent rolls from the same batch.

There is also a "slit" or "can" number that is not part of the emulsion number printed on the can label. In 35mm, this can number is usually printed on a small label stuck onto the can after labeling. In 16mm, it often appears as a two-digit number written on the can by hand in crayon. Either way, this number becomes part of the "fingerprint" of that roll, and follows that roll wherever it goes. It is written on the magazine label, on the Camera Report, and on the can label for any recan or short end.

Other information is also available from the manufacturer's label: the length of the roll, the type, pitch (distance between perforations) and number of rows of perforations, and the "wind" of the roll.

The length of the roll, obviously, is an important number to notice. The very last thing a Camera Assistant wants to happen is to run out of film in the middle of a take. It is important to check the label because it is not always what you think. You may have ordered 1000-ft. rolls, or 400-ft. rolls, but that may not be what you get. Sometimes, at the end of one of those giant rolls of film, there may be less than the requested length, so it is not unusual to get a roll direct from the manufacturer labeled "980 ft." or "950 ft." or "370 ft." So do check those numbers.

In 35mm, there are always two rows of perforations, but in 16mm, film is sold in "single perf" and "double perf" styles. The odds are that either one will run through your camera, but find out for sure. Some older cameras have sprockets with teeth on both sides. These sprockets will handle double perf film but NOT single perf, without damage to the film and possibly to the camera.

There are other reasons why you might want single perf—if you are shooting in the format known as "Super 16mm," you MUST shoot with single perf film. The additional picture negative area of Super 16mm is that area normally used for the

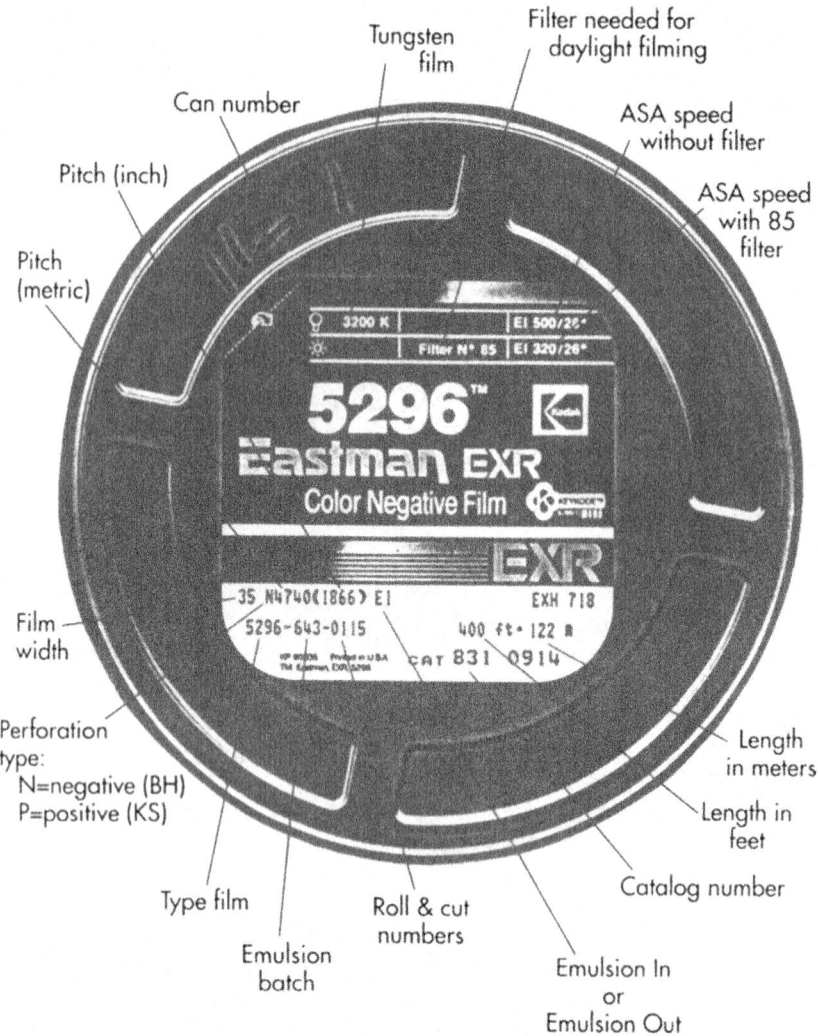

Figure 6-2 Film Can Label. The label on the film can contains a lot of useful information for the Camera Assistant. Most important is the roll's "fingerprint," its unique serial number tracing its ancestry: the Type—Batch—Roll—Cut—Can numbers. This number will follow the roll wherever it goes.

Sample Emulsion/ Batch/ Cut Number: "5247—765—432"
"5247" describes the type of film stock,
"765" is the "batch" number,
"43" is the "parent" roll number,
"2" is the "cut" number,
There will also be a "slit" or "can" number, a two- or three-digit number on an adhesive label stuck on the front of the can, or a number written on the can in crayon.

sound track area on projected 16mm film, and usually occupied by that second row of perforations in camera negative film.

There was also a time when "single-system" sound filming was common in 16mm. This process is also known as "sound-on-film," where the sound track was recorded simultaneously with the picture in special cameras designed for that purpose. Before the widespread use of videotape for television news gathering, film crews were sent out from television stations with "single-system" film equipment to shoot pictures and sound together, first with an optical sound system, recording a soundtrack by exposing that area of the film where the second row of perforations would normally be to a tiny flickering lightbulb inside the camera. This film could be processed and broadcast much faster than conventionally shot and edited film, because the sound was already attached and in sync.

Later improvements to this system utilized a stripe of magnetic material applied to the edge of specially ordered film, recorded on by a magnetic head inside the camera, as in any tape recorder. Both of these single-system technologies use single-perf film to allow for the recorded soundtrack.

We now use "double-system" sound recording virtually exclusively, recording the sound and picture material separately, and combining them in the editing stage of the production. Videotape is a "single-system" type of shooting, with audio and video signals recorded on the same strip of material simultaneously.

There are probably many of those single-system film cameras still out there somewhere, but the single-system process is not used professionally anymore.

There is also the "pitch" of the perforations to consider. Pitch is the measurement of the spacing of the perforations, measured by the distance between the beginning of one perforation and the beginning of the next one. In both 35mm and 16mm there are "short" pitch, used in original camera negative film, and "long" pitch, used in optical printers, bi-pack animation cameras, etc. Make sure you know which one you need, and which one you have.

In 35mm and 65mm, perforations also come in different shapes. There are two common choices—"Bell & Howell" or "BH" perforations, in use since the 1900s, sometimes referred to as "negative" perforations, with straight top and bottom and curved sides; and "Kodak Standard" or "KS" perforations, introduced in the 1920s and referred to often as "positive" or "print" perforations, rectangular in shape with rounded corners.

BH perforations are the most common for camera negative, but sometimes KS perforated film is used for scenes that you know are going to become opticals, or used in "Blue-Screen," rear-projection process, or other matting work. This is because of the superior accuracy and camera registration ability of the KS perforations. KS perforations are the standard worldwide for release prints, because of the durability and longevity of these perfs. KS perfs are also sometimes used for high-speed cameras, because they are better able to stand the strain of the acceleration in a high-speed startup.

Two other perforation shapes are more rare, but may still be encountered. The first is the Dubray-Howell, or "DH," perf, first suggested in 1931 as a replacement for both the BH and KS perfs, and still found on some special application films such as

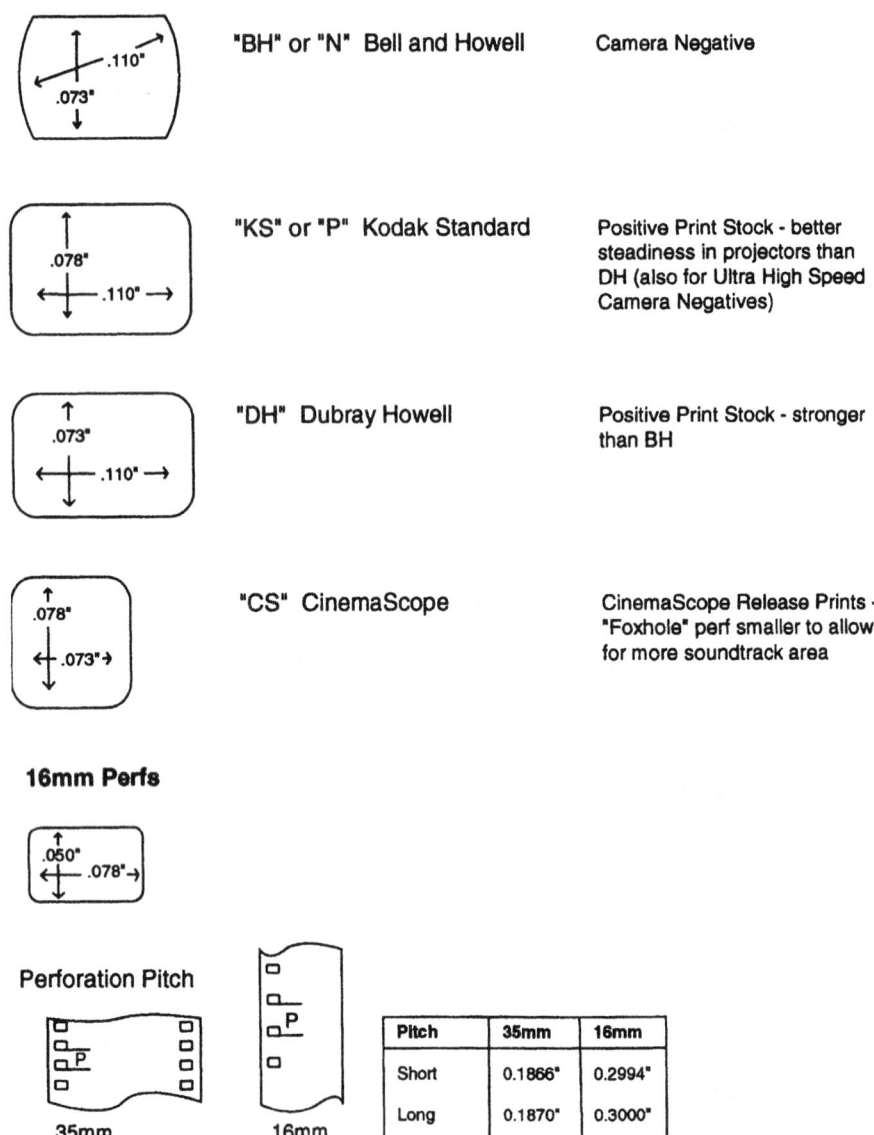

Figure 6-3 Film Perforations.

Eastman Color Intermediate Film 5243. These perfs have the same height as BH perfs, but the width of KS perfs, and with rounded corners.

The fourth perforation shape is called "CS." It was found on some Cinemascope release prints, and was nearly square in shape, and smaller than the KS perf, allowing more space for the magnetic sound tracks.

BH perforations, because of the sharp corners between the top and bottom and the sides of the perforations, sometimes tear when under stress, especially in high-speed cameras. Kodak recently announced that they had rounded these internal corners on their camera negative stocks, for added strength and resistance to perforation damage. All of the newer Eastman "EXR" film stocks use these improved BH perforations.

The can label will also let you know whether the roll of film is wound around a plastic core or onto a metal "daylight spool" (necessary for certain internal loading cameras like the Bell & Howell Eyemo 35mm and the Arriflex 16S cameras, and for some high-speed cameras like the Photosonics Actionmaster 16mm camera).

There will also be indications on the film can label of anything else unusual about the contents of that particular film can, such as when the film contained has a magnetic sound "stripe" for recording sound directly on the film as it runs through the camera ("single-system") applied on one side of the film where the second row of perforations normally go.

Once you thoroughly understand what that film can contains, and have decided that it is the right type of film for your job, you can proceed with the loading of the magazines for the shoot.

Changing Bags

The next step is to find a place to work. In a studio situation, or on a film with a real camera truck outfitted with shelves and a darkroom, there is a special little room made just for loading and unloading film magazines, called a darkroom. Obviously this loading and unloading is much easier in a darkroom, but on many jobs and locations, this will not be an option, and you will wind up using the Camera Assistants' Second Best Friend, the Changing Bag.

The Changing Bag is actually two bags sewn together one inside the other, with a large zippered opening on one side and two arm holes with elastic cuffs on the other side. The Camera Assistant places a magazine, a roll of film still in its aluminum can, but with the printed tape removed, and sometimes a film core, inside the inner bag, and zips up the two zippers—double protection against a light leak. The Assistant's arms are inserted into the cuffs from the other side and the loading can begin.

There are, of course, variations on this simple idea. Sometimes Velcro is used instead of zippers, or the bag is built like a miniature camping tent, with rods that support the material of the bag, keeping it open and out of the Assistant's way. Sometimes the bag is carried in and attached to an aluminum briefcase-style case, which is opened and supports some of the material. In the hot humid summers, the black bag becomes a hot, soggy environment, and not very pleasant to work in. Supporting the material up and away from the Assistant's hands and magazine makes the job a lot easier and more comfortable. Some bags have one side silvered to reflect away some of the ambient light and heat.

An Assistant will never use a changing bag in direct sunlight, of course, for fear of light leaking through the bag and ruining the film, and instead seeks a shady

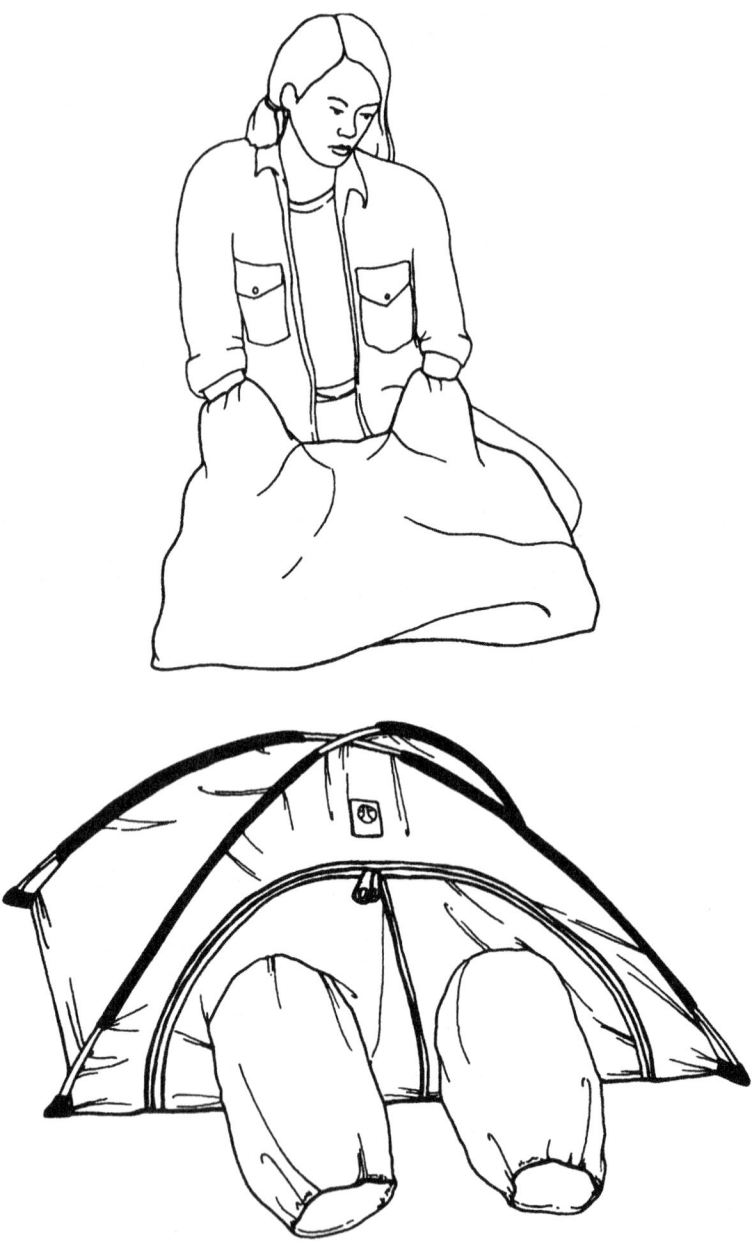

Figure 6-4 Changing Bag/Tent. Changing bags and changing tents are portable darkrooms for the Camera Assistant. Most Camera Assistants own their own, but take one from a rental house anyway. Never leave home without one!

place to work, the darker the better. Shady places are more comfortable for the Assistant to work in, also.

There are different size bags, as well. If you are going to buy your own bag (almost all Camera Assistants own their own changing bags, preferring using their own to using a rental bag), make sure you get one large enough for the largest magazine you are likely to be loading. Bags range in size from very small, used in loading small, still-film developing tanks with short lengths of still film, to very large, 36" x 45" or larger, large enough to contain with comfort a thousand-foot displacement-type magazine side-by-side with a pair of thousand-foot film cans. Naturally, the larger the bag, the better.

The changing bag should be kept clean, of course, and dry. It should also be folded neatly when not in use, and folded in a way that protects the zippered openings and the cuffs by keeping these vulnerable areas protected and away from dust, dirt, and abrasion. It is also recommended that the folded bag be stored in some other container, such as a nylon bag or case, to further protect it from the elements.

Keep in mind that the changing bag will probably be the least expensive item in the massive array of film and camera equipment on the job. But twice for each roll, on the way from the aluminum film can into the magazine and then later for the return journey, your precious film, lovingly and expensively exposed in the camera and containing the unborn photographic latent image, will be protected from ruination only by those two thin layers of cloth, and the skill and experience of the Camera Assistant.

Sometimes even when there is a darkroom on the camera truck, using a changing bag is preferable. If the shooting location is on the 27th floor of an office building and the truck is in the street, the Second Assistant will often opt for loading mags in the bag near the set, rather than disappearing for a half hour at a time and waiting for a minimum of two elevators. In such a situation, the First Assistant would probably also appreciate the Second remaining within shouting distance. I know I do.

There is nothing you can do in a darkroom that you can't do in a changing bag on a card table, or an office desk, or a kitchen table, or the floor, or even the back seat of a van or the hood of a station wagon.

Many Assistants, myself included, always pick up a rental changing bag from the equipment house when renting a camera package, even though they plan to use their own personal bags, just on the off chance that their own bags become wet, or otherwise damaged. Having a backup changing bag is the cheapest insurance you can buy. Just be sure during the Checkout that you examine the bag carefully, checking to see that the zippers are working properly, that the elastic in the cuffs is in good condition, and that there are no torn seams or other damage to either the inner or outer bag.

It is difficult to check for true light-tightness, without climbing into the bag and having someone zip you in, but an examination of the fabric on both sides, and especially the seams, zippers, and cuffs, should give you an idea about the condition of the bag. Dave suggests turning on a bright flashlight or lantern, inserting it into the bag, zipping the bag closed, and rolling it around in a darkened room. Any worn spots, loose seams, or light leaks will show up clearly.

Darkrooms

Darkrooms also come in many styles and sizes. In the camera truck, it will likely be little more than a phone booth or small closet made of plywood, sealed with black tape and/or black cloth, and painted black to minimize leaks and reflections. It will usually be too small to sit down in, and all loading will be done standing up. There might be a couple of shelves stacked with film cans, supplies, and paperwork. It might be larger, depending on who designed and built the internal fixtures of the truck.

The truck darkroom will often be storage for film stock and supplies, and sometimes even seldom-used camera equipment stored on shelves, possibly a compressed nitrogen tank with regulator, hose, and nozzle, for blowing out the magazines. There will probably be some sort of light, either battery-powered or carefully wired so that it cannot be turned on inadvertently from someone OUTSIDE the room.

Many Assistants have gotten into the habit of unscrewing and removing the darkroom light bulb and/or unplugging the power when actually working in the dark loading or unloading. This is an excellent idea, and I recommend this practice highly. Unscrewing the bulb when "in the dark" makes it impossible for someone OUTSIDE the darkroom to turn the light on while you're working, thereby ruining a roll of film. It's a simple precaution, but it might save the job.

The door will lock from the INSIDE, with a substantial barrel bolt or hook-and-eye or some other piece of hardware to prevent accidental opening of the door when something important is going on inside. The door itself will be built to overlap the door jamb, for additional light-proofing, and where the door and jamb meet will often be further protected with weatherstripping, cloth or rubber flaps, etc. to further keep the dark in and the light out.

The very first thing to check when entering a strange darkroom for the first time is whether or not it is really dark inside. Go inside, close and lock the door securely, and wait ten minutes or so for your eyes to get used to the dark. Keep looking around the inside of the darkroom for light leaks, especially around the door and along all of the interior joints—where the walls meet the floor, the ceiling, and each other. Any pinpoints or streaks or cracks of light need to be sealed with black tape or cloth before using the darkroom for any loading or unloading of film.

The usual practice is to seal both sides of a hole or crack with tape (both inside and outside the darkroom) if possible. The previous user of the darkroom may have drilled holes for electric wires, or hammered in and later removed nails for hanging up clothes or supplies, may have moved or removed a shelf, exposing previous nail holes, etc. Plug them all!

If the darkroom is in a truck, it should have been built as a single completely enclosed unit, with walls, floor, ceiling, and door. Production managers and/or head carpenters trying to save time and money sometimes try to build truck darkrooms without a floor and/or a ceiling, counting on the floor/ceiling of the truck to be light-tight. But they rarely are. The wooden floors of many trucks have small gaps between floorboards, and these gaps get wider with age.

Also, truck bodies are built to flex slightly, and this makes light-tight sealing against the truck walls and ceiling difficult if not impossible. Bouncing around in the truck may also have loosened up some of the joints. So if you have a choice, insist that the darkroom be built very securely as a complete freestanding unit.

The other problem with truck darkrooms is that they are usually built all the way forward in the cargo area, just behind the cab, and usually directly above the exhaust. Since the teamster will be spending many hours a day inside the cab with the engine running to keep warm, the darkroom will often be full of carbon monoxide and other noxious fumes. All this makes loading and unloading not a lot of fun for the Assistants and Loaders.

Studio darkrooms suffer many of the same problems, except for the carbon monoxide. Never assume that a darkroom in a studio is really dark. Check it out yourself, using the same procedure, and make whatever repairs are necessary before opening a single roll of film. More than once I have had to use a changing bag in a studio because the darkroom was in such bad condition. Studio darkrooms are also often used as clothes closets and clothes changing rooms by the construction crew building the sets before the shooting crews arrive, so they are often full of sawdust, coffee cups, paint cans, and paper bags half full of nails.

Naturally a clean darkroom is preferable to a dirty one, wherever it is located. The Second Assistant is the "housewife" of the Camera Crew, responsible for sweeping, vacuuming, and whatever else is necessary to ensure a clean place to load the film into magazines. The prop department will certainly have a vacuum cleaner available. Any dirt, dust, film chips, or other debris that gets inside a magazine, can and often does lead to scratches of the fragile film negative.

Valuable raw stock will be stored in the darkroom and a lot of companies want you to keep a lock on the darkroom door so the raw stock doesn't disappear.

Camera Trucks

A camera truck is a vehicle you are going to use on location. It will have a darkroom and shelves for your equipment cases, tools, supplies, rain gear, boots, etc. If you're lucky you can design it yourself and give the sketch to the Head Carpenter on the job and the Carpenter and Grip Departments will shelve it out the way you want.

If you're unlucky it will come from wherever the production company rented the trucks from and it will be preshelved—rarely the ideal arrangement. The shelves always seem to be in the wrong place and the wrong size, either with wasted space or not enough room. I have several different truck shelf layout diagrams for different size trucks, modified and improved periodically, so as soon as I know what size truck we'll be getting I'll send the appropriate diagram over to the carpenters.

The basic rule of camera truck loading is to follow your own common sense. Heavier items on the floor or on the lower shelves, lighter items up high. Camera bodies and particularly delicate items like lenses on the floor or on lower shelves, so they will have a shorter distance to fall should the shelves collapse (which happened to me on one job). There is generally one shelf about 3'6" high that is used as a workbench for assembling the camera and performing the morning maintenance routine. This shelf is often carpeted, or covered with a rubber mat to minimize splinters and reduce the chance of some small part from sliding or bouncing off the shelf and getting lost.

Many Camera Assistants mount a camera base plate on this shelf by drilling a hole in the shelf and bolting the base plate to the shelf from below. The base plate allows the camera to be securely mounted on the workbench when working on it, to prevent accidents. There are often worklights mounted above the workbench, and the bench provides a good writing surface for the multitude of paperwork, especially the weekly time cards. Tools and cleaning supplies are often stored on or near this workbench, for easy access.

It is essential to strap in the cases on the shelves to prevent their falling. The shelves should have been made with a lip to prevent cases sliding off, but this is not enough—use bungie cords (elastic shock cords with hooks on both ends), rope, nylon straps, whatever you can find, but strap those cases in. Bungie cords are fast and easy—just add screw eyes at each end of the shelves to hook on to, or drill holes in the vertical boards supporting the shelves.

Expendable supplies and personal bags with rain gear, etc. can go on the top shelves. Try to keep all of the magazines together, and all of the lenses together, etc. This makes things easier to find when you are in a hurry. When everything is loaded and sorted on the shelves to your satisfaction, label the shelves so you can find things and so you can return things to the right place. After a while you won't need the labels, but day players or others less familiar with the layout of this particular truck still will need the labels. Backup gear and equipment that is not going to be used very often can be stored in more out-of-the-way places, and often-used gear should be stored where it will be easily and quickly accessible.

Camera batteries are often stored together on a convenient shelf, with one or more outlet strips installed nearby so that the batteries may be charged without moving them somewhere else. When the truck gets power from the generator or from the location for lights, it also gets power for charging batteries (don't forget that battery chargers need AC power, NOT DC!)

Magazine Maintenance

The second step is starting with clean magazines. Magazines should be brushed out or blown out or both. A simple paint brush, available in any hardware store for about one dollar, 1/2" to 1" wide, with soft bristles, is just fine for brushing dirt, dust, and film chips out of magazines before putting film in.

For blowing out the magazines, aerosol cans of pressurized Freon or other chlorofluorocarbon gasses, with triggered nozzles are available from "Dust-Off" and other manufacturers, and are used by many Camera Assistants. However, these cans are not inexpensive and the material is detrimental to the environment and the atmospheric ozone, so I do not recommend indiscriminate use of it. The companies who make the stuff have started canning another material with theoretically less serious consequences, and this is becoming increasingly available, at higher cost, of course.

I have never heard an acceptable answer to the obvious question—why can't they just put compressed nitrogen, which is the safest and cheapest compressed gas to use, in a small "Dust-Off"-sized can for photographers and Camera Assistants to use?

Another disadvantage of these aerosol cans is that the early nozzle assemblies were only pressure fitted together, and often loosened enough with use to become detached and had the unfortunate tendency to shoot across the room at inopportune times. Most Assistants wrapped tape around these early nozzles to keep them together. Care must also be taken about tipping or inverting these cans when using them, as the gas can come out as a liquid from an inverted can. This liquid is very cold, and can cause injury to exposed skin and to the coatings on lenses, mirrors, and filters. This liquid, however, is very useful for erasing chalk marks from cement or blacktop.

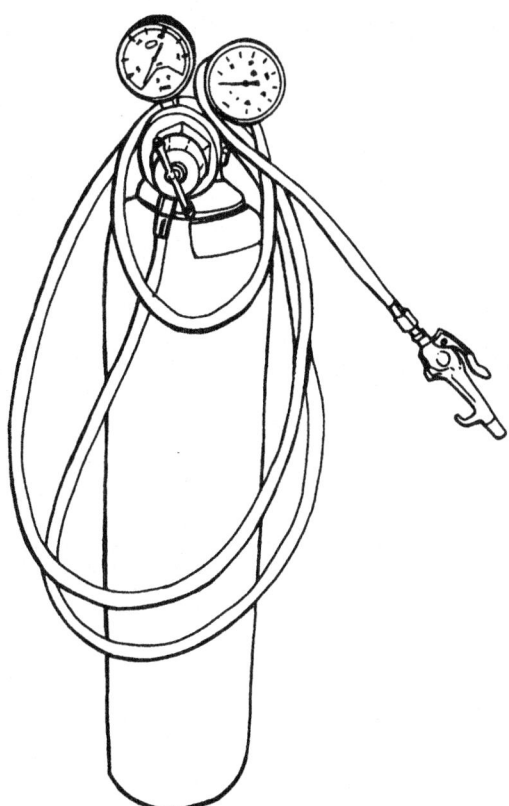

Figure 6-5 Nitrogen Tank. Nitrogen tank shown with regulator, pressure gauges, hose and nozzle. This is the most efficient and cost-effective dust remover for cameras, lenses, and magazines.

For the camera truck and for the darkroom, I prefer to use compressed nitrogen, which is available from welding supply companies in tanks of various sizes, with regulators, hoses, and nozzles.

So far, tanks of compressed nitrogen are still too large and heavy to keep in the front box under the camera, or to carry in an Assistant's kit for use on commercials or documentaries.

I've always thought that nitrous oxide ("laughing gas") would be a lot of fun to use on the set, but haven't had the opportunity to try it yet. I've been told that you need a doctor's prescription to buy the stuff, anyway.

Many Assistants carry a rubber bulb syringe or ear syringe for dusting cameras and magazines, but I have found these grossly inadequate for most purposes. They do not generate enough air pressure to move anything but the smallest and lightest dirt and debris. I haven't used one in years, but other Camera Assistants swear by them. Sometimes these syringes are available with a brush attached, as well.

Camera manufacturers recommend not using the aerosol dusters inside the camera body, because the possibility of blowing something deeper into the mechanism and causing more severe damage outweighs the benefits of blowing most debris out and away from the camera. I have been using aerosol dusters for many years in

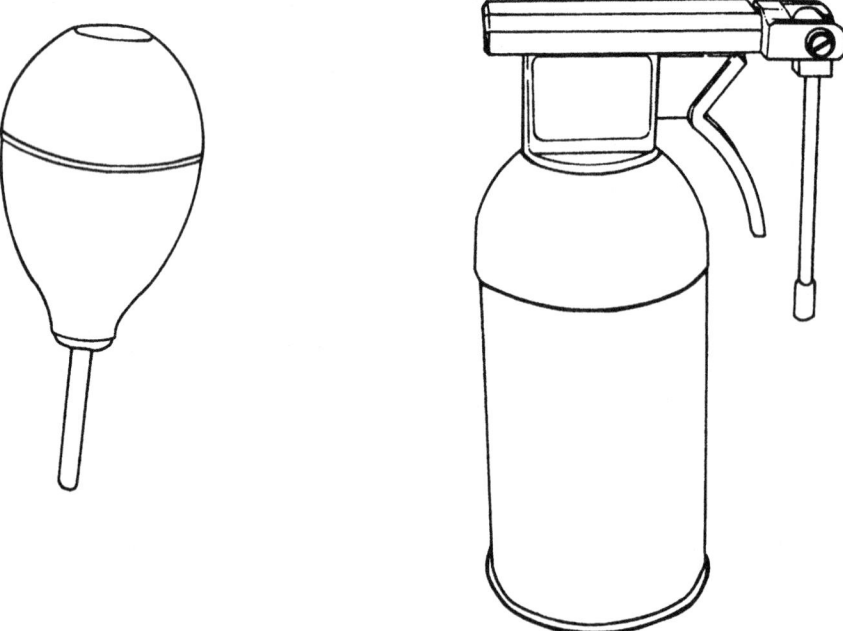

Figure 6-6 Rubber Bulb Syringe/Dust-Off Can. The Rubber Bulb Syringe, available in drug stores, is small, portable, and safe, but not very powerful. The Dust-Off aerosol can is portable and powerful, but also potentially dangerous to delicate camera mechanisms and lens coatings.

and around camera bodies, using light dusting strokes from a foot or so away from the camera, and have never had a problem, but be aware that the camera manufacturers recommend against this practice.

Certainly there is a danger of too great an aerosol pressure damaging some particularly fragile part of the camera body, such as the meter needle of a through-the-lens exposure system, or the thin pellicle or beamsplitter of a beamsplitter reflex camera, so inside the lens port I certainly support the camera manufacturers' recommendation against aerosol dusters, but around the outside of a closed camera, and inside a camera magazine, nothing works as well.

I have also been told by a representative from Arriflex that the chlorofluorocarbons in these aerosol cans can chemically damage the reflex mirror coatings.

As for other maintenance on the magazines, other than keeping them clean inside and out, there is not much to tell. I am opposed to Camera Assistants taking things apart in general, and taking apart magazines in particular. Arriflex delights in teaching Assistants about setting the torque in their magazines, and in making other adjustments inside, but I think this is a mistake on their part.

When a magazine is not taking up properly, then replace it with one that does. Send to the rental house and get a replacement, do not try and fix it yourself. Put aside that broken magazine and work with your other magazines until the replacement arrives. Then return the broken one to the rental house where competent professionals with the right tools and training can make the required repairs. For years I have avoided learning how to repair magazines, and I recommend the same philosophy for my readers.

Sometimes it may indeed be necessary to open up the throat of a 35BL or Panaflex magazine to clear a film jam, and this is another matter. By removing a few screws, the throat can be opened and the jam cleared in a few seconds, and the throat can be reassembled. The personnel at the rental house will show you how, if you ask them. Practice a few times under their supervision before trying it on your own.

For magazines with electric motor takeup, the Camera Assistant should be able to keep the electrical contacts on the magazine and on the camera body clean with a pencil eraser.

This is the extent of internal work on the magazines that the Camera Assistant should be required to know. Anything else is much more difficult, and should be left to the professional repair technicians at the rental house, who have the proper tools, the proper training, and the time to make such repairs.

An argument could be made that if the shoot is in the middle of the Kalahari Desert or some other inaccessible place, then the Camera Assistant should know how to make basic repairs to the equipment. Fine, then before going to the Kalahari, the Camera Assistant should spend some time with the manufacturer or rental house, get the proper tools and training, and learn how to repair magazines and such. In addition, before going to the Kalahari, additional backups and spares should be ordered.

For 99 percent of the shooting done in the United States, a rental house or manufacturer, and therefore replacement equipment, is only a phone call away.

The production will not want to stop and wait for repairs, anyway. They want to keep shooting. Knowledge about the internal workings of the camera and magazines is no substitute for having adequate spares, a backup camera, and enough magazines, batteries, and other items to keep shooting without interruption.

Loading Procedures

Once you have a flat, dry, and especially dark, place to work, and clean magazines to work with, you can proceed to the actual loading.

There are two basic types of magazines: single compartment and double compartment. Single compartment "displacement" magazines, such as are found with the Panavision Panaflex series of cameras, have a single, large compartment, containing both the "feed" and "takeup" rolls of film.

The "feed" roll is the unexposed film, before the film runs through the camera and is exposed behind the lens. After the film is exposed, it travels back into the magazine, and is rolled up on the "takeup" side. With the single compartment magazine, all of the loading and threading must be done at the same time, and in the dark, before replacing the magazine cover.

Double compartment magazines have separate compartments for the feed and takeup rolls, independently light-tight. These separate compartments may be side by side in the same plane, as in the Mitchell family of cameras, or they may be "coaxial,"

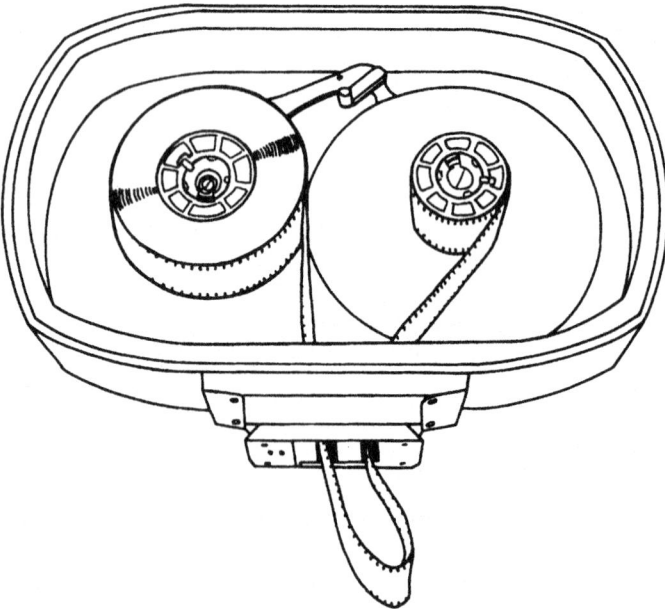

Figure 6-7 Displacement Magazines. The Panaflex magazine is an example of a displacement magazine, with both the feed and takeup rolls in a single compartment, side by side. All magazine loading must be done in the dark, of course, because everything is in the same compartment. The Arriflex IIC and III magazines are also displacement magazines.

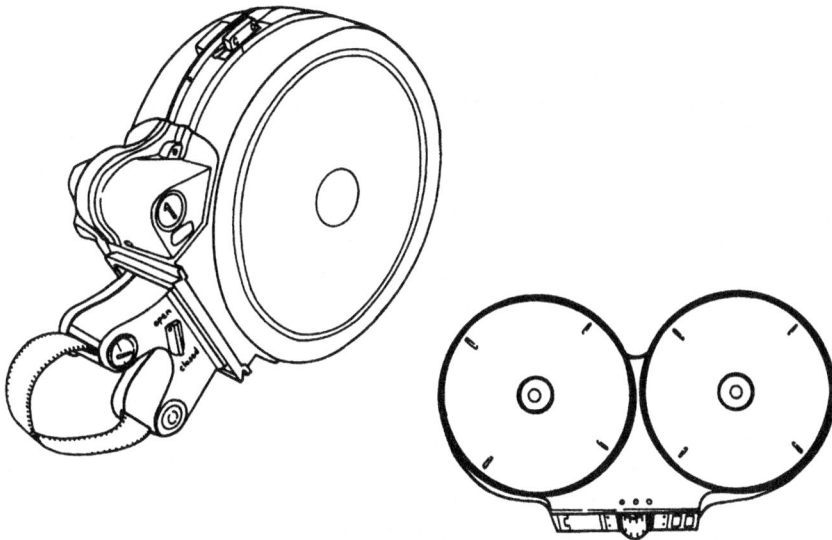

Figure 6-8 Dual Compartment/Coaxial Magazines. The Arriflex 35BL magazine is an example of a dual compartment, coaxial magazine, with the feed side of the magazine parallel to the takeup side of the magazine, one on top of the other. The Mitchell magazine is also an example of a dual compartment magazine, but is NOT coaxial, because the feed and takeup compartments are side by side in the same plane. Dual compartment magazines are generally easier to load, because part of the loading can be done in the light.

as in the Arriflex 35BL and 535 cameras, stacked one on top of the other, with their axles in line with each other, hence "coaxial."

In either configuration of double compartment magazine, the Assistant may work in either compartment without affecting the light-tightness of the other. In other words, after loading the film into the feed side, and closing the feed compartment lid, the magazine may be removed from the changing bag, or the light in the darkroom may be turned on, allowing the rest of the threading to be done in the light.

While the darkroom light is still on, or before the changing bag is zipped up, the printed tape may be removed from the film can, taking care to keep the can closed while pulling the tape off, and after the tape has been removed. Finding the end of the tape is much easier with the light on, and if you are loading in a changing bag, peeling off the tape inside the bag leaves you with about three feet of sticky tape and no place to dispose of it. So do yourself a favor and remove the tape before "going dark."

Once inside the changing bag or dark darkroom, you may open the film can. Inside, you will find a roll of film inside a black plastic or paper bag. Remove the film from this black bag. If this is a new, previously unopened roll of film, there will be a small piece of tape holding the very end of the roll from unravelling. Holding the roll of film so it will not unravel, remove this small piece of tape.

Some of the other books recommend sticking this small piece of tape INSIDE the film can, to keep it from getting loose into the magazine, and causing all sorts of trouble. However, it seems to me that INSIDE the film can is just as bad, as this is still in the line of fire, so to speak. The film can will be opened twice more in its life, once when unloading the film magazine and packaging the exposed film for shipment to the lab, and again when the lab opens the can to develop the film. This allows that small piece of tape two more opportunities to get into something and cause trouble.

I prefer to remove it forever from any proximity to the film, by sticking it to the wall of the darkroom as far from the changing table as possible (usually on the door of the darkroom, well behind me), or if using a changing bag, by sticking it to the bottom OUTSIDE of the can, until the can is removed from the changing bag, and then removing it from the can and disposing of it once and for all. This seems to me to be a far better method of keeping this troublemaker from making trouble.

If the film roll is either a "Short End" or "Recan," the previously used roll of film will probably not have the small piece of tape holding the end of the film to the roll (although I know there are Assistants who tape down the ends of short ends and recans), but it may have a torn, jagged end that makes magazine loading for certain cameras more difficult for the beginner.

After some experience, however, loading a magazine can be accomplished quickly, no matter how unevenly the end of the roll is torn. The jagged end can be cut square with scissors to make magazine loading easier, but this should not be necessary after the Assistant has loaded a few hundred magazines. I have found that if the end is really too uneven to load through the sprocket on the magazine, simply tearing off the end will make threading possible. Remember to properly dispose of the short piece of film torn or cut off, to prevent accidents.

The magazine will either have a "core adapter," a mechanical core with a lever to grab and hold the film end, and then release the end when the roll is removed from the camera, or will have a post that accepts a standard, empty, 2" film core. If the magazine has a core adapter, the Assistant need only insert the end of the film into the slot in the adapter, and then close the lever, which pinches and holds the end. The Assistant can then turn the core adapter by hand a few turns to make sure that the film will be taken up straight and flat. If the film seems to be rising up out of the magazine, disconnect and reconnect the film to the core adapter, pressing the edge of the film down into the magazine.

To attach the film to the plastic core, simply fold back about three inches of the film and align the edges of the film between your fingers as you make the fold. This makes the fold exactly perpendicular to the edges, for a more secure fit into the core slot. Then, making sure that the core is positioned so that the slot is **OPPOSED** to the direction of rotation, insert the folded end of the film as far into the slot as possible. Then fold back the double thickness of film around the core and turn by hand a few turns to secure the film.

By orienting the core slot in opposition to the direction of rotation, the film gets tighter as tension is applied, not looser. This is very important, as too loose a wind and the slot running the wrong way might allow the film to become detached from the core with vibration or as the camera torque motor applies tension. Once the film end falls out of the slot, the magazine will no longer pull the film into the magazine,

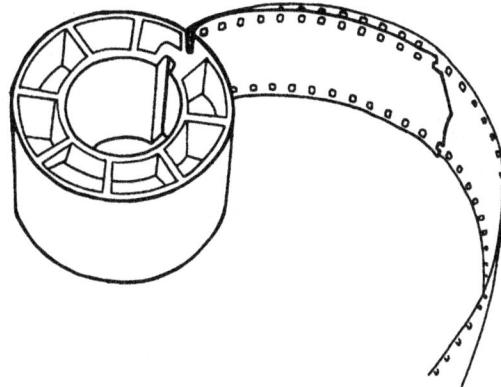

Figure 6-9 Attaching Film to Core. This is the best way to attach film to a film core in a magazine, with the film doubled over and inserted into the slot, forcing a sharp bend in the film, and holding it securely to the core. The film is unlikely to be pulled out of the slot. Some Assistants insist that this method causes a "bump" in the roll, and prefer to attach the film to the core with the slot running the other way.

and the camera will stop when the film bunching up inside finally pushes the buckle trip switch.

Some Camera Assistants insist that the core should be loaded the other way, to avoid having a lump in the roll where the film is folded back against itself. It is also claimed that this lessens the noise level of the magazine. I have never had a problem with either a "lumpy" roll or added magazine noise caused by attaching the film to the core this way. The lump disappears and the roll evens out after a few turns of film, and magazine noise is the same whichever way the core faces. I find it more reassuring that the film end is NOT going to detach from the core when the slot opposes the rotation of the roll.

One final piece of advice about loading film is that you should NOT take up the slack in a roll of film too tightly, as this can cause cinch marks. Take up the slack slightly, and let the magazine torque motor or drive maintain the tightness of the roll. If in unloading the roll, you find the roll very loose, send that magazine back to the rental house for adjustment.

The torque on Arriflex magazines can be adjusted in the field by Assistants who have been trained to do so, but do not attempt this unless you know what you are doing and have the proper tools.

Recanned Raw Stock

If the roll of film HAS been opened before, it falls into one of two categories. If the roll is still full-sized, in other words, if it has been loaded into a magazine and then unloaded again before any part of it was exposed, then it is called a "recan."

There are several possibilities for the origin of this "recan" roll. If a magazine was loaded in anticipation of shooting, and then a different film emulsion was requested by the Director of Photography, then the magazine would have been unloaded with nothing shot, and "recanned" to allow the other emulsion type to be loaded into the same magazine.

If the magazine was loaded early in the day, and the job was finished without ever getting to that particular magazine, then that roll of unused film is recanned for some other job, allowing the empty magazine to be returned to the rental house.

When the unexposed recan roll is placed back in the film can, the film can should be resealed and labeled immediately. The can should be sealed with white tape or colored tape only, signifying that the film in that can is UNEXPOSED.

When film comes from the manufacturer, it will be sealed with a tape printed with the type, emulsion, and cut number of that roll. Once that can is opened for the first time, that printed tape should be thrown away immediately. Any film can sealed with the printed tape is assumed to be a "virgin," unopened roll. Once the can is opened, if any part of that unexposed roll needs to be resealed into a can, white or colored tape should be used. Exposed film should be sealed with black tape only.

Figure 6-10 Recan Film Can Label.

This way the Camera Assistant can tell immediately from the tape around the outside of the film can, what that can contains: factory printed tape means unopened, unexposed, "virgin" film, white or colored tape means unexposed (recanned or short end) film, and black tape means exposed. Remember to color code your short ends with the same colors used for the various emulsions in your magazine labels. Pick a color code at the beginning of the job, one color for each type film you will be using. Just do it the same way every time. A system is useless if you keep changing it.

This system makes sorting short ends by emulsion type much faster and easier. Use whatever system seems right to you.

The Can Label for a Recanned Roll of Film Should Include:
1. The Word "UNEXPOSED," Large and Prominent
2. Length of the Roll
3. Emulsion Type, Batch, Cut, and Can Numbers
4. Date
5. Signature or Initials of the Camera Assistant Who Unloaded the Film

When receiving recans or short ends from another job, which often happens on commercials or on reshoots or second unit shooting for a feature film, I always check dates and the signatures on the short ends and recans. I sometimes have gotten short ends from Assistants I have worked with or trained, and once I even got my own short ends to shoot, when the commercial company I was working for had bought or borrowed some film from another company I had worked for about two weeks earlier.

If the date or signature is missing, or if the roll is older than two or three months, or if I do not know or can't read the signature of the Assistant, I show the rolls to the Director of Photography and/or production manager, and ask if they want to take a chance on the contents. This simple precaution helps protect you from the inevitable finger-pointing in the event the can is mislabeled or if there is something wrong with the film.

Film is not so expensive that you should take chances with film of dubious or unknown origin. Unless you are confident that the Camera Assistant who unloaded the film is competent, and that the film has been stored properly and is not too old, it is foolish to take the chance, no matter what the budgetary problems are. It's like Russian Roulette—if you keep pulling the trigger, eventually you will get the bullet.

Short Ends

If part of the roll has been shot, and broken off to be sent to the laboratory, and the unused part of the roll is removed from the magazine and placed in a can, then that shorter roll of unexposed film is called a "short end," because it is now "shorter" than a full roll. At what point is a short end worth saving and at what point is it better to just throw it away? Different production companies have different policies about short ends.

For the Camera Assistant, any roll shorter than about 200 feet of 35mm is just not worth saving, at least on a theatrical production. Two minutes of film is barely enough to get one take of a full dramatic scene, and frequent camera reloading wastes time and irritates actors and directors. For a commercial, short rolls are more useful, for product shots and inserts, etc.

Another reason to save short rolls is for shooting inside of cars or in tight spaces where smaller magazines must be used. There are 200-foot magazines for Arriflex cameras and 250-foot magazines for Panaflex cameras that are used for hand-held shooting or for shooting in small areas or when there is limited headroom. If the company has not ordered small rolls of film directly from the film manufacturers, then saving those short rolls for that type of shooting is necessary.

If it is necessary to spool off short rolls of film from a larger roll for use in a small hand-held camera like the Eyemo, then these rolls should be handled differently. If spooled directly off a large roll onto a 100-foot spool, the latent image edge numbers will be reversed, causing difficulties for the laboratory and negative matcher. If this "spooling off" is necessary, then the entire roll should be wound onto another reel or core, and then spooled off onto the spools in reverse, preserving the direction of the edge numbers. In many cases the laboratory will do this for you.

Another consideration for spooling off onto daylight spools is that the film should be "wobbled" back and forth while winding, so that the edges of the film are wound right up against the interior sides of the spool, preventing light from entering the spool between the roll of film and the spool side, fogging deep into the roll. This is done by film manufacturers when they make daylight loads, and the precaution should be taken when spooling your own daylight rolls.

Small rolls of unexposed film also clutter the already crowded darkroom or camera truck, use up a lot of empty film cans, make the film inventory very cumbersome, and create the false illusion that you have more film than is really usable. To the producer, looking at the inventory, having five 200-foot rolls is the same as having 1000 feet of film in one roll, but not on the set. By the time you have loaded and threaded the camera, and slated, and allowed enough leader for the laboratory at both ends of the roll, a 200-foot roll is only about 150 feet, about a minute and a half.

Some production companies have decreed that all rolls 150 feet, or even 100 feet, or longer must be saved. Somehow they feel this will save them money. In reality, it rarely works out that way, except that at the end of the job, they will have about six cases of short rolls to sell off to one of those labs that spool off movie film short ends for shooting in still cameras.

Find out at the beginning of the job from the production manager or producer, what the company policy on saving short ends is. You can fight for a 200 foot limit for saving, but be prepared to lose out to 150 or even 100. One major studio has decreed that anything fifty feet or longer must be saved. I hope that this is reflected in the time cards that go in for the Camera Assistants that have to deal with these short rolls. I know that this has resulted in many more rolls of film coming off the camera at 960 feet exposed, whether or not this is really the case!

Some companies even insist on saving the scrap film, to send out to silver recovery plants. Some individual Camera Assistants save the scrap for silver recovery. At the moment, however, silver prices are so low that it hardly seems worth the trouble. When the price of silver goes up, however, that scrap film could become very valuable indeed.

Figure 6-11 Short End Film Can Label.

The Can Label for a Short End Should Include:
1. The Word "UNEXPOSED," Large and Prominent
2. Length of the Roll
3. Emulsion Type, Batch, Cut, and Can Numbers
4. Date
5. Signature or Initials of the Camera Assistant Who Unloaded the Film
6. The Origin of the Short End:
   "Short End from Roll _____"

Every Assistant will have their own preference about shooting short ends. I try to use them up as they are made, so that they don't fill up the darkroom. If the last roll of the day is only half finished, then after canning out the exposed film for shipment to the lab, I like to thread through the five-hundred-foot short end and use that roll first the next day.

Anytime a short end roll is five hundred feet or longer, it makes sense to load it up and shoot it out, unless you know, for example, that the next scene to be shot is particularly long or difficult. If the scene involves long dialogue, or children, or if the camera is to be placed in some awkward position that might make it difficult to reload, then use a full roll. Otherwise, shoot up your short ends as they are made. It's also much easier on the paperwork.

When shooting a short end in the camera, make sure that the roll is prominently labeled with the correct footage. Many Assistants like to place a "Short End Reminder" label above or next to the footage counter, the label showing how long the roll is. Then, anytime someone looks at the footage counter, they cannot help but be reminded that the roll is not a full one, and indicating how long the original roll was. When loading the short end into the magazine, many Assistants take a short piece of tape and write the length of the roll on it, then place it on the lid of the magazine. When the short end magazine is loaded onto the camera, the reminder label can be transferred from the magazine to the proximity of the footage counter.

Magazine Labeling

Once the magazine is loaded according to the manufacturer's specifications, and closed up, it needs to be labeled as to what it contains. The magazine should also have at least one short piece of tape placed across each magazine lid latch, signifying

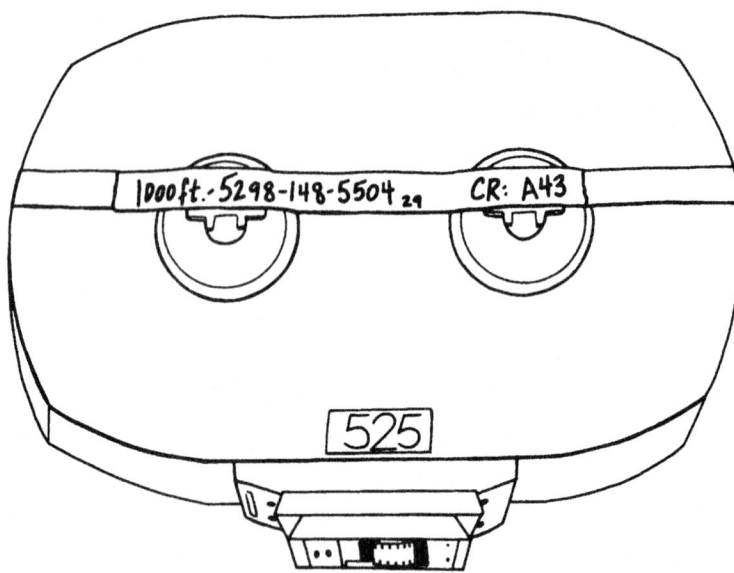

Figure 6-12 Loaded Film Magazine Label. Loaded magazine, showing the tape placed across the latches to prevent accidental opening, the magazine serial number (525) transferred to the outside of the magazine for easier reference, and the label showing the length of the roll (1000 ft.), the film type (5298), batch (148), roll (55), cut (04) and can (29) numbers, and the roll number for the production, CR (Camera Roll): A ("A" Camera), roll 43. The tape on which this information is written would be color coded for the type film being used (5298 in this case), and the same color tape would be used to tape around the seam where the lid meets the magazine, to minimize the possibility of light leaks.

that the magazine is loaded and should not be opened except in the darkroom or changing bag.

The label on the outside of the loaded magazine is very important. An unlabeled magazine or film can means real trouble for the Assistant. Can the Assistant really be sure what is inside, and can you take the chance? The easiest and best solution to this question is never let a film can or magazine go unlabeled.

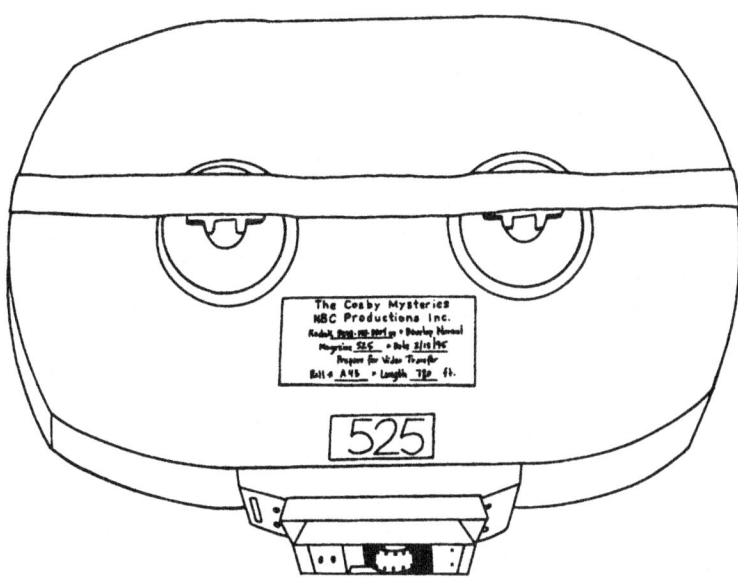

Figure 6-13 Loaded Magazine/Exposed Film Can Label. Many modern, computer-literate Camera Assistants now use adhesive labels printed on their home computer printers to label the magazine, and then transfer that label to the exposed film can for shipment to the lab.

At the very least, a Loaded Film Magazine needs a Label including the following:
1. Length of the Roll
2. Type of Film
3. Emulsion Type, Batch, Roll, Cut, and Can Numbers
4. Production Roll Number

Most Camera Assistants write a magazine label on tape, and then transfer that tape from the exposed magazine to the film can that contains that exposed roll after unloading. This label becomes the Exposed Film Can Label for shipping to the lab. This saves the Camera Assistant the time and trouble of having to write out a separate can label for the unloaded exposed roll. If you choose to go this way, the label should contain:

1. Production Company Name
2. Job Title and/or Number
3. Length of the Roll
4. Emulsion Type, Batch, Cut, and Can Numbers
5. Roll Number
6. Laboratory Processing Instructions
7. Date

Very often, especially for exterior shooting, tape is run around the outside of the magazine, along the seam where the lid meets the body of the magazine, as further insurance against accidental light leaks. This is also a good chance to further identify the contents of the magazine if multiple film stocks are being used on the job.

The First and Second Assistants can work out a color code for the tape on the outside of the magazine, blue for one stock, red for another, yellow for a third, etc. This allows the Assistants to easily identify which stock is in the magazine and inside the camera, when the magazine is placed on the camera. A simple code used by many crews is blue tape for daylight stock, white or yellow tape for slower tungsten stock, and red for high-speed tungsten stock. Simple, logical, and easy to remember—just right for a workable code on the set. Other Assistants use the same color code that Eastman Kodak recently started using for their can labels.

Magazine Case Labeling

Once the magazines are loaded with unexposed film, and the magazines properly labeled and taped up, they are placed back into their cases, and the case lids, and often the case ends, are labeled with the contents of the magazines. This can be simply a short piece of camera tape the same color as the color code for the type of film inside the magazines, with the length of the roll.

Often the Loader or Second Assistant makes up several labels, for each type of film being used on the job and one for "Empty" (often abbreviated "MT"), storing these labels on the INSIDE of the magazine case lid until needed. Then the proper label can simply be placed on the outside of the lid as the situation demands. When an exposed magazine is returned to the case, the label can be changed to read "Empty" or "MT," and then changed again when the magazine is reloaded. When the exposed magazine comes off the camera, the First Assistant will usually tear the film loop to prevent the possibility that the magazine might be mistaken for a full one.

When the magazine is placed back into the case, the broken "tails" of film can be left hanging out of the case, as a further indication that the enclosed magazine is headed for the darkroom or changing bag. The torn tails should not be wound back inside the magazine, as this allows the rolls of film to begin unravelling and loosening. Keeping the torn tails threaded through the magazine throat will help keep the rolls of film inside the magazines tight.

Film Can Labeling

Once the film is shot, it needs to be unloaded from the camera magazine and prepared for shipment to the lab. The can should be labeled so the laboratory knows what is inside the can, what they should do to it, and most importantly to the lab, who to send the bill to.

Figure 6-14 Exposed Film Can Label.

Therefore, the Exposed Film Can Label Should Include:

1. The Word "EXPOSED," Large and Prominent
2. Production Company Name
3. Job Title and/or Number
4. Length of the Roll
5. Emulsion Type, Batch, Cut, and Can Numbers
6. Roll Number
7. Laboratory Processing Instructions
8. Date

I prefer another approach to film can labeling. I have rubber stamps made, at the beginning of the job, with the production company name and the film title. I have other stamps made, with the film emulsion type and the developing instructions (99.9 percent of shooting, especially now that so many speeds of film stock are available, will be "NORMAL"). I use these stamps on plain white peel-and-stick labels available in any stationery store. I put these stamped labels onto the exposed film cans.

Lately I have started printing out exposed film can labels on my computer printer, as well as labels for short ends and recans, leaving blanks for writing in emulsion numbers, roll numbers, and footages. I know of several other computer-literate Assistants who do the same.

These stamped or computer-printed labels make the absolute best can labels, in my opinion. No one can ever say that they could not read the label or the instructions. It reduces the possibility of error at the lab. It also eliminates having to write out by hand the same information three or four hundred times for the average feature film.

Figure 6-15 Rubber Stamp Labels. Rubber stamps on peel-and-stick labels make terrific film can labels. Labels can be easily color coded by using different color stamp pads, and no one will ever complain they can't read the labels.

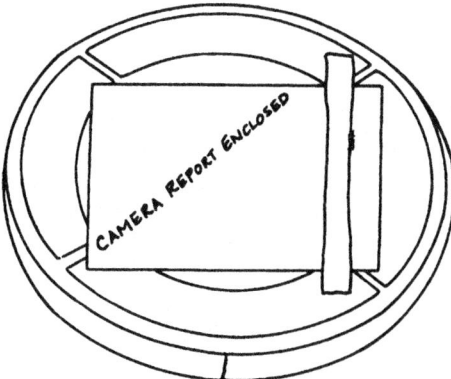

Figure 6-16 Camera Report/Purchase Order Envelopes. Camera Reports should be attached to each can by placing the report in an envelope and taping the envelope to the can. This prevents the report from being torn to shreds when removing the tape when an envelope is not used. I had two rubber stamps made up; "Camera Report Enclosed" and "Purchase Order Enclosed."

All of this information will be duplicated on the Camera Report, which will be attached to the can, either taped to the can, or inside an envelope which is taped to the can (the preferred method, so the report is not torn to shreds when the tape is pulled off). I have another rubber stamp that says "Camera Report Enclosed," and another that says "Purchase Order Enclosed," for use on these envelopes.

Every can of exposed film gets its Camera Report taped to the can, in an envelope. The stack of exposed film cans are then often taped together and the laboratory purchase order is then attached to the stack, also in an envelope. This stack of cans is then turned over to a production assistant for delivery to the lab. The carbon copies of the Camera Reports and Purchase Order are then turned over to the production office, after the Camera Assistant has removed one copy for the Camera Department files.

Multiple Film Stocks

Not so long ago, there was only one choice of film stock for color filming. Now, Eastman Kodak makes about eight 35mm color stocks, Fuji another six, and Agfa four. It is not unusual to have three, four, or even more different stocks on a job for different situations, sometimes even from different manufacturers. The more stocks there are, the more likely a mistake will be made in labeling. The Camera Assistant must be very careful with loading and unloading and particularly labeling.

The best way to keep multiple stocks sorted out is by color coding. If every magazine and short end containing Eastman 5248 is sealed and/or labeled with yellow tape, and all Eastman 5298 with red tape, and all Eastman 5297 with blue tape, etc., then even from across the room, the contents of that can or that magazine is instantly recognizable. There are many colors of camera tape (a 1"-wide cloth adhesive tape) available. Work out your color scheme before shooting begins and order as many colors of tape as you will need.

Keep in mind that a color code system only works if two basic rules are obeyed. First, the people who need to know the code must be made aware of it early. A code doesn't mean anything if it can't be decoded. If the Second Camera Assistant decides on a code to use for the particular stocks in use, then the First Assistant and the Loader and Trainee must be made aware of the code, and for those times when they are loading and/or labeling, they must use the same code.

Second, and most important, the color code must be consistent. Once you begin coding a certain stock with a certain color, stick to it! Use the same colors every time. Don't be rushed into using some other color "temporarily" because it's handier, hoping to replace it later. You've lost the continuity and you will never catch up. Do it the same way every time!

Ordering Raw Stock

Early in preproduction, speak to the Director of Photography about raw stocks. There are several questions which need to be answered immediately:

1. Which stocks are going to be needed for the production?
2. How much of each stock for the entire production should be reserved from the manufacturer, trying to get all stock of each particular type from the same batch?
3. How much of each stock will be needed immediately, during preproduction, for emulsion testing, lens tests, wardrobe tests, etc.?
4. How much of each stock will be needed the first week of shooting?
5. How much of each stock should be in 1000-foot rolls, and how much in 400-foot rolls, or other sizes, for use with Steadicam, Louma Crane, hand-held, etc.?

Once these questions have been answered, pass the information on to the production manager and/or production office coordinator. They will make the arrangements with the manufacturer or supplier, and coordinate the actual deliveries.

Try not to order more stock than you have room on the truck for, or than you will need in a week or so. Bouncing around in a truck and large shifts in temperature and humidity are not good for film, so try and keep to a minimum the amount on hand.

Get into the habit of asking the Director of Photography what stocks will be needed for the next location or for the next week of shooting. Find out when the Steadicam will be used, and when the night exterior shooting is, and order film accordingly.

Keep enough around for normal shooting, and be as prepared as possible for sudden changes of locations and for weather cover sets. Sometimes film can be stored at the production office, or at the hotel if you are at a distant location, if space is tight on the truck.

As the stock gets used in normal shooting, order more, in small (ten- to twenty-thousand-foot) lots, as required. Get in the habit of keeping accurate inventory records, and find out who, in the production office, will be handling raw stock orders, and speak to them directly. The more middlemen eliminated, the fewer mistakes will be made.

Sometimes newer stocks are so recently on the market that they are not available yet in sufficient quantity. On *Presumed Innocent*, we could only get about 25,000 feet a week of the new 5296 from Kodak and in an average week we were shooting about 28,000 feet, so we got further and further behind and were always risking running out.

Some of the black-and-white stocks are only available by Special Order from the manufacturer, and it can take six to eight weeks to get large quantities. Some stocks may also be available in 1000-ft. rolls, but not in 400-footers, or vice versa. As soon as possible in preproduction, find out what stocks you will need and if there are going to be any supply problems from the manufacturer.

Storage of Raw Stock

Common sense should prevail when storing raw stock. All photographic film is sensitive to heat, radiation, and moisture. Extremes of temperature and humidity should be avoided if possible. Camera trucks and darkrooms get hot in the sun, so keep as little stock as possible on hand. Motion picture film stretches and shrinks minutely with the temperature and humidity changes.

Humidity makes film swell up, and can cause scratching and sticking problems at the camera gate, which is set to very fine tolerances. When the film is thicker, the soft emulsion can be scraped off in the narrow gate. As this emulsion builds up in the gate area, scratches in film moving across the buildup can occur. Special care should be taken to clean away this buildup at each camera reload, using wooden or plastic implements—NEVER metal—in the gate area.

If the film is cold, it will be brittle (less flexible), and more prone to static electricity damage. If your film has been refrigerated, let it warm up slowly to near room temperature (several hours) before loading into magazines. Cold film is also razor-sharp, so be careful!

Most motion picture film will not be sitting around long enough for the Camera Assistant to have to worry about storage. In most cases there will not be anything the Camera Assistant can do about storage anyway, except for using common sense. Keep as little stock on hand as possible. Order film delivered from the manufacturer in several small lots, rather than one or two large shipments. Transfer unneeded stock out of the camera truck into the production office, or location hotel room, or other place where temperature and humidity can be better controlled than on an open truck.

Film manufacturers recommend storage for short periods at about 55 degrees F (13 degrees C) or lower, with relative humidity of 60 percent or less. These will be difficult conditions to meet, at least in any studio or location I have worked in, but a little common sense on the part of the Camera Assistant will get you through.

RECOMMENDED FILM STORAGE TEMPERATURES AND HUMIDITY

	Up to Six Months	Over Six Months
Color Negative	50° F	32° F
Color Reversal	65° F	32° F
Black and White	53° F	32° F

(Humidity always less than 60%)

SUGGESTED FILM WARMUP TIMES AFTER COLD STORAGE

Temperature Difference between Storage and Outside Temperatures (degrees Fahrenheit)	Outside Relative Humidity (Percent)	Single Rolls 16mm (hours)	Single Rolls 35mm (hours)	Case of 5 or More rolls (hours)
25°	70 %	0.5	1.5	10–12
25°	90 %	1	2.5	24
50°	70 %	1	3	16
50°	90 %	1.5	4	30
100°	70 %	2	4	24–30
100°	90 %	2.5	5	40

Refrigeration is recommended for UNOPENED, VIRGIN cans of film, but not recans or short ends. The film has been packed and sealed in controlled humidity environments at the manufacturer, but once the can has been opened in the field, and as a recan or short end resealed, there is often enough humid air trapped inside the sealed can to cause condensation and water droplets on the film when that can is refrigerated.

In general, have the film processed as soon as possible after exposure. If the film is not to be processed immediately, then store the exposed but undeveloped film in as cool and dry a place as can be found.

Shipping of Raw Stock and Exposed Film

Any raw stock that needs to be carried on or shipped by commercial air carrier should be clearly marked "**UNEXPOSED PHOTOGRAPHIC FILM—DO NOT X-RAY.**" If the exposed film needs to be shipped to the laboratory by commercial air or freight shipment, be sure to package the film securely and label the package "**UNDEVELOPED PHOTOGRAPHIC FILM—KEEP AWAY FROM HEAT OR X-RAY.**"

Large, bright, warning labels are sometimes available from the film manufacturer or from the laboratories. If you can't find any, label the cases or boxes yourself with big, red letters.

Some production companies believe the myth of hand-carried raw stock and exposed stock. When a crew is traveling by air, the Camera Assistant is often assigned the task of hand-carrying the unexposed raw stock or exposed stock as hand baggage in the cabin instead of shipping the film as accompanied baggage in the belly of the plane.

The fact is that baggage in the cargo hold is rarely in any danger of X-ray damage, but hand baggage most definitely is. Depending on which airline you're flying, and which airport you're flying from, and how recently there has been a hijacking or bombing incident, and how recently the machines have been serviced, you will never know how much X-ray energy is likely to be beamed at your precious package.

Airport security personnel and procedures do not care about the risk of your motion picture film suffering X-ray damage, and often insist on X-raying all carry-ons. If the passenger refuses to allow the package through the machine, and insists on visual inspection, the security people will be delighted to open up the cans and inspect your raw stock or undeveloped negative. This is obviously not an acceptable solution.

Assuming there is a security supervisor on duty, and that you can find him, and that you speak the same language, the odds of convincing him to allow you to hand-carry a dozen sealed film cans in a box the size of a suitcase aboard one of his airplanes are pretty small. It probably won't fit under your seat anyway. I've tried this many times, and all except once I've had to give up and check the package as baggage for the cargo hold, after long arguments, more than once through an interpreter.

The one time I was allowed to hand-carry the film, it was only because I had a changing bag with me, and a security guard and I each put one arm into the bag, and opened each of fourteen film cans in the bag to make sure that there was film inside and nothing else. By the time I had opened, examined, and resealed fourteen cans, I had missed two planes that day, but I was also on doubletime until I got home.

By far a better solution is to make your own lead-lined, X-ray-proof film shipping case, by lining a regular case with lead foil laminated in plastic, sold in either bags or rolls in many equipment supply houses. I've shipped tons of film this way without a problem in the last twenty-five years. The easiest case to do this with is the aluminum Halliburton case, as the foam lining in its bottom and lid hold the lead foil laminate in place. Just leave enough foil extending beyond the foam to overlap the other piece of foil, thus making a good seal all the way around the seam of the case. Any case can be used, as long as the laminate completely covers all sides.

I do want to pass on one horror story I heard about shipping film. A television commercial crew was traveling to some distant location by air. They landed at a small airport, and as they were walking toward the terminal building they saw the baggage train also approaching the terminal, with their camera equipment on board. There was the camera, and there was the cardboard case of unexposed film, just as it came from Kodak. The case was labeled very clearly on all sides—"**UNEXPOSED FILM—NO X-RAY!**," just as it should have been. Directly on top of the case with the film was another shipping case, about the same size, labeled equally as clearly in bright purple, "**FRAGILE—RADIOACTIVE ISOTOPES!**"

Anyway, since the crew was lucky enough to see this before shooting, they were able to order more film and shoot the job without any problems.

They did, however, run lab tests on several of the rolls that were in such close proximity to the radioactive isotopes. The film was, predictably, fogged, at least those cans closest to the isotopes. The cans at the other end of the case were fine, but they didn't know that until they got the film back from the lab. If they hadn't actually seen the two cases together, they would have shot the job on fogged film, and then have had to reshoot, at great expense to their client.

This is, however, the ONLY incident I have heard of where film had been ruined in air shipment in the belly of the plane. And if they had repacked the raw stock in a lead-foil-laminate-lined shipping case, they probably wouldn't have had any fogging, despite the proximity to the isotopes.

Dealing With Laboratories

Right from the Checkout period, the Camera Assistant should maintain close contact with the laboratory. Let the lab know that tests will be coming in, describe the tests, arrange to screen the tests at the lab's screening room, pick up your film cores and empty film cans and black bags and camera reports, etc., from the lab. Setting up a good relationship with the laboratory is important. Get to know the people there, in the Shipping Department, the Dailies Department, the Projectionist, etc.

During the regular shooting, the Second Assistant will probably spend a lot of time on the phone to the lab, passing on messages from the Director of Photography to the Dailies Timer, and back. There may be requests from the D.P. to reprint a scene with a slightly different timing, or an additional take to be printed from a scene from last week, or relaying the distressing news that there is a scratch on roll 241.

The Second Assistant will, of course, have taken great care that the Camera Report for each roll of film will be clear, explicit, and legible, but sometimes there may be questions. Hopefully, if the people at the lab are confused by any instructions or labeling, they will try and clear up the confusion before they do anything to the film. They best way for them to do this is to put in a call to the Camera Assistant or the Director of Photography. Let the lab know that this is what you would like them to do, before they call the Editing Room, or, even worse, the producer, in a panic.

Have you ever played the game "Telephone" at a party? That's the one where one person whispers a message into someone's ear, and that person passes the message on to someone else, then to someone else, etc., until the message gets back to the originator, scrambled and unintelligible. Well, this happens on the set as well.

Several years ago, one roll of our negative was being loaded into the developer tank at the lab when some sort of roller brake hardware broke off and scratched about one foot of our negative before breaking off entirely and falling free. By the time the message got to me on the set, through the Editing Room, the production coordinator, the production manager, and half a dozen production assistants, "our entire day's shooting had been ruined!" Of course, one phone call to the lab revealed that only one foot of film was scratched, and that it had happened to that piece of film between the slate and where the Director called "Action!"

What the lab should have done, and what they did from then on, was to call the production office, leave a message for me to call them, and waited until I called back to tell me what had been scratched. What they had done was just get everyone all excited for nothing.

Hand Tests ("Slop" Tests)

Decades ago, it was a common practice for Camera Assistants to develop a short length of film in a small developer tank as a test of the camera system on the job. Questions and worries about focus, framing, fogging, or other faults of the system can be answered to some degree of satisfaction by conducting a "hand" or "slop" test. Questions of exposure, color, steadiness, or registration cannot really be answered by these tests, as the image is only a black-and-white negative image and the film sample is too short to be projected at speed. This process is also used sometimes when a frame of film is needed for placement in the matte slot of the camera for accurate positioning of picture elements for an optical or blue screen shot.

Color negative film can be partially and quickly developed with ordinary black-and-white film developer and fixer, available in any camera store in the world. The tank is a standard still photographers 35mm developer tank, loaded in the darkroom or changing bag with about five feet of exposed film. I have not heard about anyone using this test in many years, and I personally have never done it, but it can be done if you really need to do it. A good description of the process can be found in David Samuelson's *Motion Picture Camera Techniques*.

Tank and chemicals can be purchased when needed, and the test done fairly quickly, following the directions for developing standard black-and-white negative film. The only extra step needed for developing color negative motion picture film is to rub the antihalation backing off of the film before viewing.

The process is crude and lacks all of the quality controls found in a real laboratory, but in an emergency, on a distant location, it is better than not knowing if your camera and lenses are working properly.

CHAPTER **7**

Lenses

Lenses in General

Photographic lenses come in many shapes, sizes, and designs, and are manufactured to fulfill many functions. The Camera Assistant need not be an optical engineer, but should know something about the way lenses work, and the limitations present in some of the wide range of lenses available to the cinematographer.

APPROXIMATE LENS ANGLE COMPARISON (ROUNDED OFF TO USABLE NUMBERS):

Horizon-tal Angle	16mm Cine Frame	Super 16mm Frame	35mm Cine 1.85:1	35mm Still Frame*	35mm Anamor-phic	65mm frame
75°	6mm	8mm	14mm	25mm	28mm	32mm
65°	8mm	9mm	16mm	30mm	33mm	38mm
55°	10mm	11mm	20mm	36mm	41mm	47mm
45°	12mm	14mm	25mm	46mm	51mm	59mm
35°	15mm	19mm	33mm	60mm	68mm	77mm
30°	18mm	22mm	39mm	70mm	79mm	91mm
25°	22mm	27mm	47mm	85mm	96mm	110mm
20°	27mm	33mm	59mm	107mm	121mm	138mm
15°	37mm	45mm	80mm	143mm	162mm	184mm
10°	55mm	67mm	120mm	216mm	243mm	278mm
5°	111mm	135mm	240mm	432mm	488mm	556mm

* also VistaVision

For purposes of our discussions, I have divided commonly used lenses into three categories; Prime Lenses (including Anamorphic Lenses), Zoom Lenses, and

Special Lenses (including Macros, Tele-Extenders, Wide-Angle Adapters, and Plus Diopters).

Prime Lenses

Prime, or single focal length, lenses are the most common type of lens used on motion picture cameras. Many different styles are available, from a great number of manufacturers. Most of the professional motion picture camera manufacturers have their own sets of lenses under their label, older lenses have been remounted with more modern lens mounts, and many still photography lenses have been converted for motion picture use.

While the conversion of still photography lenses for motion picture use may seem like a good idea, there are drawbacks to the idea. First of all, still lenses designed for the 35mm still format cover a much larger area of film negative than the 35mm motion picture frame, and the lens, while performing acceptably over the larger still frame, may not be so wonderful over the smaller motion picture frame. Secondly, it may be difficult or even impossible to adapt the still camera lens mount to the motion picture camera lens mount, because of the larger diameter of the rear elements and the differences in the flange focal depth requirements (see Chapter 10) between the two formats.

While designers strive to make lenses faster and faster to meet the demands of the cinematographers, they still have not changed the basic rule about all lenses—that lenses are never at their sharpest at their widest aperture, but are much sharper stopped down one or two stops. A T/1.4 lens might deliver acceptable sharpness at T/1.4, but will be much sharper at T/2 and better yet at T/2.8. This phenomenon is particularly evident with zoom lenses.

Other T/1.4 lenses may be "optimized" or at their best performance at T/1.4, and then get worse as the lens is stopped down. Some D.P.'s use one set of lenses for work at T/1.4 for night exteriors or other scenes that need wide apertures, and another set for shooting at smaller apertures.

Lens sharpness, while an important consideration in choosing a set of lenses, is not the only thing to look for. When considering lens sharpness, for example, look at the corners of the frame as well as the middle. A lens with more contrast appears sharper than a lens with less contrast, even if their resolving powers are very similar.

Some lenses are more prone to flare problems than others, mostly due to the type of lens coatings employed in their manufacture. Image distortion, especially in wide-angle lenses, should be considered, as well. If parallel lines photographed through a particular lens appear to be bowed out when projected, this distortion is described as "Barrel" distortion. If the reverse distortion is present, parallel lines curved inward, this is called "Pincushion" distortion.

Anamorphic Lenses

Anamorphic lenses, used in anamorphic photography processes such as Panavision and Cinemascope (35mm) and Ultra-Panavision (65/70mm), are normal lenses (prime and zoom) with an additional element added to either the front or the

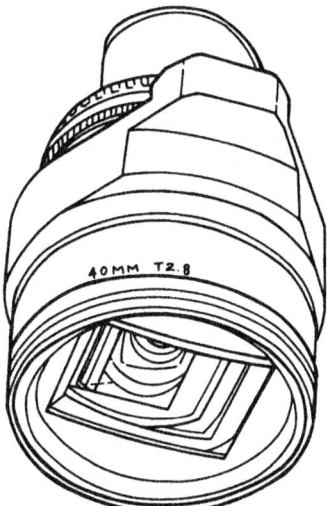

Figure 7-1 Anamorphic Photography. Anamorphic lens, showing the anamorphic (cylindrical) element in front. Other lenses may have the anamorphic element in the rear of the lens. This element compresses the image horizontally, but not vertically, allowing a widescreen image to be photographed on a standard negative.

rear. This additional element is a cylindrical, or prismatic, element that serves to compress the photographic image horizontally, but not affect the vertical reproduction of the image.

This allows a much wider image to be captured on a standard motion picture frame. The usual compression ratio for 35mm anamorphic photography is 2:1, although other ratios have been used in the past, and at least one new system is under development. The 2:1 compression ratio allows an image to be photographed "squeezed" and then the "squeezed" print made from that negative may be projected through a similar anamorphic lens, yielding an unsqueezed projected image with an aspect ratio of between 2.2:1 and 2.35:1, that is, an image that is over twice as wide as it is high. The "normal" U.S. theatrical screen aspect ratio for nonanamorphic photography is 1.85:1. The image may also be "unsqueezed" during the printing to 70mm film, and then projected through normal projection lenses for a wide-screen image.

Standard cameras are used for anamorphic cinematography, but it is much easier to use a camera that has an anamorphic-correcting viewfinder, so the Camera Operator does not need to watch a squeezed image while shooting. When eye-focusing, however, it is better to use the squeezed image without the anamorphic correction element in place. If the Operator is trying to check focus while shooting, it is not uncommon to switch off the anamorphic correction in the eyepiece.

Lens Mounts

The choice of which lenses to use on a particular motion picture project is such a subjective decision on the part of the Director of Photography that a discussion of the relative merits of one brand over another would be pointless. There are D.P.'s who

164 THE CAMERA ASSISTANT

swear by the Panavision Primo Lenses, others favor Zeiss, or Cooke, or Baltar, or Angenieux, or Nikkor, or others.

Preference for a particular brand or set of lenses has affected the choice of camera system to be used, as not all lenses are available or adaptable for use on all camera systems. There are several lens mounts available, and not all of them are interchangeable or adaptable for use on other cameras.

The Panavision lens mount is actually the same as the older Mitchell mount (with a diameter of 68.25mm), but the flange focal length is longer than on the Mitchell cameras. Mitchell cameras with the original Mitchell mount can be "shimmed" (thin sheets of metal added under the lens mount) out to the Panavision standard, allowing Panavision lenses to be used on Mitchell cameras with minimal modification.

Panavision lenses can be used on Panavision cameras, obviously, as well as modified Mitchell (S35R & MkII), Eclair (CM3), Arriflex, and other cameras that have been specially adapted ("Panavised" by Panavision) for that purpose. Panavision is Arriflex's single largest customer worldwide—hundreds of Arri III (rechristened the "PanArri"), and Arri IIC cameras have been adapted to take Panavision lenses, matte boxes, and accessories, and are used on most Panavision productions as backup, hand-held, or high-speed cameras. Panavision has ordered 50 of the new Arriflex "435" cameras, and these will become the new "PanArris."

Panavision has one lens mount for all 35mm use, a four-flange bayonet mount with a single locating pin on the bottom of the lens. This requires that the lens may only be mounted one way on the camera body. This is because certain lenses, especially wide-angle lenses, extend so far into the camera body that they have been cut or bevelled on one side so that the rotating mirror shutter does not strike the rear of the lens as it rotates. No other lens manufacturer or camera manufacturer uses the Panavision lens mount, although non-Panavision lenses, particularly telephoto and zoom lenses, have been adapted for use on Panavision cameras.

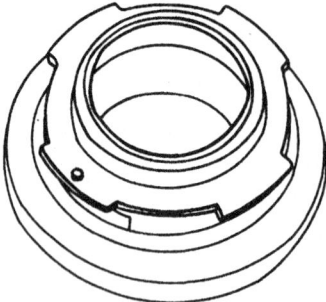 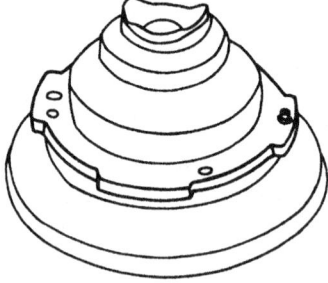

Figure 7-2 Panavision Lens Mount. The Panavision lens mount is a four-flange mount with a single locating pin on the bottom flange of the lens. The camera has a hole for this pin to slip into, and then the locking ring is turned clockwise to lock the lens onto the camera.

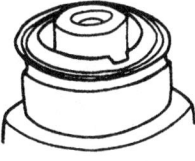 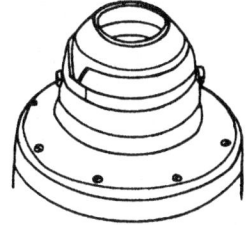 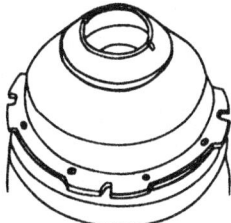

Figure 7-3 Arriflex Lens Mount. Arriflex has had three mounts in their history; the Standard mount is pretty much gone except for some elderly, privately owned cameras and lenses; the Bayonet is being phased out in favor of the PL mount in 16mm as well as 35mm cameras. With adapters, Standard and Bayonet lenses can be used in cameras with PL mounts, but not the other way. The PL mount is the current mount; a four-flange mount that can be oriented in any of the four positions, which comes in handy at times.

Arriflex has three different lens mounts for their 16mm and 35mm cameras. The Arri Standard mount is still found on many older lenses, both for 16mm and 35mm cameras, and can still be used, without an adapter, in the next newer Arri mount, the Arri "B" or "Bayonet" mount. The Arri (41mm diameter) Bayonet lenses, however, cannot be used in a camera with the Arri Standard lens port. The Arri Bayonet is also the mount currently in use for the Arriflex 16mm cameras, and in certain older 35mm cameras. The newest mount used by Arriflex for 35mm cameras is the "PL" ("Positive Lock" 54mm diameter) mount. Adapters are readily available to use either the Arri Standard or Arri Bayonet mount lenses on "PL" cameras. "PL" lenses cannot be used in Arri Standard or Arri Bayonet cameras. Beginning with the recently released Arri 16SR3 cameras, the "PL" mount will be used for 16mm cameras.

Other camera and lens manufacturers have adapted the Arri Bayonet and "PL" lens mounts for their cameras and lenses. In summary, Arri mounts are upwardly adaptable, but not downwardly. Older lenses can be used in newer cameras, but newer lenses usually cannot be used in older cameras.

Several lens manufacturers have solved the lens mount problem by manufacturing their lenses with an "unfinished" or "neutral" mount, allowing the camera and lens dealers to adapt the lens to whatever mount the customer desires.

It is very important for the Camera Assistant, during the checkout, to make sure that the lenses fit onto the camera, and that the focus scales are correct and accurate. So many lenses have been adapted from their original mounts to some other mount, and by so many individuals and dealers, that great care must be taken. Sloppy work is not uncommon, and an inaccurate focus scale can kill a job.

An incorrect focus scale, meaning a significant and consistent difference between "Eye" and "Tape" focus, is the first clue that the flange depth is not correct for that camera/lens combination. The problem might be in either the camera or in the lens mount, or both.

Zoom Lenses

A zoom lens is a lens whose effective focal length can be continuously varied, allowing a single lens to duplicate the image sizing capabilities of a whole set of lenses and more, since it can be set at focal lengths between existing prime lenses.

The focal length can be changed while filming, without changing the camera-to-subject distance. This allows the field of view to be expanded (zoomed out) or narrowed (zoomed in) without moving the camera. Theoretically, this changing the field of view is accomplished without affecting the focus or aperture settings on the lens.

Zoom lenses are compromise lenses. They trade off having many different focal lengths available for increased weight and size, decreased speed, decreased resolution, and sometimes increased minimum focusing distance. But some D.P.'s like them, and use them all the time. Modern zoom lenses are much better than older models for resolution and general image quality.

Many zoom lenses are used as variable prime lenses, affording the Director of Photography with an infinite range of focal length choices between the wide and telephoto limits of the lens, for a variety of compositions. Used this way, the lens is left at a specific focal length, and not zoomed during the shot. This method has the advantage of absolute intercutability between the shots. All shooting is done with the same lens, so color and contrast are perfectly matched between shots. The disadvantages are that zoom lenses are slower (require more light) and heavier than prime lenses.

Special Lenses

Special photographic problems and situations often require special lenses. Here are some likely to be encountered on a typical film shoot.

Macro Lenses

There are several methods available to the cinematographer to photograph objects very close to the lens. One method is to use a bellows or extension tubes between the camera body and the lens. A second is to use plus-diopter supplementary lenses on a normal lens. A third is to reverse a normal lens, mounting it so that the rear element is facing the subject. The fourth, and often the most practical, is to use a macro lens.

Macro lenses allow the cinematographer to focus on objects often as close as the front element of the lens, making photographic images that are as large (magnification 1:1) or larger than the objects themselves. In so doing, however, the user must compensate for light lost. It is comparable to adding a bellows or extension tubes between the camera body and the lens, which also requires exposure compensation, but which is much simpler and faster to use, not having to deal with the separate extension tubes.

Most of these macro lenses available for motion picture cameras have the magnification and exposure compensation required inscribed right on the barrel of the lens alongside the focus scale. Once the object is in focus, look at the compensation scale and open up the indicated number of stops from the exposure meter reading.

If your macro lens does not include such a scale, here is an approximation you can use:

MACRO LENS EXPOSURE COMPENSATION

Object-to-Image Magnification	Exposure Increase Required
1:10	1/4 stop
1:8	1/3 stop
1:6	1/2 stop
1:4	2/3 stop
1:3	1 stop
1:2	1 1/3 stops
1:1.5	1 1/2 stops
1:1.33	1 2/3 stops
1:1	2 stops
2:1	3 1/3 stops
4:1	4 2/3 stops
8:1	6 1/3 stops

For more exact exposure calculation, divide the aperture reading obtained by an incident light meter by 1 plus the magnification ratio factor. In other words, if your meter reads f/8 and you want a 1:4 image magnification, then divide 8 by 1 plus 1/4 or 1.25. This yields an aperture of T/6.4 for your shot.

Tele-Extenders

Tele-Extenders are devices that increase the focal length of the lens they are used on, at the expense of lens quality and exposure. Some of these extenders mount on the camera in the normal way, and then the lens is in turn mounted into the extender. Others are made to mount on the lens itself between the lens and the lens mount, which on some lenses may be removed easily to add the extender.

The most common extenders, usually referred to as "2X extenders," or "Two-Times extenders" double the effective focal length of the lens they are used with, at the cost of two stops light loss. For example, a 300mm T/2.8 lens with a 2X Extender becomes a 600mm T/5.6 lens. A 25–250mm T/4 zoom lens with a 2X Extender becomes a 50–500mm T/8 zoom lens.

The focus, aperture, and zoom functions perform normally, just keep in mind that the true focal length is double what is indicated on the scale, and that the aperture scale is effectively two stops LESS than what is indicated.

There are other extenders with other magnification values, such as a 1.4X Extender, that converts a 25–250mm zoom to 35–350mm, at a cost of one stop of light loss. There are also 3X extenders. Extenders may be combined for even greater magnification, but at an increased light loss and image deterioration.

Unfortunately, most of these extenders degrade the image quality considerably, especially with zoom lenses, and a 300mm lens with a 2X extender will not yield as good an image as a true 600mm lens. Also, a true 600mm lens will almost certainly have a wider maximum aperture than a 300mm lens with a 2X Extender. Aberrations present in all lenses that may not have been objectionable with the lens alone, are magnified four times when using a 2X Extender on the lens.

Despite this image quality degradation and maximum aperture loss, an extender provides a relatively inexpensive way to increase the range of focal lengths available to you on a job, in a very small package.

Wide-Angle Adapters

Wide-angle adapters are found more often for video lenses and cameras than for film cameras, but in theory, they work the same way. These wide-angle adapters are supplemental lenses attached to the front of the main lens, usually on zoom lenses, attached the same way as a filter in a sunshade might be. They reduce the focal length range of the main lens. For example, a 12–120mm zoom lens might become a 9–90mm zoom by adding one of these adapters.

These adapters are used primarily on cameras with a single fixed zoom lens, such as with video cameras and certain film cameras, such as the Canon Scoopic, to extend the possible focal length range.

While there is no light loss or exposure compensation required with these adapters, there is a trade-off. In order to get a few millimeters wider, you lose at the long end. A 10:1 zoom lens is still a 10:1, but the focal length limits have been diminished at both ends, becoming, for example, a 9–90mm zoom instead of a 12–120mm zoom. The price for those three extra millimeters at the wide end is thirty millimeters lost at the long end, but sometimes it is worth the trade-off.

Proxars (Plus Diopters/Split Diopters)

Proxars and split diopters are covered in more detail in the chapter on Focus. Basically, these are lenses and not filters, as they change the focus of the lens and not the color or imaging capabilities of the lens. These accessory lenses allow you to focus closer than the design limits of the lens itself. This permits you to photograph objects extremely close to the lens.

What you lose when using them is the ability to focus at infinity. The plus diopter lenses shift the whole focus range closer to the camera, sacrificing the long-distance focusing in order to allow close-in focus. With these supplemental lenses on your main lens, you must also disregard the focus scale on the main lens.

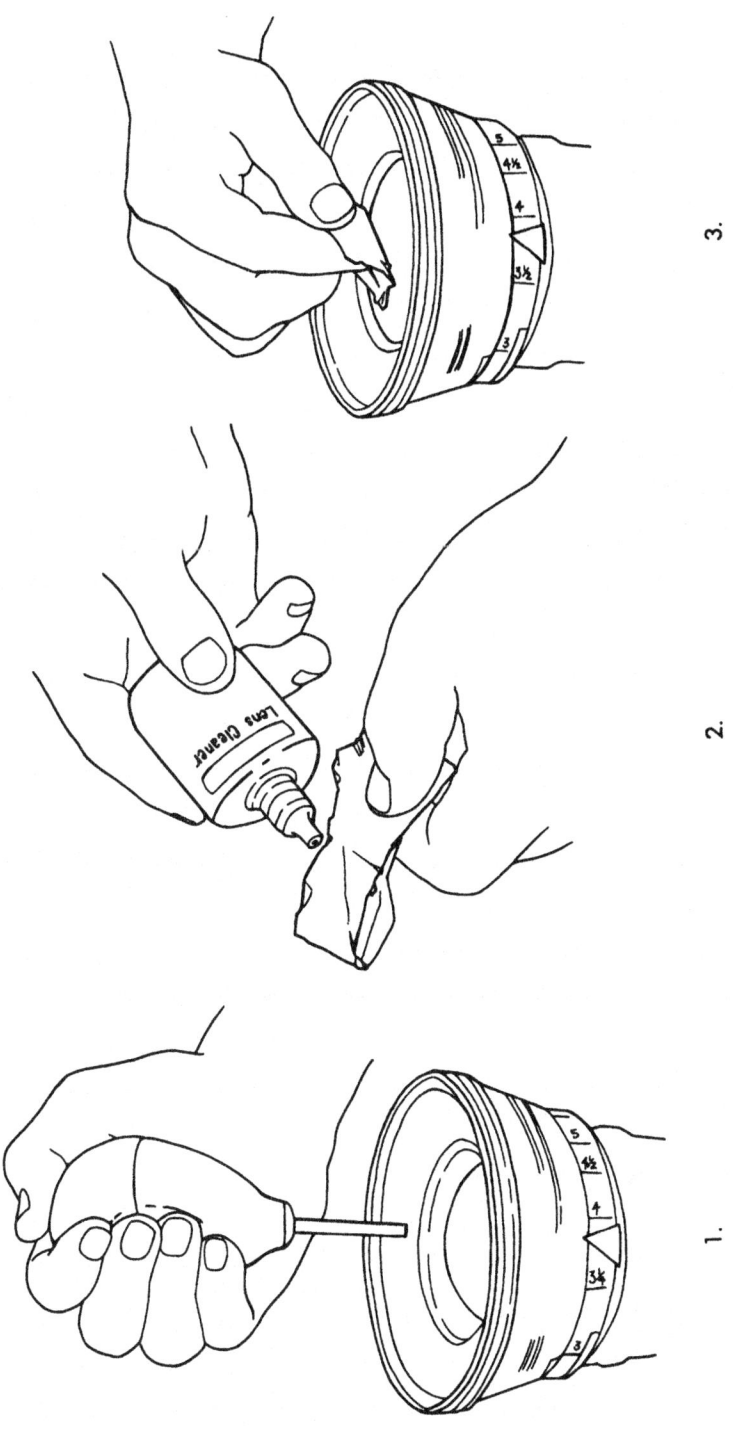

Figure 7-4 Lens Tissue/Cleaning Lenses. Three-step procedure for cleaning lenses: (1) blow away any loose dirt or dust; (2) moisten lens tissue with lens fluid (never drip lens fluid directly onto the lens itself!); and (3) wipe lens in circular motion, starting from the center and working outward. Turn or refold tissue often, exposing clean surfaces.

Cleaning Lenses

Great care must be taken in cleaning lenses, especially with the new generations of lens coatings found on modern lenses. The best advice, however, is if the lens does not really need cleaning, don't clean it.

If you have decided that the lens really needs cleaning, the first step is to blow off any solid dust with either compressed air, nitrogen, or a rubber bulb syringe. If all of the dust does not blow off, then gently brush with a soft camel-hair or sable brush reserved for use in cleaning lenses only.

If the lens surface is still not clean, and smears or fingerprints need to be removed, lens tissue must be used. The lens tissue used should be good-quality lens tissue from a recognizable name brand or rental house, but NOT the silicone-impregnated tissue or cloth sold in eyeglass stores and intended for cleaning eyeglasses. This silicone tissue can damage and remove the delicate lens coatings. Use only tissue manufactured specifically for coated photographic lenses.

Carefully fold or roll up the tissue, moisten the tissue lightly with a good-quality lens cleaning fluid, and carefully wipe the lens in a circular motion from the center outward, periodically turning or folding the tissue to expose and use a new surface. If this does not remove the smear, repeat the process with a new piece of moistened tissue. It is also recommended that lens tissue never be used dry on a lens (without lens cleaning fluid).

Use as little lens fluid as possible, and only applied directly to the tissue, not to the lens, and always start at the center of the lens and work outward in a circular motion, to minimize the chance that excess fluid will work its way into the lens housing at the edge of the glass element, and possibly loosen the elements inside.

If the smear or fingerprint still persists, try again using grain (not isopropyl or rubbing) alcohol or Xylene, which is particularly good at removing grease and oil. If the Xylene leaves a cloudy residue after removing the grease smear, use another clean tissue moistened with lens fluid or grain alcohol to remove the residue. Dave Quaid recommends grain alcohol, cut 50 percent with water.

Some Assistants use a soft, finely woven polyester cloth, sold under the brand name Luminex, to clean lenses and filters. Care should be taken to keep this cloth clean between uses, and it should be replaced when it starts to show signs of dirt or wear. Some Assistants keep it folded and enclosed in the envelope it came in, between uses, to keep it clean. I have never tried to wash one of these, but it should be possible with Woolite or other gentle cleanser.

Matte Boxes/Sunshades

Sunshades and matte boxes are attached to the front of lenses, either directly to the lens or supported on rods attached to the camera body. Sunshades can be either rubber or metal, and generally screw on or clip on to the front barrel of a lens, and their conical or rectangular shape extends out in front of the lens, blocking unwanted light from striking the lens. Sunshades often contain rings designed to hold one or more round filters in addition to the shade itself.

Lenses **171**

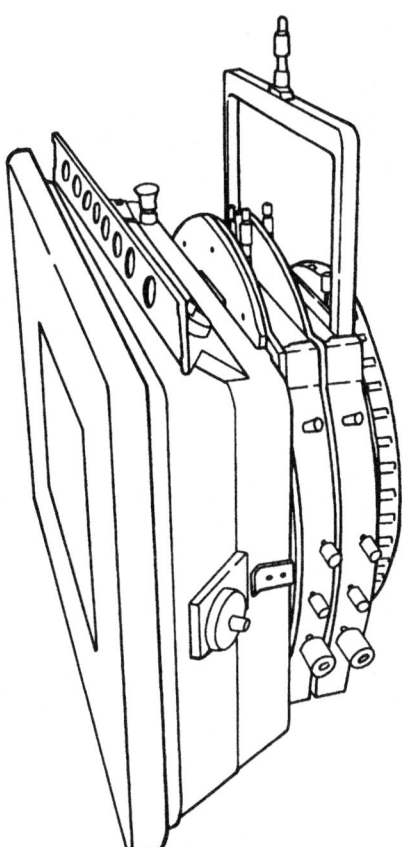

Figure 7-5 Matte Boxes/Filter Holders—Arriflex Matte Box. This model shown with matte box mask in place, bracket for French Flag on top, and filter holders for four 5" x 6" filters, two in each of two independently rotatable units. This particular box is hinged for swinging away from the lens, has an internal lens donut in the rear with a ring for mounting a fifth, 138mm round, filter. This unit also has one geared filter tray in each double filter unit, each allowing a graduated filter to be positioned higher or lower in the frame, if necessary, and allowing these filters to be moved up or down during the shot by turning the knobs, if desired.

Matte boxes generally attach to the support rods on a camera, and the better ones are built with a hinge to swing out of the way when checking the gate or changing lenses. Matte boxes are generally rectangular in shape, and masks of various sizes for various focal lengths can be used to further block unwanted light from hitting the front of a lens.

Matte boxes usually contain stages or trays for rectangular or round filters, and may also contain a rotating tray for use with polarizers or graduated filters.

Care should be taken to ensure that the matte box, especially when used with a zoom lens, does not vignette or cut into the corners of the frame, and that the matte box masks are usable for their designated focal length lenses without cropping the frame. Check for this vignetting with the lens stopped down and focused close.

Lens Flare

Lens flare is caused by unwanted light bouncing around between the glass elements of a lens, and eventually striking the film and being photographed as part of the image.

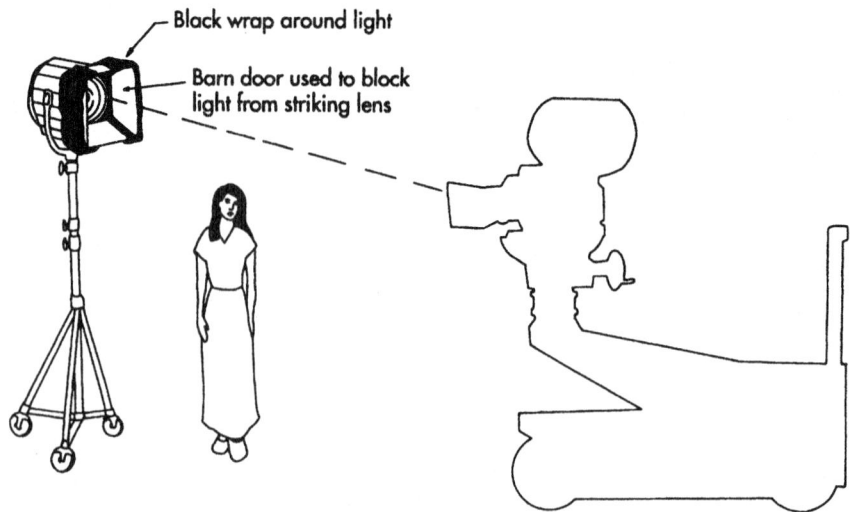

Figure 7-6 Lens Flares—Barn Doors and Black Wrap. The Electricians can often help eliminate lens flares by adjusting the barn doors on the lighting units, or by adding "black wrap" foil around the lights themselves.

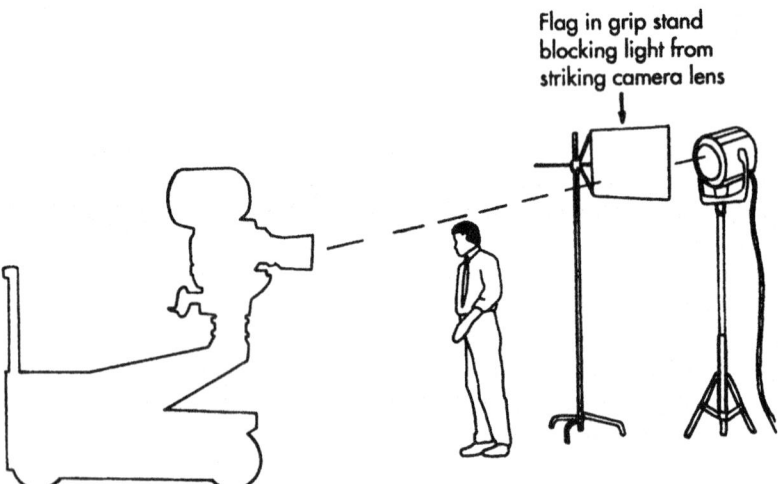

Figure 7-7 Lens Flares—Grip Stands and Flags. The Grips can help eliminate many lens flares by setting flags or cutters in grip stands, preventing set lights from shining into the camera lens. Work with the Grips and the Camera Operator to make sure that the flags eliminate the flare without intruding into the frame.

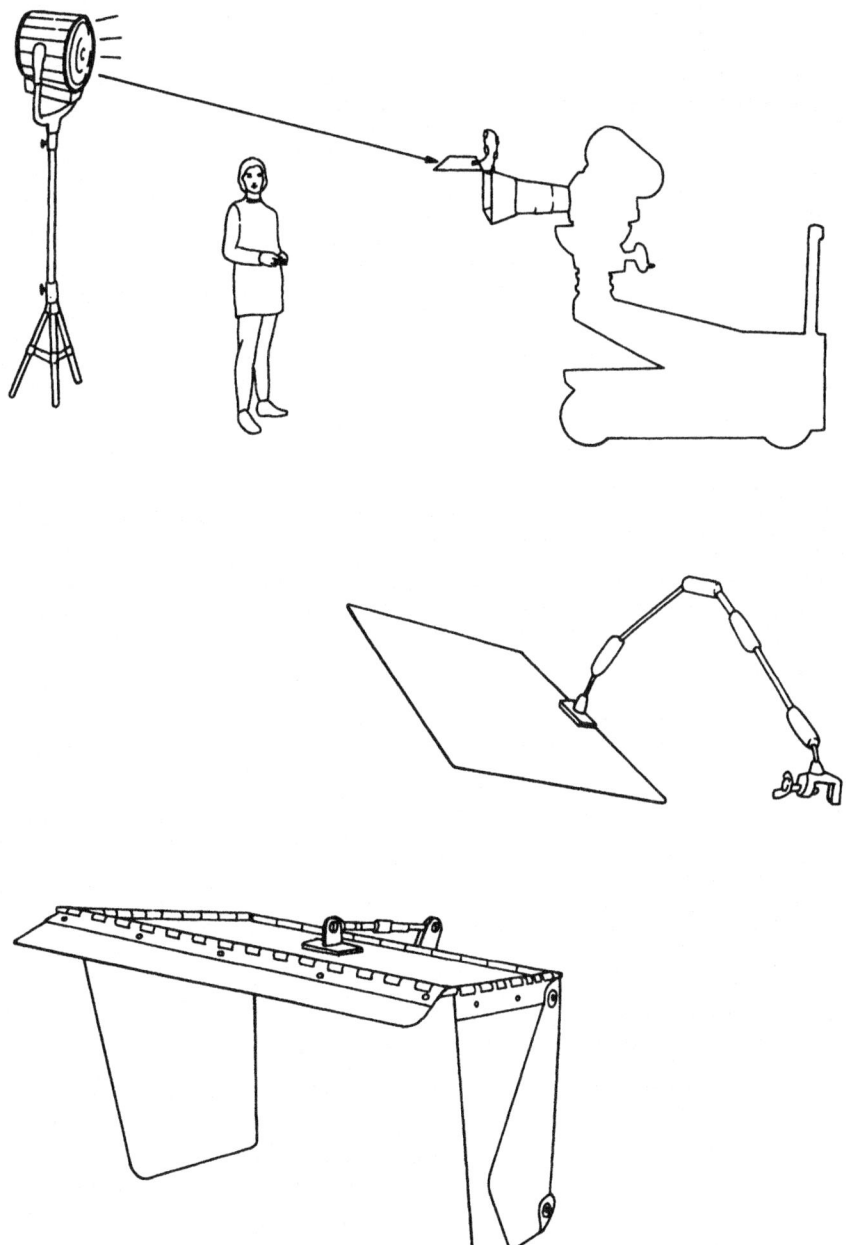

Figure 7-8 Lens Flares—French Flags and Matte Box Extensions. Lens Flares can often be eliminated by the Camera Assistant at the camera, through the use of Matte Box Extensions and/or French Flags to prevent set lights or the sun from shining directly into the lens.

Lens flares are eliminated in several ways—lens coatings, matte boxes or sunshades (including French Flags), and flagging the lights in the set or location.

Lens coatings are chemicals applied to the front elements of lenses by the manufacturer. These coatings minimize the flaring caused by off-axis light sources. Care should be taken when cleaning the lenses, as too vigorous a cleaning can remove the delicate coating.

Flagging the lights can be done in three ways, and the responsibility for such flagging thus rests with three departments. First of all, sometimes the barndoors on the lights themselves can be used to shield the camera lens from unwanted light. The Electrical Department is responsible for arranging the barndoor on the lights, or for wrapping the sides or backs of the lighting units in black foil, called Black Wrap (on some crews, the grips will wrap the lights with foil). Anything attached to the lights themselves usually belongs to the electricians.

The Grips are responsible for flagging off the lighting units from floor stands ("Grip" or "Century" Stands) with flags or cutters when the lights are seen to be causing flares in the lens. The Camera Assistant should request a flag be set by the grips whenever a light is shining into the camera lens. Anything between the lights and the camera belongs to the Grip Department. Care should be taken not to place these lens flags in such a location that they throw their own shadows from other lights into the set, or that they block some other light from lighting what it is supposed to light. When in doubt, check with the Director of Photography.

The third method of blocking unwanted light from striking the front of the lens is on the camera itself. If the light cannot be blocked with the lens sun shade or matte box with appropriate mask, sometimes the only way to block the light is with a small flag mounted on the camera itself. This device is known as a "French Flag," and is composed of a metal rectangular shade attached to a flexible (usually ball-jointed) arm with a clamp for attaching to the camera, matte box, gear head, lens support rod, or other such convenient place. When such a device is used, mounted directly on the camera or support gear, the Camera Assistant is responsible for its use. If zooming during the shot, be sure to set the French Flag so it is clear of the frame at the widest position of the zoom.

Transporting Lenses

Lenses are fragile items, and great care should be taken in packing and shipping lenses. A sturdy, foam-padded lens case, especially for heavy zoom and telephoto lenses, is an absolute necessity. Lenses should always have lens caps front and rear.

To protect the delicate iris leaves while transporting a lens, always open the iris to the maximum aperture before putting the lens away in its case. In this position, the iris leaves are supported and protected in their "cage," and the least risk is run of damage to the iris leaves during transporting in trucks and airplanes.

Further protection is afforded the lens if the focus is racked to infinity before storage and transport. This reduces the overall length of some lenses, and protects the focusing elements by ensuring that the focus group is screwed all the way into the lens barrel, affording maximum support and protection by the threaded barrel.

There is some controversy about zoom lens transport. All the sourc[es] seem to agree that the iris should be wide open and the focus racked to [?] with zoom lenses, some sources maintain that the zoom should be set [at?] mum wide-angle position, and some say to the maximum telephoto position. Since there is some disagreement among the experts about this, let's compromise and decide that the zoom should be set either at one end of its range or the other, but not in the middle. An easy way to work and remember is to turn all three zoom lens rings (focus, focal length, and aperture) to the limit in the same direction.

If the zoom group of a lens is left in the middle of the range, a bang or bump during transport could conceivably cause a bump or rough spot in the zoom track, resulting in a visible jump or pause while zooming. So zoom all the way in one direction or another. A bump at the very end of the zoom is much less likely to affect the lens' performance.

Condensation on Cold Lenses

When cameras, lenses, and filters are moved from a cold truck or exterior location into a warm, moist, interior location, condensation will probably form on the cold metal and glass surfaces. This also may occur when moving from an air-conditioned office or rental house to the hot, humid outdoors.

This condensation will disappear as the equipment warms up to the surrounding temperature, but you can speed up this warming by opening and leaving open the cases containing the equipment, by removing the lens caps from the lenses, or by removing the equipment from the cases, or by asking the Electrical Department to set up a small lighting unit and directing the light beam into the case or directly at the equipment. I sometimes use a small electric hair dryer to blow warm air over cold lenses until they clear up and dry out.

Be careful not to get the equipment too warm too quickly. If the beam of light is too hot to shine on your hand, it is too hot to shine into the equipment case. After all, you don't want to melt the lenses, you just want to clear up the condensation. Back up the light, or flood out the beam to reduce the intensity, until you can comfortably hold your hand above the equipment in the case.

Start the equipment warming process as soon as possible after entering the warmer environment, or the company will have to wait while the lenses warm up to eliminate the condensation. Running the camera without film will help the camera body warm up, as will powering the camera's internal and eyepiece heaters.

If the lens or filter is still showing condensation when you want to insert it into the camera, holding the lens in front of or above any nearby heat source, such as a lighting unit, for a few minutes, should solve the problem. Lens tissue might remove some of the condensation, but if the lens or filter is still cold, it will fog up again immediately.

Never breathe on a cold lens or filter. You will only make the condensation worse, or cause condensation where there was none before. In general, do not breathe on lenses or filters anyway. Saliva is quite acidic, so human breath can damage the lens coating, and is difficult to remove from the lens or filter surface.

Sometimes the mirror shutter fogs up when the camera is cold, or the ground-glass, or the internal viewfinder optics. After a few minutes in the warm environment, this fog will disappear.

Changing Lenses

When actually changing lenses, first make sure that the tilt lock on the gear or fluid head is securely locked, as removing the lens will change the balance of the camera, and if the lock is off, removing the lens will cause the camera to tilt back suddenly. Once the lock is on, swing away the matte box, loosen and swing away any zoom motor gear or follow focus mechanism, and remove the lens. By this time the Second should have arrived with the new lens, plus whatever rods, support gear, rubber donut, and matte box mask also need to be changed.

Get in the habit of saying out loud, "I have it," when someone hands a piece of equipment to you, to signify that you indeed have a firm grasp of the piece. I usually extend my hand out flat, and allow the other person to place the item into my hand from above. I then lift up on the item, against the other person's hand, while saying "I have it," as a double confirmation that I am not about to drop the item. Hand the Second the old lens in the same way, not letting go until you have heard, "I have it," from the Second.

Once the new lens is in your hands, always look at the rear element and the iris before putting the lens into the camera port, then make the lens secure with the locking ring. Once the lens is on the camera, look at the front element, reattach the required zoom motor and/or focus gear and control, swing back the matte box and attach the proper matte box mask.

Set the proper aperture and focus on the new lens, and the focal length if the new lens is a zoom. If filters need to be changed, do this as well, plus anything else that needs to be done, such as changing to a new battery. Once the changeover is complete, announce to the D.P. and the A.D. that the "Camera is Ready!" and proceed to make movies.

CHAPTER 8

Filters

Sizes and Shapes of Filters

Filters come in several shapes, and in several sizes in each shape. Round filters may be attached to the matte box, to the lens itself using filter rings and sunshades for use without using a matte box, and smaller sizes may be used at the rear of lenses, or even inside certain lenses in special filter holders. Common sizes for round filters for the front of the lenses are Series 8, Series 8 1/2, Series 9, 4 1/2", 138mm, and 6" round. At the rear, or inside the lenses, sizes like Series 5, Series 6, 40.5mm, 47mm, 49mm, 52mm are used.

Square and rectangular filters are made to be used in a matte box, which attaches in most cases to the same rods that support the lenses. Typical square sizes include 2" x 2," 3" x 3," 4" x 4," and the currently popular 6.6" x 6.6." Rectangular sizes include 3" x 4," 4" x 5.650" (also often referred to as "Panavision" size), and 5" x 6."

Unfortunately, instead of reducing the number of different filter sizes, lens, and camera manufacturers are increasing the number of filter sizes. Certain new lenses have their own unique filter sizes, incompatible with existing sizes.

With such a variety of filter shapes and sizes, it is very difficult for the rental houses to supply every possible filter type in every possible filter size. More and more Directors of Photography are buying their own favorite filter types in the sizes most likely to be usable with the camera and lens systems they plan to use.

How Filters Work

There are several types or classes of filters that the Camera Assistant must be familiar with. These are:

1. Color Correction Filters
2. Color Compensation Filters

3. Neutral Density Filters
4. Graduated Filters
5. Attenuator Filters
6. Diffusion Filters
7. Polarizing Filters
8. Special Effects Filters

When using filters, it is important to keep in mind that filters never ADD anything to the image that is not already there. Filters only SUBTRACT something that you do not want.

A Color Correction Filter or Color Compensation Filter subtracts light of an undesirable band of wavelengths. A colored filter permits (Transmits) light of the same color to pass through the filter uninterrupted, while preventing (Absorbing) light of other colors. A Polarizer subtracts light not "oriented" in the proper direction.

Because of this subtraction of some of the light entering the lens, the exposure must be compensated accordingly—the aperture of the lens must be opened to allow more light to enter, to make up for the light lost (absorbed) by the filter.

A Diffuser "subtracts" the inherent sharpness and contrast in a lens system, softening the image to a degree considered more pleasing to the eye. Graduated filters subtract light from some parts of the image while not affecting other parts. Special Effects filters and prisms use the existing light in various ways to create various image patterns, but in doing so, deteriorate the primary imaging capabilities of the lens.

Color Correction Filters

Photographic films are manufactured to very exacting standards of color. A photographic film emulsion manufactured for use under tungsten light sources, with a basic color temperature of 3200° Kelvin, requires light of that specific color temperature to accurately reproduce the colors of the subject on the print made from that negative. Likewise daylight film is manufactured to accurately reproduce color only under daylight color sources, with a basic color temperature of approximately 5500° Kelvin.

Color Correction Filters, sometimes called Color Conversion or Light Balancing Filters, are used to correct the color temperature of all the light sources simultaneously to the color temperature requirements of the particular film type being used.

In other words, a tungsten film used in daylight requires a color correction filter when the light source is daylight. This is the most commonly used color correction filter, and it is described as a Wratten type "85" filter. This 85 filter is orange or salmon colored, and serves to reduce the excess blue and purple (from the excess ultraviolet) light found in daylight light sources. Tungsten film exposed without a color correction filter in daylight conditions will appear very blue. Sometimes this effect is a desirable one for a particular scene, but not often.

Daylight is not the same as sunlight. Sunlight is only the light from the sun. Daylight is the combination of sunlight and skylight. Sunlight varies in color temperature from approximately 2000° Kelvin at sunrise to over 5800° at high noon, and then back to 2000° at sunset. Skylight can vary from 6000° to over 30,000° Kelvin, depending on the degree of overcast, smog content, time of day, and the latitude of the location. So there is a very wide range of color temperature to choose from.

"Photographic Daylight," in most sources, is considered to be 5500° Kelvin. "Daylight" film requires light of 5500° Kelvin to accurately reproduce color, and images will appear excessively orange if exposed under tungsten light. The filter used to correct tungsten light for use with daylight film is called the Wratten 80A filter, requires two full stops exposure compensation, and is deep blue.

Although it is possible to use either daylight or tungsten film under either lighting conditions, the exposure compensation required for the two types of color correction filters makes it much more efficient and logical to use tungsten film under daylight conditions than the reverse. The 85 filter, used on tungsten film under daylight, requires only a 2/3 stop exposure compensation, while the 80A filter used for daylight film in tungsten light requires two full stops of exposure compensation. There is rarely that much light to spare.

Color Compensation Filters

Color compensation filters are used to make smaller adjustments in the color to correct for excessive, diminished, or missing bands of light found in certain discontinuous spectrum discharge-type light sources, such as fluorescent, mercury vapor, or sodium vapor lamps sometimes found in shooting locations in factories, stadiums or sports arenas, subways, offices, etc.

These filters are available in the primary (red, green, blue) and secondary (yellow, magenta, cyan) colors of light and in various densities (05, 10, 15, 20, 30, 40, 50, etc.), to correct for various deficiencies of the light sources being used. A CC20M filter, for example, is a magenta filter with a density of 20. This magenta 20 filter is often used with fluorescent lighting, to reduce the excess green component in the light. A CC05Y is a yellow filter with a density of 5. A CC50B is a blue filter with a density of 50. These filters are often used in combination to achieve the desired effect.

Extensive testing is required to find the desired balance required for some of these strange and hard-to-predict light sources. My friend and mentor Dave Quaid is working on the definitive study of these light sources and the photographic problems they cause and solutions they require. He hopes to publish soon, and I am looking forward to his book.

Neutral Density Filters

Neutral density filters diminish the quantity of light without affecting the quality or color of the light. They work by reducing equally all colors of the light passing through.

They are gray in color, and are available in a wide range of densities, on a decimal scale beginning with 0.1 ND, with a 1/3 stop compensation required. The most common densities are .30, .60, and .90, with exposure compensation of one, two, and three stops respectively. These filters are described variously as 0.3ND, .30ND, ND3, ND.3, N3, etc., depending on the manufacturer and the packaging, but they all describe the same neutral density filter with an exposure compensation of one stop.

Neutral densities are often found in combination with color correction filters, to reduce the amount of light passing through as well as correcting the color. An 85N3 filter, for example, changes daylight to tungsten balance (with a light loss of 2/3 stop) and reduces the overall amount of light by one additional stop, for a combined exposure compensation required of 1 2/3 stops. An 85N6 requires 2 2/3 stops compensation, and an 85N9 requires 3 2/3 stops.

Neutral Density filters allow the Director of Photography to control the amount of light at the camera, instead of at the light source. The depth-of-field can be reduced to the D.P.'s preference by adding the appropriate neutral density, and the choice of aperture stop becomes the D.P.'s.

Some D.P.'s are more flexible than others about neutral density filters. Some D.P.'s choose a neutral density filter to achieve a specific stop, and are resistant to changing it. Others will allow the Camera Assistant to reduce the neutral density in use to allow increasing the Depth-of-Field by stopping down the aperture in order to ease the focus restrictions on a difficult shot or a shot with a long lens. This D.P. might give the Assistant a "basic" stop (without allowing for any ND), and allow the Assistant to use "whatever ND" he or she wants (just remember to adjust the stop accordingly). If you are having trouble with the focus on a particular shot while using a neutral density filter, ask the Director of Photography if he or she would mind reducing the neutral density to increase the depth-of-field for this shot.

Graduated Filters

Graduated filters (also called "Wedge" filters by some D.P.'s) are very common now—it's become all the rage to use colored grads all the time, especially in television commercials. It must be contagious—one Director of Photography uses them and others have to follow with even more outrageous colors. Colored grads are referred to as the "Yuppie Filter" by more than one D.P. and Assistant.

A graduated filter is a filter in which only a portion (usually half) of the filter has the color of the filter, the rest is clear glass. This can be either a sharp edge or a soft edge so it can be softly blended into the scene if necessary. It used to be that they were only available in neutral density, to cut down the quantity of the light without affecting the color. There was a choice of ND30 (one stop) to clear, and ND60 (two stops) to clear, or ND90 (three stops) to clear. One Director of Photography I worked with even had a couple of special order grads made up that were six stops neutral density to clear for use for day-for-night filming, to reduce the brightness of the sky while minimizing the amount of light needed for the foreground.

Now they come in red and blue, peach and sunset, aquamarine and yellow and almost any other color and color combination you can think of. It's not unusual for a Director of Photography to show up with a filter case that's got forty of these 6.6" by 6.6" monstrosities in all different colors.

The grad filter needs to be large enough so that if you didn't want it exactly half way across the frame you could adjust it accordingly. Filter size 6.6" x 6.6" (often referred to as simply "6 by 6") is a good size to have for grads, because it gives you plenty of leeway in all directions. Most lenses only really need a filter about two inches square in the center of this acre of glass, so with a larger filter, the grad line can be positioned where desired in the frame, without the risk of overshooting the edges of the filter. With at least one rotating stage (filter holder) in the matte box, the filter can be set in at an angle and cover only the top left corner or the bottom right corner or straight across the top, or any orientation desired.

It's even possible to use neutral density grads for night exterior scenes. On a street scene with street lamps and a car on a road, you can set the grad to cover the bulbs of the street lamps with the ND so that they're not as bright. They are still illuminating the scene, but the bulbs themselves are not so hot that they flare out.

They can also be used indoors sometimes. In a bar scene, for example, when there are a number of practical overhead lamps that are lighting the scene, and you just want to darken the bulbs themselves with the grad, without reducing their light output. It's not the same as putting lower-wattage bulbs in each of the fixtures or putting N.D.'s or nets in front of them; as they wouldn't be illuminating the scene the same way. Using a grad in this way gives you the full value of the existing lighting without the flare from having the lights in the frame.

Also keep in mind that the smaller your f/stop, the more likely the grad edge is to be in focus. This line will become sharper as the lens is stopped down. Starting off with a soft edge grad is a good idea if the lens is being stopped down a lot. It also helps to keep the grad as close to the lens as possible to further reduce the chances of seeing the grad edge. If the matte box has more than one filter tray or slot, use the slot closest to the lens for the grad unless you want a sharper grad line.

It is also possible to move the grad while panning or tilting the camera during a shot. All you have to do is mark the grad somewhere as if for a focus shift, and as the operator tilts down, for example, the Assistant can slide the grad up accordingly. Arriflex now builds a matte box with a gear-driven filter tray and knob so the Assistant can move the grad more easily during a shot.

"Attenuator" Filters

There's also a filter called an Attenuator Filter, sometimes described as "MBRA" filter. I have been unable to find out what M, B, or R stand for; if anyone out there knows, please write and let me know. These are filters that start out on one edge with heavy ND ("Neutral Density") and get lighter and lighter as you move across the filter toward the opposite edge, but with no discernable dividing line, only a continuous lessening of the neutral density effect. At one edge there would be no neutral density effect, in the center there might be one stop ND, and at the far edge there might be two stops light lost to the ND.

These come in different density ranges—it might be two stops in the center and four stops at the top or it could be one and a half stops in the center and three at the top. They are usually twice as dark at the top as they are in the center.

They are normally just called "Attenuator" or "ATN" filters, and they are normally rated by what the exposure loss is in the center. A one-stop attenuator would be one stop in the center and two stops at the darkest edge. A one-and-a-half-stop attenuator would be one and a half stops in the center and three stops at the end.

Unfortunately, I have also seen these filters labeled for the darkest part of the ND. Under this system, an ATN filter with one stop ND in the center and two stops at the darkest end was labeled "Two-Stop ATN." Be sure to take meter readings with a spot meter on all attenuator filters, to find out how they are labeled, and don't confuse the two labelling system.

These filters are useful for taking down the sky when you can't hide the grad line somewhere. You can take down the sky a lot and a little less in the middle and even less in the foreground or bottom of the frame. A Director of Photography normally takes an exposure reading for the scene and then opens up the aperture by the amount of light loss in the center of the attenuator, so the frame is underexposed above the center of the filter and overexposed below the center. It takes some practice to use successfully, but you may see them sometimes on jobs. I am surprised they are not used more than they are. For some shots, they are more useful than grads.

I've described them with the darkest part at the top, but obviously you can put it into the matte box in any configuration. Sometimes you might want to take down the sand or the snow on the ground and have less effect on the sky. Either way you use them, they do somewhat restrict panning and tilting, unless you want to move the filter during the shot.

I used to be able to say I had never heard of these being made in any color other than neutral density, but I just recently found both blue and coral attenuators at a rental house, and we actually used the coral one on that job. It would not surprise me to find out there were other colors available somewhere.

If there is no discernable dividing line between the colored and clear parts of the filter, they should properly be called "Attenuators" rather than "Grads."

Diffusion Filters

There are many different kinds of diffusion filters available, and every filter manufacturer has at least half a dozen different types, generally in sets of five strengths, with their own proprietary brand names for these filters.

Diffusion filters can be made in several ways: adding some substance to the glass or plastic to make the filter milky, texturing the glass to scatter the light rays, sandwiching a fabric net (sometimes colored) inside two thin layers of glass, or spattering the glass with colored paint. Each of these gives a different effect, some degrading (diffusing) the image without altering the color, others softening as well as adding a subtle color shading.

There are many too many different types of diffusion filters for me to try to describe all of them here. It is also a very subjective choice, and every Director of Photography will have their own favorites for different shooting situations. There are some generalizations that can be discussed, however.

Generally, the wider the shot, the less diffusion is desired; the closer the subject, the more diffusion is acceptable. Less diffusion is needed for a wide shot, because the details of the scene are already so small that even the slightest diffusion will cause the image to appear out of focus. Close-up images often look better slightly diffused, because without the diffusion there is just too much detail.

Panavision makes an interesting contraption called an "Auto-Diffuser," a motorized variable diffuser that looks like a matte box with a long, vertical, enclosed filter box that contains a long, narrow piece of glass that is clear at one end and with gradually heavier diffusion until the other end. With a zoom control gun and cable, the diffuser may be raised or lowered during the shot, increasing or decreasing the amount of diffusion in front of the lens. This is useful for such shots as a dolly in to a close-up, where the Director of Photography might want the amount of diffusion to increase as the dolly moves in.

Some lenses may accept diffusion better than others. If using a variety of lenses from different manufacturers, take care in selecting diffusion. Prime lenses can generally handle more diffusion than the same focal lengths on a zoom lens. Newer, sharper, more contrasty lenses can usually handle more diffusion than older, less sharp, less contrasty lenses.

Once a scene is started with diffusion, it is often necessary to continue using various degrees of diffusion for the rest of the scene, rather than to cut suddenly to a lens not using any diffusion. If the leading actor or actress needs a bit of diffusion to look his or her best, it is generally a good idea to use a weaker diffusion for other cast members, rather than no diffusion, which might call attention to the fact that more diffusion is being used for the leads. Intercutting between scenes with diffusion and scenes without can sometimes be difficult.

When in doubt, shoot tests.

Polarizing Filters

Polarizers are important filters. They are used primarily to take the sky down so you can see the clouds better, and to reduce the reflections from glass, water, metal, or other surfaces. Light is an electromagnetic medium that vibrates in several different planes or directions, around the axis of projection. Think of a polarizer as a gate or picket fence, only allowing light to pass through if it is vibrating in a particular direction, like between the bars of the fence. Light vibrating in another direction, across the bars, cannot pass through. There's less light passing through the filter so you do have an exposure compensation, and you can control the angle of the light passed by the filter by rotating the filter.

Using two polarizers, set with their transmission angles at right angles to each other, virtually all light can be canceled out. This is the method employed in the Panavision Panafade device, originally designed as an electronic exposure control to compensate for exposure when changing the frame rate during the scene. The initial light loss is three stops; the maximum light loss five stops.

Polarizers work best when the camera is pointed at a 90° angle to the sun, but the effect can be seen to various degrees at other angles. Polarizers are often used to darken the sky in relation to the clouds, trees, and the buildings in the frame, with only a minimal affect on the color. Polarizers tend to heighten the color saturation of the scene, and to increase contrast in the shadow areas.

Polarizers are often used when shooting through car windshields. The windshield reflects the sky up above, and with a polarizer rotated in front of the lens while looking through the camera, an orientation angle can sometimes be found where that reflection was minimized to allow seeing into the car a little better, while often retaining some of the ambient reflections of overhead trees and buildings to make the shot more realistic.

A polarizer is also often used for product shots for commercials, in close-up tabletop shooting to eliminate or at least minimize reflections off glass or plastic bottles, product packaging, and table surfaces.

Determining the exposure compensation for a polarizer is also a controversial area. Everybody does it differently. Most polarizers have between a stop and a half and two stops of compensation required. There are two schools of thought on this. One is that you can take a spot meter or light meter and read through the filter and find out how much light is lost and how much compensation you need. Some D.P.'s use that metered value in every situation when using the polarizer filter.

There are others that say it depends on the orientation of the filter. If the polarizer is angled one way, it might only be a stop and a half, if angled another way it's two stops or more. Other D.P.'s just take the one reading and believe this is good in all situations. Check with your D.P. for his or her preference. According to Eastman Kodak (*Student Filmmakers Handbook,* p.72), polarizers require an exposure increase of 1 1/3 stops, and, "This factor applies regardless of how the polarizing screen is rotated," and my experience bears this out, although 1 1/3 stops compensation seems optimistic. Always check your filters with a meter.

Special Effects Filters

Special effect filters include fog and double fog filters, star filters, multiple image prisms, diffraction gratings, false color filters, and others.

Fog filters simulate the effect of shooting through fog, diffusing the image and lowering contrast, but without the need for exposure compensation. Double fog filters also create the illusion of fog or mist, but without the loss of definition found in fog filters.

Star filters have lines etched into the filter surface in various patterns, which create a "starburst" of light centering on highlights within the frame, such as candle flames, street lights, or bright reflections off metal or glass. Parallel lines will produce a "two-pointed" star, a square grid pattern will produce a "four-pointed" star, etc. Six- and eight-pointed stars are also available. The spacing between the lines also affects the image. This spacing is usually described in millimeters; 1mm, 2mm, 3mm, etc. The best way to choose the appropriate filter is by actually viewing through the mirror reflex camera at the shooting aperture, while rotating the filter to rotate the star pattern.

Some D.P.'s have adopted a particular star filter, usually one with a very faint star pattern, for use as diffusion, and use it on the lens even when no highlights are present in the frame and no "stars" are desired. The etched lines on the filter act as diffusers, and soften the image to some degree.

Multiple image prisms are self-explanatory, creating multiple copies of the main image, either repeating images in a line, or concentrically placed around the center of the frame, or in some other pattern. These are available in several models, with two, three, four, five, six, or more images created in various patterns.

Diffraction gratings diffract, or divide, the light into its component colors, creating a rainbow of color effects in the frame. False color filters are graduated color filters with strange and bizarre colors, sometimes with several different colors in the same filter. "Varicolor" filters also produce some bizarre color combinations in the scene. These have limited use, obviously, but they do show up sometimes.

Behind-the-Lens Filters

Light comes through the lens to focus on the film plane. The lens is mounted at a very specific distance from the film plane, called the flange focal depth, or flange focal distance. That's what is measured with a depth gauge. It is a very specific distance depending on the brand of the camera.

If a filter is placed behind the lens, it will affect the way that light beam is focused. The light passing through a behind-the-lens filter is going to focus in a different plane because the filter alters and extends the optical path. The light is going to be bent a little bit differently by that additional filter. The light rays will miss the film plane and will focus behind the film plane.

This filter affects that flange focal distance by approximately 1/3 the thickness of whatever has been placed in the optical path. A rear-mounted filter elongates the effective flange focal distance by 1/3 the filter thickness.

A piece of glass 1/4" thick is going to shift that focus quite a bit behind the film plane. If using a gel filter which is very thin (approx. 3/1000" or 0.003"), the focus shift will be 1/3 of that thickness, a very minute amount (approx. 1/1000" or 0.001").

Because of the difference in depth-of-focus requirements between wide-angle and telephoto lenses, there is less of a problem with telephoto lenses than with wide-angle lenses. For zoom lenses, the widest end of the zoom requires the more critical back focus.

There are some D.P.'s who will not put a gel behind the lens for any reason believing that this will give them soft pictures. Others will use gelatin filters behind normal and telephoto lenses, but not behind wide-angle lenses.

Video cameras usually have a filter wheel inside the camera with an 85 filter, a neutral density, and a clear glass. The lens is constructed and mounted in such a way that it expects a piece of glass to be there in the optical path. That lens system works only when there is a piece of glass in that location. You can change to another filter, bring in the 85 or the neutral density and as long as that glass is the same thickness, the optical path is the same and the lens will still make sharp pictures.

186 THE CAMERA ASSISTANT

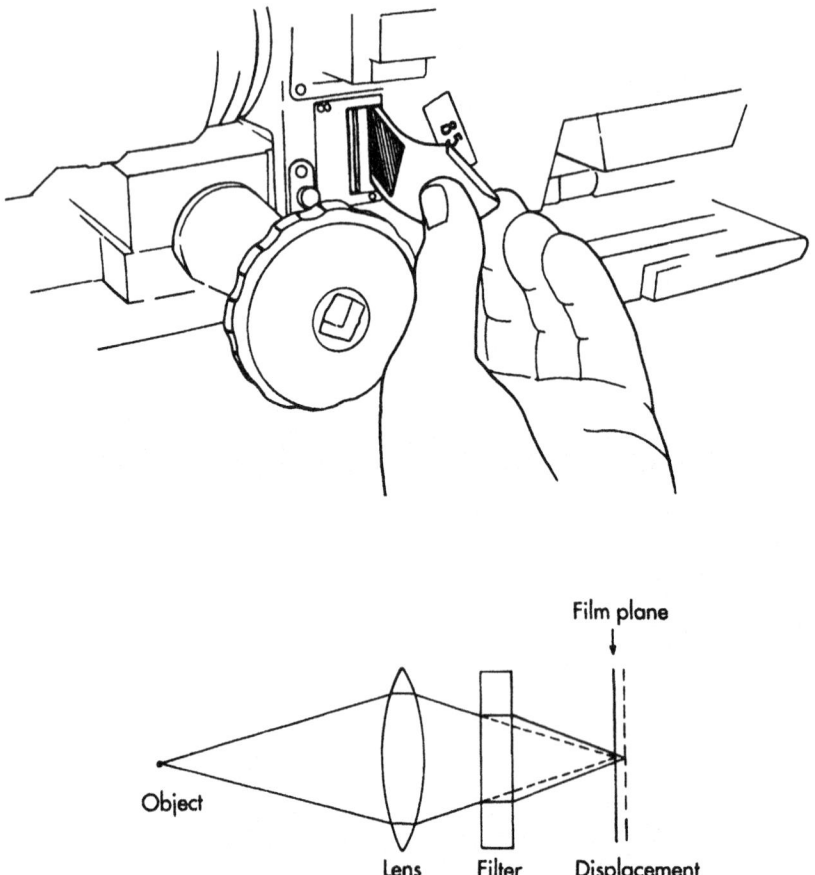

A behind-the-lens filter will alter the back focus of a lens.

Figure 8-1 Behind-the-Lens Gel Filters. Adding a gel filter behind the lens in a Panaflex camera. Be sure to label the side of the camera door near the filter slot as a reminder that a filter is inside. Do not use gel filters with very-wide-angle lenses, because of the optical phenomenon that extends the optical path behind the lens when a gel filter is added. The light is bent by the filter and is focused behind the film plane by approximately 1/3 of the thickness of the filter. While this may not be a problem with most lenses because of the Depth-of-Focus range, the wider the lens, the less the Depth-of-Focus, so using a gel with very wide lenses might cause focus problems.

Certain long telephoto lenses, such as the Canon series of 200mm, 300mm, and 400mm lenses, and the Nikon series 200mm and 300mm are also built so that an internal filter is part of the optical system. If an 85 filter is needed, a clear filter is replaced with an 85 filter of the same thickness inside the lens, and the filter becomes part of the optical system. If you're not using an 85, you replace it with an optical clear glass or neutral density filter of the same thickness. That piece of glass must be in there or your focus will be affected. The lens may still focus, but the focus scale will be off considerably.

In motion picture film cameras with an internal gel slot, like the Panavision Panaflex series of cameras, there are D.P.'s who won't use it at all, there are other D.P.'s who maintain that the shift is not important enough to worry about, and stick the gel in anyway, and there are D.P.'s who will use an internal gel filter for normal and long lenses and won't use it for the wide lenses.

A good rule of thumb is, according to David Samuelson, that for 35mm filming, if the lens is wider than 25mm, do not use a gel filter behind the lens.

There is usually enough tolerance in your depth of focus to live with a standard gelatin filter inside; adding 1/1000th of an inch to your optical system by using a gel is often within the tolerance of the depth of focus for the normal and longer focal lengths. The only problem might be with the wide-angle lenses or zoom lenses at the wide end.

Besides being lighter, faster to change, and far less expensive than glass filters, there is another advantage to using a gel behind the lens. The Director of Photography and Operator don't have to look through it when it is inserted behind the mirror shutter. If you are using the heavy 85N9 filter while shooting in bright sun, it's tough for the Operator to see through that filter—it's almost opaque. By using the gel in the filter slot behind the lens, you are also placing the filter behind the mirror shutter, so the viewfinder does not "see" the filter. The film does, but not the viewfinder.

As far as I know there is no such thing as a blank piece of gel. I've never seen one. It would seem like a logical thing to manufacture, but I've never seen it in the Kodak Wratten system. This would allow you to set up your camera's flange focal depth to allow for a gel always to be in the optical path. You could use a gel filter when needed, and when no filter is desired, a clear gel could be inserted to guarantee the correct optical path. Dave Quaid suggests using a gelatin UV (UltraViolet) filter, such as the "1A" or "2A" filter as a "clear."

If you do decide to use the gel filter behind the lens, then be sure to place a label of white camera tape identifying the filter being used on the outside of the filter slot to remind you that a filter is inside. This is vitally important! On the Panavision Platinum cameras, there is an indicator in the digital display that reads "FIL" when there is a filter in the gel slot, but this is tiny lettering and easily overlooked. The Arri 535 camera has a similar indication that a gel filter is inside. Make yourself a tape label to be sure.

It is good practice to label the Camera Assistant's side of the matte box whenever a filter is inside the matte box as well. Get in the habit of labeling the camera body or matte box as soon as a filter is inserted or changed. It only takes a few seconds, but it can prevent a tragic mistake.

Also get into the habit of removing filters and returning them to their cases as soon as the shots are finished. This prolongs the life of the filters, as well as helping to make sure that future shots are not made with unwanted or incorrect filters in place.

Behind-the-Lens Diffusion

There are a lot of Directors of Photography who like to use nets or pieces of silk stocking behind the lens for diffusion. For attaching these nets or stockings, the rental houses recommend (and insist) that you use only rubber cement because it can be removed easily without leaving a residue.

There is a peculiar tape you can use, called transfer tape (which looks and behaves like rubber cement on a paper backing), to attach the stocking to the rear of the lens. Specially machined metal or plastic rings, or even rubber bands, can be used to hold the net or stocking in place, depending on the construction of the lens. Just remember to take it off when you are done shooting.

I heard one horror story of a Camera Assistant with a Panavision camera who got tired of putting the net on and taking the net off the lens, so he took an empty gel filter holder and mounted the stocking in there, thinking that he would only have to do this once. Of course when they looked at the film they shot with this gel holder net, it looked like they were shooting through a chain-link fence. The net was right up against the film plane and it was photographed very clearly, having cast its mesh shadow on the film.

There are problems using the net behind the lens. First of all, the net might come loose from the lens and get caught in the spinning mirror. What a mess that would be! And you would never see it until you changed lenses, checked the gate, or until the camera ground to a halt.

A second and more likely problem is that with the net behind a lens, as the lens is stopped down the net becomes more and more in focus, and can become visible on the screen. This would be more of a problem with short focal length lenses than with long focal lengths, because of the increased depth-of-field with short lenses, but at the same time, the rear element of the longer lenses is usually farther from the film plane than the rear element of wide-angle lenses. Someday, someone should shoot a test and find out for sure which is worse. It is difficult to see in the viewfinder, but it sometimes looks like the scene is being shot through a fuzzy chain-link fence, especially if there is a pan or tilt. Look for this in major motion pictures—you'll see it once in a while.

Multiple Filters

When using more than one filter for a particular shot, the order in which the filters are placed in the matte box can sometimes make a difference.

Graduated filters should usually be placed as close to the lens as possible to reduce the chances of getting the grad edge in focus when the lens is stopped down.

Diffusion filters tend to flare more than other filters, due to their construction, so placing the diffusion filter where it will be the most sheltered, and where it receives the least light, will tend to reduce that flaring. This means placing the diffusion filter as close to the lens as possible, and behind the colored filter, or neutral density filter, or polarizer, in order to reduce the light hitting the diffuser. A diffuser behind a polarizer receives two stops less light than one in front of the polarizer, and will be less likely to flare.

When using more than one Proxar or plus diopter filter, the strongest one should be closest to the lens, and any other ones stacked in descending order in front of the strongest one. This may mean using more than one filter ring between them because of the curvature of the close-up lenses.

Filter Factors

The scale used to determine the amount of exposure increase needed when a particular filter is in use is the filter factor. The filter factor is the ratio of the filtered exposure to the unfiltered exposure with equal densities when developed.

$$\text{Filter Factor} = \frac{\text{Exposure With Filter}}{\text{Exposure Without Filter}}$$

Each filter has a filter factor, a number describing the number of times that the exposure need be increased to allow for the filter's absorption of a portion of the light passing through. For a filter allowing one half of the light through, the exposure must be doubled to compensate (a filter factor of 2), an exposure compensation of one stop is required. A filter factor of 2 would require that the exposure be increased, or aperture opened, one stop. A filter factor of 4 would require two stops compensation. A filter factor of 1 requires no compensation.

FILTER FACTORS AND EXPOSURE:

Filter Factor	Stops Increase	Filter Factor	Stops Increase
1	0	6	2+2/3
1.25	0 1/3	8	3
1.6	0 2/3	10	3+1/3
2	1	12.5	3+2/3
2.5	1+1/3	16	4
3.2	1+2/3	20	4+1/3
4	2	25	4+2/3
5	2+1/3	32	5

When using more than one filter, great care must be taken in compensating correctly for the exposure loss. Filter factors for more than one filter used simultaneously are MULTIPLIED together to determine the filter factor of the filter combination. The only exception to this would be with certain unusual combinations of colored filters used for black-and-white photography, and which should be tested in combination to determine the correct compensation.

Once filter factors have been converted to stops, then the stop compensations for combinations of filters must be ADDED together to yield the compensation of the combination.

To repeat the process for computing the exposure compensation needed for a combination of filters:

EITHER

1. MULTIPLY the filter factors of the individual filters, then calculate or look up the stop compensation of the combined filters

OR,

2. ADD the stop compensations of the individual filters, and set the lens accordingly.

Be careful not to confuse the two methods. Decide which method you prefer, and stick to it.

Mired Shift Value

This is a scale of measurement of color sometimes used to describe or define the color effect of a particular filter on a scene. The term MIRED refers to Micro Reciprocal Degrees, and is obtained by dividing 1,000,000 (one million) by the color temperature expressed in degrees Kelvin. Mired values for light sources, lighting gels, and camera filters are added together to arrive at the color value of the light actually being photographed.

The number may appear as a positive or negative number, and refers to the direction of the color shift and the amount of the shift. For example, a Wratten 85 filter, orange in color, has a Mired value of +112, while an 80A, deep blue in color, has a Mired value of -131, so they approximately cancel each other out. Keep in mind that the Mired value does not take into account the filter factor or exposure compensation needed when using a particular filter, only color.

Cleaning Filters

Very little is likely to happen to a glass filter, short of breaking it, that cannot be cleaned with lens tissue, either dry or moistened with a little lens fluid. Glass filters are by nature quite scratch-resistant. Some Camera Assistants use a new piece of chamois cloth for filter cleaning, although some other Assistants claim that the chamois leaves an oily residue of lanolin on the filters. The chamois, if used, must also be replaced or cleaned fairly often, as it gets dirty very quickly. Chamois can be washed by hand in Woolite, the way one might wash a delicate blouse or sweater. Some Assistants use a piece of soft, finely woven polyester cloth, sold under the brand name Luminex, to clean lenses and filters.

The worst thing that is likely to happen to a glass filter is that tape residue might be left behind after a Camera Assistant had to mount a filter to a lens with camera or gaffer tape. This happens sometimes when for some reason a sunshade or matte box cannot be used, or if filters of the wrong size are pressed into service in an emergency. This tape residue comes off easily with mineral spirits or acetone, and the solvent residue from these comes off with lens fluid or alcohol. Don't try the same solvents on plastic filters!

Care of glass filters is easy. The same cannot be said for plastic filters, made from acrylic resin or other scratch-attracting plastic, and known to Camera Assistants as "Disposable" filters or "Scratch" filters. These filters scratch very easily, and even lens tissue will scratch them, so do not use any tissue anywhere near acrylic filters. The manufacturers of these filters make their own cleaning solutions for these filters, and some recommend using only cotton balls moistened with their cleanser for cleaning. The best advice, however, is to be very careful with these filters, and never ever to have to clean them. Just blow off the dust, and keep shooting. When they become too badly scratched, just throw them away and buy new ones.

CHAPTER **9**

Focus

Overview

Focus is the second most important responsibility of the First Camera Assistant, second only to assembly and maintenance of the camera itself.

The Camera Assistant must understand not only the basic technical theory of focus, but also understand the creative choices of focus—sorting out what you want to keep in focus, what you do NOT want to be in focus, and what you don't really care about.

There is a certain degree of luck in being able to carry out your focus plan for a particular shot. Experience and skill help, of course, but the real secret is deciding on a focus plan for that shot in the first place.

What is to be the plane of sharpest focus? How, when and why will that plane of focus change during the shot? If more than one actor is in the shot, which actor shall be kept in focus?

There are so many variables that affect focus once you actually start shooting that the theory kind of gets lost. There are variables such as actors that don't hit marks, dolly grips that don't hit marks, and directors and actors that will not give you adequate rehearsal time, diffusion filters in use, lenses from different manufacturers, an aperture pull, or a zoom during the shot.

Some actors are totally oblivious to the technical problems of filmmaking. They don't even try to hit marks—they find specific marks too restrictive. With these actors, every take will be different. "Every take is an adventure into the unknown," was a remark I heard from one veteran Camera Assistant.

Other actors and directors and even Directors of Photography prefer to have technical rehearsals with "stand-ins," and then when the actual actors show up they want to shoot right away without a rehearsal. Actors just don't do things the same way stand-ins do. It's like having an orchestra practice Vivaldi just before a Mozart concert. Or, as Sean Connery says in *The Untouchables,* it's like "bringing a knife to a gun fight."

I was helping out at one workshop where the instructor Director of Photography advised the students to "wait until you see it in dailies and see if you can get away with it"—I certainly can't agree with that philosophy, because if you see it in dailies it's too late. It's on the film already. Such a philosophy can only end in unemployment.

The Camera Assistant, or "Focus Puller," should play it safe and use even higher standards of focus than are going to be noticed in dailies or you might not be working for that company the day after dailies.

Focus Theory

In any photographic situation, there will be a lens, an object (target), and an image. The variables are the focal length of the lens, the object distance (distance between the film plane and the object), and the aperture setting on the lens.

With any lens, a point focused on should yield an image point on the film negative. There is only one plane of absolute focus in front of the lens, often described as the "Principal Plane of Focus," or "PPF." There is a certain amount of APPARENT focus in front of that plane, and a certain amount of APPARENT focus behind that plane—that range is what we call "acceptable" focus, or "Depth-of-Field." Focus softens, or drops off gradually as the object moves away in either direction from the focus plane.

Photographed objects outside the exact plane of focus are not really in focus but they may be close enough so that they appear to be in focus when projected. Only objects on the exact plane of focus are really in focus.

Every photographic situation has a certain range of acceptable focus in front of and behind the focus plane. What's acceptable under one circumstance may not be acceptable in another circumstance. It depends on the type and focal length of the lens you are using. It depends on how large your film print is going to be projected on a screen, it depends on what filtration is in use, and on what gauge and emulsion type film is being shot.

Something that looks in focus on an eight-foot screen in a screening room or on a nineteen-inch television monitor might look "soft" on a sixty-foot screen in a movie theater.

"In focus" and "out of focus" are relative terms. There is no sharp, distinct, division line where an object is in focus on one side and clearly out of focus on the other. It is a gradual process, and a slight softening of the focus is sometimes hard to see.

Audiences have a tendency when watching a film to watch and concentrate on that area that is in focus on the screen. The audience is often being forced to observe a specific person or object and the filmmakers' intent is being aided by a physical or psychological law—because we tend to watch something that's in focus and ignore things that are out of focus.

If everything is in focus—yes, we could easily shoot everything with wide-angle lenses, shoot at f/11 and everything would be in focus, and the audience wouldn't

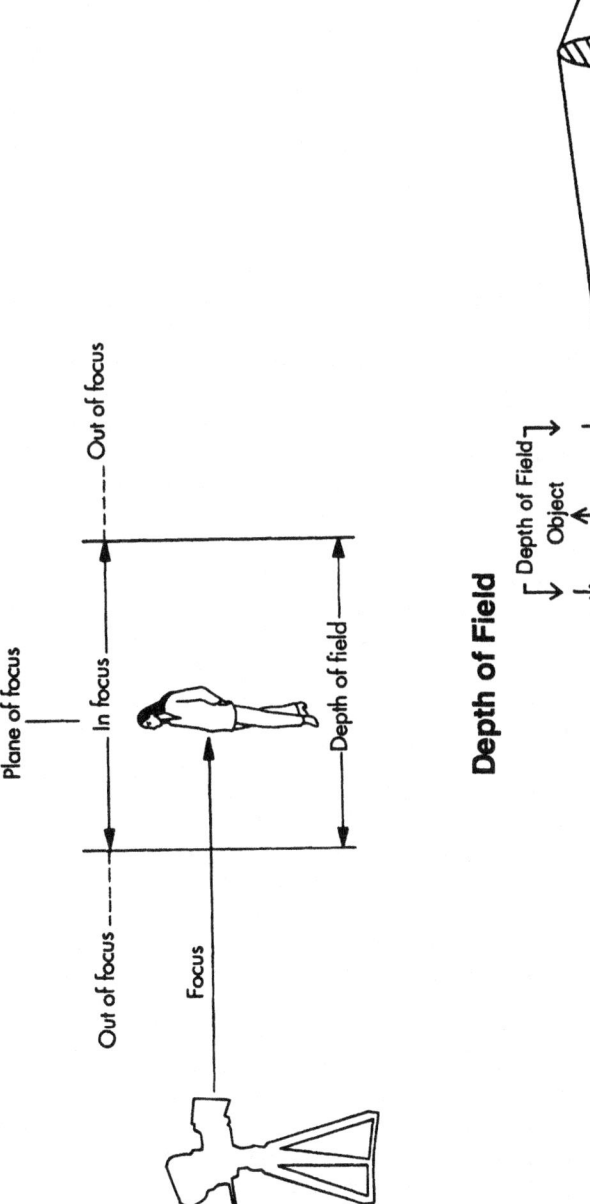

Figure 9-1 Depth-of-Field. Depth-of-Field is the range of acceptably sharp focus in front of and behind the Principal Plane of Focus (the focus setting on the lens). The focus falls off gradually in both directions from the Plane of Focus. The points at which the focus starts to look soft, in front and in back of the Plane of Focus, are the limits of acceptable focus, or the limits of the Depth-of-Field.

know what to look at—we would be giving them too much information—too much detail. So by restricting and controlling what is in focus and what is out of focus, the filmmakers are forcing the audience to pay attention to their story or what they want to get across.

A lens of a certain focal length is chosen by the director and Director of Photography for the way that lens make the image look. They have an artistic vision or composition that they want to maintain and directors in particular are often not interested in the technical problems of focus. They usually don't want to see the whole room—they only want to see a certain part of the room in focus at a time, or a part of the location, or to single out one person from a crowd of people. It's an artistic choice which sometimes causes technical problems.

Circle of Confusion

Years ago, an applicant to Local 644, while taking the written part of the Membership Test, came to the question, "What is the Circle of Confusion?" His answer: "This Test!" He passed, anyway.

If the object (target) starts to move in either direction from the plane of sharpest focus and the focus setting of the lens is not changed, the photographed image of that point is going to become a circle which will get larger and larger until it starts to look "soft" to the viewer. The diameter of that circle—the image created by that point photographed by that lens on the film, at the point at which the image begins to look "soft," or "out of focus"—is the "Circle of Confusion."

Another way to think of this is that photographic images are made up of thousands of individual points—each tiny detail and element in the target is reproduced as a tiny image point on the film. Those points exactly at the principal plane of focus will be reproduced as points on the film. Those points in front of or behind the principal plane of focus will be reproduced as tiny overlapping circles, called Circles of Confusion, whose diameter increases in direct proportion to their distance from the principal plane of focus. Photographic images made up of Circles of Confusion BELOW a certain critical diameter appear to be "sharp" or "in focus," but images made up of Circles of Confusion ABOVE this diameter are considered "out of focus" or "soft."

As long as the diameter of the image of each point of the object being photographed remains smaller than our maximum "Circle of Confusion" the image appears "sharp," or in focus, to the audience. When the diameter of the circle created on the film exceeds that of our maximum "Circle of Confusion," the audience will perceive that image as soft, or out of focus.

There is a mathematical formula (see Appendix D) for the computation of the Depth-of-Field limits for a particular focal length lens, at a particular distance, and for a particular Circle of Confusion. The point at which a point being photographed begins to look soft also changes with the format being shot. A 16mm negative is much smaller than a 35mm negative, and must be enlarged, or "blown up" much larger to fill the same size screen with an image, so the Circle of Confusion for 16mm must be much smaller than for 35mm.

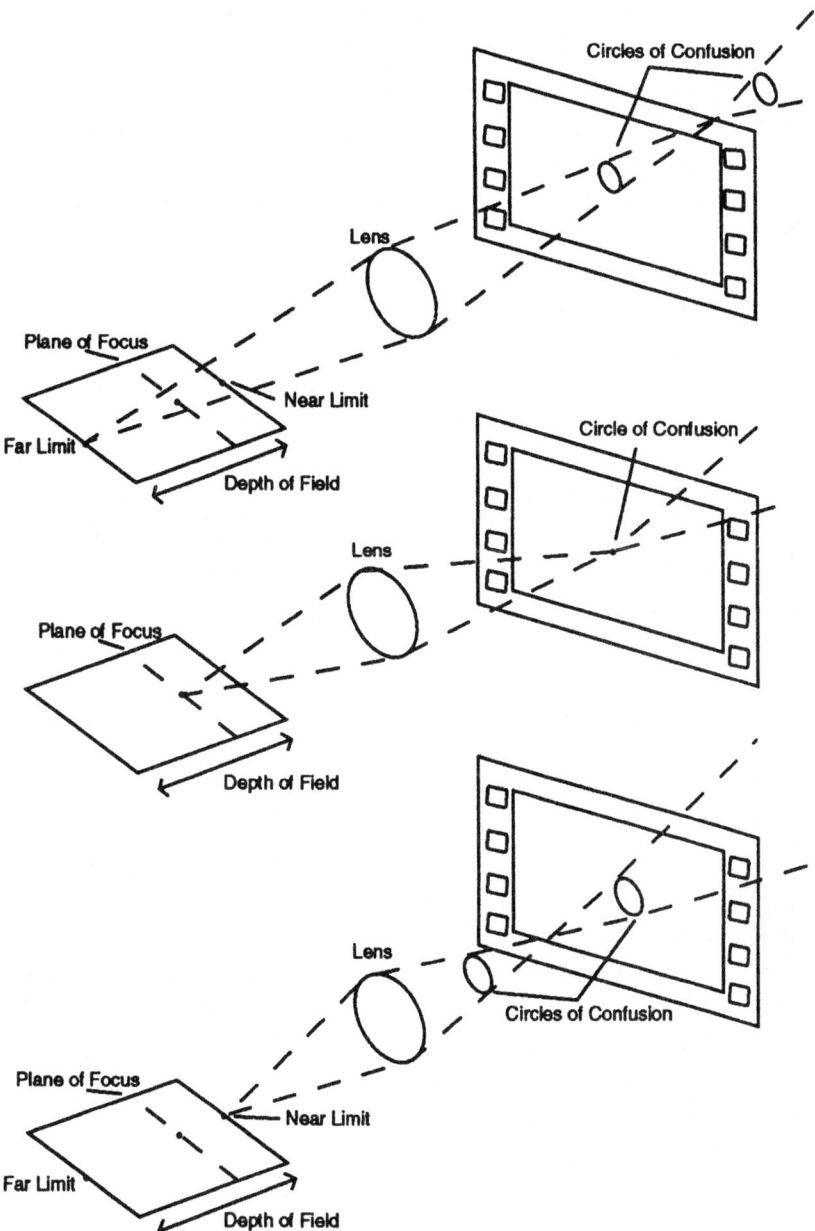

Figure 9-2 Circle of Confusion. A point at the plane of focus will be photographed as a point on the film. A point in front of or behind the plane of focus will be photographed as a circle on the film. The farther away from the plane of focus the target, the larger the image circles on the film. When the image formed by these overlapping circles first appears to be "soft" or out of focus, the diameter of one of those circles is the "Circle of Confusion."

The figures used for the maximum Circle of Confusion for motion picture photography range from 1/2000" (0.0005") or 1/1000" (0.001") for 16mm to 1/700" (0.0014") or 1/500" (0.002") for 35mm. As with so many other aspects of cinematography, there are differences of opinion on these figures, as well, but these are the numbers on which most of the Depth-of-Field charts and calculators are based.

I generally use 1/1000" for 16mm work, 1/700" for 35mm destined for the big screen, and 1/500" for 35mm work destined for television only. This is a commonly used compromise. More on this later in this chapter.

f/stops and T/stops

The relative size of the lens aperture compared with the focal length of the lens is measured in "f/stops." F/stops are mathematical computations of how much light should get through the lens, in an ideal world with an ideal lens, with perfect glass. The "f/stop" is also sometimes described as the "geometric aperture." Take the focal length of the lens being used, say 100mm, and divide by the actual diameter of the iris, say 25mm, and that's an f/4 on the lens. A 50mm lens with a 25mm aperture would be at f/2.

It's a simple formula: the f/stop equals the Focal Length of the Lens divided by the Iris Diameter.

$$f/stop = \frac{\text{Lens Focal Length}}{\text{Diameter of Lens Aperture}}$$

However, we live in a most imperfect world, no glass is optically perfect, no lens design is mathematically perfect, and no iris is perfectly round. The f/stop deals simply with the physical dimension of a hole in the diaphragm of the lens. It does not deal at all with the amount of light actually reaching the film. Some of the light passing through the lens is lost to diffraction, refraction, and reflection, before reaching the film plane.

Lenses, and zoom lenses in particular, have many elements of imperfect glass inside. The f/numbers printed on the lenses are good for theoreticians but don't have much to do with how much light actually gets to the film. Therefore, we also have "T/stops," measured with a device called a T/stop machine. This is really only a light meter with a lens mount on it, and actually measures how much light gets through all those layers of imperfect glass and through the scattering that's being done by all the air/glass surfaces inside the lens. This is much more accurate than mathematically obtained f/4, which may only be T/4.2 in reality.

T/ stands for "transmission" or "true" stop. The "T/stop" is also sometimes described as the "photometric aperture." It's the light that is actually transmitted through the lens and reaching the film plane, and will be different on every lens, depending on the design of the lens, how many elements are included, what type of glass, and what type of coatings. This is a correction, to allow more accurate and controllable exposure of the photographic image. Before zoom lenses and super-fast lenses came into common use, it was less complicated, the f/stop was an accurate enough measure of the amount of light that got through the lens. Now we've got lenses that contain many elements of glass inside, and coating on all surfaces, and it's become a lot more complicated.

We are also now more exacting in our shutter speed computations and requirements. A hundred years ago, a two or three minute exposure would be necessary to photograph a portrait or a landscape. A few seconds more or less exposure didn't make much difference. Now we've got to get 24, 30, 100, or even 500 pictures done each second with a camera. A much more accurate measurement is needed.

In prime lenses, the difference between the f/ and T/numbers is very small, because there are a limited number of elements of glass inside. Some lenses will have both f/ and T/scales on the lens. There might be two indices on your aperture scale, one for f/stops and one for T/stops. On prime lenses, the difference between the f/ and T/stops is usually less than 1/4 of a stop.

Sometimes the lens has different scales on opposite sides of the lens. On the Angenieux 12–120mm Zoom, for example, for years the standard lens for 16mm filming, the top scale has f/stops in white, and on the bottom of the lens is a T/stop scale in red.

In general, the more elements there are in the lens, the farther apart the f/ and T/numbers are going to be. The relationship between a lens' T/numbers and its f/numbers is shown in the following formula:

$$T/stop = f/stop \times \frac{10}{\sqrt{\text{Transmittance Percentage}}}$$

You can see from this formula that if the lens were perfect (a transmittance of 100 percent), the T/ number and the f/ number would be the same. For a lens with a transmittance of 90 percent, f/2 would translate to T/2.1, and for a lens with transmittance of 80 percent, f/2 translates to T/2.3, etc.

Panavision, Zeiss, and some other lens manufacturers have decided to just totally ignore f/stops on lenses. These lenses only have a T/stop scale—there is no f/stop scale anywhere.

The T/stop will always be a higher number than the equivalent f/ because light is lost inside the lens. Every time light comes to an air/glass surface, a small percentage of that light is "scattered," or refracted and reflected back. Even with a lens with only a few elements, less light gets through the lens than what entered the lens.

Every piece of glass, because there is no such thing as a perfect piece of glass, is also going to absorb a little bit of light. No glass is absolutely, perfectly, transparent. There is always some color, some impurity, in the glass. There will always be less light coming out of a lens than was put in. So T/s are always higher numbers (less light) than f/s.

There is no such thing as a light meter that will give you readings in T/stops. A meter tells you mathematically what the exposure should be and how much light needs to reach the film for proper exposure. This reading from the meter will always be in f/stops. You then set it on the lens using the T/stops. The amount of light actually reaching the film through the lens will be the correct amount, according to the exposure meter.

Any calculation of exposure must be made in f/stops. Once you have the exposure reading that you want, in order to deliver that exposure to the film you've got to set the lens to the T/stop.

When calculating Depth-of-Field, however, T/stops have no calculation value. T/stops are only a physical adjustment to allow for imperfect glass in imperfect lenses. Depth-of-Field is not affected by the amount of light lost in a lens system, but is affected by the mathematical increase in the iris diameter made to allow for this light loss.

What you are doing is opening up a little bit on your iris to allow more light through to compensate for the light lost. By increasing your iris size, you're diminishing your Depth-of-Field, which must always be computed using f/s, and not T/s.

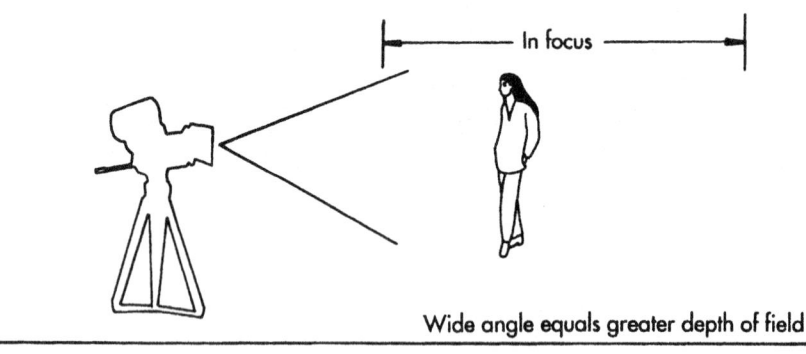

Wide angle equals greater depth of field

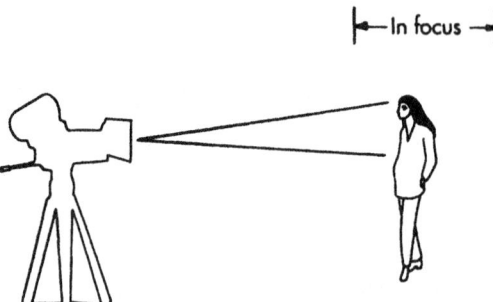

Telephoto equals less depth of field

Figure 9-3 Focal Length and Depth-of-Field. Depth-of-Field is greater with Wide-Angle Lenses (shorter focal lengths) than with Telephoto or Long Lenses (longer focal lengths), assuming the lens aperture and object distance remain the same.

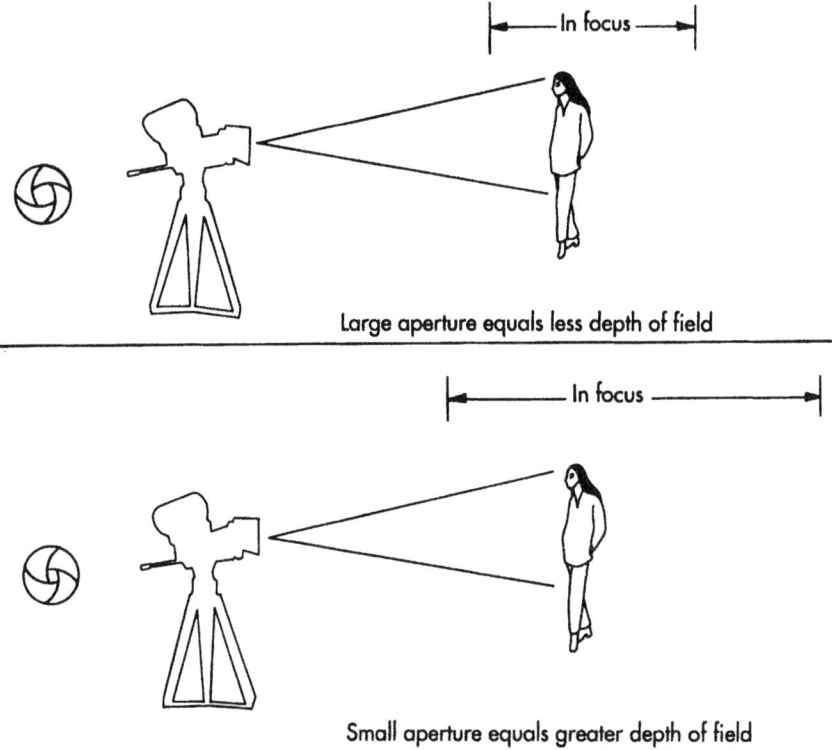

Figure 9-4 Aperture and Depth-of-Field. Depth-of-Field is greater with small apertures (stopped down) than with large apertures (opened up), assuming that focal length and object distance remain the same.

Depth-of-Field

The distance between the nearest point of acceptable focus and the farthest point of acceptable focus in a particular photographic situation is called the "Depth-of-Field," sometimes described as "lens-to-subject tolerance." After having decided on the diameter of the Circle of Confusion to be used for your application, there are three factors which affect Depth-of-Field. First is the focal length of your lens. The shorter the focal length (the "wider" the lens), the more Depth-of-Field you are going to have, assuming that nothing else is changed. The longer the lens, the less Depth-of-Field there will be.

The second factor is the lens aperture. As the aperture decreases in size, approaching a "pinhole," Depth-of-Field increases. Enlarge that hole again and the Depth-of-Field decreases.

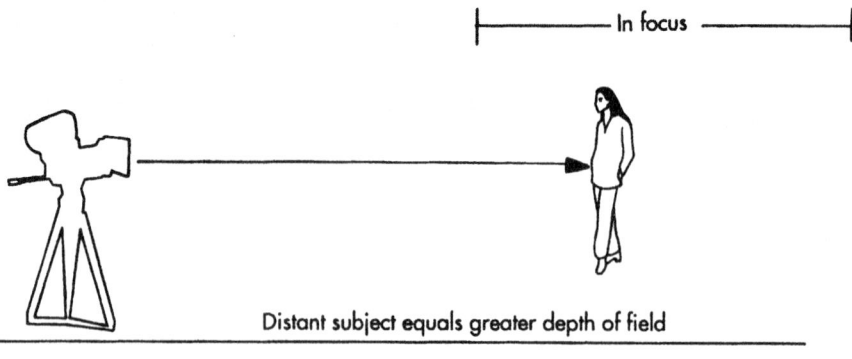

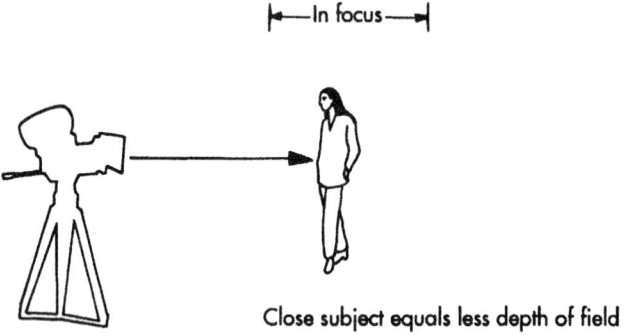

Figure 9-5 Distance and Depth-of-Field. Depth-of-Field is greater with targets farther from the lens than with targets close to the lens, assuming that the aperture and focal length remain the same.

The third factor is object distance. At a specific distance there is a specific Depth-of-Field. As the object approaches the film plane, the Depth-of-Field decreases. As the object gets further away from the film plane the Depth-of-Field increases.

These are three factors that determine Depth-of-Field. If two stay the same and one changes, then your Depth-of-Field is going to change.

There might be a situation in which two of these factors are changed, but changed in opposite directions, so that their effects are canceled out.

One of the many "Old Wives' Tales" that persists in this business is the fantasy about being able to switch to a wider lens and move in closer when two actors are too far apart to maintain both in focus. This is absolutely not true, and does not work. Switching to a wider-angle lens does increase the Depth-of-Field, but only if the other two factors remain unchanged. By moving in closer after switching to a wide lens, the Depth-of-Field decreases again.

If the image size is the same, then the Depth-of-Field is precisely the same with a wider lens in close, as with a longer lens farther away. In order to maintain the same

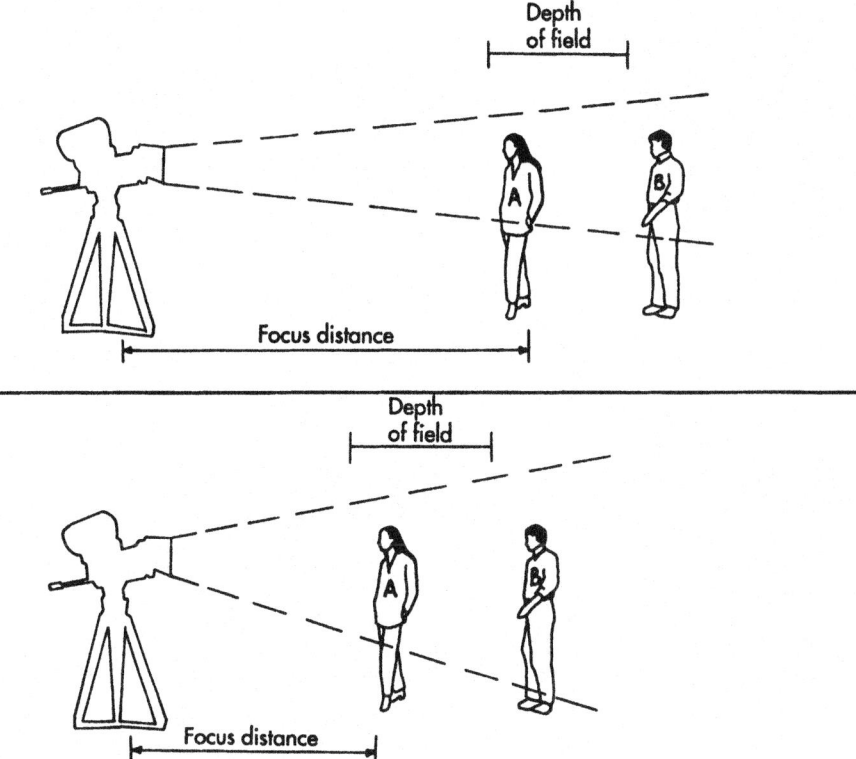

Figure 9-6 Closer and Wider DOES NOT WORK! One of the great myths of filmmaking: when Depth-of-Field is not sufficient to hold two subjects, just move closer with a wider lens. THIS DOES NOT WORK! Widening the lens (zooming out or using a shorter focal length lens) does increase the available Depth-of-Field, but moving in closer to the subjects reduces the Depth-of-Field, canceling out the gain achieved by widening the lens. If the image size of the subject in the frame is the same, then the Depth-of-Field is exactly the same.

image size, we have had to get so close with a wider lens that we canceled out that increase in Depth-of-Field by changing the object distance and it works out to be exactly the same Depth-of-Field.

Remember, the three factors that affect Depth-of-Field are Focal Length, Aperture, and Object Distance.

Macro Lens Depth-of-Field

For macro cinematography, it is sometimes easier to think in terms of image magnification than subject distance. Keep in mind that Depth-of-Field decreases as magnification increases. Depth-of-Field is extremely limited in Macro or Close-up

204 THE CAMERA ASSISTANT

Photography. For such shooting, it is not unusual to pump up the light level to f/16 or f/22 or higher to build up the Depth-of-Field to an acceptable level.

Depth-of-Focus

Depth-of-Focus is the other side of Depth-of-Field, occurring behind the lens, at the film plane. Depth-of-Focus, sometimes described as "lens-to-film tolerance," is the range between the nearest and farthest point of acceptable focus of an image in front of and behind the film plane.

The same three factors affect Depth-of-Focus, but not always the same way as for Depth-of-Field.

Depth-of-Focus is still better at smaller apertures than at larger apertures, but worse for distant objects than closer objects, and worse for wide-angle lenses than for longer lenses; the reverse of the effects with Depth-of-Field.

Factor	Depth-of-Field Increases as:	Depth-of-Focus Increases as:
Focal Length	Decreases	Increases
Aperture	Decreases	Decreases
Object Distance	Increases	Decreases

Depth-of-Focus, the opposite of Depth-of-Field, is LESS with a wide-angle lens (short focal length), and INCREASES as the focal length increases. This is why the flange focal depth of the camera is more critical with wide-angle lenses. If a zoom

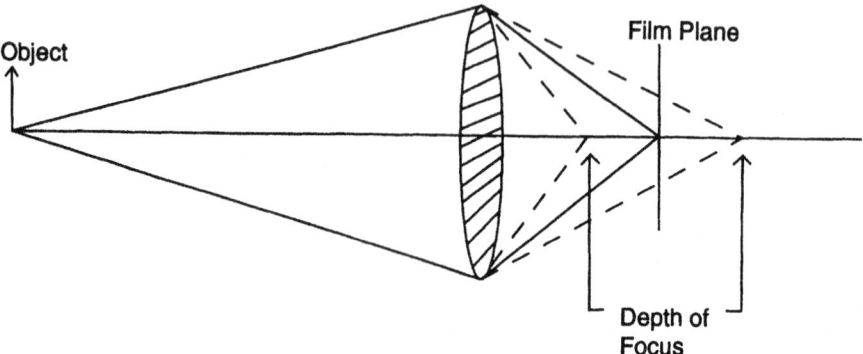

Depth of Field happens in object space
Depth of Focus happens in image space

Figure 9-7 Depth-of-Focus. Depth-of-Focus is like Depth-of-Field, except that it occurs behind the lens, inside the camera, at the film plane. Depth-of-Focus is more critical with wide-angle lenses than with long lenses.

lens, for example, ever looks soft at the wide end and sharp at the telephoto end, the first thing to check is the flange focal depth of the camera, and the lens mount itself.

This is also why behind-the-lens gel filters are usually acceptable with normal and long lenses, but with wide lenses, are sometimes unacceptable. They change the optical path behind the lens, shifting the "back focus" of the lens. The longer the focal length, the greater the Depth-of-Focus. This phenomenon is discussed in greater detail in the chapter on filters.

Smaller apertures (stopping down the lens) increase both the Depth-of-Field and Depth-of-Focus. The farther away the target, the greater the Depth-of-Field, but the less the Depth-of-Focus. The best Depth-of-Field occurs with a wide lens, a distant target, and a small aperture. The best Depth-of-Focus occurs with a long lens, a close target, and a small aperture.

Hyperfocal Distance

There are two ways to define Hyperfocal Distance. First, if the lens is focused at infinity, the Hyperfocal Distance is the nearest point of acceptable focus. Secondly, if the lens is focused at the Hyperfocal Distance, the Depth-of-Field will extend from one-half of that Hyperfocal Distance to infinity.

The Hyperfocal Distance is of limited practical use on the set, but when you want the absolute maximum Depth-of-Field possible for the particular situation, use the Hyperfocal Distance. If for some reason you do not want to or cannot follow focus on a particular shot, setting the lens at the Hyperfocal Distance for that particular aperture might give you the best overall focus for the scene.

The Hyperfocal Distance of a particular situation changes the same way that Depth-of-Field in general does—based on focal length and aperture—because the Hyperfocal Distance is in reality, a very specific Depth-of-Field situation, that in

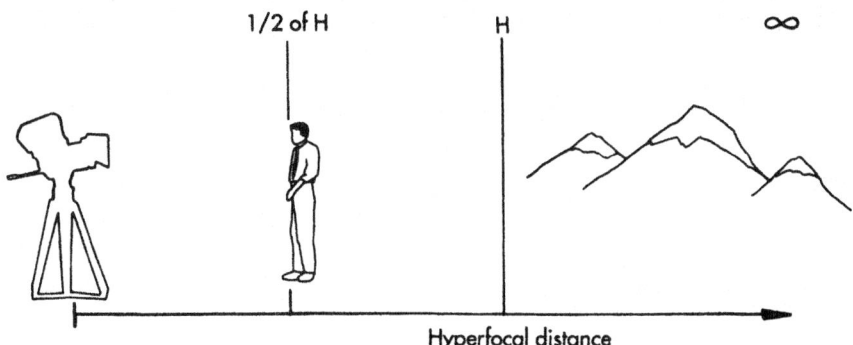

Figure 9-8 Hyperfocal Distance. When the focus scale of the lens is set to the Hyperfocal Distance for that focal length and aperture, the Depth-of-Field will extend from one-half of the Hyperfocal Distance to Infinity. When the lens focus scale is set to infinity, the near limit of the Depth-of-Field will be the Hyperfocal Distance.

which the far limit of the Depth-of-Field is at Infinity, and the actual focus at which the lens is set, is the Hyperfocal Distance. The near limit of the Depth-of-Field is found at one-half of the Hyperfocal Distance.

The Hyperfocal Distance is closer to the camera with wider-angle lenses, increasing the Depth-of-Field, and further away with longer lenses, decreasing the Depth-of-Field. The Hyperfocal Distance is closer to the camera with smaller apertures, and farther away with larger apertures, increasing and decreasing the depth, respectively.

HYPERFOCAL DISTANCES FOR .0001" CIRCLE OF CONFUSION

Focal Length	f/1	f/2	f/4	f/8
12.5mm Lens	20 ft.	10 ft.	5 ft.	2.5 ft.
17.5mm Lens	40 ft.	20 ft.	10 ft.	5 ft.
25mm Lens	80 ft.	40 ft.	20 ft.	10 ft.
35mm Lens	160 ft.	80 ft.	40 ft.	20 ft.
50mm Lens	320 ft.	160 ft.	80 ft.	40 ft.
70mm Lens	640 ft.	320 ft.	160 ft.	80 ft.
100mm Lens	1280 ft.	640 ft.	320 ft.	160 ft.
140mm Lens	2560 ft.	1280 ft.	640 ft.	320 ft.
200mm Lens	5120 ft.	2560 ft.	1280 ft.	640 ft.

Opening the aperture of the lens by two stops makes the Hyperfocal Distance twice as far from the lens. Conversely, closing the aperture by two stops reduces the Hyperfocal Distance by one half. This is a chart of Hyperfocal Distances of various focal length lenses at f/1, for a Circle of Confusion of 1/1000"; using the formula above, we can easily compute the Hyperfocal Distances for other apertures just by multiplying or dividing by two, as shown.

Values for apertures between those shown, or for focal lengths between those shown, can easily be roughly interpolated. For a Circle of Confusion of 1/500", divide all of the distances in this chart by two (a larger Circle of Confusion means a Hyperfocal Distance CLOSER to the Camera). If you can remember just the first column of distances, and the concept and the formulas above, you can construct a chart of your own at any time.

This chart gives rough values only. For really critical focus computations, please consult one of the commercially available Depth-of-Field calculators or printed chart.

Hyperfocal Distance has another interesting mathematical phenomenon. When the lens is focused on the Hyperfocal Distance, "H", the Depth-of-Field extends from infinity to 1/2 of "H". When the lens is focused at 1/2 of "H", the Depth-of-Field extends from the "H" to 1/3 of "H". When the lens is focused at 1/3 of "H", the Depth-of-Field extends from 1/2 "H" to 1/4 of "H". And this phenomenon continues, through all of the fractions of "H".

Zeiss-Planar 1.4/85 mm

Circle of confusion: 0.025 mm for 35 mm film

feet	1.4/T 1.4		2		2.8		4		5.6		8		11		feet
	from	to	from	to	from	to	from	to	from	to	from	to	from	to	
∞	672'	∞	470'	∞	336'	∞	235'	∞	168'	∞	118'	∞	86'	∞	∞
40'	37'10"	42'5"	37'	43'6"	36'	45'	34'7"	47'5"	32'10"	51'2"	30'6"	58'1"	28'	70'	40'
30'	28'9"	31'4"	28'4"	31'11"	27'9"	32'9"	26'10"	33'12"	25'10"	35'10"	24'4"	39'1"	22'9"	44'1"	30'
20'	19'5¼"	20'7"	19'2¾"	20'10"	18'11½"	21'1¾"	18'6¾"	21'8"	18'0½"	22'5"	17'4"	23'7½"	16'6"	25'4¼"	20'
15'	14'8¼"	15'4"	14'6¾"	15'5½"	14'5"	15'7½"	14'2¼"	15'11"	13'10½"	16'3¾"	13'5½"	16'11¼"	12'11½"	17'9½"	15'
12'6"	12'3½"	12'8¾"	12'2½"	12'9¾"	12'1"	12'11¼"	11'11¼"	13'1½"	11'8¾"	13'4¾"	11'5"	13'9¾"	11'0¾"	14'4½"	12'6"
10'	9'10¼"	10'1¾"	9'9¾"	10'2¼"	9'9"	10'3¼"	9'7¾"	10'4¾"	9'6"	10'6¾"	9'3½"	10'9¾"	9'0¾"	11'1¾"	10'
9'	8'10¾"	9'1¼"	8'10¼"	9'2"	8'9½"	9'2¾"	8'8½"	9'3¾"	8'7¼"	9'5¼"	8'5¼"	9'7¾"	8'2¾"	9'11"	9'
8'	7'11"	8'1"	7'10½"	8'1½"	7'10"	8'2"	7'9¼"	8'3"	7'8¼"	8'4¼"	7'6½"	8'6"	7'4¾"	8'8½"	8'
7'	6'11¼"	7'0¾"	6'11"	7'1"	6'10½"	7'1½"	6'10"	7'2¼"	6'9"	7'3¼"	6'8"	7'4½"	6'6½"	7'6½"	7'
6'	5'11½"	6'0½"	5'11¼"	6'0¾"	5'11"	6'1¼"	5'10½"	6'1½"	5'9¾"	6'2¼"	5'9"	6'3¼"	5'8"	6'4½"	6'
5'6"	5'5½"	5'6½"	5'5¼"	5'6¾"	5'5"	5'7"	5'4¾"	5'7¼"	5'4¼"	5'8"	5'3½"	5'8¾"	5'2½"	5'9¾"	5'6"
5'	4'11½"	5'0½"	4'11½"	5'0½"	4'11¼"	5'0¾"	4'11"	5'1"	4'10½"	5'1½"	4'10"	5'2¼"	4'9¼"	5'3"	5'
4'6"	4'5¾"	4'6¼"	4'5½"	4'6½"	4'5½"	4'6½"	4'5¼"	4'6¾"	4'4¾"	4'7¼"	4'4¼"	4'7¾"	4'3¾"	4'8½"	4'6"
4'	3'11¾"	4'0¼"	3'11¾"	4'0¼"	3'11½"	4'0½"	3'11¼"	4'0¾"	3'11"	4'1"	3'10¾"	4'1¼"	3'10¼"	4'2"	4'
3'9"	3'8¾"	3'9¼"	3'8¾"	3'9¼"	3'8½"	3'9½"	3'8½"	3'9½"	3'8¼"	3'9¾"	3'7¾"	3'10¼"	3'7½"	3'10¾"	3'9"
3'6"	3'5¾"	3'6¼"	3'5¾"	3'6¼"	3'5¾"	3'6¼"	3'5½"	3'6½"	3'5¼"	3'6¾"	3'5"	3'7"	3'4¾"	3'7½"	3,6"

Figure 9-9 Depth-of-Field Charts. Depth-of-Field charts, like this one from Arriflex and Zeiss, are very precise for specific focal lengths, stops, and distances, but interpolating for in-between settings is slow and inaccurate.

Depth-of-Field Calculators and Charts

There are many types and styles of Depth-of-Field Calculators and Charts available, from charts printed in the *American Cinematographer Manual*, to various calculator "wheels," to electronic hand-held computers with internal depth-of-field computer programs.

The charts in reference books, or those distributed by lens manufacturers, may be the most accurate, but are probably the slowest to use, and work only at specific focal lengths, stops, and focus distances. Any in-between focal lengths, stops, or focus distances must be "guestimated" or approximated. For example, the chart for the 50mm lens at f/4 for 10 feet might give you a depth-of-field range of from 8'11" to 11'5". But suppose you have a zoom lens and are at a focal length setting of 53mm instead of 50mm. Suppose further that you are shooting at a stop of f/3.8 instead of f/4, and that the subject is 9'9" away, instead of 10'. What now? Interpolating any or all of the three factors makes any sort of accuracy or reliability very difficult, as well as very slow. You may get faster and more accurate at guestimating with practice, but why bother when there are better and faster means available?

The "wheel"-type calculators are the most commonly used and most practical. The first one I remember was made by Birns & Sawyer, an equipment dealer and rental house in Los Angeles. There were two separate wheels, one for 35mm and one for 16mm. To use this type of wheel calculator, choose the appropriate focal length scale, line up the arrow with the focus distance, and read above the f/stops indicated on scales left and right of the arrow index. This type of wheel reduces greatly the amount of guestimating that must be done, by allowing the focus index arrow to be set between footage marks, and by allowing the reading between f/stops. The only estimating required is for in-between focal length lenses. There are scales for 40mm and 50mm, for example, but not 47mm. The more recent Guild-Kelly Calculator is of this type, as well.

Another style of wheel-type calculator is the Samuelson SAMCINE Mk. II Calculator. This calculator not only gives the user a choice of three different circles of confusion (0.001", 0.0007", and 0.0005"), but also solves the focal length problem by allowing the user to set in-between focal lengths on another scale while one part of the calculator slides up and down against another. The calculator is made of heavy white plexiglas instead of the thin plastic sheets of other wheels for more durability.

The SAMCINE II also has different scales for prime lenses and zoom lenses, because of the increased distance of the nodal point of zoom lenses in front of the film plane, compared with prime lenses, and, as if these advanced features were not enough, this is the only calculator I have seen which even mentions T/stops and allows accurate readings for lenses that have only T/stops. The SAMCINE II allows the user to "dial-in" the difference between the T/stop and the f/stop scales on the particular lenses being used, for even greater accuracy.

I have been using this type for over fifteen years with absolutely no complaints. I've had one stolen from me, and broken one (run over by the dolly), and I have worn

Focus **209**

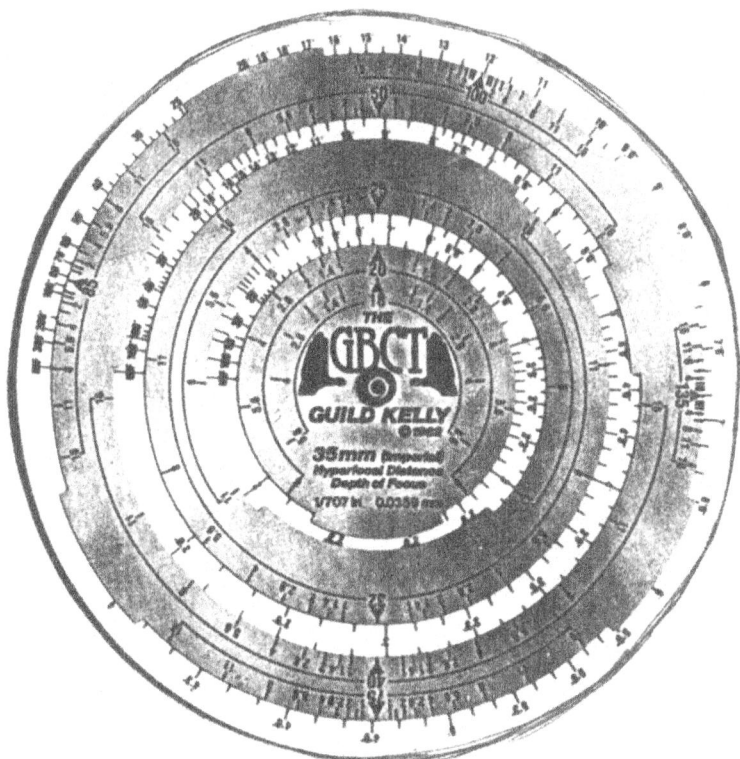

Figure 9-10 Depth-of-Field Wheel Chart. The Depth-of-Field Wheel Chart, in this case the "Guild Kelly," is compact, fast, and not expensive. It is easier to use than the printed charts, and allows quick compensation for in-between distances and stops, but not focal lengths.

off some of the lines on another through use, but I just buy new ones. The SAMCINE gets my vote for the best and fastest all around Depth-of-Field calculator.

The wheel calculators often include other useful calculator scales, for such information as field of view for particular lenses, running times, ASA/footcandle requirement scales, filter factor/aperture, shutter angle/aperture, and frame rate/aperture compensators, etc.

Several pocket-computer-type calculators have been recently introduced into the market. They allow the user to punch in to the built-in keyboard the desired Circle of Confusion, Focal Length, Distance, and Stop, and display the near and far limits of Depth-of-Field, in the user's choice of feet and inches or metric. The computer-type calculators even include such features as a time of sunrise and sunset program, exposure compensation calculator, color temperature information, image size and speed calculations, macro exposure charts, a payroll program for computing time

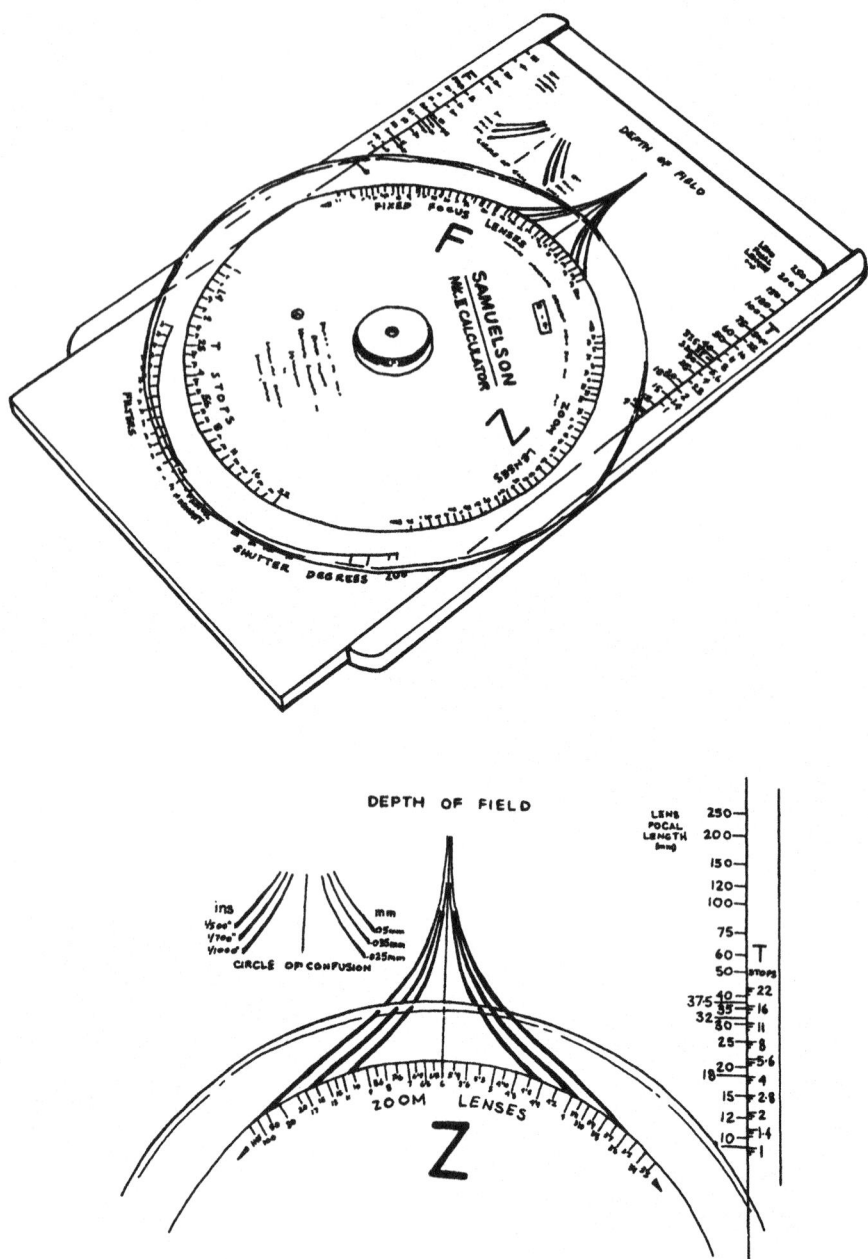

Figure 9-11 Samcine Mk. II Calculator. It is by far the most accurate, fastest, and most durable Depth-of-Field calculator on the market. Camera Assistants sometimes refer to it as the "Prayer Wheel." The detail insert shows a zoom lens set at 25mm at T/8, with the focus scale set at 6 feet. The Depth-of-Field, at a Circle of Confusion of 1/500" (.002"), would be from 3'7" to 50'. At a Circle of Confusion of 1/1000" (.001"), the Depth-of-Field would be from 4'5" to 10'.

cards, and many other useful functions. They have the added disadvantages of being rather expensive, requiring batteries, being fairly delicate, being fairly slow compared to other focus calculators, and not being waterproof, but for some Camera Assistants, those who just have to have every new gadget and toy, they are terrific.

Another problem with the printed charts and calculator wheels is that every source has their own idea of what the Circle of Confusion diameter should be for different filming formats:

EQUIVALENT CIRCLES OF CONFUSION (ROUNDED OFF TO USABLE NUMBERS)

Inch Fractions	Inch Decimal	Metric
1/2000"	0.0005"	0.0125mm
1/1400"	0.0007"	0.018mm
1/1000"	0.001"	0.025mm
1/707"	0.0014"	0.035mm
1/500"	0.002"	0.050mm

COMMONLY USED DEPTH-OF-FIELD CALCULATORS AND CHARTS AND THE CIRCLES OF CONFUSION RECOMMENDED FOR 16MM AND 35MM PHOTOGRAPHY

Chart	16mm	35mm
Samuelson SAMCINE Mk.II	0.001"	0.0014" & 0.002"
American Cinematographer Manual		
4th and 5th Edit. (1973 and 1980)	0.001"	0.002"
6th and 7th Edit. (1986 and 1993)	0.0006"	0.001"
Guild Kelly (older model)	0.001"	0.002"
Guild Kelly (newer model)	0.0005"	0.0014"
Birns & Sawyer Cine Calculator	0.001"	0.002" up to 50mm; 0.0017" for 75 & 100mm
Zeiss Super-Speed Lens Charts	0.0007"	0.001"
Angenieux Lens Charts	0.0012"	0.0012"
Rank Optics Lens Charts	0.0005"	0.00105"

The Samuelson SAMCINE Mk. II Calculator, my personal favorite, makes no real recommendations as to which scale to use, but offers the choice of 1/1000", 1/700", and 1/500". I have decided on my own to use 1/1000" for 16mm filming, 1/700" for 35mm destined for big screen theatrical release, and 1/500" for 35mm destined for television (commercials, series, or TV movies). These numbers have served me well for many years.

Whichever chart or calculator you use, you can adapt the distances given to other Circles of Confusion by reading off the Depth-of-Field as if using other apertures.

For example, if your chart shows Depth-of-Field for a 1/1000" Circle of Confusion, and you want to read the Depth at 1/700" read the figures opposite the aperture one stop smaller than your shooting aperture. A LARGER Circle of Confusion results in MORE Depth-of-Field, so read the chart at a SMALLER aperture.

If your chart shows 1/1000" and you want the figures for 1/1400", read the scale at one stop larger than your shooting aperture. A SMALLER Circle of Confusion results in LESS Depth-of-Field, so read the chart at a LARGER aperture.

Each of the figures listed in the Equivalent Circles of Confusion chart above are one stop apart on the charts and calculators. Depth-of-Field for a 1/1000" Circle of Confusion at f/2.8 is identical to Depth-of-Field for 1/700" Circle of Confusion at f/4, and to Depth-of-Field for 1/500" Circle of Confusion at f/5.6 and so on, for the figures listed above.

Camera Lens Depth-of-Field Calculator

Camera lenses themselves can be used as Depth-of-Field calculators. This is a trick I have used often on the job, to give me a quick idea of what is in focus and what is out of focus, during the shot, without having to consult the charts or calculators every time.

The readings are a bit crude, and should not be absolutely depended on, but for a quick, rough idea of where the Depth-of-Field is at a particular shot, this trick works wonders.

You may have noticed on certain 35mm still camera lenses that there are Depth-of-Field indicators alongside the focus scale index. These are often pairs of colored lines on either side of the focus scale index, and colored the same color as the aperture scale number on the aperture ring. For example, if the "2.8" is colored in yellow on your still camera lens, anything between the yellow lines on the focus scale for this lens will be in focus at that aperture.

This same principle can be applied to movie lenses. Using a chart or calculator, determine the Depth-of-Field for that lens at a particular aperture, at a specific distance. With the lens set at that distance, place two small triangles of camera tape as pointers, or two dots of white marker ink, or two white grease pencil marks, opposite the Depth-of-Field limits on the focus scale as indicated on your calculator. Now wherever you set the focus on that lens, as long as you are at the same stop, the marks you have added will show the approximate Depth-of-Field. If you are shooting a lot of the project at that aperture, you will have a built-in Depth-of-Field calculator whenever that lens is up. Do the same for your other lenses.

For example, if you have a 50mm lens up, and are shooting a lot at or near T/4 on your project, then consulting the calculator, we find that for a 50mm lens at T/4, and at a distance of 20 feet, the Depth-of-Field extends from about 15 feet to about 30 feet. So if our lens is set at 20 feet, then by adding two marks opposite 15 feet and 30 feet, we now have a rough Depth-of-Field calculator for all shooting at T/4, at whatever distances might be required. If we turn the focus knob to 5 feet, for example, the pointers we added will show an approximate Depth-of-Field of between 4'8" and 5'5".

This will not work, of course, on a zoom lens, because changing the focal length (zooming) will change the Depth-of-Field situation, and hence the spacing of the pointers; however, for prime lenses, or when using a zoom lens but not actually

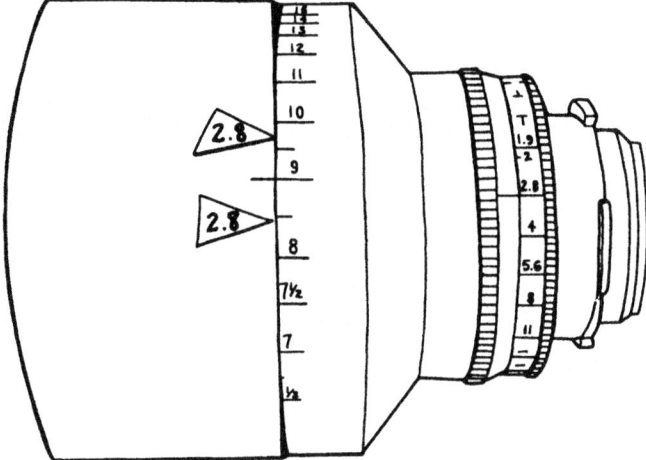

Figure 9-12 Camera Lens as Depth-of-Field Calculator. A very handy trick to know is to use the lens itself as a depth-of-field calculator. With a Depth-of-Field calculator or chart, determine the Depth-of-Field for a particular lens focal length and T/stop. With triangles of camera tape, mark the limits of Depth-of-Field on either side of the focus index on the lens. Wherever the focus barrel is turned, the tape triangles indicate the approximate Depth-of-Field at that T/stop. This will not work with zoom lenses if the focal length is changed during the shot. Remember to move the indicators appropriately if the aperture is changed.

zooming during the shot, this trick can save you time, a very precious commodity on the set, and anxiety, also a precious commodity.

Following Focus

Since we are making "Moving Pictures," our focus targets will often be moving, and focus must be adjusted during the shot to keep the main subjects or targets in focus at all times. This is called "Following Focus" or "Pulling Focus," and is a prime duty of the Camera Assistants, specifically the First Camera Assistant, on the set.

Most of the rest of the Camera Assistant's duties are accomplished while the camera is switched off. Following Focus happens while the camera is running, and nothing else going on around the camera is as important as the focus, at least for the Camera Assistant.

In order to follow the focus accurately, the Camera Assistant needs four things:

1. To be close enough to the camera to reach the lens barrel or follow-focus knob,
2. To be able to see the focus scale or marks placed on the lens barrel or focus disk,
3. To be able to see the focus target move through the set, and
4. To be able to see the natural landmarks and/or marks placed as focus references in the set.

These four conditions may not seem like a lot to ask, but it is amazing how many obstacles will appear in the Camera Assistant's path, making some of these conditions hard to achieve.

The camera may be placed so close to a wall or other obstruction that the Camera Assistant will not be able to work on the camera's left side, and must work the camera's right side, known as the "Dumb Side" of the camera, because there are often no switches, dials, counters, or other useful information on that side. On some lenses there are not even any focus or aperture scales on the "Dumb Side." Cameras are built for the Camera Assistant to work on the left side. That's where the tachometer, and the footage counter, the switch, the camera door, and other things are. The Camera Assistant is at a severe disadvantage working on the right side.

The Panavision Platinum and the Arriflex 535 cameras have finally acknowledged that sometimes the Assistant must work on the dumb side, and have made the digital display two-sided. With these cameras, at least, the tachometer and the footage counter are visible on both sides.

Some camera systems have a right-hand follow-focus knob as one of the standard accessories, and some lenses are marked for focus on the right side, or can at least be rotated in their mounts to allow positioning the marks on the right side, but not all.

Sometimes the D.P. may want to position a light right up against the left side of the camera, forcing the Assistant to work on the other side, or an actor may have to make an entrance or exit close to the camera on the left side, or an actor may have to be close off-camera left delivering off-camera dialogue in order to give the correct eye-line for the actor being photographed. Any of these things may force the Assistant to work on the "Dumb" side.

Several camera systems make "Focus Extensions," also known as "Whips," flexible shafts with a focus knob attached, that attach to the focus knob extending the reach of the Camera Assistant. A second one can sometimes even be attached to the first one to further extend the Assistant's reach.

Sometimes the Camera Assistant must position himself or herself behind the Camera Operator, and peek over the Operator's shoulder, in order to see the marks on the lens. The focus extension allows the Assistant to turn the focus knob from this position.

Finding a satisfactory place to work is of great importance to the Camera Assistant. Standing comfortably next to the camera is meaningless if the Assistant cannot see the actor or the floor marks placed in the set. Find a place where you can work, and where you can see.

While on the subject of Camera Assistant positioning, if the Camera Assistant stands exactly perpendicular to the camera axis, looking at the lens, then the action is taking place 90° to the Assistant's left. Turning the head back and forth 90° to the action and then back to the lens is time consuming. If possible, stand closer to the Operator, or over the Operator's left shoulder, and look slightly left for the lens and further left for the action. Now the angle between the action and the lens is maybe 30 to 45 degrees, which can be covered by simply flicking the eyes back and forth, instead of having to actually turn the head. This will save the Camera Assistant time and effort, and will make difficult shots easier.

Focus **215**

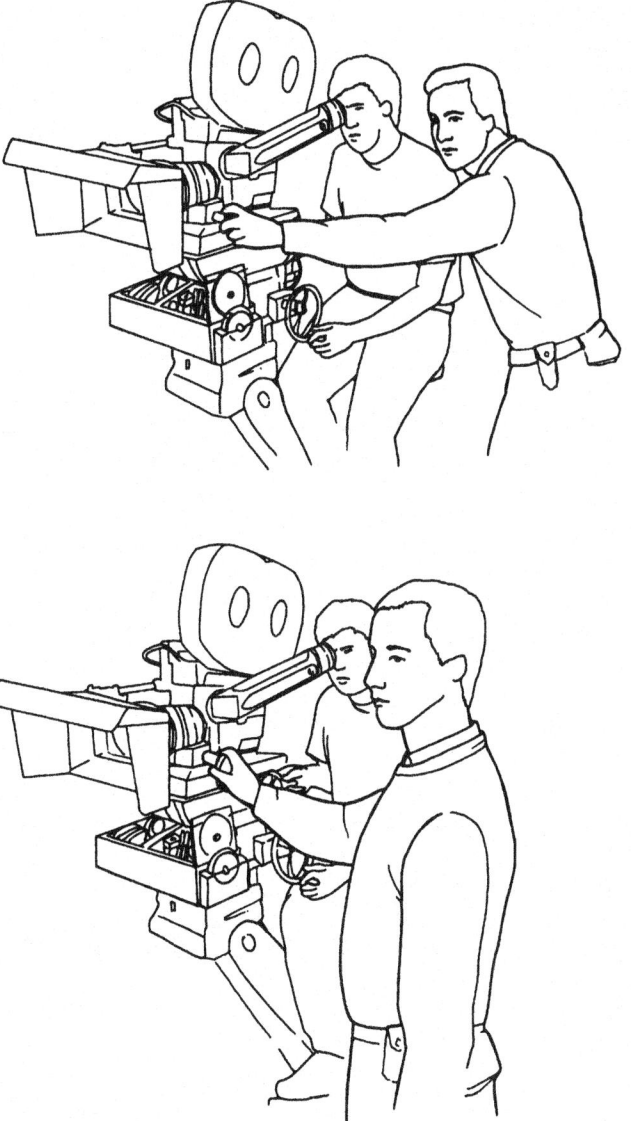

Figure 9-13 Camera Assistant Positioning. The Camera Assistant on the bottom has to turn his head to see the actors and the marks, then turn back to see the lens. This might be fine for most filming, but with fast-moving actors or vehicles, or long lenses, or critical focus situations, this is too slow. The Camera Assistant on the top is in such a position behind the Operator's shoulder that he need only flick his eyes back and forth to see both the actors and the lens, saving time and getting better focus.

Choices: Who Should be in Focus?

For 90 percent of all motion picture photography, the choice of who or what should be in focus during a particular shot is obvious, and does not need to be discussed with anyone.

With a single target in frame, focus should be kept on that target, wherever it moves during the shot. For multiple targets, most of the time it is possible to "Split" the focus between them, keeping the most important targets within the Depth-of-Field for that particular set of circumstances: Focal Length, Aperture, and Target Distance.

For that remaining 10%, however, some doubt remains. If there are multiple targets, spaced so that they cannot be contained within the available Depth-of-Field, or if the background or foreground of a particular shot are as important or more important than the focus target, or if two actors have dialogue but are placed too far apart to be included within the available Depth-of-Field, then choices must be made.

Before consulting with the Director of Photography, the final arbiter of such matters, there are some questions the Camera Assistant can ask himself or herself that might solve the problem, specifically when the shot includes more than one person:

1. Who is facing the camera? The audience has a tendency to watch the people facing the camera, and therefore facing the audience. The tendency is to establish "eye contact" with the target, even though the target is only a photographed image. It is more acceptable for the back of someone's head to be out of focus than for someone's face to be out of focus.
2. Who has the dialogue? The audience has a natural tendency to watch the person speaking. It is generally more acceptable for someone not speaking to be out of focus than for someone speaking.
3. Who is getting the largest paycheck? If you haven't already made up your mind about who should be in focus, this question should be the clincher. If a famous movie star is in a scene with a bit player or extra, like a cab driver or waiter or doorman, even if the bit player is facing the camera or has the dialogue, the audience's attention is on the star. "Stay with the money!" (or "Stay with the Lowest Number on the Call Sheet," where the Cast has been assigned a number based on their status or importance to the project, and are listed in numerical order) is often heard on the set when discussing focus.

If there is still some doubt about who to keep in focus, then confer with the Director of Photography. If the Director of Photography does not have the answer (this will not happen often), then perhaps the D.P. will want to confer with the director. Eventually, the instructions will come back to the Camera Assistant.

There are other circumstances where focus choices must be made. For example, if the actor is going to make a clean entrance into the shot, should the focus be racked from the background to the actor at the beginning of the shot, or should the focus be kept at the plane the actor is to enter into? There are reasons to do both, and the choice is not at all clear cut. Confer with the D.P.

If the shot starts with a close-up of a closed door, and the door opens to reveal the actor, should the door be in focus until the actor actually appears? If the actor is pointing a gun at the camera, for example, should the focus be on the gun, or on the actor's face? Confer with the D.P. when in doubt.

Splitting Focus

Splitting focus between two or more focus targets is often the best method of dealing with multiple targets. Splitting focus involves two steps; first, and most important, making sure that the various targets in their various positions still fit securely within the Depth-of-Field available in that situation (and with a safety margin!).

Once the Assistant is ABSOLUTELY CERTAIN that the available Depth-of-Field is sufficient for the particular shot being planned, then the placement of the actual focus plane (where the lens is focused) must be considered. If two actors are at 6' and 9' from the camera, where should the Assistant place the focus on the lens? At

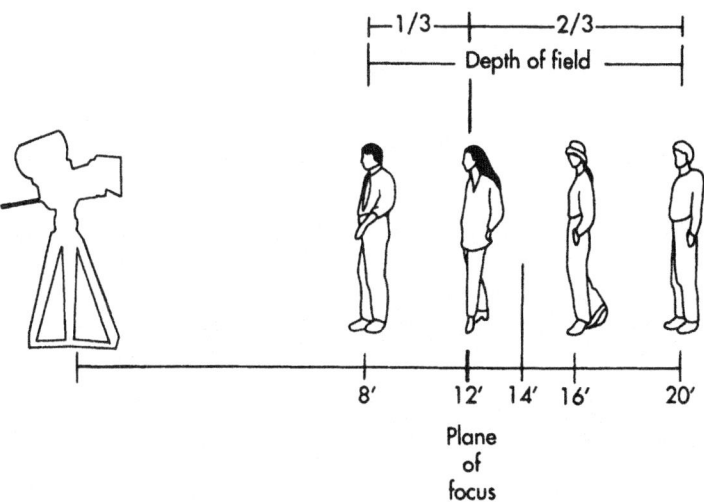

Figure 9-14 Split Focus—1/3 and 2/3 Rule. Depth-of-Field is less closer to the camera, so there is LESS Depth-of-Field IN FRONT of the Plane of Focus than BEHIND the Plane of Focus. The way this works out mathematically is that 1/3 of the Depth-of-Field range is in front of the Plane of Focus, and 2/3 of the Depth-of-Field range is behind the Plane of Focus. In this example, the best focus setting to hold the four subjects within the Depth-of-Field would be 12 feet, NOT 14 feet, even though 14 feet is mathematically halfway between the limits of Depth-of-Field.

218 THE CAMERA ASSISTANT

7'6"? That may be halfway between 6' and 9' mathematically, but in this case it is the wrong answer.

There is always less Depth-of-Field in front of the plane of focus (towards the camera), than behind it (away from the camera). The proportion between the two is 1:2; in other words, "One-third in front, Two-thirds behind." One-third of the available Depth-of-Field will be found in front of the plane of focus, and two-thirds will be behind the plane of focus.

So in our example above, the focus should be placed at 7', allowing one foot in front and two feet behind, to assure that the two actors are EQUALLY in focus, not "Favoring" either one at the expense of the other.

There will be times when one actor or target must be "favored." For example, if the available Depth-of-Field for a situation extended from 6' to 8', and the two ac-

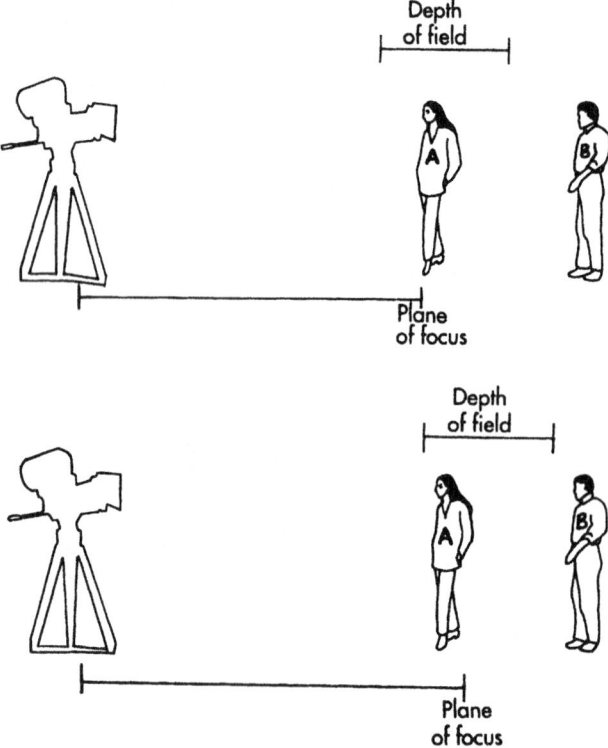

Figure 9-15 Favoring Focus. In this example, Actor A and Actor B are too far apart to keep both in focus with a split. In the top drawing, the focus is set solidly on Actor A, so Actor B is quite a bit out of focus. Another option would be to set the focus "favoring" Actor A, but pushing the depth-of-field as far toward Actor B as possible, so that Actor B is only slightly soft.

tors needed to be at 5' and 8' from the camera, respectively, then they are too far apart to both be included in the available Depth-of-Field. The Camera Assistant has three choices in this situation. Focus on actor A, focus on actor B, or split the focus between the actors, favoring one or the other.

If the focus is placed at 7', actor A at 8' will be well within the Depth-of-Field, and therefore in sharp focus, and actor B will be soft. But actor B at 5', will be in sharper focus with the focus set at 7' than with the focus set dead on actor A at 8'. This is a split favoring actor A, but still pushing the focus toward actor B, allowing B to be slightly soft as opposed to very soft.

Before deciding on this course of action, discuss your plan with the Director of Photography to be sure it's Okay. The D.P. may ask that the focus be left on actor A, or may suggest that the focus be set at 7'6", favoring actor A slightly more that if it were left at 7'. Often the D.P., in this situation, will look through the camera, with the aperture set at the shooting stop, and set a focus split by eye.

This is the best way, as none of the charts or calculators or diagrams on paper can substitute for the creative judgment of someone actually looking through the camera.

Four Categories of Shot Focus

There are four different categories of focus possibilities for motion picture photography, described below, each causing different problems and different levels of complexity for the Camera Assistant attempting to follow focus.

They may work in combination within a particular shot, but at any given moment on a shot, only one of these types will be in effect. Solve each part of the shot in turn, and combine the solutions for the complete shot. I call this process formulating the "Focus Plan" for the shot.

Type 1: The first, and easiest for the Camera Assistant, is when the camera is stationary, and the focus target is stationary. The method for dealing with the focus is obvious. Measure the distance to the target, either with a tape measure or by eye through the lens, set the focus accordingly, and be ready for the target to move unexpectedly. Murphy's Law demands that nothing is ever simple for long. If your target is a mountain or a building, it may be unlikely to move during the shot, but always be prepared for an earthquake.

If there are a number of targets within the shot, at different distances from the camera, the Camera Assistant must decide which are the most important, and where the actual focus should be placed. It is often possible to use the Depth-of-Field available for that particular situation to keep all of the desired targets in focus. The actual focus may even be placed between targets, thereby positioning the available Depth-of-Field to cover all of the desired targets. There may not be a target at the actual "plane of focus," but the overall shot might be in focus because of the Depth-of-Field.

Sometimes, for long distance scenic landscape shots, or city skyline establishing shots, the Hyperfocal Distance may be the right place to set the focus. The

220 THE CAMERA ASSISTANT

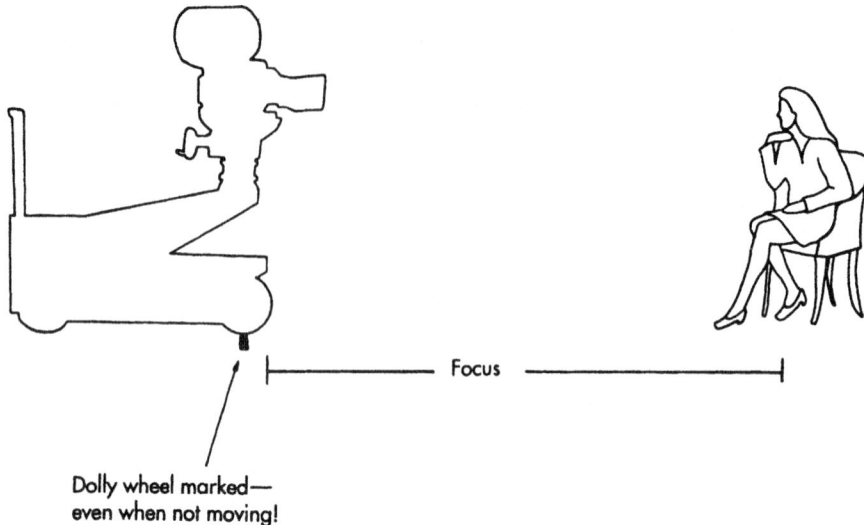

Figure 9-16 Type 1 Shot—Camera and Target Stationary. The easiest type of shot, with the Camera and Target both stationary. Just measure the distance to the target and set the focus on the lens. Just to be safe, mark the dolly wheel and the subject anyway, and be prepared for one or the other or both to move!

Hyperfocal Distance gives the MAXIMUM possible Depth-of-Field for any shooting situation with distant targets.

Type 2: The second type of shot has the camera stationary and the focus target moving. Focus marks can be set on the floor or ground, distances measured using the tape measure for most lenses, or through the lens ("Eye Focus") for long lenses or sometimes zoom lenses zoomed all the way to the telephoto end.

For lenses up to 100mm or so (for 35mm photography) tape focus is usually good enough. For lenses longer than about 100mm, eye focus is usually better.

Marks can be made on the focus wheel disk, or on the lens barrel, corresponding to the marks set on the floor. The floor marks can be labeled with the number of feet from the camera, preferably using distances appearing on the lens focus scale for better accuracy, or just numbered to correspond to the lens barrel or focus wheel marks, as in Mark #1, Mark #2, etc.

When focus marks cannot be placed on the floor because they might be seen by the lens during the shot, and cannot be "camouflaged" by making the marks a similar color to the background, then "landmarks" can be used—a chair, a doorway, a tree, a fire hydrant—anything that will not be moving during the shot, and which the focus target will be passing near during the shot.

This is often the preferred solution, with the marks on the lens barrel or focus disk coded with some easy-to-remember indication of which mark is which. "T" for

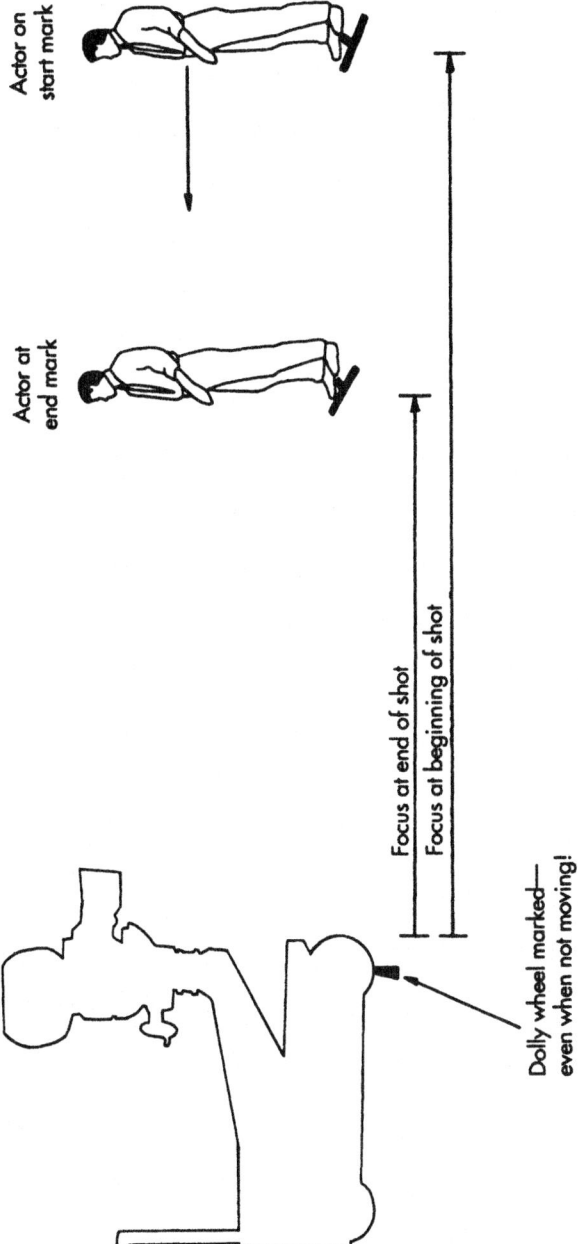

Figure 9-17 Type 2 Shot—Camera Stationary, Target Moving. When the Camera is not moving, measure the distances to the target at the beginning of the shot, and again at the end of the shot, and adjust the lens setting on the lens as the target moves from start position to end position. If necessary, get intermediate measurements for positions in between the start and end marks. Mark the dolly wheel anyway!

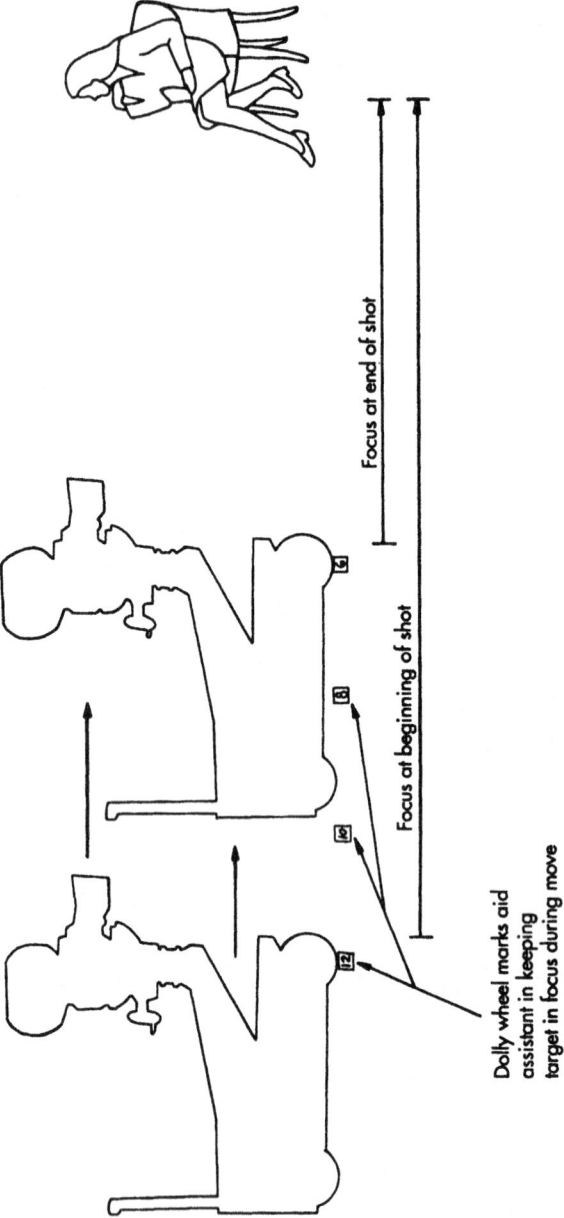

Figure 9-18 Type 3 Shot—Camera Moving, Target Stationary. When the target is still and the camera is moving, the floor in the path of the dolly can be marked in several places, where the wheel nearest the Camera Assistant passes the marks. Use as few marks as you feel comfortable with, and use the same distances for marks as are found on the focus scale of the lens.

"Tree," "H" for "Hydrant," "D" for "Doorway," "M" for "Mailbox," etc. Then as the target passes each of the landmarks, the focus can be set for the nearby landmark.

Type 3:   In this type of shot, the camera is moving but the focus target is stationary. While more difficult than TYPE 2 shots, at least the floor can be marked for the dolly, or the Steadicam, or even for the hand-held camera operator, so some marks are possible.

It is a good habit to get into always to mark one of the dolly wheels, usually the one closest to where the Camera Assistant is walking, on the floor, just as a check on the final dolly position. It doesn't do any good to have the lens on a particular focus mark if the dolly is not in the right place, and if you can't tell how far away from the mark it is, so that corrections and adjustments can be made.

Type 4:   This is by far the most difficult type of shot for the Camera Assistant, as both the camera and the target are moving, and they may not even be moving in the same direction. This shot is much more difficult because there is often no place to put a mark that means anything.

This type of shot depends much more on intuition and experience (and a bit of luck) than the other types of shots. But there are ways of positioning in-between marks where they can be of use, and for creating marks that move with you.

If the camera is on a dolly, and the dolly is on track, then in-between marks can often be positioned along the dolly track, at intervals, and marks placed for the focus target, for where that target should be at those specific dolly positions. This method can give you references during the shot, and indicate, for example whether or not the dolly is moving ahead or behind the target. If the dolly gets to the dolly wheel mark before the target gets to its mark, then the dolly is ahead of the target, and the focus should be adjusted accordingly.

A very common example of a Type 4 shot is dallying ahead of an actor or two, with the camera looking back at him or them, maintaining somewhat the same distance ahead. Although the camera and targets are moving together, in the same direction and at the same speed, there are still going to be changes in focus, because actors do not always walk at the same speed, and because the grip has a difficult job changing the speed of the dolly, because of its great weight and momentum. The focus will change, minutely. If the aperture is large, the focal length long, and the distance close, then Depth-of-Field will be extremely limited, and the focus must be constantly adjusted by the Camera Assistant.

Marks on the ground in this situation are mostly useless, so make some moving marks for yourself. The actors will generally be walking parallel to the dolly track, but OUTSIDE of it, to minimize the chance of tripping over the track or the wedges used to level the track, and also to minimize the chance of seeing the track in the shot behind the actors.

A string or cord, tied on to the dolly and trailing behind the dolly as it moves, and with bits of tape added to the cord as focus marks, will stay out from under the actors feet as they walk, yet will still provide the Camera Assistant with a traveling focus scale, and make the job of following focus much easier.

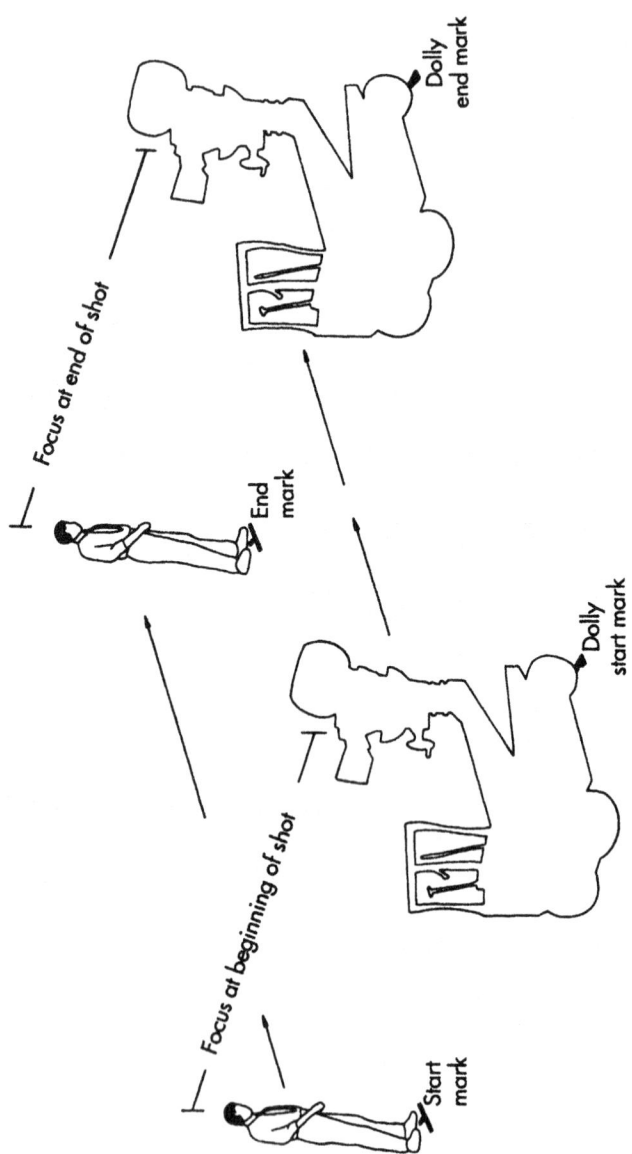

Figure 9-19 Type 4 Shot—Camera and Target Moving. When the camera and the target are both moving, marks are difficult to obtain, except for the beginning and end of the shot, because of the difficulty in getting the dolly to its mark and the actor to his mark at precisely the same time. It is sort of like putting a mark on the side of the boat so you know where to go fishing. This is the most difficult type of shot for the Camera Assistant following focus.

Focus **225**

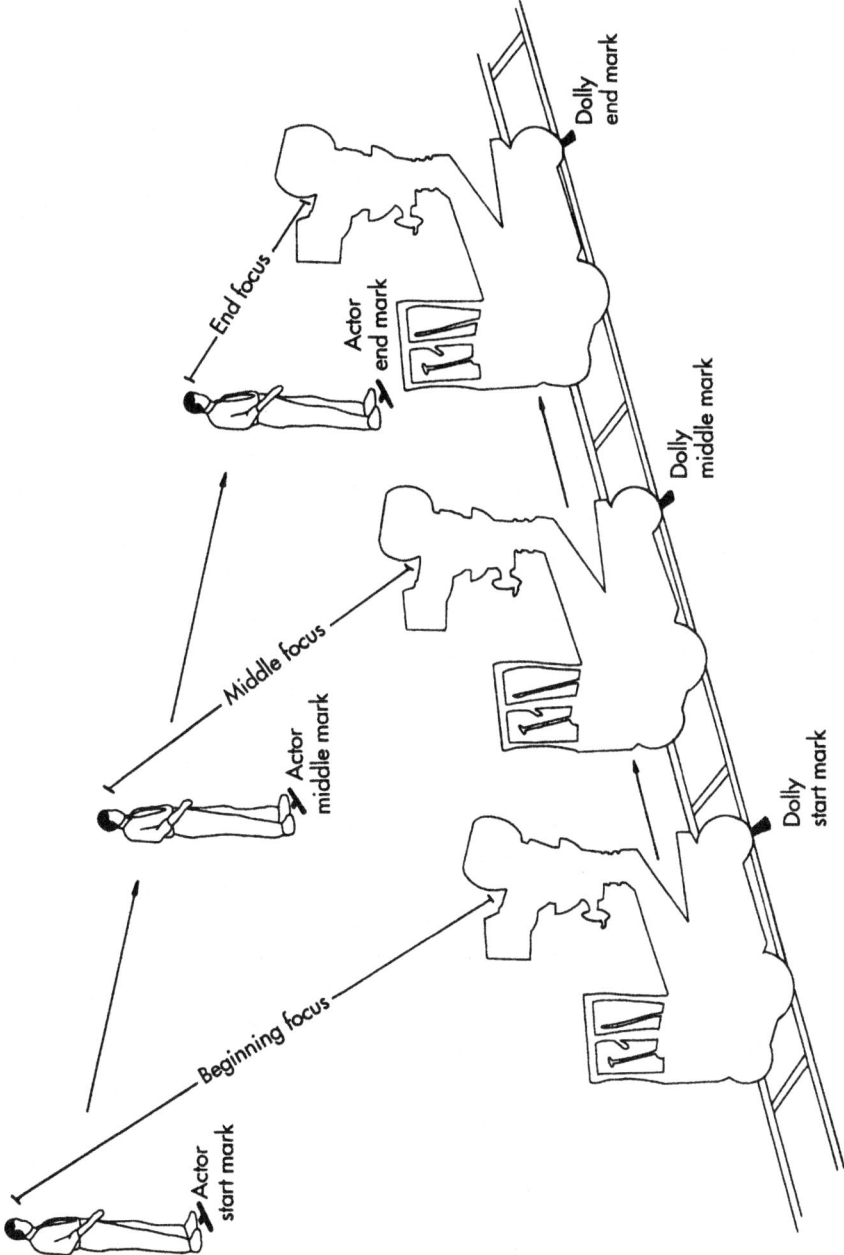

Figure 9-20 In-Between Focus Marks. It may be possible to mark the actor and the dolly in the middle of their planned moves, but be prepared to do some quick estimating and arithmetic. If the dolly reaches its mark before the actor reaches his mark, the Assistant must judge how much to add or subtract to the measured distance, and adjust the lens accordingly.

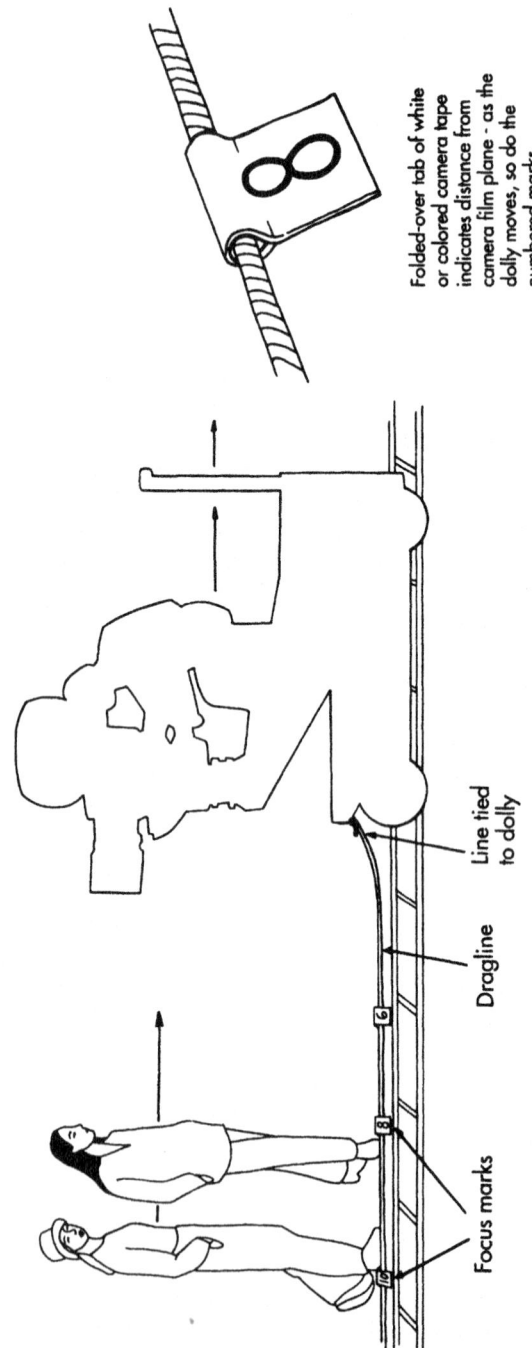

Figure 9-21 Dragline Focus Marks. Floor focus marks don't mean much if the camera is moving. The best solution is often to drag those floor marks along with the dolly, by attaching them to a "dragline" of thin cord (called "trick line" and found on most sets). Obviously this will not work if the actors are leading the dolly instead of following, or if the line gets tangled in the actors' feet.

I call this the "dragline." If the bits of tape are added to the cord at specific distances, such as 6', 8', 10', 12', etc., then as the actors are next to the 8' mark, the Camera Assistant need only set the lens focus at 8' to have the actor in focus.

This method works quite well under certain circumstances. Without dolly track, and looking straight back at the actors instead of at an angle, however, the cord is likely to be stepped on by the actor, disrupting the shot. Care must be taken to position the cord out of everyone's way. This method will not work if the dolly and the actors are on a convergent or divergent course, or if the dolly is following the actors instead of preceding them.

On one sequence, shot in a roller skating rink, I had to solve the problem another way. The dolly was to precede the actors, who were on roller skates, but there were other skaters who were scheduled to skate between the camera and our target actors, as foreground crosses, making the use of the dragline dangerous and therefore impossible. But I needed at least one traveling mark, because we were shooting with the 85mm Zeiss Super-Speed lens, wide open at T/1.4, and Depth-of-Field was extremely limited. To solve the problem, I took a flashlight with a very narrow beam, and attached it to my French Flag arm with tape. Then I attached the arm to the cam-

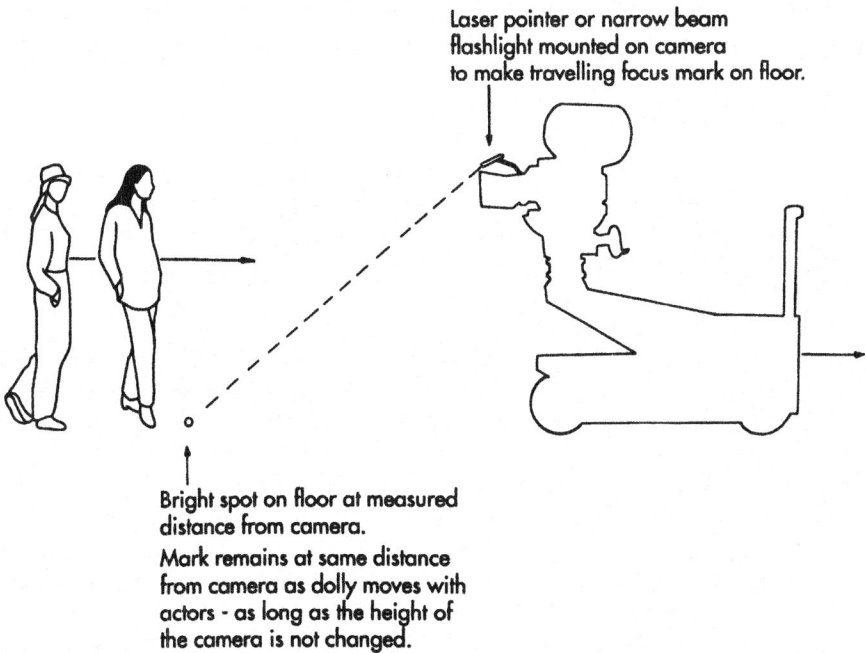

Figure 9-22 Flashlight/Laser Pointer Focus Marks. Sometimes, when floor marks are impractical or impossible, a single focus reference mark can be created with a laser pointer or spot beam flashlight mounted on the camera. The spot of light can be positioned at a specific measured distance from the camera, and that mark will travel with the camera, at that same distance.

era, and using the tape measure, I aimed the beam to strike the floor between the actors at eight feet from the camera, giving me a mark that would travel with the camera, always showing where eight feet from the camera is. And it didn't interfere with the foreground crosses.

It was easier by far to estimate the small differences more and less than eight feet than to estimate their exact distances from the camera. The shot was not perfectly in focus at all times, but it was right more often than it would have been without that traveling mark.

There have come onto the market recently small battery-powered laser units about the size of a penlight flashlight. They are used for pointers in lectures and demonstrations, and work by projecting a bright red point of light that can be used to highlight charts and slide shows. I recently had the opportunity to use one of these units for a long dolly shot in a hospital corridor. I set up the laser on the side of my front box, pointing to the floor ten feet away from the film plane of the camera as we were dollying ahead of two people walking quickly down the hallway. This gave me a single traveling mark, and the shot was easily kept in focus. The red dot of laser light is bright enough to be seen in all but the brightest sun, and serves to make this type of shot much easier. The Dolly Grip can also use the dot as a reference in attempting to maintain the same distance ahead of the actors with the camera and dolly. As long as the height of the camera is not changed during the shot, that dot of light will remain at whatever distance the Assistant has set it for.

Focus Marks

There are three kinds of focus marks: (1) those placed for actors' start and stop marks, (2) those placed on the floor at specific distances from the camera in the set, and (3) those marked on the lens barrel or focus disk. Any of these marks can be used separately, or they can be used in combination, to help the Camera Assistant keep the target in focus.

Actors' Marks The actors' start and end marks, and possibly one or more in-between marks, will have been set during the blocking of the scene, before lighting and rehearsal begin. More on these marks in the chapter on shooting procedures.

Floor Marks Actors marks are often not enough for the Camera Assistant, so additional floor marks are placed, usually small tabs of white tape, sometimes with the distance from the camera written directly on them. If chalk is used, the distance is often written near the mark, readable from the camera. As the actor passes over these intermediate marks, the focus can be set at those distances.

It is almost always better to set these marks at the distances from the camera that appear as distinct and specific markings on the lens focus scale. For example, if a lens has focus scale markings of 20', 15', 12', 10', and 8', it is better to place floor tape marks at those distances, rather than at 18', 14'6", 11'3", and 9'. If your floor marks correspond to exact scale markings, then the focus at those points is more accurate than if the Camera Assistant has to guess at where in-between marks are, especially with a fast-moving target.

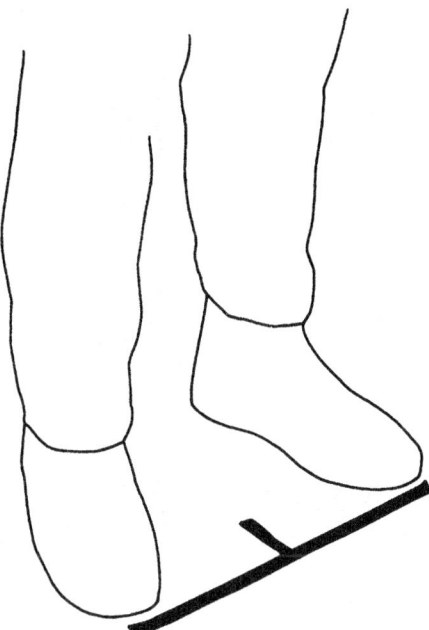

Figure 9-23 Actors' Marks. T-shaped Actors' Mark shows actors where to stand and which direction to face, and gives the Assistant a good focus reference.

A general rule for focus markings is to keep them as simple as possible, and to set as few of them as may be necessary, to minimize confusion when the camera is rolling. The faster the target is moving, the fewer marks are necessary, as the Camera Assistant will not have the time to shift his or her eyes back and forth for each of a large number of marks.

Since the Depth-of-Field decreases as the target gets closer to the camera, the Camera Assistant needs more marks close to the camera, and fewer marks farther away.

I prefer in most cases to look at the lens, and to allow peripheral vision, which is very sensitive to motion, to tell me when the various marks are being passed over.

If the marks are visible in the camera viewfinder, then they must be hidden somehow—either moved to areas not seen by the camera but still visible to the Camera Assistant, or made small enough that they are not recognizable in the viewfinder as marks but are still visible to the Assistant, or else colored or camouflaged to blend in with the surroundings yet still be recognizable to the Assistant, and visible to the actor.

You will be surprised what you can get away with. An actor standing over or near a mark can often see the mark quite clearly, yet in the viewfinder, and on the screen, the mark may be so small or well camouflaged that it is invisible.

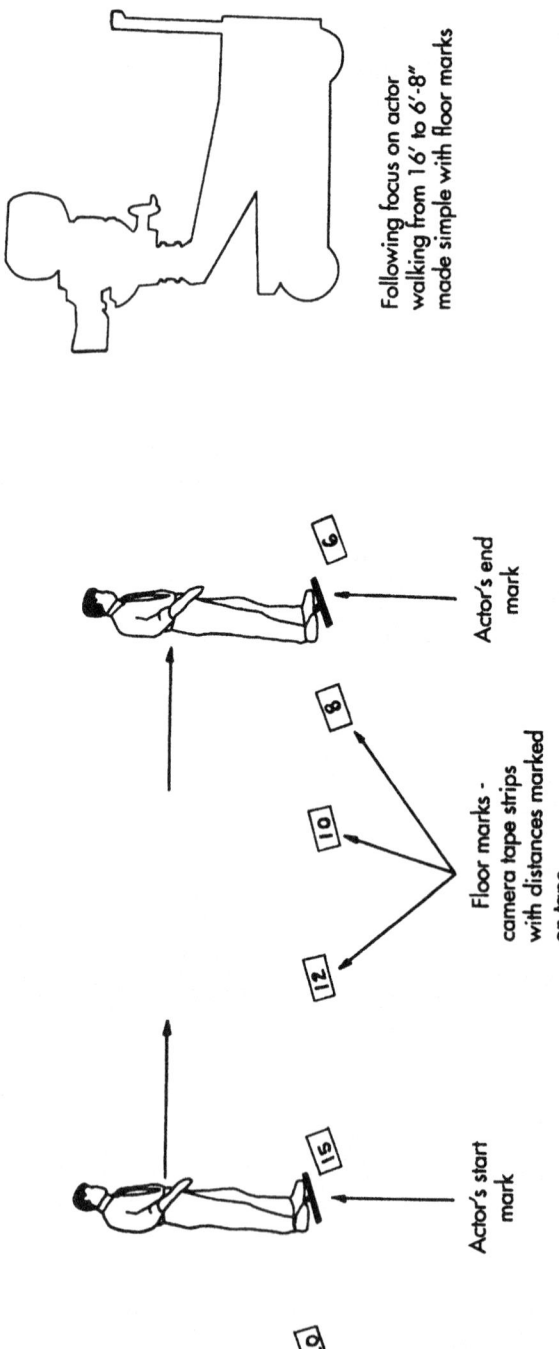

Figure 9-24 Floor Marks. As long as the camera is not moving, the floor can be marked with tape or chalk for the appropriate distances from the camera. Following focus on the lens, as the subject passes each of the indicated distances, is easy. Make sure the numbered marks are not in frame. Use the same distances that are used on the focus scale on the lens, and use as few marks as you feel comfortable with.

Focus **231**

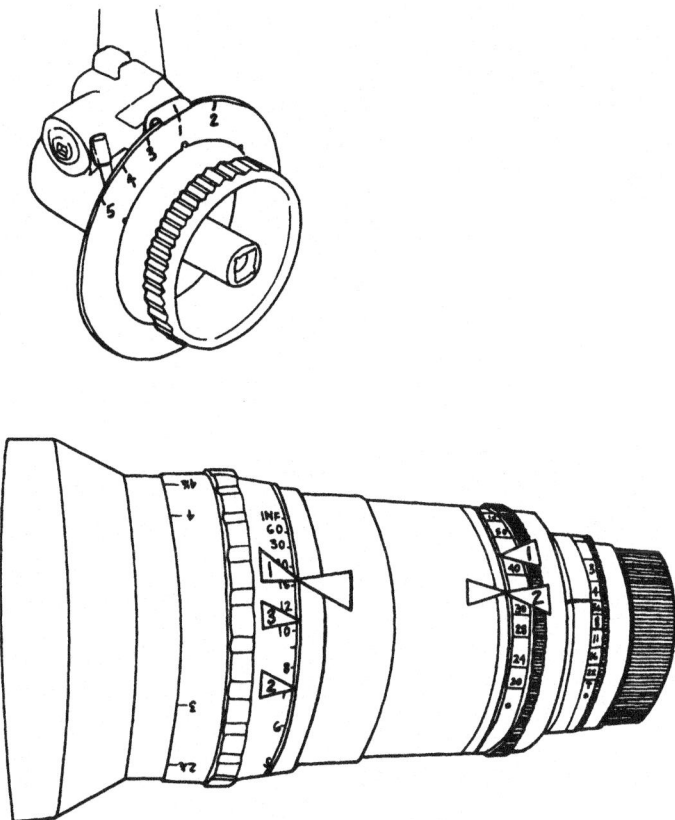

Figure 9-25 Lens Marks. Numbered tape triangles placed on the focus and zoom scales of the lens to indicate the focus and zoom moves planned for the shot. With a little practice, you should be able to watch the action, watch the lens, and make adjustments to zoom and focus during the shot. An alternative would be to mark the white plastic focus disc around the focus knob. Be sure to use a wipe-off fine-point marker or pencil, so the marks are not permanent.

Lens Marks On some shots, lens marks on the barrel or on the focus disk are preferable to floor marks. A narrow strip of artist's or draftsman's chart tape or camera tape placed over the focus scale of the lens provides a perfect place for exact marks. A mark for the actor's starting position, for example, another for the doorway the actor is walking through, and a third for the actor's end position, may be all that is required.

These marks are obtained either by tape measure or eye focus through the lens. Measuring from the camera to the actor's start and end positions with a tape measure, and also to the door frame (there is no need for the actor to actually be standing in the doorway at the time of measurement, although I have seen Assistants insisting that the actor stand there for measurement), and then transferring the distances obtained to the lens barrel or focus disk is quick and easy.

Such marks are usually numbered "1" for the start mark, "2" for the doorway, and "3" for the end mark, in such an example. Once the camera rolls, the Assistant simply starts on 1, turns toward 2 as the actor approaches the doorway, hopefully arriving at their respective marks together, and then proceeding to 3 in the same way.

If there are not too many marks, the Camera Assistant should be able to remember which mark on the lens represents which mark on the floor, even in the heat of battle. As the number of marks increases, the chances are greater that the marks will be confused, so mnemonics must be used to jog the memory.

Instead of numbering the marks consecutively, I prefer to use initials of the objects or landmarks near the marks—"T" for tree, "C" for car, "D" for door, "R" for rug, etc. This makes keeping the marks straight much easier than remembering that "1" means tree, "2" means car, "3" means door, and "4" means rug. Use common sense, and solve the problems rationally and calmly.

Eye vs. Tape Focus

Whether to use Eye Focus or Tape Focus to get your focus marks depends on several things. First of all, the focal length of the lens being used—Eye Focus is better for the longer focal length lenses, with their limited Depth-of-Field. Eye Focus marks are more accurate than Tape Focus for the longer lenses. For wide-angle lenses, accurate focus marks are harder to see through the viewfinder, and Tape Focus marks are faster and more reliable.

A good habit for Camera Assistants to get into is to mentally estimate the distance before running out the tape. Constant practice at estimating focus before actually measuring the distance will develop and refine a natural proficiency for estimating distance, an invaluable talent for a Camera Assistant to have.

Just as a rule of thumb, use Tape Focus for lenses with a focal length of 100mm or less, and Eye Focus for those lenses of 100mm or longer.

Time may also be a deciding factor. Running out the tape measure is faster, in most cases, than getting an Eye Focus mark. In other cases, Eye Focus may be faster than running out the tape. It also may be more convenient, in some cases, to use the tape measure than to change places with the Camera Operator. Sometimes the Camera Operator can give you a quick Eye Focus, but don't depend on this. Often, in the time it takes to explain to the Operator what you want to check, you could do it yourself with the tape measure.

There should be plenty of time during the lighting, or while waiting for hair and makeup, when no one needs to look through the camera, for the Camera Assistant to get to the finder and get whatever Eye Focus marks might be required. Choose your Eye Focus time sensibly, however. Don't hog the camera for long periods of time, or prevent the D.P. from looking at the lighting. It may be necessary to get one mark at a time, in between surrendering the camera viewfinder to the D.P., Director, or Camera Operator.

In certain circumstances, however, there is just no substitute for looking through the viewfinder and getting those marks yourself. No Operator should mind getting out of the way so that the Camera Assistant can get focus marks through the camera. Most Operators used to be Assistants themselves, and know the problems.

To get a quick check on focus, the Camera Operator can be asked to get a focus on a landmark in the scene. The Assistant can help by opening the stop, switching on the eyepiece magnifier, and possibly even removing the diffusion filter, and then restoring all these things after the Operator has finished focusing by eye.

If there are natural landmarks in the scene, getting eye focus marks can be done very quickly, even without the actor being present. A crack in the sidewalk, a fire hydrant, a tree, a doorway, the edge of a rug, all these things and many more can be used as focus landmarks. If there are few or no natural landmarks available, put down your own landmarks, with tape, chalk, wooden wedges driven into the ground, sandbags, or whatever else works for the particular situation.

Sometimes the Second Camera Assistant can walk the same path the actors are going to take, and can be stopped in specific places, to Eye Focus on the slate they are carrying. The high-contrast black-and-white graphics and lettering on the slate provide an ideal target for Eye Focus.

In dark interior scenes, or for night exteriors, the Second Assistant can use a flashlight pointed at the lens to give a focus target. If you have a Maglight flashlight, the Maglight lens housing can be easily unscrewed and removed, exposing the tiny bulb, which makes an ideal focus target for quick and easy Eye Focus.

Dolly Shots and Crane Shots

Once the camera is moving, getting focus marks becomes more difficult. A measured distance only becomes useful if BOTH ends of that distance are under control, and are repeatable. The Camera Assistant can get normal marks from the initial position of the dolly, and from the end position, but while the dolly is between the two ends of its path, marks are more difficult.

A common method of getting those in-between marks is to ask for a "Stop-and-Go" rehearsal, in which the Stand-ins (or even the First Team, if they are agreeable), the Camera Operator, and the Dolly Grip, walk slowly through the planned dolly move, while the Camera Assistant can hook up the end of the tape measure to the camera and can walk alongside the actors with the other end of the tape measure, making mental note of the distances obtained. Where logical and convenient, the Camera Assistant can ask everyone to stop, and can mark both the actors and the dolly wheel, providing one or more focus references during the dolly move.

The Camera Assistant must keep in mind that the actors and the dolly will probably be moving continuously, and will not be stopping at these marks, but the marks will provide a reference during the shot. If the dolly passes its mark before the actors get to theirs, for example, a focus adjustment can be made accordingly.

If the camera is on a crane, with the Camera Operator and Camera Assistant strapped into seats on the crane twenty feet in the air, it is difficult for one Camera Assistant to get adequate marks. Under these circumstances, the use of an Optical Rangefinder is often the best way to get focus marks. This device and its use is described later in this chapter.

In this scenario, perhaps asking the Operator to give you a series of Eye Focus marks, at specific points in the shot, is the best way. Tape marks can also be used from a crane—it just takes two people, one at each end of the tape. There are two ways to get Tape Focus marks from a crane. One would be to hook one end of the tape measure to the camera and toss down the rest of the tape measure to the Second. The Second can read off the distances to various targets, and call these distances to the First, on the crane.

Some Assistants, including myself, prefer to let down the "Dumb" end of the tape measure (the beginning of the tape), so that the Second can get to the actors and the distances can be read off the tape directly at the camera, by the First.

Camera Operators and Focus

While the Camera Operator is the only person actually looking through the camera when the camera is running, the Camera Operator just cannot be depended on to see if the focus is always sharp.

First of all, there are too many other things the Camera Operator is concentrating on, such as maintaining proper composition and headroom during the shot, watching for microphone booms, lights and light stands, cables on the floor, unwanted reflections, hot spots and flares, actors' eye lines, etc. All of these distractions make watching focus very difficult.

Secondly, the Operator is watching an image flickering at twenty-four or more times a second, often through various dark, colored, or diffusion filters, often on a camera with video assist stealing some of the light from the viewfinder. It is very difficult to see something as subjective as focus through such a viewfinder.

Usually by the time the Camera Operator notices that the focus is soft, it is REALLY soft. Slight missing or "Buzzing" of the focus, as it is often called, is usually undetectable to the Camera Operator under the circumstances.

If the Camera Operator DOES notice the focus as being soft, then it probably is really out of focus, and another take should be attempted immediately. As the Camera Assistant, immediately let the Director of Photography know that the focus was missed, and that you can do better next time, and ask to go again. Solve whatever problems may have caused you to miss it, and try again.

So if the Camera Operator does notice soft focus, he or she is probably right, and another take should be done. If the Camera Operator does NOT notice soft focus, this is no guarantee that the focus is good. The Camera Operator just cannot see focus under some circumstances. Dave suggests that if the Operator is concentrating on the focus instead of on the shot, then the concept of the shot is lost.

If there is the slightest doubt, get another take. Better to be safe than sorry.

Video Assist and Focus

The video assist is an even poorer indication of focus. It is virtually impossible to accurately judge focus on the typical dark, flickering, fuzzy, low contrast, black-and-white monitor images found on most sets. Color video assist is even worse for trying to see focus.

The video assist does have its advantages for the Camera Assistant, such as positioning the slate and roughly dialing slate focus before rolling the camera, and for showing where the camera is pointed and who is in frame, so that the Camera Assistant can use other marks to set lens focus by. However, for judging whether focus was good or bad on a particular take, the Video Assist just cannot be trusted for most shots.

There is another area in which the video assist is useful to the Assistant following focus. In a shot in which a focus shift or zoom cue depends on an actor just entering or exiting frame, the video assist can be used to show the Assistant exactly when to shift focus or when to zoom.

The problem will be to position a monitor so that the Camera Assistant can see it without being blocked by half a dozen ad agency and client types. There never seem to be enough monitors in the right place for the people who really could use them to help make the shot.

When I have the choice, I always position the video monitor on the camera right side, so that I can occasionally see it by looking over the lens. If there is a video assist person on the set, ask them to always position the monitor on camera right. This will give you more space on the camera left side, and will minimize the cable tangle underfoot, and positions the monitor where it could actually be useful.

Panavision "Blue Line" Lenses

Because of the optical problems with designing high-speed lenses, different manufacturers have taken different routes to solve the same problems. One of these differences is found in the aperture and focus scales on certain Panavision Primo and Super Speed lenses. On these lenses, just below the usual yellow focus "witness" or "index" mark, is a second, blue line, shorter than the yellow index. This blue line is used when setting or following focus for this lens when the aperture set on the aperture scale corresponds with aperture numbers appearing in blue. For the Primo lenses, the apertures T/1.9 (wide open) and T/2 are marked in blue, so when shooting at T/1.9 or T/2, align the focus scale opposite the blue index instead of the yellow one. All of the other T/stops, starting with T/2.8, are marked in yellow, and the yellow focus index should be used.

Panavision lenses are individually calibrated for focus at T/2.8, and the focus scale inscribed for various distances for the best possible image at that distance and aperture, and when significant differences are found between focus marks at T/2.8 and wider stops than T/2.8, then the second, blue line is added for the best possible image for those apertures. Panavision explains that the effective aperture in the view-

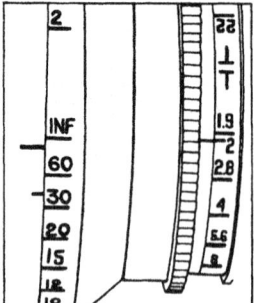 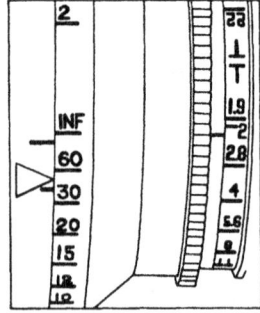 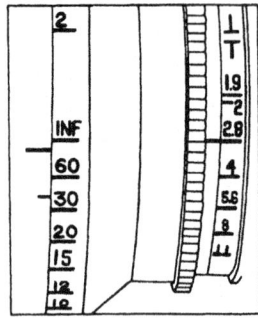

Figure 9-26 Panavision Lenses—The "Blue Line."

LEFT: For shooting at T/1.9 and T/2, use the BLUE (shorter) focus index for focusing. As a reminder, the "1.9" and "2" are engraved on the aperture scale in BLUE.
CENTER: When shooting at stops BETWEEN T/2 and T/2.8, a new focus index must be created proportionately between the BLUE and YELLOW focus indices. For example, to shoot at 1/4 stop over T/2, as in this illustration, a new focus index must be created 1/4 of the way between the BLUE line and the YELLOW line. The easiest way to do this is with a tape triangle placed on the lens.
RIGHT: For shooting at T/2.8 and above, use the YELLOW (longer) focus index. All stops from T/2.8 to T/22 are engraved on the lens in YELLOW.

ing system on their cameras is not as wide as the apertures in the lenses when wide open, so that eye focusing at these wide apertures is not necessarily correct. For these wider apertures, Panavision strongly recommends using tape focus for all work, and alignment opposite the blue line, and ignoring differences between eye and tape focus.

Panavision claims that this two-index process makes it possible for Panavision to spread out the focus scale, allowing the Camera Assistant maximum precision when setting focus. This expanded scale shows up this "aperture-related focus shift" more than on the compressed focus scales found on the Zeiss lenses used by Arriflex cameras, for example, which hide the aberration by compressing the scales so that the difference is hard to discern.

Panavision says that having a separate focus index for the very widest apertures is a "small price to pay" for a large lens barrel and an expanded focus scale.

Arriflex claims that their Zeiss lenses are "fully corrected for spherical aberrations," and therefore do not need an extra index for wide stops, and has made this controversy into an advertising issue, taking out magazine ads proclaiming this "shortcoming" in their competitor's products to the world.

I am not a lens designer, nor an optical engineer, and I do not know who is correct in this controversy, but it really doesn't matter to the Camera Assistant on the set or on location.

Personally, I do like the idea of the expanded focus scale when I work, and I am willing to deal with the "blue line" where necessary, in order to get that expanded scale. I feel much more comfortable working with a scale that has more scale references and enough space between the markings for me to estimate in-between marks. Some of the Zeiss lenses in use today have no focus marks between eight feet and infinity, and not enough space on the scale to add my own in-between marks.

For aperture settings at exactly T/1.9 or T/2 on these lenses, focus is easy. Just run out the measuring tape, and set the desired distance opposite the blue line. But what happens when the D.P. gives you a stop of T/2.3 or T/2.5? In the real world of shooting film, stops between T/2 and T/2.8 are VERY common and are encountered every day. This presents a bit more of a problem for the Camera Assistants following focus with these lenses. Focus at T/2 uses one index, focus at T/2.8 uses another. Where is the focus index for T/2.3 or T/2.5?

The answer is that a stop halfway between T/2 and T/2.8 needs a focus index halfway between the index used for T/2 and the one used for T/2.8, even though there is nothing engraved there on the lens. When a stop falls between T/2 and T/2.8, I place a small triangle of camera tape on the lens barrel, with its point on the focus scale between the yellow index and the blue index. A stop 1/3 of the way between T/2 and T/2.8 needs a focus index 1/3 of the way between the yellow and the blue lines, so move the tape triangle accordingly.

Measure the focus distances in the normal way, and set these distances opposite the tape index placed between the marks at T/2 and T/2.8.

Long Lenses

Following focus with long lenses, those lenses with focal lengths over about 150mm, with their narrow Depth-of-Field, is a difficult task. But movie photography with long lenses has been done successfully for decades, and there are tricks and solutions to these problems that the Camera Assistant can use.

First of all, put your tape measure away. This long lens photography is done at longer distances than your tape will measure, and even if you had a tape measure long enough, the information it would give you would be of little value. Even if you knew that your target was 167 feet 8 3/4 inches away, where is that on a lens that has focus marks at 100 feet and then infinity? Forget the tape measure—eye focus is essential for long lens photography.

Focus landmarks are of great use, if they are available. If not, it is often possible to make your own landmarks in the scene.

A strip of chart or camera tape on the lens barrel can be marked with eye focus marks of the natural landmarks, or of the artificial landmarks. A Walkie-Talkie becomes a valuable focus tool for the Camera Assistant. The Second takes a Walkie-Talkie and the Slate and walks the path of the target. The First can communicate over the radio, asking the Second to stop in specific spots for eye focus and placing marks on the lens barrel.

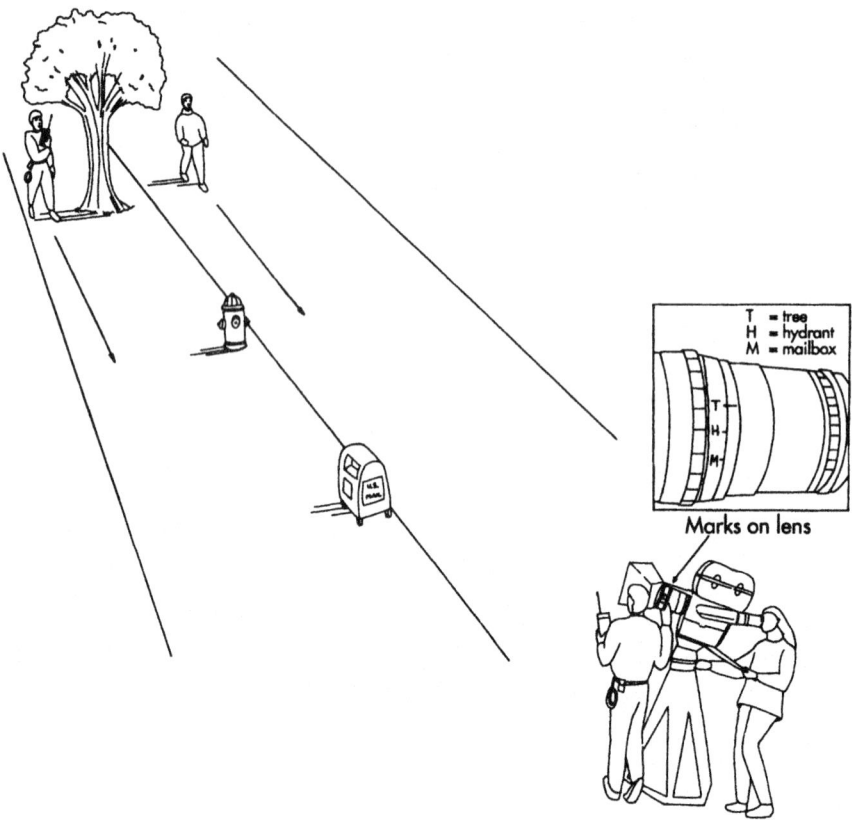

Figure 9-27 Long Lens/Walkie Talkie Marks. Walkie Talkies, plentiful on the film set, are valuable focus tools. They help the Camera Assistants get the marks, and also while shooting, allow the Second Assistant to walk along with the Actor, just out of frame, and notify the First Assistant when the Actor reaches each of the marks.

Once the camera rolls, the Walkie-Talkie can still be used. The Second can often walk or jog parallel to the actor or target, at a matching speed, but just out of camera view. The Second can announce through the radio when the target has passed Mark #1, and then Mark #2, etc. The Second often calls out the "Halfway" marks as well, meaning halfway between Marks #1 and #2, for instance, saying into the microphone "One, halfway, Two, halfway, Three, halfway, Four, . . ." as each mark is reached. The First Assistant, at the camera, can hear the Second over the radio, and can turn the lens barrel to the appropriate mark. The First need not even look at the target, when audible focus marks are coming over the radio. This is a very reliable and accurate way to follow a distant target through a long lens.

If the target is moving too fast for the Second Assistant to keep pace, it is possible to position several production assistants or other crew members, each with radios, along the route of the target, and have each in turn call out the number of the mark being passed. I used this method once on a shot of a motorcycle gang riding directly at the camera with a 300mm lens on. Once I got used to hearing six different voices giving me marks, the shot went well.

On long lenses with a focus knob instead of just a lens barrel to turn, the First can make even more accurate marks. The knob can become the mounting point for a pointer, and a dial face with a focus scale can be used for extremely accurate marks. If the lens manufacturer did not provide one, the Assistant can make his or her own pointer and dial, with cardboard "Show Card," found on most sets, gaffer-taped in position to the lens barrel. The longer the pointer, and the larger the dial face diameter, the more accurate the marks can become.

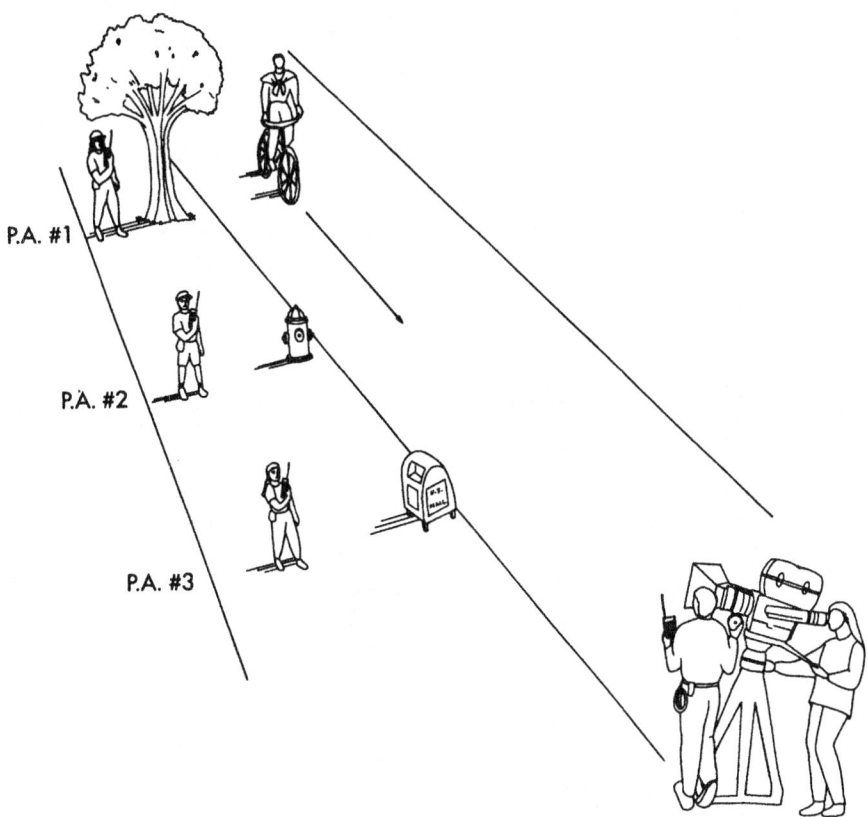

Figure 9-28 P.A./Walkie Talkie Marks. If the target is moving too quickly for the Second Assistant to keep up with, Production Assistants or other crew members with walkie talkies can be placed along the route to be taken, and can use their radios to notify the First Assistant when the target reaches each mark.

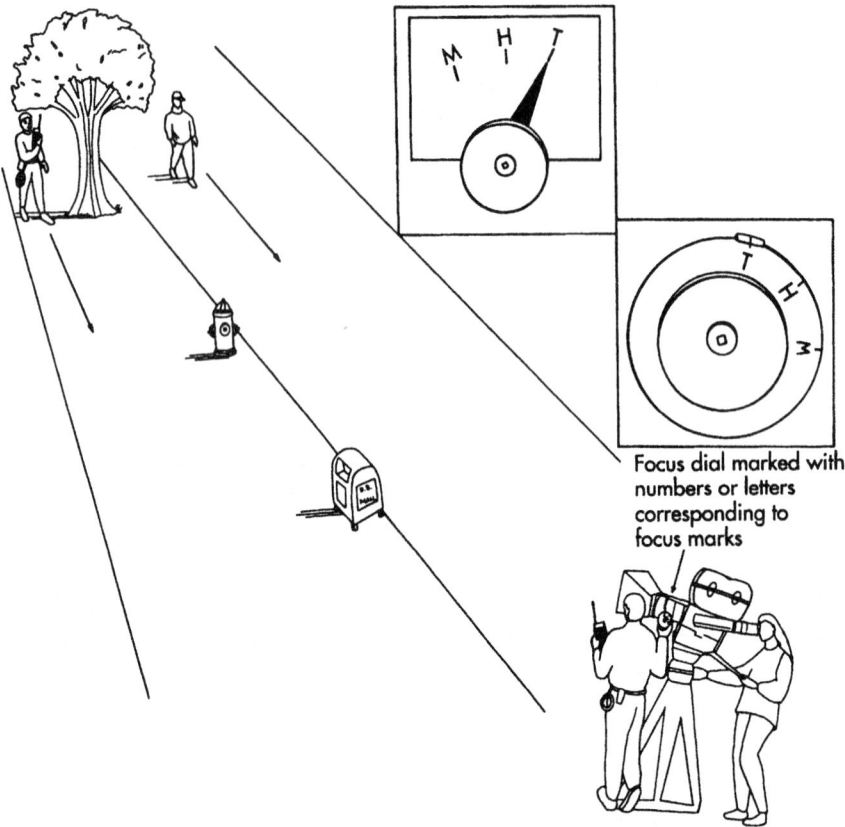

Figure 9-29 Long Lens/Pointer and Dial Marks. Some Camera Assistants prefer placing their focus marks on the focus knob dial instead of on the lens itself. For those long lenses with a focus knob but without a dial, a dial can be fashioned out of a piece of "Show Card" and mounted on the lens behind the knob with tape. A pointer can also be made out of card and attached to the knob with tape. The longer the pointer and the larger the dial face, the more accurate the marks can be.

Combining the "Pointer and Dial" method with the use of another person with a Walkie Talkie calling out marks as they are passed by the target, can tame even the longest focal length lens. All the Assistant needs is enough time to set up properly.

Zoom Lenses

Zoom lenses should be treated differently than prime lenses with respect to focus. First of all, zoom lenses include a very good means of checking focus and setting an "Eye" focus. Just zoom all the way in (toward the telephoto position), open the aperture to its widest, and focus normally through the eyepiece.

Marking the lens barrel or focus disk this way is a quick way to get the lens focus marks you may need for the shot. Set at full telephoto and wide open, the zoom lens is at its most critical Depth-of-Field, and the sharpest and most accurate focus marks should be easily obtained.

Since the zoom lens is constructed differently than a prime lens, the nodal point of the zoom lens is much further away from the film plane than that of a prime lens, and Depth-of-Field is diminished slightly because of this. The Samuelson SAMCINE Mk. II Calculator is the only chart or calculator I have seen that has different focus scales for zoom and prime (fixed) lenses to allow for this phenomenon. Depth-of-Field is always less with a zoom lens than with prime lenses, at an equivalent focal length, partly because of this phenomenon and partly because with a zoom lens, the difference between the f/ and T/stops is greater.

Finally, keep in mind that the Depth-of-Field changes with the focal length, so zooming in during the shot reduces the Depth-of-Field. If the depth is at all critical for the shot, or if you are splitting the focus between two or more targets, then the depth should be checked and the split focus set at the LONGEST focal length being used in the shot.

Aperture Pulls

If the shooting aperture needs to be changed during the shot, referred to as "aperture pulling," as when an actor crosses from sun into shadow, keep in mind that opening up the aperture decreases the Depth-of-Field, and that the depth should be checked and the split set at the WIDEST aperture.

Plus Diopters

Proxars, or Plus Diopters, are auxiliary close-up lenses. "Proxar" was a brand name for Plus Diopter lenses that stuck in our vocabularies, like "Kleenex" and "Xerox" did. It's become a generic description on the East Coast; on the West Coast and elsewhere they are usually referred to as "Plus Diopters." They are also sometimes referred to simply as "Close-up Lenses."

Every lens has a minimum focus limit. It might be two feet with a wide-angle lens, it might be five feet with a zoom lens, and it might be twenty-five feet with a long telephoto lens. Focus cannot be set any closer than that with that particular lens because the barrel won't turn any farther. The lens manufacturers could make every lens focus very close, but the lenses would all be much larger and heavier and more expensive. So in order to make lenses portable and usable, minimum focus limits exist.

If you need to photograph something that's closer than the lens' minimum focus, there are several choices. A macro lens can be used, which has an additional group of elements that will allow you to focus closer. The lens can be separated from the camera and put in an extension tube or bellows between the lens and the camera body. Both of these solutions require considerable exposure compensation.

A third choice on certain lenses is to remove the stop screw which holds the focus barrel so that the lens barrel is free to continue turning, allowing closer focus. Of course lens manufacturers and rental houses discourage this practice because it is somewhat dangerous. If the front of the lens is turned too far, it will suddenly detach from the rest of the lens, possibly dropping to the floor, or at best allowing dirt and dust into the lens. This is obviously not a good idea.

The fourth, and in most cases the preferred, solution is to add a supplemental lens in front of the lens which will allow you to bring your minimum focus closer to the lens—these supplemental lenses are called Plus Diopters. What they are doing is shifting the entire focus range of the lens closer to the camera, while very slightly increasing the focal length of the main lens.

Plus Diopter lenses look like, and are used like, photographic filters, except that they are clear. Sometimes these Plus Diopter lenses are marked with an arrow on their rings, which should be pointed toward the subject. If no arrow is marked on the rim, then the convex (outwardly curved) surface of the Plus Diopter should be placed facing the subject. It may be difficult to see on the + 1/8 and + 1/4 diopters, but the curvature gets progressively more pronounced as the strength of the diopter increases.

Image quality also decreases as the diopter strength increases. Use the longest focal length lens possible with the weakest plus diopter possible for the best images.

With one of these supplemental lenses on your camera lens, you can no longer focus the lens at infinity. The stronger the diopter you have on the lens the more of your distant focus is lost.

The "Plus One-Half" diopter brings infinity focus (the infinity mark on the lens focus scale) to two meters from the diopter lens, not from the film plane. The rest of the focus scale focuses from this two-meter mark down towards the lens. "Plus One" brings infinity to one meter. "Plus Two" focuses infinity at 1/2 meter, "Plus Three" at 1/3 meter, etc.

Plus Diopter Lens Strength	Infinity Lens Mark Focus (from Diopter Lens)	
	Meters	Feet/Inches
+ 1/8	8	26' 3"
+ 1/4	4	13' 1+1/2"
+ 1/2	2	6' 6+3/4"
+ 1	1	3' 3+3/8"
+ 2	1/2	1' 7+5/8"
+ 3	1/3	1' 1+1/8"
+ 4	1/4	0' 9+7/8"
+ 5	1/5	0' 7+7/8"
+ 6	1/6	0' 6+1/2"

As soon as one of these Plus Diopter lenses is mounted in front of the camera lens, the focus scale becomes meaningless. The Camera Assistant will have to create a new scale to use. But there is theoretically no light loss through these Plus Diopters. The lens is focusing closer but focus at the far end is lost. You will be unable to rack focus from a tree on top of a mountain to the apple two inches in front of the lens with this lens. The far end of the focus range is shortened by bringing the near end of focus closer.

The other important thing to remember about Plus Diopters is that if one is not strong enough, they can be stacked in front of the lens. The resulting combination is the sum of the powers of the two individual Diopters. If you do use more than one, however, it is important to place the strongest of the Diopters closest to the lens, and in descending order of strength going away from the lens.

Keep in mind that the stronger the Plus Diopter, the more pronounced the curvature of its front surface. In order to stack more than one in descending order it may be necessary to use multiple filter rings between the diopters so that they do not touch the next one in line.

Split Diopter Lenses

It is also possible to have a Plus Diopter which does not cover the entire lens. This is called a Split Diopter, and is used when only part of the frame needs to be in close focus. These are round filters, half of which might be a Plus One Diopter or Plus One-Half Diopter, and half of which would be clear glass or even just empty.

This Split Diopter could be positioned in front of your lens for a shot of a desk with a telephone and a door at the other side of the room, for example. It would enable both the telephone and door to be in focus even if there was not enough Depth-of-Field to do so without the Split Diopter. It would be unusual to have Depth-of-Field from two to twenty feet. on an interior. But you could use a Split Diopter on the bottom half of the frame so it would allow you to focus closer in that part of the frame so you could get this shot.

The disadvantage is that there is a division line between the diopter and the clear or open area that must be hidden someplace. If there were a dark carpet or some other convenient area in the frame the line could be hidden there. A problem would arise if you had a chair or some other object that was part in the Diopter area and part out of the Diopter. Where the object crossed the line, the change in focus would be visible.

Panavision makes a device called the Sliding Diopter Matte Box. This is a matte box that replaces the standard matte box on the camera. It still has filter slots but it has a rotating stage built to fit the Split Diopters that are mounted in trays. These trays can be positioned in the matte box and rotated to any angle, so that the desired part of the frame is covered with the Diopter. The Split Diopter might only be needed on a small specific part of the frame. The Diopter can be positioned anywhere around the frame. Dealing with the focus problem is simple. Basically what you have to do is focus through the clear part of the filter at your distant object and find the strength of Diopter

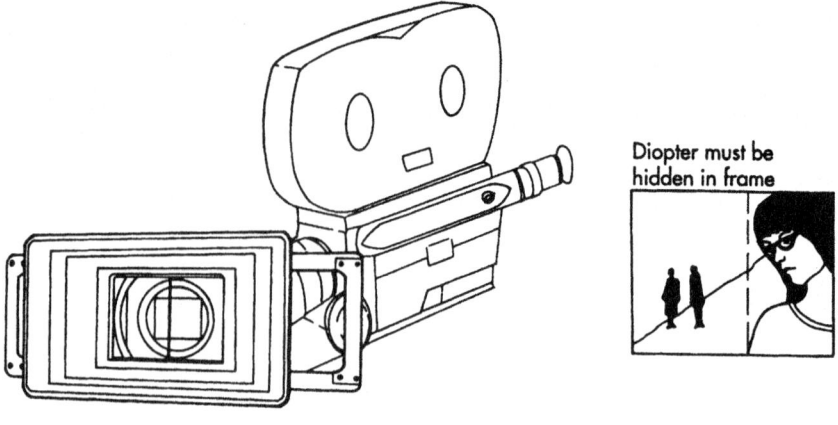

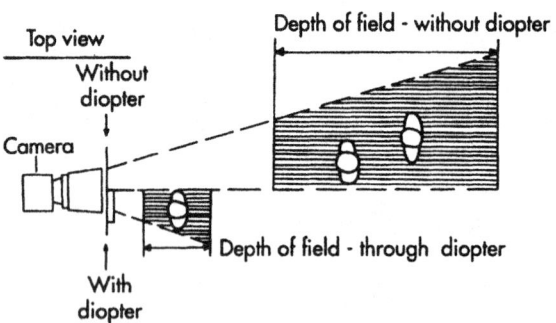

Figure 9-30 Split Diopters. The Panavision Split Diopter Matte Box shown with diopter frame in position with diopter on camera right side. To use, set the focus for that part of the frame to be seen WITHOUT the diopter, and choose the appropriate strength split diopter to bring the closer subject into focus.

that you need to get focus on your near object. Keep in mind that changing the focus during the shot changes the focus both on the distant and near objects.

Refraction or reflection of light on the cut edge of the Split Diopter could be a problem. This is generally not a polished edge. It's a rough surface that doesn't refract or reflect that much. Once the split diopter is set, the entire matte box should be wrapped in black cloth to keep all stray light from bouncing around inside and causing a flare or unwanted reflection. It takes a while to set up and generally won't be moved during the shot, although it can be moved if necessary. During a tilt or pan, the diopter tray can be slid into or out of frame while the camera is rolling.

If it must be moved during a shot, the tray can be marked where it enters and leaves the matte box so the Camera Assistant can slide the tray into or out of the frame when the camera is rolling. But it will most often be used in a stationary situation. Panning and tilting are difficult because the division line moves, and becomes even more visible.

Panatape

This is an interesting gadget, somewhat overused by some Camera Assistants, but valuable in certain circumstances. I've used it only a few times. The Panatape is a matte box with an infrared ranging system attached, getting power from the camera body, that reads and displays the distance to the target. It looks like a standard matte box with two cylinders mounted on top. One is the sender and the other the receiver of infrared pulses that measure the distance to the subject; the distance being digitally displayed on the side of the matte box.

The device must be recalibrated for each lens used, because each lens is a different length and the matte box with the Panatape attached must be moved closer to or further from the film plane to accommodate the various lenses used. This recalibration is a simple process using a slate and a tape measure to position the slate at a precise distance from the camera. The calibration knob on the Panatape is then adjusted until the display reads the same distance to which the slate has been positioned. When calibrated properly, the display gives digital distance readings in feet and tenths of feet.

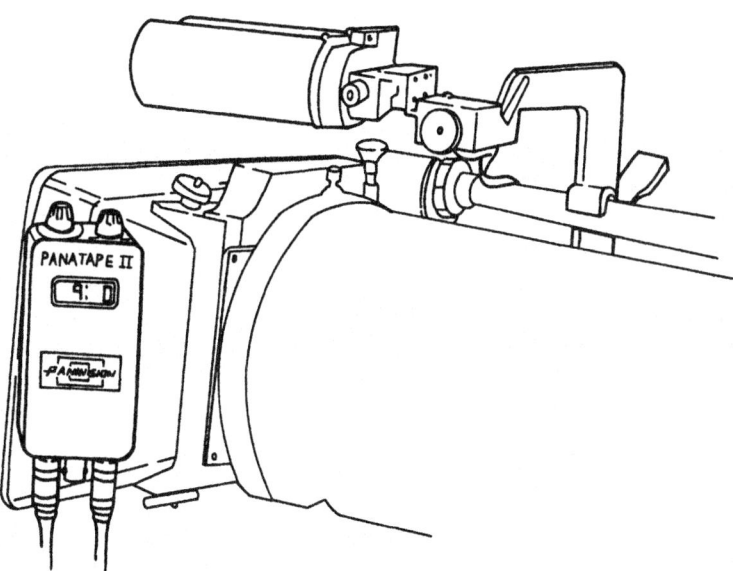

Figure 9-31 Panatape. Panavision makes the "Panatape," which uses infrared technology to display on the side of the matte box the distance to a target in front of the lens. The two tubes above the matte box are the sender and receiver.

The device does not actually change the focus of the lens—the Camera Assistant must do that. The Assistant can watch the display and set the lens focus to the reading displayed, but must be aware that the sensor may be reading the distance to the actor's chest and not to the face, or may be reading some object in the foreground or background, if the device is not aimed properly. The measured beam is quite narrow, and the device contains the means to aim it at a specific part of the frame, with both horizontal and vertical adjustment.

If you insist on using the device, use common sense as well. If an extra crosses in front of the camera, the device will read the extra, not the actor you want to keep in focus. Beware of shots through a doorway, because the device may read the doorway, not the actor beyond. You also cannot shoot through glass windows or shoot mirror reflections, because the device reads the glass and not the target.

Understanding the device and knowing when to ignore the displayed distance is as important as knowing when to believe the displayed distance. I have heard that there are some Camera Assistants who use this device on every shot, but I cannot imagine needing it that often. Maybe half a dozen shots a year would benefit from such a thing.

With practice and experience, following focus by eye and by floor marks and by educated guess becomes second nature to a good Camera Assistant. Depending on such a contraption for every shot prevents you from sharpening those natural skills. Sure, I'll ask for the Panatape when I really need it, but I don't expect that to be very often.

Rangefinders

These "Optical Tapemeasure" devices work like the viewfinder on older rangefinder still cameras. The Assistant looks through the device, sees two overlapping images, and turns a wheel to exactly superimpose the two images. The distance to the target is then displayed in a window at the top of the rangefinder.

These devices can be found in sporting goods stores and mail-order catalogs. They are used in golf and archery, apparently. They cost about $40, and have a range of about 6 to 100 feet. I have found they are accurate to about 6 inches in 10 feet, or 1 foot in 20. This is generally plenty accurate for motion picture focus. They can be, and should be calibrated every month or so, by holding one end of a tape measure flush to the back of the rangefinder, and sending the Second out in front of you with the slate and the tape measure to about 20 feet. Line up the two images to the best superimposition, and look at the display. It should read the distance to the slate. If not, the scale can be adjusted accordingly. Try this several times, to make sure you have the best alignment.

When using the rangefinder for focus marks, pick out a strong, high-contrast (light against a dark background, or dark against a light background) vertical object at the distance you want to measure. If there is no vertical target present, it may be necessary to turn the device to an angle or even 90 degrees until you can find a target easier to sight on and get an accurate reading.

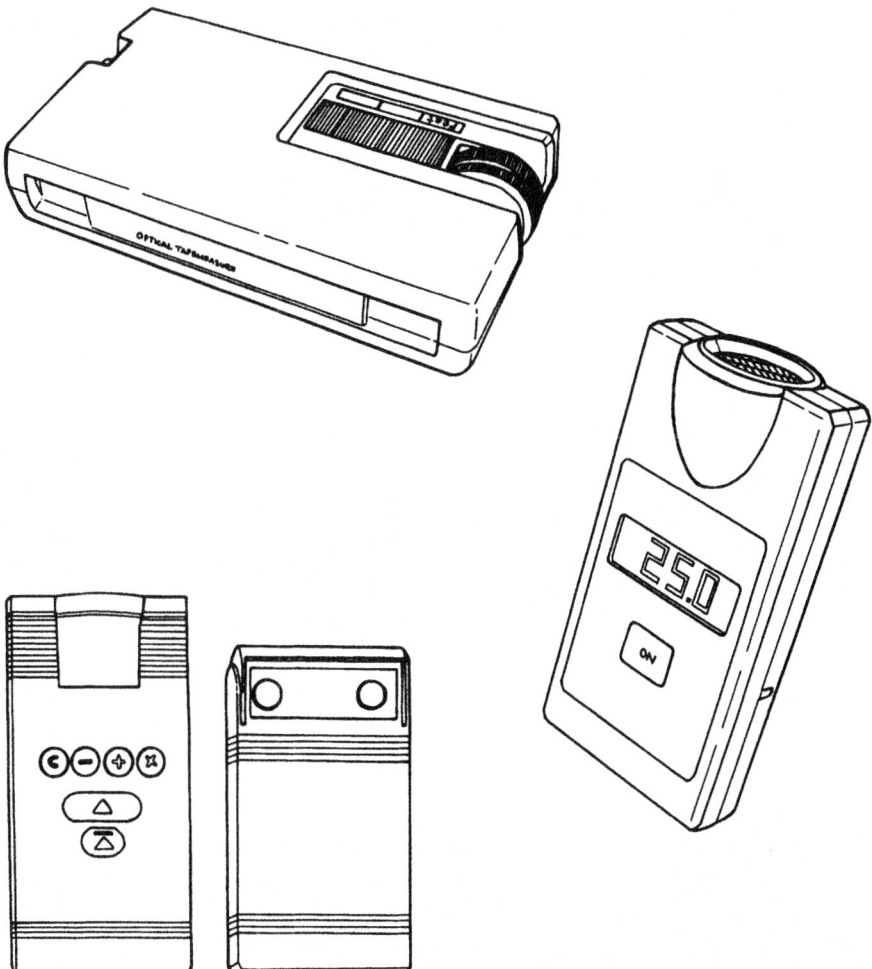

Figure 9-32 Rangefinders. The "Optical Tapemeasure" focusing tool uses a split-image rangefinder system to indicate how far away something is. This is a handy gadget to have when running out a tapemeasure is inconvenient or impossible. The "Electronic Tapemeasure" would be a terrific tool for the Assistant except for a few shortcomings: the beam is too wide, the unit takes several seconds to display a distance, the unit displays distance in feet and tenths of feet (NOT feet and inches), and the unit is too easily confused by multiple targets. It still has its uses, however, such as with the Steadicam. The "Sonin" two-piece measuring system. One unit is the transmitter and one is the receiver, which digitally displays the distance separating the two units.

Electronic Focus Gadgets

Within the past few years, several small "electronic tape measures" have been introduced by various manufacturers. They are available from hardware stores and many "Yuppie" mail-order catalogs, for between $30 and $40. They are about the size of a pack of cigarettes, and contain a permanent battery, an infrared sender-receiver, and a digital display for distance readings.

These devices use the infrared technology developed for the auto-focus Polaroid SX-70 cameras, the same technology used in the Panatape device described above. They were designed primarily to estimate the size of a room for floor tile or carpet installation, or to calculate the volume of a room to determine the size of the air conditioner that would be needed. They work fairly well for these purposes, when there is a large flat wall to measure, and there is no pressure of time to worry about, but it is less useful to the Camera Assistant.

It takes several seconds to get a distance reading, and the measuring angle is so wide that it becomes confused by multiple targets. Under certain circumstances, it is useful for focus measurements. If there is a single target, out in the open, in an area without furniture, or extras, or other obstacles, and the target is moving slowly enough, the distance readings can be useful.

I use one of these devices sometimes, when working with the Steadicam, to get periodic references during the shot. I hold it out near the camera, opposite the film plane, and point it at the target for readings. Since I cannot hook a tape measure onto the Steadicam camera for a Tape Focus reading, because of the balance problems, and because with a moving Steadicam and a moving actor, few marks are possible or meaningful; the readings from this device are better than nothing.

There is another electronic focus aid on the market, known as the "Sonin," and two models are currently available. This is a two-piece device, each piece about the size of a pack of cigarettes. One is the sender and one is the receiver. If the receiver is held or mounted at the film plane of the camera, pointed toward the target, and the sender unit is walked through the scene by the Second Assistant, the First, reading the display on the receiver, will get a sequential display of the distances between the target and the camera for the various positions the target or actor will be in during the shot. Conversely, if the sender is mounted at the camera, the First can walk the target's path himself, getting continuous readings of distances from the camera. Either way you use the device, the readings are accurate and dependable. A single rehearsal or walkthrough will give the Assistant all the reference marks needed for a successful shoot.

If not for the fact that the sender unit would have to be constantly visible, the actor would be able to carry the unit, giving the Assistant constant focus distances during the scene, wherever the actor might roam. Unfortunately, this technology will not allow for that at present, but someday the actors will be able to carry a small transmitter in a pocket or pinned under a lapel, and the Assistant will be able to zero in at anytime. But for now, we just have to do things the old-fashioned way, with some help from the high-tech toys.

The technology exists, but the market for an accurate, narrow-beam, distance-measuring device is just too small. The ideal device would resemble a spot exposure meter in size and handling. The Camera Assistant could point the device at a target using the viewfinder in the meter, and the device would display the distance to the object framed in the viewfinder. Someday . . .

There is a new laser rangefinder gadget on the market, but I haven't had the opportunity to use it yet. This device would be used to get marks during a rehearsal and not while the camera is running, as there is the tell-tale red dot projected onto the target during focus readings. This would hardly be acceptable during filming.

Use anything and everything to make your job easier. As soon as you hear about a new gadget, get one and try it out. Don't be shy!

CHAPTER **10**

Setup and Maintenance

The Morning Routine

When the Camera Assistant arrives at the studio or location in the morning, he or she has to start getting ready right away for the day's shooting. The other departments may have time for coffee and donuts, but not the Camera Assistants.

Often nothing else can happen in the morning until the camera is assembled and placed into position. This is why it is so vital that the Assistants develop the habit of punctuality. Better to be a half hour early than a half minute late. If you absolutely must have your coffee and donuts in the morning (with California crews, your "Breakfast Burrito"), or must brag to the boys and girls about your new car or your date last night, or discuss the football game, then get there early enough to do that and still start your work on time.

If the company you are working for is really on the ball, and they like to start right away in the morning and get the first shot in the can ten minutes after the call time, then the Camera Assistants must clock in even earlier so the camera is ready to roll when the company is.

This type of company is rare, however. It is much more common to show up in the morning and find the actors still in the makeup room or trailer, if they have shown up at all, and the director on the phone somewhere or else standing in the middle of the set wondering what to shoot today. The first hour after the call is known as the "Get Acquainted Hour," while the crew is drinking their coffee. On these jobs, there will be plenty of time to play with the equipment before it is needed.

Of course, on some jobs, especially episodic television series productions, or on low-budget films, every second counts because of the often impossible scheduling restraints placed on the crews, and there will be little if any slack time in the morning. Also, if you are shooting in the same location or studio set as the previous day, and the rehearsing and lighting are nearly ready to shoot, then there will not be much prep time.

Sometimes the shot is set up and lit just before the wrap the previous night, and can be ready to shoot the next morning as soon as the camera is in place. It is difficult to predict sometimes just how much time will be available in the morning, so plan ahead, and give yourself some extra time anyway.

Some companies go to great lengths to get some shot, even a meaningless insert of a doorknob turning, "in the can" as early as possible, and deliberately set up and light for some such scene the previous night. There is a space on the production forms that the Assistant Directors fill out every day for the "First Shot." Some Assistant Directors and Production Managers are determined to show as early a time as possible for this space in the form.

Apparently someone higher up "on the Coast" is easily impressed by early First Shot times, although I don't know why. It is a particularly meaningless number, and the second shot may be four or more hours later. That doesn't seem to matter, however, since there is no space on the form for the Second Shot time. Sometimes they even telephone "the Coast" to report in that First Shot time! It's hard to imagine someone being impressed by something as silly as an early First Shot time, but they are.

Warmup

Every Camera Assistant will establish his or her own "Morning Routine" of warmup and maintenance, appropriate to the type of camera equipment being used and the type of filming being done.

After sitting in a cold camera truck overnight, or even in a studio camera room, the camera should be thoroughly prepped and warmed up before starting filming. I usually arrange with the Second Assistant that the first one of us to arrive on location and into the truck will set up the camera on the bench, plug it in, and switch it on so that it can warm up.

Assemble the camera in the configuration you need for shooting, but without a magazine. Set up on the work table in the truck, or on the dolly in the studio, or on a tripod on location, it doesn't really matter, as long as the camera is securely mounted in some safe area, out of the weather, and out of the main traffic flow of crew people with coffee cups.

Although there are no hard and fast rules about camera warmup, a common rule-of-thumb is that the camera should be run without film, at the speed you intend to shoot, approximately for the length of film in the longest standard magazine you are likely to use—for 35mm filming, one thousand feet, for 16mm, 400 feet. At 24 or 25 frames per second, this amounts to about 10 minutes. Use the camera's footage counter as a guide.

If the camera is particularly cold, a longer warmup run is recommended. If really cold, it is a good idea to start the camera at some slow frame rate, if your camera allows variable speed control, then increase the frame rate as the camera warms up, until you can run at standard speed. I use as a guide the length of time that the camera takes to come up to speed when first switched on.

At normal temperatures, the camera should come to shooting speed almost instantaneously, faster even than the tachometer can react. If there is any significant delay in reaching shooting speed, then start out slow and gradually increase speed until sync speed is reached. It is not uncommon for a very cold camera to not reach sync speed for ten seconds or so. Switch off and start again in variable speed mode, at 12 frames or so, and gradually increase to sync speed. After running for a while at or near sync speed, switch back to crystal control sync speed and let the camera run for at least the length of your longest magazine.

Running the camera without film for several minutes at normal speed will not hurt the camera. Starting up a cold camera with film can be very dangerous. The strain on the cold camera motor could blow a fuse or seize up the mechanism, or the film could break and jam the movement. If you are using batteries or power supplies with fuses, then the added strain of starting a cold camera could easily exceed their rated amperage and blow these fuses. Make sure you have extra fuses for your batteries and power supplies.

Cleaning the Camera

This "Morning Routine" is also the best time for routine cleaning and lubrication of the camera. Some Assistants do their daily maintenance at night immediately after wrap, but I prefer morning maintenance, unless the camera is wet or muddy, and needs to be cleaned and taken care of immediately. Also, Assistants are worn out and tired at the end of the day, and on overtime, and often in danger of violating the "turn-around" clause of the Union contracts (a minimum rest period between the end of work one day and the start of work the next—usually ten hours), also known as "forcing the call."

There is almost always plenty of time in the morning for routine maintenance, while waiting for actors or director to show up or finish with makeup, or for the location manager to find the guy with the key to the location, or for the broken down trucks to arrive, or for a replacement generator to arrive, or for any of a hundred other reasons.

Depending on where you've been filming, "cleaning" may be nothing more than blowing off the dust. Studios are often dusty places, with forty years or more of dust in the grid just waiting to fall on your camera. A tank of nitrogen on the truck or near the darkroom is perfect for this purpose. If no nitrogen is on hand, commercially available aerosol antidust sprays usually are.

For the inside of the camera, the nitrogen and aerosol sprays are often of too high a pressure, and could damage delicate camera mechanisms, so they are not recommended. For the nitrogen tank with adjustable regulators, do not use more than about 25 lbs. of pressure for blowing around the outside of the camera. Rubber bulb syringes and a soft brush are generally sufficient for interior dusting.

Cotton applicator "Q-tips" are useful for interior cleaning. The kind with the six-inch wooden stick are better than the ones with the cardboard stick, and are longer, for a better reach. I suggest that you pull off about half of the cotton, to make the pad smaller, and that you twist the remaining cotton tight with your fingers before using it inside the camera, to reduce the chances of cotton fibers being left inside. If there are some loose fibers, blowing them out with the syringe is often enough. You also might try wrapping the end of the Q-tip with lens tissue to reduce the chance of stray fibers being left behind.

There are other applicators on sticks made for cleaning audio and video recording heads that use a foam pad instead of cotton, so they do not leave loose fibers behind. You can find these at electronics stores and places like Radio Shack. I have found that these are often too thick to penetrate some of the places I want to get to, and quite expensive, but decide for yourself.

The camera gate, if it can be removed easily, should be removed, inspected, and wiped with a piece of lens tissue, applicator, or lintless paper wipe. The camera pressure plate should also be removed and wiped.

The lens mount should be checked and cleaned, if necessary, with a Q-tip or wad of lens tissue moistened with alcohol or lens cleaning fluid. Some assistants use Xylene, or acetone, or lighter fluid (naphtha), or other such solvent, but I have never found the need for more than plain grain alcohol. Other solvents are overly strong, and if spilled, can take the paint off the camera or dissolve plastic parts. It just is not necessary to use anything that strong. Some of these solvents are toxic and/or flammable, so be careful. Use them only in ventilated areas, and don't smoke. (Camera Assistants should not smoke around the equipment, anyway!)

The mounts on the lenses should be periodically cleaned as well. Alcohol or even lens fluid on a wad of lens tissue is usually enough to clean out the lens mount, unless there is something horrible like tape residue that might require some acetone or mineral spirits.

Make it a habit to examine the rear element, the iris leaves (by looking into the rear of the lens), the lens mount, and the front element every time you put a lens on the camera. The iris leaves can become stuck or loose, and this can adversely affect the exposure of the film. After a while it will become automatic to perform this check, and you won't even have to think about it. Routines like this make a good Assistant better.

Viewfinder

Another part of the camera to check every day as part of the "Morning Routine" is the viewfinder. Look through the finder, without a lens, but with the lens port cap removed. Shine a flashlight into the lens port if necessary. Is the ground glass clean? Are the viewfinder optics clean? Are the ground glass markings level with the camera? Does the viewfinder light trap close the viewfinder completely? Is the magnifier working? How about the anamorphic correction? Are the viewfinder contrast viewers working and are they clean? Check all these things, just as in a checkout.

All of these questions can be answered in a minute or two. If the viewfinder optics are dirty, there are some surfaces that the Assistant has access to—the rear eyepiece surface is the one most likely to accumulate dust or fingerprints. Clean this with lens tissue moistened with a bit of lens fluid.

If the eyepiece disconnects from the extension tube, or if the viewfinder tube disconnects from the camera, that gives access to more surfaces for cleaning. If there are problems with any of the other parts of the viewing system, the camera should be returned to the rental house for cleaning or repair. These are not things the Camera Assistant can do anything about in the field without proper training and tools.

The ground glass should be protected enough in its position inside the camera that the only cleaning that should be necessary is an occasional dust-blowing. If more strenuous cleaning is required, treat the ground glass as you would a lens or a filter—with care. Lens tissue and lens fluid should be all that is needed. Be especially careful with ground glasses that have illuminated markings, as the markings may be scratched or removed by too vigorous a cleaning.

The mirrors in reflex cameras are particularly delicate, being just a thin coating of aluminum or silver, and softer than some lens coatings. Cleaning should only be attempted if the mirror is really smudged, and then with great care, using a quality lens fluid and soft, lintless tissue. Don't get crazy about cleaning the mirror, because, after all, any smudge or dust on the mirror will not be photographed. The same with the viewing system—dust inside the viewing system may be annoying, but it is not serious, because it does not affect the negative being photographed.

If absolutely necessary, have the rental house technicians clean the viewing system, but never attempt dismantling this in the field.

Lubricating the Camera

Some cameras require no lubrication, others should be oiled or otherwise lubricated often, depending on temperature, running speed, or the amount of film run through the previous day. Find out from the camera manufacturer what the recommended lubrication schedule is.

I have found that daily oiling of the movement of cameras such as those from Panavision that require oiling is a simple item on my "Morning Routine," with repeat oilings as needed through the day. Normal feature film shooting in studios or on location averages between 5000 and 8000 feet of 35mm film per day. Daily oiling is just about the right interval. If you are shooting a lot more film, or shooting high speed, then more frequent oiling is recommended. The Panaflex cameras have a dozen or so oiling points inside the movement, illustrated on the threading diagram inside the door of the camera, or found in one of the several excellent books on camera hardware available.

Some high-speed cameras require oiling with every magazine reload or even after each take. Find out what the manufacturer recommends, and then lubricate even more often. High-speed cameras are usually rented with a small bottle of the appropriate oil in the case. Over-oiling will not hurt a camera as much as under-oiling will. Normal camera oil is generally light in color; high-speed oil is generally dark. If possible, run the camera at high speed after oiling and discard the film that has run through the camera, as the camera will spit or spray excess oil onto the film the first time it is run after oiling. This excess oil can contaminate the developer chemicals, and the labs would prefer not to have to replenish too often.

Black-and-white filming requires more frequent lubrication, because the black-and-white film stock does not have the lubrication layer that the color film stocks do. The increased friction causes the camera to run hotter, requiring more frequent oiling. On black-and-white jobs, oil the camera in the morning and again after lunch, or some other convenient point during the day.

The Panaflex cameras also require application of silicone lubricant on the two felt pads in the pull-down claw race. Add a drop of silicone (supplied by the rental agent with the camera) whenever you oil the movement. Don't use the silicone anywhere else on the camera movement, but you might consider using it on the gear head balance plate dovetail or tilt wedge dovetail.

There is another Old Wives Tale about using "nose grease" on the gate. Rubbing your fingertip along the sides of your nose will indeed collect some skin oil, but I can't believe there is enough of it to make any difference to the film running through the camera.

I do, however, recommend that when it is hot and humid, or cold, or if you are shooting black-and-white film, that the gate should be occasionally siliconed, with the Panavision liquid silicone. A single drop on each side rail of the gate, spread along the length of the side rail with a finger, and then nearly rubbed off with lens tissue or the heel of the hand, is enough, once or twice a day.

Flange Focal Depth Checking/Film Gap Setting

Some cameras allow the adjustment in the field of the Flange Focal Depth (usually called just the "Depth") and the Film Gap. The Flange Focal Depth is the distance between the rear mounting flange of a lens and the film plane.

This distance varies from camera system to camera system, but is a specific critical distance, measured in ten-thousandths of an inch.

Here are some of the depth settings for various cameras:

FLANGE FOCAL DEPTH

Metric	Inches	Camera
17.52mm	0.6898"	Standard "C" Mount
38.10mm	1.5000"	Cinema Products (16mm)
40.00mm	1.5748"	Aaton (16mm)
46.50mm	1.8310"	Nikon
48.00mm	1.8898"	Eclair
51.98mm	2.0465"	Arriflex (Aperture Plate)*
52.00mm	2.0472"	Arriflex (Groundglass)*
57.12mm	2.2488"	Panavision (Aperture Plate)*
57.15mm	2.2500"	Panavision (Groundglass)*
61.47mm	2.4201"	Mitchell BNCR
73.50mm	2.8937"	Arriflex 765 (65mm Camera)

* Different distances given for the Arriflex and Panavision Groundglass and aperture plate depth because the latest theory and policy is that the depth should be set so that the exact focus plane should be not on the surface of the film, but below the surface, to ensure optimum focus on all three emulsion layers, not just the top layer. The Groundglass is set to the full flange focal plane depth.

The "Depth" of certain cameras can vary during the shooting day, due to vibration or temperature shifts, and when using these cameras, the Depth should be checked every day with an instrument called a Depth Gauge, and more often if the camera experiences a considerable shift in temperature or a lot of vibration.

Checking the Depth takes only a minute or so, but if it needs adjustment, this can take considerably longer. This is why I prefer to check it every morning during the Morning Routine. If it does need adjustment, it is easier and faster to do it without a hundred people watching and waiting. I have decided that the length of time it takes to check and set the depth is directly proportional to the number of people watching.

I have found that checking the depth once each and every morning is quite sufficient for normal filming. If we are filming outside in the cold, and then come into a warm interior for more filming on the same day, however, I would check it and reset it again once the camera warms up to room temperature.

The depth would also have to be checked and reset every time the camera movement has been removed from the camera and replaced after cleaning. I do this twice a week on a job, usually on Monday and Thursday, but you will have to determine your own schedule. On the Panaflex cameras, the movement can be removed by simply loosening two screws in the camera interior. Removing the movement makes cleaning much easier, with lens tissue and/or cotton applicator, but then you will have to set the depth with the gauge after reinstalling the movement in the camera body. I prefer not to have to do that every day.

The Film Gap can also be adjusted, but will rarely, if ever, need to be. This is the distance between the camera's film gate and pressure plate, and is set very close to the thickness of the film, so it forces the film to lie flat during exposure. Modern motion picture film is generally 0.0065" thick, and the film gap setting on the camera is generally 0.0067", so there is not much tolerance. Black-and-white film used to be thicker than the color negative stocks, but this is no longer true. All of the commonly used color and black-and-white stocks I know of are the same thickness now.

An excellent description of the flange focal depth and film gap checking process can be found in David Samuelson's *Panaflex Users' Manual* (pp.150–151).

Shutter Opening

The "Morning Routine" should include checking the variable shutter, if your camera has one, to make sure that it is set where it is supposed to be, and that if you have changed it during the previous day's filming, that it has been properly reset. The shutter is such an easy thing to overlook and forget to reset after a change, that I have included checking it in my routine.

Whenever the shutter is changed, a piece of tape "reminder" should be placed on the side of the camera to remind the Director of Photography to take the change of shutter angle into account in the exposure calculation, and to remind the Camera Assistant to reset the shutter to the normal position after completing the scene for which a change was requested.

Every Director of Photography has his or her own idea what a "normal" shutter position is. On the Panaflex cameras, for example, the shutter can be varied from 200 to 40 degrees. Some D.P.'s prefer that the shutter be set at 200 degrees, its maximum, while others prefer to set it at 180 degrees, which yields an exposure time of 1/48 of a second, which is what most professional light meters are set for. Find out what your Director of Photography prefers, and remember to reset to that setting after every change.

Other reasons to adjust the shutter might be to freeze the action in individual frames if a freeze-frame optical is to be made (the smaller the shutter angle, the shorter the exposure time and the sharper the image on each individual frame), or to attempt to minimize the roll bar on the TV or computer monitor in the frame (144° for filming at 24 frames per second), or to simply decrease the exposure without using neutral density gels or without changing the aperture.

Movement Phasing

This is a simple test that can be done whenever you feel insecure. I recommend it during the Checkout, and about once a week after that. It would be a good little test to perform after a camera jam, an airplane flight, or a rough truck ride, as well, just to reassure you that the movement is still in sync, or in phase, with the shutter.

A strip of film with a wavy line drawn with a marker pen and threaded in the camera can be used to see any camera movement phasing error. By inching the camera movement by hand while looking through the lens port, individual frames of film and line segment are seen. The visible segments of the line should have stopped moving before the shutter opens, and remain stationery until the shutter closes completely.

Take a piece of film about two feet long. With a Sharpie or other felt-tip pen, draw a wavy line on the emulsion side of the film, between the perforations. Poke a loop of the film into the camera from where the magazine would be, and thread up the camera normally. Remove the lens or lens cap, and look into the lens port at the gate, and turn the inching knob to clear the shutter.

You will see one frame of the film, with one frame of the wavy line. Turn the inching knob of the camera while watching the gate through the lens port. You will see a succession of single frames of the wavy line.

As the shutter turns, and alternately blocks and clears the gate, you should see that the wavy line you see, a different piece of wavy line for each frame, does not move while you can see it, as you turn the inching knob. The film should be held motionless while the shutter is open and you can see the gate, and should advance to the next frame only after the shutter closes completely. By the time the shutter opens again, a new frame of film should be in the gate, and should be held motionless as long as the shutter is open.

If you see the film move in the gate before the shutter closes completely, then the shutter is out of sync, or out of phase, with the movement, and the images photographed with that camera will streak as the film moves during exposure. These streaks will show up more over the darker areas of the frame.

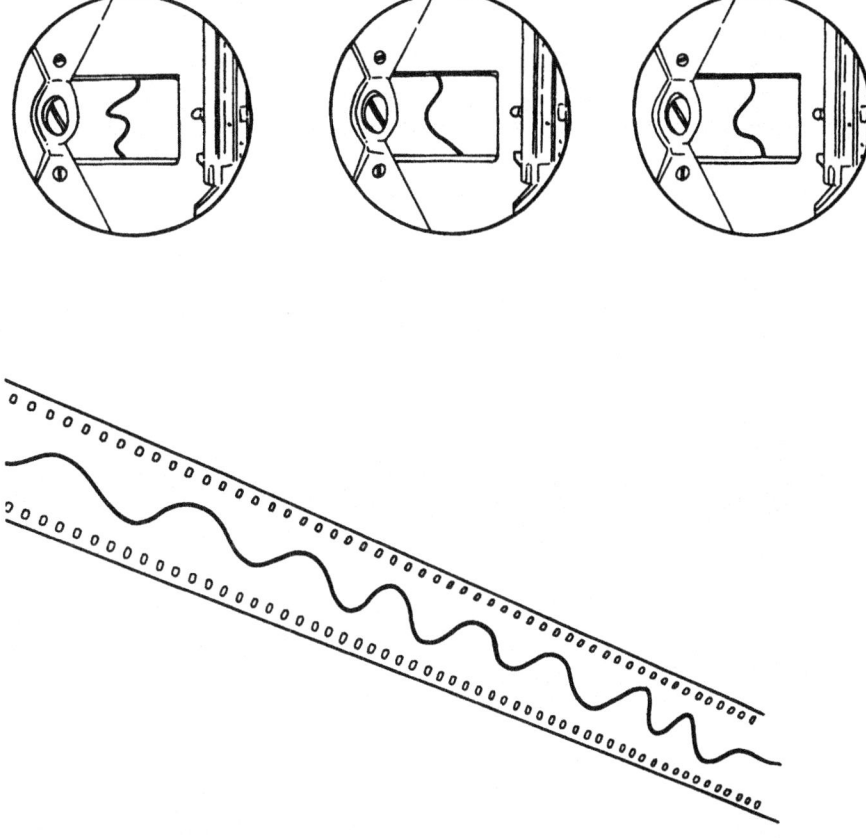

Figure 10-1 Movement Phasing. A strip of film with a wavy line drawn with a marker pen and threaded in the camera can be used to see any camera movement phasing error. By inching the camera movement by hand while looking through the lens port, individual frames of film and line segment are seen. The visible segments of the line should have stopped moving before the shutter opens, and remain stationary until the shutter closes completely.

Stop filming immediately with that camera body and rush it to the repair shop. This is not a repair you can do in the field.

Setting Up

Once you are satisfied with the cleanliness, lubrication, depth, shutter setting, and movement phasing of the camera, you can get to work.

If you know for sure which emulsion to load first, do so. If you don't, ask the Director of Photography. He or she may not have decided yet, so that can wait. If you have a long short end (over 500 feet) of the emulsion you need, load that first.

It's always a good idea to use up those short ends when you can. Otherwise they pile up in the darkroom and make the inventory a nightmare.

If you know what the first setup is, get the camera set up as soon as the grips get the dolly or tripod into position, get the proper film stock threaded up, get the right lens in place, and let the Director of Photography know that the camera is ready. Don't forget the little things, like a battery, power cable, eyepiece leveler, filters, etc. If you have the misfortune to be using a Video Assist, get that hooked up as well.

Another source says to put up the widest lens you have first, so the Director of Photography can get a look at the whole set through the camera, but I find this an unnecessary waste of time. If the scene has been blocked properly, you will know what lens to put up, or ask the D.P. If your Director of Photography uses the zoom lens all the time, then by all means put up the zoom, and set the zoom at the wide end, unless you know what the planned focal length is.

Open the aperture of the lens either to the widest opening, or to the anticipated shooting stop, depending on your Director of Photography. Some D.P.'s always want the lens set up wide open, so they can see what is going on. Others prefer the lens to be set at the anticipated shooting aperture, f/2.8 or f/4 or whatever, so they can watch the lighting progress through the right aperture, and see the expected depth-of-field. Ask the D.P. which he or she prefers.

I once worked for a Director of Photography who loved to look through the camera for hours at a time, and once he got a hold of that camera, he never let go of it long enough for me to thread up, or check focus, or tweak the Video Assist, or anything else, until he was ready to shoot, and then I was always behind and had to rush to catch up.

After the first week, I solved the problem. My solution was to do everything else I needed to do to that camera before I put the lens up. As soon as the lens was up, his eye was glued to the finder, his hands on the wheels, and I lost that camera. But by then, everything I needed to do was done. He never complained, and he has called me back to work with him since that job, so I guess my solution to the problem was the right one.

For other D.P.'s, however, get the camera set up with the lens as soon as possible, so they can look. Hopefully, after a while they will let go of the camera and go away so you can get the rest of your work done.

Service Carts and Handtrucks

While the First Camera Assistant is busy with the morning camera routine, the Second Assistant has morning chores as well. The first priority should be to unload the truck. The equipment that will be needed for the first shot or sequence needs to be unloaded and brought to the shooting location. Obviously, moving all of those heavy cases fifty times a day would be easier if they were on wheels, so many Camera Assistants own and use handtrucks or service carts.

Several manufacturers of handtrucks have models available that fold down into four-wheeled carts for moving cases, and then fold back to upright two-wheeled configuration for storage and travel, and for hauling cases up a flight of stairs. Harper and Magliner are the two most common brands available. The second pair of wheels are usually too small, however, and the four-wheel configuration is often too long for some elevators and the wheelbase too narrow for good stability on uneven surfaces, but the reduced storage size is sometimes worth these inconveniences, especially if you are travelling by air or sometimes need to load everything into a station wagon or van. Several times I have sent a folded up handtruck as baggage when flying, with no problems. It is certainly worth the added shipping cost, to have the convenience of wheels when you get to location.

For general shooting on exterior locations or in large interiors like studios, warehouses, and office buildings, I prefer the service cart solution. Service carts are like hotel room service carts, four wheels, and two or more flat shelves. The most popular model is from Rubbermaid, believe it or not, and is called the Model 4520, 24" by 36" in size. They have a smaller model as well, but it is really too small for most uses. These units are made from high-density plastic, and the larger one is the perfect size for the Camera Assistant's purposes.

It is large enough for a couple of lens cases, or a lens case and a filter case, on the top shelf, and three or four magazines and a pair of batteries on the bottom shelf.

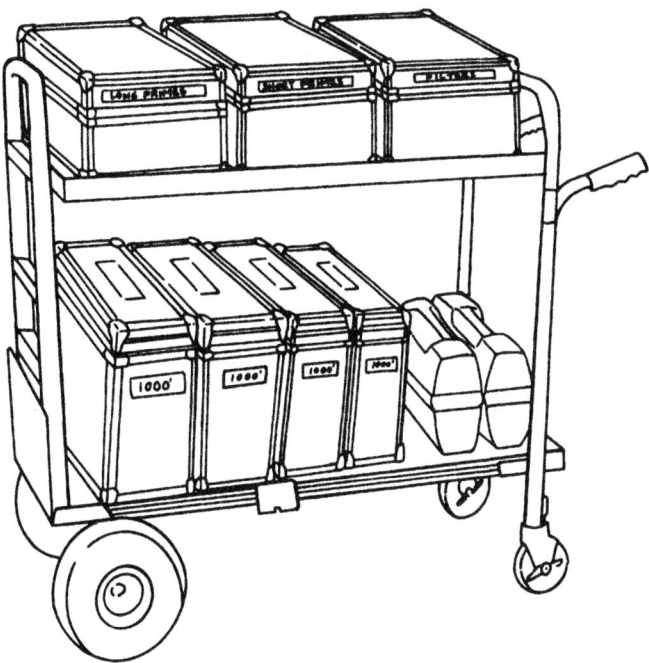

Figure 10-2 Handtrucks. Two-wheel/Four-wheel convertible hand truck with upper shelf added makes a handy equipment carrier.

It is also small enough to fit through narrow aisles and hallways, and into elevators, with ease. When empty, it is light enough for one robust Camera Assistant to carry up or down a flight of stairs, and when loaded, it is sturdy enough to carry the film, lenses, filters, batteries, and accessories that you need to shoot with for a few hours at a time.

Some camera trucks can be rigged by removing one or more of the lower shelves so that the service cart, fully loaded, can be stored without having to be unloaded. This makes for a quick offload in the morning and a quick wrap at night. If the cart is properly bungied in for safety, there is no reason not to store it this way. If the truck shelves cannot be removed, and the service cart must be left in the aisle after the equipment is put away, then I do not advise leaving it loaded.

I often set up the gear head on a high hat on the upper shelf, and mount the camera aboard for moving in to the location, when the dolly is not available. The upper shelf is also the perfect working height for mounting up the lens and matte box on the camera, and for threading up the first magazine, or for other chores. With care, and with one hand on the camera at all times, the cart is fine for getting the camera and the most essential gear from the truck to the shooting site. Two people can maneuver the cart through even the toughest obstacle course, including up and down curbs and single steps. For longer stairs, the cart must, of course, be unloaded, and carried empty up or down the stairs, and then loaded again.

The cart does require some modifications, however, to be really useful. Throw away the tiny casters it comes with and buy some big wheels! Larger wheels, at least six inches in diameter (and better at eight or ten inches), are essential for wheeling over the hundreds of electric cables that litter all film sets, as well as for other broken and uneven surfaces like an average New York City sidewalk. Large casters are usually available from the same places that sell service carts and handtrucks, or you can find a specialty hardware store in the phone book.

Be prepared to spend more for the wheels than you spent for the cart. The last time I bought one of the Rubbermaid carts, a few years ago, the cart came to about $120, and I went out and spent $140 for a set (two fixed and two swivel) of casters, eight-inch pneumatic wonders. Pneumatic casters (that pump up with air, like small automobile tires) make the ride much smoother than the hard rubber wheels, and eight inches in diameter is just right for most cable-hopping and curb-climbing.

In order to mount the new casters, I persuaded the grips to cut me a piece of 3/4" plywood the same size as the bottom of the cart, and I had to drill a few new holes. You will also have to buy longer bolts, washers, lock washers, and nuts, to put the thing together, but the result is worth the expense and the time. The cart is now a bit heavier, and a few inches higher, but it sure makes the job easier.

You should also drill four small holes, one in each corner of the upper and lower shelves, diagonally downward from the inside of the cart to the outside. These holes are for drainage when working in the rain, to prevent rainwater from collecting and forming a lake inside the cart. By drilling a hole in each corner, you guarantee that no matter how uneven the terrain, one hole will always be at the low point, and will work as a drain.

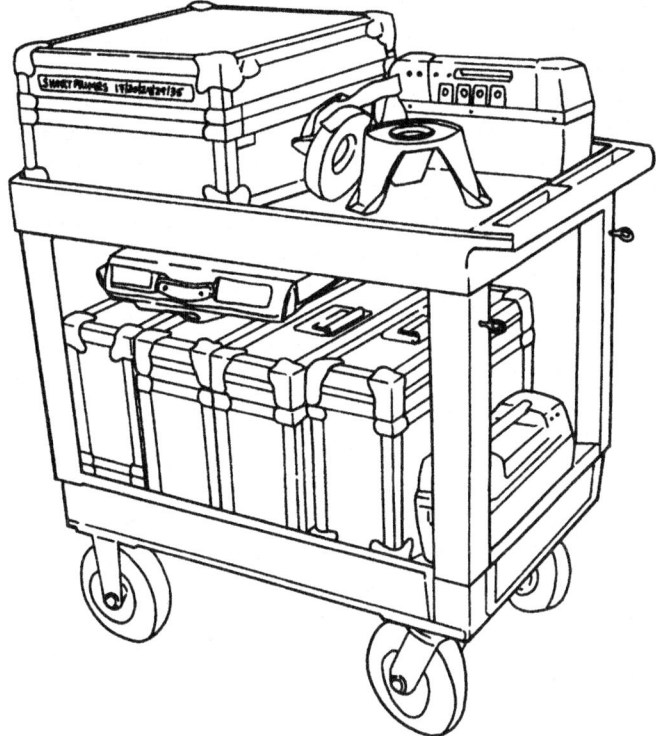

Figure 10-3 Camera Assistants' Service Cart. Heavy-duty plastic service cart from Rubbermaid with extra-large wheels added makes ideal equipment carrier.

Bringing Equipment to the Set

There are two schools of thought among Camera Assistants about what to bring to the set. Some Assistants feel they must bring everything they or the company owns or rents with them to every shot. This is fine for the young and foolish, who don't mind having to load and unload their carts over and over again with cases they will never use, and then trying to find enough space on the set between the grips and the electricians and their hampers, grip stands, and sandbags.

I prefer a more logical (and a more lazy) approach. Bring along only absolute essentials, like the prime lenses and film magazines, and pieces most likely to be used, like spare batteries. But I won't bring the 600mm lens and the intervalometer into an office building to shoot a dialogue scene in the elevator, and I won't bring the 10:1 zoom lens out to the set for a night exterior, unless the D.P. specifically requests that I do.

After a short time on the job, it will become obvious what lenses are likely to be needed, and what accessories. If in doubt, ask the D.P. I try to corral the D.P. early, and ask what sort of shooting to expect at that location and what equipment (and especially which film stocks) we will most likely use. This information can save a lot of running around later.

This is also a good time for the Assistant to "scout the location;" to find out which rooms you are actually going to shoot in, which rooms or areas would be good for equipment storage, where the elevators are, where the loading dock is, where the phones and the rest rooms are, etc.

If something is subsequently needed that you have not loaded onto the carts, then it can usually be fetched very quickly. A clever Camera Assistant will soon be able to anticipate such needs in plenty of time to send the Second or the Loader or Trainee back to the truck.

Morning Chores

In addition to the camera maintenance and truck unloading chores, the Camera Assistants can do other things to prepare for the day's shooting. These include, but are not limited to, updating the raw stock inventory, ordering more raw stock to be delivered from the manufacturer or production office, filling out time cards, changing the date on the slates, phoning the rental house to order or check on additional equipment or needed repairs, changing over loaded magazines to a different type stock, filling out the top of the camera reports, sweeping out the camera truck, bringing batteries into the location to charge, and any of a thousand other things that will save time or energy later.

CHAPTER **11**

Shooting Procedures

Set Etiquette

There are only two rules of Set Etiquette for Camera Assistants (and everybody else on the crew):

Rule #1: Keep Your Mouth Shut!
Rule #2: Stay in Your Own Department!

Unfortunately, I never mastered these rules, and am constantly getting myself into trouble. Maybe you will have better luck.

Rule #1 has more to do with career insurance than etiquette, but it is an important concept to understand. I have rarely been able to resist the temptation to let some fool know that I know he is a fool. I often do this loudly, and in front of witnesses. Tact was never my strong suit, and neither is tolerance for incompetence or injustice.

Unfortunately, these demonstrations of honest indignation have a nasty habit of coming back to haunt me. The parking P.A. or location manager you yell at for screwing up somehow will cross your path again a year later as the production manager, and again a year after that as producer, and again a year after that as the owner of some major studio. What some of these people lack in intelligence and common sense they make up for in long memories.

Try negotiating a better day rate for yourself with a production manager who remembers you yelling at him in front of the crew years ago when he was a location manager on some job for arranging camera truck parking six blocks from the shooting location. This happened to me once.

The production department is the only place on the film set where the lack of experience, honesty, or common sense is no impediment to advancement or promotion. But it is bad luck for a lowly crew person to let them know that you know this. Don't get me wrong—not many production people fall into this category—but a few do. A much better approach, and the one I recommend to you all, is to collect all that overtime and laugh at them all the way to the bank.

Eighty percent of the expensive delays on film sets are due, in my opinion, based on 26 years in the business, to Production Department screw-ups of some sort. (Another 10 percent is due to mechanical breakdowns, usually generators or special effects rigs, and the final 10 percent is due to the weather.)

The most common production screw-ups are: unrealistic or downright impossible scheduling, "economizing" in the wrong places, failure to pass on information to the people who need to know, failure to heed the advice of more experienced people on the crew, coddling prima donna actors and directors, and not doing one's "homework" before arriving on the set.

Producers and production managers are very strange animals. Before the job begins, they are doing everything possible to make the job happen. Once shooting starts, they seem to be doing everything possible to PREVENT the job from happening. I've never understood this phenomenon, but have seen it demonstrated countless times.

I know this chapter will get me in even more trouble with certain production types, but it needs to be said.

Rule #2; "Stay in your own department!" is also an important concept. It is a natural tendency to want to help out fellow crew members, but 90 percent of the time, other departments do not need or want the help. Responsibilities on the film set are very specifically assigned, and the members of the various Departments take great pride in being able to do their own jobs without help from "outsiders." It is also possible to make things worse by trying to help. There may be factors unknown to you that you may be upsetting.

For example, the table that is in your way on the set may be an antique that falls apart when moved improperly. Wait for the Prop Department to move furniture out of the way. The flag you want to set to keep a distant light out of the lens may cast a shadow on part of the set from another light. Let the Grip Department set all flags. A cable next to a stage box may look like it has been accidentally kicked out, but it may have been removed on purpose, and putting it back may turn on an unwanted light. Let the Electrical Department handle all cables.

In simple terms: Stay in your own Department. An often-heard phrase, "Tell me what to do—Don't tell me how to do it!" describes the situation well. All departments have their own pride of profession. Let them do their jobs their way. There is a great deal of logic and common sense in craft lines and department divisions.

Don't make things worse by trying to help. You wouldn't want the grips to set the aperture on the lens, or the electricians to add a filter without letting you know—don't do the same to them!

The only exceptions to this basic rule I can think of are if someone asks for your help, or if someone is about to be injured, it is certainly all right to cross craft lines. Since I am usually next to the dolly, I am the first in line to help out when the dolly needs to climb a step or curb. And certainly if the wind is about to blow over a light or grip stand, no one will object to your helping out to prevent an injury. But otherwise, wait to be asked to help.

Chain of Command

Obviously, you're working for the Director of Photography as an Assistant, but you are also working for the production company. The problem is that everyone thinks they are in charge. The Assistant Directors think they are always the ones in charge. The Directors think they're in charge. The Production Managers think they're in charge. The Producers think they're in charge. But as far as the Camera Assistants are concerned, only the Director of Photography is in charge.

The Director of Photography has to be the source of all Camera Department decisions. What equipment shall we carry? What stock shall we shoot? How many cameras shall we use? All of these questions must be answered by the Director of Photography.

If there is some budget or equipment or personnel problem, then the Director of Photography has to be the one to battle it out with the Producer or Production Manager. The Camera Assistant should avoid getting caught in the middle of this battle. If the Production Manager complains about how many lenses or magazines are on rental, and wants some returned to reduce the rental bills, let the Director of Photography decide. Don't let yourself get caught in a situation where the D.P. asks for something and you have to say that the Production Manager made you send it back.

If you know that multiple cameras are being scheduled, confer with the Director of Photography about ordering extra cameras and lenses, and about recommending additional crew for those extra cameras. The Director of Photography may have certain Camera Operators and Camera Assistants that he or she might want to use for those days, or, more importantly, may have certain Operators and Assistants that he or she NEVER wants to work with or see on the set, because of some problem in the past.

I generally try to call the Union to find out who is available before speaking to the D.P. about extra crew. This eliminates the step of choosing people and then finding out they are not available for the days you need them.

Never Distract Director or Actors

On the set, actors and directors are each going to have their own personalities and egos and they are going to be upset by different things. Try not to be a distraction on the set. If temperamental or nervous actors are doing intimate things, the best advice for a Camera Assistant is to be invisible and silent.

The best Assistants are those who can do their jobs quietly and efficiently, without fuss or fanfare. They get their focus marks with a minimum of dialogue, they reload quickly, change lenses quietly, etc., with a minimum of bother and distraction.

It is vital that the actions and movements of the Camera Assistant should not distract the actors from their performances. All too often, the Camera Assistant is the crew member most likely to be in the actor's line of sight. The Assistant is standing or sitting just to the right of the camera, usually in plain sight. The Operator is hidden by the camera, the director and other crew members are usually behind the camera or at least partially hidden in the darkness, but the Camera Assistant is right there in full view.

Any rapid or jerky motions by the Camera Assistant in that position might be very distracting to the performers. The Assistant can usually figure out very early in the shoot which actors are the most likely to be spooked, and should tread lightly when shooting a scene with those actors.

I heard one story about an Assistant that used to make faces when he missed a mark or was a bit late on a zoom cue. He was totally oblivious to the scowls and grimaces he was making, but the actors sometimes noticed and once stopped in the middle of the scene being shot to ask if something was wrong. Finally the D.P. figured out what was happening and spoke to the Assistant about masking his emotions a little better.

You'd be surprised to hear about actors with dozens of pictures under their belts still being distracted by the simple movements of the Camera Assistant just doing his or her job.

More than once I have asked the grips to put up a flag between me and the actors so they cannot see me as well, or to use the focus extension and step away from the camera either behind the operator or behind a light or piece of furniture, for added camouflage.

No Eye Contact With Actors

The worst possible distraction for an actor is to inadvertently make eye contact with someone other than the other actors in the scene. It is human nature to look at the eyes of another person, but as an Assistant, don't do it. Don't ever look at the face of a performing actor—look at their shoes, or belt buckle, or chest, or hands, or some other part, but never at the face. If the actor should happen to turn his head and find you staring into his eyes, that moment of eye contact could easily ruin the performer's concentration and ruin the take.

Even the D.P. needs to find a place to stand that is out of the actors' eyelines and out of distraction range.

Never Leave Camera Unattended

This is a very important part of the Camera Assistant's job. Dave Quaid would say a good Camera Assistant is never further than a double arms' length from the camera. If you have a Second Assistant on the job that's often possible to do. The First can be within range of the camera at all times, and let the Second do all the running, but if you're the only Assistant it's not going to be possible.

The Dolly Grip will very often be near the dolly most of the time. Before I leave the camera for any reason, I make sure the Second Assistant and/or the Dolly Grip knows that I'm going and that the camera is in their charge temporarily. This is for many reasons—tripods get kicked, cameras fall over, people carrying scenery or furniture through the set can bump into the camera, it suddenly starts to rain, or if the camera is front-heavy or back-heavy on the head and has not been properly balanced, then the camera may suddenly droop over.

The safety and security of the camera is a prime responsibility of the Camera Assistant.

Unplug and Cover the Camera

Also, when going to lunch, or leaving the set or location while the actors are rehearsing, or even while leaving the set to answer the call of nature, unplug the camera and cover it over with a weather protector or rain cover.

It is impossible to predict what the weather might do, and what other people might do. You don't want someone to hit the switch by accident and shoot 800 feet of a set being lit, or of the director picking his nose, or of the inside of a lens cap, which has happened many times on sets, I'm sure. When this does happen, it is generally listed as a "Motor Test" on the Camera Report.

If it is cold enough to be using the built-in heater in some cameras, then leave the heater plugged in while going to lunch, or when leaving the camera for any length of time, but unplug the camera power.

Also make sure the video assist tap is switched off or unplugged if leaving the camera for any length of time. Nothing drains a battery as fast as the video assist.

Moving the Camera

Once the camera is on the dolly, it is often very convenient to leave it on the dolly and wheel over to the location of the next shot. The Camera Assistant should keep at least one hand on the camera at all times while the dolly is moving between locations, walking alongside as the dolly travels. If the street, sidewalk, or ground is rough, then it might be advisable to remove the camera from the gear head and hand carry it to the next location. At the very least, remove the lens, especially if the lens is a zoom or heavy telephoto.

I sometimes keep a high hat on the service cart we use to transport equipment, and the gear head and camera can be transferred from the dolly to this high hat and wheeled to the next location on the service cart, which with its larger, softer tires, provides a smoother ride for the camera and lens.

I also use Gear Head Carry Rods to transport the gear head, camera, lens, mag, etc. These are stainless steel rods about 32 inches long that fit into holes in the cradle of the Panahead (these holes also can be found in the cradle of the Arri Gear Head, but the diameter is different—just to annoy Camera Assistants, I'm sure!) and allow two persons to carry the whole package together as if carrying a stretcher to an ambulance. The advantage is that nothing needs to be removed from the camera before transport, except to disconnect the power cable from the battery. This is the absolutely fastest and safest way to transfer the head and camera from the dolly to a high hat for a low-angle shot, for example, or to move from a tripod to a dolly, or from the dolly to a crane.

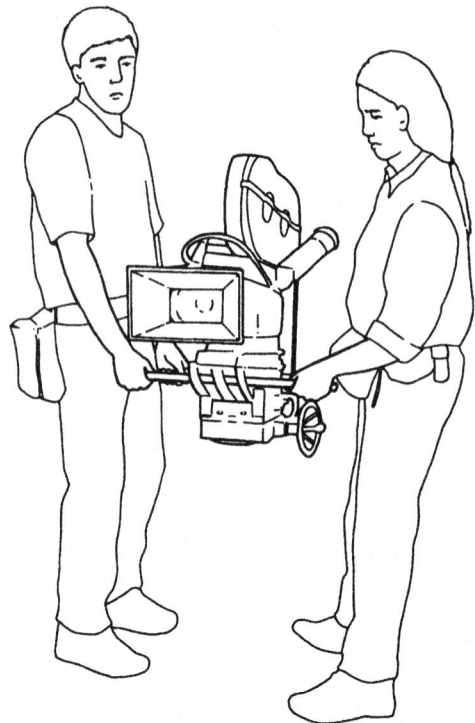

Figure 11-1 Gear Head Carry Rods. Gear head "Carry Rods" make transporting gear head, camera, lens, magazine, matte box, etc., easy, without the need to dismantle and re-assemble. This is the fastest and safest method of transferring the camera from tripod to dolly, or dolly to hi-hat, etc.

If you do not have, or cannot get Gear Head Rods, then it is still possible to move the head and camera together with two people, but it is a lot less comfortable. Two persons, standing on the camera left and right sides, can grasp the cradle of the gear head and shift the entire package from the dolly to the tripod, etc. Lift by the cradle of the head, not by the camera.

When changing from the dolly to a high hat, there is an additional trick to make the transfer even easier. Once the tie-down is removed from the gear head, two people can grab the gear head cradle and lift the head and camera straight up, while a third person sets the high hat onto the dolly, between the dolly and the gear head, aligning the keyway with the key on the gear head. The camera can then be lowered onto the high hat and the tie-down attached. The whole package can then be carried to wherever it needs to go, and set down in position.

We have all seen pictures of a Camera Assistant with a tripod, gear head, and full camera with magazine, lens, and matte box slung over his shoulder, walking from one location to another. While this may have been popular and possible in the past, it is not a good idea, from a health standpoint, or from a camera safety standpoint.

First of all, this combination is VERY heavy, and none but the largest and strongest Camera Assistants should even try to do this. Secondly, when the whole rig is on your shoulder, you cannot even see the camera, and it is just too dangerous to travel this way. It is difficult, if not impossible, for anyone to walk behind such a procession as a safety. They certainly cannot help with the weight. I have also seen the screws holding the base plate onto the gear head shear off with a sudden shock. Fortunately, I caught the camera before it could fall from the dolly and hit the ground. If this were to happen while the camera is being transported over your shoulder, I hope you have a back-up camera.

I have never understood how some Assistants, who insist on walking alongside a dolly with a hand on the camera while it is riding right side up on a dolly, can hoist the whole thing up on their shoulders and walk along with the camera suspended sideways six feet in the air with nothing underneath except cement. This is infinitely more risky. It is hard to imagine a situation where a safer means of transportation of the camera is not possible or advisable. It is difficult to imagine being in that much of a hurry between setups, either.

If you do not have gear head rods, then whenever possible, remove the camera from the gear head, and carry the thing in two pieces. The First can carry the camera, and the Second can carry the gear head and legs, and it is every bit as fast and a whole lot safer. I suppose there will always be those macho Assistant types who insist on carrying the cameras, heads, and tripods on their shoulders, but you won't find me doing it very often.

Of course, there has to be an exception. When I was working on one film, we had to film a football game in the semifrozen mud of a prison yard. There was no way to use a dolly or even a service cart in the six-inch deep mud, so carrying the camera, gear head, and tripod in one piece was the only way we could work. It was tough, especially in the deep mud, but we were lucky and didn't have any accidents dropping cameras.

If you absolutely must travel in one piece this way, then make sure the camera is secured to the head, the balance plate and base plate locked off, the pan locked, and then turn the tilt wheel all the way to the right, tilting the camera all the way up. It also helps to extend one tripod leg, the one directly under the lens, so that it is a few inches longer than the others. Then use the tripod shoulder pad hanging between the tripod legs up between the front of the gear head cradle and your shoulder. Set your feet, crouch down a bit, grab the two shorter tripod legs, tilt back as you lift, putting the weight first on the extended leg, and then onto your shoulder, and there you go. BE CAREFUL! Get someone to walk nearby, and get some help again to set the rig down. Set the longest leg into the ground first, the leg that was directly beneath the lens when you picked up the tripod, then spread out the other legs as you rock the weight forward onto the other legs.

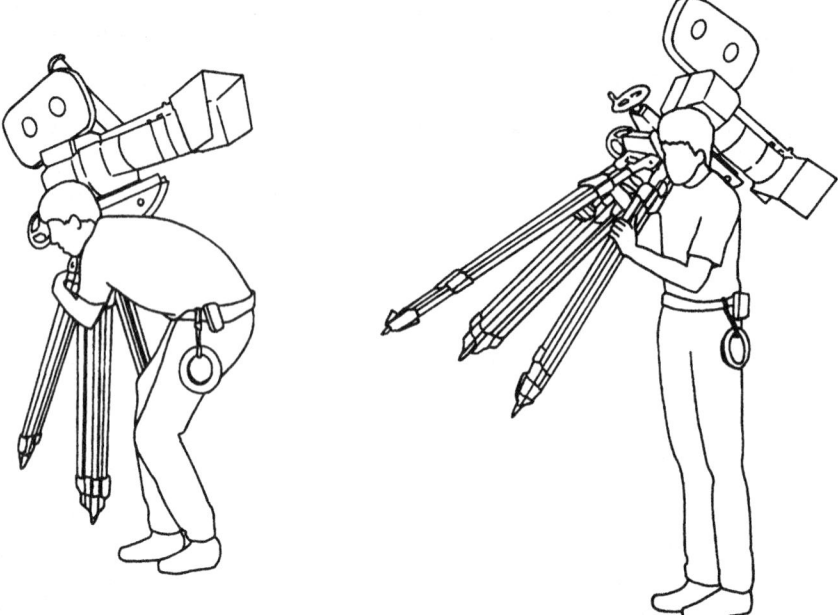

Figure 11-2 Camera, Head, and Tripod on Shoulder. I cannot recommend carrying the camera this way, but if you absolutely must do it this way, do it safely for you and safely for the camera. Be very careful.

Scene Blocking

Scene Blocking consists of finding a position in which the camera will be set up for shooting a scene, and of positioning and marking the various actors, vehicles, furniture and/or props that will be needed for the scene. A by-product of this process is that the crew finds out what is going to happen in the scene.

For some Directors and Directors of Photography this process of scene blocking will be very involved and detailed, with specific marks laid down with tape or chalk, and numbered for different positions within the scene, sometimes blocking several shots at one time for an entire scene or sequence, and sometimes for a whole day's work. For other directors and D.P.'s, scene blocking will consist of a vague hand gesture pointing, "Over there, somewhere."

If done right, Scene Blocking works something like this: the Director and the Director of Photography, having discussed the script scene by scene, and having seen all of the locations during preproduction, and having in their minds a good idea of what they want, take the actors into the set or location, possibly with the script supervisor and assistant director, to rehearse the scene and block the action. The crew is busy at this time unloading the trucks and setting up the equipment. At this time, no equipment is inside the set or location.

When they have worked out roughly what happens—where the camera should be, where the actors are moving during the scene, and how to break up the scene into individual shots, they call for the "Marking Team" to join them inside. The Marking Team consists of the Dolly Grip, the Camera Assistants, the Gaffer, the Propmaster, the Sound Mixer, and possibly other department heads, who may benefit from a preview of what is going to happen.

The Director of Photography holds the director's finder where the camera will go, and the actors are in position. When the D.P. is satisfied that everyone is in the right place, the Grip measures the height of the finder off the floor. The First Camera Assistant places a piece of tape on the floor, directly under the rear of the finder, writing on the tape the number of the shot, the focal length of the lens desired, an arrow showing which direction the camera is looking, and the lens height, obtained from the Grip. The Script Supervisor might also be keeping this same information in list form for future reference. I usually try and keep my own list, as well.

The Second Camera Assistant, possibly with the Trainee to help, marks the actors' positions with the appropriately colored tapes. Hopefully the actors will stand still long enough to be marked. A lot of actors see the Assistant approaching with the tape, and step out of the way before the tape can be placed. It is hard to mark shoes that are not there anymore. Try to impress on the actors how important it is to stand still in place until accurately marked.

The Prop crew marks essential furniture and other key props the same way the Assistants mark the actors. The Stand-ins for the actors in the scene should be watching, at this point, to see where and when the actors they are standing in for move from position to position during the scene. Once the actors leave, for wardrobe and makeup, the Stand-ins will duplicate these moves, and assume the same positions for lighting, dolly rehearsal, focus marks, etc.

Once everyone has opening marks, the actors will walk through the scene, moving as they will be moving when the camera is rolling. At each stopping point, the Second will put down another mark. If the camera is moving as well, the First and the Dolly Grip will mark each camera position—lens, height, and direction. If the shot involves a zoom, the First makes note of that information as well. The shots are numbered—#1, #2, etc. They will be given real scene numbers later by the script supervisor.

The individual shots will probably be laid out in chronological script sequence, although they might not be shot in that order. The Director of Photography, conferring with the Director and often the Assistant Director, determines the shooting order for the shots laid out, depending on the lighting requirements and other considerations.

By laying out a whole scene, or a whole location's work, or a whole day's work at one time, much time and effort is saved. Everyone who needs to know what is going to happen finds out at the same time, and all the questions get answered—questions about necessary furniture, about where to hide cables, about which windows need to be gelled, about which lenses will be needed.

Now that everyone knows what is happening, the dolly, camera, and lights can be brought into the room, and the real work can begin. Once the camera is in place, the fine-tuning can begin.

This is how it COULD go, but rarely does. It would be a real joy for everyone involved to work out the blocking this way. There is less screaming, less changing of minds, less misinformation, less wasted effort, and everything fits together like the precision machine it could be.

Unfortunately, most jobs do not work this way. Every Director/ D.P. team works differently in their scene blocking styles, depending on whether or not the Director has done his or her homework, or is working "off the cuff."

Sometimes the Director has never seen the location before arriving there with cast, crew, and equipment, and must "improvise" on the spot. Sometimes the Director cannot "see" more than one shot in his or her head at a time. Disinformation is the name of the game. No one knows what is happening in THIS shot, let alone the NEXT one. The work progresses at the speed of a glacier, and schedules fall farther and farther behind.

Some Directors and Directors of Photography can only block a scene through a camera, moving the camera and the actors aimlessly around the room in search of a shot. This is a slow and painful way to work, but it is very common.

Some Directors and Directors of Photography insist on blocking the scenes using the Stand-ins instead of the First Team. This almost always ends in disaster. The actors often have ideas in their own minds of how to play the scene, when to move, and where to move to. The Stand-ins, moving about the set at the direction of the Director, cannot possibly guess what the actors are planning to do.

When the actors do show up on the set, they will often want to change the blocking of the scene, forcing the crew to re-light, or move the dolly track, or get new focus marks, in short, to redo everything they have done in the past hour. All of that could be avoided by blocking the scenes with the First Team.

Sometimes the cast members have an influence on the scene blocking process. Some actors find it too confining and restricting to be marked precisely for exact scene planning, and prefer to be "spontaneous," a word which should strike terror into the heart of the Camera Assistant who has to keep this tremendous talent in focus.

That usually means that the actor will be all over the room, unpredictably, and will do each take differently. Even more distressing is that some directors let these actors get away with that sort of foolishness. This may be all right for stage plays, but for motion pictures, where intricate dolly, zoom, and focus work depends on cooperation among all the Departments, including the Acting Department, this "spontaneous" stuff makes for poor composition, soft focus, short tempers, and numerous reshoots. To me, it separates the professionals from the amateurs. There is another word for "spontaneous" movies—"documentaries."

Directors' Finders/Real Lens Finders/Camera-as-Finder

There are three styles of "director's viewfinders" for finding camera positions and actor marks. Since the Camera Assistant is the one who ends up carrying and handling the finders, I have divided the types into weight categories; "Three Pound," "Hundred Pound," and "Thousand Pound" finders.

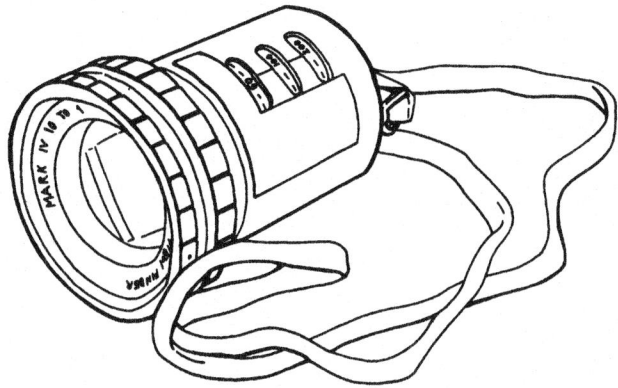

Figure 11-3 Three Pound Finder. The Directors Finder approximates the view through a wide range of camera lenses in a small, pocket-sized unit. This is a fast and easy system, but is also the least accurate.

The first, and most practical and portable, is the "Three Pound" finder. Also called a "Director's Finder," this unit is smaller than most motion picture camera lenses, but approximates many lenses. Several models are available, with different ranges of lenses. The best of these units approximates the 10:1 zoom lens (25mm through 250mm lenses, for 35mm photography), and simulates aspect ratios from Academy (1.33:1) to 1.66:1 to 1.85:1 to 2.35:1 for anamorphic photography, all in one small, light-weight, unit, perfectly sized and shaped for meter cases, front boxes, or jacket pockets. Changing focal lengths or aspect ratios involves simply turning the appropriate ring on the finder.

There are no focus adjustments on these "Director's Finders" (except on the eyepiece to correct for the user's eyesight), so they are not useful for viewing anticipated Depth-of-Field, but for reasonably accurate camera positioning, they are just fine. Unfortunately, some Directors and Directors of Photography feel that it is not accurate enough, or does not yield a large enough image.

The next category of finder I describe as the "Hundred Pound Finder," or "Real Lens" finders. These devices, resembling a camera eyepiece attached to the appropriate lens mount, are exactly that, with the appropriately marked ground glass installed inside, and actually use the camera lenses mounted to the finder to look through.

Since the actual camera lenses are used, the finders are as accurate as the camera would be, and because the camera-style eyepiece magnifies the image just as the camera does, the image is bright and clear, and must be focused by turning the lens focus barrel, just as on a camera.

Arriflex and Panavision both make these, as do other companies. They may be either "in-line" (straight) or "right-angle," and each style has its pluses and minuses. The in-line ones are good for most purposes, but for a low-angle shot, in order to look through it in position, the user must lie down on the floor or ground.

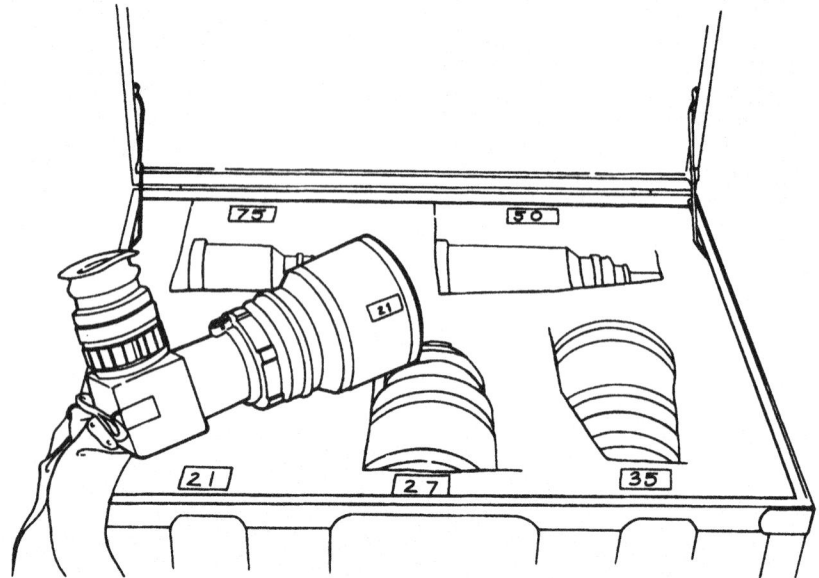

Figure 11-4 Hundred Pound Finder. The "Real Lens" finder uses actual camera lenses to find camera positions. Less convenient than pocket-sized Director's Finder, but more precise.

The right-angle finder, with an internal prism, is better for this type of shot, requiring only that the user sit or kneel to see a low-angle shot, but is less useful for setting an "eye-level" shot, forcing the user to stand on an apple box or a lens case in order to position the head to look through the lens at eye-level from the ground.

In order to go off searching for a shot with one of these "Hundred Pound" finders, the scouting party must include at least one Camera Assistant, and must carry with them the actual lenses that are to be used, at least one lens case, sometimes two or more, hence the description "Hundred Pound" finder. It is also much slower and clumsier to have the Camera Assistant actually change lenses on the finder than to just turn a ring on the finder, but for really accurate camera positioning, such as looking for a wide shot in a small set or location, where camera placement is a problem, it is the right tool. Another disadvantage is that the lens focus must be constantly adjusted in order to keep the actors or targets in focus. Focus must be "followed," just as when the camera is in place.

Unfortunately again, there are Directors and D.P.'s who seem unable to use even these "Real Lens" finders, preferring the "Thousand Pound" finder; a complete camera package mounted on a gear head on a dolly, and all lenses in their cases, as well as a Dolly Grip or two and a Camera Assistant or two, hence the description "Thousand Pound" finder. The bigger and heavier the finder gets, the slower it is to move and use, but sometimes, with some directors, it is the only way they can work.

Another type of finder some directors prefer, although fewer and fewer of them are around these days, is the offset side viewfinder from an old Mitchell camera, with

Figure 11-5 Thousand Pound Finder. Complete camera package with production dolly (and crew members) used as Director's Finder. Slowest, most cumbersome and least efficient system, but very common.

its masks for various lenses. This viewfinder provides a large clear image, and several directors still use these finders, even though the cameras they belong to are rarely seen anymore. These finders belong in the "Three Pound" category, I suppose, although they are slightly heavier than that.

Still another option is to use a small, hand-held camera body, such as an Arri IIC or even an Arri III, as a viewfinder, without a magazine, but with a real camera lens. This gives you a fairly light and portable viewfinder system without having to deal with the dolly, the gear head, and the full production camera.

Marking Actors

Marking actors is a basic and simple part of blocking the scene. The actor will be given a start mark, and if the actor needs to move somewhere during the shot, there will be an end mark, and possibly one or more intermediate marks. The Camera

278 THE CAMERA ASSISTANT

Assistants will simply mark the actors' shoes on the floor or ground. Actors' shoe marks may take different forms, and every Camera Assistant will have a personal preference for style, but they all serve the same purpose.

These marks are not only used by the actors, but also by several members of the crew. The Director of Photography needs the "Stand-ins" (also known as the "Second Team") on those marks for lighting, usually while the actual actors (the "First Team") are having their makeup and hair done, and getting into wardrobe. The Camera Operator needs the actors to be on those marks in order to maintain the proper composition for the shot, as specified by the Director of Photography and director during scene blocking. The dolly grip often depends on actor position to cue the dolly move.

The actor marks are used by the Camera Assistant for focus reference. The Camera Assistant will have taken measurements, and will know how far it is from the camera to each actors' mark, and will be adjusting focus accordingly during the shot. If the actor is not at the mark, the Camera Operator, the Dolly Grip, and the Camera Assistant cannot do their jobs properly. They must start estimating and guessing, and compromising, and the shot and the whole scene will suffer.

Some actors are better than others about being marked and hitting marks. I'll use initials instead of names, to protect the guilty. "W" is the best I've ever worked with. He could back up into a mark and hit it within two inches. "R" never came

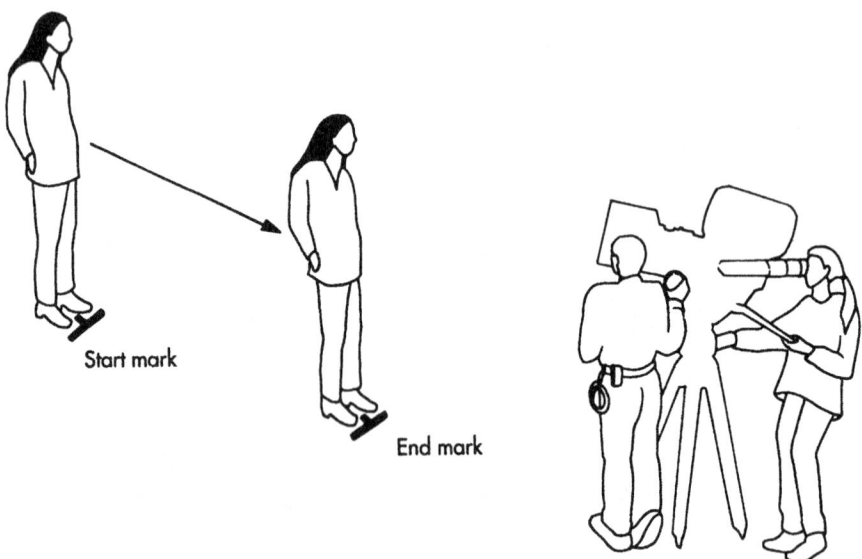

Figure 11-6 Actors' Marks—Start and End. An actor's starting position can be marked with a "T"-shaped mark in tape or chalk, and then another mark placed for the end position. The Camera Assistant can measure the distance to each mark, and adjust the focus accordingly as the actor moves from mark to mark.

within a foot of a mark in his life, and likes to do each take differently, which makes it very difficult for the Assistant and the Operator. "T" never came anywhere near a mark—she knew where they were and seemed to be purposely avoiding them. "A" would plant his feet on the marks, and then lean about two feet in every direction, constantly leaning and shifting his weight throughout the scene. I don't know how he did this without falling over. "K" will see a mark and will consistently stop six to twelve inches behind it. "J" would do the opposite, stopping consistently about six inches in front of the mark. You'll get to know how the different actors on your job work very quickly, and will adapt to their idiosyncracies. It is often absolutely unpredictable.

The most common actor shoe mark is a "T"-shaped mark, with the cross-bar running from shoe tip to shoe tip, and the short stem between the shoes, showing the actor which side of the cross-bar to stand on. A second style of mark runs from shoe tip to shoe tip, and then angles back on both ends. A third type is two "U"-shaped or "V"-shaped marks, one for each shoe tip. A faster version of the shoe marks uses two short straight pieces of tape, one for each shoe tip. Any of these styles establish the actor's position fairly precisely. An "X" on the floor or ground is useless. It does not show which direction the actor needs to be facing, nor does it show the width of the actor's stance, both important for precise placement.

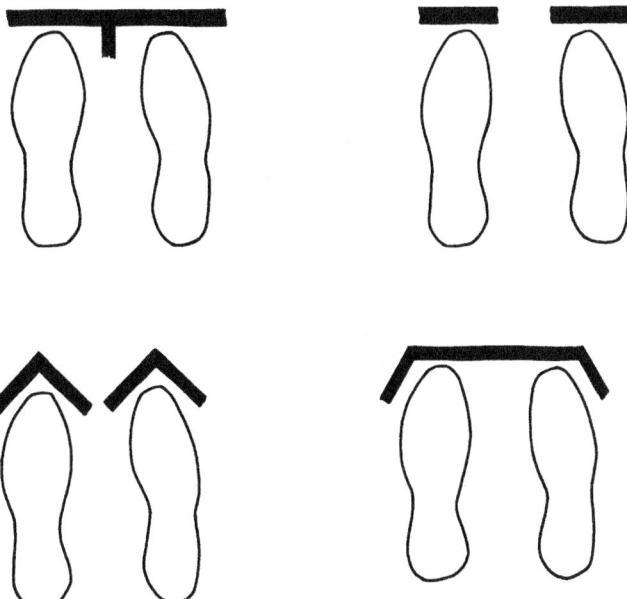

Figure 11-7 Actors' Toe Marks—Four Styles. Four styles of Actors Toe Marks, using tape or chalk. Color coding the marks for specific actors makes it easier for the actors and for the Assistant.

280 THE CAMERA ASSISTANT

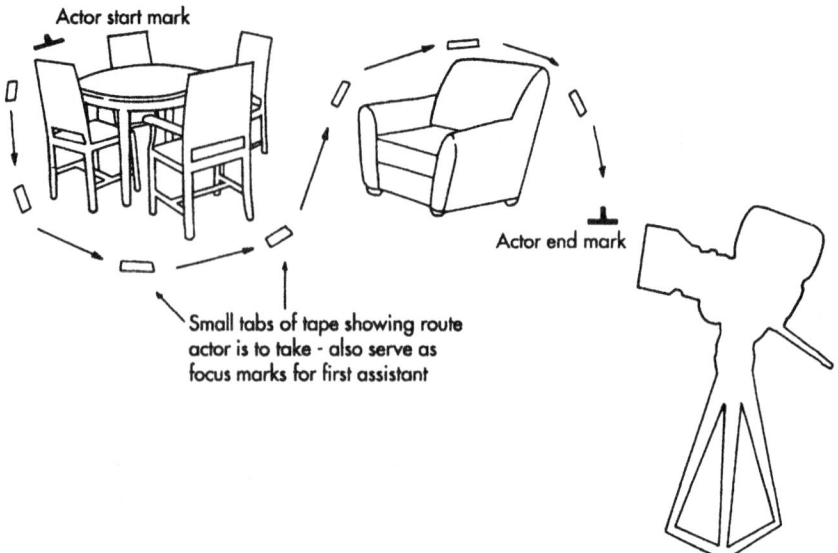

Figure 11-8 "Follow the Yellow Brick Road." Make a path for the actors to follow, using tape or chalk. Use some of those same marks for focus reference as well. As long as the actor stays on the path, you will have your focus references.

If the actor's walking path needs to be precisely marked for composition, lighting, and/or focus or for any other reason, make a trail for the actor to follow, with strips of tape or short chalk marks placed between the actor's feet as he walks. Then all he has to do is follow the dotted line.

Actor's marks can be made with tape, or chalk, or crayon, or wooden wedges or "T"s, or even sandbags. Anything that establishes an actor's position, and is not likely to blow away or get kicked out of position, can be used. It also depends on the surface being marked. For wooden or tile floors, or for carpeting, colored tapes are the best material. They stay where they are placed, and are easily removable, without leaving a residue.

On cement or blacktop, chalk is probably the best, unless the surface is wet, in which case, use something more durable, like lumber crayon (thick crayons available in hardware stores). Keep in mind that marks sometimes have to be hidden and/or removed, so don't make them too permanent. Some colored chalk is very difficult to remove from cement or brick, even with water.

Outside, on dirt or grass, wooden wedges or plastic tent stakes, driven into the ground until only the very top shows, or wooden or rubber "T"-shaped marks are used, nailed down into the ground with spikes to prevent their moving around.

Actor's marks are generally color coded, at least for the principal actors. At the beginning of the job, the Camera Assistants should decide on a color code to be used for the various lead actors in the picture. Generally the brighter colors of marks are used for the key actors—yellow, white, red, and orange. Once a color has been

Shooting Procedures **281**

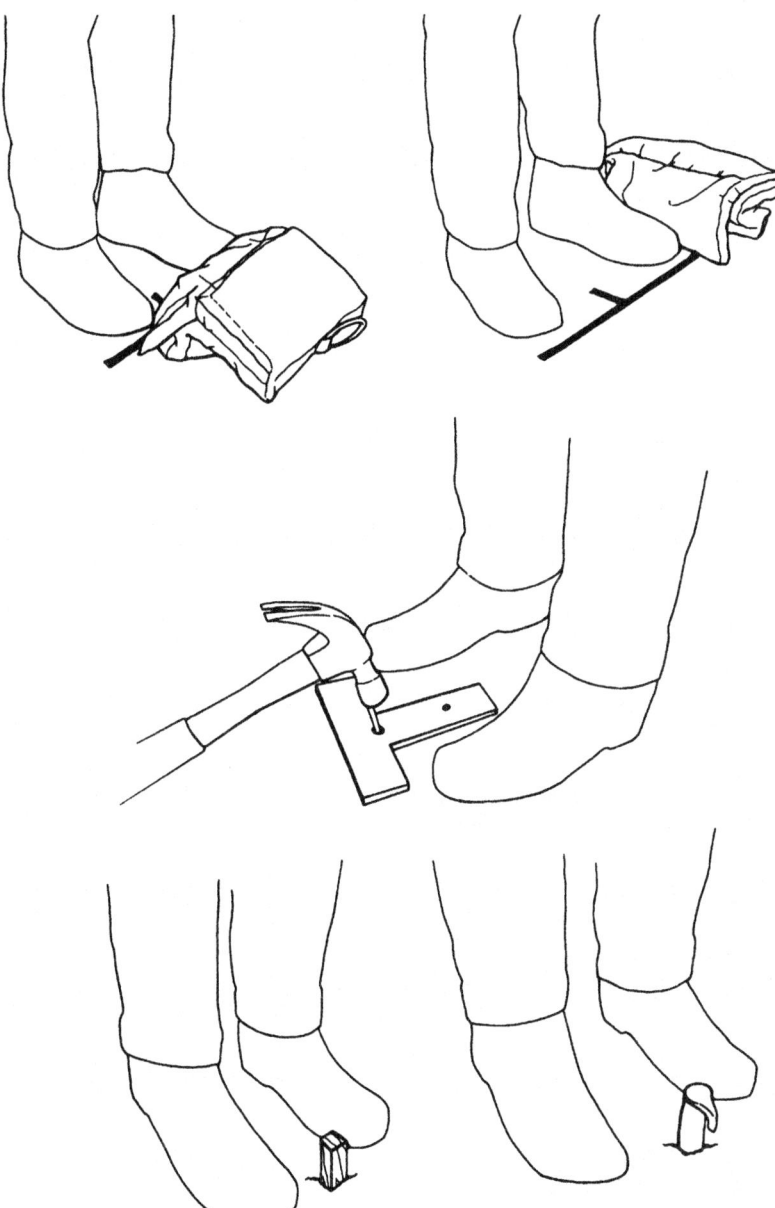

Figure 11-9 Other Actors' Marks—Sandbags, T-Marks, etc. Sandbags placed in front of or alongside of tape or chalk marks help actors find the marks without looking down for them. Tape and chalk are the best methods for marking actors on floors, cement, or other hard surfaces. When working on exterior locations, on dirt, grass, sand, etc. other methods must be used. Wooden wedges or plastic tent pegs driven into the ground work very well, and the exposed tops can be color-coded with tape. Wooden or rubber "T"-marks can also be used, and anchored to the ground with nails, if necessary, to prevent them from being kicked out of position.

decided upon for each actor, stick to it for the run of the job. For actors appearing in only a few scenes it doesn't really matter what color is used.

The lead actors will get used to looking for marks of their assigned color, and the Camera Assistants will be able to decipher the road map of marks that most sets become after a while. Colored tape and chalk, "T" marks of wood or rubber painted with the actors' colors (two sides; two different colors), anything that helps distinguish between actor A's marks and actor B's can be used.

Hiding Marks

Marks may have to be hidden if they are visible in the frame, because of a wide lens or a dolly move. In this case, try to rehearse the scene with the full-sized, colored marks, and then, just before filming begins, make the marks disappear.

If you do have to hide an actor's mark, by changing its size or color, always let the actor know that you are doing that, so they know what to look for.

Making the marks smaller may be enough to hide them. If not, change the color to some color that more closely matches the background. If this doesn't work, either, try reducing the mark to a small black dot with a marker or tape, large enough for the actor and the Camera Assistant to see, but small enough so that the camera does not. You'll be surprised at what you can get away with.

The more colors of tape you have, the more likely that you will have one that can be hidden in the scene. Brown is a great color to hide on a wood floor, even if the brown is not exactly the right shade.

If you do not have a color of tape that closely matches the floor color, here is a trick used sometimes. Get a piece of plywood or some other such material, and lay out on it parallel strips of white 1/2" tape. Then ask the company scenic artist to paint the tape the same color as the floor. The standby scenic artist will always have a can of whatever colors might be necessary for quick touchups. This will give you tape that will be virtually invisible to the camera, but visible to the actors and to the Camera Assistants who are using the marks as focus guides.

Coffee, rarely in short supply on a film set, makes a very good chalk remover. If you need to wet the surface in order to remove marks, do it early enough so the surface can dry before everyone is ready to shoot! Dust-Off, or other brands of compressed camera cleaning gas, also makes a good chalk eraser, if the can is held upside down and the liquid is sprayed directly onto the chalk mark.

Numbering the Marks

If there are several actors in the scenes, or if actors have a large number of marks to hit within the scene, or if several shots are being blocked out at one time, it is usually desirable to number the marks. The best way to do this is to give each mark a two-part number: the shot number and the number of the mark within that shot. In other words, the first yellow mark for actor A in shot #4 would be numbered "4-1." The next yellow mark would be "4-2," followed by "4-3" and "4-4." Shot #5 would begin with yellow mark "5-1," etc.

Shooting Procedures **283**

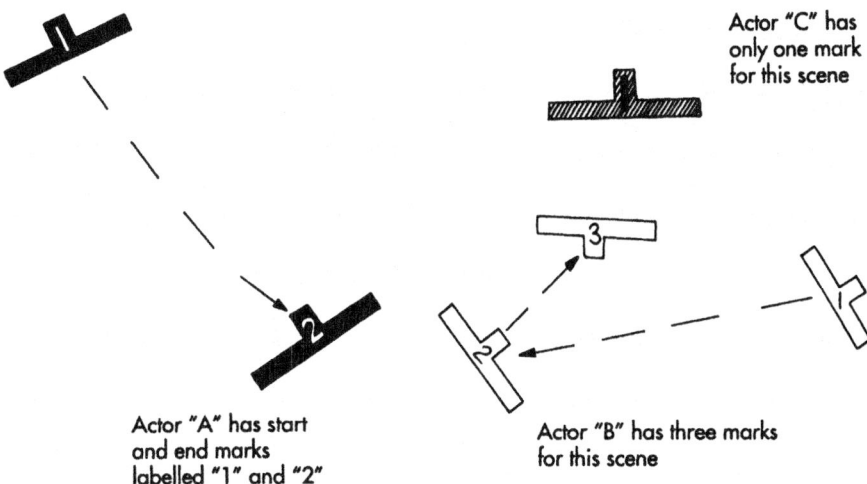

Figure 11-10 Numbering Marks. When actors have several positions to take during the shot, numbering their marks consecutively eliminates much confusion. Color coding the marks for specific actors helps also.

If actor B (red marks) confronts actor A (yellow marks) at position "4-2," then the red mark would also be labeled "4-2". Using this system, the scene can be easily broken down into its smaller components, lit, rehearsed, and then reconstructed for shooting.

Removing the Marks

One might think that after the shot is done, the actors' marks could be pulled up, but sometimes this is not a good idea. Quite often, two or more shots later, or the next day, the D.P. or the Director might ask where actor A was standing during the master shot for a certain line of dialogue, or how far away the camera was from actor B during his close-up. Leaving the marks from previous shots on the floor until the entire scene is completed is a good idea, or at least until those marks are in some other shot and must be removed.

On some jobs with certain Directors and D.P.'s we used large rolls of tracing paper to save marks laid down for entire scenes, so that the marks could be recreated days or weeks later, if necessary. These "overlays" of tracing paper were laid down over the marks, and the marks traced onto them, with notes about mark color and numbers, and also camera position marks with notes about the focal length and lens height.

Color Charts and Gray Scales

Some Directors of Photography will ask for a color chart or gray scale to be photographed at the head of every roll of film, or at least one per day or one per location, to give the lab some help in color printing and matching. The D.P. may have a favorite chart or scale to use, or may ask that the Assistant obtain one. They are often available from film laboratories, rental houses, film stock manufacturers, or other sources.

This will usually need to be shot under controlled lighting situations, with unfiltered or unaltered tungsten light, or daylight. Ask the Electricians for a small lighting unit to be set up near the camera, and establish a routine for the other times the chart needs to be shot.

Sometimes the scale or chart is actually attached to the slate, to be photographed with every shot, but this system seems particularly useless, as the lighting on the slate is rarely if ever ideal for such a chart. A chart photographed two stops underexposed in mixed daylight and tungsten cannot be of much use to the timer.

Dave Quaid explains that the only function of color film is to accurately reproduce gray. All of the information needed to obtain an accurate color scene is found in the standard Kodak 18 percent gray card and the 80 percent white card. Photographing the gray card at the beginning of the scene is all that is required to give the lab a printer reference.

Setting the Eyepiece

Before shooting, the eyepiece must be set to match the vision of the person looking through the viewfinder. Even if the camera lens is in focus, the viewfinder image will appear out of focus if the eyepiece itself is not properly focussed on the ground glass for the viewer's individual eyesight.

The best way to do this is to remove the lens from the camera, and looking through the viewfinder at a reasonably bright background, and turning the eyepiece adjustment, either the eyepiece itself, or on some cameras a knob on the camera body, to yield the sharpest image possible of the center crosshair or frameline mark on the ground glass.

This process may also be done without removing the lens from the camera, to save time. Open the aperture of the lens to its widest to allow the most light to enter, and pan or tilt the camera toward a bright area of background or sky. If using a zoom lens, zoom to the longest focal length to further limit the depth-of-field. Then defocus the image—usually by turning the focus knob or ring all the way to the close limit of focus for that lens. This will remove the distraction of the image from the finder, and make the ground glass markings more clear against a soft, out-of-focus background. Then focus the eyepiece on the crosshair or ground glass markings normally.

Once the image is as sharp as can be obtained, the Camera Assistant should place a mark on a strip of tape placed on the eyepiece or in some other convenient place near the moving knob or eyepiece. Repeat the process a few times to check the

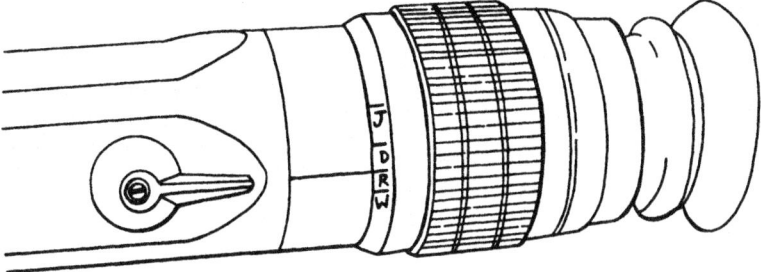

Figure 11-11 Eyepiece Marks. Eyepiece marks show diopter correction for the Director of Photography, Camera Operator, Camera Assistant and Director, using their initials for easy reference.

accuracy of this mark to make sure the ground glass is as sharply in focus as possible. Some cameras have a white plastic ring on the eyepiece for making such marks.

The Camera Operator, the Director of Photography, the Camera Assistant, and the Director will all have to look through the camera at various times during the day, so at least those four distinct eyepiece focus marks should be placed on this strip of tape, with some indication as to which mark represents whose vision, such as an initial.

The Camera Assistant should attempt to set the eyepiece on the correct mark for each of the people who might be looking through the camera, preferably before they begin looking. This saves time, and minimizes the discomfort of looking at an out-of-focus scene when first looking through the camera. As soon as someone approaches the camera to take a look through, the Camera Assistant should set the eyepiece to his or her mark. A good habit to get into is to return the eyepiece to the D.P.'s mark whenever anyone else is finished looking through. That way, the camera is always ready for the D.P. to look through.

It will not always be possible to set the eyepiece for the viewer's vision before they get there, as the Assistant has a great number of other things to do and to think about, but it is a gesture appreciated by those people who do need to look through the camera often. The less experienced people who look through the camera often think that the image is soft, when in reality, only the eyepiece needs adjustment.

Keeping the Camera Quiet

Whether or not it is the Camera Assistants' fault (and it very rarely is) that the camera is noisy, it is the Camera Assistants' responsibility to do whatever is necessary, short of redesigning the camera, to keep the camera quiet enough to satisfy the sound mixer. When the Sound Department complains about camera noise, all eyes turn to the Camera Assistant, as if there were some miracle about to be performed.

There are only three ways I know of to keep a camera quiet: lubrication, pitch adjustment, and blimps or barneys.

Lubrication

The lubrication should have been performed by the rental house technician before you arrive for the Checkout. You may or may not have to relubricate the camera during the shoot, depending on the length of the shoot, depending on your shooting conditions and the manufacturer's recommendations, the type of shooting (frame rate, amount of film shot), and the particular camera equipment in use.

If you expect to have to lubricate your camera, then make sure you have the oils and lubricants the manufacturer recommends for your climate and camera type. The rental house will often include with the camera accessories, at no charge, an oiler filled with the proper lubricant. This is especially necessary for high-speed cameras, not to keep them quiet, but to keep them running!

Pitch Control

Pitch adjustment was discussed earlier, but just keep in mind that not all cameras have a pitch control, and here we are in the late 20th century! The pitch is the distance between the perforations, which unfortunately changes with changes in temperature, humidity, and the age of the film stock. The pitch control varies the distance between where the registration pins enter the film perforation, and where the pulldown claw enters the perforation. By listening to the noise made by the running camera while turning the pitch control back and forth, it is an easy task to settle on the quietest position for the knob.

Adjusting the pitch control is part of the reloading procedure. After the new magazine is on board and the film threaded, the camera's counter is reset to zero and the camera switched on. While the camera runs enough film leader into the take-up side of the magazine for the head of the roll, the Camera Assistant can adjust the pitch for this particular roll of film. The odds are that the pitch will not have to be adjusted again for that roll, but if it is required, it takes only a few seconds to adjust again.

Blimps and Barneys

It used to be that noisy cameras were placed in soundproof (or at least semi-soundproof) metal or plastic boxes, with little windows for eyepiece, lenses, footage counters, etc. These lead- and foam-lined metal or plastic monstrosities were called blimps, and I hope you never ever have to use one.

For a time the cameras were judged "quiet" enough, but the lenses were enclosed in metal, glass, and plastic blimp housings which attached to the front of the camera, because camera noise is often projected out the front of the lens like shouting through a megaphone.

Once the camera manufacturers started making quiet or semi-quiet cameras, these large, heavy, rigid camera housings were replaced with soft leather, nylon, or other fabric, jackets, often quilted with sound-deadening padding, which wrapped around the camera and/or magazine and fastened with zippers, snaps, or Velcro. These soft covers are called "Barneys," according to one source, after comic strip character Barney Google's horse, who was usually seen wearing a tattered horse blanket.

They do somewhat muffle the noise generated by the camera, especially if they contain a layer of lead foil, which many do. But they are inconvenient for the Camera Assistant. It takes time to encase the camera or magazine in a barney, and the zippers are always jamming or breaking. And as soon as the Camera Assistant has to change lenses or reload film or even check the gate, the barney must often be removed first and then replaced for shooting.

Sometimes the barneys cover the magazines only, sometimes the whole camera. If you have to have barneys on the job, make sure they fit and that the zippers, snaps, or Velcro fasteners are working properly.

Magazine Noise

Sometimes the magazine makes some mechanical noise, a scraping or knocking sound, generally caused by the film being taken up unevenly, or "dishing" inside the magazine. Often the best solution to this is what we used to call "corporal punishment," a sharp slap to the side of the magazine. Some Assistants hit the magazine from both sides simultaneously, others hit a particular place on one side of the magazine, and you will find your favorite spot. I usually run the camera and hit the magazine while the camera is running.

Loaded magazines, especially those loaded with thousand-foot rolls of film, should always be transported and stored on edge, the way that the cases are built to contain them. If loaded magazines, especially single compartment magazines (like Panavision), absolutely need to be transported on the flat, then at least lay the case down so that the magazines are right side up as you load them—for Panavision, this means lay the case down with the hinge of the lid facing up and the latches facing down. This puts the magazine down on the torque motors, with the roll of film lying flat on the flange, where it is supported and less likely to "dish."

If a Panavision magazine is noisy when first loaded onto the camera, the most likely reason is that the magazine has been stored or transported on the wrong side, and the roll of film is lifted off of the flange and onto the inside of the lid. A sharp hit on the lid of the magazine either before or after loading onto the camera, can solve the problem. As a matter of habit, every time the Second hands me the new magazine, I hit the "P" of "Panavision" on the lid sharply with my closed fist. I have found that this pushes the roll back against the flange and makes for a quieter magazine. It also shows the magazine who is "Boss."

Setting the Aperture

Yet another of the areas in which the film industry refuses to standardize is in the names given to intermediate aperture stops. Some D.P.'s work in quarter and half stops, others in one-third stops. Every reference book seems to have different names for the quarter, half, and third stops. Some D.P.'s have invented their own scale, not related to any known scale of intermediate stops. And the capper is that we now have electronic exposure meters that give readings in tenths of stops. It is actually possible to have a Director of Photography give the Assistant a stop of "Two-point-eight-point-four!" To those of us who took classical mathematics in school, this just boggles the mind!

There is even some disagreement about the names of the full stops, although hopefully this can be credited to different ways of rounding off the exact calculated values. For example, the stop after "8" actually calculates to "11.3," and some sources list it as such, but no one actually calls it "11.3" in common usage, and I have never seen "11.3" inscribed on a lens. Everyone just says "11."

Here is an attempt at charting the quarter-stop and third-stop scales, just to add to the confusion. Reading straight down the scales gives a one-stop difference. Reading across gives one-third and one-quarter stop differences respectively.

ONE-THIRD STOP SCALE:				**ONE-QUARTER STOP SCALE:**				
Full	1/3	2/3	Full	Full	1/4	1/2	3/4	Full
0.7	0.8	0.9	1	0.7	0.75	0.8	0.9	1
1	1.1	1.3	1.4	1	1.1	1.2	1.3	1.4
1.4	1.6	1.8	2	1.4	1.5	1.6	1.8	2
2	2.2	2.5	2.8	2	2.1	2.3	2.5	2.8
2.8	3.2	3.6	4	2.8	3	3.2	3.6	4
4	4.5	5	5.6	4	4.2	4.5	5	5.6
5.6	6.3	7.1	8	5.6	6	6.3	7.2	8
8	9	10	11.3	8	8.5	9	10	11
11.3	12.7	14.2	16	11	12	12.7	14	16
16	18	20	22.6	16	17	18	20	22
22	25	28	32	22	24	25	28	32
32	36	40	45	32	34	36	40	45

These scales are from two different editions of the *American Cinematographer Manual* [6th Edition (1986) and 4th Edition (1973) respectively], and you can see the problem—several of the same numbers appear on both the one-third and the one-quarter stop scales. So find out from the Director of Photography what scale he or she intends to use, and stick with it.

Just in case there are not enough numbers here to memorize, here are a few more:

To find a 1/3 stop increase, multiply T/ stop by 1.1225
To find a 2/3 stop increase, multiply T/ stop by 1.26
To find a 1/4 stop increase, multiply T/ stop by 1.07
To find a 1/2 stop increase, multiply T/ stop by 1.1892
To find a 3/4 stop increase, multiply T/ stop by 1.26

Some D.P.'s prefer to set the aperture on the lens themselves. Others prefer the Camera Assistant to set the aperture. It is the Camera Assistant's responsibility to find out from the Director of Photography what scale will be used, and to make sure that the Camera Assistant knows precisely where on the lens the D.P. intends the stop to be set, and whatever the D.P. calls those intermediate stops. If the Director of Photography calls out "4.5," he or she expects a specific place on the aperture scale. Is T/4.5 a third of a stop closed from T/4, or is it a half stop closed from T/4? The Camera Assistant has to know where the D.P. thinks it is.

To make things worse, there are even less specific instructions likely to come from the D.P. Very often the Camera Assistant will hear, "Heavy 8," or "Light 4.5," or "2 lines heavy from 2.8," ("2 lines" meaning twice the thickness of the etched lines on the scale) or some other such vague description. How "heavy" is "heavy?" How "light" is "light?" On some lenses the stops are very close together. "Two lines heavy" might be a quarter of a stop on such a lens, and might be only a tenth of a stop on a lens where the numbers are further apart. At the beginning of the job, get together with the Director of Photography and decide what each of these things will mean.

If a Camera Assistant works with the same Director of Photography on job after job, he or she will get used to the scale that the D.P. uses, but then when working with some other D.P., the Assistant must reeducate himself or herself to the new scale of numbers.

A very common practice and one that is good for the D.P. and Assistant as well is that when the D.P. tells the Assistant the stop to set, the Assistant repeats the stop back to the D.P. out loud, not just "Yes" or "Okay." If the Director of Photography says "5.6," the Assistant should say "5.6" back. It gives him or her a chance to know that you have heard them correctly, and it gives them a chance to say, "Wait a minute—I don't really mean 5.6, I meant 6.5." If the D.P. hears it, it gives him one

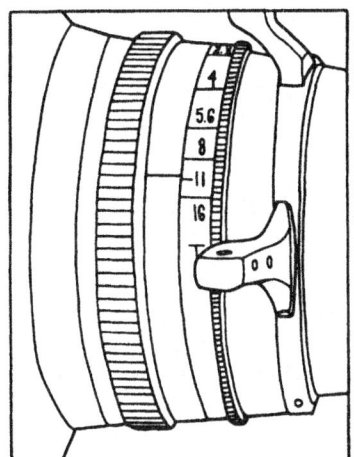 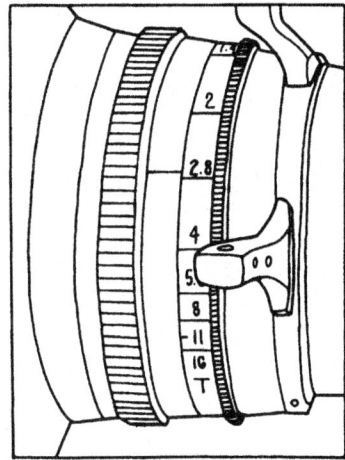

Figure 11-12 Two Lines Light? Where is That? On some lenses or at some stops "Two Lines Light" might be one-quarter of a stop or more. On other lenses or stops "Two Lines Light" might be only one-eighth of a stop. Discuss with the D.P. exactly what "Two Lines Light" should mean, if he intends to use such descriptions.

more chance to change his mind before committing to film and the same works with filters or frame rate or whatever else may apply.

If the Director of Photography says "T/3.8 with an 85N6 at 32 frames per second," then the Assistant should repeat back the instruction in its entirety. Anything that helps eliminate possible chances for error should be done whenever possible. If the Assistant does this often enough, it will become routine and automatic. It's very helpful to everyone.

An even better idea is to repeat the instructions back slightly differently. If the instruction is "4.2 with an 85," then the Assistant might repeat back "Straight 85, one quarter closed from 4," which is the same thing in a different way. The D.P. will let you know what his or her preferences are. Whatever can be done to eliminate possible sources of confusion and error should be done.

Remember also that to change the aperture on a lens, it is always better to stop down to the desired aperture, because of the possibility of play in the aperture linkage. If you are at T/4 and need to stop down to T/5.6, just stop down one stop. If you are at T/5.6 and need to open up to T/4, always open the aperture farther than your destination, and stop down to T/4 from the open side. This practice will help keep your exposures consistent, and will compensate for any play or slippage in the aperture ring. Modern lenses are manufactured with very close tolerances, and generally will not have any appreciable play, but this is still a good habit to develop.

Camera Cases

Somehow the practice got started that camera equipment cases should be secured with only one latch when they are actively being used, and secured with two latches when they are not being accessed. I wish I could stop this practice, but all I can do is give you my reasons why I think this is a bad idea. First off, I agree that every case should be latched at all times and that cases should never be left open or unlatched. The possibility that someone in a hurry might come by and unknowingly pick up an unlatched case, spilling its contents, is too horrible to contemplate! So latch all cases, but latch them completely.

If a case has two latches, close them both. You should never be in such a hurry that you cannot spare the time to open and close both latches when getting something from an equipment case. The extra security is well worth the fraction of a second it takes to open and close the second latch.

Also, if the case is on the floor or the ground, then an open latch presents several sharp corners that can tear clothing and cut skin if encountered unexpectedly, especially in the dark. I have scars on both ankles from such open latches, as does every Camera Assistant I have ever spoken to about this. Open latches also catch on electric, video, and sound cables being pulled through the area.

And the best reason to close both latches is that with most foam-lined cases, the lids must be pushed down against the foam in order to close the latches, so leaving one latch open puts a lot of strain on the latch, on the hinge, and on the lid itself.

A case secured with only one latch is also often open enough to let in rain, smoke, dust, or other contaminants. So close all the latches!

Troubleshooting: What to Do When the Camera Stops

The first and most important thing to do if the camera stops unexpectedly, or will not run at all, is NOT PANIC. This is a machine, not a magical device, and there must be a logical reason for its not working properly.

The first thing to check is the power source: batteries, cables, and power supplies are the most likely source of trouble. Fortunately, problems with these are easily solved—get another one. Change batteries, use a different power cable, make sure the battery voltage is correct, and that the voltage switch, if there is one, is in the right position; check the fuses in power supplies; check the outlet or cable that the power supply is plugged into.

If any of the electrical functions of the camera work, then the power source is probably not at fault. If the electronic footage counter works, for example, then the camera is getting the proper voltage, and the problem must be elsewhere. Check the internal buckle trips, look for other switches that might not be in the correct position, try inching the movement by hand.

Check the threading of the camera. Check the camera speed setting. If none of these solves the problem, you may have to change the internal camera fuse or circuit boards.

If the film is jammed or broken inside the camera, clear out the film, blow out the camera to remove film chips, check the gate and the pressure plate for emulsion build-up, and try inching the camera by hand. Then switch on the camera without film. Only then, after successfully inching and running the camera, should you put on another magazine.

A very good **Camera Troubleshooting** checklist is included in David Samuelson's book *Motion Picture Camera Data*.

Once the Camera Is Rolling

So far, everything mentioned above in this chapter can be and should be done before the camera starts to roll. Once the camera is running, there are a whole new group of things that need to be done by the Camera Assistant.

Before actually turning on the camera, the Camera Assistant has one last chance to take a deep breath and mentally go over the hundred or so factors and elements needed for successful filming, and to consider one more time: "Is everything ready?" One source suggests the following mnemonic for Camera Assistants: "F-A-S-T," meaning "Focus—Aperture—Shutter—Tachometer," four of the most important settings for the Camera Assistant to remember to set for each shot. Run through the requirements for the shot in your head, and make sure that these settings are correct, and don't forget the other "F"—Filters!

Following Focus

Following Focus is a lot easier if the Camera Assistant is positioned well, and comfortable. This means finding a place to stand or sit (ask the grips for an applebox), where the marks and the actors can be seen easily, and where the focus knob can be reached comfortably. With a bit of patience, the grips can be trained to make two appleboxes appear (one for the Operator, one for the Assistant) whenever the camera height for the shot is below a comfortable standing height.

It also helps to "unwind" into a shot. By this I mean position yourself for the END of the shot, then contort yourself or do whatever you have to do to get the BEGINNING of the shot. As the shot progresses, you will be "unwinding," and will get more comfortable as the shot goes on. This is especially good advice for the Camera Operator as well.

A much more detailed discussion of following focus appears in the chapter on Focus.

Zooming

Before attempting a shot involving a zoom, especially the first zoom shot of the day, turn the zoom barrel back and forth from one limit to the opposite a few times by hand, to distribute the lubrication evenly.

Many times the zoom lens is used as a "variable prime" lens, and the Director of Photography and Director may not want the audience to be aware of a zoom or change in focal length during the shot. In this event, any zooming is done during a pan, tilt, or dolly, or some combination of the three, and the zoom is hidden. If the zoom is moved slowly and smoothly enough during such a camera move, and the zooming has stopped before or just as the camera move stops, then the audience may never even be aware that the focal length has changed.

With some rehearsal, and possibly with a soft verbal cue from Camera Operator or Director, the Camera Assistant should be able to make these moves imperceptibly. When a verbal cue is not possible, a cue in the actor's dialogue or a mechanical cue can often be used, such as beginning the zoom just as the dolly starts to move or just as the Operator starts to pan. Some directors like to cue the zoom themselves, and if a verbal cue is not possible, by standing near the Assistant, the Director can cue the zoom by lightly tapping the Assistant's arm or shoulder.

Nearly all professional zoom lenses these days come with a zoom motor and speed control, but sometimes zooming by hand is still preferable. Zoom controls need some practice to get used to, but once you are used to them, the smoothest zooms become easy. The zoom control is especially good for very slow "creeping" zooms, which would be bumpy and irregular without the zoom motor.

Many Camera Assistants, especially if they need to zoom and focus together during the shot, put a "brake" on the zoom barrel of the lens with a strip of camera tape attached to the lens and the support rods at the end point of the zoom. This strip of tape will stop the zoom barrel from rotating further when the tape becomes taut, so the Assistant can concentrate on the focus and let the zoom take care of itself. Just remember to remove the tape brake before the next shot!

If hand zooms are desired or necessary, a zoom handle sticking out of the lens barrel is usually preferable to grasping the barrel itself, and the longer the zoom stick or handle, the better for leverage and smoothness, especially when a slow zoom is required. The handle can be extended by taping a length of wood or metal to the handle. I used to carry an eight-inch length of copper tubing which would just fit over the zoom handle, but I lost it somewhere and never got around to replacing it.

There is a clever tool available for Camera Assistants from the kitchen department of your local K-Mart or similar store for only a few bucks. It is sold as a jar opener, but can be used as a neat little zoom or focus handle for zoom or other lenses. It is an eight-inch plastic handle with a tightening knob at the end and an adjustable metal strap that can be placed around a lens before the lens is mounted on the camera. When tightened, the metal strap holds the handle in position perpendicular to the lens, making a solid zoom or focus handle long enough to make nice smooth moves.

For fast hand zooms, a strip of tape can be attached to the zoom barrel and wound up by turning the barrel. Then on the zoom cue, the tape can be pulled quickly, turning the barrel as it unwinds. It would be a good idea to fold the tape lengthwise after the first few inches attached to the lens, with the adhesive on the inside of the fold, so that you are not fighting the adhesive during the unwinding. Just be careful not to pull so hard that you pull the camera away from the operator's control!

Aperture Pulls

If an aperture change ("pull") is required during the shot, for example, during a dolly move in which we travel from bright sun into shadow, or vice versa, then this is also performed by the Camera Assistant. The Director of Photography will have instructed the Assistant at what point the move should be started and by what point the move should be finished, and established the two respective settings.

Some camera and lens combinations have an aperture knob, much like a focus knob, for making such changes, or even an electric aperture control motor, but these are rare. Most likely the move will have to be done by hand, turning the aperture ring on the lens barrel. With practice and a few rehearsals, the move should be able to be accomplished without the audience being aware. Most such moves are a stop or less, but on occasion there might be a much larger stop change.

Shutter Changes

If the shutter needs to be changed for a shot, make the necessary adjustment to the shutter, and then immediately make up a label for the Camera Assistant's side of the camera body, showing the new shutter angle. This will serve to remind you that the shutter has been changed, and that it needs to be reset to its normal setting after the shot or sequence. When using the Panavision cameras, a good habit is to place a second label with the new shutter setting on the shutter adjustment dial itself, on the back of the camera. This is an additional reminder, and one placed where the Director of Photography and/or Camera Operator can see it as well.

Some D.P.'s use the variable shutter for exposure control, closing the shutter down to a smaller angle as an actor crosses from shade into sun, for example. On some cameras, the shutter can be changed while the camera is running, and this presents the D.P. with another tool for exposure control. The one thing to watch out for is that the shutter gets returned to where it should be for the next take or the next shot. D.P.'s sometimes get distracted and forget such details.

Simultaneous Moves

Oftentimes the zoom and focus must be changed simultaneously. Since the First Camera Assistant generally has two hands, most zoom and focus moves can both be made by the First. If the focus is especially critical, or if the line of sight of the Assistant is obscured, or if the aperture must also be pulled during the shot, then the Second Assistant may be asked to help. How the various jobs are distributed between the First and Second will depend on the situation and the personalities and the experience of the two Camera Assistants. I generally keep the focus for myself, no matter what, since that is really one of the prime functions of the First Assistant.

If the zoom or the aperture has markings on the camera right side (the "Dumb Side"), then that often determines which function the Second will perform. If the work can be done from the other side of the camera easily, then the Second is better off on that side, to be out of the way of the First Assistant and of the Camera Operator.

One of the most difficult shots I have ever had to do on a film was a pan-tilt-boom down-dolly-zoom-focus shift-aperture pull combination. An actor was coming out of a revolving door under a hotel marquee, walked down the steps right past the camera and out into the brightly sunlit street, then got into a taxi which drove away and around the corner.

The zoom had to go from 50mm to 20mm then to 100mm; the focus had to go from 20 feet to 5 feet and then out to infinity; the aperture had to go from T/3 to T/5.6 and then to T/11. And while this was going on, the camera tilted down, boomed down, and panned around to the right at least 270 degrees, all while the dolly was moving on track for about 40 feet. We had our hands full.

I handled the zoom and focus, and at one point I had to duck under the lens and come up on the other side without missing a mark. My Second had the aperture pull, and had to climb over the chassis of the dolly and get off as the dolly started to move. But it looked great on film. We had about four rehearsals and about six takes. I only had my foot run over by the dolly once.

There is no such thing as an impossible shot. There are only easy shots and difficult shots. Do whatever you need to do to get the shot. There are no rules.

Filming in the Cold

Potential equipment problems while shooting in the cold have been discussed elsewhere in this book. Here are a few pointers and suggestions about procedures while shooting in the cold.

First of all, if you know in advance that you will be shooting in the cold for an extended period, try to find overnight camera equipment storage space outdoors, or at least in a camera truck left outdoors. You will be better off if the camera equipment remains cold between shooting days, than to constantly change temperature. This will minimize the condensation problems of moving from a cold environment into a warm environment. Except for batteries, cold weather generally will not cause equipment problems, if cameras are properly maintained and lubricated. If the shooting schedule calls for several days of cold exteriors, then leave the cameras, lenses, magazines, etc., in a cold truck overnight.

If it should be necessary to shoot part of the day outdoors and part indoors, consider using different cameras, leaving one camera cold, and bringing another camera body indoors several hours before starting filming indoors, to allow adequate warmup time. When and if you go outdoors again, use the outdoors camera.

If you do not have the luxury of two cameras, and it is necessary to move from the cold into the warm with a single camera, you should expect condensation to form immediately on a cold camera. Sealing the camera in a plastic bag before bringing it inside will help, as the condensation will form on the outside of the bag. Once the camera has warmed up to room temperature, the condensation will evaporate and the bag may be removed and the shooting begun. That is the theory, anyway. In reality, production schedules will not allow you several hours for the equipment to warm up. So, you will often have to warm up and dry off cameras other ways, such as with heat lamps or studio lights, or more often with paper or cloth towels. Running the camera without film will help with the warmup process, as will opening all the doors and removing the lens and magazine port covers. If your camera has a motor cover that is easily removable, such as with the Panaflex camera, remove it as well. In a half hour, a subfreezing camera can be warmed and dried enough to continue shooting without problem.

At the same time, open all lens, filter, magazine, and accessory cases so their contents can warm up and dry off as well. Remove the front and rear lens caps, and rest the lenses on top of the foam in the lens cases, if this can be done safely, to speed warmup.

Moving from a warm interior to a cold exterior should not present any problems, as no condensation will form on warm cameras, but if it is snowing outside, great care must be taken to cover the cameras and other gear, as the snow will melt on a warm camera and moisture will collect inside the camera and will eventually freeze when the camera temperature drops far enough, potentially causing great damage to the electronics and/or movement. Using barneys and weather protectors will help keep the heat in and the water out.

Moving Cameras

Once the camera is moving during the shot, the Camera Assistant is faced with additional problems. Space must be found to keep up with the camera, by walking alongside or by riding the dolly, always keeping the lens and the target in sight, and the focus knob within reach.

Dollies

Virtually all feature film productions will have some sort of camera dolly as standard equipment. There are probably twenty different dollies available, from various manufacturers, and the selection of which ones you might encounter depends on availability, D.P. preference, and budget.

All dollies will have one thing in common—they have wheels, and will move. They might have a hydraulic center post or arm for smooth vertical movements during the shot, they might have seats for the Camera Operator and/or Camera Assistant, they might have "running boards" that make it easier to ride, they might be rolling on track, or simply on plywood, wooden planks, or shelving boards.

A very common way of using the dolly outdoors over rough terrain is to place the entire dolly on top of another dolly, known as a "sled dolly" or "pipe dolly," which is generally a large flat dolly with four pairs of double wheels, itself running on rails of steel pipe, held at the proper spacing by notched wooden "ties" or "spreaders."

These dollies have several advantages. The first is speed—several hundred feet of track can be laid and levelled very quickly. The second advantage is smoothness. The double wheels smooth out the joints between rails much better than single wheels, and using twenty-foot lengths of pipe for rails means much fewer joints than using eight-foot lengths of regular dolly track. It is also possible to stagger the joints of the pipe rails, so that only one side of the dolly passes a joint at a time, instead of both sides. The wider stance of the sled dolly helps stabilize and smooth out the move as well. The sled dolly, its rails and spreaders also store in a much smaller volume than the equivalent length of regular track.

These sled dollies are also larger and more comfortable to work and ride on for the camera crew. With regular dollies on track, I usually prefer NOT to ride the dolly during a dolly shot, opting for walking alongside with a hand on the focus knob, or with a Focus Extension "Whip" if necessary, unless the dolly is moving so fast that I can't keep up and still watch the marks and the actors, or unless the ground under the dolly track is so rough I can't walk without watching where I'm going. With a sled dolly, however, I generally can ride in comfort, if the shot calls for it.

Cranes

Cranes are used a lot on films—budget allowing. A crane is basically a truck with an arm on it. At the end of the arm is a circular platform to put a camera with a fluid or gear head and seats for a Camera Operator and a Camera Assistant and possibly a Director. This weight is balanced with lead counterweights on the other side, or by pumping mercury from the center outward.

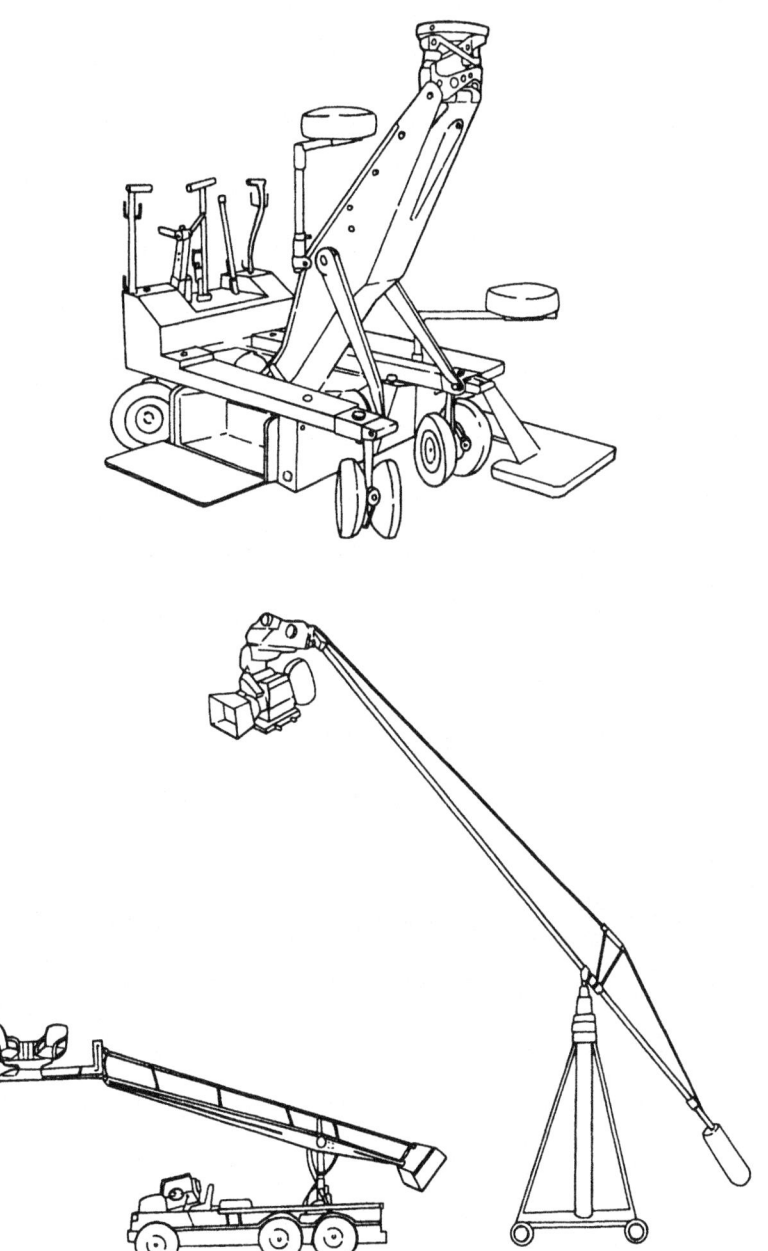

Figure 11-13 Dollies and Cranes. There are many types of dollies and cranes that might need to have a camera mounted on them. Each one has its own advantages and disadvantages

298 THE CAMERA ASSISTANT

Once you get onto a crane, you are stuck there for some time, so make sure you have everything needed before mounting up. Once a crane comes onto the set, the Key Grip is in charge of safety. The grips will let the Camera Assistant know when to put the camera onto the arm, and when to get on themselves.

Once on, use the seat belts, not only to keep yourself from falling off, but also to remind you not to voluntarily get off until the grip says it is O.K. The most dangerous thing you can do when working with a crane is get off unexpectedly, because any sudden change in weight upsets the delicate balance. Getting off suddenly can be very dangerous, the arm could suddenly swing up, and injure someone. The grips need to remove some of the counterweights before a person can get off.

On a big-budget picture, safety is usually not a problem. There will be an experienced grip crew that has worked with all this equipment. They know how it runs and how to do it safely. The problem is in low-budget pictures where the crews are less trained or experienced where they are trying to cut corners by having fewer people and it can be very dangerous. The guy that drives the crane should know how to operate the thing safely, but don't even count on that. Be careful.

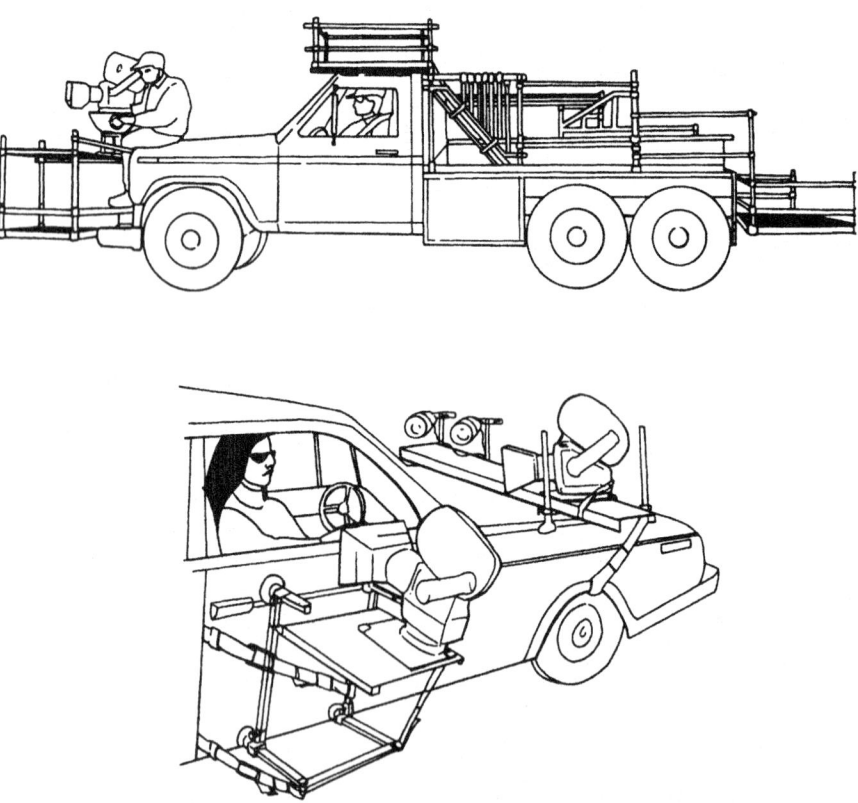

Figure 11-14 Insert Cars and Car Rigs. Insert cars offer a wide variety of camera positioning possibilities. It is not unusual to have several cameras mounted and filming simultaneously.

Insert Cars

"Camera cars," often referred to as "Insert Cars," are vehicles with various platforms built on to handle the placement of cameras and crews. They are used for filming other vehicles moving, or for filming the points-of-view of characters riding in a vehicle. They often have generators built in for lighting units, and are usually rigged to tow the vehicles being photographed, either from the rear or side of the insert car.

Some of these vehicles may have a crane-type arm for shooting with a remote-controlled camera. They usually have front platforms, rear platforms, and roof platforms—all movable to some extent, for a wide variety of camera mounting possibilities.

The major problem with these vehicles is that everyone wants to ride, and they become very overloaded, and therefore unsafe. For a typical two-camera setup, a director, two operators, two assistants, a script person, a sound mixer, a VTR person, the D.P., the gaffer, the key grip, and the driver—12 people, plus two cameras and other equipment, on a pickup truck chassis.

At least with the newer specially designed Insert Cars, the chassis and suspension and brakes can handle the expected weight, hopefully, but most of these vehicles seem to be the Key Grip's pickup truck with a few Speed-Rail platforms bolted on. Be careful.

Steadicam/Panaglide

Assisting for the Steadicam is always an interesting experience. First off, the professional Steadicam Operators usually hired for work on feature films generally own their own Steadicam rigs, and have customized them in various complex, and sometimes bizarre, ways. They often bring their own Camera Assistants with them to the job, Assistants who they have worked with before, and who are familiar with their particular Steadicam rig.

If for some reason these Steadicam Operators are not bringing their own Assistants with them, and the regular shooting crew Assistants are going to be assisting for their Steadicam, the Operator will usually have to work closely with the Assistant, in assembling and tuning up the Steadicam rig and camera. Some Operators don't let the Assistant do anything, preferring to do it all themselves.

The camera being used on the Steadicam may have come from any of a number of sources. It may be a camera owned by the Steadicam Operator, that maybe will use just the lenses and film stock from the job, or it may be a camera specially ordered from the camera rental house. Several Steadicam operators have bought their own Moviecam Compact cameras for use on their Steadicam. Others will request the Moviecam Compact when they are hired for a job. For Arriflex jobs, Steadicam Operators prefer to use the older 35BL cameras, because they are lighter than the later versions, and certainly lighter than the Arri 535. For Panavision jobs, there are a few specially modified lightweight Panaflex camera bodies. These are for the dialogue scenes. For M.O.S. shooting, Arri IIC and Arri III cameras are preferred, with whatever lens mount might be required. The Moviecam Compact camera is being touted by some as the ideal Steadicam camera for both dialogue and M.O.S. shooting because of its small size, light weight, and versatility.

Lens choice is also dependent on weight. The Zeiss prime lenses are nice and light, as are certain Panavision primes. Others are very heavy, especially Panavision Anamorphic lenses. Check with the D.P. and Steadicam Operator about lenses for Steadicam use.

Steadicam shooting is almost always done with 400-foot rolls of film. There may be lightweight magazines available for the camera system you are using. There may also be magazine extension throats available for the Arri IIC camera, which position the magazine farther back and lower, making the Steadicam with camera slightly more maneuverable and easier to balance.

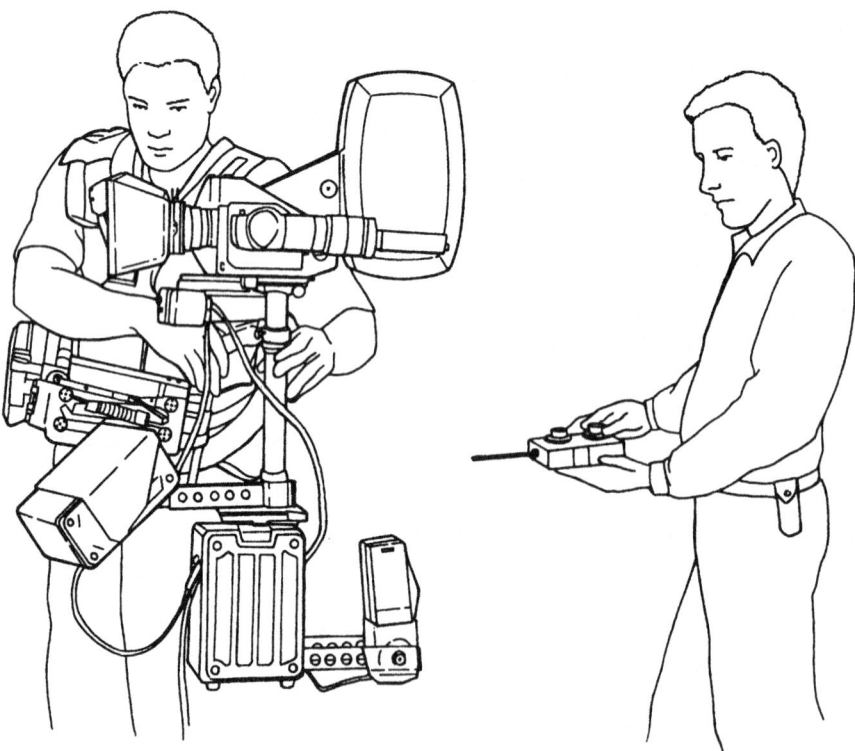

Figure 11-15 Steadicam. Steadicam Operators need Camera Assistants, too. This Assistant is using a remote focus control to follow focus for a shot. This radio control unit uses small servo motors mounted on the camera and meshed to geared rings on the lenses. Zoom and aperture controls are available as well. Cable ("Hard-Wire") units are also available, used mostly as backups for the wireless versions.

Once assembled, and loaded and with lens and filters attached, the rig needs to be carefully balanced. An experienced Steadicam Operator can accomplish this in minutes, and will periodically adjust the balance while shooting. Since balance is so important to the operation of the Steadicam, it is recommended that only factory 400-foot rolls of film be used, and not short ends canned out from the job, because the weights of the factory rolls will all be the same, but not the weights of the short ends.

The follow focus arrangement for the Steadicam is tricky. The Assistant cannot turn the lens focus ring or knob normally, by hand, because this would upset the balance of the camera, so must rely on a remote focus controller, either radio controlled or hard-wired. These remote focus systems work with a small motor mounted on the lens or camera body, and geared to the focus ring, much like the zoom motors commonly used. The Camera Assistant has a control box with a knob marked like a focus knob, and by turning the knob to the desired focus setting, the motor turns the lens to the same setting, after proper calibration.

The hard-wired units are generally used only as backups, as the wires often get in the way and impede the Operator's movements. There are several radio controlled units, some of which have more than one channel, which can be used for controlling focus, aperture, and zoom, on such lenses that are properly geared and motorized. The Steadicam Operator will show you how to set these units up and calibrate them for the anticipated requirements.

Batteries are another problem with the Steadicam. The Steadicam uses a lot of batteries, to run the camera, the video viewfinder, and the remote focus, and they must be changed frequently. Keep the chargers handy and close, and immediately charge a discharged battery. As soon as the Operator and the equipment arrive on the set, get those batteries charging and keep them close. A common practice is to rehearse a scene with one set of batteries, and then change to fresh batteries for the shoot.

The Steadicam Operators often work with tape or chalk marks on the floor or pavement, and these same marks can be used for focus. It is sometimes difficult to get tape focus marks, because the tape measure cannot simply be hooked onto the camera and run out to the target, without pulling the Steadicam Operator off balance. For this reason, a steel tape held in position by the Assistant near, but not touching the camera, and run out to the target for a measurement, is often used. A cloth or fiberglass tape measure could be used this same way, but a second person would be required to hold the other end.

This is a case where one of those small hand-held infrared units might be useful. If the focus target is out in the open, without other distracting targets nearby, these electronic tape measures can sometimes be used, held close to but not touching the camera and pointed at the target. Keep in mind that these units take a few seconds to give a reading, during which time the target or the Steadicam may have moved, and that their viewing angle is fairly wide and easily confused by other objects.

Some of the older Panaglide cameras still in use, and in some cases very popular with Operators, have a pellicle (beamsplitter) instead of a rotating mirror. This gives an uninterrupted video image (without the flicker from the rotating mirror) which the Operators love, but at the cost of the 1/2 to 2/3 stop exposure compensation necessary for the pellicle. This can present a lighting problem for the D.P., especially on night exteriors.

Camera Reports

Once shooting begins, Camera Reports need to be kept up to date. Each take will generate a scene and take number, and an end footage, all of which need to be recorded on the Camera Report for that roll of film. If there is a Second Assistant on the job, the chore of keeping such records falls to the Second. Once shooting begins, slating and report keeping can fill up the Second's time. When magazines need to be reloaded, or equipment fetched from the truck, then the slating and report keeping chores may revert temporarily back to the First Assistant.

After each take, hopefully during a lull in the cacophony of noise and voices that seems to happen every time the camera is turned off, the First can call out to the Second the end footage as displayed on the footage counter on the camera. It may be possible for the Second to position him- or herself where they can see the display and read for themselves, especially now that the Platinum and 535 cameras have such displays on both sides of the cameras, but if not, the First should call it out, and the Second should repeat back the number, so the First knows that the Second heard it correctly.

There are hand signals for the numbers involved, but I have very rarely found these necessary. The First looks at the counter, and calls out the number, rounding up (yes, I said rounding up—I prefer going to the next higher ten feet, rather than rounding down) to the nearest 10 feet and dropping the last digit, for the sake of brevity and easier mathematics—a counter reading 315 becomes "32," 764 becomes "77," etc. The Second repeats back what he or she heard, and the whole process takes less than five seconds. After a while working together, the Second will be able to single out the First's voice from among the sea of voices.

Many Assistants attach the Camera Report to the back of the slate, but I do not particularly like this practice—the report is too easily torn, rained on, or dirtied, and one of the main advantages to using the plastic slate is lost, the ability to see the scene and take numbers with backlight through the plastic even when the front light is too dim.

I much prefer keeping the camera reports in an aluminum clipboard-type box, often called the "report tin" even though it is made of aluminum. These form holders are available in a dozen or so sizes from large office supply stores or by mail order. The reports stored this way are kept clean and dry and undamaged, and therefore always neat and readable.

Safety on the Set

Don't put yourself in an unsafe position. You read every once in a while that somebody in a film crew gets killed when a camera insert car rolls over or a helicopter crashes, and we've all heard of *The Twilight Zone* tragedy, and in the intensity of the situation, safety considerations often get shoved aside. It only takes a moment of carelessness to cause an accident.

Shooting Procedures **303**

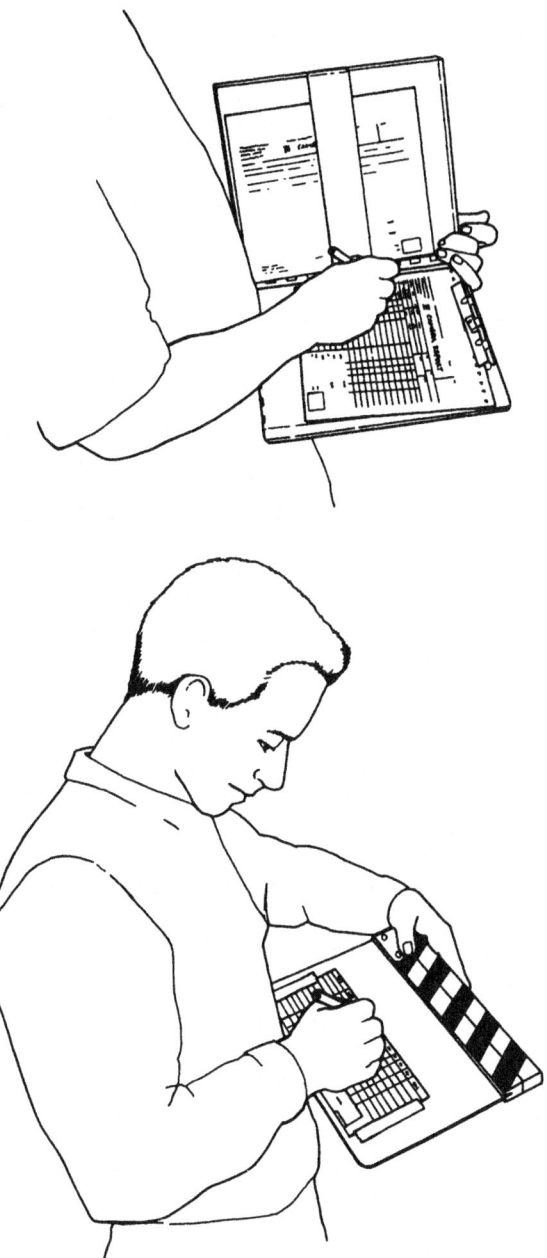

Figure 11-16 Camera Report Tin/Back of the Slate. Camera Reports can be attached to the back of the slate with tape, or can be used and stored in an aluminum clipboard, called the "Report Tin," for added protection.

There are hazardous conditions and locations found often in film schedules—coal mines, volcanos, construction sites, airport runways, helicopters, racetracks during a race, high scaffolding, hanging off the side of a building, inside oil tankers, and a hundred others.

There are dangerous situations which can be made less dangerous by a little careful planning and having the right crew and equipment on the job. The basic rule would be one hand for yourself and one for the job. If you've got a safety rail, hold onto the rail and then do your work with the other hand.

Safety lines or harnesses can either be good or bad—they are restrictive. Camera Assistants sometimes have to dash around the other side of the camera to plug in a new battery or something. Don't let the excitement of shooting interfere with common sense and safety.

Grips are often responsible for safety on a set as far as construction, scaffolding, camera positioning, and crew safety, and it is the Electricians' responsibility to make sure there's no loose electricity running around.

As far as electricity goes it's not unusual to have both AC and DC power on the job. Arc lights require DC. HMI lights require AC. If you are in the rain, or near water, DC is a lot safer than AC—it generally will not kill you although it may burn you.

Electricians are responsible for making sure that stage boxes and cables are not sitting in puddles. Grips are responsible for making sure that there are walkways and railings and that any kind of parallels or scaffolding are properly assembled and braced off.

If you are doing stunts then there is often a stunt coordinator who is responsible for that stuff, including explosions and collapsing sets. It is the coordinator's job to know when and where things are going to explode, and how big those explosions are going to be, and where it is safe to place cameras and other equipment and where it is safe for people to be.

The company is responsible for providing any kind of safety equipment that may be required; hard hats, safety belts, earplugs, flameproof suits, goggles. If there are explosions to be filmed they will often issue hard hats and goggles and put up safety screens, etc. If you are in a construction site or a mine, often the construction contractor or the mining company will insist that you wear steel-toed boots and hard hats and goggles to enter the location.

Some hard hats have a full face shield, and if you are doing explosions these are better than goggles. Wearing one of these, you will still have peripheral vision which is very important for an Assistant when pulling focus is necessary.

If you feel uncomfortable with the situation, let the company know. There is nothing wrong with demanding additional safety hardware or precautions. No job is worth getting hurt on.

Checking the Gate

The "gate" is that little rectangular area inside the camera where the film is held behind the lens and where the picture is actually taken.

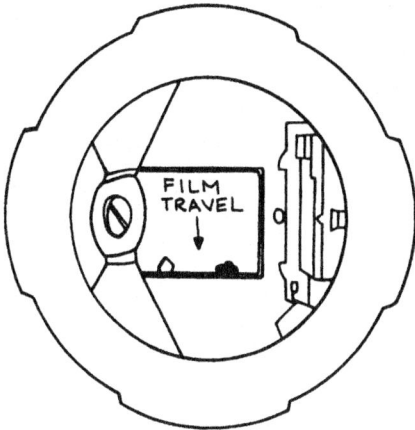

Figure 11-17 Checking the Gate. Sometimes when filming, a piece of dirt, or a film chip, or other debris will find its way into the worst possible place in the camera for it to be—the gate, where the picture is actually taken. Objects that come to rest in the gate leave their shadows permanently on the film, and may causes scratches on the soft emulsion surface. Keep the camera as clean as possible, and check the gate for "hairs" and other undesirable material often.

If dust or dirt gets trapped in there it will be seen along the bottom edge of the gate, which is the top of the negative, and then on the print made from that negative. Depending on what aspect ratio is being shot, dust or dirt in the gate area may or may not be in the final projected picture.

Checking the gate for debris is very important. Depending on your situation, and how much time you have, it's a good idea to check the gate fairly often. It can be very inconvenient sometimes. Every Assistant and D.P. should work out a schedule and routine for when this should happen. The most common time to check the gate is after each scene, before moving on to the next scene, so you know nothing has been deposited into the gate that might ruin the scene just completed.

It is a lot easier and cheaper to reshoot a scene while all the lights and dolly track and other things are already set up and working, than to set everything up again the next day or the next week.

Since most cameras use a Full Aperture Gate, there is usually a margin of safety around the frame, where some debris lodged in the gate will be OUTSIDE of the Academy, TV, 1.85 or other format being used.

If something is discovered there, running the camera while looking through the lens port at the frame will show whether the debris will be inside the necessary format or not, by showing the debris position against the reflection of the ground glass markings on the mirror as the shutter turns.

If you're shooting for television, or for 1.85:1, you have quite a bit of leeway around the outside so even if something is in there it may not be in your usable picture area. If you're shooting Cinemascope (anamorphic) you have almost no

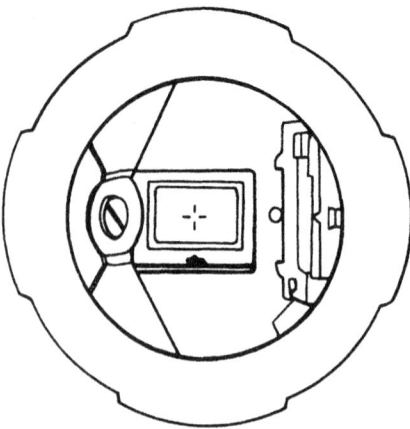

Figure 11-18 Checking the Gate—Outside of Academy. This film chip or piece of dirt is shown at the bottom of the gate, where it would occur. By switching the camera on briefly while looking through the lens port, the Assistant will see first the piece of dirt, then the reflection of the ground glass in the mirror shutter, then the dirt, then the ground glass, etc., alternately 24 times a second. By observing the dirt in relationship to the ground glass markings, the Assistant can determine if the dirt is outside of the Academy marking (as in this illustration), or if it is invading the Academy frame. With most filming formats, enough safety area exists inside the Silent Aperture gate but outside of the usable film area that most hairs or film chips will not be serious problems. Anamorphic filming has the LEAST safety area, so the gate should be checked more frequently. After deciding whether another take of the scene is necessary, the dirt should be removed with a plastic or wooden implement—NEVER METAL!

tolerance area at all. Anything that's in there has been photographed and will be huge on the screen.

Some Assistants check the gate even more often, such as after every printed take. If you're using, for example, a film stock that is notoriously soft and scratches and builds up in the gate, and especially if the humidity is high, then check even more often. Some film stocks are worse than others, and some cameras are worse than others. High humidity is often a factor, as is blowing dust, sand, smoke, etc.

I generally check after each setup before moving on to the next, but also with every camera reload, and sometimes at additional opportunities during the shooting, such as when makeup is being touched up, if, for example, there have been a lot of takes in a scene since the last gate check.

Under normal shooting conditions, I usually figure to get something serious in the gate about once a year. As of this writing, we have been shooting "The Cosby Mysteries" for nine months, and have run over 1,000,000 feet of 35mm film through two Panavision Panaflex GII cameras. We have yet to have a hair in the gate! Of course, now that I have said that, I'll probably get one tomorrow morning.

There are three ways to check the gate in a motion picture camera. They each have their advantages and disadvantages. It won't take long to decide on your favorite.

Pull the Lens

The first (and my personal preference), is the "Pull the Lens" method. The matte box is swung aside, the lens is removed, the shutter and mirror are inched out of the way, and the Camera Assistant looks into the lens port with a small flashlight, directly at the gate. Anything that is there will be seen clearly. If the gate is clean, the lens is reinserted, the matte box swung back into place, and the camera switch momentarily turned on and off, to move the mirror shutter back into the viewing position.

The advantage to this method is that there are no obstructions in front of the gate, and the clearest possible view of the gate is seen by the Assistant. If something is there in the gate, the Camera Assistant is already in the best position to do something about it.

The disadvantage of this method, according to some people, is that it takes too long. After a few tries, however, a Camera Assistant can do this procedure in just a few seconds.

Another possible disadvantage is that in a windy location, some dust or sand or other debris may be blown into the camera while the lens port is open, making the situation worse instead of better. Sometimes in such a situation I deliberately do not check the gate, until a sheltered area can be found, or at least until the wind dies down.

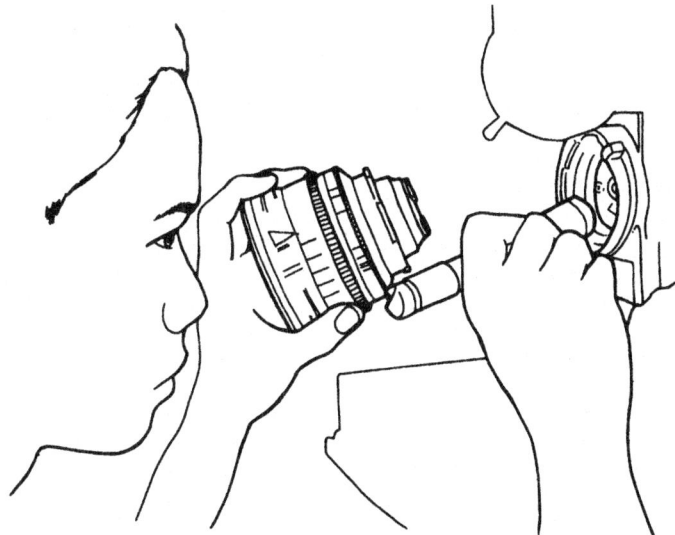

Figure 11-19 Checking the Gate—Pull the Lens. Pulling (removing) the Lens to check the gate is the best way, as it shows a clear, unobstructed view of the gate area. Some Assistants claim it takes too long, but with practice it only takes a few seconds to pull the lens, check the gate, and replace the lens.

308 THE CAMERA ASSISTANT

Through the Lens

The second method is the "Through the Lens" method. The matte box is swung out of the way, the lens focus racked to infinity, the lens aperture opened, the mirror shutter inched out of the way, and the Camera Assistant looks into the front of the lens with a flashlight. This method works best with lenses above about 40mm focal length.

If the lens is a zoom, it helps to zoom to full telephoto. The lens acts as a magnifier, and by holding the flashlight close to the eye, the Camera Assistant can trace the outline of the magnified gate and ensure its cleanliness. If the gate is clear, the lens aperture, focus, and zoom must be reset, the mirror shutter moved to the viewing position, and the matte box swung back.

The advantage to this method is that the lens magnifies any debris that may be present, so nothing is missed. The disadvantage is that this method takes too long, and the placement of the Assistant's eye and flashlight in relationship to the lens is so critical that it takes a lot of practice to get it right. Then if there is something there, the lens must be removed anyway. Also, this method does not work well with wide lenses.

I also don't like changing the focus, aperture, and zoom settings of the lens, and then having to reset them to continue shooting. This opens up too many possibilities for mistakes.

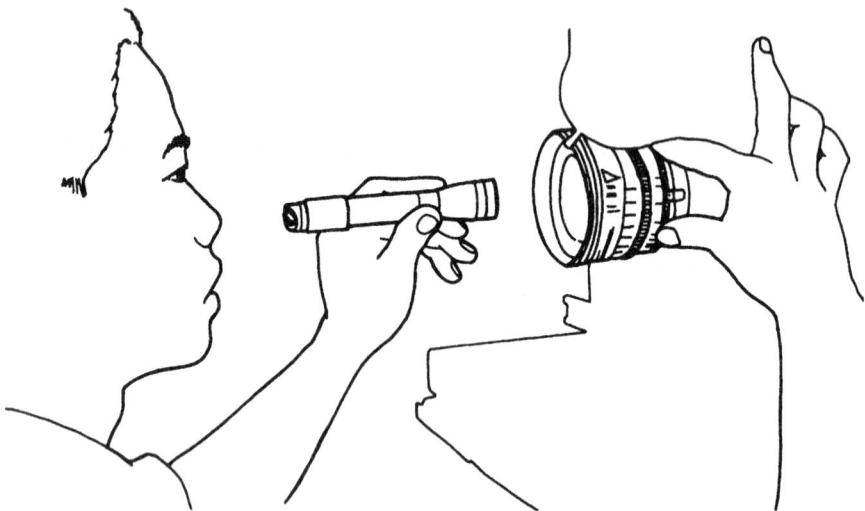

Figure 11-20 Checking the Gate—Through the Lens. Some Assistants prefer to check the gate through the lens, using a flashlight. The lens acts as a magnifier. This method works best with longer lenses (above 40mm).

Pull the Gate

The third and final method is the "Pull the Gate" method. This is the least preferred of the three, as it involves opening the camera door, unthreading the film from the movement, removing the gate for inspection, then replacing the gate, rethreading the film, and closing the door.

The problem is that in unthreading and removing the film, anything that might have been in the gate stands a good chance of being dislodged, and the clean gate the Assistant inspects leaves no indication about what might have been there during the shot. For me, checking the gate in this way accomplishes nothing. The whole point of checking the gate is to find out if the previous takes and scenes are free of gate debris. This method cannot tell you that with any degree of certainty. It also takes a lot longer to unthread and rethread the camera than it does to pull the lens out and replace it.

The only time I used this method was years ago, on a feature using two early Arri 35BL cameras that required the use of lens blimp housings to keep the noise down. One of our cameras had a zoom lens in a zoom blimp housing, and it would have taken ten minutes to get the lens out of the blimp for a real gate check, and another ten to get it back in, so I opted for the "Pull the Gate" check for that camera. The

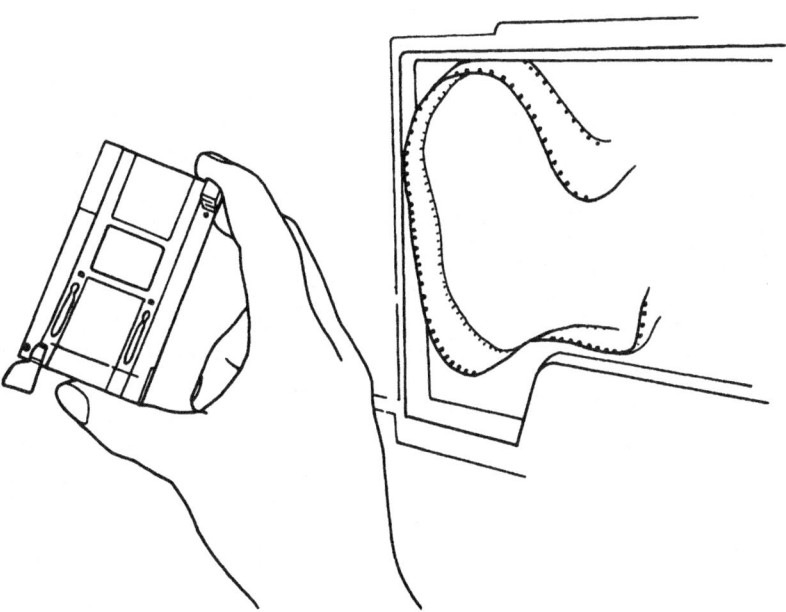

Figure 11-21 Checking the Gate—Pulling the Gate. The "Pull-the-Gate" method is the slowest and least reliable method of the three, because any dirt in the gate area will probably fall out when the gate is removed, so you won't know if something was there during the shot. Also, the film must be unthreaded and then rethreaded again, which takes time.

lens housings were so difficult to work with that we left the zoom lens permanently mounted on one camera body for three months, preferring changing to our other camera body whenever we had to change from the zoom to prime lenses.

Cleaning the Gate

If there is something in the gate, or something close to the gate, that doesn't belong there, it must be removed immediately. If it is already in the gate, first find out if it is in the picture area for the format being used. Do this by running the camera while looking through the lens port (without a lens) at the gate. You will see the debris in the gate and the reflection of the ground glass markings in the shutter mirror. The position of the hair or debris in relation to the ground glass image will let you know if the picture area of the previous scene has been invaded by the debris.

If so, remove the debris, run a few feet through the camera, then check the gate again. Once the gate is clear, then shoot a few more takes of the scene, just to be sure that you have a clean take or two. There is no way to know exactly when the object first appeared—all you can be sure of is that it appeared between the last two gate checks. Maybe only one take has the hair, maybe all of them since the previous check. So check often, and if you find something in there, check even more often.

The easiest way to remove a foreign object from the gate is with an orangewood stick, Q-tip stick, or toothpick (wood or plastic only—NEVER metal near the gate area), moistened by touching it to your tongue. Whatever is there should come away easily. If not, unthread the camera and remove the gate for a more thorough cleaning with lens tissue or wooden or plastic implement.

Reloading Etiquette

First of all, never run out of film during a shot, because it makes the whole Department look foolish. It is also generally unnecessary. By keeping accurate Camera Reports, and by checking the lengths of the takes by looking at the footage column on those Reports, you should be able to predict when to reload before running out. If a scene takes 200 feet of film, don't even attempt another take if there is only 200 feet left in the camera. Don't even try it with 220 feet left. That is too small a safety margin.

Look at several recent takes and use the longest one for a comparison, then add a safety factor of at least 20 percent of the length of the longest take, or 50 feet, whichever is less. For a 200-foot take, allow an additional 50 feet. For a 40-foot take, allow that same additional 50 feet. It is always better to be safe than sorry.

It's sometimes difficult to predict, especially when you get halfway through a scene that you figured you had enough film to finish and the director says to the actors, "Start again." You have to do some quick computation—are we going to make it or not? You have to be very fast and let them know if you will not be able to make it. If there is any doubt at all, if you're coming within 50 feet of the end, don't even try it.

When you rehearse the scene, either ask the script person to time the rehearsal, or time it yourself to see how long it runs. A two-minute scene with only 300 feet in the camera will only give you one take. So reload before going into the new scene.

Reload before beginning a long scene because it can be upsetting to actors and directors if a reload must occur in a new scene after the first or second take. It's better to start off with a new load—you can get three or four or more takes to build up a momentum. Those are often the best takes for the actors because they are fresh.

When it is time to reload, call out as soon as the last scene is cut, "Camera Reload!" The Second Assistant, keeping the camera report, will know often before the First that the camera needs a reload, and should have a magazine already out of the case, already labeled with the next roll number, standing by. The First should run off some safety film, with a hand in front of the lens, to let the lab know not to print this piece. Ten to twenty feet is the usual amount, plenty for the lab to thread their developing machines.

The First opens the camera, unthreads the film, and breaks the loop (tears the film), so that magazine will not be accidentally threaded up as a fresh magazine. A magazine with a torn loop indicates that the roll is exposed and is waiting to be unloaded. It is often placed in the case and the case lid closed with the torn end of the film sticking out of the case, indicating that the magazine case contains a spent magazine awaiting reloading.

After removing the film from the camera, the First often removes the gate and inspects it for cleanliness and emulsion build-up. It is a good idea to always remove the gate for inspection when reloading the camera, especially if the tail end of the previous magazine has been pulled through the gate before the camera was switched

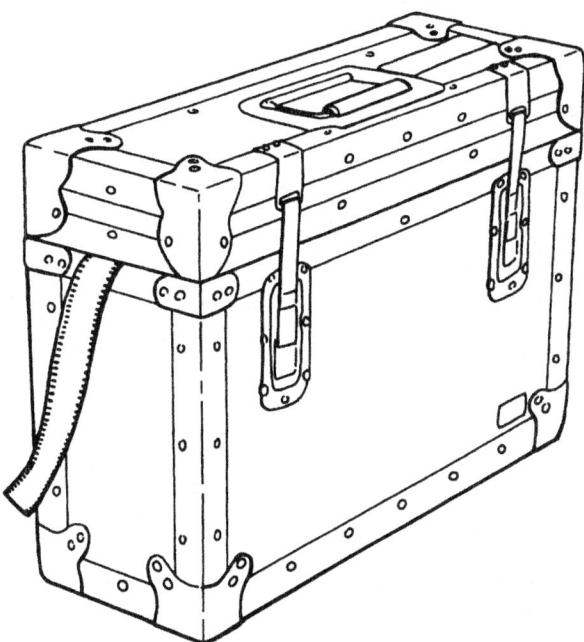

Figure 11-22 Exposed Magazine in Case. Magazine Case with tail of film hanging out, indicating that this magazine has been shot and awaits reloading.

off. When this happens, tiny bits of film are often broken off the tail and will come to rest somewhere inside the camera. Most often these fragments end up at the bottom of the camera just below the gate, but once in a while one gets stuffed inside the registration pin hole or in some other place that could cause problems. Blow these chips out of the camera with your blower bulb. The First also checks for debris in the gate itself. If the gate is clean, it is reinserted into the camera, and the camera is blown out with the bulb syringe.

The new magazine can then be attached to the camera, and then threaded. The footage counter is reset to zero, the pitch set, and the door closed. It is important to reset the counter **before** setting the pitch, as some film will be used during the pitch setting, and if the counter is reset afterwards, the real length of the roll can be quite a bit shorter than the counter indicates. The camera is then run up to at least 10 or 15 feet, as safety at the beginning of the new roll, again with the hand held in front of the lens.

If there is something else that needs to be done, such as a change to a new battery, this is the best time to do that. If the eyepiece leveler was detached for the reloading, it is reattached, positioning the eyepiece at the same height it was at before the reload. Once the camera is absolutely ready to continue shooting, the First calls out "Camera Ready!" and the action can begin again. This whole process should take less than a minute, unless there are other factors to consider, such as being on a crane or vehicle, or on top of a parallel, or such other inconvenient position.

While the First Assistant is reloading the camera, the Second is nearby, receiving from the First the exposed magazine, and handing to the First the new magazine, properly labeled with the new roll number. After placing the exposed magazine safely in its case, the Second is free to catch up on the paperwork, finishing up the Camera Report for the exposed roll, and filling in the information for the new roll—film emulsion number, batch, cut and can number, date, magazine number, beginning scene, and take number, if this has not already been done.

Some Camera Assistants prepare a Camera Report well in advance, as each magazine is loaded, complete with emulsion, batch, cut and can numbers, and magazine number, and place that Camera Report in the case with the magazine, either taped to the magazine or loose in the case, ready to be used when that magazine is loaded onto the camera.

Film Break-Off

Sometimes if you're a long way from the lab and the film will have to be shipped to the lab on a plane, there will be a film break-off point during the shooting day. Everything shot up to a certain time has to be canned out, packed in some sort of shipping case (properly labeled "EXPOSED UNDEVELOPED FILM—DO NOT X-RAY"), and rushed to the airport to catch a plane to the lab in order to be developed and printed before the next day.

You may continue shooting that day or night, but at least some of your film must be sent off to the lab. Find out well in advance if there is a film break-off time, and be prepared to reload at that time, even if only a small fraction of the magazine has been shot.

This film break-off also means losing the services of the Second Assistant for as long as it takes to can out all exposed rolls in magazines, do the paperwork, and prepare the package of film cans for shipping. Murphy's Law dictates that this will always happen at the most inconvenient time of the shooting day, when the most difficult and complicated shot of the day is being done, when having the Second nearby to help is most desirable and necessary.

Footage shot after the break-off time usually does not go into the lab until the next day, at the following day's break-off time. This makes the paperwork a terrible mess at the beginning, with the film shot each day going to the lab on different days and exposed film from the previous day waiting for a later shipment, but you will get into the routine soon enough.

Recordkeeping—Shot Notebook

Keeping a record of lenses, filters, exposure, height, scene, film type, roll number, and other factors for each scene filmed is of varying importance to various crews. Some D.P.'s will want this information saved for future reshoots or for matching scenes shot out of sequence. Every D.P. will have their own system. Some D.P.'s prefer to do it themselves. Most prefer the Camera Assistants to keep the book. Sometimes the First does it, sometimes the Second. I prefer to keep the records myself, and keep the notebook in the front box, readily accessible. I made a rubber stamp to use in the notebook, listing the factors I want to record, one page for every shot. Other Assistants have had larger notebooks printed up with several shots per page.

Multiple Camera Shooting

Multiple cameras shooting simultaneously make things more difficult in some ways, but easier in others. As far as the Camera Assistants are concerned, multiple camera shooting involves more film, more equipment, more batteries, and more paperwork; on the other hand, however, there are more Camera Assistants to do this extra work, in most cases.

When several cameras are involved in a day's shooting, it is a good idea to assign each camera to a specific First Camera Assistant, and for that Assistant to stay with that camera, wherever it goes and whoever is operating. This process will allow one Assistant to concentrate on a single camera package, and familiarize himself with the accessories, lenses, and filters associated with that camera. This is safer and more efficient. It may not always be possible in the heat of battle, but it is a good goal to shoot for.

Most procedures on the set are exactly the same, no matter how many cameras are running. Cameras still have to be assembled, mags loaded, batteries charged, focus marks taken, etc.

Slating is a bit more complicated with multiple cameras, and care must be taken when placing actor and focus marks in the set, as they might be seen by the other cameras with wider lenses or a higher point of view. Whenever placing a mark in the scene, check with all of the other cameras to make sure your marks are hidden from their view.

See the next chapter for a discussion of slating for multiple cameras.

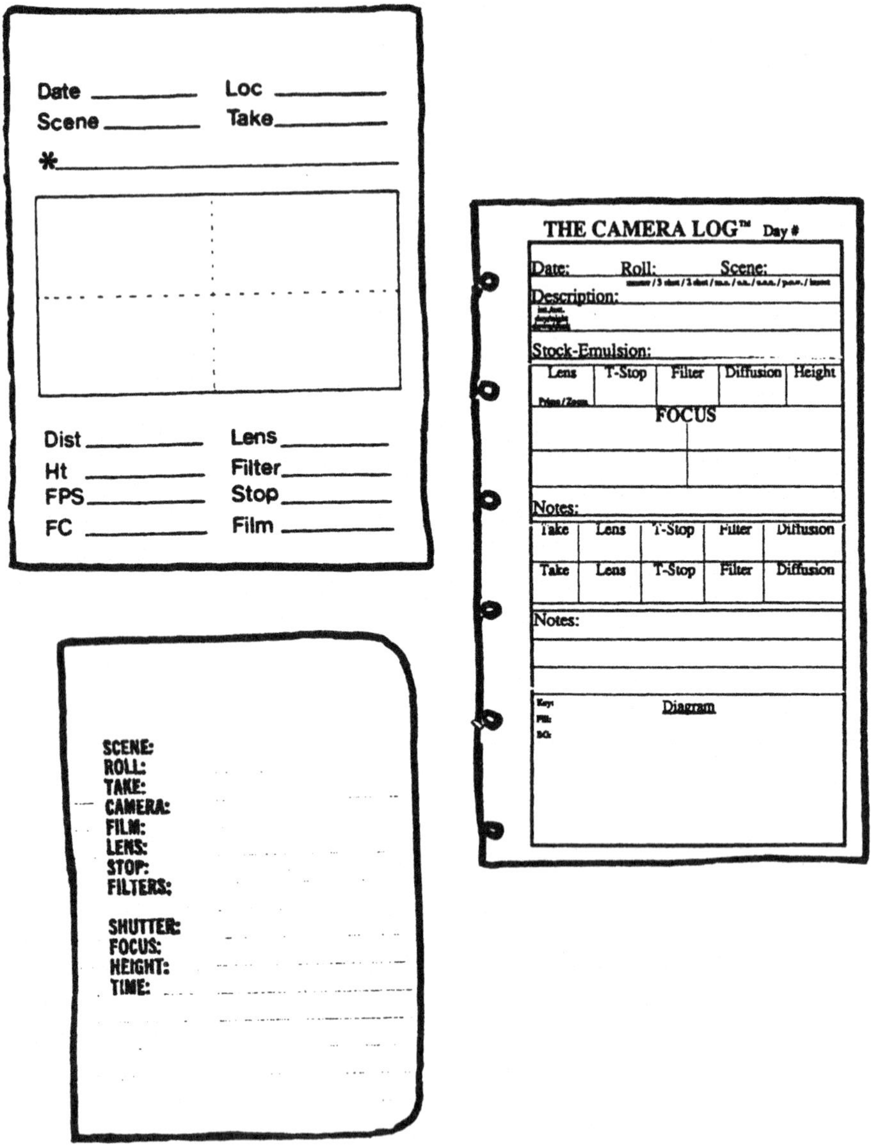

Figure 11-23 Shot Notebook Pages. Three examples of the "Shot Notebook" or "Camera Log." On the right is a commercially printed log book; on top left is one created by a Camera Assistant; and bottom left is the format I used for many years, made by using a rubber stamp on each page of a dime-store notebook. I had the stamp made up with the categories I would write in for each shot, one shot to a page.

Efficiency on the Set

Efficiency is vitally important for the Camera Assistant. If you have to go to the truck to get something, like a lens, take something back with you, like a magazine that needs reloading or a battery that needs charging. Don't make two trips, make one trip. I'm constantly surprised by crews not remembering to think about things like this.

Do your homework. Plan ahead. Read the call sheet. Discuss things with the Director of Photography and the Production Manager. Make notes for yourself about things that need to be done. Get a shooting schedule at the beginning of the job. If you know there are going to be multiple cameras working on the 10th, don't wait until the 9th to start ordering equipment and looking for a crew. Anticipate and solve problems before they become problems.

There are many areas where problems can be solved by the Assistant without even getting the D.P. involved, without getting the production company involved—you just do it and the best compliment they can give you as an Assistant is that they didn't even know you were there—things just seem to happen without a lot of commotion or trouble.

One of the highest compliments I ever got on my work as Camera Assistant was from a Production Manager and an Assistant Director who came up to me after a day of twelve cameras shooting a huge stunt (exploding building). I had been responsible, as First Assistant on the "A" Camera, for organizing the extra crew and equipment needed for this stunt. Everything had gone flawlessly, despite having four different types of cameras with their different (and incompatible) magazines and batteries. One high-speed camera had stopped during the shot, but AFTER the explosion (a film jam due mostly to the cold, I think), but the other eleven had worked fine. The Production Manager said to me at the wrap, "It was just like shooting with a single camera!" He said he had never been on a multiple camera shoot "that went this smoothly." This was a high compliment, indeed!

Looking at Dailies

I go to see dailies as often as possible, and I recommend this for all Camera Assistants. This is the best way to learn from the experts. Seeing the film you have worked on as dailies the next day, while it is still fresh in your memory and before it has been chopped, scrambled, repositioned, matted, colorized, transferred, etc., is essential.

Unfortunately, the Camera Assistants often cannot get to dailies in time. As soon as "Wrap!" is called, the D.P. and the Director hop into a station wagon and dash off to the lab or other screening room. The Camera Assistants still have to put the cameras and other toys away, can out the day's film, set up batteries for charging, etc. By the time they can wrap up and get to the screening room, dailies are usually over.

Of course it would be possible for the First Assistant to dash off with the D.P., leaving the poor Second Assistant with all of the work, and some Firsts do this all the time, but I don't think it is fair or proper to do so. I have done it a very few times, but only when there is something that I really need to see, such as after we have gotten a report about soft focus or a camera scratch. I certainly would not make a habit of abandoning the Second with all the wrapping up. As I stated in the beginning of this book, the job of the First Camera Assistant is not over until all the equipment is disassembled, put into appropriate cases, and put back into the truck or studio camera room.

Once at dailies, the Director and D.P. generally sit together in the very back row so they can talk over the previous day's work and communicate with the projectionist. At a lab or a professional screening room, there is usually a telephone or intercom hookup between the back row and the projection booth.

Everyone attending dailies screenings is looking for different things. The Director is looking for performance, the D.P. is looking at the lighting and the composition, the Art Director is looking at the sets and furnishings, the Script Person is looking for continuity errors and dialogue accuracy, etc. Some of the things for the Camera Assistant to watch for at dailies, besides the obvious, like soft focus or bumpy zooms or bad headroom or microphones in the shot, are dirt, edge fog, static marks, registration problems, vignetting, cinch marks, and scratches.

Film Handling and Camera Problems

Dirt or dust on projected film can be either white or black, and the color of the dirt helps determine the source. Black dirt is less noticeable and less objectionable than white dirt, but it shouldn't be there, whatever the color! Dirt on projected dailies, workprint or release prints, or dirt on reversal film originals, shows up as black. Dirt on black-and-white or color original negative shows up as white.

Dirt on prints can usually be cleaned off, but dirt on camera negative probably cannot be cleaned without making the problem worse by adding scratches. The actual dirt may not even be there on the negative anymore, and what we are seeing is the photographic "shadow" of the dirt, after development. Negative dirt can originate in the darkroom, in the magazines, in the camera body, or at the lab, so keeping your equipment and work areas clean and dust-free is very important.

Dirt in the camera gate, sometimes called "hair" in the gate, appears as an irregular white blob on the screen, generally on the top of the projected image, which is the bottom of the camera gate, since the image is photographed upside down in the camera. It may appear and get worse as the shot progresses, and then may disappear suddenly. It may be accompanied by a scratch. Like scratches on the negative, it may last a few feet or an entire roll, which is a good reason to check the gate frequently! Dirt in the projector gate is black on the screen, and can simply be blown away.

Edge fog is the result of a light leak before the film is processed. It can be caused by leaks in your darkroom or changing bag, or by a loose magazine lid or camera door, or a loose connection between the magazine and the camera body. It can also result from inadvertently opening a film can or loaded magazine. Edge fog is sometimes mistaken for lens flare, but an examination of the negative will answer that question. If the fog extends through the perforation area to the edge of the film, it is edge fog. Lens flare will be restricted to the frame area only, and the frame lines will be clearly seen. It usually appears on the right side of the image if the leak occurred in the camera or magazine, because the right side of the image is the side closest to the magazine lid and camera door. Edge fog can be any color, depending on the color of the light leaking in and the type of film, and can vary in width in the frame based on the intensity of the leak and the speed of the film. The only solution, besides reshooting, is to optically reposition the image, but this, of course, compromises the original composition, and will only be considered in an extreme emergency. Edge fog is almost always the result of Camera Assistant error—it is the Assistants' responsibility to ensure that the magazine lids and camera doors are light-tight.

Cinch marks are diagonal scratches caused by improper film handling, such as forcing a dished, core-wound, roll of film flat or by pulling the end of an unraveled roll of film tight. This is a problem more likely occurring at the laboratory than on the set or in the darkroom. Careful handling when loading and unloading the magazine will minimize the "dishing" problem, and be careful not to pull too tight when taking up the slack at the end of a roll. Scratches can originate in the magazine, in the camera body, or at the lab. Negative scratches are usually white or yellow in color, but can be other colors depending on how deep they are. Print scratches are usually black or dark in color. "Buffing" the negative and/or liquid gate printing can sometimes eliminate or minimize the scratches. Scratches and cinch marks show up more clearly with a thin (underexposed) negative than with a thick (overexposed) negative, and will be more visible in the darker areas of the projected frame than in the lighter areas.

Static marks look like miniature lightning bolts or tree branches on the film, usually blue or violet in color, and usually occur in cold, dry conditions found on location. Static electricity is unlikely in the laboratory, where temperature and humidity are more controlled. Static marks can be minimized by careful and slow handling of the film when working under conditions of cold and low humidity. Rapid removal of the tape sealing a film can or magazine can generate enough static electricity to affect the film in that can or magazine. Try this experiment yourself—in a darkroom, rip off the tape on a film can as fast as you can, while watching the area where the tape meets the can. You can actually see the blue sparks as the tape is removed! This is static electricity, and the best thing the Camera Assistant can do to minimize the problem is to slow down when loading or unloading in cold, dry locations, and to use a darkroom instead of a changing bag. Even more careful handling of the film than normal is warranted under these conditions, especially with black-and-white negative film, which has a much higher tendency to show static marks.

"Breathing" is another problem sometimes seen in dailies, when the image seems to go in and out of focus. This also can have a variety of causes. If the camera negative is improperly threaded into the camera, or if the pressure plate is missing or if the retaining spring for the pressure plate is too weak to hold the film flat, breathing can occur. If the processed negative or print stock is improperly threaded into the optical printer, or if the print is improperly threaded into the projector, breathing can occur. If the problem is in the print, another print can always be made, but if the problem is on the negative, it can't be fixed by reprinting.

If the camera shutter and movement are out of sync, called a "timing" error or "movement phasing" problem, a partial, vertical, ghost-like blurring may be seen. A test for this condition is discussed in the chapter on Setup and Maintenance. Registration problems are discussed in the chapter on Shooting Tests.

Camera negative is very fragile, and handling problems abound. The film is handled several times, by the Camera Assistants when loading the mags, threading the camera, unloading the mags, and by the lab people loading into the developer machine, loading onto the printer, etc., and later by the editor or negative cutter. Those few people who actually handle the film can never be too careful with the original negative!

Raw Stock and Processing Defects

It is difficult, sometimes, to tell the difference between film stock manufacturing defects and laboratory processing defects, as their symptoms are often identical. Mottling of the images, uneven exposure density, chemical stains, spotting, or streaking, can all be either manufacturer or processing defects.

"Reticulation" breaks up the images into cell-like patterns. This is caused by sudden temperature changes in the processing chemicals. Exhausted chemicals can leave an image looking very flat (low in contrast) or uneven in density. Improper drying of the negative or print can result in spotting or streaking. Using out-of-date negative stock, or stock that has been improperly stored, can show up as increased fog and grain, and/or by decreased contrast and film speed.

Some of these problems are the fault of the Camera Assistants, while others can be blamed on the lab or film manufacturers, but fixing the blame is not the point, and does not solve the problem! If there is a problem, the laboratory and/or the film manufacturer will, at best, replace the raw stock or refund the cost of the processing, but this hardly reimburses the filmmakers for the equipment, cast, and crew costs involved in reshooting. By working in a thorough, careful, and conscientious way, the Camera Assistants can avoid many of these problems and help their employers get the shot without problems. That's the key. Get the shot—whatever it takes!

CHAPTER **12**

Slates and Slating

Why Slate?

Why do we slate?
The "slate" itself is simply a rectangular board of plastic, masonite, plywood, or aluminum, on which various information is written. The slate is photographed, usually at the very beginning of the scene, so the information it contains becomes a part of the scene being photographed. The top part of the slate is the section known as the "clapsticks," or just "sticks." These "sticks" are just two pieces of wood (or plastic or aluminum, or some other material) hinged together at one end and usually painted in black and white diagonal stripes. The contrasting stripes aid in their being seen against any type of background, in nearly any lighting conditions.

The words and numbers written on the slate provide essential information to the laboratory and to the film editor, such as the scene and take number, the camera roll number, the date, the camera letter, etc., and the "sticks" make a distinct, sharp sound when snapped closed quickly and forcefully by the Camera Assistant, giving the editor a noise easily distinguished against the background noise.

When photographed by a motion picture camera and recorded by the sound tape recorder, the noise of the sticks closing and the picture of the sticks closing, give the Editor a visual and audio "sync point," with which to ensure the synchronization of the sound with the picture. All the Editor needs to do is line up the first frame of the picture in which the sticks are closed with the frame of the transferred soundtrack in which the sharp "sticks" sound is heard, and from that point on, until either the camera or sound recorder is stopped, as long as the camera and recorder are running at the correct speed, as long as the two strips of material are moved in synchronization with each other, the sound will remain in "sync" with the picture.

The Scene Number and Take Number (or sometimes "Sound Number") will have been spoken out loud either by the Camera Assistant or by the Sound Mixer, and recorded by the Sound Department, so as the sound track is played on the editing

320 THE CAMERA ASSISTANT

Figure 12-1 Sync Slate, Insert Slate, and Time Code Slate. White Plexiglas Standard Sync Slate. Insert Slate without sticks, and Time Code Smart Slate with internal Time Code Generator.

machine, the Editor can hear the spoken scene and take numbers and see the written scene and take numbers on the slate, and can quickly line up the two strips of film at the single frame of each where the sticks close together, and achieve synchronization until either the camera or the sound recorder are shut off.

Generally, the Second Camera Assistant, when there is one, is going to be operating the slate on the set. If not, then the slate belongs to the First Camera Assistant. Sometimes, if the Camera Assistant has other things to do with his or her hands during the shot, some other crew person can be drafted into helping out with the slate.

Slates and Slating 321

Figure 12-2 Slates and Sync Sound. All the editor has to do is match up the film frame when the sticks first close with the sound of the sticks closing to establish synchronization ("sync") between picture and sound.

When necessary, even most actors can do their own slates, such as with scenes photographed inside a moving car, where it would be difficult if not impossible for the Camera Assistant to lean into the car to operate the sticks.

Single System/Double System

When filming in "Double System" style, that is, when the picture and sound are being recorded separately, on two different machines on two different types of recording material, there must be a method to get the two media back into synchronization in the editing room.

Once the camera and sound recorder are both rolling, and their running speed is either locked together by a common AC power source, or by electronic pulses in a cable connecting the two machines ("cable sync"), or independently controlled by oscillating crystals ("crystal sync") or digital clocks ("time code") of some sort, then all that is needed is a single frame of each media that can be positively identified as belonging exactly with the corresponding frame on the other media. The way to get that "sync point" is to use a slate and clapsticks.

This is not necessary in "single-system" recording of picture and sound together on the same strip of film or tape, as in videotape recording or in the old single-system 16mm filming systems of Auricon, CP-16, and similar cameras that recorded the sound and picture simultaneously inside the film camera along one edge of the film, either optically with a tiny, flickering lightbulb, or magnetically on a narrow stripe of magnetic recording media applied to the film.

Information on the Slate

The slate displays much useful information. The name of the production company, the title of the production, the scene number, take number, camera roll number, date, Director's name, Director of Photography's name, etc., all are useful information and will fit on the slate.

This information helps keep your film from getting lost at the lab, and also lets the lab know who to send the bill to. The camera roll number, scene number, and take numbers allow the Editor to find the correct piece of soundtrack to align with the pic-

Figure 12-3 Slate Information. Information usually found on the slate includes: Production Company and/or Project Title, Production Number (if there is one), Director's Name, Director of Photography's Name, Date, Scene Number, Take Number, Camera Roll Number (in this case, roll number "10-A45," standing for episode 10, camera "A", roll 45, the system we have been using for this TV series) and Camera Letter (this slate is for the "A" Camera).

ture for proper sound synchronization. The scene and take numbers also allow the Director of the film to pinpoint and describe exactly which of the individual takes are the preferred takes for inclusion in the finished film.

The presence of the slates between takes lets the laboratory personnel know where in the roll to start and stop their optical printer machines when making the workprint or the video transfer from the original camera negative.

So it is important for the Camera Assistant to make sure that the correct information is written on the slate, and that the slate is properly in frame, in focus, and at close to the right exposure so that it is legible to all those who need to refer to the information it contains.

Types of Slates

There are many types of slates found in the industry. The white Plexiglas slates are the most common now, used with temporary, wipe-off markers that make nice fat, black lines which are easily visible, and will erase quickly and easily. Another advantage to these slates is that if you are in back light or dim light you can still read the numbers against the brighter background of light coming through the back of the translucent plastic.

Some Assistants like to attach the Camera Reports on the back of the slate, making it impossible to read through. I prefer to keep the Camera Reports separate so that when you need it you can read the scene and take numbers through the plastic.

White plastic isn't the only material. Slates used to be and still are made of black masonite, a pressed wood product—you could use chalk on them, or numbers and letters written on white tape. Slates are also made with Velcro fronts and Velcro-backed numbers and letters to arrange in the proper sequence.

There used to be slates made with segmented numbers built in, with little doors that can be opened and closed on individual segments, revealing black or white rectangular shapes for spelling out the correct numbers, similar to the segmenting of characters on a pocket calculator. The Assistant need only open and close the proper doors to spell out the required numbers and letters. I haven't seen any of these lately.

All of these types of slates have their advantages and disadvantages. The white plastic slates, while in themselves waterproof, do not work well in the rain because the ink in the special dry-erase markers does not erase very well when wet, or when the cloth eraser is wet. The solution to this problem is to use black crayon or china marker instead of the wipe-off marker when working in the rain. The white plastic is also prone to breaking if dropped or stepped on (or run over by the dolly, which happened to one of mine not too long ago).

The black masonite or wooden slates, while more break-resistant than the Plexiglas, are harder to read, because the chalk numbers are thin and faint, and repeated erasings smear chalk dust across the background of the slate, making the chalk markings even harder to read. Occasional wiping with a damp cloth or sponge will get rid of the chalk dust. Using numbers written on tape will increase the legibility, but the adhesive on the tape will take its toll on the surface of the masonite, eventually tearing off the smooth surface and leaving the surface pitted. The tape numbers will also start to fall off as the adhesive wears out, and must be continually replaced. The tape numbers won't stick very well in the cold or rain either.

The Velcro slates work as well in the rain as in bright sun, as the Velcro is unaffected by water, but the Velcro makes noise (the sound of ripping cloth) while being changed, sometimes disturbing to actors and others, and the numbers silkscreen printed on the back of the Velcro strips eventually wear off and the strips themselves often get lost. Replacing them is neither convenient nor easy, and the Assistant sometimes needs to write something on the slate that is not already preprinted on the Velcro strips.

The plastic segmented number slate is really too fragile for the rigors of film production, with the little plastic doors breaking off or jamming, making it difficult to change the numbers. Also, there are a specific number of characters available on the slate, and they only spell out numbers and certain letters, with any legibility, so any lengthy scene description or alphabetic characters that need to be on the slate have to be added with white tape anyway.

I also used to have an aluminum spring-loaded slate, black on one side and white on the other, made to be written on with crayon or china marker. The spring-loaded sticks could be locked open and released by pushing on the spring release, snapping the sticks closed. That one is now in my museum of obsolete and silly equipment.

Slates also come in various sizes, from pocket-sized to the standard 9" by 12" to giant-sized, for use in the variety of circumstances that a Camera Assistant might encounter. The small ones, sometimes described as "insert slates," are useful in close-up filming or tabletop work, where a large slate cannot be backed away from the camera far enough to fit the frame being photographed. The standard size slate is good for nearly all circumstances, and is conveniently sized for storage in a slot found underneath most gear-head "front boxes" used by Camera Assistants or carried in tool cases and bags.

Extra-large slates or just the "sticks" portion (two to four feet long) are useful in multiple camera slating, being positioned where several cameras can photograph it simultaneously, and in scenes where it is not convenient to be close to the camera with a smaller slate.

Roll Slates

Roll slates are more often found on documentary shoots than on feature or commercial shoots. At the beginning, or "head" of the roll, the common practice on documentary filming is to "slate the roll," photographing the slate in order to ensure the proper identification of the production company and production title and whatever other information might be desired is photographed on the film so the roll is not lost in the lab.

This is only really necessary if there will not be any other slates photographed on the remainder of the roll, if, for example, only a flashing light slate or microphone taps will be used for sound synching purposes, documentary style.

Often when this is done on documentary productions, a color chart is also photographed as part of the roll slate. This color chart, a standardized collection of colored squares or rectangles, allows the color timer at the laboratory to balance the workprint for proper color, by comparing the color chart on the photographed negative with a chart kept at the laboratory.

By adjusting three color filters (red, green, and blue) the timer can correct for minor color variations brought about by mixed or unusual lighting sources, or by filming early in the morning or late in the afternoon when the sun is much redder than at midday. Color charts are sometimes used in feature and commercial productions, in the same way—photographed at the head of the roll or at the beginning of the shooting day, depending on the Director of Photography, and used as a reference by the color timer when printing the workprint.

There are times, also, when roll slating is desirable on feature or commercial productions. If the very first take on the roll is going to be a tail slate, for instance, it is a good idea to get some identification at the very head of the roll with a head slate. If shooting silent scenes (without recording sync sound), and the decision has been made to print the entire roll instead of printing individually slated takes, then a roll slate makes even more sense, as it will probably be the only slate on that roll.

Tail Slates

Slates at the beginning of the scenes are always preferable, but not always possible or convenient. When the footage comes back from the lab and is screened, it is

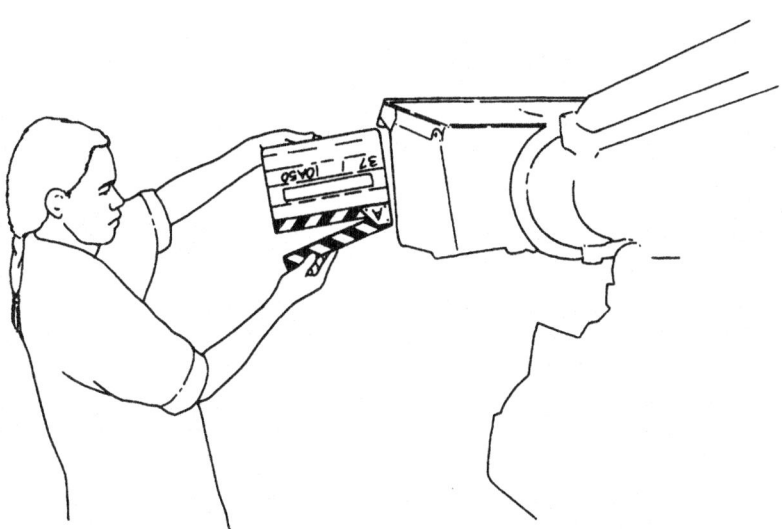

Figure 12-4 Tail Slate. Tail Slates are always photographed upside down at the end of scene being photographed. To save film, snap the sticks closed first, so the camera can be shut off, and then announce the scene and take number, and be sure to announce "Tail Slate" for the sound recorder.

much more convenient to have the scene number and take number displayed at the beginning of the scene, even though the actual sync "sticks" are at the tail of the scene.

A tail slate is distinguished from a head slate by being photographed upside down in the frame. When the lab or the Editor sees an inverted slate, they know immediately that it is a tail slate at the end of the scene. Any slate photographed right side up is assumed to be at the head of the scene.

There are several reasons why the sticks might be recorded at the end of the scene instead of at the head. First off, if the scene being filmed involves young children, animals, or even nervous nonprofessional actors, then a slate at the tail of the scene is less disruptive or distracting to these performers.

Secondly, if the blocking of the scene makes it difficult for one of the Assistants to get the slate in frame at the head of the shot, such as if the shot begins on a close-up of a doorknob and then pulls back to see the room, a tail slate is much easier.

Sometimes there is not enough time after the camera begins rolling to get a slate, as in a shot of an unexpected or difficult to predict event. The camera can be switched on, the event photographed, and then, as long as neither the camera nor the sound recorder has been shut off, the sticks can be photographed anytime after the event, at the crew's convenience.

Tail slates are also useful if the camera is going to be started later than the sound, which sometimes is desirable when filming a long dialogue scene in which the Director only needs the end of the scene for a particular shot, but wants the actors to act out the entire scene in order to build the rhythm and emotion of the scene. The Director can indicate to the crew when to roll the camera, either in response to a cue in the dialogue, or by tapping the Camera Assistant on the shoulder or otherwise signaling the Assistant to start the camera. After the scene, keep the camera rolling long enough to photograph the slate.

Whenever possible, when you know that a particular scene is to be tail slated, shoot a head slate with the scene and take numbers, right side up, so that the person operating the printing machine at the lab can find more easily where to turn the printer on as the negative runs through. This also gives the Director and the Editor screening the dailies an easy way to identify the take being screened. This is often referred to as "Getting an I.D." slate (for "Identification").

When tail slating, it is a good idea to call out "Tail Slate," "End Sticks," or other such indication as soon as the sound recorder is turned on at the head of the scene to announce your intention to tail slate, and then again as soon as the scene is cut, to remind everyone that the scene still needs to be slated, and to remind the sound mixer not to shut off the recorder until the slate is taken. Often, as soon as the scene is cut, everyone starts talking at once and walking into the frame, which makes slating difficult.

It is also a good practice when tail slating to hit the sticks together first, then announce "Tail Marker," because after the sticks close, the camera can be shut off, saving expensive film. The announcement can be recorded on the sound tape after the camera is shut off for a fraction of the cost.

Second Sticks

Despite the best of intentions and experience, sometimes things just go wrong. If the First Assistant is a bit slow on starting the camera, or if the Second Assistant holds the slate a bit too far left or too low, and it is out of the frame, then sometimes the sticks are missed by the camera. In this event, the Camera Operator, who can best see the sticks through the lens, or the First Assistant, if he or she notices that the camera started late, should call out "Second Sticks" as quickly as possible. This alerts everyone that the sticks were missed by the camera, and that the Second Assistant should put the slate back in and try again. The camera should be switched on again and the slating procedure continued, using the same take number, and with the Second Camera Assistant calling out "Second Sticks" before hitting the sticks together. This alerts the Editor that the second clap of the sticks is the one to use for synching up sound to picture.

When "Second Sticks" is necessary, make sure to indicate that on the Camera Report, and make sure that the Script Supervisor has made that note as well, for the benefit of the Lab and the Editor.

False Starts

Sometimes the slating is completed, and the Director calls "Action" but then something goes wrong and the scene is cut. In this instance, the take number is advanced to the next in sequence, and the slating process starts over again. Keep in mind that with a "Second Sticks" situation, the take number remains the same, since you never got beyond the slating process. For the "False Start," the take number changes to the next number, because the slating was actually finished.

Silent Slates

The same sort of "ID" slates used to indicate an upcoming tail slate are good for "silent" filming, as well, filming without sound, or "M.O.S." ("Mit Out Sound," as the legend goes). We usually add the initials "MOS" to the slate, in addition to the scene and take numbers, so that the Editor does not go looking for the sound for that shot.

This "ID" or "M.O.S." slate can be filmed anytime before the scene begins, and as there is no need to clap the sticks together for a silent scene, the camera can be switched off between photographing the slate and filming the scene. This can save some time, as the slating can be done while the actors and directors are talking about the scene, or the makeup is being touched up, or even while the set is still being lit.

Then when all is ready, the Assistant can switch on the camera and just say "Speed!" or "Rolling!" out loud to let everyone know that the camera is rolling at the correct speed and that the scene may commence.

The usual method for M.O.S. slating is to hold the slate in frame with the sticks closed, although I have worked with Camera Assistants and Script Supervisors who

Figure 12-5 M.O.S. ID Slate. M.O.S. Slate photographed at head of scene to label film with scene and take numbers. There is no need to hit the sticks, as sound is not being recorded for M.O.S. shooting.

have insisted that the sticks should be open for a silent slate. It makes more sense to leave them closed for silent slating and beginning with the sticks open for sync sound slating so the Editor can differentiate instantly between the two. There is also some current foolishness about having the Assistant place his or her fingers between the sticks when photographing an M.O.S. ID Slate. I can't imagine what this would accomplish, and I have never heard an Editor request this, so forget it. Sometimes this nonsense gets started for no apparent reason, and spreads like wildfire because no one stops to ask why. Everyone is afraid to say that the Emperor has no clothes, I guess.

Whichever system you decide to use, be consistent.

Getting Started

Once everything on the set is ready to begin filming, the Assistant Director takes one last look around the set, hopefully, and then says out loud "Roll Sound!" In England, the phrase is "Turn Over!"

Whatever the phrase is for where you're shooting, what it means is that the Sound Mixer should turn on the sound recorder. The recorder takes a few seconds to come up to speed, much slower than the camera takes to get to speed, so the sound recorder is started first. Also sound tape costs only pennies a foot, so it is much more financially efficient to begin the sound recording first.

Once the Mixer has started the recorder, and the recorder comes up to speed, the Mixer calls out "Speed!" If the Mixer has set up the sound equipment at any distance from the set, such as in another room or in the hallway, then the Boom Person, who generally has a pair of headphones on and can hear the Mixer even if the rest of the crew can't, echoes out "Speed!" for the shooting crew.

If recording the video assist picture, then keep in mind that the video recorder often takes even longer than the sound recorder to come up to speed. Often the Assistant Director calls out "Roll Video," or "Roll Tape," before "Roll Sound," to allow the video recorder the time to come up to speed. Some A.D.'s call out "Roll Tapes," for both Sound and Video to begin recording.

Once the word "Speed" is heard by the Camera Assistant, the camera can be switched on. Modern sync cameras reach speed almost instantaneously after being switched on. Most Camera Assistants prefer to switch the camera off and on themselves, rather than to have the Camera Operator switch on and off, for several reasons. First off, the Camera Operator, if using a geared head, must remove one hand from the wheel in order to hit the switch, and then must grab the wheel again and steady himself (herself) for the scene, possibly having to reframe for the opening of the shot.

Secondly, Camera Operators often get so involved in what they are looking at that they forget to hit the switch, which sometimes results in missing the slate and having to ask for the dreaded "Second Sticks!", or even worse, that they switch off the camera so quickly at the word, "Cut!", that the tail slate is missed. This means additional work for the editor.

The Camera Assistant is less likely to miss the slates than the Camera Operator, in the heat of battle, and most Camera Assistants prefer to have the camera switch under their control.

Once both the sound recorder and the camera are rolling at the correct speed, the Second Assistant can read off the scene and take number (or scene and sound number for a commercial) and hit the sticks together. Some cameras have a small beeper installed that announces that the camera is rolling, and the beep stops when the proper speed is reached. On other cameras without the beeper, often the Second Assistant can hear the click of the switch as the First Assistant switches on. Either of these audio signals cues the Second Assistant to begin reading out the slate information.

On cameras with quiet switches, or in locations with so much background noise that the switch cannot be heard, the First Assistant should work out with the Second a system of visible signals, such as a nod from the First after the camera is running, to serve as a slating cue. After a while the Second Assistant learns how long to wait after "Speed!" to begin the slate. With such a camera, if there is any delay in switching on after "Speed!", the First Assistant should be prepared to signal or to call out to the Second to delay the slate until the camera is rolling properly.

Sometimes the sound mixer, particularly with a West Coast sound crew, will have set up a microphone at the sound cart or table, and "pre-slated" the sound tape with the scene and take numbers by rolling the tape and reading the information into the microphone. Then after "Speed!", the camera is switched on and the Second Assistant need only call out "Marker!" and hit the sticks together.

The reason "Marker!" is called out is to alert the sound transfer house and the editor that the next sound heard on the tape or on the soundtrack will be the sound of the sticks coming together. This is to prevent some other sound, such as a door closing or a footstep from being mistaken for the sticks, and the scene sunk (past tense of "sync"? or should it be "synched"?) up improperly.

Don't laugh—it happens! I was once on a job when we got a panic phone call from the editor in California (we were filming in Georgia and shipping film each night to the lab in Los Angeles). The editor told us that a long master scene we had filmed of a gun battle the previous day (we were making a Western) was totally out of sync. The editor was of the opinion that the camera motor was somehow at fault. This was in the early days of crystal sync, and crews always feared crystal motor failure, after years of fairly reliable cable sync. The editor's phone call, as such calls often do, went to the producer, who panicked, instead of to the Director of Photography or the Camera Assistant, who might have been able to diagnose the problem without any lost production time.

Anyway, we were told to stop filming, and since we did not have a back-up sync camera on this job (never a good idea not to have a back-up—a false economy), we shot a sync test with the camera and rushed it out to the lab, and then we just sat around the hotel until the previous day's workprint and soundtrack arrived that night for us to look at. Because of the airline schedule, our sync test arrived at the lab and was pronounced perfect by the editor before the workprint arrived at location.

Once the film arrived, and was set up in the local movie theater we were using to screen dailies, and the scene was run, it was immediately obvious that the editor had sunk up the picture of the slate sticks closing to the sound of the first gunshot instead of to the sound of the sticks. Of course everything was out of sync. The starting point for the picture was not aligned with the starting point for the sound.

The Camera Assistant had properly called out "Marker!" but the microphone boom was so far away from the Assistant that the word "Marker!" was barely audible. Sometimes despite the best intentions and the proper procedure, mistakes happen. This mistake cost the production more than a day's work.

If the Camera Assistant had called out "Marker!" louder, or if the Boom Man had swung the microphone closer to the slate, or if the Mixer had boosted the gain on the recorder during the slate, or if the producer had allowed the rental of a back-up camera, or if the editor had looked at the film again and listened more carefully, instead of jumping on the phone, the problem might have been averted without losing a day. As it worked out, we all got a day's much needed rest, at the company's expense.

Slating Procedure

Always try to give the editors slates in focus, properly exposed, and in some reasonable size so they can see it and read it. After a short time, the Second Assistant will begin to know where to place the slate so it is readable in the frame. A simple rule of thumb for 35mm filming is to divide the focal length of the lens by ten. For example, if filming with a 40mm lens, slate four feet from the camera. If using a 100mm lens, slate at ten feet. For 16mm filming, divide the focal length by 5.

Don't make the Camera Operator search for the slate. Get the slate properly into the frame, asking the Operator or the First Assistant where the frame is, if necessary. If the Operator has to pan or tilt away from the action in order to slate, then the frame must be reset before "Action!" is called. This wastes film and time. Prepare yourself for the slate position well in advance, to discover a good place to hold the slate, giving the First a chance to see where you will be so the focus can be rolled back to the slate before the scene commences, and to prepare your escape route after slating.

Get used to tilting the slate forward, to eliminate the possibility of a reflection on the shiny surface of those white plastic slates. Lights behind and above the camera could reflect back off the slate and obscure the scene and take numbers written there. By tilting the slate forward, the odds of this are greatly reduced. This is a good habit to get into—just tilt forward every time and pretty soon it will be simply a reflex.

The First Assistant should plan to roll the focus forward for the slate, and then to roll back for the scene focus. After a while, this will become automatic. If the area where the slate will be is dark, as it often is in a studio, or on a night exterior, the Electrical Department should be asked for a "slate light," a small lighting unit set up near the camera to illuminate the slate and then get shut off before the scene starts. An Electrician will generally man the switch of this light, and will adjust the intensity of the light to a level somewhat similar to the lighting of the scene. If necessary, the assistant director should be notified that a moment will be needed after the slate to reset the focus for the scene and/or switch off the slate light, before calling "Action."

These efforts at keeping the slate in frame, in focus, and properly exposed will be appreciated by the director, the editor, and the lab.

Getting the slate into the frame at the beginning of the shot is only half the battle. After the sticks come together, the Camera Assistant has to get the slate and himself (or herself) out of the frame and out of the actors' way and sightlines. It's very important for the Assistant to have an "escape route" planned well in advance before getting out there for the slate, an escape route that does not involve crossing in front of the lens, an escape route that is fast and quiet.

There's nothing more embarrassing than going out there to do a slate, closing the sticks smartly, and then not being able to get out of the way. There are actors and gripstands and lights and furniture and other obstacles just waiting to catch the Assistant and trap him or her in the frame. Every new Assistant does it once and then forever after that embarrassment, plans an escape route carefully. Many times the Second just can't get in front of the camera and then out again because of the obstacles. Sometimes the First Assistant can operate the sticks more easily and less disruptively.

The First Assistant can do the slate and sticks, hopefully, and the Second Assistant who may be trapped behind the camera or behind the set someplace will do the Camera Reports. Sometimes, if the First has his hands full with focus and zoom, then the slate can be handed to the Second quickly after the sticks, allowing the First to get on with being the First. The Second can change the slate to the next number and stand ready to hand it back to the First for the beginning of the next take.

A slate should at least be stationary at the moment the sticks close. A common mistake made by new Camera Assistants is to start to move the slate out of the frame before the sticks actually close. A moving target is hard for the editor to line up on, because the individual frames are blurred if the target is moving, so hold it still for the sticks to close, pause for a split second, and then get out quickly. This is especially important with the "Smart Slate" used for Time Code Slating. The slate must be held stationary long enough for the editor to read the digital display before the sticks close, and then long enough to read the other digital display after the sticks have closed. Doing a sloppy slate too fast is almost worse than no sticks at all.

In certain rare instances, you may be unable to get into the scene with a proper slate and almost anything that makes noise will do as a sync slate, such as a tap on the microphone or a hand clap, preferably with hands held in profile, so the camera sees the hands come together, and the microphone hears the sound of the clap.

I once worked with a French Canadian crew who insisted very noisily that on a sync sound slate the sticks had to begin open, then close, and open again before removing the slate from the frame. This, to me, is totally wrong, makes no sense, takes too long, and makes more work for the editor. With what I consider a "normal" slate, being open when the camera switches on, then closing and remaining closed as it is removed from the frame, when the editor is working away at the editing table, looking at any individual frame of the slate, the editor will be able to tell instantly whether the actual frame of the sticks closing is forward or backward on the roll.

With the French Canadian system, the editor cannot tell if a frame with the sticks open is before or after the "clap" and the odds are 50-50 that the editor will try the wrong direction first. It would take longer to find the exact frame of sticks closing with this system. Why make more work for the editor? I don't know if that was an isolated incident, or if this is common practice in some areas, but it shows that there should be a good reason for any procedure. Don't just do something because someone else does. Think it through and have a reason for every procedure.

With European slates, sometimes the sticks are on the bottom of the slate instead of at the top. One Italian crew I worked with in New York had a slate where the sticks were on the bottom and the moveable stick extended past the slate. They would do slates by slapping down the part that stuck out, and it would snap closed and then fall open again.

Etiquette of Slating

It is always the Camera Assistants' responsibility to prevent the slating procedure from distracting or disturbing the actors and/or director. Professional actors and directors will of course recognize the necessity of slating, but might still be distracted by what I call "impolite" slating.

Examples of this impolite slating would be holding the slate so close to the actor's face that it is uncomfortable, holding up the slate in front of the actor while the actor is still talking to the director, or calling out the scene and take number very loudly just before a quiet, intimate scene. All of these things can be avoided with a little thought and consideration, and should be avoided.

The Camera Assistant can, in a very short time, develop a sense of etiquette about the slating procedure. Put yourself in the actor's place. Never surprise or frighten actors by swinging the slate quickly at their faces or startle them by shouting out the scene number right in their ears.

Some directors or actors are so put off by the slating that they might request the Assistant to tail slate some of the more intimate scenes, or scenes demanding the most concentration by the actors. Some directors even tail slate everything, on the theory that head slating destroys or at least damages the spontaneity of the performance.

Perspective and Timing

Knowing exactly when and how loud to slate is important. Common sense should provide this information. Think about the scene and deal with the peculiarities of each scene.

Don't slate a scene if the director and actors are still talking to each other about the scene. Don't slate a scene if the Camera Operator is trying to get the Boom Man to lift the microphone out of the frame. Don't slate a scene if you hear a jet airplane or motorcycle nearby. It is only a waste of film to begin a scene under such situations. It is better to wait until the situation resolves itself before beginning the slating and shooting procedure.

The same goes for the First Assistant. Don't even switch on the camera if the director and actors are talking to each other or if a plane is overhead. Film is expensive and you should save it for really essential shooting whenever possible. Waiting will not only save the producer money but will minimize the reloading and the paperwork. When things quiet down or the director finishes talking, then proceed. An assistant director who is paying attention will realize that things are not 100 percent ready to film, and will call out "Hold the Roll!" as soon as he or she sees that the director is not ready to call "Action!"

On a quiet, intimate two shot or close-up, the microphone will likely be hovering just above the frame line, less than a foot from the slate. Don't shout out the scene number and slam the sticks together. The director, the actors, and the Sound Department will appreciate your consideration. The same is true for a scene with young children or animals, or even amateur actors, who might be startled by a loud slate. This is what I mean by perspective.

The reverse is true also. If the scene is a huge wide shot and the actors are a block away inside a car, then shout out the scene number and slam those sticks together. Watch for the microphone. If you don't see the microphone, then ask the Sound Department where the mikes are hidden.

The Camera Assistant should address the microphone when slating, not the camera. This is a difficult concept to master for the beginner. The tendency is to face the camera and speak out the scene number to the camera. You should be directing that toward the microphone, especially if the microphone is behind you or at some distance away.

Sometimes the Sound Department will utilize an additional microphone solely for the slate. If, for example, the dialogue is taking place between two actors sitting in a car, while the camera is some distance away, the inside of the car will be "miked," and the boom person might be standing near the camera with the boom mike just to get the

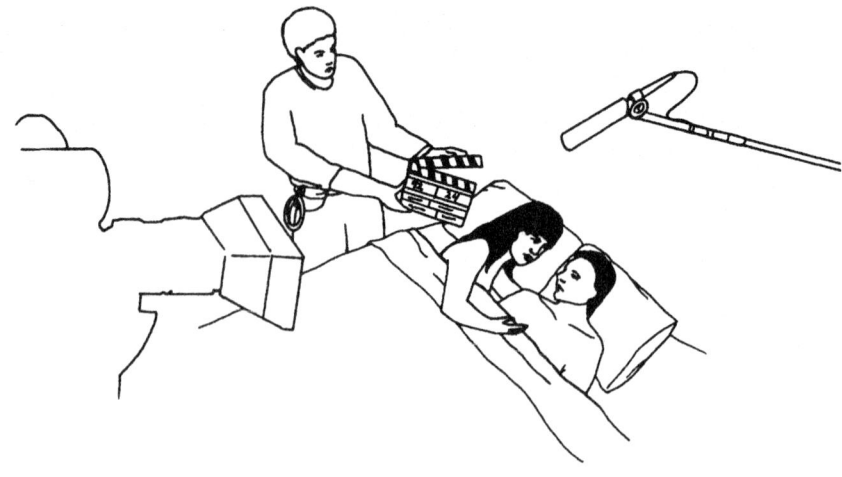

Quiet sticks!

Loud sticks!

Figure 12-6 Slate Perspective. Use a little common sense when slating. There are occasions when quiet sticks are recommended and other situations when loud sticks are called for. Be sure to notice where the microphone is, and how much ambient sound there is in the area before slating.

sticks at the head of the scene. Sometimes the Sound Department places a wireless microphone on the Second Camera Assistant just to pick up the sticks.

Quite often if walking actors are radio-miked, the boom mike will be in use also to pick up the natural ambient sound of the location, and will be used for the slating as well.

The Sound Department is also eager to give the editors good slates, so they will gladly work out with the Camera Assistants a slating procedure adequate and satisfactory to the shooting situation. Sometimes they might request the Second to give "Loud Sticks" if they are some distance away from the camera. Or there might be a situation where it might be easier to get better sound if the scene is tail slated instead of head slated.

Also make sure that the Script Supervisor and the Assistant Director are aware of any changes in the normal slating procedure that you have planned, such as if a scene is to be tail slated, or if additional time is needed to reset the camera or microphones after the slate but before "Action!"

Documentary Slating

Normal slating procedures are often impractical under most documentary situations. Documentary filming requires its own procedures.

Often the only written slates photographed on documentary productions are roll slates, brief identification at the head or each roll of film for the laboratory, listing the title, company name, and roll number, and often the date. For sync sound, the normal slate board is often not used. Instead, other types of less disruptive and time-consuming slates are used.

The most common type of documentary slate is probably the flashing light slate, or beep slate. This is a device normally worn on the neck strap or carrying case for the sound recorder, carried by the Sound Mixer. Various commercial models are available, and many sound recordists have made their own, but the concept is quite simple. The device consists of a small box connected by cable to the sound recorder, with either a lightbulb or an LED (light emitting diode) that flashes when a button on the box is pressed by the recordist. The camera is turned momentarily toward the sound recorder and the recordist presses the button. The film camera photographs the light flashing on and off, and at the same time the light flashes, the little box sends an electronic signal to the recorder which is recorded as a "beep" on the sound tape. This "beep" is heard only by the sound recordist through the headphones, and is not heard by anyone not wearing headphones.

The editor then has only to line up the first frame of the film in which the light is on with the first frame of the sound track in which is heard the beep. From then on, as long as the camera and sound recorder are both crystal-controlled, and were both turned on and running, the picture and track will remain in sync.

Variations on this idea may range from a simple light with a small pad of paper attached nearby with consecutive numbers written on consecutive pages. This allows a sequential sound number to be photographed with each successive slate photographed. The sound recorder simply tears off a page after each slate. Fancier models of the beep slate have multiple LEDs spelling out sequential numbers in segments, either manually or automatically advancing to the next number after each flash.

Slates of this type can be used quickly and silently, without disrupting the situation or calling attention to the filmmaking process.

Time Code Slating

Slating via time code is a process found more and more often in documentary filming, and has been making inroads into commercial and theatrical filming as well, but much more slowly. Time code is particularly useful where electronic postproduction (editing on videotape) is planned.

For documentary filming, time code is the ideal method. Just turn on the camera and sound recorder and begin filming. No special procedures need be taken, after making sure that the internal clocks in the camera and sound recorder are synchronized.

Time code involves installing very accurate electronic clocks in both the camera and the sound recorder. These clocks produce intermittent electronic signals which are recorded photographically on the edge of the film itself and on the sound tape at specific and identical intervals. These clocks must be periodically synchronized with each other by briefly connecting them to each other by cable, or by connecting them each in turn to a third clock, resetting them to the clock designated "master" clock. Various manufacturers have different methods of achieving synchronization. Once synchronized, the clocks boast accuracy of 1 frame in 8 hours continuous running.

On film, the signal is recorded by small flashing LEDs shining through a tiny window near the aperture opening, on the very edge of the film as the film runs through the camera. When the film is developed, the flashes of light become visible. This recording may be either "machine-readable" or "user-readable," that is, either as a bar-code type pattern coded for a machine to read, or displayed as tiny numbers representing hours, minutes, seconds, and frames, visible along the edge of the developed film. For the Panavision Aätoncode system, the machine-readable code appears alongside each frame, except for where the "user-readable" print appears once each second (every 24 frames). There is space for additional information as well, such as a date and roll number, production number, camera number, cameraman's initials, or some other such information, described in "techno-babble" as "user bits."

On the sound tape, the time code is recorded as intermittent electronic pulses or beeps that can be read by the tape transfer machine and printed along the edge of the workprint soundtrack.

The editor only has to line up identical clock displays on the film and track, and sync is achieved. This can even be done totally by machine, saving hours of work.

Another advantage to time code slating is that any number of multiple cameras can be used without any special additional equipment or trouble, as long as each camera's time code clock is synchronized to the master clock.

The disadvantages to time code slating are the high cost of the electronic clock modules, the added weight of the additional electronics, especially if the cameras are to be hand held, time lost to long and unnecessary "prerolls," and the general orneriness

Slates and Slating **337**

and unpredictability of the complex electronics. In other words, the more electronics that are being used, the more things there are that can go wrong. Batteries drain faster, rain or humidity can cause unusual problems, and cameras and sound recorders become even more fragile and delicate.

Several times during the early days of time code development I have started a time code job and have had to disconnect the time code clocks and revert to normal

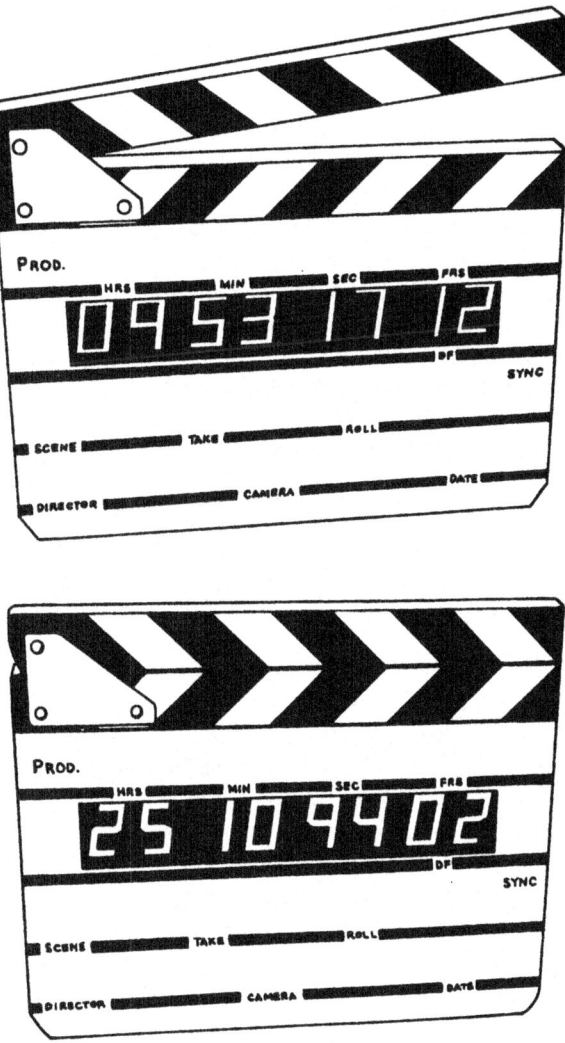

Figure 12-7 Time Code "Smart Slate." The Time Code Smart Slate displays Hours, Minutes, Seconds, and Frames when the sticks are open, and then the User Bits entered by the Sound Mixer when the sticks close.

slating methods after a few days, when the electronics died or the clocks began drifting out of control. Hopefully these bugs are all worked out by now.

There is another time code method that needs to be mentioned here. It is sort of a hybrid, somewhere between the time code method described above and "normal" slating. In this method, only the sound recorder has to have the time code clock installed. The camera only needs a regular crystal-controlled motor.

There are two styles of time code slates, both externally resembling a normal slate, but containing a digital LED display, showing hours, minutes, seconds, and frames, and then displaying user bits programmed in by the Sound Mixer, that may be the date, camera number, roll number, production number, etc. One of these slate styles is known as the "dumb slate," because it must be connected by cable or wireless link to receive clock information from the time code generator in the sound recorder. The other is called the "smart" slate, because it has its own time code generator that can be synchronized ("jammed") periodically with the sound recorder time code generator by briefly connecting them with a cable. The manufacturer of the "dumb slate" has since made available a small time code generator which can be attached to the "dumb slate," making it a "smart slate," without the need for a cable or wireless link between the slate and the sound recorder.

These time code slates have space for the picture title, director and D.P., date, scene number, take number, etc., just as on a normal slate, and there are normal sticks. When the sticks are opened, the digital readout displays the running time code. When the sticks are closed, this time code display freezes for three frames and then changes to display the user bits that have been programmed in.

The camera need only photograph a few frames of the digital display slate at the head of the scene. The manufacturer of these slates recommends one second of camera rolling before closing the sticks, but I keep running into editors that insist on five or more seconds of "preroll." One New York transfer house claims they need ten to fifteen seconds of "preroll," an outrageous delay when doing serious shooting under tight schedules.

According to the manufacturer, Sound needs 5 to 10 seconds of preroll, but the Camera should need only one second. Nothing slows down production or annoys actors and directors more than having to wait for the damned time code slate preroll. One commercial director I have worked for insists that all slating be tail slating, because he can't stand waiting for the preroll.

The identical time reading is simultaneously recorded as described above on the soundtrack, and synchronization is easy.

The manual for this slate also recommends against tail slating, and especially against turning the slate upside down during tail slating, "because the editor cannot turn over his monitor." Film editors have been using upside down tail slates for over fifty years without turning over their Moviolas or Steenbecks—why should time code tail slates be any different?

This method of slating works fairly well, and is becoming more and more common, but it has its disadvantages. The slate now weighs over three pounds, needs batteries, has to be connected by cable to the sound recorder periodically, probably won't work in the rain, and costs over a thousand dollars. This is progress?

Commercial Slating

For some reason lost to time, commercial slating is different from feature (theatrical) slating in scene and take nomenclature. While theatrical slating uses a scene number and a take number, commercial slating usually uses a scene number and a consecutive sound number.

Take numbers start at "One" for each scene, and progress sequentially for as many times as the scene is filmed. When the next scene is to be slated, the scene number is changed, and the take number goes back to "One." Sound numbers, on the other hand, start at "One" for the first scene shot on the job, on the first day of shooting, and progress sequentially throughout the job, never returning to "One."

For example, if scene 101 is filmed ten times, and the next scene is 102, the sound number for the first attempt at filming scene 102 will be sound 11. If scene 102 is filmed 12 times, the first attempt at the next scene will be sound 24. The sound number keeps climbing until the end of the job. On a long commercial shoot, sound numbers up to 400 or 500 are not unusual.

But then, what about M.O.S. filming (without sound) in commercials, as with most product shots? Using the "commercial" slating system, we would have to use a scene number only, with no sound number, since we are not recording sound, and all takes would have the same number, with no way of telling them apart.

But no—for M.O.S. filming, we just switch back to that "other" slating system, the one using scene and take numbers—that system that wasn't good enough to shoot

Figure 12-8 Commercial Slating. Slating for Television Commercials uses Scene and consecutive Sound numbers instead of scene and take numbers. The Sound numbers continue in sequence from the first shot of the job to the last shot of the job, so that each sound take has a unique number.

a 15-second commercial with (only multimillion dollar feature films) but that all of a sudden becomes necessary in order to do the M.O.S. shooting. We use scene and take numbers for the M.O.S. stuff, then switch back to where we left off with the sound numbers when sound recording starts again. If I were reading this in a book without having experienced it hundreds of times, I wouldn't believe it either. How these things get started, we'll probably never know.

The only scenario I can imagine that would explain this seeming contradiction is that when television commercial shooting first began, in the late 1940s and early 1950s, the people doing this work were the documentary filmmakers, rather than feature filmmakers, and this type of slating more closely matches documentary slating than feature slating. Since documentaries by definition are not scripted, how can you have a scene or take number? But you do record sound, so consecutive sound numbers does make sense as a slating method. If the scripted commercials were being made by the documentary crews, they might stay with a slating system they were used to and were comfortable with. How's that for pure conjecture?

Commercials are also often filmed in batches, making several lengths or versions of the commercial, or filming several scripts at the same time. It would not be unusual to make a 30-second and a 15-second version of the same commercial simultaneously, or to make an East Coast version and a West Coast version simultaneously, or a Caucasian and a Black version or even an English language and a Spanish language version simultaneously on the same set or location, but with different actors.

For this reason, scenes are numbered so that they can be sorted out as to which commercial version they belong with. For example, all scenes belonging to the 30-second version of the commercial might be numbered starting with 101. The scenes for the 15-second version start with 201. If there are more versions to contend with, they will start with 301, and 401, and 501, etc. Since it is highly unlikely that there will be over 100 shots for a commercial, scene number duplication is unlikely. The editor can easily sort out the 100s from the 200s, no matter what order the scenes are filmed in.

All the Camera Assistant need worry about is finding out from the script supervisor what numbering system is to be used, and keep the slates and Camera Report records accordingly.

Multiple Camera Slating

Slating for multiple cameras takes a little longer, and involves more planning on the Camera Assistants' part, but really should be no problem.

First off, each camera filming simultaneously gets a camera letter. The primary camera is always "Camera A," the next is "Camera B," then "Camera C," etc. This camera letter is incorporated into the camera roll number: camera rolls A12, A13, A14, A15, etc., for the A Camera; rolls B6, B7, B8, for B Camera. This is sometimes written as 12A, 13A, 14A, etc. It doesn't really matter whether the camera letter leads or follows, as long as it is there. I prefer A13 to 13A, myself. Find out what the script supervisor wants to do, and be consistent. Once you start with a system of roll numbering, keep to it.

The camera letter also gets posted on the slate for that camera. Each camera should have its own slate, and the Camera Assistant with that camera should "ID" slate each scene with the camera's own slate, with the camera letter clearly shown on the slate, as well as the scene and take number.

Whenever possible, a "common marker," or single clap of the sticks, should be used to establish sync for multiple cameras. A common marker saves time and film, both important commodities on the set. Sometimes a large set of sticks, two to four feet in length, and painted with the black and white diagonal stripes, but without the slate part with the numbers, is used, because it may be visible from greater distances from the camera. Common marking will not always be possible, depending on where the cameras are located, what lenses are being used, and what they are pointed at.

If two cameras are close together, with lenses reasonably close in focal length, and pointed somewhat in the same direction, then a common marker should be easy.

Individual slates at each camera for scene and take numbers.
Common marker only for sticks.

Figure 12-9 Common Marker. Using a "Common Marker" when slating multiple cameras saves time and film. After slating each camera individually with the scene and take number, another slate can often be positioned somewhere in the set so that it can be seen by more than one camera, and can provide the sync "sticks" for both cameras together.

Each camera shoots its own ID slate with scene and take number, then waits for sound speed to start rolling and when both cameras are rolling (Camera Assistants at each camera call out "A speed" and "B speed" to indicate they are rolling) then the Second Assistant can call out the scene and take number (if the sound mixer has not already preslated), then "Common Marker, A and B Cameras," or "A and B Cameras, Common Marker," and then snap the sticks together.

If the camera positioning or lenses being used or other circumstances make it difficult to find a place to slate the two cameras with a common marker where both cameras can see the slate sticks clearly and legibly, then separate sticks are necessary. "A" camera slates first, then "B," etc., in alphabetical order. The A Camera Assistant calls out the scene number and take number, then "Camera A marker," and then the sticks.

The B Camera Assistant does not need to call out the scene and take number—they are already on the sound tape, read out by the A Camera Assistant, so the B Assistant need only say "B Camera marker" and hit the sticks. This would continue for the "C Camera marker," "D Camera marker," and so on, if necessary. Try and slate as quickly as possible, so the action may commence.

The circumstances may require a combination of common marker and separate markers for multiple cameras. For example, A and B Cameras may be able to utilize a common marker, and C Camera may have to be done separately.

Whatever the plan you work out, let the other Camera Assistants know, and let the Script and Sound Departments know, and let the Assistant Director know, so there will be no surprises once the cameras start to roll.

Obviously, the procedures for Second Sticks and Tail Slates are exactly the same for multiple cameras as for a single camera, as long as the Assistant includes the camera letter as part of the solution; in other words, calls out "B Camera—Second Sticks," or "Tail Sticks—C Camera."

When involved in a multiple camera sequence, having been slating "A Camera" and "B Camera" for several scenes in a row, and then reverting back to single camera filming for a close-up or some other shot, it is a good idea to slate saying "A Camera ONLY," so that the Editor knows that only one camera is rolling for this particular shot.

CHAPTER **13**

Paperwork

No Shortage of Paperwork

If you are interested in becoming a Motion Picture Camera Assistant to avoid some "civilian" ("noncinema") occupation because of all the paperwork, then you have made a BIG mistake.

There is plenty of paperwork here, more than enough to go around! Also, the bigger the budget, the more paperwork there will be. It must be some sort of punishment for wanting to work on the big-budget feature films.

The Second Camera Assistant's first duty is to assist the First Assistant with all the duties listed in an earlier chapter for the First Camera Assistant, but in addition, he or she must do all the paperwork, and there's a great deal of paperwork on a feature; Camera Reports, Film Raw Stock Inventories, Laboratory Purchase Orders, Daily Film Reports, Petty Cash Forms, Meal Money and Per Diem Forms, Payroll Start Cards, W-4 and I-9 Forms, lists of equipment taken from and returned to the rental house, receipts for expendable supplies, etc.

The Second Assistant is also responsible for that most important piece of paper—the Weekly Payroll Time Card. Generally the Second Assistant does the time cards for the entire Camera Department (except maybe the Director of Photography, who is often working on a weekly flat fee). This is partly because the Second Assistant is the last one to leave the set or location. Magazines have to be downloaded and reloaded, batteries have to be charged, other paperwork completed, etc. The Second Assistants are the last people in the Camera Department to get off the clock. They are the ones who know when everyone else in the Department has gone off the clock, since they are still there. Their job isn't over until all the film is accounted for, truck is locked up, and paperwork delivered to office, so they get the Time Cards, as well.

Camera Reports

Almost as important as the Time Cards are the Camera Reports. Every roll of film that goes through the camera will have a Camera Report. There is no such thing as a roll of exposed film without a Camera Report. Dialogue, Lens Test, Insert, M.O.S., whatever type of shooting is being done, that roll, and every roll, gets a camera report.

The Camera Report tells the laboratory, which is the next destination of that roll of film after it has been unloaded from the camera magazine, what type of film has been shot, how much film is on the roll, what processing that film should get, what takes should be printed, and how they should be printed.

The Camera Report tells the Assistant Editor, the next destination after developing and printing in the laboratory, what scenes are on the roll, what order they are in, whether the shooting was M.O.S. or sync sound, what type of slates (if any) were used for that roll, and any other synching instructions.

There are as many different styles and types of Camera Report forms as there are laboratories—maybe more. Here is yet another example of an area that the film industry has been unable to standardize. Every laboratory prints up their own forms, apparently without ever looking at their competitors' forms. The laboratories distribute these blank Camera Report forms without charge to film production companies and/or Camera Assistants.

After seeing and using several forms from different laboratories, you will undoubtedly find one to call your favorite. It is quite acceptable to send exposed film to the lab with Camera Reports from another lab. In fact, I often do it on purpose, just to annoy the labs, who can't seem to standardize on a single form.

Some Camera Report forms are larger than others. On the West Coast, for example, labs seem to prefer small, skinny reports with a single column for takes. Unfortunately, this small report means that you are almost assured of needing a second or even a third page, before finishing a 1000-foot roll, especially on a commercial, where the takes are usually shorter. East Coast reports almost always have two columns for entries, on a larger form, and we rarely need to go to a second page.

Some major film studios print up their own forms, thereby enforcing some sort of standardization at least on their own productions. Some of these forms are even serial numbered, for some bizarre reason. We had a lot of fun once using these reports chosen at random from the stack they sent us—no two reports had consecutive numbers.

Camera Reports are almost always multipart forms, that is, they have built-in carbon copies. Some of the older forms still have real carbon paper between the copies, but most of the forms are now "carbonless" forms. Camera Report forms also come with different numbers of carbon copies. Some have two carbons after the original, others have three or four.

The original, or top copy, ALWAYS goes to the laboratory with the film. This is simply because the top copy is the clearest and easiest to read. The laboratory, after all, is going to do something to that film that cannot be undone. They are going to open that can and develop that film hopefully following the directions on that Camera Report. If the laboratory personnel cannot read the instructions, you and the film are in trouble. They need the very best copy, which is the original.

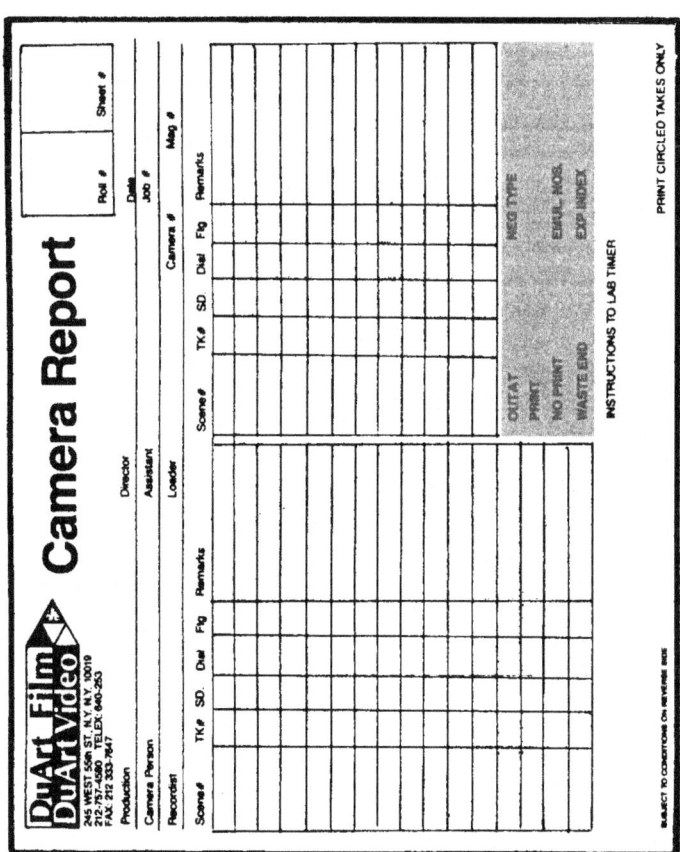
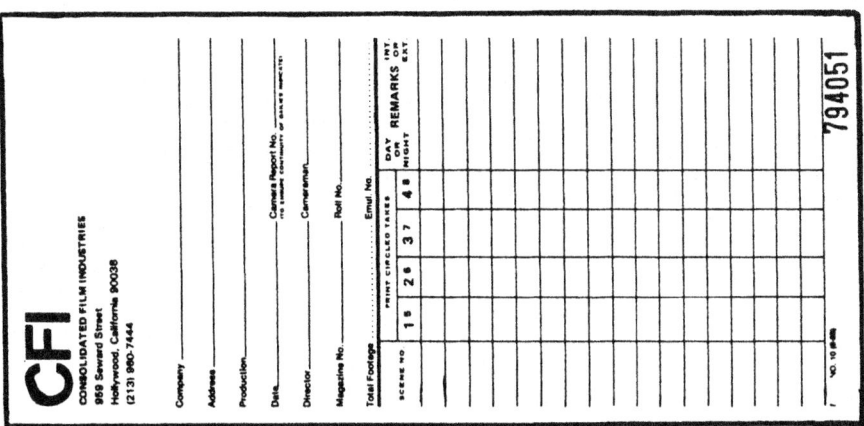

Figure 13-1 East and West Coast Camera Reports. Here is another of those annoying geographical differences that seem to make no sense and have no reason—on the East Coast, laboratory Camera Reports are large, two-column forms, while West Coast Camera Reports are usually longer and skinnier, with a single column.

Speaking of being able to read the Camera Reports, a Camera Assistant will have to develop a legible handwriting to survive as an Assistant. If you can't write legibly, print in block letters—in capital letters, if necessary. And press hard while writing, to get through all those copies. If you can't print legibly, then do yourself and the industry a favor and go to medical school and become a doctor, where you are expected to have lousy handwriting. A Camera Report that can't be read by the people that need to read it is useless. There might as well not be one.

One copy goes to the production office to be forwarded to the Assistant Editor for use in synching up the dailies. One copy stays with the Camera Assistant. I always take the bottom carbon copy to keep in my files, based on the theory that if I can read the bottom copy—the worst copy—then the lab, the editor, and the production office should be able to read copies further up the stack. If there are any additional copies of the reports, they should be sent to the production office, where they just love more paperwork.

Every report, whatever lab it is from, should have three distinct sections. I call these sections "Identification," "Contents," and "Instructions."

Identification

The first section, generally at the top of the form, identifies the roll. Typical entries might be:

the Name of the Production Company,
the Title of the Production or Production Number,
the Roll Number,
the Date the Roll was Shot,
the Name of the Director of Photography,
the Name of the Director,
the Name of the First Camera Assistant,
the Name of the Person who Loaded the Magazine,
the Date the Magazine was loaded,
the Emulsion Type of the Film,
the Camera that Shot this Particular Roll, and
the Magazine Number.

The laboratory is mostly interested in who to send the bill to, but for the Camera Assistant, the important numbers are emulsion type, the roll number, the camera number, and the magazine number.

Should there be a problem with that roll—a scratch, a light leak, a registration problem, etc., the Assistant must be able to immediately identify the camera body and the magazine used for that roll to help track down the problem so it can be corrected and prevented from happening again. It also might be important to find the short end that came from that roll, which is possible if the can number has been noted on the report and on the can label, along with the emulsion and batch numbers.

It is better to list the camera serial number, rather than the temporary camera description "A" or "B" camera, on the Camera Report. The actual camera body used

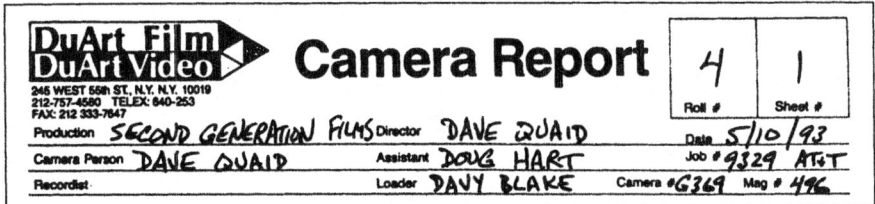

Figure 13-2 Camera Report—Identification Section. The Identification section of the Camera Report contains information about the roll of film such as the name of the production company, names of D.P., Director, and Assistant, roll number, camera number, date, etc.

for the "A" camera may change at some point during the job, due to required repair work, or some other reason. The serial number is a permanent and unique description of that camera, and will never be confused with any other camera body.

The same goes for magazine numbers. I have seen Camera Assistants renumber magazines "1," "2," "3," etc., ignoring the magazine serial numbers, but this is not a good practice. If one of the magazines is sent back for repair and replacement, and the replacement magazine is numbered with the number from the old magazine, then continuity is lost and the numbers are meaningless. All magazines have serial numbers, and these are the numbers that should be recorded on the Camera Reports. Some magazines have their serial numbers on the inside, or on the throat where it is invisible after it is loaded with film or placed on the camera. Many Assistants transfer the number to a piece of tape on the outside of the magazine where it can easily be seen and copied onto the Camera Report.

Contents

The second section contains the take-by-take entries—the Scene Number, the Take Number, the Sound Number, the Dial Footage, the Take Footage, and usually a column for Comments.

This is the "Table of Contents" for that roll of film. For each scene number filmed, there will probably have been several takes, each with a take number (or sound number, if the production is a commercial or documentary, but NOT BOTH a take and sound number).

Each of those takes will have used a certain number of feet of film. And each of those takes will either be printed by the lab, or not printed. The laboratory will need to know where on the roll to find each of the takes to be printed. All of this information is on the Camera Report.

Usually on a feature film production, shots are described by scene and take numbers. On television commercial productions, Scene and Sound numbers are generally used.

If using take numbers, the numbers start at "Take 1" for each new scene, and count consecutively for as many takes as are shot. The next new scene will begin with Take 1 again.

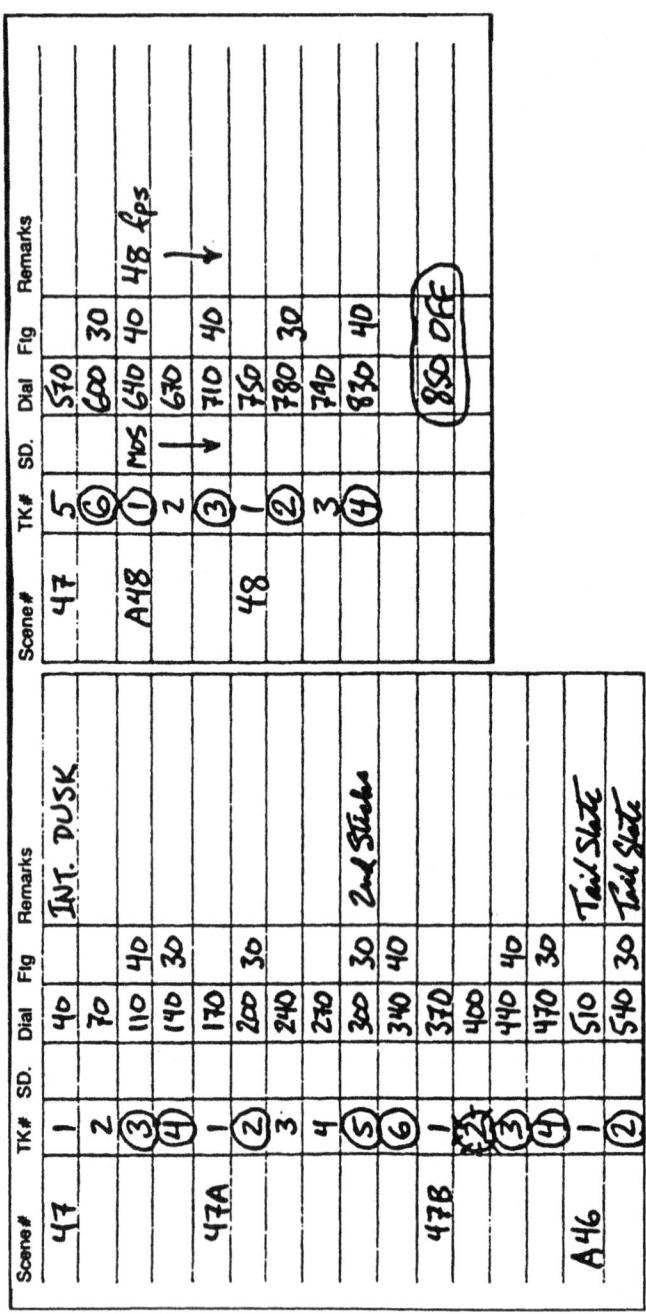

Figure 13-3 Camera Report—Contents Section. The Contents section contains information about each scene and each take of that scene; scene number, take number, length of the take, whether or not the take is to be printed (circled take numbers) and any other pertinent information the lab or editor might be interested in ("Tail Slate," "2nd Sticks," "48 fps," etc.).

For productions using sound numbers, the sound numbers run consecutively from the first scene shot on the first day of the job, right through to the last scene shot on the last day, regardless of when the scene number is changed.

Most modern cameras have digital footage counters that start at "0" with a new magazine (if the Camera Assistant remembers to reset the counter when loading the camera), and count up from "0" toward the end of the roll. These are "Additive" counters. After each take, the number shown on the display represents the amount of footage shot since the beginning of the roll, and is written on the Camera Report in the "Dial" column.

For those cameras without a digital counter, the only counter may be the "Footage Remaining" counter on the magazine. These are "Subtractive" counters, starting at the length of the roll on the feed side of the magazine, and counting back toward zero.

If this is the only counter available, the Assistant must do some arithmetic before writing down the "Dial" footage. If the roll started at 400 feet, and the counter now shows 320 feet, then the footage shot is 80 feet, and "80" should be written on the report. If after the next take, the counter reads 220 feet, then 180 feet have been shot on the roll (400 − 220 = 180), and "180" should be written on the reports after take 2. Writing down "320" and "220" is incorrect. What the lab needs to know is how many feet have been shot from the beginning of the roll, not how much film is left in the magazine. They use these figures to determine how far into the roll to switch on their printing machine, and then when to turn it off. Listing how much film is left in the magazine does them no good at all.

For 35mm filming, this number is usually rounded to the nearest ten feet, to make the mathematics simpler and faster. This number is only a reference and exact accuracy is not necessary. For 16mm filming, many Assistants round off to the nearest five feet, for those cameras having a counter.

The "Dial" column on the Camera Report shows the total footage expended since the beginning of the roll. The number written on each line in that column is the footage at the END of that take.

The lab uses the Dial column footages to find the slates between the takes, and uses the slates as starting and stopping points for the printer.

The next column, headed "Footage" or sometimes "Ftg.," refers to the footage used on that single, particular take, and is derived by subtracting the end Dial footage of the previous take from the end Dial footage of this take. This difference is the length of the take.

Some Assistants do this computation for every take, and this is useful for determining the average or maximum length of the takes, to make sure there will be enough film in the magazine for another take.

Other Assistants, including myself, prefer to compute the take length footage for only those takes actually being printed. Then when it comes time to add up the total footage being printed on each roll, which is needed for the Daily Film Report, all that needs be done is to add the numbers in that column.

A prime reason to keep a camera report is to keep track of how much film is used on each take, and when a reload will be required. Give yourself plenty of safety margin. Film is the cheapest commodity on the set. It is cheaper than time, it is cheaper than energy, and it is cheaper than worry. If in the slightest doubt about having enough film for the next take, reload.

After the last take on a Camera Report, when a roll is taken off the camera and another roll put on, It is a good idea to write the "Off" or "Out" footage, which includes the film run off for laboratory leader, known as "Safety."

The lab needs a certain amount of film to thread the developing tanks, and the Camera Assistant should be sure to run the camera with a hand or slate blocking the lens for at least ten feet at the head of the roll when the roll is first put onto the camera, and at least ten feet at the end of the roll, before removing the roll from the camera. Fifteen or twenty feet would be better, if perhaps a bit extravagant.

Some Camera Reports contain spaces for the Out, Print, No Print, and Waste/Short End footages for that roll. These are the footages needed for the Daily Film Report. The "Out" footage is the total amount of film exposed or used, including the "Safety" at both ends of the roll. The "Print" footage is the total amount to be printed, found by adding together the individual lengths of the takes on that roll actually being printed. The "No Print" footage is the difference between the "Out" footage and the "Print" footage. This is the total film NOT being printed from that roll.

The "Waste"/"Short End" footage is the film left unexposed on the roll when that magazine comes off of the camera, obtained by subtracting the "Out" footage from the original length of the roll. If this length is less than the "Waste Cutoff" established at the beginning of the job, then that footage is considered "Waste" and is thrown away. Waste Cutoff length is discussed in the chapter on Loading. Rolls of unexposed film less than a certain length (that length determined by the production company), are not worth saving and not worth shooting.

If the "Waste"/"Short End" footage is more than the Cutoff, then that roll is considered a "Short End," and will be either removed from the magazine and placed in a film can for use later in the production, or threaded through the magazine for use the next day. There is EITHER "Waste" or "Short End" left from a particular roll—THERE CAN NEVER BE BOTH. Just to confuse things further, at least one major studio considers the "Safety" rolloff at the tail of the roll "Waste" instead of "No Print," so at least on their paperwork, it is possible to have both "Waste" and "Short

Figure 13-4 Camera Report—Summary Section. The Summary section contains the following information which will be used in the Daily Film Report; length of roll, amount to be Printed, amount Not Printed, amount Waste, or amount Short End.

End" on the same roll. The best and easiest solution to this situation is simply to refuse to use their paperwork. Throw it out and use your own forms.

Quite often the "Waste" film is recycled to get the silver out. Another possible use for these short rolls of unexposed film is to spool them off into 35mm still cassettes and shoot them in a still camera. There are companies that do this with movie film short ends, or it can be done with a film loader for your own use. Still a third possibility is to tape off the ends of these short rolls so they don't unwind, and to ship them to the camera equipment rental house, for use by Camera Assistants in scratch testing camera magazines during the Checkout. Rental houses always seem to be short of scrap film for magazine testing, so they will certainly appreciate donations.

Every crew uses the "Comments" column differently. The D.P. may request that a scene be singled out for different printing instructions than the rest of the roll, or there may be something special about that scene, such as that it was shot at a different frame rate, or with a different filter, or some other change that might want to be referred to later. Some D.P.'s want as little information given to the lab as possible, to prevent confusion and possible mistakes.

The Comments column is also a good place to indicate that a take was slated with a Tail Slate, or that a "Second Sticks" slate should be looked for. I also like to use this column to indicate after which takes a "Gate Check" was performed, placing a little "x" in this column, my own little code.

If a scene is filmed without recording sound ("M.O.S."), then that should also be indicated, either in the "Sound" column or under "Comments," by writing "M.O.S."

Quite often the script supervisor, after giving the Camera Assistant the takes to be printed, comes back later and changes the list of takes to be printed, based on the director's changing his or her mind. It is no problem to circle a previously uncircled take, but sometimes it is necessary to "Un-print" a take. Since the take has already been circled, and it is difficult to "Un-circle," short hatch marks drawn through the circle indicate that the take is NOT to be printed. This is an age-old convention that all the labs understand, but it is not uncommon to write "No Print" in the Comments column as well, just to be sure.

If shooting without keeping a shot record book, the comments column can be used to record lens, filter, and aperture information. I sometimes do this on commercial shoots, for my own reference, making such notations as "45/85N6/4.5/30," standing for 45mm on the zoom, 85N6 filter, T 4.5, and 30 frames per second.

Instructions

The third section contains instructions for the laboratory. It tells the lab what to do to that roll in developing. It tells the lab what parts of the roll to print, if any, and how to print them.

The instructions on how to develop the roll will come from the Director of Photography. The D.P. may tell you to write "Develop Normal," or "Push One Stop," or some other instruction. With all of the different film stocks available now, "Push" processing is becoming quite rare, but what it means is that the D.P. wants the film

DEVELOP NORMAL — PRINT AT 28-36-32
INSTRUCTIONS TO LAB TIMER
PRINT CIRCLED TAKES ONLY

Figure 13-5 Camera Report—Instructions Section. The Instructions section tells the lab what to do to the film; how to develop ("Normal"), what to print ("Circled Takes"), and how to print ("PRINT AT 28-36-32"). Alternates might be to write out "Print for Late Afternoon," "Print for Blue Moonlight," "Print for Gray Scale at Head of Roll," "Prepare for Video Transfer," "Print ALL," etc.

slowed down in the developer, to allow the developer more time to work on that film. This has the effect of making the negative thinner, so more light can be pumped through it in printing. In effect this changes the effective ASA rating of the film to a rating higher than the one the manufacturer recommends. It is also possible to "pull" process, or under-develop, the negative by speeding up the film's travel through the developer, but this is not done very often.

The instructions of what to print should come from the Director by way of the Script (or Continuity) Supervisor, and will usually be indicated to the lab by simply circling those takes to be printed, or by writing "Print All" at the bottom of the Camera Report.

If your job is shooting film that is being transferred to videotape for editing, an increasingly common practice in commercials and TV series, you might be asked to write, "Develop Normal and Prepare for Video Transfer."

The Printing Instructions also come from the Director of Photography and may range from "Print for Warm Sunny Afternoon," to "Print for Blue Moonlight Effect," to "Print for Fluorescent," to "Print for Gray Scale at Head of Roll," or even "Print at 32-41-36," for those D.P.'s who determine through pre-production testing of that particular emulsion batch what printing lights they want for specific scenes.

Often the Director of Photography will telephone the laboratory timer directly after the day's shooting or early the next morning and discuss the day's work, giving more specific instructions than are possible on a Camera Report, so that the lab timer knows what to expect and what the D.P. wants to see in the dailies screening.

Camera Reports for Short Ends

If the roll of film in the magazine is not a full roll, then it is a short end, and the camera report for the short end is kept exactly the same as if the roll were a full load, with the following exceptions.

Somewhere on the camera report form, usually at the top, possibly in the space marked "Loaded" or even "Recordist" or "Microphone," since this space is not needed for that item of information, the size of the roll should be noted.

As a further reminder that this roll is not a full load, a single diagonal line is drawn from the lower left to upper right corners of the Contents section of the camera report form.

Data can then be entered normally, but the diagonal line is a constant reminder that this roll is not a full roll, or is not the normal size for this magazine.

Daily Film Reports

The Daily Film Report is a summary of the Camera Reports from a particular day's filming. This Report shows the number of rolls of film shot on that day, and for each roll, the length of the roll when placed on the camera, the amount exposed, the amount printed, the amount not printed, the waste, and the short end left over after the roll was removed from the camera. Separate reports are filled out for each different film stock type in use that day.

Each of these columns is totalled, and those totals transferred to something called the Daily Production Report which is filled out in the production office. Some of these totals will be used to prepare the Daily Film Inventory, which is submitted with the Daily Film Report to the production office. These reports are generally filled out in duplicate, with one copy sent to the production office and one retained by the Camera Department.

The Daily Film Report and Daily Film Inventory are generally not used for productions other than feature films.

DAILY FILM REPORT

DATE: 5/10/90

LENGTH OF ROLL	ROLL #	EXPOSED	PRINT	NO PRINT	WASTE	S.E.
1000	A 29	850	450	400	150	—
1000	A 30	900	520	380	100	—
1000	A 31	640	600	40	—	360
850	A 32	420	420	—	—	430
350	B 7	300	280	20	50	—
400	B 8	280	190	90	120	—
1000	C 2	870	410	460	130	—
200	TEST 29	200	200	—	—	—
5800	TOTALS:	4460	3070	1390	550	790

ASSISTANT CAMERAMAN: DOUGLAS C. HART

Figure 13-6 Daily Film Reports. The Daily Film Report has a line for each roll of film shot during that day's shooting, and breaks that roll down into amount Exposed, amount Printed, amount Not Printed, Waste and Short End.

Daily Film Inventory

The Daily Film Inventory Form helps the Camera Assistant and the production company keep track of the ever-changing inventory of unexposed film. There are spaces for the amount of unexposed film on hand at the beginning of each day, new stock received that day, the amount expended that day, and the amount remaining on hand for the next day.

```
                DAILY MOTION PICTURE FILM INVENTORY
                ==================================

FILM TITLE:        "REVENGE OF THE KILLER TOMATOES"
PRODUCTION COMPANY: XYZ FILMS INC.
CAMERA ASSISTANT:  DOUG HART              DATE:   5/10/90
FILM TYPE:         5297          EMULSION: 039-427
        (Separate inventory to be submitted for each film type)

***** TODAY'S OPENED FOOTAGE: **********************************
1   (a)   4  rolls ( 1000 foot) Opened Today  +     4000
    (b)   2  rolls (  400 foot) Opened Today  +      800
    (c) ____ rolls (_____ foot) Opened Today  +     ____
    (d) TOTAL NEWLY OPENED TODAY              =     4800
2   SHORT ENDS (from earlier days)            +     2150
3   TOTAL OPENED NOW (Check against Line 8)   =     6950

***** TODAY'S EXPOSED FOOTAGE: **********************************
4   EXPOSED (Check against Line 11)                 4460
5   WASTE                                     +      550
6   TOTAL USED TODAY (Enter on Line 13)       =     5010
7   SHORT ENDS UNEXPOSED                      +     1940
8   TOTAL OPENED TODAY (Check against Line 3) =     6950

***** TODAY'S PRINT FOOTAGE: ************************************
9   TODAY'S PRINT FOOTAGE                           3070
10  TODAY'S NO PRINT FOOTAGE                  +     1390
11  TOTAL (Check against Line 4)              =     4460

***** TODAY'S UNEXPOSED FOOTAGE: ********************************
12  PREVIOUS UNEXPOSED FOOTAGE ON HAND              12490
13  FOOTAGE USED TODAY (From Line 6)          -      5010
14  NEW UNEXPOSED RAW STOCK RECEIVED TODAY    +     10000
15  TOTAL UNEXPOSED FOOTAGE NOW ON HAND       =     17480

(c) DOUG HART 1987
```

Figure 13-7 Daily Film Inventory. A typical Daily Film Inventory form includes spaces for film on hand, new film received, film used today, total film used, balance on hand, etc. Separate inventories should be completed for each film stock in use on the production.

There are often spaces for the total amount of film received from the manufacturer since the job began, and for the total amount expended on the job to date.

Separate inventories are kept for each different type of film stock in use on the production. These reports are also made in duplicate, one copy for the production office, and one kept by the Camera Department.

Combination Forms

The Daily Film Report and the Daily Film Inventory are sometimes combined into a single form. Here are two samples of such combination forms, each with space for two different emulsion types; one designed on a home computer by my good friend Denise Brassard, who helped me set up and teach the first few Camera Assistants Workshops in Maine many years ago, and the second designed and sold by another friend and Camera Assistant, Ron Coons, who also has a Camera Assistants' tools and supplies mail-order business called CamWare.

Purchase Orders

A Purchase Order normally accompanies the exposed film to the lab. This authorizes the film lab to do the specified work to the rolls of film sent in, and to send the bill for such services to the production company.

The Purchase Order includes such information as the company Name, Billing Address, Phone Number, Contact Person's Name, Job Title or Number, and instructions for developing and printing the film.

The usual wording on the Purchase Order goes something like this:

"Submitting (Number) Rolls of (Film Type),
Total Footage (Amount) Feet
Camera Rolls (Roll Numbers)
Develop Normal
Assemble Rolls in Numerical Order
Print Circled Takes
Printing Instructions on Camera Reports
Hold Negative and Release Print to Messenger"

Of course there may be variations on this typical form. The Instructions might read "Push One Stop" instead of "Develop Normal." It might say "Print All" instead of "Print Circled Takes." The Printing Instructions might be written out in full on the Purchase Order instead of or in addition to being in the Camera Reports. And if the editing of the project is to be done on video instead of film, it might say, "Develop Normal and Prepare for Video Transfer," or even "Develop Normal and Transfer to Video," if the lab has their own transfer facilities.

Separate Purchase Orders will be filled out for each Developing Process required for that day's footage. One Purchase Order is usually sufficient for all "Develop Normal" footage, even for multiple stocks and stocks from different manufacturers. The Normal Development for all of the common color stocks is exactly the same—same chemicals, same temperature, etc.

Page #	Production	Day #	Date

FILM TYPE:		FILM TYPE:	

Roll Number	Amount Loaded	Print	N.G.	Waste	Short End	Roll Number	Amount Loaded	Print	N.G.	Waste	Short End

1000's	400's	Short Ends				1000's	400's	Short Ends
				Beginning Stock On Hand				
				Raw Stock Received Today				
				Sub Total				
				Raw Stock Used Today				
				Ending Stock On Hand				

Previous Shot To Date			Total Shot To Date Both Stocks
Shot Today			
Total Shot To Date			

Figure 13-8 Combination Film Report/Film Inventory Form #1.

A separate Purchase Order would be required if some of the rolls of exposed film needed to be "Pushed One Stop," or if some other special process were being requested from the lab. Keeping the orders separate for different lab processes helps minimize the possibility of a mistake being made with the film.

Paperwork **357**

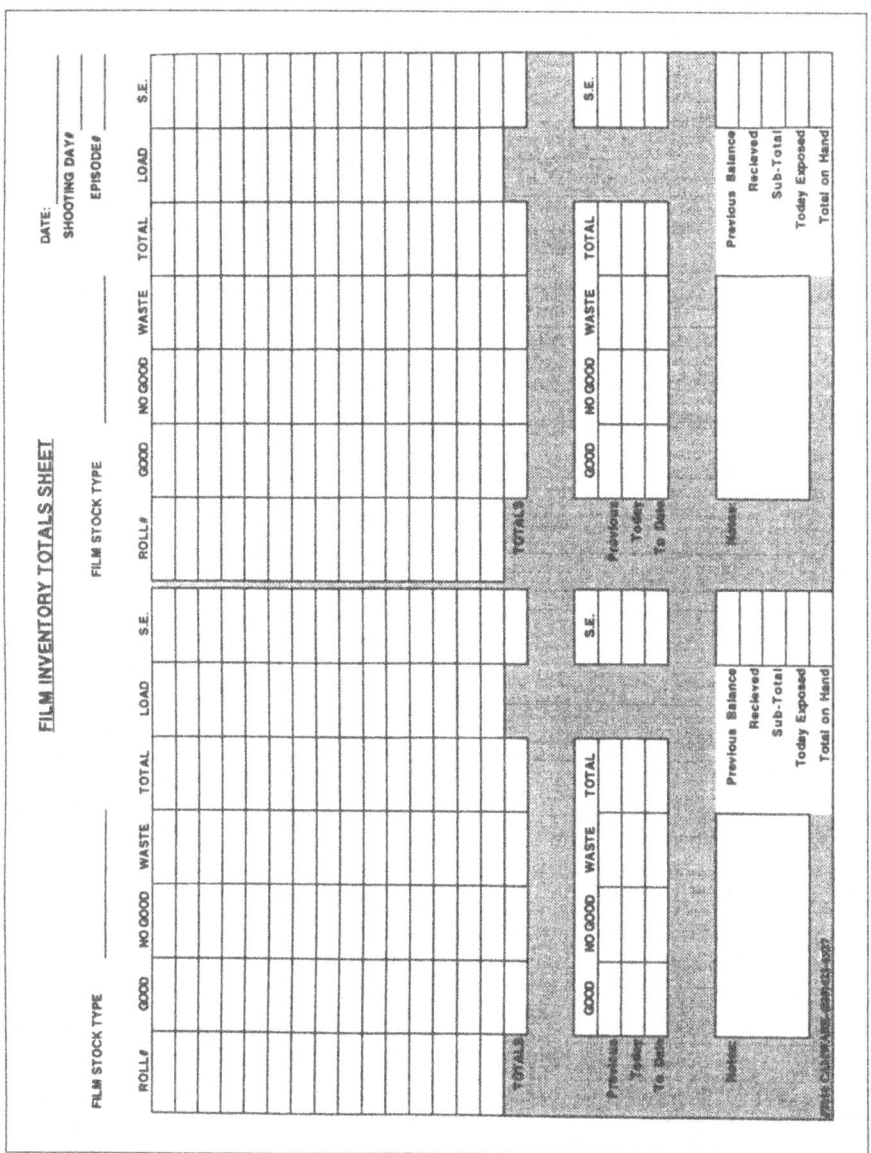

Figure 13-9 Combination Film Report/Film Inventory Form #2.

Keep in mind that "Push" footage is developed last, at the very end of the developing day, and there is a chance that this "Push" footage will not be ready in time for the dailies screening.

Of course, if you are shooting black-and-white stock and color negative stock on the same job, or color negative and color reversal stocks, or other such unusual combinations, separate Purchase Orders should be prepared.

For feature film productions, at least one of these Purchase Orders will be needed each day of filming, so the production offices often type them out in advance, leaving blanks for the Camera Assistant to fill in the number of film cans, film type, roll numbers, total footage, etc. With a computer word processor and daisy-wheel or dot-matrix printer (because of the carbon copies), or even a memory typewriter, this is easily done. The Camera Assistant might even do this himself or herself, on a home computer.

As with the other paperwork, there will be carbon copies of the Purchase Order. The original is placed in an envelope, attached to the bundle of film cans, and then sent to the lab. The bottom copy remains with the Camera Department, generally stapled to the copies of the Camera Reports for the rolls submitted that day and kept safe for future reference. Many Assistants keep a looseleaf or other binder type to keep the Camera Department copies of this paperwork neat and tidy. The remaining copies go to the production office, for the accountant or auditor.

Time Cards

As keeper of the Time Cards for the Camera Department, the Second Camera Assistant needs to be familiar with the many and sometimes impossibly complicated union contracts or other employment deals that the crew may be working under.

As the payroll representative of the Department, numerous discussions must be held with the bookkeepers or payroll company representatives or production auditor, and possibly the union office, if problems arise. The Second needs to be a tough negotiator.

Many Second Assistants make copies of the hours from the time cards and distribute these to the appropriate Camera Crews members for their records, in addition to keeping their own record of the hours in a notebook of some sort, to check on the accuracy of the paychecks when they do arrive once a week.

In addition to the Time Cards, there are other employment forms that must be filled out—the familiar W-4, the infamous I-9, the elusive Start Card/Deal Memo—all are received from and submitted to the production office by way of the Second Assistant.

When multiple cameras roll, there is a veritable blizzard of paperwork for all new additional crew members, often referred to as "Day Players," since their employment is on a day-to-day basis.

Equipment Lists

The inventory of Camera Equipment in the Assistants' charge starts with a copy of the rental contract from the rental house, but doesn't end there. Hopefully the copy of the rental contract you have is readable, but since the rental house normally gives the Camera Assistant the 19th carbon copy, there is usually no writing on the form. If this is the case, ask for a photocopy of the original.

There will inevitably be changes and additions to the list, caused by repairs, replacements, and special equipment needs that come up nearly every day. Every item returned for repair or replacement will generate another piece or pieces of paper, and certainly every new equipment order will sport a new rental contract. All of these papers should be collected and filed away for the inevitable "Check-In" day at the end of shooting, when all of these pieces must be surrendered or at least accounted for at the rental house.

An even better method of keeping track of the equipment is for the Second Assistant to maintain a "Diary" of equipment changes—a daily list of returns, replacements, and additions received. This will make the ultimate reconciliation much easier, and may even make it possible to find out what happened to magazine number #2536, which somehow disappeared during the third week of shooting!

Don't trust your memory—keep a diary!

Call Sheets

The Call Sheets are distributed by the assistant directors and/or production assistants at the end of each day, and contain such valuable information as where to report for work the next day, and what time to get there.

The Call Sheet will also describe the next day's shooting—scene number, description (Day/ Night/ Interior/ Exterior), cast members needed, special effects or additional equipment needed, etc., and will usually list what is planned for the following day, and maybe even the day after that.

Although it is the production department's responsibility to make sure that the entire crew is notified of the next day's call time and location, the Camera Assistants should double check this, making sure the D.P. and Camera Operator get Call Sheets, and also that any additional crew needed for the next day get phone calls telling them where and when to report.

The Call Sheet is a good source of valuable information, but only if it is read. If the company is planning Steadicam shooting for Thursday, are there enough 400-foot loads of film on the truck for the Steadicam magazines? If the plan is to shoot with four cameras for the big stunt scene Friday night, has the extra equipment been ordered? Has the extra crew been hired? Has anybody been hired to check out that additional equipment? If the underwater scene has been changed from Tuesday to Monday, has the rental house been notified of the change?

So READ the Call Sheet!

Keep Copies of Everything!

I can't stress enough the necessity for keeping copies of all paperwork originating in the Camera Department or just passing through.

First off, you never know when you will need to check some of that information. Months later you may need to know what day such and such a scene was shot, or how many takes for another scene were printed, or what day the 1000mm lens was returned, or what magazine Roll 98 came out of, or how much 5297 stock was received a week ago last Monday. All of this information should be quickly retrievable.

Sometimes it is also necessary to defend yourself. If Take 7 of Scene 112 was requested by the Director, but was somehow not printed, the Production Manager needs someone to blame. Was it the Script Supervisor's fault, the Camera Assistant's fault, or the lab's fault? Checking the Camera Department copy of the Camera Report might answer that question. If the take was circled on the carbon copy, but not printed, then the lab is at fault. If the take is not circled, then it was either the Script Supervisor or the Camera Assistant that screwed up. I know this is silly, but you wouldn't believe how much time is spent on such nonsense once the job starts.

So make it easy on yourself and keep the paperwork organized, complete and accessible.

CHAPTER **14**

Video Assist Systems

The Theory and Practice of Video Assist

The theory behind video assist is that it takes too long to process and print and view film, and that a video camera mounted piggyback-style on a film camera, looking at the ground glass image in the camera viewfinder, offers "instant dailies," allowing the director to decide instantly whether or not the scene just shot is acceptable and whether the company can move on to the next shot.

The theory continues; if the director can see immediately what the finished shot will look like, without waiting for the lab, then fewer takes need be made, less film will be shot, less time will be needed to film a particular scene, and the producer will save money and time, which also really means money. Sounds pretty good, doesn't it?

The reality is quite different. The video camera makes the film camera heavier and bulkier, burns through batteries at an alarming rate, and steals a lot of light from the viewfinder, making the D.P.'s and the Camera Operator's job more difficult. The viewfinder is darker because light is being diverted from the viewfinder to the video camera.

The camera is also less mobile, because of the video cable connecting the video assist camera to the video recorder. After all the time and energy spent developing the crystal sync system, freeing the camera from the sync cable connection to the sound recorder, we now have to reattach the cable to get a video picture.

The video picture just does not look like the resulting film picture, anyway. Video cannot accept the wide contrast range of film, and does not show the subtleties of focus, the effect of diffusion filters, and certainly cannot match the resolution of the film that is in the camera.

It also costs a great deal more to rent a video assist camera package, sometimes as much as double the rental of the film camera alone, depending on the particular equipment involved.

361

The video camera also needs power, from either batteries or a power supply, and must be connected to either a monitor or a video recorder by a cable, or by a video transmitter, which would also need a power supply or battery. More batteries, more cables, more electronics to have trouble with. All this makes the Camera Assistant's job much more difficult.

And if the company wants record and playback capability, another person must be added to the crew, another salary paid, and more equipment rented (recorders and monitors).

The picture delivered by the video assist camera is usually poor—dark, grainy, with a strong flicker from the camera shutter—generally, it is hard to see what was happening in the frame, let alone showing the subtleties that the video assist audience wants to see.

In the early days of video assist, most video assist cameras were little more than supermarket surveillance cameras, in black-and-white, capable of delivering only marginally acceptable pictures at best. When faster film stocks and faster lenses were introduced, these video cameras were almost totally useless, because they were not getting enough light to yield a decent picture.

Advancing video technology has solved many of these problems, with better tubes that require less light, and with no tubes at all (the CCD "Charge-Coupled Device" cameras), and with various electronic "Flicker-Free" systems, but the video assist theory is still far from being met by the technical and practical realities.

Unfortunately, this same advancing technology has also led to color video assist, which is a classic example of a bad idea out-of-control. The color is rarely if ever going to be right, and every color monitor in use will have different color. The NTSC ("Never Twice the Same Color") video system used in this country just does not allow accurate enough color reproduction. The agency and client will always be complaining about the color of their shampoo bottle on the monitor. I dread jobs with color video assist.

As for shooting fewer takes and using less film, this is certainly not true. I would estimate that in the last decade of using video assist, especially on TV commercial shoots, the average number of takes shot and the amount of film shot has at least tripled, and quadrupled is probably closer to the truth. This is because playing back the recorded video assist takes for the client and agency people (as many as a dozen additional people on the set) results not in their agreeing on which take is best, but in disagreements leading to more and more takes, in an attempt at getting one perfect take that everyone will love.

Back in the "B.V." ("Before Video") days, clients had to trust the agency to deliver the best commercial possible; the agency had to trust the director, and the director had to trust the Director of Photography and/or the Camera Operator. All this trust is gone, now that video assist gives everybody access to the camera ground glass image. Each of the agency and client people needs to be satisfied individually. In doing this, many hours are spent playing back and rewinding and playing again, in search of the perfect take. Hours lost on the set and more takes shot translates to costs of many thousands of additional dollars spent on commercials, for film, lab costs, and crew overtime.

Another problem is in the checkout of the video assist system. If the company is going to be recording the video assist picture, then there will be another person on the set, usually one who owns his or her own monitors and recorders and is renting them to the company. But the company does not want to put that person on the payroll for the checkout day, so the Camera Assistant and the rental house video department set up the video assist camera and adjust it to give an acceptable picture on the test monitor at the rental house, a monitor that will be staying at the rental house when the camera package is delivered to the set or location. This is like putting a cast on a broken arm, and then leaving the cast at the hospital when the patient goes home.

The first time the video assist is hooked up to the actual VTR person's recorder and monitors is on the set. Since no two monitors are alike, there is almost always some "tweaking" and adjustment that needs to be done, and done while a dozen agency and client people are trying to see what is going on.

Once the shooting begins, the first piece of equipment most likely to break down is the video assist (unless there is a generator on the job, in which case the generator is the first to break down and the video assist is second). Out come the little plastic screwdrivers, the volt meters, the soldering irons, and the oscilloscopes. Hopefully the VTR person knows something about video, but this is not always the case. Very few Camera Assistants know enough about video to be of much use in repair of the system (this is not an accident—I have tried for years to learn as little as possible about the little buggers). After trying another battery, and another cable, and turning all the little screws ("pots" in video lingo), there is nothing left to do but call the rental house for another one.

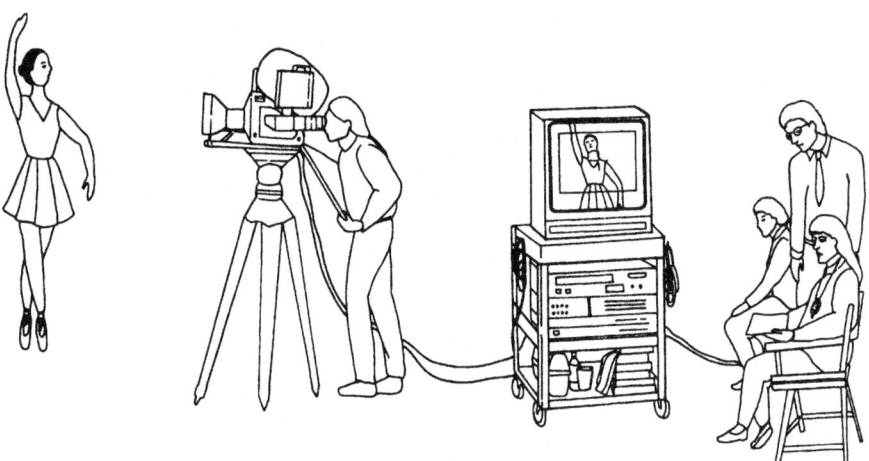

Figure 14-1 Video Assist System. The theory behind the Video Assist System is simple. Without the Video Assist, only the Camera Operator sees what happens in the camera viewfinder. With Video Assist, many people can see what the camera sees, by watching the monitor. The television commercial industry was the first to use the Video Assist this way, as the various client and agency representatives wanted to see what was going on.

Video Assist—Help or Hindrance?

Don't get me wrong, now. There are times when the video assist is very useful. If it is working, and if there is a monitor within range of sight, a video assist is useful to the Camera Assistant for showing when the slate is in frame appropriately, and when it is in approximate focus.

It can also be of use to the Camera Assistant if there is to be a zoom or focus shift as something enters or leaves the frame, by enabling the Camera Assistant to see exactly what the camera is seeing, finding that cue and reacting to it quickly.

If the camera is mounted on a vehicle, or helicopter, or in some other place where there is no way, either for safety or for space reasons, a Camera Operator or a Camera Assistant can work at the camera while it is shooting, video assist is vital to determine if the desired shot has been achieved.

For some special pieces of equipment, such as the Steadicam, Louma Crane (and Hot Head, Cam-Remote, etc.), the only way they can be used is if the camera has a video assist system installed. For these systems, the Camera Operator must use a video assist monitor to see what the camera sees. The optical viewfinder is unavailable or inaccessible.

When shooting for blue screen or split screen or some other special effect, it can be very useful for setting position and size of various elements in the frame, if the system is set up to allow switching between previously recorded video sources and live picture.

When the director is also the actor in a scene, it is very useful in allowing the director/actor to see what is happening in front of the camera.

Video Assist Flicker and Flicker-Free Video

Most video assist systems consist simply of a video camera looking at the camera ground glass. Since the rotating shutter in a mirror reflex motion picture camera makes the ground glass image flicker at a rate equal to the frame rate the camera is running at, then the video image flickers as well at that same rate.

The Camera Operator has to watch a flickering image, and anyone watching the video assist monitor has to watch a flickering image. Since the human eye and the video camera react differently to light, the flicker is not a serious impediment to the Camera Operator, but the video image, depending on the lighting in the scene, can be virtually unviewable because of the flicker. In a strong backlight situation, such as on a beach or against a snowy background, or a silhouette scene, the video camera and monitor cannot handle the wide range of brightness and contrast differences between the bright background and the darkness of the closed shutter. The resulting video monitor image is very difficult to watch.

Newer video assist systems, especially those with CCD (Charge-Coupled Device) cameras, have brought this situation under control, and allowed for the development of "Flicker-Free" video, in which the video image is electronically duplicated and repeated to fill in the black spaces when the camera shutter is closed. This makes the video monitor image much easier to watch, especially in certain lighting situations. The Panavid CCD system, and the CEI VPIII and VPIV systems are current examples of this "Flicker-Free" video assist.

There is another option for "Flicker-Free" video assist. On the Panavision family of cameras, the normal mirror shutter can be replaced with a "fixed-pellicle" beamsplitter, such as in the early Mitchell BNC reflex conversions, and certain 16mm cameras, so that the viewfinder image (and consequently the video image) does not flicker.

This is a system used, for example, when filming the Muppets movies, where the puppet operators or puppeteers needed to see a high-quality, flickerless, video assist picture to aid in their performances. This pellicle system does, however, require an exposure compensation for the light reflected away from the film and into the viewfinder and video camera, whereas a normal rotating mirror video assist system does not require an exposure compensation.

Video Assist on the Set

There are some things for the Camera Assistant to watch out for on the set while using the video assist.

When the video assist picture starts getting larger (I know that sounds like a mistake, but it is true), the battery needs to be replaced. I don't know why this happens—it would seem more logical for the picture to get smaller as the battery dies, but it does get larger.

At the first sign of picture failure, try another battery. This is the most likely cause of the problem. If possible, use a power supply (transformer) for the video assist instead of batteries. A battery will only power the video assist camera for a couple of hours, since the video camera is on almost continuously through the shooting day.

It is a good idea to shut off the video camera between setups, during the lighting adjustments, and other times when it is not being used, but under combat conditions, it is not easy to remember to do so.

A film camera might run all day on one battery, because it is only actually running for short spurts, but the video stays on all day, draining lots of batteries. If you know you will not be able to obtain or use a power supply, then get extra batteries if video assist will be used on the job. Don't forget to get spare fuses for the power supply. Even if you do have a power supply, get extra batteries for when the power supply dies.

Some power supplies allow the running of both the film camera and the video camera, but not all of them will do this. Sometimes when using a power supply for both video and film cameras, there is interference on the video when the film camera is switched on. This can be caused by a grounding problem in the power supply, or motor brush noise from the film camera motor causing this interference, or some other cause, but the effect is that sometimes you cannot use both the film and video cameras when they are both plugged in to some power supplies.

The Video Assist Beamsplitter

The way the video assist works is to steal some of the light traveling through the viewfinder before it reaches the Camera Operator. This is done by placing a beamsplitter in the optical path between the ground glass and the eyepiece. Most of the light continues through to the eyepiece, but some is diverted to the video camera. There are different types of beamsplitters, allowing for different amounts of light to be diverted to the video. The most common type is called "70/30," meaning that 70 percent of the light goes to the eyepiece and 30 percent to the video, but there are other ratios available. Panavision cameras use a "70/30" video beamsplitter as standard, with "80/20" available as an option. The Arri 535 camera allows the Assistant to switch between 80/20, 50/50, and 10/90 (90 percent going to the video tap camera) anytime, right on the camera, by turning a knob. This is the only camera I know of that offers this option.

The light lost to the video is of serious concern to the Director of Photography and the Camera Operator, who may be working in low-light situations to begin with. To have additional light lost through the use of video assist is unfortunate. The jobs are tough enough with a bright viewfinder. Often, if video assist is not requested on the job, the D.P. or Camera Operator will request that the unneeded video beamsplitter be removed from the optical path, to allow the maximum amount of light to get through to the viewfinder.

These video tape cameras have a tough job. Since the video assist is only receiving about 20 percent of the viewfinder light, and since with faster lenses and faster film stocks less light is needed on the set, the video assist cameras are really "pushing the envelope" of light levels.

CHAPTER **15**

Tools and Supplies

Assistant's Tool Kit

It is possible to be a Camera Assistant with very few tools. You can almost do this job with these three items: (1) Swiss Army Knife, (2) Cloth Tape Measure, and (3) Flashlight.

The job is easier and more fun, however, with a few additions to this meager list. Every Camera Assistant is going to have his or her own set of tools that they carry. It will also vary from job to job.

I have broken my list into two sections, **Essential** and **Optional**. Have fun customizing your own tool kit.

Keep in mind the one basic rule about tools:

ALWAYS USE THE RIGHT TOOL FOR THE JOB.

There is also yet another codicil of Murphy's Law that applies to the Camera Assistants' tools:

NO MATTER HOW MANY TOOLS YOU OWN OR BRING TO THE SET, YOU WILL ALWAYS NEED SOMETHING YOU DO NOT HAVE.

Cameras are delicate and temperamental, and using the wrong tool can damage small screws and parts. If the work requires metric tools, then use metric tools.

Essential Items

Swiss Army Knife   There are many different models to choose from, with different blades and tools, so have fun choosing one just right for you. I've carried one with me everywhere for so long now that I can't imagine a Camera Assistant working without one. I suppose it might be possible, but why would anyone want to? For size, weight, and versatility, there is just no equal.

Tape Measure   Please get a cloth or fiberglass tape measure and not a steel one for your main focus tool. A cloth or fiberglass tape is quieter, easier to use, and above all, safer. The edges of a steel tape are sharp and can give you or someone else a nasty cut. Beheading an actor or poking his eye out with a tape measure is messy and not recommended. There are always people that will walk into your tape. In fact, sometimes I think they wait until they see the Assistant run out the tape before they decide to walk across the set. Twenty-five feet will be plenty long enough for most of your work, but consider a fifty footer for your first purchase. It's only a few dollars more, and only a tiny bit bigger and heavier, but for those times you need the extra length, you'll be glad you have it. Cloth tapes shrink more than fiberglass, and will eventually need to be replaced. The ideal cloth tape would have feet and inches one side and meters on the other, using the same start mark, but good luck finding one.

Steel Tape Measure   A steel tape is also useful at times, for when you cannot physically reach the object you want to measure. Look for the one-inch-wide size, sixteen to twenty-five feet long. The blade of the one-inch models will stay erect better when extended than the smaller sizes, allowing you to extend the end out and away from you. This will permit you to stand at the camera and measure the distance to an actor or other subject matter beyond the length of your outstretched arms, which you would otherwise not be able to do with a cloth tape measure.

Depth-of-Field Calculator or Charts   Discussed in detail in the chapter on Focus. Several models are available—it won't take long to find your favorite.

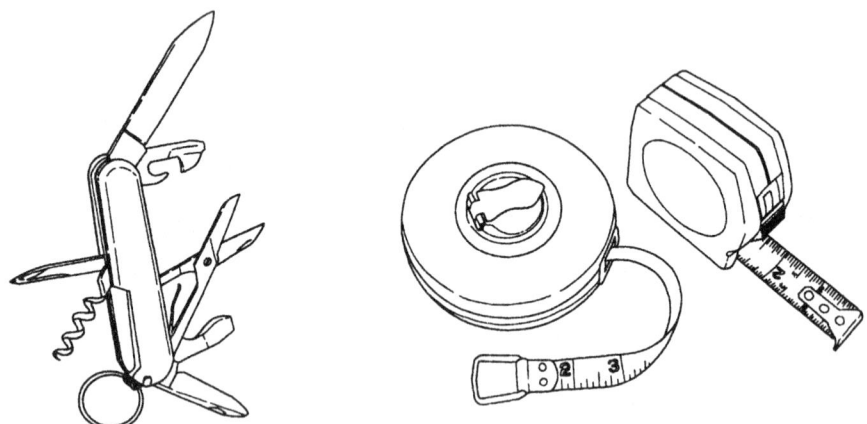

Figure 15-1   Swiss Army Knife/Tape Measures. It is hard to imagine any Camera Assistant without a Swiss Army Knife, one of the most versatile and convenient combination tools ever made. A cloth or fiberglass tape measure (25 or 50 feet) and a steel tape measure (12 to 25 feet) fulfill different measuring needs; both are needed by the Assistant.

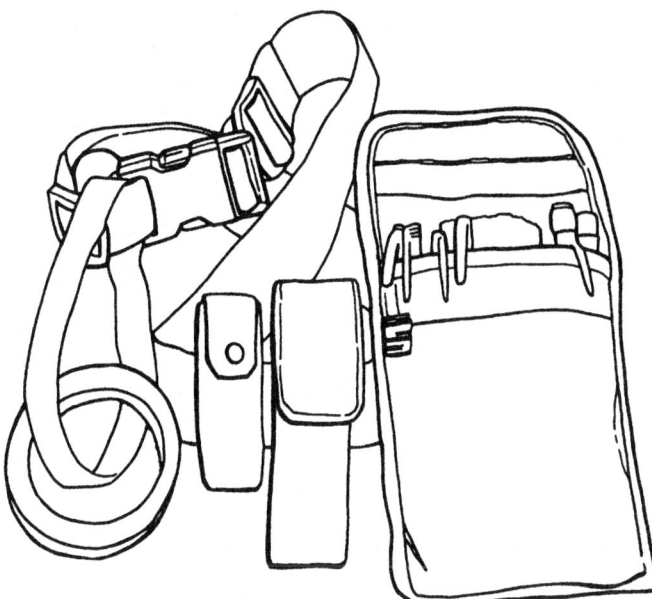

Figure 15-2 Belt Pouch. Most Camera Assistants use some sort of belt system for carrying basic tools and supplies. Mine includes a roll of white camera tape (preferably a half roll or less. Save those half rolls from the darkroom for use on your belt), a Leatherman combination tool (I already have a Swiss Army Knife attached to the belt that holds up my pants!), a Maglight flashlight, and a pouch of pens, markers, chalk, lens tissue, slate marker, etc. Customizing your own "Utility Belt" is fun, but do yourself a favor and don't load yourself up with a lot of stuff you don't absolutely need to have in immediate access. Even a minimal belt gets heavy after a long day! Often when I have a well-stocked front box available right at the camera, I don't wear my utility belt at all.

Film Footage, Frame Rate, Filter Factor, Field-of-View Calculator These are often found in reference books and manuals, or as part of a Depth-of-Field Calculator. These are discussed in chapter on Focus.

Belt Pouch Most Assistants use a belt pack or pouch of some sort to keep their pens and chalk and flashlights and stuff. Many camping supply stores and Army/Navy stores have these, as well as many mail-order catalogs in various sizes, materials, and colors.

Front Box The Camera Assistant's best friend on the set—a place to put tools, markers, pens, depth-of-field calculator, chewing gum, tape measure, etc. All modern gear heads have the mounting bracket for a front box (I am happy to report that on this, at least, a standardized bracket does exist!) Many rental houses have also installed this bracket on their fluid heads. Most modern front boxes have a slot underneath for the slate. Unfortunately, some Directors of Photography think that the Front Box is for the D.P.'s stuff. This should be gently discouraged if possible.

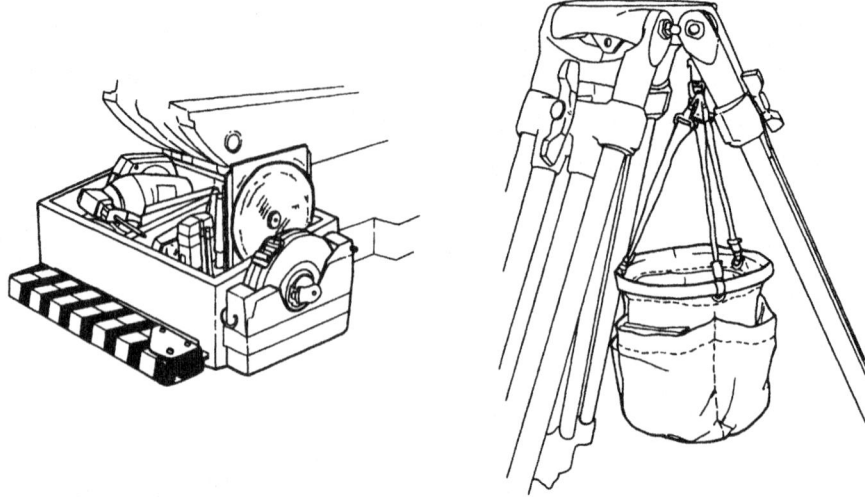

Figure 15-3 Front Box and "Ditty Bag." The Front Box mounted on the gear head under the camera holds the Camera Assistants' most essential and frequently used tools and supplies. An alternate would be the "Ditty Bag" hanging below the tripod or dolly.

Ditty Bag For those jobs without a gear head, using a Front Box may not be worth the trouble. Many Assistants use a canvas or nylon bag with pockets and a snap-hook, called a Ditty Bag, for their small tools and supplies. The Ditty Bag can be hung below the camera on the tripod or dolly or in some other convenient place.

Larry Bag, Rapport Bag, Kangaroo Bag, L.L.Bean Boat Bag, etc. Several companies make these nylon or canvas bags, useful for holding the 50 pounds or so of accessories and supplies needed to service the modern production cameras. It won't take long to find one you like. The problem is that these bags tend to get very heavy, once all the bits and pieces have been added. Look for a bag that is waterproof and has a cover, so your toys won't get lost or wet.

Basic Tools

Screwdrivers (Slot, Phillips, and Jewelers)
Pliers (Needle-Nose, Slip-Joint, Wire Cutter)
Adjustable Wrench
Vice-Grip Pliers (Large and Small)
Allen Wrenches (also known as Hex Key Wrenches) in both Inch and Metric sizes, especially 2mm size for Arriflex shutters, etc.
Tweezers/Forceps/Hemostats
Hirschmann Forceps (Arri Ground glass Puller)
Arri Magazine Tension Gauge (expensive, and therefore optional. I've never owned one, nor needed one, but many Assistants carry one in their kit.)

 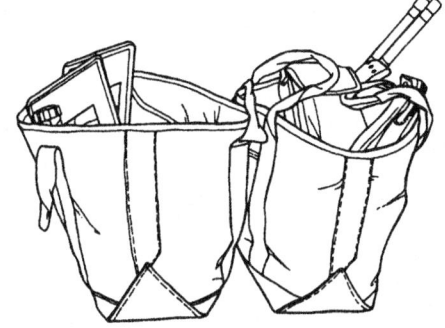

Figure 15-4 Larry Bag/Boat Bag. The "Larry" Bag, designed and marketed by New York Camera Assistant Larry Huston is very popular among Camera Assistants. Canvas or oilskin "Boat" bags or utility bags carry accessories better and more accessibly than cumbersome and heavy accessory cases.

It's usually about here that Murphy's Law comes in—you never have the size Allen Keys or screwdrivers you need, but you always have the sizes you don't need and never use. This is true of the little sizes especially.

Lens Tissue and Lens Fluid   Rental houses often have their own brand of tissue and fluid, and some camera manufacturers make their own. I advise sticking to the big name brands, if the rental house brand is not available: Kodak, Tiffen, Rosco, Panchro, etc. At all cost avoid the tissue made for eyeglasses and sold in eyeglass stores. This tissue often is impregnated with a silicone compound that can harm the coatings on lenses.

Orangewood Sticks   Available at the cosmetics section in pharmacies and department stores. Useful for removing hairs and emulsion build-up from the gate area of motion picture cameras.

Pin-Point Oilers and Camera Oil   Very little oil is needed in these cameras, and the best way to dispense and control that small amount is with a hollow needle point, like a hypodermic syringe, that places one drop of oil specifically where you want it—very good for oiling the Mitchell and Panavision cameras. A second oiler might contain silicone for the felt pads at the bottom of the pull-down claw channel. If pin-point oilers are not available, a hypodermic needle is often used, after rounding and blunting the point with a file, sharpening stone, or grindstone, to prevent accidents. The camera oil usually comes from the rental house or from the camera manufacturer. If you are really stuck, in an emergency, any high-quality, light, fine machine oil, such as sewing machine oil, will work, although the camera manufacturers might disagree.

Camera Grease   For Arriflex and Mitchell Cameras, usually available from the rental house, often without charge when a camera is going out.

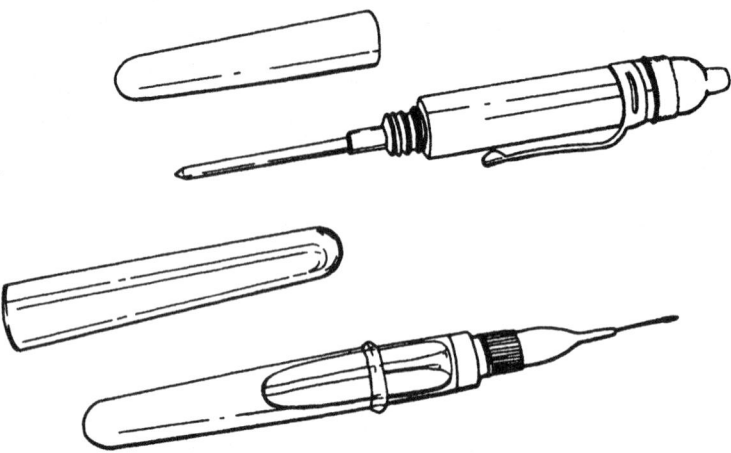

Figure 15-5 Precision Oilers. Pin-point oilers make oiling Panavision and other cameras a cinch. One oiler (bottom) holds light camera oil; the other (top) works best with thicker materials such as the silicon liquid used for Panavision cameras on the felt pads below the pull-down claw. Both lubricants are available from the Panavision dealer.

Flashlights   I prefer rechargeable flashlights, such as the one made by Sanyo, but there are many fine battery lights as well. Plastic flashlight bodies are more comfortable than metal ones to hold in your teeth, which is a common pose for Camera Assistants, especially when threading the camera in the dark. Assistants are often seen in that configuration, with both hands full. Mag lights are very popular and useful because you get not only a good strong beam but it's focusable, flood to spot. Some Assistants use a coalminer's or climber's headlamp—a battery flashlight with a strap to attach around the head. This works fine but looks a little foolish. If you have a battery light, make sure you have plenty of spare batteries. Murphy's Law of Flashlights will get you if you don't!

Magnifying Glass or Illuminated Magnifier   Good to have for checking the gate, examining film for scratches, looking at film clips or mattes, and in general for seeing little things.

Scissors   A small pair of quality scissors is important. Film, gelatin filters, paper, cardboard, electrical insulation, etc., all need to be cut. Fiskars are probably the best. They stay sharp and have comfortable handles. Blades about 2 inches long are best, preferably with rounded tips, so you don't stab yourself or somebody else.

Markers and Pens   You will need to have an assortment of pens, pencils, and markers in various sizes and colors, depending on your working methods and color code system. You will need ball point pens for Camera Reports and some other paperwork because you are writing through several carbons. Unfortunately, there is no one pen that's good for everything. A fine-tip

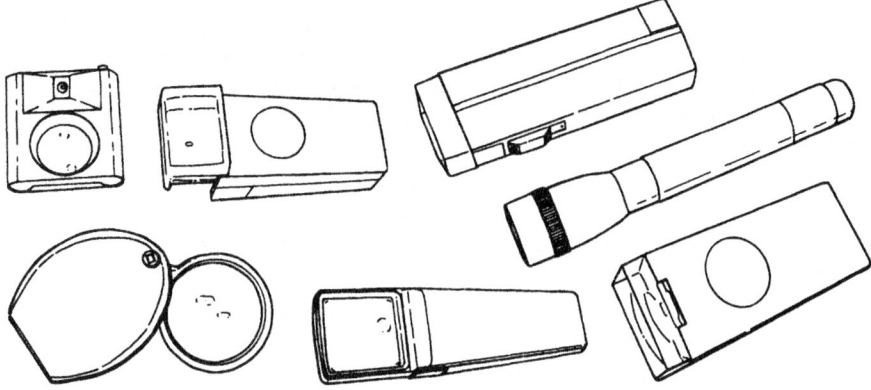

Figure 15-6 Flashlights and Magnifiers. Many styles of flashlights and magnifiers and illuminated magnifiers are available for Camera Assistants, either rechargeable or battery powered.

marker that writes on camera tape for focus and zoom marks, a medium-wide marker for labeling magazines and making notes, a wide marker for labeling cases, grease pencils (china markers), ordinary lead pencils (useful for making temporary marks directly on lens barrels), and wipe-off slate markers, will all be useful to the Camera Assistant. Don't forget a cosmetics powder puff for erasing the slate marker from the slate between takes and scenes.

Chalk and Chalk Holders For marking actors' and camera positions and setting focus marks for yourself. Available everywhere from toy stores to art supply stores and hardware stores. Get several colors, plus white. Also available in large sticks, that won't break apart on you. Use aluminum chalk holders or wrap the chalk in paper masking tape to minimize chalk dust on hands and in pockets. The paper tape will wear away by itself as you use the chalk on cement and blacktop.

Chart or Pinstripe Tape This narrow tape, usually 1/8" to 1/4" in width, and available in art supply stores, is used for focus marks on lenses. White and yellow are the best colors, and if the surface is glossy, some pens and markers will be erasable, which is desirable for making temporary focus marks on lenses.

Blower Bulb Available in pharmacies, as ear syringes. I personally am not crazy about these things. It is difficult to get enough air volume or velocity to be of much use, but it is safer to use inside of delicate cameras than the compressed-gas-type aerosol can. Some Assistants swear by them.

Dust-Off Available in three styles; Old style (chrome), New style (black plastic), and the new Environmentally Safe model (gray plastic). The cans and nozzles are not interchangeable. If you have the old type chrome nozzle, wrap it securely with tape to prevent the pieces from being blown across the room.

They have a habit of detaching—they are apparently just pressure-fitted, and come loose with age. The New style has a locking collar on the nozzle to prevent accidental discharging while travelling, etc. The newest, Environmental, model is theoretically nonharmful to the ozone layer, and has a handy swivel nozzle that will bend in almost every direction, but it is also quite a bit larger, and doesn't fit in the front box as well as the older models.

Lens Brush   These soft sable or camels' hair brushes are available in camera stores, and look like lipstick tubes when closed. The brass or chrome housing protects the brush and keeps it clean. Do not use this brush for anything other than lenses, and keep capped when not in use.

Magazine Brush   This brush should have stiffer bristles than the lens brush, for easier and more efficient magazine brushing. I use a simple 1" paintbrush from a hardware store, and keep it in a Zip-Lock Bag when not in use. It costs about $1.

Clear Nail Polish   This is good to have for repairing cracks in plastics, sealing in small screws, etc.

Transfer Tape   A lot of D.P.'s like to use ladies' stocking material mounted behind the lens. There is a tape available in art supply stores called "transfer tape," resembling rubber cement with a paper backing, that works superbly for this purpose, allowing you to attach the material and is still removable without permanent damage and without leaving a residue.

Batteries   Batteries for the D.P.'s light meters are very important. Find out at the beginning of the job what meters the Director of Photography will be using and get a full set of spare batteries. It makes you a hero when all of a sudden batteries go dead. Batteries for flashlights, color temperature meters, crystal checking meters, lanterns, and other devices will also be needed.

Fuses   Murphy's Law of Fuses: They always blow when it is least convenient. Fuses of various types and amperages will be needed for cameras, camera batteries, power supplies, battery chargers, etc.

Voltmeter   A small and inexpensive voltmeter and continuity tester, sometimes called a "Volt-Ohm-Meter" or "VOM," or "Multimeter," is very important for checking batteries, bulbs, fuses, switches, cables, wall outlets, battery chargers, and other electrical apparatus. These are available in hardware stores and electronics supply stores. Radio Shack has several inexpensive models.

Q-Tips (Cotton Applicators)   The short two-ended ones with the cardboard or plastic stick are not good for our purposes. You often need a longer reach, and with the single-ended models with a six-inch wooden stick you can use the wooden end as well, for removing hairs and film emulsion build-up in the gate area. There are also foam-tipped applicators available that eliminate the possibility of leaving cotton fibers behind when using a cotton-tipped applicator. The foam ones are more expensive, but are a good idea. They are available at places like Radio Shack, having been designed for use cleaning audio and video recorder heads.

Tools and Supplies **375**

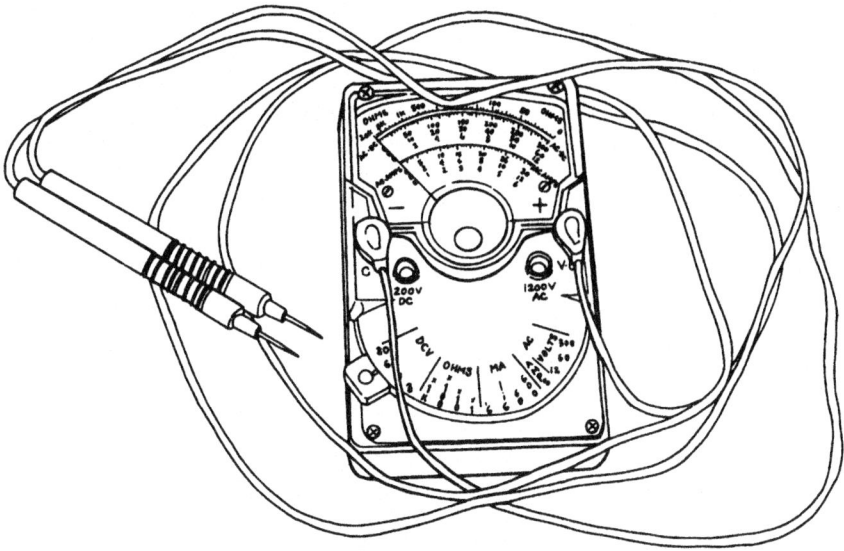

Figure 15-7 Multimeter (Volt-Ohm-Meter). Multimeters or Volt-Ohm-Meters are useful for checking fuses, cables, switches, batteries, power supplies, and anything electrical.

Level   A small, pocket "torpedo" or "target" or "bulls-eye" bubble level is useful for leveling the camera. Some are shaped like a ball-point pen, others are circular about the diameter of a poker chip or silver dollar, available in hardware stores.

Grounding Adapters   A good thing to have in your kit. Battery chargers often come with a three-prong plug and hotel rooms often come with two-prong

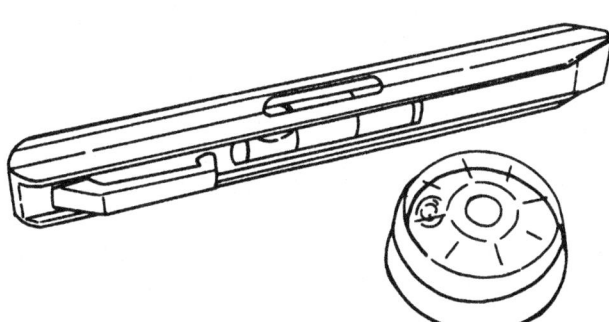

Figure 15-8 Levels. Small levels, either "torpedo" or "bullseye" styles, are used to make sure the camera is mounted or placed level with the horizon.

outlets. There are two solutions for that particular problem, but probably the way the equipment houses would prefer you to solve the problem is to use one of those adapters.

Cube Taps and Outlet Strips I always carry a cube tap or outlet strip when I travel on a job. It's essential if you have more than one battery charger and only one outlet. You always can tell the Camera Assistant's hotel room on location—it is the one lit up like a Christmas tree—the one with the little orange lights when the battery chargers are on. I can't go to sleep at night on location unless I am surrounded with lots of those little orange lights.

Small C-Clamps 1" or 2" C-Clamps often come in handy for securing the Hi-Hat or Sliding Base Plate or other uses.

Camera Mounting Bolts 3/8" x 16 (3/8" diameter; 16 threads per inch) bolts of various lengths from 1/2" to 3", flat head and hex head, with nuts and washers, for mounting the camera onto unusual surfaces.

Spare Film Cores and Black Lab Bags Keep spares handy.

Production Slate Many Camera Assistants own their own slates, although often for feature films, new slates are purchased.

Insert Slate Small slate for close-up and tabletop filming. They usually do not have sticks, but most close-up inserts, and tabletop shooting are M.O.S.

French Flag This is a rectangular metal flag on an articulated arm mounted on a clamp, and attached to the camera to shade the lens from the sun or lighting unit. I carry two different sizes.

Earplugs A good thing to have when working on music videos and concerts, or even in factories, power stations, subways, etc.

Gray Scale and/or Color Chart Many D.P.'s like to shoot these standardized gray scales or color charts at the head of each roll, or once each day, or once each location, to give the lab a standard reference for timing the workprint. Kodak sells these, and sometimes labs give them away free.

Gray Card 18 percent Gray Card, useful for reflected light exposure readings and for laboratory printer reference. Kodak sells these, but you may be able to get one for nothing from a film lab.

Optional Items

Leatherman There is an interesting combination tool gadget called the Leatherman. It consists of pliers, a knife blade, several screwdrivers, a file, Phillips screwdriver, can opener, etc. It folds up in a nice compact package and is better than the Swiss Army Knife because of the pliers, although the knife blade is not as good, and it doesn't have a corkscrew!

Dental (Inspection) Mirror A good thing to have. You can't always work on the right side of the camera. Sometimes you have to work the "dumb" side. With the mirror I can still see the aperture scale or footage counter and tachometer, although some practice was needed to get used to reading the numbers backwards. Mine came from the automotive hardware section at Sears, has a telescoping handle, and is called an "Inspection Mirror."

Tools and Supplies **377**

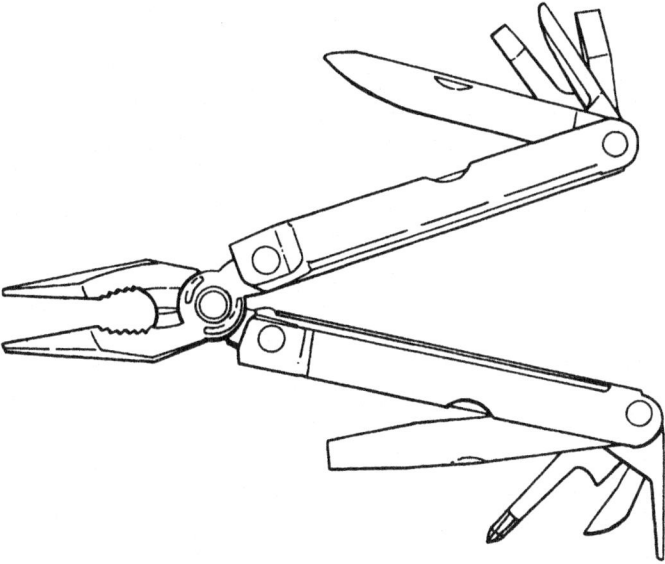

Figure 15-9 Leatherman. The "Leatherman" is a useful combination tool built around a plier instead of a knife, like the Swiss Army Knife. Gerber and "S.O.G." make similar tools.

Lens Handle (Jar Opener) Here is a good example of something designed and sold for one purpose, but very useful for a totally different purpose. This device is intended as a jar opener—it is a plastic handle with an adjustable metal strap that can be tightened or loosened by turning a knob on one end of the handle. It can be found in the kitchen departments of hardware or department stores. It can also be used as an auxiliary focus or zoom handle for a cinema lens. Slip the open strap around the lens before putting the lens on the camera, then tighten (not too tight!) around either the focus or zoom ring of

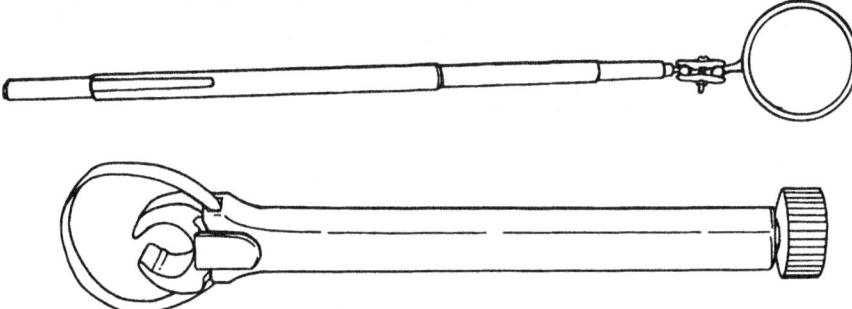

Figure 15-10 Inspection Mirror/Lens Handle. Also useful is an inspection mirror (this one with telescoping handle) and an adjustable jar opener used as an auxiliary zoom lens or focus handle.

the lens. The handle will stick out perpendicularly to the lens, and makes a nice firm handle for smooth hand zooms or focus moves. The longer the handle, the smoother the zooms, especially slow zooms.

Spanner Wrench Useful sometimes, but not essential. A spanner wrench is used to dismantle lenses, eyepieces, and other such optical apparatus. This type of work is not recommended in the field, and certainly not by anyone who has not been thoroughly trained in such work. I use mine to tighten those rings that have become loose through vibration, especially on filter rings.

Emery Paper and/or Crocus Cloth These are abrasive papers and cloths like super-fine sandpaper. I confess that I carried these for many years without ever finding a use for them, simply because they were included in the "Essential Tools" listings in other sources. One day I needed to clean the corrosion off some electrical contacts, and this stuff was perfect. This is also good for rust removal (on the OUTSIDE of the camera and gear head).

Tweezers, Forceps, and/or Hemostats Available from medical supply stores and some hardware stores. Useful for holding, picking up, and securing small pieces and screws. Some Assistants use hemostats for inserting and removing the ground glass.

Twine/Cord Useful for tying up and securing equipment, such as securing batteries and cables on an insert car, for a focus drag-line (see the section on drag-line focus marks in the chapter on Focus), but is usually available from the Prop, Electric, or Grip Departments when you need it. This is also sometimes called "trick line."

Black Velvet or Duvateen Cloth About 2 feet by 2 feet, for preventing light from entering the matte box through the filter slots, for blacking out unwanted reflections off car windshields, covering the magazine to prevent reflections in a window or mirror, etc. If you are really ambitious and own a sewing machine, make a black bag that will fit over a Panavision magazine, to eliminate reflections of the light gray magazine in windows and mirrors on location.

Stat-Ban It is made for eyeglasses by Bausch & Lomb, but also keeps camera eyepieces from fogging up. This product should NOT be used on camera lenses or filters.

Silicone Spray, Teflon Spray, and/or WD-40 Spray Multipurpose lubricants for tripod legs, gear head dovetails and balance plates, etc. DO NOT USE ON OR IN CAMERAS!

Compass For finding the sunrise or sunset, and for finding the location when the call sheet directions are not so great.

Wooden Wedges For leveling the camera or marking actors.

T-Marks Made from wood or rubber, for marking actors. Often used with nails or spikes to prevent the mark from being kicked away by actors with big feet. The two sides can be painted different colors to distinguish between actors.

Misc. Small Tools and Supplies Razor Blades, Alligator Clips, Insulated Wire, Spare Fuses, Rubber Bands, etc.

Rangefinder Works the same way as rangefinder on a Leica camera. Two images are seen and you turn the wheel until the images are superimposed. This item is discussed in the chapter on Focus.

Digitape Electronic measuring device using the infrared technology from the Polaroid instant cameras. It gives a digital readout of the distance, but takes several seconds to give a reading and is easily confused by multiple targets. Discussed in further detail in the chapter on Focus.

Space Blankets Costs $8 to $10 at sporting goods stores. They are just the right size to cover a camera or an equipment cart to protect against rain, sun, dust, and the ravages of nature.

Gooseneck Flashlight With an adjustable neck if you don't feel like holding it in your mouth, you can clip it somewhere and point it where you want it to shine—it can be taped to the camera so that it shines on the lens and illuminates the focus marks. Some camera manufacturers make a lens light that mounts on the camera and gets power from the camera body. I built my own. Soon you will start customizing and inventing your own things.

Cold Weather/Rain Gear Never skimp on rain gear or cold weather gear or boots. Get the best that money can buy. The production company will buy $3 rain ponchos, but these are guaranteed to rip after five minutes. If you are going to be out in the cold or wet for any period of time, you want a good set of rain gear (jacket and pants), cold weather gear, and especially good boots. It's very important to have good stuff. Anyone can stand the cold for the few minutes it takes to get from the house to the car, or from the car to the office, but if you are working on a film, you will be out in the cold all day or all night long. No one does their best work if they are cold, wet, and uncomfortable. And if you get wet and cold, you might get sick, the worst thing that can happen to a freelancer.

Soldering Iron A soldering iron is a good thing to have for absolute emergencies, but don't ever break it out on the set! Have enough back-up power cables so that it is not necessary to use it on the set. When you get back home or to the hotel room you can solder to your heart's content, on your own time. Nothing brands an Assistant as "Inexperienced" faster than a smoking soldering iron on the set.

Eyepiece covers Made of foam or chamois or both—Panavision's are round; Arri's can be either oval or round, depending on the camera in use.

Hand Warmers There are several different types available. Some use a solid stick of fuel like charcoal that you light before closing up the unit. Others use liquid fuel like lighter fluid, but some people don't like the smell. (Be careful refilling and lighting these. I once nearly set fire to the camera truck! That would have been very embarrassing!) Some new disposable ones are available that use intermixed chemicals for heat, but they don't last very long. There are also reusable chemical heaters, but they only work for about 2 hours, and then must be boiled for 20 minutes between uses to reset them.

They all work fairly well at keeping people warm, they are less successful at keeping cameras warm. A handwarmer placed as close as possible to the motor of a camera, and wrapped in aluminum foil (no foil between the handwarmer and the camera motor, of course), will work wonders for keeping the camera running in the cold. A second handwarmer near the zoom motor, also wrapped in foil, should keep the zoom motor running. A few more in the Camera Assistant's pockets, will keep the Assistant working, as well. Don't forget to give a couple to the D.P., Camera Operator, and Still Photographer.

Assistant's Supplies

Solvents While a tempting solvent to use everywhere, acetone has the unfortunate tendency of removing paint and enamel, and dissolving plastic. Keep acetone away from camera bodies and lenses. I have used it on glass filters to remove camera tape residue. Use it for tripod legs or other such nondelicate items. Great care should be taken when using solvents. Other commonly used solvents include xylene, naphtha (lighter fluid), mineral spirits, benzene, and trichloroethane (nonflammable but hazardous if inhaled—use only in ventilated areas). Grain alcohol (not isopropyl or rubbing alcohol) is much gentler and almost as effective a solvent as acetone, and will not harm plastics or most painted surfaces. It is rare that anything stronger will be needed.

Lubricants Camera manufacturers and rental houses should be the source of any oil or grease for use inside the cameras. If the manufacturer does not make their own lubricating oils, they will recommend one. Arri recommends Isoflex PDP-38 oil and Petrolon Slick-50 Teflon Grease, for example. Many rental houses will give you the oil and/or grease you need for the cameras you are taking from them, in an attempt to ensure that only the correct oils and lubricants will be used. If they don't have it to give you, they probably have it to sell to you. This is certainly true about high-speed cameras like the Panavision Panastar, Mitchell Mark II, and the Image 300. For other lubrication needs, many Camera Assistants swear by WD-40 or CRC-556 cleaner/lubricants. They work, but are slightly oily. LPS-1 is a better moisture-displacer/lubricant, and is not oily. Break-Free is another product in this line. Silicone or Teflon spray lubricants are good for tripod legs, spreaders, and gear heads, but not around cameras.

Adhesives Clear nail polish, Crazy Glue, contact cement, Duco Cement, Rubber Cement, epoxy, all have their uses on the set as adhesives to make quick repairs.

Traveling Heavy vs. Traveling Light

You will have to decide for yourself how much and what to bring with you on the job. The more you bring, the more prepared you will be, but the more you must carry.

On a feature, with a truck carrying the camera equipment and serving as home base for months at a time, many Camera Assistants travel heavy, bringing all sorts of tools and supplies with them, being ready for any emergency.

On a commercial or other short job, much smaller kits are carried, as the odds for something going wrong decrease dramatically with the shorter shooting schedules.

CHAPTER **16**

Education of a Camera Assistant, and Finding Work Afterwards

How does one train for a career as a Camera Assistant? There are several ways to learn about the cameras themselves, and several ways to learn the other techniques the Camera Assistant needs and uses.

Film School

If you are in a film school, and I don't mean a liberal arts college with one Film Aesthetics or Film History class, or if you intend to go to film school someday, and want to get more involved in Cinematography, then take advantage of the opportunities that film schools present.

A real film school, with courses in Film Production, Photography, Lighting, Sound, Direction, Editing, Screenwriting, Animation, and all the rest, can give the aspiring cinematographer a first chance at getting his or her hands on amateur and professional cameras, usually only 16mm. They may be only Bolexes or Arri 16S cameras, but all of the same rules apply, whatever the brand name.

Film schools, with very few exceptions, are geared toward graduating potential directors, writers, and critics, and only incidentally a few cinematographers, editors, and sound mixers slip through. Film schools play up the glitz and glamour of directing and writing, and play down the technical end—the getting-your-hands-dirty, working-for-a-living, actual making of films. It's a shame, really. The potential for turning out really good cinema technicians has never really been realized in film schools, except in rare instances.

The large majority of the "Directors" and "Writers" that graduate from film schools never make it in the real world of the movie business. They wind up as frustrated film critics for local newspapers, and as frustrated instructors in film schools. There are a few exceptions, of course, but only a few.

The few film school graduates who do survive in the business seem to have made good mostly in the technical areas—Camera, Sound, Editing, Animation, etc., because they took advantage of the opportunities that film schools offer—the chance to make films, the chance to get to know the equipment (despite the limitations of that equipment), and the chance to make mistakes and learn from those mistakes, and the chance to improvise and solve production problems.

When I was in film school, at the School of Visual Arts in New York, almost everyone else in my class was determined to become the next Orson Welles or C. B. DeMille, and they didn't even try to learn the nuts and bolts of the way things work. As a result, out of 60 students, only 18 of us finished the three-year program SVA had at the time, and only about six of us are still in the business, and all in the technical crafts. Those six were the ones who got right into the technical stuff and wound up working on everyone else's student films.

For the Camera Assistant, film school represents the first opportunity to change a lens, load a magazine, and thread a camera. So what if the camera is a Bolex and not a Panaflex or an Arri 535. A camera is a camera, and needs to be treated with the same respect, and fed the same ingredients, film, power, and TLC.

Magazines still need to be loaded, film shipped to the lab, filters changed, and focus followed. The basic techniques are there to be learned, and learned in a much more easy-going, laid-back low-pressure atmosphere than you are likely to find on a professional film set. And the consequences of making a mistake do not include getting fired or ending your career.

Scenes still need to be slated, film cans labeled, and lenses cleaned. All of the elements are there—just take advantage of the opportunity.

Equipment Rental Houses as Training Grounds

Training new Assistants, and showing new equipment to established Assistants, is a secondary, but no less important function of the rental houses. When a new camera or lens comes out, the Assistant can find one to play with at the rental house. When the new Assistant applies for union membership, where better to practice with the equipment applicants are tested on than at the rental houses?

Rental houses generally don't mind this equipment training, if you approach them carefully and at the right time. Call first, and ask (politely) if they're willing to let you come in and practice with the equipment. If the rental house refuses, it is generally for one of the following reasons: either the equipment is not available, or the rental house itself is too busy on the day you want to come in, or they don't have personnel available to show you the equipment. Don't just show up and expect them to roll out the red carpet.

In general, don't call or try to make an appointment on a Friday afternoon or Monday morning, for these are traditionally the busiest and most chaotic times at rental houses. Don't come in and expect them to drop everything to show you every piece of equipment they own. Ask for specific cameras and items you need to familiarize yourself with, and make sure they are available for demonstration.

Do your homework first. Read up on that equipment in one of the technical manuals or cinematography magazines. If you can find someone (preferably a Camera Assistant) that the rental house knows and trusts to bring you in, introduce you around, and show you the equipment so the hands-on training doesn't involve any of their personnel, so much the better. I have done this several times for people.

It is also to the rental house's advantage to train new Assistants. First of all, they are creating a future customer, who will remember the rental house that helped them get started, and who will come back to rent equipment when they are famous D.P.'s.

Secondly, it is to every rental house's advantage to properly train the people who will be using their equipment because then the equipment will be used correctly and treated with the proper respect, and there will be less down time for repairs and maintenance on that equipment.

Working at a Rental House

Many of the best Camera Assistants got their start working in a rental house. Where better to learn the equipment from the inside out?

It is true that at most rental houses, the entry level position is usually cleaning cases or counting C-clamps in the Grip Department, but when the openings in the Camera Rental Department appear, be ready to pounce on it.

Not only is the rental house the best place to learn the equipment, but it is the best place to meet and get to know the people who make films in your area—the Camera Assistants, the Gaffers, the Grips, maybe even a D.P. or two. When you finally enter the freelance world, knowing these people, especially the working Camera Assistants, can be a great advantage. When they need a loader or an additional Second, they will be more inclined to hire someone they know, and someone they know who knows the equipment.

Visit and Learn

Rental houses help educate Camera Assistants in another way, besides taking a job in one. Prospective or established Camera Assistants frequently visit the rental houses in their area to become acquainted with the latest in camera gear, newly arrived and on the market.

Rental houses are generally happy to show off their new toys to the people who are going to be using them in the future, so don't be shy—call up and arrange an educational field trip to the local rental house.

Student Films

Student films are a good training ground for future film techies. If there is a film school in your area, then there are student films being made all the time—they just don't get the publicity *Rambo XII* would if they were shooting in your town. Student films are always looking for crew to help out. If you have even the tiniest bit of professional or semiprofessional film experience, then you probably have more than any of the students, so you should be able to get yourself involved in the filming with no trouble.

Get yourself down to the college, find the Film Department, and put up an announcement on the bulletin board advertising your services, then hurry home to start answering the phone. You might also look in the "trades" for casting notices for student films. You will probably not get paid for this work, but the experience gained will be well worth the effort.

Ads in the Trade Press

Many industry newcomers have gotten jobs on sets by answering ads or notices found in the "Trade Press," publications such as *Variety*, *Hollywood Reporter*, *BackStage* (on the East Coast), and *Dramalogue* (on the West Coast). If a low-budget picture has published a casting notice, they are probably also looking for a crew. Call them, FAX or mail a resume—who knows? You might just get lucky. A lot of the success going around in this business has to do with being in the right place at the right time.

Work as Production Assistant

The best way to learn the business is to watch the pros at work. If you can get paid to watch the pros work, so much the better. Okay, so what is the entry-level position on the film set? The production assistant, or PA, of course. Every motion picture production company needs PAs, for the office, crowd control, drivers, craft service, etc. Nobody stays a PA very long, so the turnover in PA hiring is pretty high.

The pay may not be terrific, but the chance to watch the big kids play at movie making is worth it. So what if they keep sending you out to look for designer water for some prima donna movie star, or to chase tourists away from the location. You are on the payroll, and get to watch what goes on.

After a while, you might approach the boss, or producer, and ask about getting a bit closer to the set, possible as a "Camera P.A." Many jobs have a PA designated as the Camera PA, generally to keep the Director of Photography supplied with coffee, and sometimes to avoid hiring a Loader or Camera Trainee. If the Camera Assistants on the job are amenable, you might wind up helping with the mountain of camera cases, or doing the slates and camera reports, or other such activity.

After you have spent some time with the Camera Assistants on the job, and demonstrated to them your deep interest and eagerness to learn and help out, they might be persuaded to let you practice loading a mag with some scrap film. From there, the sky is the limit.

Workshops and Seminars

If you can afford them, workshops and seminars are an excellent chance for you to get your hands on professional camera equipment and learn from the professionals. Of course, I'm prejudiced, because I founded and continue to teach the Camera Assistants Workshop in Rockport, Maine, given twice every summer.

We have Arriflex, Panavision, Kodak, Tiffen, and many others as sponsors, so we have the largest range of equipment available in one place that I have ever seen. I don't even know of any rental houses that have this extensive a range of cameras.

The sessions offer extensive hands-on opportunities for the students. This may be the ONLY week-long Camera Assistants Workshop in the country, or even the world. I've never heard of another. The Workshop has 30 to 35 students per session, and divides its week-long schedule between lectures on Camera Assisting, Focus Theory, Lenses, Camera Maintenance, Formats and Aspect Ratios, Following Focus, Paperwork, etc., and hands-on sessions with top line state-of-the-art camera systems from Arriflex, Panavision, Moviecam, etc.

Sometimes camera rental houses or manufacturers or producers' associations offer one-day or weekend seminars or workshops for certain specific cameras or camera systems, and these are very good, although they rarely offer much in the way of hands-on time for the students. There just isn't enough time or equipment available in one-day seminars. They are good for learning the features of a new camera or lens, but for real hands-on, I recommend a longer term workshop.

Equipment shows, such as the SMPTE, ShowBiz Expo (East and West), or the NAB shows are good for finding out what is available in new equipment, but they are mostly for salesmen, and you may have trouble getting your technical questions answered if you are not planning to buy something.

Arriflex runs a series of seminars for Camera Assistants, teaching the maintenance and repair for Arriflex cameras. I think they have it on both the East and West Coasts, and it lasts six or eight three-hour sessions. Call Arriflex for more information.

Trainee Program

Some unions and large film companies have trainee programs for prospective Camera Assistants. The requirements may be difficult to meet, such as passing the test for union membership, or having an uncle who owns the company, but these programs exist out there, if you can find them.

I helped start the Local 644 Trainee Program, about fifteen years ago. This is an invaluable experience for a new Assistant and new union member. The theory is that new union members, who have taken and passed the union entrance examination (written and practical exams) and theoretically know the equipment, often do not have the necessary set experience, having come from rental house or documentary film backgrounds, or being recently out of film school.

The program currently provides for a new union Camera Assistant who expresses an interest in the program to work for twenty weeks or two films, whichever comes first, as a Camera Trainee. The union also suggests that the two films be for different camera crews, to maximize the exposure and learning experience for the trainee, and to meet and work with more people.

I recommend the trainee program highly; even though the salary is not wonderful, the learning experience is. I wish there had been such a program when I was just getting started. Not all of the various unions in the industry have such a program, but some do.

Finding Work

I wish there were an easy answer to the question, "How do I find work?" Unfortunately, there isn't. The only answer is "Any way you can."

Learn all you can, meet people, ask questions, visit rental houses and seminars, attend workshops, make a pest of yourself on the phone to the people you meet, answer ads in the "trades," work as a P.A., visit sets and watch what is going on, ask more questions—all of these will help get you known in your area as a dedicated, interested, and determined potential Camera Assistant.

Freelancing

Freelancing is a tough way to make a living. Except in very small areas of this country, and for a very few large companies, staff employment for Camera Assistants is rare. Not many production companies shoot often enough to justify keeping Camera Assistants on the payroll on a staff basis. Almost all employment for Camera Assistants is on a freelance, project-to-project, day-to-day, or week-to-week basis.

The shooting schedule on an average feature film is eight to twelve weeks, with a two-week checkout. For a television movie or pilot, four weeks (18 to 20 days) shooting, with maybe a three- to five-day checkout. For a commercial, it might only be a single day shooting, plus a day for the checkout.

Even the most experienced Camera Assistants live with the uncertainty of freelance employment. A freelance Camera Assistant is never certain where the next paycheck will come from. We get our jobs by phone, by having a telephone answering machine, by employing an answering service, by carrying a beeper, and now by using a cellular phone.

We depend for jobs on people we have worked with before, and on referrals or recommendations of our friends when they are not available to take a job.

In between paying jobs, it may be possible to collect your state's Unemployment Insurance Benefits, although qualifications and benefits vary greatly from state to state. This money is not welfare, or charity. This money comes from taxes levied against the employers who employed you for various periods of time within the past year. In effect, it is a penalty the employers pay for not keeping you employed full-time. Only jobs in which taxes are withheld from the paychecks count toward the qualifying period for unemployment payments.

If you take work as an Independent Contractor, no taxes are taken from your checks, and those jobs do not count toward qualifying for Unemployment Insurance. As an Independent Contractor, you are responsible for paying your own City, State, and Federal Taxes, either annually or quarterly. You are not avoiding taxes by working as an Independent Contractor, you are only postponing them.

I suggest you put that amount of your Contractor checks that you would have been paying in taxes, into a savings account, for when that tax bill becomes due. It may be necessary for such independent contractors to file quarterly, estimated tax forms and payments. The IRS also watches Independent Contractors very carefully, and keeps changing the rules so that whatever you do is wrong.

Another disadvantage of working as an Independent Contractor is that under certain circumstances you may not be covered by the employers' medical or liability insurance. If you are injured on the job, you may not be insured. Some states require that Independent Contractors have their own Workmens Compensation and/or Disability Insurance. This coverage is not cheap.

As an Independent Contractor, you also may not be protected by the union contract. If there is a problem with your salary or fringe benefits payments from the employer, the union may be powerless to help, since you are technically not an "employee" working under a union contract if taxes are not being withheld from your paychecks.

Getting the full paycheck may sound like a great idea, but consider the consequences before proceeding. The laws are constantly changing as well.

IATSE

Everyone should belong to a union, in the motion picture industry and in every other industry. Every job should be a union job, and the workers should be protected by a union contract. There should be negotiated minimum wages, benefits, and working conditions for every job. There should be job safety requirements, as well. Workers should be covered by health and pension plans, and they should be protected against crooked producers.

In the United States and Canada, the primary motion picture union is the IATSE, also known as the IA, the Alliance, or the International Alliance of Theatrical Stage Employees and Moving Picture Machine Operators of the United States and Canada. This is a large union, covering theatrical stagehands and projectionists as well as the motion picture and television production crafts.

There are nearly 800 locals in the United States and Canada, with a total membership of about 60,000. This is the union that has the contracts with all of the major film producers and many of the smaller independents.

In the United States there are three different locals covering motion picture and television camera crews; Local 644 in New York, Local 666 in Chicago, and Local 659 in Los Angeles. The country is divided roughly in thirds east to west, for the respective jurisdictions of these locals. In Canada, Local 667, based in Toronto, covers the eastern half and Local 669, based in Vancouver, the western half of Canada. Local 644 has fifteen states along the East Coast, Maine to Florida.

There are sometimes other, smaller unions that do some film work. Until September of 1990, Local 15 of NABET (The National Association of Broadcast Employees and Technicians) also covered some film and television work in the United States. That summer (1990), plans were finally completed to merge the members of this small but important local union into the IATSE, and the vote was taken in August, overwhelmingly in favor of the merger. The members were distributed among a half dozen East Coast locals of the IATSE, including Local 644. Just recently, Local 531 of NABET merged with the West Coast IATSE unions.

This merger is a wonderful victory for unionized filmmakers, and will prevent the producers from shopping around between unions for the best concessions. The East Coast, at least, now has a powerful union containing the very best and experienced crews available.

Together, we as camera crew craftsmen and union members can now work on the non-union productions going on all the time, organizing them into union jobs, and accepting their crews into membership.

To me, and to Local 644, there are only two types of jobs, union jobs that already have a signed contract, and jobs in the process of being organized and becoming union jobs.

Non-Union

On the West Coast, unfortunately, there is a tremendous amount of non-union work, as much as 75 percent by some sources, most being done by union members in violation of their oaths and obligations as union members, and in violation of every principle of logic and common sense and good unionism.

On the East Coast, thanks to aggressive organizing by Local 644, non-union work is for the most part limited to the very lowest-budget feature, documentary, or commercial production. This work is done by crews with very little experience, because as their experience grows, so does the desire to join a union and be protected by its contracts and benefits. Non-union film work is the training grounds for union members, and this is how it should be. Once those crew people are trained, however, they should be recruited into the unions in aggressive organizing campaigns. They should not be allowed to continue to work non-union after they acquire the basic skills and experience for their crafts.

In California, however, bigger-and-bigger-budget films, a few television series, and nearly all television movies are being made without union contracts, but with union members in the crew. This is a very bad policy.

With unions that actively and aggressively seek to organize non-union productions, and take the non-union personnel into membership, non-union work is kept to a negligible minimum. If a producer wants an experienced crew, he must come to the unions and sign a contract.

If unions do not police their memberships and do not punish members who work outside the union, to the union's detriment, then the unions lose control of their memberships, and lose power and influence. Their contracts with the producers suffer, and become more and more slanted toward the producers, because there is less and less reason for the producer to sign a union contract, as long as union members are willing to work non-union without a contract.

This is exactly what has happened in California. They work under a very bad contract, with wages and working conditions much less than they could be, if they changed their policies and starting behaving like a union. Unfortunately, the locals in California allow, if not actively encourage, their members to work non-union, against everything that makes unions work. As a result, every three years when the contract comes up for renewal, the union finds itself competing for contracts and jobs with its own members working non-union, so more and more concessions must be given on the contract. The contract is slowly spiraling itself into the ground. Wages, overtime, and benefits are reduced every negotiating session, getting closer to non-union costs.

Union members must be educated by their locals into working to make their locals and unions stronger and more united, for it is only through unity that unions can survive and prosper. We can only hope that someday they will clean up their act, before unions elsewhere in the country suffer.

The opinions expressed herein are my own, of course, and do not necessarily reflect the official policy of Local 644, IATSE, of which I happen to be a former President and former Executive Board member. I have made my views public on many occasions, so they are no secret to Local 644, to Local 659, to Local 666, or to the IATSE.

Membership Procedure

Every union and local of that union has its own membership and testing procedure, but in general it works like this for a Camera Assistant applicant to International Photographers Local 644, IATSE. This procedure is, of course, subject to change.

After making the initial contact with the union, the applicant is sent a Preliminary Application, which is filled out and returned to the union. It is reviewed by the Membership Committee and the applicant is invited to an Interview Session.

Based on the preliminary application, the applicant is questioned about his or her education and experience in the motion picture field. On being convinced that the level of the applicant's experience in the field is adequate, the applicant is given the regular Application, which is filled out and returned to the union with an application fee, a copy of the applicant's Birth Certificate, and three letters of recommendation by people working in the film industry.

This Application is referred first to the Membership Committee, where it is checked for completeness and accuracy, and then forwarded to the Executive Board of the local, which by vote approves the applicant for Testing.

The Test for applicants to the union is a combination of written test, generally given at the union offices on a Friday night, and a practical test, usually held at a camera rental house all day the following Saturday. The written test is usually composed of multiple choice, true/false, and fill-in-the-blanks questions, about camera systems, photographic theory, filters, film stocks, procedures, etc.

The practical test is the assembly, threading, operation, and disassembly of various camera systems, whatever is commonly used and available at the time. Members of the union, mostly Camera Assistants, act as proctors for the practical exam, and applicants are scored for general knowledge, competence, and speed, as they assemble, thread up, and disassemble the various cameras.

Some cameras are worth more points than others, based on their degree of difficulty and their commonness in the industry. In other words, a Panaflex counts for more points than an Arri 16S.

The tests are not held on a strict schedule, but are scheduled when enough applicants are ready to take the tests and make it worthwhile having one. This usually amounts to about 10 to 12 applicants per testing session, which works out to about twice a year that these tests are held. There is a testing fee paid by the applicants, which covers the expenses of holding the tests, opening the rental house on a Saturday, shipping and insuring any cameras that need to be brought in from elsewhere, etc.

Once the test scores are totaled and checked, those applicants receiving the minimum score or higher, are referred to the Executive Board of the local, and recommended for acceptance into membership. These applicants are voted on by the Executive Board, and those passing the vote are accepted into membership. Upon payment of the first third of the initiation fee to the union, the applicants are sworn into membership. They have a three-year payment schedule to pay the remaining initiation fee.

The amount of the initiation fee is tied to the feature film contract in effect at the time. The way the initiation fees are computed is by the formula, four weeks pay at union feature contract weekly scale for whatever category is applied for.

The whole process might take as long as a year, or as short as six months. This is the present process for membership in Local 644. The other camera locals have different requirements, different application procedures, different testing procedures. Contact them directly for further information.

Union Organizing

It is also possible to gain entrance to the union through the union's organizing efforts. If a crew is working on a production when the producer signs a union contract for the job, then those crew members may be taken directly into the union as part of the organizing process.

A few unions, like Local 644, actively pursue non-union productions we find in our jurisdiction, and try very hard to get a contract with the Producer. Getting a contract begins, hopefully, a long-term relationship with the Producer for future jobs done in the jurisdiction, which benefits the union and its members. Camera crew members employed by the company when the contract is signed become members and are protected by the contract, which is good for the members. The Producer gains access to the finest pool of experienced and talented camera personnel anywhere in the world. Everybody wins.

All that needs to happen for this process to begin is for one of the camera crew people to call the union office. If the members of the camera crew want to be represented by the union in dealings with the employer, then representation cards are signed. Once the union business representative or organizer has signed cards from the majority of the Camera Department, he contacts the employer, lets the employer know that the union has been authorized by the camera crew to represent them, and begins negotiations on their behalf. The employer must, by law, negotiate with the union if the majority of the members of the crew have authorized the union to represent them. The employer is never told who made the original call.

Seems simple, doesn't it? Well, it is. The union usually gets the contract, the camera crews get their union wages and benefits, and future jobs by that producer are done with union crews.

Sometimes a union, in an attempt to recruit all of the qualified camera people in a certain area in order to control the industry in that area offers reduced initiation fees or reduced entrance requirements for a specific length of time for new applicants living and working in the target area. This is another good way to get membership in the union.

Membership in a union generally means health insurance coverage, pension benefits, protection of the union contract for wages, overtime and other conditions, and most important, it means that the union will represent the member in dealings with the employer—from salary disputes to safety issues. Sounds like a good deal to me.

Union members, if offered jobs on non-union productions, should accept the jobs, then call the union and cooperate in the attempt to organize the job and get a contract. There is nothing to lose from attempting to organize a job. The union's attempt at getting a contract is not always successful, but the benefits of a contract far outweigh the risks. The worst that can happen is that the organizing attempt will not be successful and the job will continue on a non-union basis.

Union members must be educated in the process of organizing their jobs, and the benefits of succeeding in a serious organizing campaign nationwide. They must be persuaded to cooperate with organizing efforts and must be educated in the philosophy of unionism and solidarity. This is the great failing of many unions, including my own. Hopefully, the members of the film unions in this country will eventually get fed up with the lack of representation by their leaders, and will make some changes to correct the situation before it is too late for us all.

Did I Leave Something Out? Got a Better Way?

I have attempted in this HANDBOOK to collect information and procedures from a variety of sources, mostly from the professional experience of myself and other motion picture Camera Assistants working in the motion picture industry in this country.

I have tried to create a HANDBOOK that Camera Assistants could carry in their kits, along with the *American Cinematographer Manual* and *The Professional Cameraman's Handbook*, and that they could use for quick reference in the field, as well as for further study into areas of the Camera Assistants' work they may not be thoroughly familiar with.

Until now, there has never been a textbook for aspiring and practicing Camera Assistants to perfect their skills and theoretical knowledge of the job. Since there are no regular classes or schools teaching the theory and the skills needed by Camera Assistants, except for my workshop in Maine, this book is necessary. It has been a big job compiling all of this.

I am sure, however, that despite my efforts at completeness, there are procedures and precautions that I have overlooked. I am sure there are regional differences I have not mentioned. I am sure there are other ways of doing some of the things discussed in this book. I am sure there are more efficient, faster, more practical and less expensive ways of doing some of the things discussed in this book. I am sure that there is new equipment and tools I haven't used yet.

There may even be factual or theoretical errors in this book that need to be corrected, but hopefully not many.

I am the first to admit that I have not worked in ALL of the possible areas within the Camera Assisting field. I have never worked in the big "Hollywood" studio back lots, and I confess to not knowing how they do things in those "factories."

I have never worked at Industrial Light and Magic or in other such special effects houses. My experience with blue screen and matte work is limited. I have worked some with Vistavision cameras, and the footage was used for rear projection. I also worked briefly on one IMAX job.

I am sure that my Southern California brothers and sisters will have much to say about this HANDBOOK, and not all of it will be kind, but I'll gladly take the heat. Maybe some of them will be inspired to write to me and offer some constructive criticism. Great!

I'm also sure that I may have ruffled the feathers of certain Production Managers, Assistant Directors, and maybe a Director of Photography or two, but I don't know how else to say what I believe and feel about the industry, other than the honest truth. No one has ever accused me of being reluctant to speak my mind. I did make a conscious effort, however, not to mention names or to make it too easy to guess who I am writing about.

I have not worked in the documentary field in several years, and I am sure there have been changes in the way things are done. I make no claims at expertise in electronics, or video, or even photography. I do work, however, in the industry as a Camera Assistant, and I have for over twenty-five years, on major features, minor features, documentaries, and commercials.

Send it to me for the Second Edition!

I am depending on you, my readers, whether working Camera Assistants, Directors of Photography, film school students, or workers in other crafts interested in the Camera Department, to send me these additions. I welcome any and all comments, suggestions, alternatives, additions, and corrections.

These suggestions and additions will be combined with the present text and will be included in future editions of the HANDBOOK. Help me make this HANDBOOK even more complete and valuable to this and future generations of Camera Assistants.

Write to me in care of the Publisher, Focal Press. Their address is printed in the beginning of this book. All letters will be acknowledged and answered if possible. I am interested in hearing from you.

Tell me what you think of the HANDBOOK, and how you think it can be improved.

APPENDIX **A**

Bibliography

AMERICAN CINEMATOGRAPHER MANUAL, published by the American Society of Cinematographers, Hollywood, 1986, 1993.

PROFESSIONAL 16/35mm CAMERAMAN'S HANDBOOK, by Verne and Sylvia Carlson, Amphoto, New York, 1981.

PANAFLEX USERS MANUAL, by David W. Samuelson, Focal Press, Boston & London, 1990.

THE ARRI 35 BOOK, by Jon Fauer, Arriflex, Blauvelt, New York, 1989.

"HANDS ON" MANUAL FOR CINEMATOGRAPHERS, by David W. Samuelson, Focal Press, Boston & London, 1994.

THE 16SR BOOK, by Jon Fauer, Arriflex, Blauvelt, New York, 1986.

THE CAMERA ASSISTANT'S MANUAL, by David E. Elkins, Focal Press, Boston & London, 1991.

STUDENT FILMMAKER'S HANDBOOK, Eastman Kodak, Rochester NY, 1991.

CINEMATOGRAPHER'S FIELD GUIDE, Eastman Kodak, Rochester NY, 1992.

MOTION PICTURE CAMERA DATA, by David W. Samuelson, Communication Arts Books, New York, 1979.

MOTION PICTURE CAMERA TECHNIQUES, by David W. Samuelson, Communication Arts Books, New York, 1984.

MOTION PICTURE CAMERA & LIGHTING EQUIPMENT, by David W. Samuelson, Communication Arts Books, New York, 1986.

CINEMA WORKSHOP, by Anton Wilson, A.S.C. Holding Corp., Hollywood, 1983.

INDEPENDENT FILM MAKING, by Lenny Lipton, Straight Arrow Books, San Francisco, 1972.

CINEMATOGRAPHY, by J. Kris Malkiewicz, Van Nostrand Reinhold Company, New York, 1973.

THE LENS IN ACTION, by Sidney Ray, Communication Arts Books, New York, 1976.

THE LENS AND ALL ITS JOBS, by Sidney Ray, Communication Arts Books, New York, 1977.

MOTION PICTURE FILM PROCESSING, by Dominic Case, Focal Press Media Manuals, New York, 1985.

PHOTOGRAPHIC THEORY FOR THE MOTION PICTURE CAMERAMAN, compiled and edited by Russell Campbell, A.S. Barnes & Co., New York, 1970.

PRACTICAL MOTION PICTURE PHOTOGRAPHY, compiled and edited by Russell Campbell, A.S. Barnes & Co., New York, 1979.

YOUR FILM AND THE LAB, by L. Bernard Happe, Communication Arts Books, New York, 1983.

PROFESSIONAL CINEMATOGRAPHY, by Charles G. Clarke, American Society of Cinematographers, Hollywood, 1968.

PRINCIPLES OF CINEMATOGRAPHY, by Leslie J. Wheeler, Fountain Press, London, 1971.

MASCELLI'S CINE WORKBOOK, by Joseph V. Mascelli, Cine/Grafic Publications, Hollywood, 1973.

THE WORK OF THE MOTION PICTURE CAMERAMAN, by Freddie Young and Paul Petzold, Communication Arts Books, New York, 1972.

THE FIVE C'S OF CINEMATOGRAPHY, by Joseph V. Mascelli, Cine/Grafic Publications, Hollywood, 1968.

BASIC PRODUCTION TECHNIQUES FOR MOTION PICTURES, Eastman Kodak Company, Rochester, 1971.

OPTICS AND OPTICAL INSTRUMENTS, by B. K. Johnson, Dover Publications, New York, 1960.

PHOTOGRAPHIC OPTICS, by Arthur Cox, Focal Press, New York, 1971.

THE FILMMAKER'S HANDBOOK, by Edward Pincus and Steven Ascher, New American Library, New York, 1984.

INTRODUCTION TO FILM, by Robert S. Withers, Barnes & Noble Books, New York, 1983.

BASIC FILM TECHNIQUE, by Ken Daly, Focal Press Media Manuals, Hastings House, New York, N.Y., 1984.

A PRIMER FOR FILM-MAKING, by Kenneth H. Roberts and Win Sharples, Jr., Bobbs-Merrill Educational Publishing, Indianapolis, Indiana, 1971.

GUIDE TO FILMMAKING, by Edward Pincus, New American Library, New York, 1972.

AN INTRODUCTION TO CINEMATOGRAPHY, by John Mercer, Stipes Publishing Co., Champaign, Illinois, 1979.

BASIC FILM-MAKING, by Dana H. Hodgdon & Stuart M. Kaminsky, Arco Publishing, New York, 1981.

ELEMENTS OF COLOR IN PROFESSIONAL MOTION PICTURES, Society of Motion Picture and Television Engineers, Scarsdale, New York, 1974.

PRINCIPLES OF COLOR SENSITOMETRY, edited by Roderick T. Ryan, S.M.P.T.E., Scarsdale, New York, 1974.

CONTROL TECHNIQUES IN FILM PROCESSING, S.M.P.T.E., Scarsdale, New York, 1965.

THE FILM EDITING ROOM HANDBOOK, by Norman Hollyn, Arco Publishing, New York, 1984.

MOTION PICTURE AND TELEVISION FILM - IMAGE CONTROL AND PROCESSING TECHNIQUES, by D.J. Corbett, Focal Press, New York, 1968.

APPENDIX **B**

Expendable Supplies Shopping List

Equipping a major motion picture shooting for six months in the mountains of Tibet is obviously different from equipping a one-day commercial in a studio in midtown Manhattan involving only tabletop shooting, but start with a complete list and eliminate what you won't need. Experience and developing your own working style will further refine the list.

Some of these items are available from the rental house where the cameras are coming from, usually at inflated prices. Some are available free from the laboratory. Other places to shop are a camera store, a stationery store, a hardware store, a pharmacy, and a sporting goods or camping store.

Sometimes the production company will want everything purchased through purchase orders and/or charge accounts they have established with various stores in the area, but often it is easier for everyone if the Camera Assistants purchase the items themselves and turn in receipts for reimbursement. Check with your Production Manager before spending any money.

Talk to the Director of Photography about what gelatin filters you may need, what color chart or grey scale he or she prefers, if any, and about what batteries are needed for the D.P.'s light meters.

Camera Assistants love to color code things. They color code accessories to match them to a particular camera body. They color code actors' marks so the actors get used to looking for the same color mark all the time. They color code magazines and magazine cases to remind them which film stock is inside. They color code unexposed film cans so they can separate different stocks for the darkroom. This is why I have so many different colors of tape and markers and chalk on the list. Develop your own system, and refine this list into your own list.

I have not listed any quantities of the items on the list, because every job is different and every crew is different. Order or purchase enough of these things to get started on the job. You can always order more of whatever you need once the job is underway.

There will be things left over at the end of the job. These leftovers are traditionally divided among the Camera Assistants (known as the "Division of the Spoils"), and the stuff winds up in their basements and garages, unless the Production Manager wants everything left over at the end of the job delivered to the production office, where it will disappear into someone else's basement and garage. Usually, though, the companies don't have the time to bother with collecting extra rolls of tape and things, and don't have the storage facilities. It's easier to start from scratch for the next production.

Expendable Supplies Shopping List

Adhesive Tapes

Gaffers Tape (2" Cloth Tape)
    Black
    Other Colors (White, Gray, Red, etc.)
Camera Tape (1" Cloth Tape)
    Black
    White
    Red
    Other Colors—Blue, Yellow, Orange, Green, etc.
Marking Tapes (1/2" Cloth Tape, for marking actors)
    Key Colors: Yellow, Orange, Black, White, Red
    Other Colors: Green, Blue, Brown
Masking Tape (Paper Tape; Dull Surface, Opaque)
    Black 2"
    Black 1"
Chart (Pinstripe) Tape
    White and/or Yellow
    Widths from 1/16" to 1/4"
Plastic Electricians Tape
Fiberglass Strapping Tape
"Exposed Film"/ "Open in Darkroom Only" Warning Tape

Stationery Items

Writing Supplies
    Ball Point Pens—Black plus other colors
    Sharpie Markers—Black, Blue, Red, plus other colors
    Wide-Point Markers—Black, Blue, Red, other colors
    Erasable Slate Markers—Black
    Pencils
    Erasable Fine-Point Markers for chart tape on lenses
    Chalk—White and colors
    Grease Pencils ("China Markers")—White and colors
    Lumber Crayons (thick, permanent—several colors)
Stationery Supplies
    Large Envelopes (9" x 12") for paperwork
    Small Envelopes (3 5/8" x 6 1/2") for attaching Camera Reports and Purchase Orders to film cans
    Peel-and-Stick Labels for film cans
    Rubber Stamps (for Film Type and Lab Instructions)
    Rubber Stamp Pads—Black and colors
    Desk Stapler and Staples
    Three-Hole Punch
    Looseleaf Binder for copies of Camera Reports, Purchase Orders and other paperwork
    Small Notebooks for Shooting Notes
    Yellow Pads
    Clip Boards
    Vinyl Stick-On Letters for Slates

Batteries

For Flashlights, etc. (Sizes D, C, AA, AAA)
For Light Meters, Crystal Checkers, etc. (Check meters for required sizes)
For Lanterns (6- or 12-Volt Lantern Batteries)

Lens Cleaning Accessories

Lens Tissue (NOT SILICONE-IMPREGNATED !!!!)
Lens Cleaning Fluid (stick to recognizable brand names: Kodak, Tiffen, Rosco, rental houses)
Dust-Off Nozzles and Refills (Environmentally Friendly, of course)

Hardware

Electrical Hardware for Truck Lighting systems
- Zip Cord
- Light Sockets
- Light Bulbs/ Heat Lamp Bulbs
- Plugs, Cube Taps, Grounding Adapters, Wire Nuts, etc.
- Power Strips

Hardware
- Nails, Screws
- Screw Eyes, Eye Bolts
- Staple Gun and Staples
- Flat Head/Hex Head Bolts, Nuts, Washers (3/8" x 16 and 1/4" x 20, various lengths)
- Emery Paper—various grits
- Single-Edge Razor Blades
- #4 Sash Cord (Venetian Blind Cord)
- Bungie (Shock) Cords—(measure shelves for sizes)

Spray Paint
- Flat Black
- Flat White
- Other Colors
- Dulling Spray

Lubricants
- Camera Oil
- Camera Grease
- Liquid Silicone
- Machine Oil (3-in-1 type)
- Spray Teflon or Silicone
- WD-40 or Break-Free type (spray)
- Powdered Graphite

Adhesives
- Clear Nail Polish
- Crazy Glue
- Rubber Cement
- Contact Cement
- Duco Cement
- White Carpenters' Glue

Solvents
- Acetone
- Mineral Spirits
- Grain Alcohol

Space Blankets or Plastic Tarps

Plastic Bags
- Heavy Duty Garbage Bags
- Zip Lock Bags

Flashlights and Lanterns (with spare batteries and bulbs)

Miscellaneous

Gelatin Filters
- Color Conversion Filters
  - 85/ 85N3/ 85N6/ 85N9/ 85C/ 81EF
  - 85B/ 85BN3/ 85BN6/ 85BN9
- Neutral Density Filters—ND3/ ND6/ ND9
- Color Compensation Filters
  - Blue—CC05B, CC10B, etc.
  - Yellow—CC05Y, CC10Y, etc.
  - Magenta—CC10M, CC20M, etc.
  - Red, Green, and Cyan also available

From the Lab (no charge)
- Camera Reports
- Empty Film Cans and Bags (400-foot and 1000-foot)
- Film Can Labels (some labs have them)
- Film Cores

Miscellaneous Supplies
- Chamois Cloths
- Luminex Cloth (for lens and filter cleaning)
- Chamois or Foam Eyepiece Covers
- Color Chip Charts
- Gray Scale Charts

Miscellaneous Supplies, continued
- Antistatic Eyepiece Defogging Spray (Stat-Ban)
- Orangewood Sticks
- Powder Puffs (for erasing Slates; check with Makeup Dept.)
- Cotton Swabs (long wooden stick)
- Production Slates (generally purchased new for each feature production)
- Insert Slates
- French Flags
- Changing Bags
- Adhesive-backed Velcro Strips (especially if working with Steadicam!)
- Depth-of-Field Charts or Calculator
- Paperwork (either the Camera Assistant's own, or from the Production Office; enough copies for the entire job)
- Laboratory Purchase Orders
- Daily Raw Film Stock Inventory Forms
- Daily Exposed Film Reports
- Payroll Time Cards
- Other Employee Paperwork (Start Cards, Deal Memos, I-9 and W-4 forms)
- Petty Cash Forms or Envelopes
- Per Diem/Meal Money Sheets

APPENDIX **C**

Camera Equipment Checkout Checklist

© Douglas C. Hart 1994

I. The Camera Body
  A. Video Assist
    1. Acceptable Picture
    2. Cables - Power and Video
    3. Power - 110 Volt/ Batteries
    4. Adjusted for Picture Size and Shape
    5. Adjusted for Contrast and Brightness
    6. Flicker-Free
  B. Check for Obvious Damage
    1. Broken or Missing Knobs and Switches
    2. Missing Screws
  C. Run Camera
  D. Switches and Controls
    1. On/Off Switchesa.
      a. Main Power Switch
      b. Remote On/Off Switch
    2. Tachometer steady
      a. Accurate at Crystal Speeds
      b. Range of Variable Speeds
    3. Footage Counter and Reset
    4. Crystal & Hertz Settings
    5. Variable Speed Control
      a. Adjusts throughout Range
      b. Minimal Drift
    6. Variable Shutter
      a. Adjusts throughout Range
      b. Locks
  E. Electrical System
    1. Buckle Trips (stops and resets)
    2. Fuses (location and spares)
    3. Circuit Boards and Modules
    4. Battery Condition Meter
    5. Heaters
      a. Heater Power Cables
      b. Eyepiece Heater
      c. Magazine Heaters
      d. Heater Electrical Contacts
    6. Magazine Torque Motor Electrical Contacts
    7. Motors
      a. Types
      b. Power Requirements
    8. Bulbs/ LEDs
      a. Camera Running
      b. Sync Warning
      c. Battery Condition
      d. Film Jam Warning
      e. Low Film or Out-of-Film Warning
      f. Frame Marking
      g. Edge Marking
    9. Power Cables
    10. Batteries/ Chargers
      a. Correct Voltage
      b. Adequate Amperage
      c. Batteries Hold Charge
    11. Power Supplies/ Battery Eliminators
  F. Movement
    1. Clean
    2. Gate (aperture)
      a. Correct Aperture
      b. Easily Removable
      c. Clean
      d. No Rough Edges
      e. Locks Securely
      f. Gate Masks
    3. Pressure Plate
      a. Easily Removable
      b. Clean
      c. No Rough Edges
      d. Locks Securely
    4. Flange Focal Depth/Film Gap
      a. Checking

        b. Adjustment
    5. Shutter Sync (Phasing)
    6. Registration Pins
        a. Operational
        b. Retract Smoothly
        c. Registration Test
    7. Lubrication
    8. Free Rollers
    9. Pitch Control
        a. Working
        b. Quiets Camera
    10. Scratch Test
G. Viewing System
    1. Groundglass
        a. Correct Aspect Ratio
        b. Accurate Markings
        c. Illuminated Markings
        d. Installed Correctly
        e. Depth Correct
    2. Clean
    3. Stops in Viewing Position
    4. Diopter Correction
        a. Working
        b. Adequate For Job
    5. Illuminated Groundglass Dimmer
    6. Viewfinder Magnifier
    7. Contrast Viewing Glasses
        a. Correct Filters
        b. Clean
    8. Eyepiece Extension
        a. Functional
        b. Clean
    9. Periscope
    10. Video Assist Door
    11. Rotating Eyepiece
        a. Functional
        b. Clean
    12. Viewfinder Masks
    13. Matte Slot
H. Miscellaneous
    1. Door Latches & Seals
    2. Gel Filter Slot
        a. Slot Empty
        b. Gel Holders
        c. Cut Gels for Holders
    3. Camera Lockdown Screw
I. Accessories
    1. Hand-Held Accessories
    2. Speed Control Accessories
        a. Variable Crystal Speed Controllers
        b. Time Lapse/Single Frame Controllers
        c. High-Speed Controls
    3. Sync Control Accessories
        a. Field/Frame Synchronizers
        b. Projector Synchronizers
        c. Television/Monitor Synchronizers
    4. Eyepiece Levelers
    5. Weather Protectors/Rain Covers
    6. Matte Punch
    7. Lens Lights
    8. On-Board Video Monitor
    9. Carrying Handles
II. Lenses & Filters
    A. Lens Mount
    B. Lens Support
        1. Adequate Support
        2. Correct Rods
        3. Correct Brackets
    C. Iris
        1. Moves Smoothly
        2. Leaves Flat and Regular
        3. Minimal Play
    D. Focus
        1. Infinity
        2. Focus Marks
            a. Enough Marks
            b. Marks Accurate
            c. Feet/Meters
        3. Follow Focus Gear
            a. Mounts correctly on Lenses
            b. Smooth over Full Range
            c. Minimal "play"
        4. "Blue Line" Lenses
        5. Sharp across Frame
    E. Zoom Lenses
        1. Tracking Straight
        2. Holds Focus throughout Zoom
        3. Zoom Motors
            a. Smooth at all Speeds
            b. Smooth throughout Zoom Range
            c. Mounting Bracket and Rods
            d. Lens Gears Correct and Solid
            e. Power - Correct Voltage
                1. Batteries/Chargers
                2. Power From Camera Body
                      a) Power Available
                      b) Cables and Backups
    F. Coatings
    G. Filters
        1. Materials
        2. Sizes
        3. Types

H. Sunshades/Filter Rings
  1. Sizes
  2. Quantities
I. Matte Boxes
  1. Sizes
  2. Support Rods
  3. Holders for Filters
  4. Adapters for Different Size Filters
  5. Motorized and Geared Matte Box Trays
  6. Tilting Filter Stages
  7. Extensions
  8. Masks
  9. Check for Cutoff with Wide Lenses
  10. Swing Out Matte Boxes
J. Donuts for Lenses
K. Lens Housings

III. Magazines
  A. Sizes
  B. Quantities
  C. Locks Securely on Camera Body
  D. Clean
  E. Latches and Seals
  F. Torque Motors/Belts/Brakes
  G. Clutch Tension Adjustment
  H. Footage Counters
    1. Working
    2. Accurate
    3. Feet or Meters
    4. Additive or Subtractive
  I. Heaters
    1. Electrical Contacts Clean
    2. Indicator Lights
  J. Hand-Held Capability
    1. Light Weight
    2. Sizes
  K. Steadicam/Louma/Hot Head Capability
    1. Extension Throats
    2. Light Weight
    3. Sizes
  L. Scratch Testing
  M. Cores or Core Adapters

IV. Support Equipment
  A. Heads
    1. Types
      a. Geared
      b. Fluid
      d. Friction
      e. Special
        1) Underslung
        2) Remote Control
      f. "Dutch" head
    2. Camera Mounting
      a. Quick-Release
      b. Balance Adjustment
      c. Camera Attachment Screws
    3. Controls
      a. Locks Securely in all Positions
      b. Drag/Tension Adjustment
      c. Spring Settings
      d. Smooth Gear Shifting
      e. Balancing Ability
    4. Mounts
      a. Mitchell Standard
      b. Ball Leveling
  B. Tripods & High Hats
    1. Mounts (Topcasting)
      a. Matches Casting of Heads
      b. Ball Level Adapters
    2. Materials
      a. Wood
      b. Fiberglass
      c. Carbon
      d. Stainless Steel
    3. Sizes
    4. Smooth Length Adjustment
    5. Locks
    6. Head Lockdown Screw Fits
  C. Bridge Plates/Risers/Geared Wedges/ Rocker Base
  D. Spreaders/Rugs
    1. Matches Legs
    2. Smooth
    3. Locks
  E. Dollies
  F. Autobase and Special Mounting Hardware

V. Miscellaneous Accessories
  A. Changing Bag
  B. French Flag
  C. Slate
  D. Barney
  E. Lens Light
  F. "Real-Lens" Finders
  G. Spray Deflectors
  H. On Board Lights
  I. Dynalens and Image Stabilizer
  J. Low-Angle Prism
  K. Panatape
  L. Lightflex/ Panaflasher
  M. Panatate & Pananode
  N. Shallow Water Housing

APPENDIX D

Useful Formulas and Charts

USEFUL FORMULAS

1. Exposure Time:

$$\text{Exposure Time} = \frac{\text{Shutter Opening}}{360 \times (\text{frames per second})}$$

2. f/stops:

$$\text{f/stop} = \frac{\text{focal length of lens}}{\text{diameter of lens opening}}$$

3. Image Size:

$$\frac{\text{Object Size}}{\text{Image Size}} = \frac{\text{Object Distance}}{\text{Focal Length}}$$

4. Hyperfocal Distance:

$$\text{Hyperfocal Distance} = \frac{\text{focal length}^2}{\text{f/stop} \times \text{Circle of Confusion}}$$

5. Electrical Current (Amperage):

$$\text{Amperes} = \frac{\text{Watts}}{\text{Volts}}$$

6. Screen Time:

$$\text{Screen Time (sec)} = \frac{\text{Camera Running Time (sec)} \times \text{Frames/Sec}}{24}$$

7. Macro Exposure Compensation:

$$\text{Lens Aperture} = \frac{\text{Incident Meter Reading}}{1 + \text{Magnification Ratio}}$$

8. Film Length/Time Conversion Factors:

35mm to or from 16mm:	2.5
65/70mm to or from 35mm:	1.25
24 fps to or from 25 fps:	0.96

9. Footcandle Requirements:

$$\text{footcandles} = \frac{25 \times (\text{T/stop})^2}{(\text{ASA Rating}) \times (\text{Shutter Speed})}$$

Here's a shortcut: To compute the number of footcandles required for a T/2.8 exposure, simply divide 10,000 (ten thousand) by the ASA (Exposure Index) of the film stock being used. (This only works for T2.8!) From this number, you should be able to interpolate the footcandles required for other T/ stops, multiplying the T/2.8 value by two for every stop above T/2.8 and dividing by two for every stop below T/2.8:

Sample: For EI 400 film, the footcandles required for a T/2.8 exposure is

$$\frac{10,000}{400} = 25 \text{ footcandles}$$

For a T/4 exposure, multiply 25 by 2 for 50 footcandles;
For a T/2 exposure, divide 25 by 2 for 12.5 footcandles.

10. Depth of Focus:

$$\text{Depth of Focus} = \frac{\text{Focal Length} \times \text{f/stop}}{1000}$$

11. Depth of Field (Near Limit):

$$\text{Near Limit} = \frac{\text{Hyperfocal Distance} \times \text{Camera to Object Distance}}{\text{Hyperfocal} + (\text{Object Distance} - \text{Focal Length})}$$

12. Depth of Field (Far Limit):

$$\text{Far Limit} = \frac{\text{Hyperfocal Distance} \times \text{Camera to Object Distance}}{\text{Hyperfocal} - (\text{Object Distance} - \text{Focal Length})}$$

USEFUL CHARTS

CAMERA SPEED IN FEET PER MINUTE:

Speed (frames/sec.)	16mm Film (feet/min.) 40 frames/ft.	35mm Film (feet/min.) 16 frames/ft.	65mm Film (feet/min.) 12.8 frames/ft.
8	12	30	37.5
12	18	45	56.25
16	24	60	75
20	30	75	93.75
24	36	90	112.5
25	37.5	93.75	117.1875
30	45	112.5	140.625
32	48	120	150
36	54	135	168.75
48	72	180	225
60	90	225	281.25
72	108	270	337.5
96	144	360	450
120	180	450	562.5

CAMERA SPEED VS. EXPOSURE TIME (SHUTTER SPEED)
(with 180° Shutter)

Camera Speed (frames per second)	Exposure Time (Shutter Speed) (rounded off)	Exposure Adjustment (from 24 fps)
6 fps	1/12 sec.	close 2 stops
8 fps	1/16 sec.	close 1 1/2 stops
12 fps	1/24 sec.	close 1 stop
16 fps	1/32 sec.	close 1/2 stop
24 fps	1/48 sec.	-
25 fps	1/50 sec.	-
32 fps	1/64 sec.	open 1/2 stop
48 fps	1/100 sec.	open 1 stop
64 fps	1/125 sec.	open 1 1/2 stops
96 fps	1/200 sec.	open 2 stops
128 fps	1/250 sec.	open 3 stops
250 fps	1/500 sec.	open 4 stops

SHUTTER ANGLE VS. EXPOSURE TIME (SHUTTER SPEED)
(at 24 fps)

Shutter Angle (degrees)	Shutter Speed (from 180°)	Exposure Adjustment
5.6°	1/1536 sec.	open 5 stops
11.3°	1/768 sec.	open 4 stops
15°	1/576 sec.	open 3 2/3 Stops
22.5°	1/384 sec.	open 3 stops
30°	1/288 sec.	open 2 2/3 stops
45°	1/192 sec.	open 2 stops
60°	1/144 sec.	open 1 2/3 stops
90°	1/96 sec.	open 1 stop
120°	1/72 sec.	open 2/3 stop
144°	1/60 sec.	open 1/3 stop
172.8°	1/50 sec.	open 1/10 stop
180°	1/48 sec.	none
200°	1/43 sec.	close 1/6 stop

OPTIMUM SHUTTER ANGLES AND RUNNING SPEEDS FOR FILMING WITH HMI LIGHTING EQUIPMENT

Frames Per Second	Shutter Opening at 60 Hz	50 Hz
12 fps	72°	86.4° & 172.8°
18 fps	108°	129.6°
24 fps	144° & 180°	172.8°
25 fps	150°	180°
36 fps	106°	129.6°
48 fps	144°	172.8°
50 fps	-	180°
60 fps	180°	-
72 fps	-	-
96 fps	-	-
100 fps	-	180°
120 fps	180°	-

APPENDIX E
Film Magazine Takeup

This chart describes the film emulsion take-up position for normal magazines and internal loads, if applicable. "Emulsion In" means that the emulsion side of the film faces the inside of the roll, "Emulsion Out" faces the outside of the roll.

EMULSION IN
ARRIFLEX—all
MOVIECAM—all
ULTRACAM

AATON—all
CINEMA PRODUCTS—GSMO
ECLAIR—GV16, ACL (English)
AURICON
FREZZOLINI
BOLEX
BEAULIEU
CANON SCOOPIC

EMULSION OUT
PANAVISION—all*
MITCHELL—all
CINEMA PRODUCTS—
    CP16, XR35, FX35
ECLAIR—CM3, NPR, ACL (French)

*Of course, there has to be an exception: The special "Reverse Running" magazines for the Panavision Platinum and Panastar cameras take up EMULSION IN, on the left side of the magazine.

APPENDIX F

Screen Time/Camera Running Time

This is a useful chart for computing screen time when the camera is running at a speed other than normal speed (24 frames per second).

To use the chart, find your camera running speed along the top of the chart, and go down that column until you find the length of the shot, in seconds. Then trace to the left edge to find the actual screen time.

If you know how long the event takes, and how long it needs to be on the screen, but need to know the running speed to set the camera at, find the needed screen time on the left, then trace across that row until you find the event length. Then follow that column up to find the necessary camera running speed.

The chart gives screen time in one-half-second intervals up to 20 seconds, and then uses ten-second intervals up to 60 seconds. I did it this way to get the chart on a single page. To find the running time for 36 seconds, for example, add the values for 30 seconds and 6 seconds.

To find the running time for screen times over 60 seconds, multiply out the one minute values, or use the formula in Appendix D.

SCREEN TIME VS. CAMERA RUNNING TIME

Seconds of Screen Time (Script Time)	4 fps	8 fps	12 fps	16 fps	18 fps	20 fps	24 fps	30 fps	32 fps	36 fps	40 fps	48 fps	64 fps	72 fps	96 fps	120 fps
0.5 sec	3.0	1.5	1.0	0.75	0.67	0.60	0.50	0.40	0.38	0.33	0.30	0.25	0.19	0.17	0.13	0.10
1.0	6.0	3.0	2.0	1.50	1.33	1.20	1.00	0.80	0.75	0.67	0.60	0.50	0.38	0.33	0.25	0.20
1.5	9.0	4.5	3.0	2.25	2.00	1.80	1.50	1.20	1.13	1.00	0.90	0.75	0.56	0.50	0.38	0.30
2.0	12.0	6.0	4.0	3.00	2.67	2.40	2.00	1.60	1.50	1.33	1.20	1.00	0.75	0.67	0.50	0.40
2.5	15.0	7.5	5.0	3.75	3.33	3.00	2.50	2.00	1.88	1.67	1.50	1.25	0.94	0.83	0.63	0.50
3.0	18.0	9.0	6.0	4.50	4.00	3.60	3.00	2.40	2.25	2.00	1.80	1.50	1.13	1.00	0.75	0.60
3.5	21.0	10.5	7.0	5.25	4.67	4.20	3.50	2.80	2.63	2.33	2.10	1.75	1.31	1.17	0.88	0.70
4.0	24.0	12.0	8.0	6.00	5.33	4.80	4.00	3.20	3.00	2.67	2.40	2.00	1.50	1.33	1.00	0.80
4.5	27.0	13.5	9.0	6.75	6.00	5.40	4.50	3.60	3.38	3.00	2.70	2.25	1.69	1.50	1.13	0.90
5.0	30.0	15.0	10.0	7.50	6.67	6.00	5.00	4.00	3.75	3.33	3.00	2.50	1.88	1.67	1.25	1.00
5.5	33.0	16.5	11.0	8.25	7.33	6.60	5.50	4.40	4.13	3.67	3.30	2.75	2.06	1.83	1.38	1.10
6.0	36.0	18.0	12.0	9.00	8.00	7.20	6.00	4.80	4.50	4.00	3.60	3.00	2.25	2.00	1.50	1.20
6.5	39.0	19.5	13.0	9.75	8.67	7.80	6.50	5.20	4.88	4.33	3.90	3.25	2.44	2.17	1.63	1.30
7.0	42.0	21.0	14.0	10.50	9.33	8.40	7.00	5.60	5.25	4.67	4.20	3.50	2.63	2.33	1.75	1.40
7.5	45.0	22.5	15.0	11.25	10.00	9.00	7.50	6.00	5.63	5.00	4.50	3.75	2.81	2.50	1.88	1.50
8.0	48.0	24.0	16.0	12.00	10.67	9.60	8.00	6.40	6.00	5.33	4.80	4.00	3.00	2.67	2.00	1.60
8.5	51.0	25.5	17.0	12.75	11.33	10.20	8.50	6.80	6.38	5.67	5.10	4.25	3.19	2.83	2.13	1.70
9.0	54.0	27.0	18.0	13.50	12.00	10.80	9.00	7.20	6.75	6.00	5.40	4.50	3.38	3.00	2.25	1.80
9.5	57.0	28.5	19.0	14.25	12.67	11.40	9.50	7.60	7.13	6.33	5.70	4.75	3.56	3.17	2.38	1.90
10.0	60.0	30.0	20.0	15.00	13.33	12.00	10.00	8.00	7.50	6.67	6.00	5.00	3.75	3.33	2.50	2.00
10.5	63.0	31.5	21.0	15.75	14.00	12.60	10.50	8.40	7.88	7.00	6.30	5.25	3.94	3.50	2.63	2.10
11.0	66.0	33.0	22.0	16.50	14.67	13.20	11.00	8.80	8.25	7.33	6.60	5.50	4.13	3.67	2.75	2.20
11.5	69.0	34.5	23.0	17.25	15.33	13.80	11.50	9.20	8.63	7.67	6.90	5.75	4.31	3.83	2.88	2.30
12.0	72.0	36.0	24.0	18.00	16.00	14.40	12.00	9.60	9.00	8.00	7.20	6.00	4.50	4.00	3.00	2.40
12.5	75.0	37.5	25.0	18.75	16.67	15.00	12.50	10.00	9.38	8.33	7.50	6.25	4.69	4.17	3.13	2.50
13.0	78.0	39.0	26.0	19.50	17.33	15.60	13.00	10.40	9.75	8.67	7.80	6.50	4.88	4.33	3.25	2.60
13.5	81.0	40.5	27.0	20.25	18.00	16.20	13.50	10.80	10.13	9.00	8.10	6.75	5.06	4.50	3.38	2.70
14.0	84.0	42.0	28.0	21.00	18.67	16.80	14.00	11.20	10.50	9.33	8.40	7.00	5.25	4.67	3.50	2.80
14.5	87.0	43.5	29.0	21.75	19.33	17.40	14.50	11.60	10.88	9.67	8.70	7.25	5.44	4.83	3.63	2.90
15.0	90.0	45.0	30.0	22.50	20.00	18.00	15.00	12.00	11.25	10.00	9.00	7.50	5.63	5.00	3.75	3.00
15.5	93.0	46.5	31.0	23.25	20.67	18.60	15.50	12.40	11.63	10.33	9.30	7.75	5.81	5.17	3.88	3.10
16.0	96.0	48.0	32.0	24.00	21.33	19.20	16.00	12.80	12.00	10.67	9.60	8.00	6.00	5.33	4.00	3.20
16.5	99.0	49.5	33.0	24.75	22.00	19.80	16.50	13.20	12.38	11.00	9.90	8.25	6.19	5.50	4.13	3.30
17.0	102.0	51.0	34.0	25.50	22.67	20.40	17.00	13.60	12.75	11.33	10.20	8.50	6.38	5.67	4.25	3.40
17.5	105.0	52.5	35.0	26.25	23.33	21.00	17.50	14.00	13.13	11.67	10.50	8.75	6.56	5.83	4.38	3.50
18.0	108.0	54.0	36.0	27.00	24.00	21.60	18.00	14.40	13.50	12.00	10.80	9.00	6.75	6.00	4.50	3.60
18.5	111.0	55.5	37.0	27.75	24.67	22.20	18.50	14.80	13.88	12.33	11.10	9.25	6.94	6.17	4.63	3.70
19.0	114.0	57.0	38.0	28.50	25.33	22.80	19.00	15.20	14.25	12.67	11.40	9.50	7.13	6.33	4.75	3.80
19.5	117.0	58.5	39.0	29.25	26.00	23.40	19.50	15.60	14.63	13.00	11.70	9.75	7.31	6.50	4.88	3.90
20.0 sec	120.0	60.0	40.0	30.00	26.67	24.00	20.00	16.00	15.00	13.33	12.00	10.00	7.50	6.67	5.00	4.00
30.0 sec	180.0	90.0	60.0	45.00	40.00	36.00	30.00	24.00	22.50	20.00	18.00	15.00	11.25	10.00	7.50	6.00
40.0 sec	240.0	120.0	80.0	60.00	53.33	48.00	40.00	32.00	30.00	26.67	24.00	20.00	15.00	13.33	10.00	8.00
50.0 sec	300.0	150.0	100.0	75.00	66.67	60.00	50.00	40.00	37.50	33.33	30.00	25.00	18.75	16.67	12.50	10.00
60.0 sec	360.0	180.0	120.0	90.00	80.00	72.00	60.00	48.00	45.00	40.00	36.00	30.00	22.50	20.00	15.00	12.00

Camera Running Time

Index

Academy format, 28
Adapters, wide-angle, 168
Anamorphic lenses, 162–163
Anamorphic systems, 26–27
Aperture pulls, 241, 293
Aperture setting, 287–290
Arriflex lens mounts, 165
Aspect ratios (film), 23–36
Astigmatism, 113
Attenuator filters, 181–182
Auto-Diffuser (Panavision), 183
Autocollimator, 111–112
Axial drift (zoom lens), 108

Bags, changing, 97, 131–133
Barneys, 286
Barrel distortion, 113, 162
Batteries, 59–63
Beamsplitter, 301
Beep slate, 335
Behind-the-lens filters, 185–188
Blimps, 286
Blocking, 272–274
Blue Line lenses, Panavision, 235–237

Calculator, camera lens Depth-of-Field, 212–213
Calculators, pocket-computer-type, 209
Calculators and charts, Depth-of-Field, 208–212
Call sheets, 359
Camera Assistant, 1–5
    responsibilities, 7–22
        First Camera Assistant, 9–11
        Second Camera Assistant, 11–12
Camera department, 8–12
Camera equipment checkout, 37–102
Camera equipment checkout checklist, 47–100, 402–404
    camera body, 48–77
        check for obvious damage, 50
        electrical system, 57–64
        movement, 64–66
        run camera, 50
        switches and controls, 50–57
        video assist, 48–50
        viewing system, 66–71
    lenses & filters, 77–88
        coatings, 83–84
        donuts for lenses, 86–87
        filters, 84
        focus, 79–82
        iris, 78–79
        lens housing, 88
        lens mount, 77
        lens support, 78

Camera equipment checkout checklist,
lenses & filters, matte boxes,
(continued)
    sunshades/filter rings, 84
    zoom lenses, 82–83
magazines, 88–93
    clean, 89
    clutch tension adjustment, 89
    cores or core adapters, 93
    footage counters, 89–90
    hand-held capability, 90
    heaters, 90
    latches and seals, 89
    locks securely on camera body, 89
    quantities, 88–89
    sizes, 88
    scratch testing, 90–93
    Steadicam/Panaglide/Louma/Hot Head, 90
    torque motors/belts/brakes, 89
miscellaneous accessories, 97–100
    Arri Varicon/Panaflasher, 99–100
    barney, 97
    changing bag, 97
    Dynalens and image stabilizer, 98–99
    French flag, 97
    lens light, 97
    low-angle prism/inclining prism, 99
    on-board lights, 98
    Panatape, 99
    Panatate and Pananode, 100
    real-lens finders, 98
    slate, 97
    spray deflectors, 98
    water box (shallow water housing), 100
support equipment, 93–96
    autobase, 96
    bridge plates/risers/geared wedges/rocker base, 96
    dollies, 96
    heads, 93–95
    spreaders/rugs, 96
    tripods and high hats, 95–96
Camera equipment rental houses, 38–47, 384–385
Camera power cables, 60–62
Camera reports, 19, 153, 302–303, 344–353
Camera running time, 406, 408–409, 410–411
Camera trucks, 135–136
Case labeling, 101–102
CCD (Charge-Coupled Device) cameras, 362–364
Changing bags, 97, 131–133
Charts, useful, 408–409
Checking the gate, 304–310
Checkout
    availability problems, 40
    camera equipment, 37–102
    camera equipment checklist, 47–100
    importance of camera equipment, 37–38
    philosophy, 42–44
    shooting tests during, 103–124
Chromatic aberration, 113
Cinch marks, 317
Cine-Check meter (Cinematography Electronics), 52
Cinemascope, 27
Cinemascope/Panavision 35, 33
Cinemiracle (obsolete), 34
Cinerama formats (obsolete), 29, 33
Circle of Confusion, 196–198, 206
Cleaning lenses, 170
Close-up lenses, 241–243
Cold weather, 295
Collimator, 111–112
Color charts, 284
Color coding (multiple film stocks), 153–154
Coma (lens aberration), 113
Compressed nitrogen, 137–138
Condensation on cold lenses, 175–176
Contract, rental, 100–101

Crane shots, 233–234
Crystal checkers, 50–52
Curvilinear distortion, 113

Dailies projection leaders, making, 111
Dailies screening, 3
Daily Film Inventory, 354–355
Daily Film Report, 353
Darkrooms, 134–135
Depth-of-Field, 194, 200–205, 407
Depth-of-Field calculators
    camera lenses used as, 212–213
    and charts, 208–212
Depth-of-Focus, 204–205, 407
Diffraction gratings, 185
Diffusion, behind-the-lens, 188
Diffusion filters, 122, 182–183, 189
Diopter lenses
    plus, 168, 189, 241–243
    split, 168, 243–245
Director's finders, 275
Dirt
    in the camera gate, 316
    on prints, 316
    on projected film, 316
Distortion
    barrel, 162
    pincushion, 162
Documentary slates, 335–336
Dolly
    and crane shots, 233–234, 296–298
    grips, 16–17, 228
Double-system sound recording, 129
Dragline, 227
Dumb slates, 338
Dynalens, 98–99

Edge fog, 316
Emulsion tests, 118–120
Equipment lists, 358–359
Equipment rental houses, 38–47, 384–385
Equipment shows, 387
Extenders, two-times, 167

Eye focus, 165, 220, 240
Eye vs. tape focus, 232–233

F-A-S-T (Focus-Aperture-Shutter-Tachometer), 291
f/stops and T/stops, 198–201, 406
Field curvature, 113
Film can labels, manufacturer's, 125–131
Film formats and aspect ratios, 23–36
Film magazine takeup, 409
Film
    aspect ratios, 27
    break-off, 312–313
    can labeling, 151–153
    daily inventory, 354–355
    daily reports, 353
    emulsion tests, 118–120
    gauges, 23–24
    handling, 316–318
    loaders, 12
    manufacturer's can label, 125–131
    multiple stocks, 153–154
    ordering raw stock, 154–155
    perforations, 129–131
    recanned raw stock, 143–145
    schools, 383–384
    sealing cans of, 144–145
    shipping of raw stock and exposed film, 156–158
    short ends, 145–148
    storage of raw stock, 155–156
    student, 385–386
    wide screen, 29
Film school, 383–384
Filters, 84, 177–191
    ATN, 182
    attenuator, 181–182
    behind-the-lens, 185–188
    cleaning, 190–191
    color compensation, 179
    color conversion, 178–179
    color correction, 178–179
    diffusion, 122, 182–183, 189

416 Index

Filters, (continued)
  diopter, 189
  disposable, 191
  factors, 189–190
  false color, 185
  fog, 184
  graduated, 180–181, 188
  light balancing, 178–179
  MBRA, 181
  mired shift value, 190
  multiple, 188–189
  neutral density, 179–180
  polarizing, 183–184
  sizes and shapes of, 177
  special effects, 184–185
  star, 184–185
  tests, 122
  wedge, 180
  Wratten 80A, 179
  Wratten type "85", 178–179
Finders
  director's, 275
  hundred pound, 275–276
  real lens, 275–276
  right-angle, 276
First team, 278
First unit, 13–15
Flange focal depth, 256–257
Flare, lens, 171–174
Flashing light slate, 335
Flicker tests, 109
Focus, 193–249
  apparent, 194
  camera operators and, 234
  choices, 216–217
  Circle of Confusion, 206
  Depth-of, 204–205
  Depth-of-Field, 201–205
  electronic gadgets, 248–249
  eye, 165, 220, 240
  eye vs. tape, 232–233
  following, 213–214, 292
  hyperfocal distance, 205–206
  laser pointer focus marks, 227–228
  long lenses, 237–240
  marks, 228–232
  multiple targets, 217–219
  splitting, 217–219
  tape, 165, 232–233
  theory, 194–196
  video assist and, 235
  zoom lenses, 240–241
Focus marks, 228–232, 285
  actors' marks, 228
  floor marks, 228–230
  lens marks, 231
Following focus, 212–215, 292
Formats
  16mm, 30
  35mm anamorphic, 33
  35mm anamorphic and horizontal, 33
  35mm nonanamorphic (spherical), 30–33
  65mm anamorphic, 35
  65mm nonanamorphic (spherical), 34
  Academy, 28
  Cinerama (obsolete), 29, 33
  film, 24–25
  IMAX, 24
  Lazy 8, 24
  OMNIMAX, 24
  3-perforations, 32
  VistaVision 24, 32–33
  wide-screen, 28–29
Formulas and charts, useful, 405–408
Freelancing work, 388–389
French flag, 97
Full aperture, 27

Gate checking, 304–310
Gel filters, 185–188
Geometric distortion, 113
Graduated filters, 180–181, 188
Gray scales, 284
Ground glass markings tests, 109–111
Ground glass position, determining, 111–113

Hand (slop) tests, 159
Hand trucks, 261–264

HDTV (high definition TV), 35–36
HMI lighting, 120
Horizontal formats, 32–35
Hundred pound finders, 275–276
Hyperfocal distance, 205–206, 406

IMAX format, 24
Insert cars, 298–299

Lab continuity tests, 123–124
Labeling
    case, 101–102
    film can, 151–153
    magazine, 148–150
    manufacturer's film can, 125–131
Laser pointer focus marks, 227–228
Lazy 8 format, 24
Lens aberrations, 113–114
    astigmatism, 113
    barrel distortion, 113
    chromatic aberration, 113
    coma, 113
    curvilinear distortion, 113
    field curvature, 113
    geometric distortion, 113
    pincushion distortion, 114
    spherical aberration, 113
Lens color, 117–118
Lens mounts, 77–78, 163–165
Lens sharpness, 114–117
Lens-to-film tolerance, 204
Lens-to-subject tolerance, 201
Lenses, 77–84, 161–176
    anamorphic, 162–163
    changing, 176
    cleaning, 169–170
    close-up, 241–243
    color tests, 117–118
    condensation on cold, 175–176
    flares, 171–174
    in general, 161–162
    long, 237–240
    Panavision Blue Line, 235–237
    prime, 162
    sharpness tests, 114–117
    special, 166–168
        2X extenders, 167
        macro lenses, 166–167
        Proxars (plus diopters/split diopters), 168
        tele-extenders, 167–168
        two-times extenders, 167
        wide-angle adapters, 168
    split diopter, 243–245
    transporting, 174–175
    zoom, 166, 240–241
Light balancing filters, 178–179
Long lenses, 237–240
Lubricating the camera, 255–256, 286

M. O. S. (mit out sound) filming, 327, 328, 339, 340, 351
Macro lens Depth-of-Field, 203–204
Macro lenses, 166–167, 407
Magazine maintenance, 136–140
Magazines, 88–93
    coaxial, 141
    displacement, 140
    labeling, 148–150
    loading procedures, 140–143
    loading/unloading, 125–159
    noise, 287
    scratch testing, 91–93
Maintenance
    magazine, 136–140
    setup and, 251–264
Makeup tests, 122–13
Manufacturer's film can label, 125–131
Marking actors, 277–283
Matte boxes/sunshades, 84–88, 170–171
MBRA filters, 181
Meters
    Cine-Check (Cinematography Electronics), 52
    P. O. M. (peace of mind), 52
MIRED (micro reciprocal degrees), 190
Mitchell lens mount, 164
Moire patterns, 105
Morning routine, setup and maintenance, 251–252

Movement phasing, 109, 258–260
MTF (modulation transfer function), 114
Multiple camera shooting, 313–314
Multiple film stocks, 153–154
Multiple image prisms, 185

Neutral density filters, 179–180
Nitrogen, compressed, 137–138

OMNIMAX format, 24
Optical tape measure, 246–247

Panaflasher, 98–100
Panatape, 99, 245–246
Panavision 35/Cinemascope, 33
Panavision Blue Line lenses, 235–237
Panavision lens mounts, 164
Panavision Super 35, 31
Paperwork, 343–360
    call sheets, 359
    camera reports, 344–352
    combination forms, 355
    daily film inventory, 354–355
    daily film reports, 353
    equipment lists, 358–359
    keeping copies of everything, 359–360
    payroll time card, 343, 358
    perforations, 129–131
    purchase orders, 355–358
Pellicle (beamsplitter), 301
Perforations, 129–131
Phasing (shutter/movement timing test), 109, 258–260
Photographic daylight, 179
Pincushion distortion, 114, 162
Pitch, 129, 286
PL lens mounts, 165
Plus diopters, 241–243
Polarizing filters, 183–184
P.O.M. (peace of mind) meters, 50–52
Power cables, 60–62
Prayer Wheel, 210
Prime lenses, 162
Principal plane of focus (PPF), 194

Printers, weaving, 108
Printing lights tests, 120–122
Prints, dirt on, 316
Prisms, multiple image, 185
Projector Line-Up Leader, 109–111
Proxars, 168, 241–243
Purchase orders, 355–358

Quiet, keeping the camera, 285–287

Rangefinders, 246–247
Ratios, aspect, 23–36
Raw stock and processing defects, 318
Real lens finders, 98, 275–276
Recan, 143–144
Registration tests, 103–109
Reloading, 310–312
Rental contract, 100–101
Rental houses, 38–42, 44–47, 384–385
Report tin, 302–303
Reports, camera, 19, 344–352
Responsibilities, 7–22
Reticulation, 318
Right-angle finders, 276
Roll slates, 324–325
RSI (responsibility: salary index) scale, 5

Safety, 302–304
Scene blocking, 272–274
Scratch testing, 91–93
Screen time, 410–411
Second camera crews, 13
Second Second Camera Assistant, 12
Second sticks, 327
Second team, 278
Second unit, 13–15
Service carts, 261–264
Setup and maintenance, 251–264
    bringing equipment to the set, 263–264
    cleaning the camera, 253–254
    film gap setting, 256–257
    flange focal depth checking, 256–257
    lubricating the camera, 255–256

the morning routine, 251–252, 264
movement phasing, 258–259
service carts and handtrucks, 260–263
setting up, 259–260
shutter opening, 257–258
viewfinder, 254–255
warmup, 252–253
Shooting procedures, 265–318
aperture pulls, 293
camera cases, 290–291
camera problems, 316–318
Camera Reports, 302
chain of command, 267
checking the gate, 304–310
cleaning the gate, 310
color charts and gray scales, 284
Directors' Finders/Real Lens Finders/Camera-as Finder, 274–277
efficiency on the set, 315
film break-off, 312–313
film handling, 316–318
filming in the cold, 295
following focus, 292
hiding marks, 282
keeping the camera quiet, 285–287
magazine noises, 287
marking actors, 277–282
moving the camera, 269–272
moving cameras, 296–299
multiple camera shootings, 313
numbering the marks, 282–283
once the camera is rolling, 291
recordkeeping - Shot Notebook, 313–314
reloading etiquette, 310–312
removing the marks, 283
safety on the set, 302–304
scene blocking, 272–274
set etiquette, 265–266
setting the aperture, 287–290
setting the eyepiece, 284–285
shutter changes, 293–294
simultaneous moves, 294
Steadicam, 299–302
troubleshooting: when the camera stops, 291
unplug and cover the camera, 269
zooming, 292–293
Short ends, 145–148
Shutter, variable, 55–57, 257–258, 293–294, 406, 409
Siemen's Star targets, 105
Silent aperture aspect ratios, 27
Silent slates, 327–328
Single-system sound filming, 129
16mm formats, 30
65mm Anamorphic Formats, 35
65mm Nonanamorphic (Spherical) Formats, 34
Slate light, 331
Slates and slating, 319–342
beep, 335
commercial slating, 339–340
documentary, 335–336
double system, 321–322
dumb, 338
etiquette of slating, 322–333
false starts, 327
flashing light, 335
getting started, 328–330
information on the, 322–323
multiple camera slating, 340–342
perspective and timing, 333–335
reasons for having, 319–321
roll, 324–325
second sticks, 327
silent, 327–328
single system/double system, 321–322
slating procedure, 330–332
smart, 338
tail, 325–326, 338
time code slating, 336–338
types of, 323–324
Slop tests, 159
Smart slate, 332, 338
Special effects filters, 184–185
Spherical aberration, 113
Split diopter lenses, 243–245

Splitting focus, 217–219
Stand-ins, 278
Star filters, 184–185
Static marks, 317
Steadicam, 298–302
Stock (film)
    ordering raw, 154–155
    storage of raw, 155–156
Sunshades, 170–171
Super 16, 29–30
Super 35, Panavision, 31
Superscope (obsolete), 31
Supplies, expendable, shopping list, 398–401

T-shaped mark, 279–282
T/stop machine, 198
T/stops, 198–201
Tail slates, 325–326, 338
Tape focus, 165, 232–233
Tape measures
    electronic, 248
    optical, 246–247
Techniscope, 32
Tele-extenders, 167–168
Tests
    actors' screen, 123
    camera registration test, 103–109
    checkout shooting, 103
    emulsion, 118–120
    filter, 122
    flicker, 109
    ground glass markings, 109–111
    hand, 159
    lab continuity, 123–124
    lens color, 117–118
    lens sharpness, 114–117
    makeup, 122–123
    registration, 103–109
    shooting, 103–124
    slop, 159
    specifying printing lights, 120–122
    wardrobe and makeup, 122–123
Thousand pound finders, 276–277

35mm anamorphic and horizontal formats, 33
35mm miltistrip systems, 33
35mm nonanamorphic (spherical) formats, 30–33
35mm Panavision Super 35, 31
Three pound finders, 275
Time cards, 358
Time code slating, 336–338
Tools and supplies, 367–381
    assistant's supplies, 380
    assistant's tool kit, 367
    essential items, 367–376
    optional items, 376–380
    traveling heavy vs. traveling light, 380–381
Trainee programs, 387–388
Training
    equipment rental houses, 384–385
    student films, 385–386
Transfer tape, 188
Transmission stop, 198
Troubleshooting, 291
Trucks, camera, 135–136
True stop, 198
Two-times extenders, 167

Ultra-Panavision, 27
Unions, 389–393
    IATSE, 389–390
    membership procedures, 391–392
    NABET (The National Association of Broadcast Employees and Technicians), 389
    organizing, 392–393

Variable shutter, 55–57, 257–258, 293–294, 406, 409
Varicon, 99–100
Vertical formats, 30–34
Video assist, 48–50
    beamsplitter, 366
    flicker and flicker-free video, 364–365

and focus, 235
help or hindrance, 364
on the set, 365
systems, 361–366
theory and practice, 361–363
Viewing system, 66–71, 254–255, 284–285
VistaVision (Lazy 8) format, 24, 32–33

Walkie-talkies, 237–240
Wardrobe and makeup tests, 122–123
Wedge filters, 180
Whips (focus extensions), 214
Wide-angle adapters, 168
Wide-screen formats, 28–29

Work
  finding, 388
  freelancing, 388–389
  joining unions, 391–392
  non-union, 390–391
  placing ads in the trade press, 386
  as a Production Assistant, 386
  trainee programs, 387–388
  union, 389–393
  union's organizing efforts, 392–393
Workshops and seminars, 386–387
Wratten 80A filter, 179
Wratten type "85" filter, 178–179

Zoom lenses, 166, 240–241
Zooming, 292–293, 294

CPSIA information can be obtained at www.ICGtesting.com
Printed in the USA
BVOW06*0539010716

454123BV00003B/5/P